D0820654

PHILIP V OF MACEDON

Silver Attic Tetradrachm from Macedonia (obverse).

Silver Attic Tetradrachm from Polyrrhenia in Crete
(obverse) showing Philip V idealised as Apollo.

Philip V of Macedon from contemporary coins in the British Museum (enlarged)

PHILIP V
OF MACEDON

by
F. W. WALBANK

Rathbone Professor of
Ancient History and Classical Archaeology
University of Liverpool

THE HARE PRIZE ESSAY 1939

ARCHON BOOKS
1967

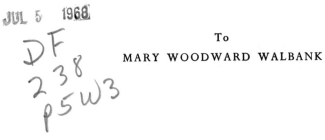
To

MARY WOODWARD WALBANK

FIRST PUBLISHED 1940

REPRINTED 1967 WITH PERMISSION
CAMBRIDGE UNIVERSITY PRESS

WITH A NEW FOREWORD

LIBRARY OF CONGRESS CATALOG CARD NUMBER: 67–12981
PRINTED IN THE UNITED STATES OF AMERICA

CONTENTS

ILLUSTRATIONS

PLATES

MAPS

FOREWORD

Writing in 1913 Maurice Holleaux indicated the need for a series of monographs devoted to the more outstanding Hellenistic monarchs, and looked forward to the time when 'on se décidera enfin à écrire une histoire équitable de Philippe V'. The following pages are an attempt to fill this gap with a study of Philip, not solely as a figure in the history of Roman imperialism, but, as far as is feasible, from the aspect of Macedon itself. It is scarcely necessary to-day to emphasise the extent to which such a work is inevitably indebted to Holleaux's own studies. In particular, it is to Holleaux that we owe the elucidation of the actual role of the Senate in the story of Roman expansion. From his work emerges the picture of a body very imperfectly acquainted with the Greek world, slow to take decisions, easily thrown into panic at unreliable rumours, and the victim of prejudices which the more astute among Hellenistic politicians were quick to exploit. Yet behind it there stands the whole weight of the Roman legions and of the invincible war-machine, that had been built up in the sixteen years' struggle with Hannibal.

What had frequently been taken for a consistent and long-sighted senatorial policy was in fact, Holleaux showed, very little more than a superiority of Roman arms; and the real causes behind the eastern advance of the Roman army were to be sought, not merely on the banks of the Tiber, but also in the diplomatic and military inter-relations, and even in the internal social and economic conditions of Egypt, Syria, Macedonia and the Greek states. Here, in the Near East, in the clash between power and power, class and class, there occurred those periodic political crises—a classic example is the Syro-Macedonian pact of 203–2 against Egypt—which afforded the Senate the occasion and the incentive to intervene with the Roman legions. In this world the Senate's role was always decisive, but not always predominant. Hence a study of the years from Cannae to Pydna cannot but suffer from being cramped within the conventional limits of 'Roman History'; it is, indeed, only by a careful analysis of the parallel objectives and policies of the Hellenistic states, and in particular of the men who directed them, that one is able to reach satisfactory conclusions about this complicated period of Roman expansion.

For the years covered by the reign of Philip V a vast literature exists, from which it is not easy to separate what concerns Macedon from what is, so to speak, common ground. My primary debt to Holleaux will be apparent on almost every page; for the rest, I have tried to make my individual acknowledgements in the footnotes, and must be satisfied here with mentioning the last two volumes of De Sanctis's *Storia dei Romani*. I have, however, the pleasant duty of acknowledging personal obligations. To Mr G. T. Griffith, who, as one of the examiners for the Hare Prize, 1939, read these pages in their first form, I owe many valuable suggestions and criticisms which have led to the clarification and amplification of more than one passage. Both Dr W. W. Tarn and Dr J. V. A. Fine generously allowed me to read in manuscript and make full use of important forthcoming articles, dealing with Philip's parentage and the background of the Social War respectively. Mr C. F. Edson has given me the benefit of his recent work on the Macedonian inscriptions and has kept me informed of fresh material. And my friend Dr Piero Treves has helped me ungrudgingly in the thankless task of proof-reading. I owe many last-minute corrections, emendations of detail and changes of emphasis to his keen eye and his wide and sensitive knowledge of the Hellenistic world. To all five I take this opportunity of tendering my sincerest thanks. Lastly I am grateful to the University of Liverpool for financial assistance towards the cost of the plates and maps, and to the Syndics and staff of the Cambridge University Press for their constant help and courtesy during the time this book was in their hands.

One word more. I am under no illusion of having drawn a picture of Philip V that is in any way final. Every year new discoveries are constantly helping us to fill in this and the other feature, to sharpen the perspective and even to remove the accretions of a faulty tradition. Historical science, no less than history itself, represents a continual process of integration; and the validity of any formulation is directly related to the contemporary state of knowledge. Realising this, all I venture to hope, therefore, is that I have assembled and in some degree synthesised what is at present known about Philip V of Macedon.

F. W. W.

Liverpool

February 1940

FOREWORD TO THE 1967 EDITION

Published in a limited edition in the early days of the Second World War, this book was very soon out of print and it has been virtually unobtainable for almost twenty years. I am grateful to Archon Books for reprinting it and also for giving me the opportunity to correct a few misprints and errors which I have noted over the years. Since the book was first published a certain amount of new material has become available. For example, new light has been thrown on Philip V's religious policy by the publication of the letter to the Athenians on Lemnos, mentioned on p. 288 (n. 1 A (k))[1]; more is now known about Philip's relations with Olympichus, who is shown by various newly discovered inscriptions to have been active from the beginning of Philip's reign (p. 116)[2]; the discovery of a copy of the Romano-Aetolian treaty from the First Macedonian War (p. 83) has supplemented our literary sources and created new problems[3]; a recent study of the topography of

[1] Cf. Accame, *Riv. fil.* lxix, 1941, 179–93; Fraser and McDonald, *JRS*, xlii, 1952, 81–3.

[2] Cf. A. Vogliano, Acme, 1948, 389–90; J. Crampe, *Opusc. Atheniensia*, 3, 1960, 99–104; (Nine Greek inscriptions of Labraunda' in A. Westholm, *Labraunda: Swedish Excavations and Researches*, i. 2 (Lund, 1963), 121–33.

[3] G. Klaffenbach ,*S.-B. Berlin*, 1954, no. 1; *IG*, ix.^{2}1.241; *SEG*, xiii. 382; McDonald, *JRS*, xlvi, 1956, 153–7.

Epirus has led to a revised account of the campaign and battle in the Aous narrows between Philip and Flamininus (pp. 148–53)[4]; and the events between the Peace of Phoenice and the outbreak of the Second Macedonian War, together with the motivation of Roman policy, have received continual attention.[5] It would have been tempting to revise *Philip V of Macedon*, taking all these and other points into account; but the method of reproduction necessarily adopted excludes the possibility of extensive changes, and the loss is perhaps not serious, for when it is added up the new material hardly alters other than marginally the picture which I have attempted to draw of Philip's character, aims and achievement—a picture which still seems to me to be valid and convincing. In any case, if anyone wishes to be brought up to date on details and to be advised of more recent bibliography, he will find both in my *Historical Commentary on Polybius* (Oxford: Clarendon Press), one volume of which appeared in 1957 and a second, going down to the outbreak of the war between Rome and Antiochus, is due to appear almost immediately.

F. W. W.

Liverpool, 1967

[4] Cf. N. G. L. Hammond, *JRS*, lvi, 1966, 39–54.
[5] See e.g. my discussion in *JRS*, liii, 1963, 1–13.

CORRECTIONS

P. 16, n. 1, line 1: *for* iv, 85, 6 *read* iv, 85, 3.

P. 18, n. 2, line 2: *for* Tarn *read* Holleaux.

P. 40, n. 4, line 2: *for* 219 *read* 220.

P. 45, n. 4: *for* 178, n. 1 *read* 176, n. 1.

P. 48, line 16: *for* Dyme *read* Pharae.

P. 57, line 29: *for* 1300 *read* 2200.

P. 61, line 28: *for* try to execute *read* try and execute.

P. 88, n. 1, lines 2–3: *read* cf. Niese, II, 48, n. 3; Holleaux, 16 seq.

P. 94, line 21: *for* Boeotia *read* Euboea.

P. 116, n. 5, line 1: *for* Perinthus *read* Cius.

P. 132, n. 1: omit the reference to Cretan coins, which belong to the first century: cf. Raven, *Num. Chron.* 1938, 133–58.

P. 153, n. 1, line 1: *for* XXXII, 4, 3 *read* XXXIII, 4, 3.

P. 186, n. 1, line 1: *for* XXX, 20, 8 *read* XXXIII, 20, 8.

P. 189, n. 7: *for* Diod. XXVIII. 13 *read* Diod. XXVIII, 12.

P. 218, n. 3: *for* XXI, 45, 9 *read* XXI, 46, 9.

P. 236, n. 4: *for* XLII, 12, 12 *read* XLII, 12, 10.

P. 278, line 16: *for* hostages *read* detainees.

P. 290, n. 3: omit the reference, XVI, 19, 7.

P. 291, line 3: *for* fleet *read* dockyards.

P. 293, line 6: *for* Polyb. VII, 13 seq. *read* Polyb. VIII, 13 seq.

P. 295, n. 7: *for* Tarn *read* Holleaux.

P. 300, n. 7, line 2: *for* III, 2, 44 *read* III, 2, 414 and 440.

P. 311, line 24: *for* *prevastato* read *pervastato*.

P. 347, lines 27–8: omit the words 'in Pelagonia'.

P. 353, line 1: *for* Aymard, G *read* Aymard, A.

Chapter I : Introduction

§1. THE REALM OF MACEDON[1]

FOR fifty years after the death of Alexander the Great, the Eastern Mediterranean with its adjacent lands was undergoing the birth-pangs of a new age. When at length the unwieldy empire of Alexander settled down into its new form, Macedon itself proved to have changed far less fundamentally than either of the rival kingdoms which had been set up in Egypt and Syria. There Macedonian dynasties had had to impose their government upon foreign subjects, differing from themselves in culture and economic and social development; but the Antigonids acquired a Macedon not vitally different from that of Philip II, and a people of their own blood and outlook;[2] and if the wars had been a severe drain on the man-power of the land, many had returned rich,[3] and the gaps in a prolific population had to some extent been filled.[4]

The predominance of the monarchy in Macedon goes back to the fifth or early fourth century, when one of the kings— his identity is uncertain[5]—instituted a popular infantry force of πεζέταιροι from among the free yeomanry who composed the mass of the people. In this force the king acquired not only an instrument of Macedonian expansion, but also a check on the power of the aristocracy, whose cavalry had hitherto provided

[1] For this section see in particular Beloch, IV, I, 272 seq.; Tarn, 167 seq.; Geyer, P–W, 'Makedonia', cols. 680 seq., 769 seq.; P. Zancan, 110 seq., 130; Momigliano, Athen. XIII, 1935, 3 seq.

[2] For the survival of national Macedonian characteristics under the Antigonids see Kaerst, II, 330 seq.

[3] Cf. Arrian, VII, 12; Diod. XVIII, 16, 4; Justin. XII, 12, 7–10 for the 10,000 men sent back with a talent each by Alexander.

[4] Tarn, Greeks in Bactria, 70, n. 5, thinks Macedon was perhaps irremediably depopulated.

[5] Anaximenes of Lampsacus (FGH, II, A, 72, F. 4) ascribes the institution of both ἑταῖροι and πεζέταιροι to 'Alexander'; this may be Alexander II (369–8)—so Jacoby, FGH, II, C, 107, and Granier, 9—or (more probably) Alexander I Philhellene (c. 480), as is assumed by Ferguson, Gnomon, XI, 1935, 520, Costanzi, Athen. VIII, 1930, 164, and Momigliano, ibid. XIII, 1935, 3; Filippo il Macedone, 8 seq. Emendations have, however, been suggested, to 'Philippos' (Kaerst, I, 193; Plaumann, P–W, ''Εταῖροι', col. 1378) or 'Archelaos' (Köhler, Berlin S.B. 1893, 493 seq.: Beloch, III, I², 23; Geyer, P–W, 'Makedonia', col. 713). In any case, Ferguson, loc. cit., is right in regarding the ἑταῖροι as the earlier body (cf. Granier, 6).

the only military force.[1] The strength which this new citizen-army afforded the monarchy[2] was reflected in the popular right, which it inherited, to acclaim each new king upon his accession,[3] even though in practice the throne was hereditary; and further, custom gave it the power to act as a supreme court in cases of high treason.[4] Nevertheless, with foreign policy in his own hands, a strong king did not need to pay great attention to its embryo powers.

The administration of Macedon, moreover, was centralised in Pella, and the local governors were appointed directly by the king; thus it is, as Tarn observes,[5] incorrect to describe the system as feudal. Under the Antigonids *strategoi* controlled the outer provinces of Macedonia proper, and *epistatai* (helped by *dicastai*) the subject districts and the important towns, Greek and Macedonian.[6] The royal council itself—Alexander's οἱ ἀμφ᾽

[1] Geyer, *op. cit.* col. 712 *seq.*; Momigliano, *Athen.* XIII, 1935, 8–9.

[2] This citizen-army was called up at need; but permanent garrisoning, etc., was usually entrusted to mercenaries; cf. Griffith, 67 *seq.*

[3] Appian, *Syr.* 54; Plut. *Demet.* 18; cf. Beloch, IV, 1, 379–80.

[4] Cf. Arr. III, 26; IV, 14, 3; Diod. XVIII, 37, 2; XIX, 51, 1; Plut. *Alex.* 55, 3; *Eumen.* 8, 3; Curt. VI, 8, 25; Polyb. V, 27, 5 *seq.*; 29, 6. See Tarn, *Ant. Gon.* 189 ('certain obscure rights'); *CAH*, VI, 390; Granier, 42 *seq.*; cf. however Ferguson, *Gnomon*, XI, 1935, 522, 'The kings did not submit cases of alleged treason to it (*sc.* the Macedonian army) when they thought it unsafe to do so. It took no action when...Philip V executed Apelles and Leontius without trial.'

[5] *Op. cit.* 190, against Wilamowitz, *Staat und Gesellschaft²*, 1923, 143.

[6] The *strategos* was primarily a military officer in a specific area, though he might operate with a town as his sphere (cf. Heuss, *Stadt und Herrscher*, 17–29); the term *epistates* covers officers with functions varying from place to place (cf. Holleaux, *BCH*, LVII, 1933, 26 *seq.*; Heuss, *op. cit.* 29–35). For the evidence relating to Macedon see Tarn, 195. Under Philip a *strategos* (*praetor*) is mentioned for Paeonia (Livy (P) XL, 21, 9; 23, 2); and this position is probably referred to elsewhere, e.g. Polyb. V, 96, 4: Ἀλέξανδρος ὁ τεταγμένος πι τῆς Φωκίδος (cf. *Syll.* 552); Polyb. XXII, 13, 3: Ὀνόμαστον τὸν ἐπὶ Θράκης τεταγμένον. (Heuss, *loc. cit.*, claims that the Jason who in 218 was placed by Alexander in charge of Phanoteus (Polyb. V, 96, 4) was also a *strategos*; but it seems improbable that the authority to make such appointments was delegated.) For *epistatai* under Philip see Polyb. V, 26, 5 (Thessaly and Macedonia); perhaps Polyb. XXII, 13, 4 (Cassander at Maronea); Makaronas, *AE*, 1934–5, 117 *seq.* (Archippus, *epistates* at 'Greia' (otherwise unknown); inscription found between Kosane and Verria, at Koilada); Livy (P) XXVIII, 6, 1 (Plator, probably *epistates* at Oreus). Pelekides, 6, has an inscription mentioning (line 23) an *epistates* at Thessalonica, and also *dikastai* (cf. *IG*, XI, 4, 1053 (Thessalonica), where Pelekides also restores οἱ δικασταί); and another earlier example of an *epistates* with a Macedonian city as his sphere of operation is the Harpalus, governor of Beroea, to whom Demetrius II addressed a letter, while crown prince (*Syll.* 459; cf. Edson, *Harv. Stud.* XLV, 1934, 227 *seq.*; Pelekides, 12, n. 3). Philip also left *epistatai* in Caria; cf.

αὐτὸν ἑταῖροι and the φίλοι of the Antigonid court—formed an advisory body and in some respects a civil service;[1] but it had no rights beyond those of advising, and under a forceful king could be rendered of little importance.

Nevertheless, the king of Macedon was not an absolute monarch, but had his powers increasingly modified by other sources of authority within the state. Of these the most important was the army-assembly, which had exerted its influence in the chaotic years following Alexander's death;[2] and since it was recruited by districts, it seems probable that it encouraged the persistence of some kind of regional patriotism. For while it is true that, by the time of Alexander, the absorption of the outlying districts into Macedon was almost complete,[3] there is evidence of a strong regional sense in these parts which potentially, though by no means inevitably, conflicted with national loyalty. Thus as late as the time of Sellasia[4] a man could describe himself as an inhabitant both of Elimiotis and of Macedon; and the support given to Pyrrhus in 288 by the western provinces points to a degree of separatism at that time.[5]

Early in Antigonus Doson's reign, the army-assembly succeeded in obtaining constitutional recognition of its semi-independent authority inside the state, probably as the result of a mutiny which took place shortly after Doson assumed the guardianship of the young heir, Philip.[6] Confronting the mutinous army, Doson pointed out his services in subduing Dardania and recovering the greater part of Thessaly from the Aetolians,[7] and threatened to 'hand back the state'. The bluff succeeded,

Holleaux, *BCH*, xxviii, 1904, 346 and 358; Persson, *BCH*, xlvi, 1922, 395 (doubtful, cf. Roussel, *REG*, xxxvii, 1924, 355); and a recently found inscription (Laumonier, *BCH*, lviii, 1934, 291–8; see below, p. 116, n. 3) shows a native dynast, Olympichus of Alinda, acting there as his *strategos* (*c.* 201).

[1] E.g. the post of Megaleas under Philip (Polyb. iv, 87, 8: ἐπὶ τοῦ γραμματείου). The ἑταῖροι did not survive the break-up of the empire; their place is taken under the Antigonids by φίλοι: Polyb. v, 2, 1; 16, 5; 22, 8; xxvii, 8, 1 (cf. Ferguson, *Gnomon*, xi, 1935, 521). On one occasion Philip employs the φίλοι as a court for high treason (v, 16, 5–8); and a recently found inscription (Roussel, *Rev. Arch.* iii⁶, 1934, 39 *seq.*, col. iii) shows them acting as judges in the distribution of booty.

[2] Cf. Zancan, 35 *seq.*; on the army-assembly in general see Granier.

[3] Tarn, 177.

[4] *GDI*, 2765 (date: 222, Pomtow).   [5] Tarn, 185.

[6] Justin. xxviii, 3, 11 *seq.*; Plut. *Aem. Paull.* 8; Porphyry, *FGH*, ii, B, 260, F. 3, 14.   [7] See below, p. 11.

4   INTRODUCTION

the army withdrew its opposition and Doson became king. However, the evidence of inscriptions which appeared shortly afterwards suggests that Doson's triumph was less complete than Justinus would have us believe; for these speak not merely of βασιλεὺς Μακεδών or βασιλεὺς Μακεδόνων, but also of βασιλεὺς καὶ Μακεδόνες,[1] thus giving official recognition to the Macedonians as a constituent body. Now admittedly this change brought no increase of real power to the army-assembly;[2] but by recognising it constitutionally as an element in the state, it set the seal of authority on such powers as it already enjoyed. 'A divergence that had been traditional now acquired the sanction of law.'[3]

It was probably at the same time that the Macedonians obtained recognition as a 'league'. A Delian inscription[4] refers to τὸ κοινὸν Μ[ακε]δόν[ων], thus showing that in some form or other the Macedonian people were, towards the end of the third century, a 'league';[5] and Tarn associates the founding of this κοινόν with the incident of Doson and the mutinous army.[6] Earlier dates have been proposed; thus Zancan follows Beloch[7] in placing its institution at the time of the anarchy which followed the death of Ptolemy Ceraunus. But the only other evidence for the existence of the κοινόν is the entry of the Macedonians into

---

[1] Evidence: *Syll.* 518 (Doson's dedication on Delos after Sellasia), Polyb. VII, 9, 1; cf. 9, 5; 9, 7 (Philip's treaty with Hannibal), and four non-Macedonian records, *OGIS*, 283 (Attalus's dedication after Chios), Polyb. XVIII, 46, 5 (the Isthmus proclamation) and two Latin inscriptions commemorating the defeat of Perseus (*Dess.* 8884: *L. Aimilius L.f. Imperator de rege Perse Macedonibusque cepet; CIL*, I², p. 48, XXVII (acta triumph. Capit.); *L. Aimilius...ex Macedon. et rege Perse*). Two other inscriptions, *AJA*, XI, 1896, 582 *seq.*, no. 67, and *GDI*, 5043 (probably dating to Doson's reign; cf. Tarn, 471), also show traces of this formula, but are very fragmentary; and Plut. *Moralia*, 197 F: τοῦ πρὸς Περσέα καὶ Μακεδόνας πολέμου is perhaps in a different category; see further Dow and Edson, *Harv. Stud.* XLVIII, 1937, 128 *seq.*
[2] Ferguson, *Gnomon*, XI, 1935, 522: 'It (*sc.* the army-assembly) was...an organisation dependent on the king for its convocation and agenda, and destitute of constitutional remedies when its rights were ignored.'
[3] Zancan, 111.
[4] *Syll.* 575 (restored by Dittenberger); cf. Durrbach, *Choix d'insc. de Délos*, I, 71, no. 55.
[5] See Tarn, *Hellen. Civil.*² 45; *CAH*, VII, 751; *JHS*, XXIX, 1909, 269; *CQ*, XVIII, 1924, 21; Zancan, 110 *seq.*; Treves, *Athen.* XII, 1934, 395; XIII, 1935, 52-4. De Sanctis's argument (IV, 1, 9, n. 26; cf. *Riv. Fil.* LXIII, 1935, 421) that the κοινόν was an association of Macedonian residents on Delos is to be rejected.
[6] *Ant. Gon.* 54, n. 36; 390, n. 61; *JHS*, XLI, 1921, 16-17; cf. Treves, *Athen.* XIII, 1935, 53-4.   [7] IV, 1, 383.

the Symmachy of Leagues set up by Doson in 224–3,[1] and certainly there is nothing to support so early a date as Beloch's for its foundation. Equally uncertain is the exact meaning of the word κοινόν in this context. A recent theory[2] connects this Macedonian League with the old army-assembly, but assumes some influence from the urban centres which, as we shall see, had arisen as a hybrid element, half Macedonian and half Greek. Probably, too, it is to be associated with the regionalism, which played so important a part in economic developments during the last decade of Philip's reign, when the local units—corresponding roughly to the cantons of the leagues of north Greece[3]—were granted, along with the cities, special autonomous rights of coining.[4]

The cities, however, formed an exceptional category within the general economy of Macedon. The majority of the Macedonian population were free peasant cultivators or cattle farmers,[5] as yet largely unaffected by the wide spread of slavery,[6] which was common to the whole of the Greek world after Alexander.[7] The possession of land in Macedon rested upon a grant from the king, and carried with it the duty of serving in the army.[8] Once there had been vast royal estates, and, in spite of the many gifts of Philip II and Alexander,[9] large remnants of these, farmed by tenants, existed in the time of Perseus;[10] it has been suggested that the 100,000 *medimni* of corn given by Queen Chryseis to Rhodes, after the great earthquake of *c.* 227,[11] and the corn accumulated by Perseus,[12] came from these private lands. But,

[1] Polyb. IV, 9, 4 (rejected unnecessarily by Treves, *Athen.* XIII, 1935, 52).
[2] Zancan, 113.   [3] Tarn, 52–3.
[4] See below, pp. 224; 265 *seq.*   [5] Tarn, 190.
[6] Cf. Beloch, IV, 1, 304, for the growth of slavery even in the more backward districts. For the existence of some slaves in Macedon under Philip V cf. Polyb. XXIII, 1, 11.
[7] The sending back of captured Greek mercenaries to work in the Macedonian mines (Arrian, 1, 16, 6) is a special case which does not affect the general rule.
[8] This was a general duty; cf. Momigliano, *Athen.* XIII, 1935, 3 *seq.*, for a criticism of Hampl's legalistic attempt to distinguish between wars of defence which involved the whole people, and foreign wars, in which, he claims, the people fought for the king virtually as mercenaries.
[9] Cf. Plut. *Alex.* 15, 2; *Syll.* 332.   [10] Cicero, *de leg. agr.* II, 19, 51.
[11] Polyb. V, 89, 7; cf. Beloch, IV, 1, 343; Holleaux, *REG*, XXXVI, 1923, 480–98 (=1, 445–62); Hiller v. Gaertringen, *P-W*, Suppl.-B. V, 'Rhodos', col. 785.
[12] Livy (P) XLII, 12, 8; Plut. *Aem. Paull.* 8, 8; 28, 2.

by the third century, lots had become alienable,[1] and the way was open, as at Sparta, to the accumulation of land in a few hands. The failure of the nobles to attain any such political power as belonged to the Athenian *pentacosiomedimni* at the time of Solon suggests, it is true, that this power had not advanced very far; on the other hand, it is significant that land was possessed by cities such as Beroea.[2]

In essentials, then, the social organisation of Macedon in the third century was that of a self-sufficient agricultural community, still scarcely affected by the impact of foreign trade. From the military point of view, this meant that large-scale operations of the citizen-army could only be carried out at the expense of the country's agriculture (for though women might to some extent deputise in the fields, the probability is that, as in the Balkans to-day, adequate cultivation required the constant attention of both sexes). Hence the Antigonids were always reluctant to prolong their campaigns, and winter demobilisation was the rule;[3] and since, moreover, the comparative poverty of Macedon was an automatic check on the enrolling of mercenaries, this economic factor assumed peculiar importance during any period of continuous campaigning.

To this self-sufficient agricultural system there were, however, already important exceptions. Two main sources of income in Macedon were the mines and forests, and both were state (i.e. royal) monopolies.[4] Admittedly, the alluvial gold, which had been so great a source of wealth in the fourth century, had now given out;[5] though some gold may still have been mined inside Macedon,[6] the chief mineral products were now silver, iron and lead.[7] But the extraction of these metals and the trade in timber and pitch from the forests were left mainly in the king's hands,[8] and constituted an important part of the national revenue; at the same time this retarded the rise of a trading class and the

---

[1] Cf. *Syll.* 332 (Cassander's decree).

[2] The letter sent by Demetrius II, when crown prince, to Harpalus, probably the *epistates* of Beroea (see above, p. 2, n. 6) refers to πολιτικαί πρόσοδοι.   [3] Cf. Griffith, 65, 67–8.

[4] Beloch, IV, 1, 343 *seq.*; Geyer, *op. cit.* col. 680 *seq.*; Tarn, 187 *seq.*; Glotz, *REG*, XXIX, 1916, 318 *seq.*   [5] Perdrizet, *Klio*, X, 1910, 1; 25–7; Tarn, 188.

[6] There was still gold to be mined in Macedon in 167; cf. Livy (P) XLV, 29, 11: *metalla quoque auri atque argenti non exerceri, ferri et aeris permitti*.

[7] Cf. Polyb. v, 89, 6–7.

[8] For the monopoly trade in timber and pitch see the epigraphical and literary material quoted by Geyer, *op. cit.* col. 680.

development of the usual features of third-century Greek economy.

It was inside this system that the cities of Macedon formed a group of economic enclaves. Ever since the fifth century, when the Macedonian kings had begun to stress their connections with Argos and had adopted a philhellenic policy,[1] towns such as Beroea, Pella and Edessa, on the Hellenic model, had existed in Macedon; and though nothing is known of their original status, by the third century they were enjoying a semi-autonomous position inside the kingdom. Pella, for instance, could pass decrees in its own name;[2] and, as we saw, cities might possess land.[3] At the same time their citizens remained Macedonians, and inscriptions bear the name of the city or the nation, quite arbitrarily;[4] and though they may have served as focal points

[1] Cf. Geyer, op. cit. col. 698; Thuc. II, 99, 3.

[2] Pella granted ἀσυλία to the temple of Asclepius at Cos (cf. Tarn, 184). L. Laurenzi, Historia, v, 1931, 620–21 (cf. Segre, Riv. Fil. LXI, 1933, 367, n. 3; LXII, 1934, 181) has now found evidence for similar grants by Amphipolis, Cassandreia and Philippi, dated 242 (Gonatas's 41st year). On the degree of civic independence shown in these decrees, see P. Collart, Philippes, ville de Macédoine (Paris, 1937), 181–2.

[3] See above, p. 6, n. 2. Immediately before the third Macedonian war with Rome, civitates Macedoniae sent embassies to offer Perseus contributions of corn and money (Livy (P) XLII, 53; cf. Costanzi, Athen. VIII, 1930, 161); this may be evidence of the independent status of the Macedonian towns: on the other hand, the civitates may be the Greek coastal towns (Tarn, 184, n. 54).

[4] Tarn, 184, n. 54. From the point of view of the cities themselves a distinction was apparently drawn between the local citizen and the Macedonian from another part of the kingdom. Philip's letter to Archippus (see above, p. 2, n. 6) grants Nicanor, a tetrarch, the land of Corrhagus, son of Perdiccas, τῶν ἐγ Γρήιαι μετοίκων. What is the meaning of μέτοικος in this context? It might be argued that in a letter from Philip it represents a status inferior to full Macedonian citizenship, and that Greia has a purely local significance. But it is difficult to see how Corrhagus, son of Perdiccas (both well-attested Macedonian names: cf. Berve, Das Alexanderreich, II, nos. 444–5, 626–8), could be anything but a full Macedonian citizen. It therefore seems probable that his inferior status relates to Greia, and that as a stranger from another part of Macedon, cultivating (it appears) neighbouring royal land, Corrhagus was reckoned a resident alien in the city. This certainly suggests a degree of independence in a very insignificant Macedonian city not elsewhere attested, and rather recalling the position inside federal states (cf. Busolt-Swoboda, II, 1315, for οἱ ἐν Αἰτωλίᾳ πολιτεύοντες (IG, XII, 2, 15; 5, 526), Aetolian citizens not attributed to any town; Aymard, Assemblées, 110 seq. for Achaea); it also prompts the query whether every Macedonian had normally a πόλις or ἔθνος citizenship as well as his national rank as a Macedonian. On our present evidence these questions cannot, perhaps, be satisfactorily answered. Meanwhile there is no foundation for Welles's suggestion (AJA, XLII, 1938, 248) that by accepting Greian citizenship Corrhagus would have lost status as a Macedonian. See further, below, p. 265.

for the local patriotism, which obtained its recognition in the κοινὸν Μακεδόνων,[1] there is no evidence of any divergence of interest between these cities and the monarchy.

The position of the Greek towns was rather different. Originally independent, they had been forcibly absorbed into Macedon, where they continued to form social and economic, if no longer political units. In general they were loyal to the king, and on occasions their inhabitants called themselves Macedonians;[2] but their peculiar status is shown by the fact that whereas the usual tax throughout Macedon was based on land,[3] from the fourth century onwards harbour dues existed as an additional impost for these coastal cities.[4] After Alexander new towns appeared. Cassander established his large port at Cassandreia and amalgamated twenty-six villages farther up the coast to form Thessalonica;[5] and though the Antigonids were not famed as founders of cities, a few were set up by Gonatas as centres of administration rather than trade. However, Greek or Macedonian, all these cities fall together into a special category, with interests different in kind from those of agricultural Macedon; and this cleavage was subsequently to prove a factor of some political importance.[6]

The citizen-army, the regional areas with their κοινόν, the cities—these were the main checks on absolutism, when Philip succeeded to the throne of Macedon. They presented him with three possible courses of action. By strength of personality he might dominate his people and prevent their theoretical rights

[1] On the close connection between the Macedonian city and the surrounding countryside see Hampl, 79. Edson, *Harv. Stud.* XLV, 1934, 236 *seq.*, has an interesting analysis of the part played by Beroea in its separatist support of Pyrrhus in 288.

[2] E.g. *GDI*, 2762 (Arethusa); *GDI*, 2764 and *IG*, XII, 9, 199 (Amphipolis); *AE*, 1914, 183, no. 242 ('Αρκυνία: if indeed this otherwise unknown town is Greek and not Macedonian). But the essentially Greek nature of these towns persisted, as can be seen from the worship of Philip V in the Greek manner at Amphipolis (Perdrizet, *BCH*, XVII, 1894, 416: inscription in which Alcaeus, son of Heracleides (i.e. a Greek), couples Philip with Isis and Sarapis).

[3] Plut. *Aem. Paull.* 28, 6; Livy (P) XLV, 18, 7; 29, 4; though direct evidence is lacking, this tax must plainly have been of ancient standing. Its yield was small.

[4] *Syll.* 135; [Aristot.] *Econom.* II, 22, 1350a; cf. Momigliano, *Filippo*, 51 *seq.*

[5] *Cassandreia*: Diod. XIX, 52, 1; Strabo, VII, 330, fr. 25; Pausan. V, 23, 2; Steph. Byz. *s.v. Thessalonica*: Strabo, VII, 330, fr. 21. 24; Steph. Byz. *s.v.*

[6] See below, pp. 265 *seq.*

from growing into a real political force; he might weakly allow the κοινόν and the regionalism which it embodied to develop into something approaching the genuine leagues of Greece; or, finally, he might continue to acknowledge its rights on paper until such time as he could utilise them to his own ends, and by well-timed concessions secure new forms of support to consolidate his position and his policy. This was Philip's main political problem within his own realm. But at the same time he inherited very close associations with Greece, in part complementary to his position at home, in part obscuring the questions of internal policy with a series of new problems, which often had their focal point outside Macedon. In the next section, therefore, we must consider shortly the foreign policy of Philip's immediate predecessors, and the frontiers of the Macedon they bequeathed to him.

§ 2. PHILIP'S EARLY YEARS[1]

Late in 240 or early in 239 B.C. Demetrius II succeeded Antigonus Gonatas on the throne of Macedon;[2] and about the same time Pyrrhus's son, Alexander, died, leaving the kingdom of Epirus in the weak hands of his widow and half-sister Olympias and her two sons. Threatened by the Aetolians, Olympias turned for aid to Macedon, and Demetrius sealed a compact to help her, in a marriage alliance which brought her daughter Phthia (or Chryseis, as she was familiarly known) to Pella as his queen. However, neither this marriage, nor yet a second between the princess Nereis and Gelon of Syracuse, could save the house of Pyrrhus; its remnants were swept away in the republican revolution of 233, Phthia's sister Deidamia was butchered by the people of Ambracia, and the young son of Demetrius and Phthia, the prince Philip, born in 238,[3] was

---

[1] References in this section have been restricted in general to standard modern works.

[2] Cf. Tarn, *Ant. Gon.* 409; *CAH*, VII, 744; Beloch, IV, 2, 121. In *Phthia-Chryseis* (to be published in 1940) Tarn points out that Gonatas's death cannot be accurately dated to any month in 240-39; in assigning it definitely to 240 Dinsmoor (p. 108) is basing his calculations on Beloch's discredited theory (IV, 2, 113; 256) that in about 200 the Roman consular year ran from August to August.

[3] For this date see below, Appendix III, p. 295. If the alliance was a reply to the Aetolian move on Acarnania, it will not have preceded Gonatas's

soon the only surviving member of the Epirote line outside Sicily.

Demetrius's reign had been one of constant warfare, first against the Aetolians and the Achaeans, and then on the northern frontier, in the struggle against the Dardanians, which eventually cost him his life.[1] When in the spring of 229[2] he died, leaving as sole heir a boy of eight, it was a critical situation for Macedon. Fortunately the country found its saviour in Antigonus Doson, a cousin of Demetrius, who assumed the guardianship of Philip, married his mother Phthia-Chryseis[3] and, as *strategos*,[4] set about the immediate task of reorganisation. First he had to expel the Dardanians from the northern districts;[5] and though he contented himself with clearing the lower Axius valley, and left the barbarians in possession of Bylazora, the capital of Paeonia,[6] he evidently secured a decisive victory. At any rate, there is no record of further trouble on these frontiers until Doson is occupied, some six years later, in the Peloponnese; and even then it was the Illyrians, and not the Dardanians, who burst into the northern provinces.[7]

The Dardanians were not, however, Doson's only neighbours

death (cf. Tarn, *CAH*, VII, 733); and as Philip was born in 238, the marriage must have been in 239. On Philip's parentage see Tarn, *CQ*, XVIII, 1924, 17 *seq.*; *Phthia-Chryseis*; Fine, *CQ*, XXVIII, 1934, 99 *seq.*; Treves, *Athen.* XII, 1934, 408–9; Dow and Edson, *Harv. Stud.* XLVIII, 1937, 127–80. The ancient authorities (Justin. XXVIII, 3, 9–10; Plut. *Aem.Paull.*8, 3; Euseb. *Chronica* (ed. Schoene), I, 237, 238; Porphyry, *FGH*, II, B, 260, F. 3, 14; *Etym. Magn. s.v.* Δώσων) all suggest that Philip's mother was Chryseis, whereas inscriptions make it clear that she was Phthia; in his forthcoming paper Dr Tarn shows to my satisfaction (and, as Mr Edson kindly informs me by letter, to his also) that Phthia and Chryseis were one and the same person, Chryseis being a familiar nickname that won popular currency and eventually ousted the princess's real name in the majority of the written sources.

[1] On Demetrius see Treves, *Rend. Linc.* 1932, 167–205.
[2] See below, Appendix III, p. 295.
[3] According to Plut. *Aem.Paull.*8, 3, Doson was married to his predecessor's widow by οἱ πρῶτοι Μακεδόνων, who feared anarchy; Justin. XXVIII, 3, 9–10, suggests that the marriage was a move of Doson himself, who *regem se constitui laborat*. It is difficult to say which of these two indifferent sources is the more accurate. But, at least, Tarn's exposure of the worthlessness of Eusebius (in *Phthia-Chryseis*) makes it no longer possible to prefer this writer's account that Doson married Chryseis only when he was elevated to the throne.
[4] Plut. *Aem. Paull.* 8, 3.   [5] See Bettingen, 17 *seq.*
[6] Bylazora is probably about the site of the modern Köprülü; cf. Geyer, *op. cit.* col. 661–2.
[7] Polyb. II, 70, 6.

to take advantage of the dynastic crisis. Boeotia wavered, torn between rival factions, Athens declared her independence, and a number of Peloponnesian tyrants resigned their power and united their cities to the Achaean League.[1] Worse still, the Aetolians, already foes to Macedon, hastily annexed the Thessalian provinces of Phthiotic Achaea, Phthiotis, Thessaliotis and Hestiaeotis;[2] and though Doson recovered the three latter districts almost at once,[3] the agreement which he made with Aetolia left Phthiotic Achaea in her hands for the rest of his reign. These events appear to have been followed, probably in the late winter of 228–7,[4] by the mutiny in the Macedonian army already described;[5] and as a sequel to this outbreak, which may have been due to war exhaustion,[6] Doson assumed the full rights of kingship. The concessions which he made to the Macedonian people have already been indicated.

Meanwhile the eastern and western frontiers remained quiet. On the east Macedon stretched as far as Mt Rhodope, on the west it reached Lake Lychnidus, and, beyond that, included certain Dassaretian towns, in particular Antipatreia (mod.

---

[1] Cf. Holleaux, 121; Flacelière, 248 seq.

[2] Beloch, IV, 2, 409, 412–17.

[3] See Fine, TAPhA, LVIII, 1932, 133 seq.; CW, XXXII, 1938, 91; Treves, Athen. XII, 1934, 396, 407–8; contra Lenschau, Bursian, 1936, 166; Klaffenbach, Klio, XXXII, 1939, 201, n. 1. For the agreement with Aetolia see Polyb. II, 45, 2. An echo of this fighting in Thessaly may have survived in Frontin. Strat. II, 6, 5; cf. Droysen, III, 2, 67; contra, Niese, II, 287 and Bauer, 66, n. 1.

[4] Dow and Edson, Harv. Stud. XLVIII, 1937, 172 seq. argue plausibly for the view that Doson was strategos (and not king) for three years, this fact being the source of the error in Eusebius, who states that Doson reigned twelve years (i.e. three years as strategos added to nine for the reign as a whole). Tarn's criticisms of Eusebius's account do not, it should be observed, apply to his chronology, weak though that often is. But to accept Dow and Edson's thesis does not necessarily mean bringing Doson's elevation to the throne down to autumn 227 (as they claim). If we assume that the Macedonian calendar was at this time running true to the sun (see below, Appendix III, p. 297, n. 2), Doson's first year as epitropos or strategos would end in September 229, and his second in September 228; any subsequent months would be reckoned as part of his third year. Therefore the seditio of Justin. XXVIII, 3, 11, may have occurred at any time later than September 228; and since, as Fine has convincingly shown (AJPh, LXI, 1940, 143 seq.), Doson's Carian expedition was in 227, and he will hardly have left Macedon as late as July, his assumption of the crown was probably about the end of winter 228–7.

[5] See above, p. 3.

[6] So Fine, AJPh, LXI, 1940, 143. He points out that the Macedonians had been fighting constantly for some years. 'The proposed Carian expedition in 227 was the final straw.'

Berat).[1] The upper valley of the Aous, covering the districts of
Parauaea and Tymphaea, was in the friendly keeping of Epirus,
and not actually part of Doson's possessions;[2] it formed a wedge
between Macedon proper and Atintania, which, after the First
Illyrian War (229–8), constituted part of the Roman protectorate
in Illyria. This war the Romans had undertaken as a piece of
necessary police work against the piracy of Queen Teuta; and
to ensure the permanence of the results, they had decided to
control both shores of the Adriatic, by annexing not only certain
islands, like Issa and Corcyra, but in addition a strip of mainland territory, stretching from just below Lissus in the north to
a point somewhere above Phoenice in the south, and including
the whole valley of the Drynos, southwards from Antigoneia
(mod. Tepeleni).[3] This protectorate, about 120 miles in length
and from 20 to 40 miles in width, marched with Macedonian
territory at one point only, at Antipatreia; and there is no evidence that Doson ever regarded it as a threat.[4] At any rate,
early the very next year (227),[5] he set out in the opposite direction, on a naval expedition to Caria of which both the objects
and details are exceedingly obscure.[6] Most probably it was
intended as a move against Egypt, the old enemy, whose

[1] Fine, *JRS*, xxvi, 1936, 24–7. See also below, p. 291, n. 9.
[2] Fine, *TAPhA*, lviii, 1932, 126–9; *contra* Lenschau, *Bursian*, 1936, 166.
For the older view that the Aous valley was Macedonian from the time of
Pyrrhus see Beloch, iv, 2, 378 *seq.*; Tarn, *CAH*, vii, 96; Fluss, *P–W*, 'Teuta',
map at col. 1147–8. Fine has shown that it cannot be proved that this valley
above the confluence of the Aous and the Drynos ever went back to Macedon.
[3] Holleaux, *Rome*, 104 *seq.*; *CAH*, vii, 835–7; Larsen, *Economic Survey*,
iv, 261–3.
[4] Holleaux, *loc. cit.*, claims that the protectorate was designed partly to
block Macedon; however, the Roman embassies to Aetolia, Achaea, Corinth
and Athens cannot be shown to be anti-Macedonian in intention. Moreover,
Doson was too occupied at this time in Paeonia and Thessaly to give the
Romans much thought, still less cause for alarm. On this see the excellent
remarks of M. Cary, 406. For a recent and extreme form of Holleaux's thesis
see Treves, *Athen.* xii, 1934, 380–411; xiii, 1935, 22–56.
[5] For the date see Fine, *AJPh*, lxi, 1940, 143 *seq.*, who refutes Dow and
Edson's attempt to bring it down to 226. The first Achaean appeal to Doson
was in winter 227–6, and since the speech of the Megalopolitan envoys implies
that Boeotia was at that time friendly towards Macedon (Polyb. ii, 49, 6; cf.
Dow and Edson, *Harv. Stud.* xlviii, 1937, 179–80), their visit to Pella must
have been later than the Carian expedition, which coincided with a Boeoto-
Macedonian rapprochement (cf. Polyb. xx, 5, 7 *seq.*).
[6] See Beloch, iv, 1, 683; 2, 548 *seq.*; Tarn, *CAH*, vii, 722; Nicolaus, 79–80;
Bettingen, 21 *seq.*; Treves, *Athen.* xiii, 1935, 37 *seq.*; the expedition is rejected
by Kolbe, *GGA*, 1916, 459–62; Holleaux, *REA*, xxv, 1923, 344, n. 8; *Rev.
Phil.* l, 1926, 56, n. 1; E. Meyer, *Die Grenzen d. hell. St. in Kleinasien*, 161.

activity in Thrace was a constant irritation;[1] but in any case it argues a lack of interest in the Adriatic coast.

This Carian expedition had few lasting results, and what conquests were made Doson probably surrendered a little later to Ptolemy Euergetes, as a bribe to cease his subsidies to Sparta.[2] In the islands, too, there was little activity. Macedonian were Euboea,[3] Peparethos (and Sciathos)[4] and possibly Lemnos (with Imbros),[5] and among the Cyclades Syros, Amorgos, Poiessa on Ceos and the important religious centre of Delos;[6] there is evidence too that Doson possessed Cos;[7] while farther south, in Crete, defensive alliances were struck between Macedon and the towns of Hierapytna and Eleutherna,[8] similar to that between Gortyn and Demetrius II.[9] In addition there may have been other isolated, unrecorded moves. But there was certainly nothing like an attempt at Macedonian suzerainty over the islands; on the contrary, Doson's declining interest in this region is reflected in the rapid decay of the Macedonian fleet after the Carian expedition.[10] For the explanation of this sudden abandonment of a naval policy in the Aegean, it is necessary to turn to the Peloponnese.

Macedonian influence in the south of Greece had never recovered from Gonatas's loss of Acrocorinth to the Achaeans in 243. Ten years later, Demetrius's general Bithys had penetrated the Peloponnese and defeated the Achaeans at Phylace;[11] but

---

[1] Tarn, *CAH*, VII, 719; Treves, *loc. cit.*, regards it as an anti-Syrian move, but cf. Aymard, *REA*, XXXVIII, 1936, 266.

[2] Tarn, *CAH*, VII, 722; against Beloch's view that Doson's Carian conquests were permanent see Nicolaus, 71 *seq.* (with the criticisms of Treves, *Athen.* XIII, 1935, 41). But Macedon may have maintained some connections with Caria, which were strengthened with the decay of Egypt towards the end of the century; see below, p. 116, n. 3.

[3] Polyb. II, 52, 7.   [4] Polyb. X, 42, 1; Livy (P) XXVIII, 5, 10.

[5] For Lemnos see Livy (P) XXVIII, 5, 1, and below, p. 270, n. 6. Imbros usually shared the fate of Lemnos (cf. Fredrich, *P-W*, 'Imbros', col. 1106).

[6] Holleaux, *BCH*, XXXI, 1907, 104; Bettingen, 28–33; Bikerman, *REA*, XL, 1938, 380.

[7] Segre *apud* Treves, *Athen.* XIII, 1935, 56; but on the inconclusiveness of *GDI*, 3611, see Segre, *Riv. Fil.* LXII, 1934, 183–4.

[8] Doublet, *BCH*, XIII, 1899, 47, nos. 1 and 2; cf. Tarn, *JHS*, XXIX, 1909, 268, c; Cardinali, *Riv. Stor. Ant.* IX, 1904, 91–3.   [9] Tarn, 471.

[10] Tarn, *Ant. Gon.* 391; *CAH*, VII, 352; Bettingen, 32; Niese, II, 466; Holleaux, *Rome*, 23; 158–9; *BCH*, XXXI, 1907, 107; *Rev. Phil.* L, 1926, 56, n. 1; 203, n. 2; De Sanctis, III, 1, 298; Pozzi, *Mem. Acc. Torino*, s. II, LXIII, 1912–13, 385; Ormerod, 136, n. 1.

[11] On this battle see Beloch, IV, 2, 529–30; Walbank, 64 *seq.*; Treves, *Athen.* XII, 1934, 401–2; XIII, 1935, 28.

the Dardanian war soon required Macedonian forces in the north, and Demetrius died without recovering anything of what Gonatas had lost.[1] Furthermore, Athens seized the opportunity of his death to declare herself independent, Diogenes, the commander of the garrison, readily surrendering the fortress in return for the 150 talents needed to pay off his mercenaries.[2] At the same time Doson was faced, as we saw, with the defection of a large part of Thessaly to the Aetolian League, while the Boeotians, cut off from Macedon, turned once more towards the Aetolians.

Meanwhile, however, events at Sparta conspired to assist the Macedonian cause in Greece.[3] The spectacular rise of the revolutionary king Cleomenes rapidly developed into a serious threat to the Achaean League. In 229 Cleomenes occupied the Arcadian cities of Tegea, Mantinea, Caphyae and Orchomenus; in 228, having fortified the Athenaeum on the Megalopolitan frontier, he directed raids on Achaean territory and forced the League into a declaration of war. And the next year (227) he further weakened the Achaeans by two victories at Mt Lycaeum and Ladoceia, and followed up his success with a social and political *coup d'état* in the autumn.

Thoroughly alarmed and seeing the need for outside help, Aratus of Sicyon now instituted semi-private negotiations with Doson, through the agency of two Megalopolitans, Cercidas and Nicophanes, who visited Macedon during the winter of 227–6.[4] The crisis which had developed in the Peloponnese, and the possibilities which it possessed for Macedon, thus clearly indicated why Doson should abandon his naval policy in Caria before he had had time to reap its fruits. The weakness of Achaea provided an opportunity to restore Macedon to her old

[1] Boeotia temporarily joined Macedon (Polyb. xx, 5, 3), but wavered for some years. Phocis and Opuntian Locris were Macedonian allies in 224 (Polyb. IV, 9, 4; XI, 5, 4), but they may have gone over after Doson's accession; cf. Flacelière, 280–81; Fine, *AJPh*, LXI, 1940, 151, n. 92.

[2] Tarn, *CAH*, VII, 748; Ferguson, *Hellen. Ath.* 206; Flacelière, 256–7.

[3] On the Cleomenean War see Tarn, *CAH*, VII, 752 *seq.*; Walbank, 72 *seq.* (with the criticism of Treves, *Athen.* XII, 1934, 328); Flacelière, 278–88; Treves, *Athen.* XIII, 1935, 33 *seq.*; Porter, introd. lix *seq.*; Fine, *AJPh*, LXI, 1940, 129 *seq.* Fine has a good criticism (*op. cit.* 135, n. 25) of Treves's attempt to show (*Athen.* XII, 1934, 409–11) that the Cleomenean War was engineered by Antigonus Doson.

[4] Polyb. II, 47 *seq.* For the date see Bettingen, 36, n. 3; Porter, lxxii–lxxiii; Fine, *AJPh*, LXI, 1940, 140, n. 47.

supremacy and to undo the mischief of Gonatas's last years; and in guarded terms Doson gave the Megalopolitans the required assurances. The next year (226) saw the Achaeans defeated once more at Hecatombaeum in western Achaea; and the following nine or ten months were spent in protracted negotiations between Cleomenes and the League. Simultaneously, however, three Achaean representatives, including Aratus's own son, were at Pella, secretly making final arrangements for Macedonian intervention; and Antigonus was able to propose and obtain the most drastic concessions—nothing less than the return of Acrocorinth itself. Early in 224 he received the actual signal to march south. Hampered by the latent hostility of the Aetolians, who closed Thermopylae against him,[1] he shipped his troops across to Euboea, and by this route reached the Isthmus of Corinth.

Two campaigns served to drive Cleomenes back into Laconia, but not to crush him; this was clear from the offensive which he was still able to level against Megalopolis and the Argolid. But meanwhile Antigonus, taking advantage of the abandonment of his eastern policy, opened negotiations with Ptolemy, and laid the foundations for an agreement between the two old enemies, Macedon and Egypt.[2] As a result, when in July 222[3] Cleomenes faced the united army which Antigonus commanded, at Sellasia, he did so knowing that his Egyptian subsidies were at an end.[4] The battle was a decisive victory for the Macedonians; Cleomenes fled to Egypt, the Macedonian army marched into Sparta and Doson found himself in the long-coveted position of arbiter of the Peloponnese.

With foresight Antigonus had already created the instrument of Macedonian domination.[5] During the winter of 224 he had set up a new organisation, the Symmachy, based upon the confederations of Alexander and Demetrius Poliorcetes, but having as its units, not cities, but leagues.[6] Its members were the

---

[1] Polyb. II, 52, 8.   [2] Cf. Treves, *Athen.* XIII, 1935, 40 *seq.*

[3] See below, Appendix III, p. 296, n. 5.

[4] Plut. *Cleom.* 22, 7; Polyb. (=Phylarchus) II, 63.

[5] Cf. however, Treves, *Athen.* XIII, 1935, 37, who maintains that the Symmachy was primarily an instrument of anti-Roman policy.

[6] On the Symmachy see Beloch, IV, 1, 712 *seq.*; Ferrabino, 71; 109–11; Walbank, 104 *seq.*, 158; Tarn, *CAH,* VII, 759; Zancan, 117; Ferguson, *Greek Imperialism,* 242–5; W. Schwahn, *P–W,* 'Symmachia', col. 1133–4; Fine, *AJPh,* LXI, 1940, 151–2, n. 92; Treves, *LEC,* IX, 1940, 160 *seq.*

Achaeans,[1] Macedonians,[2] Thessalians, Epirotes, Acarnanians, Boeotians, Phocians, Euboeans and perhaps the Opuntian Locrians.[3] These leagues, and inside them the individual cities, did not, however, surrender their autonomy. The Council, or Synedrion, of the Symmachy, could be summoned by the king of Macedon in his capacity of president, and had the power to decide questions of war and peace, the voting of supplies and the co-opting of new members; moreover, the king of Macedon was *ex officio* commander-in-chief. But the Symmachy possessed no treasury, and all decisions were subject to ratification by the legislative bodies of the separate leagues,[4] which thus maintained a considerable measure of independence.

How far this loose organisation was Doson's own creation, and how far he was inspired by Aratus,[5] it would be difficult to say. Eventually, the Symmachy was to prove a failure; but what should have been immediately clear was that, so long as the king of Macedon was prepared to abide by its terms, the domination which it offered him was largely illusory; on the other hand, Achaea and the other small federal states would profit by Macedonian military protection, without sustaining any appreciable loss of autonomy. With the crushing of Cleomenes, the threat from Sparta, which had first turned Aratus to Macedon, was gone; but meanwhile the Aetolian League was a force to reckon with, and against Aetolia Macedonian help was invaluable.

[1] Two passages in Polybius (IV, 85, 6; V, 1, 6) suggest that at this time the Achaeans passed a law enjoining the magistrates to summon an assembly whenever the king of Macedon (as president of the Symmachy) required them; see Aymard, *Les assemblées de la confédération achaienne*, 200. The evidence of Livy (P) XXVII, 30, 6, on this question is indecisive, since it is left uncertain whether an Achaean assembly or a conference of members of the Symmachy is meant (see below, p. 90, n. 2).
[2] Polyb. IV, 9, 4; Treves, *Athen.* XIII, 1935, 52, argues that the Macedonian *people* remained outside the Symmachy.
[3] Polyb. IV, 9, 4; 15, 1; XI, 5, 4. It is, however, possible that the Opuntian Locrians, like Megara since 225, were at this time part of Boeotia; cf. Oldfather, *P–W*, 'Lokris', col. 1224; Niese, II, 275; 375; Holleaux, *BCH*, XVI, 1892, 468; Klaffenbach, *Klio*, XX, 1926, 83 and n. 3; Flacelière, 280. The Euboeans were perhaps directly subject to Macedon; cf. Niese, II, 336; Täubler, I, 218, n. 1. Sparta was allied to the Symmachy (cf. Polyb. IV, 9, 6), but whether as a full member (so Heuss, *Stadt und Herrscher*, 30) is uncertain.
[4] References: Polyb. IV, 9, 3; 16, 1; 22, 2; 25; 26, 2; V, 102, 9; 103, 1; 103, 7; 105, 1; 105, 2.
[5] Plut. *Arat.* 42, 2–3; the later anti-Aratean policy of Apelles is not evidence for Doson's attitude towards the Achaean (so Treves, *Athen.* XIII, 1935, 36).

Economically, too, the Symmachy fulfilled a function more
directly in the interests of Achaea than anyone else; for, in
crushing Cleomenes, Doson and his allies were crushing that
spectre of social revolution which haunted third-century Greece;[1]
and, beyond doubt, social revolution constituted an infinitely
greater threat to the oligarchic Achaean League than to the
semi-feudal monarchy of Macedonia.

It is doubtful, however, if Doson perceived these weaknesses
in the Symmachy; and he had at least established Macedonian
garrisons at the three key positions of Acrocorinth, Orchomenus
and Heraea,[2] thus extending Macedonian influence far beyond

---

[1] See Tarn, "The Social Question in the Third Century" in *The
Hellenistic Age* (Cambridge, 1923), 108.

[2] *Orchomenus:* Plut. *Arat.* 45, 1; Polyb. IV, 6, 5; cf. Hiller von Gaertringen
on *IG*, V, 2, p. 69, lines 71 *seq*; *Corinth:* Polyb. II, 52, 4; IV, 6, 5. *Heraea* was
taken by Cleomenes in 227; but Philip held it in 208, when he offered to
restore it to the Achaeans (Livy (P) XXVIII, 8, 6), a promise carried out
eventually in 199–8 (Livy (P) XXXII, 5, 4). The probability is that Doson
garrisoned it after its submission to him in the campaign of 223 (Polyb. II,
54, 12). This view is contested by Aymard, *Premiers Rapports*, 25–7, n. 5;
59, n. 53, who argues that whereas in 208 Philip promised to restore Heraea,
Triphylia and Alipheira to the League, he failed to include Orchomenus, an
inheritance from Doson. Hence Heraea must have been captured by Philip
himself; and Aymard invokes Philip's well-known reluctance to cede any
of his *ancestral* territories, as opposed to those personally acquired (Polyb.
XVIII, 7, 1; Livy (P) XXXII, 10, 4; Diod. XXVIII, 11). Aymard has therefore to
assume that the Aetolians took Heraea during the first Macedonian war (our
records for the Social War are too full to have omitted such an incident) and
that Philip recaptured it before 208. This hypothesis encounters considerable
difficulties. The Aetolians did not enter the war until summer 211 (see below,
Appendix III, p. 301 *seq*.) and their movements for the remainder of that year
are adequately accounted for (see below, p. 84); if they took Heraea in 210 (and
there is no trace of an Aetolian army in the Peloponnese that year) it is most
improbable that this should not have been mentioned in the Achaean appeal
to Philip in 209 (Livy (P) XXVII, 29, 9) or the subsequent discussions at Aegium
(*ibid.* 30, 10 *seq*.). Moreover, we have a full account of Philip's activities in
the Peloponnese in 209 and 208, which leaves no room for the recapture of an
important town like Heraea. A further argument brought forward by Aymard
in favour of his hypothesis is that it explains the Aetolian claim to Heraea in
196 (Polyb. XVIII, 42, 7; Livy (P) XXXIII, 34, 9; cf. Polyb. XVIII, 47, 10 (with
lacuna); see below, p. 178, n. 1). But an occupation of at most a few months
would constitute a ludicrous claim to a city which the Aetolians could only
approach through Elean territory, and which would have been a member of
the Achaean League (with one short break) from 236 to *c.* 210. On the other
hand, it is dangerous to reject as corrupt a text which was accepted unques-
tioningly by Livy. Is it possible that the Aetolian claim rested on a promise
of the town by Philip in the separate peace of 206 (just as he promised but
never handed over certain towns in Thessaly: see below, p. 100, n. 1)? Whatever the explanation here, Aymard's theory involves too many unlikely as-
sumptions to be accepted.

the limits envisaged by Antigonus Gonatas. Moreover, Doson's organisation was a war-time measure, built up hurriedly before Cleomenes had been defeated. He had not yet had time, nor was he in a position to face the detailed internal problems, that were later to reveal themselves in the war with Aetolia. His immediate task was threefold: first, to establish a military foothold in Greece; secondly, to obtain a legitimate position, which would enable him to play a decisive role in Greek politics; and thirdly, to defeat Cleomenes and extirpate social revolution. Two of these objects he accomplished completely, the third partially;[1] but before he could even approach the question of what was to be the future of the Symmachy, outside events called him away.

For, while he was still at Sparta, he received news of an Illyrian invasion of Macedon.[2] Rapidly he marched north and defeated the barbarians; but in the excitement of the battle he is said to have burst a blood-vessel with fatal effect. At the time of Sellasia, Antigonus was already suffering from an advanced stage of consumption,[3] and it seems highly probable that the exertion of the march and second battle brought on an internal haemorrhage. Returning home, however, he lingered on until the following summer (221);[4] and the intervening year he devoted to the question of the succession, and in particular to the Greek Symmachy, which was established but untried. Philip's extreme youth, the difficulties he was likely to encounter in adjusting the conflicting interests of Greece and Macedonia, the need to leave the boy reliable advisers, these were the problems that Doson had to solve before he died.

Philip was only sixteen when his stepfather returned from defeating the Illyrians. Of his youth we have no records; of his personal appearance only the later coin-representations,[5] which

[1] That social revolution proved to have been only temporarily suppressed, was due to factors inherent in the economic causes of the movement.

[2] This invasion was not instigated by Rome, as Droysen claimed; cf. Tarn, *CAH*, VII, 843, n. 1. The Illyrians concerned were not those under Demetrius of Pharus, who fought with Antigonus at Sellasia, but more probably rebellious tribes farther east, akin to the Dardanians, whose land they bordered; cf. Fine, *JRS*, XXVI, 1936, 25.   [3] Plut. *Cleom.* 30, 2.

[4] Plut. *Cleom.* 16, 7 (cf., for consumption in antiquity, Tarn, *Greeks in Bactria*, 215); 30, 2 (later version that he died in battle). For the date, see below, Appendix III, p. 295 *seq.*

[5] See frontispiece: the beardless version on the coins of Polyrrhenia is probably an idealised representation.

show him in the prime of life, a bearded figure with a straight, finely formed nose, slightly beetling brows—a characteristic more pronounced in his son Perseus—moustache and strong chin; his mouth is firm and his eyes wide and intelligent. The confidence and skill with which he carried out his early campaigns point to an excellent training in military strategy and

tactics; but whether he had accompanied Doson on the Greek or Illyrian campaigns is unknown,[1] and he was probably too young to go to Caria in 227. Now, within a year at the most, he would have to take over the dual position of King of Macedon and

[1] The group representing Antigonus Doson and Philip, crowned, which the Eleans set up at Olympia (Pausan. VI, 16, 3), is not evidence that Philip shared in the victory over Cleomenes, still less (cf. Swoboda, *Hermes*, LVII, 1922, 529) that he was ever co-regent with Doson; cf. Tarn, *CQ*, XVIII, 1924, 21 *seq.* (It is, however, interesting as evidence for an Elean move towards Macedon during the interval between the Cleomenean and Social Wars.)

General of the Hellenic Symmachy. Doson's solution revealed the breadth of vision to be expected from the founder of the Symmachy, and also his genuine desire that the Greek Alliance might prove a permanent instrument of Greek unity, and not only a means to Macedonian hegemony in Hellas.

First, Doson made a will appointing guardians for Philip and filling all the higher court positions from among his most trusted counsellors.[1] The most important of these guardians was Apelles; and the other appointments were Leontius as Captain of the Peltasts, Megaleas as Secretary of State, Taurion as High Commissioner for the Peloponnese,[2] and Alexander as Chamberlain.[3] All these men were tried leaders, who would understand and further the interests of the kingdom. But the only man who had co-operated with Doson in planning the Greek Symmachy was Aratus, the Achaean. Accordingly, in the winter of 222–1, the young prince was sent into the Peloponnese, with orders to attach himself to Aratus, and by his help to acquaint himself with the problems and outlook of the Achaeans.[4] This he did, and when in the spring of 221 he returned to Antigonus, it was with a new enthusiasm for Aratus and for Greece.

The same summer Antigonus Doson died, leaving Macedon a more firmly welded and prosperous country than the one he had saved from ruin eight years before. To the north and northwest, the Dardanian and Illyrian tribes of the interior were cowed, if not friendly; on the Adriatic coast the Illyrians under Demetrius of Pharus were his allies;[5] to the south Thessaly, except for Phthiotic Achaea, was in his hands; and finally, three garrisons and the newly formed Symmachy guaranteed the fidelity of the Achaean League. Against these gains were to be set the decay of the Macedonian fleet and the renunciation of the

---

[1] Polyb. IV, 87, 6.

[2] Perhaps the equivalent of ὁ ὑπὸ τῶν βασιλέων ἀποδεδειγμένος στρατηγός who commanded the garrison on Acrocorinth under Poliorcetes; cf. *IG*, IV², 68, III, 71–2 (16–17); Treves, *Athen.* XIII, 1935, 54.

[3] Polyb. IV, 87, 8: Ἀλέξανδρος δ' ἐπὶ τῆς θεραπείας; cf. Polyb. XV, 25a, 3, where the θεραπεία and Royal Hypaspists are coupled together. θεραπεία is the official organisational term for the court: see H. Berve, *Das Alexanderreich auf prosopographischer Grundlage*, I, 25.

[4] Plut. *Arat.* 46, 2–3.

[5] Demetrius and 1600 Illyrians fought at Sellasia on the allied side (Polyb. II, 65, 4–5); but this is no evidence for a Macedonian 'western policy' (so Treves, *Athen.* XIII, 1935, 46).

Carian schemes. On the other hand, history had shown and was to show again that Macedon lacked the resources to maintain a vigorous policy simultaneously by land and sea; hence the decay in sea power was no unmixed evil. More disquieting was Doson's failure to solve the Aetolian problem. He had been content to recover Hestiaeotis, Thessaliotis and the district round Pharsalus, and had allowed his enemy to keep Phthiotic Achaea. Yet the passive hostility of the Aetolian League was plain in 224, when it closed the pass of Thermopylae against Doson; and with the founding of the Symmachy, this hostility was mingled with alarm, as the Aetolians found themselves surrounded by potential foes. Epirus, Acarnania, Phocis, Opuntian Locris, Boeotia and Achaea were all members of the new alliance, and to the north lay Thessaly and Macedonia itself. In the Peloponnese too, where Messenia, Elis and Phigaleia were their sole remaining allies, the Aetolians saw a clear threat in the Achaean ambition to dominate the peninsula. In Messenia power was already in the hands of a party that was well-disposed towards Achaea;[1] and in Elis too there is slight but positive evidence for a move towards the Symmachy after Sellasia,[2] probably under the influence of Amphidamus, who was subsequently exiled as pro-Achaean.[3] Thus on every side Aetolia was faced with a coalition which might prove overpowering, once it had had the opportunity to feel its own strength and taste the fruits of unity. On the other hand, Doson was dying, and a boy of seventeen would shortly succeed to the leadership of the Alliance and the throne of Macedon. To the Aetolians the moment seemed ripe to challenge the Alliance while it was disorganised, and they began to look around for the most favourable opening.

Thus Philip inherited from Doson a two-fold legacy, a Symmachy created by a tempered idealism which he fully shared, and—less apparent—an opposition in Aetolia, which was determined to put this Symmachy to the test of war. Meanwhile, in the background stood the figures of Apelles and his fellow-counsellors, loyal to their king, yet suspicious, perhaps, of this new Hellenic policy, initiated by Doson under Achaean

[1] See below, p. 24; also Fine, *AJPh*, LXI, 1940, 150–65.
[2] See above, p. 19, n. 1.
[3] See below, p. 49 (events of winter 219–18).

influence, at a time when his health was already failing, and
favoured now by the young Philip, who had returned from the
Peloponnese full of Greek ideals, when he might have been
devoting his whole attention to the needs of Macedon. And in

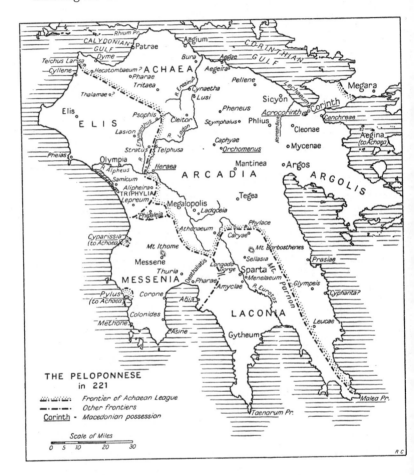

THE PELOPONNESE
in 221

·······   *Frontier of Achaean League*
—·—·—   *Other frontiers*
Corinth -   *Macedonian possession*

Scale of Miles
0   5   10   20   30

Achaea, as if to balance the picture, was the crafty Aratus, who
saw, probably clearer than anyone else, the political forces then
operating in the Greek world. With the aid of Doson he had
built up the structure of the Symmachy, to be a defence for an
oligarchic Achaea; he had won the confidence, first of Doson,

then of Philip, and was prepared to use either for that defence of class and country which was his sole criterion.

Philip succeeded to the throne in the summer of 221. About the same time changes were taking place in the other Hellenistic kingdoms. In Egypt Euergetes had died a few months previously, leaving the crown of the Ptolemies to his degenerate son, Philopator;[1] and some two years before, Syria had come into the hands of another boy, Antiochus III. In the western Mediterranean the powers of Rome and Carthage were confronting each other for the long struggle of the Hannibalic War. It was the point of time which Polybius was later to select for the opening of his history of how the whole of the civilised world passed under the hands of Rome; in short, it was one of those moments of general crisis, which afterwards stand out as marking the end of one era and the birth of another. It is, however, unlikely that the significance of the moment was apparent to Philip, who had probably only a limited knowledge of Rome and the most general interest in her affairs. The later 'cloud in the west'[2] was still below the Greek horizon; and the only meaning of the expression in 221 would have been to indicate the now imminent threat from the Aetolian League.

[1] For the date see below, Appendix III, p. 296.
[2] Cf. Polyb. v, 104, 10; IX, 37, 10.

Chapter II : Philip Looks South

THE SOCIAL WAR (221–217)

AS soon as Doson was dead, the Aetolians began to move in the Peloponnese; and their immediate victim was Messenia. At this time Messenia, like Elis, enjoyed friendly relations with Achaea; though she had (most probably) taken no active part in the war against Cleomenes,[1] she had shown her friendship by affording sanctuary to the Megalopolitan refugees in 223[2] and after Sellasia had been rewarded with the district of Denthaliatis, between Kalamata and the Langada Gorge.[3] Operating from the town of Phigaleia, which had been an Aetolian ally since about 244,[4] Dorimachus of Trichonium, one of the younger and more violent leaders of the Aetolian war party, now directed a series of raids on the Messenians, though nominally they were also allied to Aetolia;[5] and when they retaliated with personal insults, he returned to Aetolia to organise a more regular expedition. Such is Polybius's account. Followed strictly, it suggests an entirely unprovoked marauding expedition directed by a small group of Aetolian leaders, acting in a private capacity against a friendly people. But in fact the affair had its political side.[6] Polybius admits that Dorimachus was present in Phigaleia on public business (κατὰ κοινόν); and there can be little doubt that the whole Aetolian policy was directed towards countering Achaean influence in Messenia. This done, the Aetolians could go ahead with their plans to use Messenia as a base from which they could unite Elis and Sparta against the Achaean League.

On reaching Aetolia, Dorimachus found the new general,

---

[1] Pausanias's statement (IV, 29, 9) that there were Messenians fighting at Sellasia has been generally rejected or ignored; cf. Niese, II, 411–12. Fine, *AJPh*, LXI, 1940, 155–6, considers the point at some length, and makes a number of points in favour of accepting Pausanias's assertion. On the whole, in view of Polybius's silence, I am inclined, however, to reject it.

[2] Polyb. II, 55, 1 *seq.*; Plut. *Cleom.* 24, 1 *seq.*   [3] Tacit. *Ann.* IV, 43.

[4] *Syll.* 472; cf. Walbank, *JHS*, LVI, 1936, 68, n. 30.

[5] Polyb. IV, 3, 9.   [6] See, in general, Fine, *AJPh*, LXI, 1940, 150 *seq.*

Ariston, ill,[1] and his power conveniently delegated to Scopas of Trichonium, the other war leader—a situation which enabled him to dispense with the authority of the assembly[2] in pushing ahead with his plans against the Symmachy. Helped by the fleet of their allies in Cephallenia,[3] the Aetolians not merely pillaged the coast of Epirus, but even seized one of the few remaining vessels of the Macedonian navy off Cythera and sold it with all its crew.[4] Meanwhile, on land they attacked Thyrrheum in Acarnania and, in the Peloponnese, seized the fortress of Clarium,[5] in Megalopolitan territory, and used it for raiding parties, until Taurion, the Macedonian commissioner, and Timoxenus, the Achaean general for 221–20, drove them out.

The following spring (220) this policy of consistent aggression reached a climax, when a force of Aetolians under Scopas and Dorimachus[6] crossed the Corinthian Gulf to Rhium and, advancing through the middle of Achaea, once more established themselves at Phigaleia.[7] Complaints at once poured into Aegium, where an assembly of the Achaean League was in session;[8] and when Timoxenus, the retiring general, proved reluctant to satisfy either the petitioning cities or the Messenians, who were requesting Achaean help, Aratus stepped into the breach. Taking over the seals of office five days before the authorised date, he summoned the army of the League to assemble at Megalopolis,[9] and there gave a further hearing to the Messenians. It was decided to refer their request for membership of the Symmachy to the other allies, as the constitution of

[1] Polyb. IV, 5, I.   [2] Polyb. IV, 5, 9 seq.
[3] Polyb. IV, 6, 2. Cephallenia had apparently entered into isopolity with Aetolia since Demetrius's death, probably c. 226; cf. Beloch, IV, I, 719, n. 3; Klaffenbach, IG, IX, I[2], introd. p. xxiii; Flacelière, 258; 284.
[4] Polyb. IV, 6, 1–2.
[5] Polyb. IV, 6, 3. The site of Clarium is unknown, but it probably lay between Phigaleia and Megalopolis.
[6] Polyb. IV, 6, 8: πανδημεί: it is, however, improbable that Aetolia was left undefended. More likely the size of the expedition is exaggerated by Polybius or his source to excuse Aratus's subsequent defeat.
[7] Polyb. IV, 6, 9. The route was probably through Elis, not Arcadia; cf. Walbank, 115, n. 1.
[8] The date was probably about the middle of May; cf. Aymard, Assemblées, 253, n. 6.
[9] Polyb. IV, 7, 10. On these incidents, and in particular the legal aspect of the Achaean army acting as the equivalent of an assembly, see Aymard, Assemblées, 220 seq.

the Symmachy required;[1] but in the meantime the Achaeans made a special alliance with Messenia, to meet the emergency.[2] They were awake to the danger of trusting her too far. The recent Achaean acquisition of Pylus and Cyparissia[3] had alienated many of the oligarchic party in Messenia, and had caused the failure of one set of negotiations for an alliance.[4] It was external necessity that had now driven Messenia to seek help at Aegium, and accordingly the Achaeans felt they must be protected against any wavering of policy.[5] Accordingly, the Messenians were required to deposit hostages; and these Aratus lodged at Sparta, planning in this way to maintain the wavering support of that city.[6] Meanwhile the Spartans had sent a force to the frontiers of Megalopolis to await events.[7]

The Achaeans now despatched an ultimatum to Scopas and Dorimachus; they were to evacuate Messenia and not set foot in Achaea, otherwise they would be treated as enemies. This firm step met with apparent compliance, but in fact Aratus found himself outmanœuvred; for after shipping their booty at Pheias (mod. Katákolo)[8] in Elis, the Aetolians suddenly turned inland and forced him to a battle with depleted forces near Caphyae.[9] Aratus foolishly delayed attack until the enemy were ascending the opposite slopes, a tactical error which resulted in an Achaean rout; the Aetolian freebooters were thus able to make their way home through the heart of Achaea and across the Isthmus.

In this battle the Achaeans had had the support of Taurion,[10] the Macedonian commissioner, who had already helped to expel the Aetolians from Clarium. Thus clearly a series of alarming reports must already have reached Philip at Pella: shortly afterwards these were reinforced by an embassy from the Achaeans,

---

[1] Cf. Heuss, *Stadt und Herrscher*, 160–1.

[2] See Fine, *AJPh*, LXI, 1940, 160, n. 141. It is nowhere specifically stated that an Achaeo-Messenian alliance was concluded; but Polybius's narrative favours this view (cf. IV, 9, 7; 15).   [3] Cf. Niese, II, 411, n. 1.

[4] Polyb. IV, 5, 8 (not very good evidence, since it comes from a report of Dorimachus's agents).

[5] Later events justified the Achaeans: e.g. Polyb. IV, 31 (Messenian reluctance to support the Symmachy).   [6] Polyb. IV, 9, 5.

[7] Polyb. IV, 9, 6: Λακεδαιμόνιοι κατὰ τὴν συμμαχίαν ἐξεληλυθότες.

[8] Polyb. IV, 9, 9: εἰς τὴν Φειάδα καλουμένην νῆσον. But cf. F. Bölte, *P-W*, 'Phea', col. 1913.

[9] Polyb. IV, 9, 8–12, 14. See Leake, *Morea*, III, 122–8; Walbank, 117–18.

[10] Polyb. IV, 10, 2.

who, after a natural revulsion against Aratus's mismanagement of the recent campaign, had been brought round to his policy of an appeal to the Symmachy.[1] Aratus realised that the Aetolian threat to Achaea and the peace of Hellas could be smashed only by the combined forces of the Alliance. Accordingly he had persuaded the Achaeans to send embassies to Philip and the other members of the Symmachy, to complain of the double invasion of Achaea and to ask for the assistance to which she was entitled. At the same time they sponsored the Messenian application for membership; and at home, meanwhile, they pledged themselves to assist Messenia, if she were invaded, and made provision for the raising of a force of 10,000 foot and 1000 horse—an inadequate figure, which points to a neglect of the military arm in Achaea since the defeat of Cleomenes.[2]

The Aetolians, on their side, were equally awake to the dangers of the war, if the whole Symmachy should be effectively marshalled against them. This was, indeed, the contingency which they had hoped, by striking at once, to avoid; and notwithstanding their offences against Macedon and Epirus, a general war was more than they cared to envisage. The fact was, the Aetolians were a race of freebooters, too apt to act first and think afterwards. And now, at their general assembly, they awoke suddenly to the need of localising the conflict to Achaea, and the Messenian question: accordingly they passed a resolution to remain at peace with everyone else, including Sparta and Messenia, and with Achaea too, if she abandoned the Messenian alliance: otherwise they would consider themselves at war with Achaea. Behind this decision was evidently a fear lest Messenia should be absorbed into the Achaean League; for, significantly, it was not against the admission of Messenia into the Symmachy, but against her separate alliance with Achaea that the Aetolian complaints were levelled.[3] The resolution, not unnaturally, made no reference to Scopas and Dorimachus, whose brigandage,

---

[1] Polyb. IV, 15, 1.
[2] Polyb. IV, 15, 5–7; cf. IV, 7, 7. This force, moreover, included the levies from Messenia and Sparta; its small numbers prompt the query whether the socially disaffected and, from the oligarchic standpoint, unreliable elements of the population in the various cities were in fact far greater than our sources suggest. Or were the Achaeans relying on Philip?
[3] In either case, of course, Messenia would become an Achaean ally: but the Aetolians hoped to 'buy off' the other members of the Symmachy, by making the issue one between themselves and Achaea only.

like the piracy of the English sea-dogs of Elizabeth's time,[1] was evidently regarded as no business of the government.

The replies of the other members of the Symmachy appear to have been inspired by Philip:[2] Messenia might enter the Symmachy, but, for the rest, they preferred to remain at peace with Aetolia. The acceptance of the Achaean proposals on Messenia was an admission that the Achaean cause was the cause of the rest, including Macedon; on the other hand, while the diplomatic phrasing of the reply was designed to throw the responsibility of the next move on to Aetolia, a certain weakness was evident in the omission of any reference to the assaults already made by the Aetolians on Achaea. It appeared as though Philip was prepared to forget these, if Aetolia could be cajoled into keeping the peace and abstaining from further aggression.[3] However, Aetolia could not[4] or would not take the hint. After the decision of the allies, she did for a time cease her attacks on Messenia; but the aggression against Achaea was soon resumed in a more flagrant manner than before. And this time Aetolia found an ally.

One of the terms imposed by Rome on the Illyrians after the First Illyrian War had been an undertaking that no Illyrian warship should sail south of Lissus.[5] Now, in the summer of 220, the Illyrian princes Scerdilaidas and Demetrius of Pharus set sail with a fleet of ninety ships and, passing Lissus, embarked upon a piratical expedition.[6] They began with an attack, in conjunction with the Aetolians, on Pylus, an Achaean town[7] on the Messenian coast; and when this failed, Demetrius continued into

---

[1] Cf. Tarn, *CAH*, VII, 763.

[2] Polybius (IV, 16, 1) gives only the replies of Philip and the Epirotes; but the agreement of the other members is implied. Holleaux has assumed from this coupling of Philip's name with the Epirotes that Philip was at this time (summer 220) in Epirus (*Rome*, 141, n. 4). This may be true: it cannot, however, be proved, and, as Fine shows (*JRS*, XXVI, 1936, 38–9), it is quite improper to assume with Holleaux that such a visit had necessarily any connection with the affairs of Illyria and Rome.

[3] On Philip's reluctance to embark on a war with Aetolia, see Holleaux, 149, n. 1, where, however, many of the examples quoted admit of other explanations.

[4] In judging Aetolian policy, one must always bear in mind the lack of resources, which drove the Aetolians to piracy and mercenary-service (cf. Griffith, 81; 121; 258).   [5] Polyb. II, 12, 3.

[6] On the motives behind this breach of the treaty see Holleaux, 132 *seq.*

[7] See above, p. 26, n. 3; this action shows that the expedition was not instigated by Philip, as Holleaux, 141, contends; cf. Fine, *JRS*, XXVI, 1936, 31.

the Aegean with fifty of the ships, pillaging and looting in the Cyclades, while Scerdilaidas returned towards Illyria. On the way, however, he put in at Naupactus, and there struck a bargain with Agelaus, a prominent Aetolian, for a joint raid on Achaea, in return for a share in the spoils. The combined forces crossed the gulf, marched up the Erasinus to Cynaetha and, helped by traitors within, seized and sacked the town; from here they advanced to Cleitor, but failed to take it and so marched back to Cynaetha, which, after the Eleans had declined it, they burnt before returning home via Rhium.[1]

The identity of the Cynaethan 'traitors' is probably to be sought among the anti-oligarchic faction, which, in the various cities of Achaea, had welcomed Cleomenes five years previously. For the career of Cleomenes had raised in an acute form in Greece a problem that transcended frontiers. The discontented elements which had rallied to his programme had not been confined to Sparta; and the sensational collapse of Achaea had been due, partly, it is true, to military weakness, but even more to the sympathy of the common people for a movement which they mistakenly believed to be about to bring them abolition of debts and a redistribution of the soil.[2] Sellasia had crushed social revolution in Sparta, but its supporters still lived on in the various states, an intransigent opposition to the oligarchic authorities, now entrenched behind the defences of Doson's Symmachy. In view of this class alignment throughout the Peloponnese, it seems extremely probable that the Aetolian action at Cynaetha was part of a bid to exploit revolutionary sentiment throughout the Peloponnese,[3] and links up with a simultaneous attempt to secure the adherence of the Cleomenean faction at Sparta.[4]

---

[1] Polyb. IV, 16, 6–21, 12. The sparing of the temple of Artemis near Lusi on this raid is probably to be connected with the Aetolian grant of 'asylia' to that town (*IG*, IX, I², 135; cf. F. Poulsen and K. Rhomaios, *I. vorläufiger Bericht über die dänisch-griechischen Ausgrabungen von Kalydon*, Danske Videnskabernes Selskab, XIV, 1927, 3, 45). [2] Plut. *Cleom.* 17, 3.

[3] So Ferrabino, 142 *seq.* The indiscriminate murder of friend and foe alike in Cynaetha was perhaps due to excess of zeal in the rank and file: it was scarcely calculated to assist Aetolian policy, but is no argument against its existence. For the acuteness of the class struggle inside Cynaetha cf. Polyb. IV, 17, 4.

[4] It is noteworthy that in 205 it was Dorimachus and Scopas, the present leaders of the Aetolian war party, who attempted a social revolution in their own country (see below, p. 109, n. 2).

For already, at the time of the first Achaean appeal to the Symmachy, certain Spartans were in secret communication with Aetolia.[1]

Meanwhile the task of defence fell upon Philip; for Aratus, whether from fear or policy,[2] made no move against Agelaus, beyond despatching further appeals to Philip, as president of the Hellenic Confederacy. And either in response to orders from Pella, or on his own initiative, Taurion now took steps against the Aetolians. Demetrius of Pharus had suddenly appeared at Cenchreae, pursued by the Rhodians; following the Aetolian cue, Taurion struck a bargain with him, by which the Illyrian fleet should be dragged across the Isthmus at Macedon's expense and in return should lend assistance against the Aetolians and Demetrius's late confederate, Scerdilaidas. Unfortunately, the move came too late, and after a few raids on the Aetolian coast, Demetrius returned to Corinth.[3]

By this time Philip was quite awake to the gravity of the situation. Influenced as much, no doubt, by the news of the Aetolian compact with Scerdilaidas,[4] as by the appeals of Aratus, he now marched south to Corinth. Instead of taking the chance offered by the recent Macedonian decision, the Aetolians had bought the help of one of his own neighbours. Unwilling to ignore such a challenge, Philip, on arriving at Corinth, at once issued notices to all the allies to send representatives to a general council. Equally important, he now came once more under the influence of Aratus, whose policy was gradually being adopted; and very soon an incident occurred which served to reveal the strength of that influence.

For some time the position at Sparta had been unsatisfactory. Even at the time when the Messenian hostages were lodged there,[5] in the hopes of countering the hostile faction, the Spartan

---

[1] Polyb. IV, 16, 5: the reference to φιλίαν...καὶ συμμαχίαν seems, however, to be an exaggeration at this date.

[2] Polyb. IV, 19, 11; Aratus acted πολιτικώτερον ἢ στρατηγικώτερον: for a discussion of this phrase see Walbank, 122.

[3] Here again Holleaux, *CAH*, VII, 848, detects evidence of a Macedonian anti-Roman policy; refuted by Fine, *JRS*, XXVI, 1936, 34.

[4] The Aetolians had collaborated with the Illyrians at Pylus as well as Cynaetha; cf. Polyb. IV, 25, 4; IX, 38, 8.

[5] In spite of the objections of Ferrabino, 121 *seq.*, the subsequent support afforded by Achaea suggests that the hostages were given as required.

levies were, in the words of the Megalopolitan historian, 'more in the position of reserves and spectators than of allies';[1] and the movement towards an agreement with Aetolia has already been noticed.[2] Now upon his arrival in Corinth Philip learnt that the pro-Achaean and pro-Aetolian members of the Ephorate had come into open conflict.[3] He at once decided to visit Sparta, while the representatives of the Symmachy were assembling. At the news of his approach the Aetolian party tried to mobilise the youth against him, and when an opponent spoke against this, he and a number of his group were assassinated. Such was the account conveyed to Philip when he was met, somewhere between Argos and Tegea, by delegates of the two factions, both accusing each other of trying to betray the town to Aetolia.

Philip ordered responsible representatives to be sent to him at Tegea; and after hearing their excuses he hesitated for some time as to how he should treat the city. In what was perhaps his first decision of any magnitude the young man naturally placed reliance upon the advice of those about him. Three points of view were expressed. To Apelles and his friends Sparta appeared an intractable enemy, and they were only divided on the method of punishing her. Should she be wholly wiped out, as Thebes had been wiped out by Alexander? Or should Philip remove the guilty ephors and put the city under the control of those friendly to Macedon? Philip did neither; instead, he followed the third counsel, that of Aratus, and contented himself with reprimanding Sparta and administering new oaths. Sending one of his Friends, Petraeus, with this decision to Sparta, he himself returned to Corinth. Aratus's motives were clearly to try to win over Sparta by clemency; mild punishment would drive her nearer to Aetolia, while annihilation, by altering the balance of power in the Peloponnese, might create internal problems within the Achaean League itself. There was always a potential rivalry between Achaea proper and Arcadia, and the disappearance of Sparta would have rendered Megalopolis less vulnerable and so more influential. To the young Philip, however, Aratus's solution was in full accordance with the generous ideals of Hellenism, with which he had been inspired on his visit of eighteen months before.

[1] Polyb. IV, 9, 7.   [2] See above, p. 30, n. 1.   [3] Polyb. IV, 22, 3–24, 9.

At Corinth Philip found the representatives of the allies waiting with a series of accusations against Aetolia. From Boeotia, Phocis, Epirus, Acarnania and Achaea came stories of attacks[1] on cities and temples, and ravaging of land, all in time of peace. Unanimously it was decided to make war on Aetolia, and the programme of aims showed the new aspect from which the question was being approached. The Symmachy was no longer seeking mere reparations; it was pledged, instead, to the recovery of all cities and territories occupied by the Aetolians since the death of Demetrius II of Macedon, in short since the end of their alliance with Achaea;[2] and its members undertook to liberate and reinstate in their traditional forms of government all independent states that had been coerced into the League. Finally, to give their campaign the added aroma of a sacred war, Delphi and the Amphictyonic Council were to be freed from the Aetolian yoke. In the event of success, Epirus would recover Ambracia and Amphilochia,[3] Acarnania her traditional limits west of the Achelous, where Aetolia at present held Stratus, Phoetiae, Metropolis and Oeniadae,[4] and Thessaly Phthiotic Achaea.[5] Phocis, Locris and Boeotia would benefit concretely under the second clause or, at the least, in added security; and finally Macedon would naturally take over the useful machinery of the Amphictyony as a second instrument for controlling Greece.

There was enough in this programme to commend it to Philip's counsellors, Apelles, Leontius and Megaleas; to Aratus it was the bribe by which he bought the support of the Symmachy for Achaea, but to them it was undoubtedly a step towards a still greater Panhellenic Federation more firmly under the control of Macedon. Thus already the clash of interests was implicit in the march of events; but as yet it was far from the surface. The war could begin with complete unanimity in the allied camp.

In the meantime, the alignment of forces was not restricted

[1] Polyb. IV, 25, 1–4 (and perhaps IX, 34, 11). The attack on Megalopolis in company with Illyrians is mentioned along with the attack on Pylus, and probably occurred on the same expedition.

[2] Polyb. IV, 25, 6 *seq.*

[3] Polyb. IV, 61, 6; cf. Beloch, IV, 2, 384; Flacelière, 252, n. 1. Cassope may also have gone with Ambracia.

[4] Polyb. II, 45, 1; IV, 63, 7 (Phoetiae); 63, 10 (Stratus); 64, 4 (Metropolis); 65 5 (Oeniadae); cf. Beloch, IV, 1, 596, n. 1.

[5] Cf. Fine, *TAPhA*, LVIII, 1932, 133 *seq.*; see above, p. 11.

to mainland Greece, but quickly displayed itself in a local conflict that had already begun in Crete.[1] Here, the town of Lyttus,
after successfully resisting an attempt of Cnossus and Gortyn
to establish a joint hegemony over the whole island, had gathered
around herself the nucleus of an opposition group of cities.[2]
The Cnossians, however, had an agreement with Aetolia, and
having obtained 1000 Aetolian troops by virtue of this, were able
to put down a revolt in Gortyn and raze the city of Lyttus to the
ground. These events were previous to the time with which we
are concerned (summer 220);[3] and it was possibly to this same
council at Corinth that representatives came from the anti-

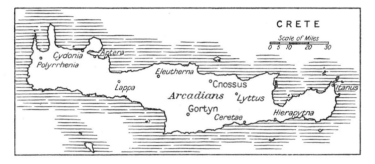

Cnossian cities, to ask Philip and the Achaeans for assistance.
Philip saw the advantage of occupying as many Aetolians as
possible in Crete; probably, too, the appeal flattered him with
its possibility of extending Macedonian influence in a district
in which both Doson and Demetrius had shown their interest.[4]
The cities in question—Polyrrhenia, Ceretae and Lappa, together
with the Orii and the Cretan Arcadians [5]—were received into the
Symmachy (presumably as a league) and a force of 400 Illyrians,
200 Achaeans and 100 Phocians was sent out to help them.[6]

[1] On this war see Cardinali, *Riv. Fil.* XXXIII, 1905, 519 *seq.*; Pozzi, *Mem. Acc. Torino*, LXIII, 1913, 386, n. 3; Klaffenbach, *IG*, IX, I², introd. p. xxv; A. Scrinzi, *Atti dell' Istituto Veneto*, IX, 1897–8, 1509 *seq.*; M. van der Mijns-brugge, 60 *seq.*

[2] Polyb. IV, 53–5.   [3] Polyb. IV, 53, 3: βραχὺ πρὸ τούτων τῶν καιρῶν.

[4] See above, p. 13, nn. 7 and 8.

[5] On these two confederacies see M. Guarducci, *Riv. Fil.* LXVI, 1938, 50–55.

[6] This alliance is reflected in the coinage: a silver tetradrachm from
Polyrrhenia, dating from this period, shows a male, beardless head, which
almost certainly represents Philip V idealised as Apollo; see frontispiece and,
for discussion, W. Wroth, *NC*, IV³, 1884, 54; Hill, no. 78.

Behind this policy, as in the decision at Tegea, was to be seen the hand of Aratus;[1] and in its results it was wholly justified. For within a very short time Eleutherna, Cydonia and Aptera had joined the coalition against Cnossus, and not only did Philip extend his influence in Crete, but the Symmachy received some 500 men from the Polyrrhenians to balance in some degree the 1000 with which the Cnossians shortly afterwards repaid their debt to Aetolia.[2] From now on, notwithstanding Rhodian assistance to Cnossus, the war in Crete went rapidly in favour of Philip's allies.[3]

Meanwhile the decree passed at Corinth was at once sent for confirmation to all the allies; Philip, moreover, despatched a copy to the Aetolians, with an offer to meet them, if they had any justification to offer.[4] The object of this move is uncertain. Philip may have hoped to postpone the official breach until the next spring,[5] or merely to put the onus for it upon the enemy. The Aetolians, however, regarding it as a bluff, fixed a rendezvous at Rhium, and then, hearing that Philip was on his way there, failed to keep it. This minor comedy over, Philip proceeded to Aegium, where an Achaean assembly now passed the war measure; in an address to the gathering, Philip impressed everyone very favourably, and the Achaeans now renewed in person with Philip the relations which had existed between them and his predecessor.[6] Aratus's influence with the young king appeared to be unchallenged.

At their autumn assembly the Aetolians replied to the allied

---

[1] Plut. *Arat.* 48, 3; Polyb. VII, 14, 4.   [2] Polyb. IV, 55, 5; cf. 61, 2.
[3] Polyb. VII, 11, 9; cf. Deiters, *Rhein. Mus.* LIX, 1904, 565 *seq.*
[4] Polyb. IV, 26, 3 *seq.*
[5] That he still sought to avoid the war (so Holleaux, 149, n. 1) is, however, improbable.
[6] Polyb. IV, 26, 8: τὰ προϋπάρχοντα φιλάνθρωπα τοῖς προγόνοις ἀνενεώσαντο πρὸς αὐτὸν τὸν Φίλιππον. Doson is the only one of Philip's predecessors with whom friendly relations had existed, but the plural πρόγονοι is used elsewhere of a single person; cf. *Syll.* 434/5 (Ptolemy I); *OGIS*, 222 (Antiochus I); see Tarn, *The Greeks in Bactria*, 450, n. 3. The phrase τὰ προϋπάρχοντα φιλάνθρωπα may include the renewal of such privileges as the annual Achaean oath of loyalty to the king of Macedon (Livy (P) XXXII, 5, 4), the king's right to summon an Achaean assembly (see above, p. 16, n. 1) and the law forbidding the proposal of any measure contrary to the Macedonian alliance (Livy (P) XXXII, 22, 3). See Aymard, *Premiers Rapports*, 54 *seq.*

ultimatum by electing Scopas general, a proceeding which arouses the partisan fury of Polybius.[1] About the same time, Philip returned with his army to Macedon, to make his own domestic preparations for the war. The excellent impression created by his philhellenic policy and willingness to take Aratus's advice is echoed in the praise of the Achaean historian, who writes[2] of the 'fair hopes of a mild reign and of the magnanimity of a true king'. However, the president of the Hellenic confederacy had not forgotten that he was first and foremost king of Macedon. One of his first acts on reaching Macedon (September 220) was to send a letter to the people of Larisa,[3] the key to Tempe, whose ambassadors had recently visited him, in which he urged them to make up their citizen body by enrolling resident aliens. It was an emergency measure, Philip explained; for he was already awake to the dangers of an Aetolian invasion of Pieria through Thessaly and the narrow pass of Tempe. The approaching winter (220–19) he spent levying troops and securing his northern frontiers against the ever-present threat from the Dardanians;[4] and, perhaps more important, he saw Scerdilaidas in person, and by a combination of boldness and clever diplomacy[5] bought his support for an annual subsidy of twenty talents. Cheated of his share in the booty from Cynaetha, the Illyrian readily undertook to use his fleet of thirty ships against his former employers.[6]

In Greece one state alone hesitated to ratify the allied decision. Whether alarmed at Philip's leniency towards her old enemy, Sparta, or whether, indeed, her decision merely reflected a

---

[1] Polyb. IV, 27, 2: ὑπὲρ ὧν οὐκ οἶδα πῶς χρὴ λέγειν. Soteriades, Ἀρχ. Δελτ. I, 1915, no. 18, attributes to this assembly certain decrees granting 'proxeniai' to citizens of Megalopolis, Aegium and Bura (cf. Klaffenbach, *IG*, IX, 1², 12; 13); and S. Schebelev, *Comptes rendus de l'Académie des Sciences de l'U.R.S.S.* 1930, 488–9 (in Russian: report by E. Bickermann, *Phil. Woch.* 1931, 1575) sees in these an attempt to win over the disaffected sections in Achaea. However, Klaffenbach, *loc. cit.*, shows clearly that the Scopas under whose generalship they were passed is not this one, and that they are to be dated a little before 271; cf. also Flacelière, 291, n. 3.

[2] Polyb. IV, 27, 10: καλὰς ἐλπίδας ὑποδεικνύων πρᾳότητος καὶ μεγαλοψυχίας βασιλικῆς.

[3] *Syll.* 543; see below, Appendix III, p. 297, for the date.

[4] Polyb. IV, 29, 1 *seq.*

[5] Polyb. IV, 29, 3: τολμηρῶς δοὺς αὑτὸν εἰς τὰς χεῖρας.

[6] Scerdilaidas may also have sought Philip's help in securing the title of king; cf. Zippel, 59.

change in the balance of parties (as Polybius suggests),[1] Messenia now put forward as a pretext for non-co-operation the presence of the Aetolian garrison at Phigaleia—the very factor which had given rise to the war. In north-west Greece Acarnania ratified the decree at once, but the Epirotes, according to Polybius, tried to play a double game and compromise with Aetolia.[2] Sparta, too, presented the usual difficulties.[3] Learning nothing from Philip's clemency at Tegea, she dismissed the envoys of the confederacy unanswered. Shortly afterwards, the pro-Aetolian opposition were strong enough to compel the Ephors, who favoured the Symmachy, to grant an interview to Machatas, an Aetolian representative, though not strong enough to carry their policy of an alliance. Soon, however,[4] news of the death of the late king Cleomenes in Egypt cleared the way for a new leader, and under a certain Lycurgus the royalists murdered the Ephors, installed Agesipolis and Lycurgus himself as kings, recalled Machatas and struck the long-awaited alliance with the Aetolians. It was arranged that the Spartan offensive should open against Achaea in the next spring (219).

The Spartan alliance was a diplomatic triumph for Aetolia, and stood out as the chief move in this year of manœuvres and preparations. The Aetolians had been above all anxious to take away the war from their own threshold into the Peloponnese; this was the reason why, faced with the hostility of the combined Symmachy, they had nevertheless refrained hitherto from the obvious move of an attack on Epirus or Acarnania—a move which Epirus's temporising attitude shows to have been widely anticipated. In addition, they were determined to exploit the social dissatisfaction which existed everywhere throughout the fruitful soil of the Peloponnese, hampering and demoralising Achaean attempts at united resistance. Philip, on the other hand, had sponsored the admission of Messenia into the Symmachy, and had showed clemency towards the Spartans in the hope of confronting Aetolia with a united Peloponnese. Now, by

---

[1] Polyb. IV, 31, 2; cf. 4, 3. The change, if any, was within a single class; the new ephors, though severely criticised by Polybius for their neutrality, are described as oligarchs, and did not align themselves with Sparta and Aetolia.

[2] Polyb. IV, 30, 2–7. Envoys were also sent to Ptolemy, requesting his non-intervention in the war (Polyb. IV, 30, 8).

[3] Polyb. IV, 34, 1–11. [4] Polyb. IV, 35, 1–36, 3.

Messenia's relapse into her traditional neutrality[1] and the *volte-face* of a Sparta under revolutionary control, the situation had become very similar to that at the opening of the Cleomenean War; and the resemblance was completed when Machatas shortly afterwards persuaded the Eleans to join the Aetolian confederacy.[2]

To keep the war out of the Peloponnese had been a policy that appealed equally to the interests of Philip and of the Achaeans; but the new situation contained within it the seeds of a clash between the two. Philip might still feel that Aetolia was better dealt with by a direct offensive in the north-west; but Aratus would unquestionably call for the support without which (as he knew from the Cleomenean War) the Achaean League would be a broken reed. This was indeed the situation that rapidly developed. For Lycurgus, after a swift raid in which he recovered the Laconian towns of Polichna, Prasiae, Leucae and Cyphanta, which lay east of Parnon, from the Argives, returned to Sparta, declared war on Achaea[3] and, in May, emulated

[1] Cf. Polyb. IV, 32, 5 *seq.*   [2] Polyb. IV, 36, 6.
[3] Polyb. IV, 36, 5: ἐπεκήρυξαν τὸ λάφυρον κατὰ τῶν Ἀχαιῶν.

Cleomenes by seizing the Athenaeum on the Megalopolitan frontier; and a little later Alexander and Dorimachus shipped 1200 Aetolians across from Oeantheia in the Crisaean Gulf and attempted a raid on Aegeira, in central Achaea, which failed only through recklessness.[1] On the Elean front, meanwhile, Euripidas, the Aetolian in charge, defeated an Achaean force and seized Teichus Larisa, and another fort of uncertain name near Telphusa.[2] So demoralised were the Achaeans by these attacks, that before the end of the season the western cities of Dyme, Pharae and Tritaea were withholding their federal contributions, and using them to hire their own mercenaries; in short, the League was nearer collapse than it had been since 225.[3] Yet all that the federal government could do was to send appeals to Philip.

He, meanwhile, was spending the summer of 219 in the coastal area west of Aetolia. After a detour through Thessaly,[4] with the purpose, no doubt, of following his letter to Larisa with a personal visit, he led a force of some 16,000 men[5] over the Zygos Pass, and through Tymphaea into Epirus, where he received the whole Epirote levy, 300 Achaean slingers and the 500 Cretans sent by the Polyrrhenians in gratitude for the help given them the previous winter.[6] With this united force he descended into Ambracia, where, Polybius states,[7] the Epirotes persuaded him to spend forty valuable days blockading Ambracus, a fortress lying on a lagoon immediately north of the Ambracian Gulf, and commanding the alluvial plain of the rivers Oropus and Arachthus.

Polybius censures Philip for letting himself be turned aside in this way from a direct invasion of Aetolia.[8] However, if the Aetolians held Ambracus and Ambracia, they also controlled the head of the Ambracian Gulf. For an invasion of Aetolia,

---

[1] Polyb. IV, 57, 2–58, 12.

[2] Polyb. IV, 60, 3: the MSS. give γόργον: 'Gortyna' and 'Stratus' have both been suggested (cf. Polyb. IV, 73, 2). See Klaffenbach, *IG*, IX, 1², introd. p. xxvi.

[3] Polyb. IV, 60, 4–10.

[4] Polyb. IV, 61, 1. Polybius gives no reason for the detour, but this is easily deduced from the general context of events, and from Philip's policy at Larisa. His further route follows from the reference to Thessaly.

[5] On Philip's forces this summer see Holleaux, 146, n. 3.

[6] See above, p. 33.   [7] Polyb. IV, 61, 5.

[8] Polyb. IV, 61, 3.

therefore, the best point of attack—if Philip was not to fight his
way along the narrow and difficult Amphilochian coast road—
was to disembark at Limnaea (as in fact he did in his campaign
of 218). But in 219 he had no fleet available for such an expedition, and there is no proof that he ever contemplated it.[1] There
is, indeed, good reason to question Polybius's criticism of the
Epirotes as responsible for Philip's delay at Ambracus. For at
the very outset Philip learnt of an Aetolian invasion of Thessaly
and Pieria, in the course of which crops had been ravaged and
the shrines at Dium pillaged by Scopas and his men;[2] nevertheless, he persisted in the long and arduous siege, thus displaying
his conviction of its strategical value.

After its fall, Philip presented Ambracus to the Epirotes; then,
taking his army along the coast of the gulf, he ferried it over
to Actium in Acarnania, and from here advanced rapidly, with
the addition of 2200 Acarnanian troops, against Phoetiae, an
Acarnanian town now held by the Aetolians. After two days it
surrendered, and after ambushing and destroying a force of 500
Aetolian reinforcements, Philip turned east towards Stratus and
the Achelous; it was while he was ravaging this district that he
received the Achaean appeal to march south at once, cross the
gulf at Rhium and invade Elis.[3]

Apparently in response to this appeal, Philip continued south
to Metropolis, and after taking this town, crossed the Achelous
and advanced to the capture of the Aetolian frontier towns of
Conope and Ithoria. At the river itself the Macedonian peltasts
showed their excellent discipline by crossing company by company, in strict formation and with shields interlocked, in the
face of strong opposition from the Aetolians, who controlled the
ford. From here Philip continued slowly south to Oeniadae,
provisioning as he went and destroying the Aetolian forts which
threatened the district.[4]

The Achaeans had urged Philip to cross the gulf at Rhium;
but the king had plans of his own. Having carefully dismantled

---

[1] Polybius's criticism recalls his similar misunderstanding of the issue in
201, when he censures Philip for not sailing on Alexandria after his victory
at Lade (Polyb. XVI, 10).

.[2] Polyb. IV, 62.

[3] Polyb. IV, 63, 3–64, 2; cf. B. Powell, *AJA*, VIII, 1904, 143.

[4] Polyb. IV, 64, 3–11; cf. Woodhouse, 159–61.

the well-constructed town of Paeanium, he floated the material down the Achelous to Oeniadae, which he soon captured and, after a short raid on Calydon, proceeded to fortify with a wall connecting the harbours and dockyards with the citadel.[1] But, while he was engaged here, news reached him of an imminent Dardanian invasion. At once he dismissed the Achaean envoys with promises of help as soon as it was practicable, and returned up the west coast to Macedon.[2] On the way a minor event occurred which was destined to have the most widespread consequences for Philip's future career; for at Actium he was met by Demetrius of Pharus, seeking refuge from the Romans, who had driven him out of Illyria. Philip greeted him kindly and sent him by the eastern route to Macedon. At Pella, however, learning that the Dardanian invasion had not materialised, he dismissed his citizen army to gather in the harvest, and himself spent the rest of the summer and autumn at Larisa in Thessaly.[3] Scopas's raid on Dium had shown clearly that this town, the strategical point for both Thessalian plains, still lay open to Aetolian attacks. Since, therefore, a letter and a hurried visit had not proved adequate, Philip was prepared to give the district the detailed attention that was only possible in a stay of two or three months. The time was well spent: a frontier dispute between the key citadels of Heracleium and Gonnus[4] was settled shortly after this visit, and though the internal problems of Larisa were not yet completely solved, there is no record throughout the remainder of this war of any Aetolian invasion through Tempe.

What were Philip's motives in his campaign of 219? We have already rejected the view that he contemplated an immediate invasion of Aetolia. If, on the other hand, his objective was, throughout, the Peloponnese, is his failure to reach it to be

---

[1] Polyb. IV, 65. In 212 (cf. Polyb. IX, 39, 2; Livy (P) XXVI, 24, 15) Oeniadae belonged to the Acarnanians; it is uncertain at what date Philip handed it over to them; cf. Holleaux, 160, n. 2. For two tiles with the inscription ΦΙΛΙΠ[ΠΟΥ] (which probably go back to this refortification), discovered at Oeniadae, see Powell, loc. cit. 170.

[2] Polyb. IV, 66, 1–5; ἐποιεῖτο τὴν ἐπάνοδον ᾗπερ καὶ τὴν παρουσίαν ἐπεποίητο. Presumably, however, he went direct from Epirus to Macedon.

[3] Polyb. IV, 66, 6–7.

[4] Arvanitopullos, AE, 1913, 43–6, no. 173, cf. 46, no. 174. The settlement is dated to Philip's third year, i.e. it is subsequent to September, 219.

attributed to an Aetolian opposition stronger than Polybius admits?[1] Or was Philip in fact deliberately delaying his march south in order to keep his eyes on the expedition with which the Romans were, this very summer, punishing the Illyrian breach of the last peace?[2] The latter is the view of Tarn[3] and Holleaux;[4] in its extreme form, which holds Philip in part responsible for the outbreak, it has been adequately refuted by Fine.[5] Philip had at no time committed any aggressive action against Rome, direct or indirect, nor had he ever displayed aggressive intentions. On the other hand, he must have been at least interested, if not alarmed by the Roman operations in Illyria, and this interest may possibly have been a contributing factor in the undoubted slowness which he showed in his advance on Oeniadae. Oeniadae itself, moreover, is not so excellently placed for crossing to the Peloponnese as Polybius claims;[6] it faces the Ionian Sea rather than the Corinthian Gulf, and lies nearer 200 than 100 stades from the nearest Peloponnesian port. It was, however, a good naval base for action in the north-west, such as took place the following summer; and, well fortified, it would be an adequate centre for co-operation with Achaea.

The difference between the merits of Oeniadae and the short crossings farther east is in fact the difference between the Achaean hopes and Philip's intentions. For whatever Philip's attitude towards Illyria, the systematic nature of his advance shows more than a mere desire to delay. From the persistent siege of Ambracus, which commanded the crossing of the Ambracian Gulf at Actium, to the expedition into Calydon, where he dismantled the fortress of Elaus, which Attalus of Pergamum had built for the Aetolians,[7] Philip's object revealed itself as the systematic opening up of a western coast route through the friendly territories of Epirus, western Ambracia and Acarnania. All the important fortresses along that route were seized or dismantled, and at Oeniadae, where the route necessarily narrowed, additional security was achieved by the

---

[1] So Ferrabino, 156.
[2] See above, p. 28.
[3] *CAH*, VII, 765.
[4] *Rome*, 140 *seq.*; so too Nicolaus, 52–3.
[5] *JRS*, XXVI, 1936, 35 *seq.*
[6] Polyb. IV, 65, 8: τὴν εὐκαιρίαν τοῦ τόπου πρός τε τἆλλα καὶ μάλιστα πρὸς τὰς εἰς Πελοπόννησον διαβάσεις.
[7] Polyb. IV, 65, 6.

possession of the Aetolian frontier towns and the ravaging of
Calydon. Thus Philip was looking beyond the immediate
expedition; he was not prepared to register a few successes
against the Aetolians and then cross over into the Peloponnese:
he sought rather to build a strong line of communications down
the west coast, which would at once consolidate his influence
among the western allies, and render it easier to reach Achaea
from Macedon. Oeniadae, at the terminus, was a well-placed
naval base, where a fleet could be built to operate against Aetolia
in either the Ambracian or the Corinthian Gulf. This scheme
was ruined by the threatened Dardanian invasion; the fortifi-
cation of Oeniadae remained unfinished,[1] and when the next
year the naval policy was taken some steps further, it assumed
a somewhat different form.

The summer's campaign, welcome though it no doubt appeared to Philip's counsellors, had nevertheless its price.
Thessaly and Macedon itself had suffered from Aetolian raids;
Achaea had been strained to breaking point under the combined
attacks of Aetolia, Sparta and Elis; and, notwithstanding their
considerable losses on their western frontiers, the Aetolians had
not yet sustained a decisive defeat. Quite plainly, another such
summer must mean the end of the Achaean League; and, whatever his plans against Aetolia, Philip could not afford this.
Accordingly he resolved to implement his promises by the novel
scheme of a winter campaign in the Peloponnese.

The Aetolians had apparently rounded off the campaigning
season with a raid on the shrine of Zeus at Dodona,[2] and it was
already the winter solstice, when suddenly Philip appeared with
nearly 6000 men at Corinth.[3] Like Doson in 224,[4] he had been
obliged by the Aetolian occupation of Thermopylae to make a
detour through Euboea—an immediate confirmation of his
wisdom in seeking to acquire a western coast route. Secrecy

---

[1] Polyb. iv, 66, 1; the part played by Oeniadae in Philip's scheme seems to
have been suggested when he saw the position of the city, and was not part
of the original plan; cf. Polyb. iv, 65, 8.

[2] Polyb. iv, 67, 1–5. A Macedonian coin depicting Zeus of Dodona
probably commemorates Philip's rebuilding of the shrine after the war: cf.
Mamroth, *ZN*, xlii, 1935, 225, no. 4.

[3] Polyb. iv, 67, 6–7; there were 3000 hoplites, 2000 peltasts, 300 Cretans
and 400 horse-guards.

[4] See above, p. 15.

was of the essence of Philip's plan. The gates of Corinth were closed and patrolled, lest news of his arrival should spread,[1] Aratus was summoned from Sicyon and instructions were despatched to the various cities of Achaea, fixing a rendezvous at Caphyae. This done, Philip moved south and encamped near the temple of the Dioscuri in the territory of Phlius. Here some of his Cretans, who were sent out plundering in the early morning, fell in with a band of Aetolians who were on their way to raid Sicyon.[2] Euripidas, the Aetolian leader, beat a hasty retreat, in the hopes of reaching the high ground beyond Stymphalus, but Philip pursued and brought him to a battle in a narrow pass near that town. Euripidas escaped, but of his 2000 men about 800 perished and the rest were sent back as prisoners to Corinth, along with the captured arms. Meanwhile Philip advanced over the difficult snow-covered pass of Mt Olygyrtus to Caphyae. Then, after two days' rest and the arrival of enough Achaean reinforcements, under the younger Aratus, to bring his forces up to 10,000, he continued through the territory of Cleitor against the strong fortress of Psophis, which, so long as the Eleans held it, menaced the western parts of both Achaea and Arcadia.

Polybius has a vivid description of the apparent impregnability of this fortress, which lay in the fork between the Erymanthus and a violent torrent which joined it, and was protected on its northern side by a hill, artificially fortified.[3] It was Philip's first attempt at taking a large town by assault, and at first the difficulties somewhat took him aback. Having resolved to make the attempt, he approached the town boldly in the early morning, and having by the unexpectedness of this move slightly shaken the morale of the defenders, who began to fear treachery within, he divided his forces into three columns, set up his ladders (gathered from various places *en route*) and by hard fighting got a footing on the walls. Simultaneously his Cretans drove back a mercenary force, which had come out of the city, and were able to pursue their retreating opponents within the walls. Euripidas and some of the inhabitants took

---

[1] Polyb. iv, 67, 8.
[2] Polyb. iv, 68, 1–69, 9; cf. Leake, *Morea*, iii, 132–3.
[3] Polyb. iv, 70; cf. Leake, *Morea*, ii, 245–8.

refuge in the citadel and made terms with Philip, who, while giving up the town to pillage, took special care to safeguard the lives of the inhabitants. He remained at Psophis for a few days, held up by snow, and then, handing over the fortress to the Achaeans, continued his march south.[1]

Before his triumphant advance the Eleans abandoned the garrisons of Lasion and Stratus, near the Erymanthus, and these Philip restored to the Achaeans and Telphusans respectively.[2] Five days later he reached Olympia, and after sacrificing to Zeus, proceeded to ravage Elis far and wide from two successive centres at the temples of Artemis and the Dioscuri. Intensive agriculture and farming on a slave basis were more advanced in the rich lowlands of Elis than in any other part of the Peloponnese;[3] and the wealthy squires who lived there now, as they had done in the time of Xenophon, supplied valuable plunder for Philip's never too richly endowed war. chest. A vast body of refugees had taken shelter, along with their slaves and cattle, in a secluded valley, known as Thalamae (the Recess),[4] and this assembly Philip trapped and compelled to surrender. The total yield amounted to 5000 Eleans, 200 mercenaries and large numbers of cattle and movables. Highly satisfied, Philip returned to Olympia.

Financially the expedition had been a complete success; in planning and execution it was typical of the tactics which Aratus favoured,[5] and which were eventually to make Philip renowned— the swift, sharp thrust, carefully organised and delivered when and where it was least expected. By this Elean expedition something had been done to recoup Philip for both his military expenses and the destruction done by Scopas in his raid on Thessaly and Pieria. On the other hand, the policy of handing over his conquests to Achaea could scarcely please Apelles and the court circle, to whom the Symmachy was an instrument for the political and financial aggrandisement of Macedon. Philip, indeed, was in no sense blind to Macedonian interests; the

---

[1] Polyb. IV, 71–2.
[2] Polyb. IV, 73, 2.   [3] Polyb. IV, 73, 5–75, 1.
[4] Situated, according to Curtius, II, 38 *seq.*, in north Elis, near the Achaean frontier; cf. Leake, *Morea*, II, 204.
[5] E.g. in his attacks on Sicyon (251), Corinth (243), Cleonae (235) or Mantinea (227).

difference was that under the influence of the generous philhellenic sentiments which Aratus had inspired, he did not interpret those interests as including territorial expansion in the
Peloponnese. The court circle, however, seeing the question
from the standpoint of Macedonian landowners, who must have
been called upon for large contributions to the privy purse, did
not care to have their money squandered to increase the power
of a league which they knew to have been built up on a policy
of hostility to Macedon.[1] Above all they mistrusted Aratus, and
envied the influence which he exercised over the king. The result
was a movement which began as a personal campaign against
Aratus, and ended as high treason against Philip.

This conflict of aims and personalities must have been in
existence for some time, when the first open clash came at
Olympia.[2] A number of Achaeans came to Aratus to complain
that Apelles had taken to ejecting them from their billets to make
room for Macedonians, that he had confiscated their share in the
booty and had even had those flogged or enslaved who remonstrated against this entirely unauthorised treatment. Realising
that behind this attempt at military subjugation there certainly
lay a threat to the Achaeans' political status, Aratus at once
appealed to Philip, who readily promised that such incidents
should cease; on the other hand, no action was taken against
the responsible ministers, and it was soon apparent that their
influence was on the increase, while that of Aratus was temporarily
on the wane.

This became clear from the sequel. For after setting out from
Olympia towards Pharae,[3] as if his goal were the west of Achaea,
whose claims had been only partially satisfied by the recent
expedition, Philip suddenly turned south again at Telphusa,
descended the Ladon, and held a sale of his Elean booty at
Heraea. The change in route evidently reflects a change in plan;
and it seems highly probable[4] that Philip's intention of assisting
Achaea had in fact been overruled by the advice of Apelles. The
proof of this is to be found in the short and brilliant campaign
in Triphylia.

The successor of the unfortunate Euripidas in Elis was a

[1] Cf. Treves, *Athen.* XIII, 1935, 35-6.   [2] Polyb. IV, 76.
[3] Polyb. IV, 77, 5: ἐπὶ Φαραίαν.   [4] So Ferrabino, 178, n. I.

certain Phillidas, who brought with him 600 Aetolian reinforcements.[1] With these, together with a little over 1500 Eleans,
natives and mercenaries, Phillidas now came to the help of
Triphylia, but on his arrival somewhat foolishly split up his
forces between the towns of Lepreum, Alipheira and Typaneae,
thus facilitating Philip's task. Leaving his baggage, the king
marched due south to Alipheira, and at sunrise on a cloudless
winter's morning set up his siege-ladders against its precipitous
walls.[2] The occupants were taken completely by surprise, and
after the mercenaries had fled to the citadel, he allowed them to
surrender this in exchange for their lives. On hearing of the
disaster, Phillidas evacuated Typaneae and joined his Elean
troops at Lepreum, whereupon Typaneae and Hypana not unnaturally surrendered without further resistance. Simultaneously the Phigaleians took a long-desired revenge by expelling the Aetolians quartered on them, and offered their city to
Philip.

At this favourable juncture Philip was able to split up his
forces; sending Taurion with one division to take over Phigaleia,
he himself advanced west on Lepreum, where an internal rising
already threatened Phillidas and his troops.[3] Upon his approach
Phillidas abandoned the town, and leaving his Spartan mercenaries to find their way home through Messenia, retired north
on Samicum. Philip was too late with his light troops to prevent
his taking refuge in the town, but upon his threatening a siege,
Phillidas begged for terms, and was finally allowed to withdraw
with his arms to Elis.[4] The remaining towns[5] now all surrendered
voluntarily, and Philip was able to return to Lepreum as master
of Triphylia. His conquest had lasted six days![6] From Lepreum
he marched back to Heraea for his heavy baggage, and continued to Megalopolis, arriving there in mid-winter.[7]

[1] Polyb. IV, 77, 6.
[2] Polyb. IV, 78, 2; for this campaign see Leake, *Morea*, II, 76–8.
[3] Polyb. IV, 80, 1; 80, 4. These troops consisted of 1000 Eleans, 1000
Aetolians, including the freebooters from Phigaleia, 500 mercenaries and 200
Spartans, making 2700 in all. Since the mercenaries brought by Phillidas had
been sent to Alipheira, where Philip took them prisoner, these 500 must be
another corps.
[4] Polyb. IV, 80, 5–13.
[5] These were Phrixa, Stylagium, Aepium, Bolax, Pyrgus and Epitalium.
[6] Polyb. IV, 80, 14.   [7] Polyb. IV, 80, 16; μέσου χειμῶνος.

More interesting than the actual conquest, however, was the settlement that followed. For instead of handing over the district to Arcadia, or even granting it an autonomous regime with membership in the Symmachy, Philip set it under a Macedonian *epimeletes*, Ladicus of Acarnania, and placed garrisons in the towns.[1] This reversion to the garrison system of Doson[2] may have been justified militarily by the necessity for thrusting a strong wedge between Aetolia and her Spartan allies, or even as an inducement to Messenia to join in the war; it is indeed significant that Philip's conquest included that ancient plague spot, Phigaleia.[3] But, whatever the justification, the policy adopted clearly demonstrates the ascendancy of Apelles and his group.

Philip's arrival at Megalopolis caused great alarm at Sparta, where a short-lived coup by a certain Cheilon had brought about a general fall in morale and the dismantling of the Athenaeum;[4] he continued, however, to Argos, there to be acclaimed with the greatest enthusiasm.[5] The mythical connection between the Argeads and the Temenids had always rendered that city a warm supporter of the Macedonian monarchy.[6] And now, for the majority of the Achaeans, Philip's brilliant campaigns[7] closed their eyes to the dangerous new precedent established in his settlement of Triphylia. The stage was set for Apelles's next move against Aratus. So long as the army was in winter quarters at Argos, he sedulously cultivated Aratus's personal enemies throughout the League, introduced them to Philip as likely tools of a policy of subjugating Achaea, and in general carried on a

[1] There is evidence for Lepreum, Polyb. IV, 80, 15.
[2] Evidence: Polyb. II, 54, 1 (Corinth); Polyb. II, 54, 10; Plut. *Cleom.* 23, 1; *Arat.* 45, 1 (Orchomenus); Polyb. II, 54, 12; Livy (P) XXVIII, 8, 6 (Heraea).
[3] The fate of Phigaleia is, however, uncertain. But one text (Pausan. VIII, 30, 5) suggests that it was handed over to Achaea, and this is confirmed by its issuing Achaean coins (Head, 418); cf. Aymard, *Premiers Rapports*, 58, n. 51.
[4] Polyb. IV, 81. King Lycurgus had apparently proved insufficiently revolutionary for some of his Cleomenean supporters; and Cheilon, under the slogan of social revolution, had murdered the ephors and caused Lycurgus to flee. Later, when Lycurgus returned, Cheilon took refuge in Achaea: but there is no evidence for the view (Ferrabino, 179) that Cheilon was supported by Philip.
[5] Polyb. IV, 82, 1.
[6] The coinage of the Antigonids (who claimed kinship with the Argeads) stresses the connection; cf. Mamroth, *ZN*, XL, 1930, 287; and below, pp. 258–9.
[7] For the effect in Greece cf. Polyb. IV, 69, 9; 77, 1; 82, 1.

campaign against Aratus's re-election as *strategos* for 218–17;[1] and Aratus's confidence was apparently so badly shaken that, contrary to his usual practice, he did not contest the office, but instead put up a nominee, Timoxenus. Apelles's campaign bears the marks of a very subtle and successful attempt to unite two quite different strands of Achaean opposition. Aratus's enemies in the various cities[2] were most probably those socially dissatisfied elements for whose support Aetolia had been angling, and who were only to be won over to support of Philip, if they believed him to be ready to modify his patronage of the established order. Alone, these sections were not strong enough to oust Aratus: Apelles's skill lay in combining their opposition with that of the western cities, who were by this time quite desperate at the failure of the League to give them adequate support against Elis, and in persuading both discontented parties to unite in support of a single candidate, Eperatus of Dyme. Thus Apelles, who was himself responsible for deflecting Philip to Triphylia, now thrust the blame for the neglect of western Achaea on to Aratus; and his master stroke was Philip's arrival at Aegium, with his army, at the time of the elections, on his way to succour these cities by means of a new expedition.[3] The voting was close: but Eperatus was elected by a small majority.

Philip had now to fulfil the more concrete half of his election pledges. Advancing along the coast through Patrae and Dyme, he forced the surrender of Teichus Larisa, the Achaean fort on the Elean frontier,[4] which Euripidas had recently seized and garrisoned. Handing this over to Dyme, Philip continued into north Elis, and returned very soon with rich plunder, having justified Eperatus's election and replenished his own war chest. On the strength of this success, Apelles now proceeded to a personal attack on his rival. Among the prisoners taken at

[1] Polyb. IV, 82, 1–7. By custom Aratus was elected *strategos* every other year, successive generalships being illegal (Plut. *Arat.* 24, 4); as general in 220–19, he would normally have been re-elected in 218–17. In 225, similarly, Timoxenus had stood in Aratus's place (Plut. *Arat.* 38, 2; *Cleom.* 15, 1).

[2] Polyb. IV, 82, 4: ἑκάστους ἐκ τῶν πόλεων ἐπεσπάσατο. Note that Apelles's headquarters at this time were at Argos, and the record of Argos, both in the Cleomenean War and later (see below, p. 165, n. 1), suggests that it harboured many of the popular opponents of Aratus. On the acuteness of class-feeling in Argos, even in the fourth century, see Diod. xv, 57, 58; Isoc. *Philip.* 52.

[3] Polyb. IV, 82, 7–8.

[4] Polyb. IV, 83, 2: σπεύδων δὴ τοῦτο κατὰ πάντα τρόπον ἀνακομίσασθαι τοῖς Δυμαίοις.

Thalamae was Amphidamus, the Elean general; after an interview at Olympia, this man had undertaken to try to bring over Elis to the allied side, and had been sent back without ransom to convey to his countrymen Philip's offer to restore all booty and prisoners free if they would join him.[1] However, the Eleans had rejected Amphidamus's proposals, and Apelles now claimed to have proof that the failure was due to the machinations of Aratus, who, in his jealousy of the growing influence of Macedon in the Peloponnese, had persuaded Amphidamus not to press the matter. Philip heard the accusation and the defence, but left the question undecided for want of adequate evidence. But now, by the irony of fortune, Apelles's main tactical success, the campaign against northern Elis, proved the means of exonerating his rival; for the Eleans, in a war panic, chose this moment to impeach Amphidamus as a traitor; and he, learning what was afoot, fled to Philip at Dyme, to be triumphantly produced by Aratus as a witness for the defence.[2]

The vindication of Aratus was a slight setback for Apelles; but it is clear from Polybius[3] that Aratus's reinstatement was only partial. Moreover, his earlier experience had led Philip to identify Greece with Aratus. With the eclipse of Aratus, the first flush of Philip's philhellenism was now over; henceforward his dealings with the Symmachy would evidently be governed more strictly by Macedonian policy, and this no longer excluded the acquisition of key positions in south Greece. This increase in Macedonian claims was reflected in the growth of separatism in Achaea and the discrediting of Aratus; but two winter campaigns had staved off disruption in the Peloponnese by the ingenious device of winning over the disruptive, dissatisfied elements to the side of Philip. These campaigns had provided Philip with a valuable political lesson, as well as military experience and a certain necessary addition to his financial resources. The drain on the slender income of Macedon had been, in fact, considerable. Even though the citizen army had been able to reap the harvest[4] and Elis had yielded such adequate

[1] Polyb. IV, 84, 4: ἐὰν ἕλωνται τὴν πρὸς αὐτὸν φιλίαν. Presumably they were to join the Symmachy.
[2] Polyb. IV, 86.   [3] Polyb. IV, 86, 8.
[4] See above, p. 40.

plunder, the prospect of another expensive season's campaigning, coming immediately after the summer and winter expeditions of 219, filled Philip with some alarm.[1]

In May Eperatus took office,[2] and Philip soon discovered his weak character and lack of genuine influence in Achaea. His willingness as a tool was nullified by his complete ineffectiveness; and so Philip turned once more to Aratus. Having persuaded the League officials to transfer a special assembly from Aegium to Sicyon, he there came to terms with Aratus, and it was decreed[3] that as soon as he struck camp Philip should receive fifty talents and 10,000 bushels of corn to last him for the next three months, and after that seventeen talents a month so long as he remained in the Peloponnese. This agreement no doubt wore a different aspect to Apelles, Philip and Aratus. The dilemma which the last year's campaigns had presented to Achaea was either to collapse internally through failure to meet the attacks of Elis, Sparta and Aetolia, or, alternatively, to obtain help from Macedon at the expense of seeing an unwelcome growth of Macedonian power on her frontiers. However, with Elis and Sparta weakened, it seemed that if Philip could be induced to guarantee the Peloponnese as an Achaean sphere of influence and, in the meantime, concentrate on attacking Aetolia, Achaea might struggle on alone. To Aratus, beyond doubt, the financial arrangement represented such a guarantee. To Apelles, on the contrary, it must have appealed as a means of taxing Achaea, while Macedon established still firmer roots in the Peloponnese. Finally, to Philip it was an immediate subsidy and a guarantee against future Achaean appeals for charity, in the form of a Macedonian army. The immediate use of this two-edged weapon must turn inevitably on Philip's plans for the year 218.

At a meeting of his Friends, held shortly after the conference at Sicyon, Philip revealed his determination to institute a strong naval policy against Aetolia.[4] Only by the command of the sea

---

[1] Polyb. v, 1, 6: ἐνδεὴς ὢν σίτου καὶ χρημάτων εἰς τὰς δυνάμεις.

[2] Polyb. v, 1, 1; cf. Beloch, IV, 2, 220; Aymard, *Assemblées*, 252, n. 3.

[3] Polyb. v, 1, 11–12; cf. Aymard, *Assemblées*, 252, n. 4, who, with Casaubon, rightly takes the words εἰς τὴν πρώτην ἀναζυγήν to mean *quo die primum castra rex moveret*, and not, as Schweighäuser (and Paton in the Loeb translation), *pro prima expeditione*.

[4] Polyb. v, 2, 1–3.

could the communications of Sparta, Elis and Aetolia be cut; with a fleet he could fall upon each member of the coalition in turn, and so divide and conquer. This scheme, which involved the resuscitation of a fleet that had been allowed to decay since Doson's Carian expedition of 227,[1] had been foreshadowed and half-formulated in the previous summer's struggle to open up the western coast road and fortify Oeniadae; but now it emerged as a clear plan of action.

Moreover, behind the naval policy there stood a new figure— Demetrius of Pharus, who had joined Philip at Actium the previous summer[2] and may have accompanied him on the winter expedition in the Peloponnese. His growing influence was to be apparent throughout the approaching campaign, and in view of his later activity, there can be little doubt that the responsibility for the naval policy was his. On the other hand, there is no reason for concluding that so far Philip looked forward to anything more than the suppression of the Aetolian coalition, and perhaps an increased influence in Epirus and Acarnania; certainly there is no evidence for reading into this naval policy any formulated programme of hostility towards Rome.

While the actual preparations were going busily ahead at Lechaeum, the Apelles group took counsel. To Apelles, who remembered the Carian incident, the assembling[3] and maintaining of a fleet must have seemed an expensive and hazardous project, likely to put an intolerable strain upon the Macedonian budget, and so upon the large landowners, who were represented by Philip's Friends; moreover, taken in conjunction with the financial agreement, it appeared to involve the surrender of most of the advantages of his recent attack on Achaean autonomy. Indeed, Apelles and his group, with their eyes on the Peloponnese, seem to have been bitterly opposed to any move towards the north-west. With longer memories than Philip, they may have remembered the Peloponnesian policy of the early Antigonids, pursued with the connivance of a friendly Aetolia.

---

[1] See above, p. 12.   [2] See above, p. 40.

[3] The fleet was in fact assembled from Macedonian and Achaean sources; but from Livy (P) xxviii, 8, 14 (date: 208) it is clear that Philip built no new vessels, and Holleaux has shown (*Rome*, 158, n. 6; 159, n. 1) that in all he could muster only a dozen cataphracts and some forty light vessels. The crews consisted of specially trained phalangites.

Moré and more their plans began to envisage a diversion of the war from Aetolia, and further inroads on Achaean independence. Philip, however, was adamant; and accordingly Apelles, Megaleas and Leontius took a further step and formed a conspiracy to sabotage the naval scheme.[1] First, it was decided, they would continue in their efforts to traduce Taurion, the Commissioner of the Peloponnese, and Alexander, the Chamberlain;[2] and secondly, Apelles was to retire to Chalcis and from there organise a systematic interference with Philip's supplies, while his fellow-conspirators remained with the king to obstruct whatever was afoot in the camp. This scheme was put into operation; and, whether through its efficiency or because of the natural strain of a naval programme, Philip was very soon driven to the pitch of pawning his family plate.[3]

It was early June when the fleet was ready to sail.[4] With the supplies received from the Achaeans Philip paid and provisioned his troops, and set out with a force of 6000 Macedonians and 1200 mercenaries to Patrae. The news caused some alarm in Elis, where Philip was generally supposed to be making for the Elean coast town of Cyllene. This would indeed have been the natural continuation of the expedition which saw the capture of Teichus Larisa; and Cyllene would be a useful counterpart to Oeniadae across the Calydonian Gulf. It was at present the headquarters for communications with Aetolia,[5] and the Aetolians, sharing the general alarm, despatched two officers with 500 Cretan mercenaries[6] to Elis, and fortified the place. However, Philip had quite different plans. Leaving a mixed force of Achaeans and Galatian and Cretan mercenaries to defend the frontier near Dyme, he himself put out from Patrae, and sailed to Pronni in Cephallenia, where he had already instructed the

---

[1] Polyb. v, 3, 7-8.   [2] Polyb. iv, 87, 1; 87, 5.

[3] Polyb. v, 2, 10. Apelles had himself appointed governor of Euboea; S. B. Kougeas claims that a record of his activity there survives in the inscription published in Ἑλληνικά, vii, 1934, 177-208 (= IG, xii, Suppl. 644). However, C. B. Welles, AJA, xlii, 1938, 245-60, is probably right in regarding this as part of a general army code, not connected with Apelles.

[4] Eperatus entered office at the beginning of May; the subsequent events occupy at least a month.

[5] Polyb. iv, 9, 9.

[6] Polyb. v, 3, 1; Polybius calls them 'Neocretans', probably with reference to some special type of arms; cf. Griffith, 144, n. 2.

Messenians,[1] Acarnanians and Illyrians under Scerdilaidas to meet him.

The island of Cephallenia was an important base for anyone who wished to operate in these waters;[2] in alliance with the Aetolians, it provided them with a fleet for plundering expeditions in Epirus and Acarnania, and also for communications with the Peloponnese.[3] Philip began by setting up his siege-works outside Pale, on the western side of the island, and succeeded in breaking down the walls; but, whether through the influence of Leontius, as Polybius reports,[4] or for some other reason, the Macedonians were driven out of the town, and, after consultation with his Friends, Philip abandoned the siege.

The next move was hotly debated. News had arrived of a large-scale invasion of Thessaly by half the Aetolian army under Dorimachus; and the Acarnanians, from not wholly disinterested motives, urged Philip to sail north and force their withdrawal by an invasion of Aetolia. The newly converted Messenians, on the other hand, urged him to make use of the Etesian winds to sail swiftly south, and bring help against Lycurgus, who was once more safely installed upon the throne of Sparta. Leontius naturally supported the Messenian plan, hoping thereby to see Macedonian domination still further established in the Peloponnese, at the cost to Achaea of seventeen talents a month! Unable to return north with any ease in the face of the prevailing winds, Philip would be obliged to concentrate on the complete subjugation of Sparta. That Leontius looked forward with relish to the continued ravaging of Thessaly and Epirus by the Aetolians is, notwithstanding Polybius's accusations, less likely.[5]

Aratus was equally anxious to keep Philip in the north; the force at Dyme was some sort of check on Elis, and temporarily the Spartans had found another victim in Messenia. This was the more acceptable policy to Philip; he had not, after all, built a fleet solely to operate in Messenia, and he was eager to follow up his previous summer's successes. Accordingly the Achaeans were bidden to send help to Messenia, and the Macedonians

---

[1] The capture of Phigaleia had brought the Messenians into the war; Polyb. v, 4, 5.
[2] Polyb. v, 3, 9–4, 1.
[3] See above, p. 25, n. 3.
[4] Polyb. v, 4, 7–13.
[5] Polyb. v, 5, 7–8.

sailed north between Leucas and the mainland to Limnaea, the Acarnanian port at the head of the Ambracian Gulf.

Reinforced by Acarnanians (the Epirote levy was late in arriving) and encouraged by Dorimachus's absence in Thessaly, Philip had decided on a typically bold and striking step—a swift blow at the very heart of Aetolia, the federal and religious centre of Thermum.[1] Leaving all his heavy baggage behind, under a guard (as in his assault on Triphylia), he set out in the evening, continued all through the night and, by daybreak, had reached the Achelous, a little south of Stratus. Here, once more trying to ruin the expedition, Leontius urged Philip to rest his men; but the king preferred to follow the advice of Aratus, which matched his own inclinations, and pressed on to catch the enemy unawares. Crossing the Achelous, he advanced along the south shore of Lake Trichonis, plundering the country; and he occupied the town of Metapa with a garrison of 500 men, before venturing through the narrow coastal pass between there and Pamphia.[2] From Pamphia he turned north-east to Thermum, and reaching the holy place in the evening he at once set about plundering in good earnest. Thermum was full not only of corn, but also of the precious goods assembled in preparation for the autumn festival;[3] it was systematically pillaged, and what could not be removed was destroyed.[4]

But Philip went still further. In revenge for the looting at Dium and Dodona the previous year, he now destroyed the temple colonnades, razed the sacred buildings to the ground, and shattered any statues not actually representing or dedicated to gods. And on the walls the Macedonians scrawled the grim jest of the poet Samus, Philip's foster-brother, with its punning

[1] For the topography of the invasion see Woodhouse, 228–286, with the criticisms of Bölte, *P-W*, 'Lysimacheia (1)', cols. 2552 *seq.*; Rhomaios, Ἀρχ. Δελτ. II, 1916, append. 45; Plassart, *BCH*, XLV, 1921, 62, n. 3; Klaffenbach, *Berlin S.B.* 1935, 715; Flacelière, 6–7.

[2] Polyb. v, 8, 1–2 puts the pass between Pamphia and Thermum. Woodhouse, 257 *seq.*, attributes the confusion to a contamination of two sources, Aratus's *Memoirs* and Nicander of Trichonium, whom Polybius will have met at Rome. However, the *Memoirs* ceased in 220 (cf. Polyb. IV, 2, 1); hence the cause of the confusion must lie elsewhere.

[3] Polyb. v, 8, 4–9.

[4] A contemporary reference to the sack of Thermum survives in a letter to the Parians (?), *IG*, XII, 5, 125; it is too fragmentary for its authorship to be determined with certainty.

reference to Dium: ὁρᾷς τὸ δῖον οὗ βέλος διέπτατο.[1] Polybius is strong in condemning this sacrilege, and blames Demetrius of Pharus, who was undoubtedly prominent in Philip's counsels at this time.[2] He may be right; but it would be rash to exonerate Aratus completely. Aratus must have felt a far keener hatred of the Aetolians than Demetrius, and he had, like Philip, the memory of past Aetolian outrages to influence him. But, in any case, Philip was not acting against his nature; the suggestion met with a ready response from the great-grandson of Pyrrhus, who now revealed an aspect of his character with which the Greeks were soon to become only too familiar.

On the other hand, sacrilege apart, the attack on Thermum showed decided method. Psychologically, the destruction of their hitherto impregnable centre was calculated to depress the morale of the Aetolians; furthermore, the double programme by land and sea, to say nothing of Apelles's attempts at sabotage, was proving a drag upon the treasury, and, as had been widely recognised by military leaders from Philomelus to Scopas, the sacred places were the most profitable to plunder. Like his teacher, Aratus, Philip was inclined to ignore the rising tide of feeling, which, throughout the third century, sought to invest these places with the rights of inviolability and asylum;[3] and in fact it was this quality of calculating ruthlessness which, more than any other, rendered Philip so unsympathetic a character in Polybius's eyes. It has been claimed[4] that in giving way to his passions at Thermum Philip acted against his own interests, by closing the way to reconciliation with Aetolia. This estimate fails to take account of the speech of Agelaus of Naupactus the next year.[5] But, more important, it is not so certain that Philip desired reconciliation; the savagery which he showed may have been planned to force the Aetolians to accept a dictated peace.

From Thermum Philip covered his retreat with great care; loaded with plunder, he anticipated an attack from those Aetolian troops who were not in Thessaly. In the face of the immense Macedonian numerical superiority (Philip had over 10,000

---

[1] Polyb. v, 9, 5. The line is adapted from Euripides, *Suppl.* 860, and as Dow and Edson, *Harv. Stud.* XLVIII, 1937, 156, observe, its point lies not only in the pun but also in giving Philip the role of Zeus.
[2] Polyb. v, 12, 5–8.
[3] Cary, 242–3.   [4] Tarn, *CAH*, VII, 767.   [5] See below, p. 66.

men),[1] the Aetolians dared not come out into the open, but once the retreat began, they attacked the Macedonian rear. However, Philip took care to screen his own men by the use of mercenaries,[2] and routed them with slight losses; and the march proceeded without further incident (save the burning of the towns they passed) until Stratus was reached. Here the enemy had massed their forces and, refusing to be tempted out, waited until Philip was marching past the town to engage him in a rearguard action; nothing came of this, however, and Philip reached Limnaea without further incident.

The most remarkable feature of the attack was its speed and lack of precedent. In a little over twenty-four hours Philip had covered the distance from Limnaea to Thermum,[3] and this, together with his superior numbers, had paralysed the opposition. The actual route, except for a few miles along the lake, is an easy one; as in the taking of Triphylia, speed and numbers had done the work almost unaided, and immense booty had been collected. On the other hand, no decisive blow had been delivered against the Aetolian army; and it is not entirely impossible (though this cannot of course be proved) that Leontius's attempts to delay Philip had the object of provoking a regular conflict.

Certainly the opposition of the Apelles group now became more pronounced than ever. Returning to his tent after dinner, Aratus was stoned by Megaleas and a friend named Crinon;[4] and this time Philip took action. The two courtiers were fined twenty talents each and imprisoned until they paid; and Leontius failed to secure their release. The incident is of interest as showing Philip in a new and autocratic light: for in claiming to try and sentence men of high rank, he was undoubtedly encroaching upon custom, if not upon the rights of the army-assembly.[5]

---

[1] 7200 Macedonians (Polyb. v, 2, 11), the Acarnanians πανδημεί (Polyb. v, 6, 1–2), i.e. perhaps 3–4000. The Aetolians had about 8000 men, unless the 3000 at Stratus are different from the 3000 at Thermum (Polyb. v, 13, 3; 14, 1); the forces left in Aetolia were half the total levy (Polyb. v, 6, 4; 17, 5–7).
[2] Cf. Tarn, *Hellenist. Milit. and Naval Developments*, 26.
[3] Cf. Polyb. v, 6, 5; 8, 3–4.
[4] Polyb. v, 14, 8–16, 10.
[5] See above, p. 2; any rights proper in such cases were vested not in the Friends, but in the army-assembly; cf. Polyb. v, 27, 5; 29, 6. But see below, p. 61, n. 4.

When the fleet reached Leucas, however, he called together his
Friends and gave the two men a form of trial. Aratus, as accuser,
brought forward not merely relevant evidence, but charges going
back into the reign of Doson,[1] that of having carried out a
massacre at Argos being calculated to appeal to Philip's Argive
sympathies. The Friends confirmed Philip's sentence, Crinon
was left in prison and Megaleas was freed on Leontius's surety.
Aratus had apparently recovered his old position with the king.

On the other fronts, meanwhile, activity was at a minimum.[2]
Both in Messenia and in a raid on Tegea, Lycurgus had failed.
The Eleans, it is true, had outwitted both the force at Dyme and
Eperatus, who proved too incompetent to protect even his own
western cities, and they had secured important Achaean prisoners;
but in Thessaly Dorimachus had met with substantial Macedonian opposition, and had been obliged to return to Aetolia,
too late, however, to catch Philip. For Philip, meanwhile, was
already planning a third spectacular campaign. From Leucas
he sailed quickly to Corinth, pausing only to plunder the land
of Oeantheia on the Crisaean Gulf; and on reaching Lechaeum,
he sent out notices mobilising the Peloponnesians at Tegea for a
fixed day.[3] Four days later—less than a fortnight after leaving
Thermum[4]—Philip appeared with his new levies on the hills
east of Sparta, having taken a circuitous route so that his arrival
might be unexpected.

For some days he pillaged the Laconian plain systematically,
first in the rich district near Amyclae, and later as far south as
Taenarum and Malea.[5] With 4000 troops against Philip's 10,000,[6]
Lycurgus was at a grave disadvantage, and wisely restricted
himself to attacking a contingent of 1300 Messenians who, like
the Epirotes at Limnaea, had arrived late at Tegea and gone on
into the district east of Parnon.[7] These Lycurgus surprised near

[1] Polyb. v, 16, 6.   [2] Polyb. v, 17, 1–4.
[3] Polyb. v, 17, 8–9.
[4] Polyb. v, 18, 9–10. For the chronology of this journey see Holleaux,
157, n. 8.
[5] Polyb. v, 19; cf. Leake, *Morea*, I, 138 *seq*.
[6] Polyb. v, 21, 1; it may be assumed that the 2000 men with whom Lycurgus
occupied the Menelaeum represented about half his total forces. As the
Sellasia campaign shows (Polyb. II, 65, 7) Laconia was capable of a much
greater contingent than this.
[7] Polyb. v, 20, 1–3; cf. Leake, *Morea*, I, 273.

Glympeis and carried off all their equipment to Sparta; and arriving here he began to prepare for Philip's return north.[1]

By occupying the Menelaeum, on the left bank of the Eurotas, with a force of 2000, and flooding the plain, so as to limit the ground over which Philip could advance, Lycurgus hoped to neutralise the Macedonian cavalry and force Philip to proceed in a long column open to flank attacks from either side. However, Philip was able to seize the Menelaeum without difficulty; having tired out its garrison with mercenary assaults, he followed up with his peltasts, while the Illyrians attacked the flank. The Spartans broke and ran, and Philip was able to cover his phalanx from a cavalry attack from Sparta, until, under the command of Aratus, it had negotiated the dangerous passage.[2] That night he encamped on a plateau north of Sparta, and the next day inspected the famous battlefield of Sellasia, before returning to Tegea. Here he held a sale of booty, and finally marched back to Corinth.

The apparently overwhelming success of these rapid and sensational raids[3] could not, unfortunately, cloak the comparative failure of Philip's policy. The rich plunder from Thermum and south Laconia was swallowed up in the overhead costs of the naval squadron, so much so that the army grew dissatisfied at its share; and meanwhile Leontius and Apelles continued their intrigues to such effect that for the first and last time in his life Philip was faced with a mutiny of his troops.[4] He was busy at Lechaeum with naval matters, including a proposed visit to Phocis, when he was recalled to Corinth by the news that some of the peltasts and troops of the *Agema* were plundering the royal apartments and the tents of the Friends. At a mass meeting in the theatre Philip succeeded in quelling the sedition, at least for the moment; whereupon Leontius, who had been the prime mover in the rising, decided to recall Apelles. Since he left the court Apelles had been exercising autocratic power in Thessaly and south Macedonia to an extent unknown since Alexander's command at Corinth, in the time of Gonatas.[5] But Aratus,

---

[1] Polyb. v, 20, 4–12.   [2] Polyb. v, 21–3.

[3] For the general effect of Philip's generalship see Polyb. v, 18, 7; 18, 10; 29, 2; 102, 1. On a possible further source for these events see below, p. 352, n. 1.

[4] Polyb. v, 25.   [5] See above, p. 52, n. 3.

meanwhile, had recovered Philip's favour and used it to effect against his rival;[1] hence, when Apelles reached Corinth, he found the magnificent reception given him by the troops, under Leontius's influence, nullified by an unexpected rebuff from the king. Whereupon Megaleas, sensing an approaching storm and conscious that he had not yet paid the money he was fined at Limnaea, prepared for flight.

Apelles, however, was now made to accompany Philip on an expedition to Phocis, the purpose of which Polybius does not reveal.[2] It took Philip by ship from Lechaeum and later up country as far as Elatea, where the plan, whatever it was, seems to have foundered. It has been suggested that Apelles had been stirring up unrest and opposition to Philip's concentration on the west coast;[3] this is possible, but if so what were Philip's plans and how did they fail? Far more probably Philip's main concern, as in Acarnania the previous year, was to open up swift communications with the Peloponnese, this time with his new naval base at Corinth. True, the Aetolians still held Ther-

---

[1] Polyb. v, 26, 6: ἅτε καὶ παρὰ πλευρὰν ὄντος ᾿Αράτου καὶ πραγματικῶς ἐξεργαζομένου τὴν ὑπόθεσιν.

[2] Polyb. v, 26, 16.   [3] Ferrabino, 212 seq.

mopylae; but if for the tedious march through Boeotia there could
be substituted a safe route through Phocis to Cirrha or Anticyra,
there connecting with the fleet from Lechaeum, Corinth would
become twice as accessible as before. And, in addition, a move
would have been made towards shaking the Aetolians' grip on
Delphi. For such a route Philip must be able to rely completely
on Elatea; preferably he must acquire some direct control over
the town. Yet it would be fatal to arouse the hostility of the
Phocians. It was probably on the failure to solve this delicate
problem that the Phocian expedition foundered.[1]

Returning to Cirrha, Philip sailed across to Sicyon and put
up at the house of Aratus.[2] The Achaean's return to favour is
one of the most remarkable features of this summer's campaigns.
The raid on Laconia was, in fact, wholly to the benefit of Achaea,
since Philip had shown no signs of the policy of increasing direct
Macedonian control. Similarly, the naval activity from Corinth
would check the enemy in what had been for many years an
Aetolian lake, without offering any threat to Achaea. Now,
significantly, it was from Aratus's house that Philip took the
swift steps necessary to finish with the opposition group. Apelles
was sent on to Corinth; Leontius's peltasts were despatched to
Triphylia and their leader arrested as the surety for the runaway
Megaleas. A deputation from the peltasts, urging a public trial
and, alternatively, offering to subscribe the sum forfeited by
Megaleas, merely enraged the king, and Leontius was executed.[3]

Apparent evidence of Megaleas's treachery now came to hand.
A short time previously, on his return from Sparta, Philip had
been met at Corinth by neutral ambassadors from Chios and
Rhodes,[4] offering to arbitrate between Aetolia and the Symmachy,
and had sent them on to the Aetolians under the pretext that he
had always been quite ready to make peace. This was of course a
diplomatic lie, as Polybius tells us;[5] the sensational if not very
solid successes of this summer had given him no reason to

---

[1] For complete success in such a scheme Philip would have needed
Epicnemidian Locris, since so long as this remained Aetolian (Klaffenbach,
Klio, xx, 1926, 82) he could not land further west than Cynus. Meanwhile
he may have been encouraged by the strong pro-Macedonian feeling along
the Cephisus and near Elatea (cf. Flacelière, 286).

[2] Polyb. v, 27, 3.   [3] Polyb. v, 27, 4–8.   [4] Polyb. v, 24, 11.

[5] *Ibid.* Holleaux, 149, n. 1, assumes that Philip had played a reluctant part
all through the war, and has therefore to reject Polybius's evidence here.

modify the policy he had been following since 220. Aetolia and Sparta, on the other hand, if not defeated, had suffered considerably from Philip's raids; and the ambassadors soon returned to Sicyon, announcing that the Aetolians desired peace[1] and would meet Philip on a certain day at Rhium. It was at Patrae, on his way to this meeting, that Philip now received certain letters from Phocis, which, it was claimed, Megaleas had sent to the Aetolians, urging them to press on with the war. The king acted quickly: he sent Apelles back to Corinth and there had him executed along with his son. And Megaleas, learning of this at Thebes, forestalled a similar fate only by committing suicide.[2]

So ended the Apelles conspiracy. Whether the Phocian letters were genuine or not there is no longer the evidence to decide. They may have been forged by Philip to counter the expected opposition of the army; or again they may have been a genuine attempt by Megaleas to reinforce Aetolian opposition, so that Philip might be tempted back into the easier field of the Peloponnese;[3] or finally Polybius may be right, and the long-rankling jealousy of Aratus may have turned Doson's trusted counsellors into traitors. However, Aratus's personal triumph turned out, somewhat ironically, against the interests of Achaea. For the Aetolians, taking heart at the apparent disorganisation of Philip's court, put off the date of the peace conference; whereupon Philip threw aside the mask of peacemaker, cancelled negotiations and urged the worn-out allies to new efforts. Having sent his Macedonians home through Thessaly for the winter, he then returned by sea from Cenchreae, pausing at Demetrias on the way to try to execute Ptolemaeus, the last of the Apelles group.[4]

Meanwhile, the arrival of winter saw Achaea reduced to desperate straits, with an Elean detachment stationed on the

---

[1] Cf. Polyb. v, 29, 1.   [2] Polyb. v, 28, 4 seq.

[3] That Megaleas believed Philip's professions of peace, and thought to thwart them, as Tarn seems to suggest (CAH, VII, 767), is highly improbable in view of the conspirators' long record of interference with Philip's war against Aetolia.

[4] Polyb. v, 29, 6. Ptolemaeus, alone of the conspirators, was tried ἐν τοῖς Μακεδόσιν—by the army-assembly, according to the usual view; cf. Granier, 127 seq. But the army had been sent home by land to Macedon (Polyb. v, 29, 5); and though it may have met Philip by arrangement at Demetrias (it would have come via Euboea), it cannot be considered certain that the court at Demetrias was a regular army-assembly.

Panachaean Mountain above Patrae, and raiding the country as far as Rhium and Aegium. The federal contributions ceased and, when the following spring Aratus took over the command from Eperatus, the League was on the verge of collapse. A desperate remedy was needed; and Aratus to some extent saved the situation with a new system of regional organisation, designed to counter the secessionist movement of the western cities. Indeed, under a vigorous leader, Lycus of Dyme, these cities had some success during the succeeding spring and early

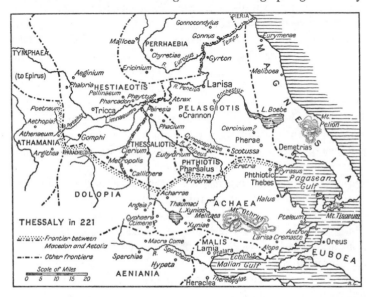

summer (217).[1] In the north-west of Greece there were raids and counter-raids between Aetolia, Epirus and Acarnania, without decisive results; and in Phocis, Philip's commander Alexander succeeded in capturing a hundred picked Aetolian troops, who were persuaded to enter the fortress of Phanoteus, in the belief that it was to be handed over to them.[2] On all sides it was a year of weakness and small enterprises; yet the Aetolians had declined peace and the allies were dependent on Philip.

So far Philip had, rather strangely, made no move against Aetolia from the Thessalian frontier. His attention to Larisa

---

[1] Polyb. v, 94; 95, 5–12.   [2] Polyb. v, 96.

and Phocis was, of course, designed as a check on his enemy in
the north-east and east; but it had not been enough. In particular,
Philip felt the difficulty which the continued Aetolian occupation of Thermopylae and Phthiotic Achaea[1] presented to his
communications with the south,[2] apart from the threat from this
province to Magnesia, Thessaly and the narrow outlet to the
Pagasean Gulf at Demetrias.[3] Now the chief outpost of Aetolian
power in Phthiotic Achaea was Demetrias's ancient rival,[4] the
city of Phthiotic Thebes; and it was therefore against this town
that Philip's main plan for 217 was directed.

He opened the season, however, with a preliminary campaign
in the north. Philip had not forgotten the Dardanian threat of
219; but, unfortunately, his almost continuous activity in Greece
since the essential winter campaign of 219–18 had given him no
time to rectify the position on his northern frontier. Now, in
the spring of 217, he continued Doson's work by seizing Bylazora,
the town in Paeonia commanding the pass over into Dardania.[5]
Then, with a typical exhibition of speed and organisation, he
assembled the citizen levies from the various provinces at
Edessa, and marched south to arrive in Larisa on the sixth day.[6]

Philip's first scheme for the taking of Phthiotic Achaea was
evidently based on the now famous Triphylian campaign. He
planned to drive a wedge between the province and Aetolia, and
from this base to advance east and so proceed systematically to
the capture of Thebes. However, his attack upon Melitaea, the
base selected, failed, mainly because the siege-ladders were too
short,[7] and Philip, evidently changing his plans,[8] advanced to the
assault on Thebes without delay. In all, the operations lasted
fifteen days, and the townspeople finally surrendered when the
Macedonians had undermined the wall and brought down a

---

[1] See above, p. 11.

[2] Philip's activity in the north-west and in Phocis is evidence of this.

[3] Polyb. v, 99, 3–4; XVIII, 11, 6–7.

[4] Demetrias was synoecised by Demetrius Poliorcetes (Strabo, IX, 5, 15;
perhaps in opposition to Thebes; cf. Diod. XX, 110, 3); see Stählin, 67; 173;
Ernst Meyer, *Pagasai und Demetrias*, 178 *seq.*; 194.

[5] See above, p. 10, n. 6.   [6] Polyb. v, 97, 1–4.

[7] Did Philip rely on finding these *en route*, as in his attack on Psophis?
(See above, p. 43.) Polybius has two contradictory accounts of the attack on
Melitaea: v, 97, 5–6; IX, 18, 5; cf. Niese, II, 457, n. 2.

[8] This seems the most probable explanation of Philip's movements, prior
to his attack on Thebes.

large section in ruins. However, their surrender availed them
little, for with complete ruthlessness Philip sold the whole
population into slavery and, rechristening the town Philippopolis, established a Macedonian colony there.[1]

The fall of Thebes was an important step towards the conquest of Phthiotic Achaea; but news of the revolt of Scerdilaidas
prevented Philip from following it up. Dissatisfied with his
subsidy from the depleted Macedonian treasury, the Illyrian
had seized four of the ships Taurion had at Leucas, and he was
reported to be buccaneering with these off Malea.[2] With a
hurriedly marshalled fleet of fifty vessels, mostly light,[3] Philip
at once sailed through the Euripus to Cenchreae, and sending
his eight decked ships round the peninsula he dragged the rest
of his fleet across to Lechaeum. From his actions it is plain that
his eyes were still on Aetolia;[4] and though he had sent a second
group of neutral ambassadors from Chios, Rhodes, Byzantium
and Egypt to the Aetolians[5] with the old plea that the Symmachy
was always ready for peace, he was clearly bluffing.

Suddenly Philip's whole policy was reversed. As he sat at the
Nemean games at Argos, which he visited from Lechaeum, he
learnt from a messenger from Pella that Hannibal had won a
sensational victory over the Romans at Lake Trasimene in June.[6]
At first Philip showed the letter to Demetrius of Pharus alone,
and the Illyrian exile at once advised him to bring to an end the
Aetolian war and turn his full attention to the west. Plainly
Philip had for some time had his eyes on the Hannibalic War;
the messenger who reported the Roman defeat was obviously
one of several who had kept the court at Pella posted with news

[1] Polyb. v, 100, 1–8; Diod. xxvi, 9; cf. Tscherikower, 4. Hiller von Gaertringen, *Hist. Gr. Epig.* 104, records a twelve-line hexameter verse from the
tomb of an Antigenes, son of Sotimus, from Demetrias, who fell on Philip's
side in this campaign (cf. A. J. Reinach, *REG*, xxiv, 1911, 320). Some of the
inhabitants who escaped found refuge in Thronium, now Aetolian (Livy (P)
xxviii, 7, 12).
[2] Polyb. v, 95, 1–4; 101, 1 *seq.*
[3] Polyb. v, 101, 2; cf. Holleaux, 159, n. 1.
[4] Polyb. v, 101, 2: σπεύδων μὲν καταλαβεῖν καὶ τοὺς Ἰλλυριούς, καθόλου δὲ
μετέωρος ὢν ταῖς ἐπιβολαῖς ἐπὶ τὸν κατὰ τῶν Αἰτωλῶν πόλεμον διὰ τὸ μηδέν πω
συνεικέναι τῶν ἐν Ἰταλίᾳ γεγονότων.
[5] Polyb. v, 100, 9–11: αὐτὸς δὲ τῆς μὲν διαλύσεως ὠλιγώρει, τοῦ δὲ πράττειν τι
τῶν ἑξῆς ἀντείχετο.
[6] Polyb. v, 101, 6; for the date see De Sanctis, iii, 2, 119 *seq.*

from Italy. But this is far from saying with Tarn[1] that Philip
had already plans for joining in that war, or admitting the
existence of a 'fixed idea, inherited from Antigonus, of driving
the Romans from Illyria'.[2] On the contrary, it is clear from
Polybius that the spirit behind Philip's western policy was
Demetrius.[3] His influence had already appeared in the events
at Thermum, and naturally Philip must have consulted him first
and foremost in anything that concerned the west coast. Thus
Philip's plan for a naval expedition against Scerdilaidas was
essentially a project to receive the approbation of Demetrius;
and in the news of the Roman crisis, the latter at once saw the
chance to recover his kingdom. To Philip his advice was simple:
let him end the Aetolian war, and devote all his attention to the
reduction of Illyria (including incidentally his own kingdom);
this done, he could send an expedition to Italy, and later still
take further steps towards world domination![4] In the meantime
Greece would be subservient, the Achaeans through preference
and the Aetolians through the weakness that must follow the
present war.

To the young king the advice was most welcome.[5] Hitherto
his eyes had been in the main turned south towards Greece,
where he had fought to extend Macedonian influence, both
directly and through the Symmachy. But as the war dragged on
indecisively, he was not sorry to be reminded that he was
descended from Pyrrhus as well as Antigonus Gonatas, and to
be encouraged to embrace a new and exciting western policy,
which would take him away from the little stage of Greece into
the greater arena, where Hannibal and the Senate were, in
effect, deciding even now the fate of the Hellenistic world. This
plan for a western expedition was rash; it bore all over it the
marks of haste, of a young man's surrender to flattery rather than
a cool calculation of the factors involved. But it served to bring
the war of the Leagues to a sudden end.

At a meeting of his Friends Philip encountered no opposition;
and Aratus, now that the war was going in his favour, preferred,
typically, to realise any advantages that could be obtained from

[1] *CAH*, vii, 765.
[2] Holleaux, *CAH*, vii, 853; cf. *Rome*, 139 *seq.*; *Rev. Phil.* L, 1926, 201 *seq.*
[3] Polyb. v, 102, 1.   [4] Polyb. v, 101, 8–10.   [5] Polyb. v, 102, 1.

a negotiated peace. So, ignoring the neutral embassies, Philip despatched an Aetolian prisoner,[1] Cleonicus of Naupactus, directly to the Aetolians, and brought his fleet to Aegium. Meanwhile, not to prejudice his bargaining power by an apparent over-eagerness for peace, he marched over Erymanthus to seize a fort near Lasion;[2] and while negotiations were actually in progress he made a short expedition to gain control over Zacynthus, which occupied an important position for any western scheme.[3]

At length, after some exchange of messengers, Philip met the Aetolian leaders on the shore near Naupactus, and peace was made on the basis of the *status quo*. Of the various speeches delivered, Polybius reproduces as most significant that of Agelaus of Naupactus, the leader of the Aetolian peace party[4] and a representative exponent of the Greek point of view. This was, in essentials,[5] an invitation to Philip to undertake a benevolent guardianship over Greece, and, adopting an attitude of defensive watchfulness, to wait and see if eventually an opportunity should arise for securing world sovereignty. For all its tactful phrasing, the speech was fundamentally a request to Philip not to hurl himself thoughtlessly into a war with Rome. At the same time, the danger from Rome, the 'cloud in the west',[6] was fully recognised, and before it the Greeks must compose their difficulties while there was still time.

There was no longer a war party; by waiting, Philip had been able to impose his peace at the moment he desired. On the other hand, the war had brought few gains to the Symmachy.[7] The Epirotes and Acarnanians had won a few slight advantages at the expense of Aetolia, and the Achaeans had gained Psophis and Phigaleia. But the main fruits of the war, Triphylia, Phthiotic Thebes and Zacynthus, had gone to Macedon, whose power was once more dominant in the Peloponnese and the

---

[1] Polyb. v, 95, 12. For an analysis of the negotiations leading up to the peace, from a juridical aspect, see Heuss, *Stadt und Herrscher*, 140 *seq.*

[2] Polyb. v, 102, 2–6.   [3] Polyb. v, 102, 10.

[4] Cf. Holleaux, 162 and n. 4.

[5] Polyb. v, 104. The speech in Polybius, notwithstanding rhetorical elements (cf. De Sanctis, *Riv. Fil.* LXII, 1934, 108–9), bears the mark of a true version based on a contemporary record; cf. Holleaux, 18, n. 2.

[6] Polyb. v, 104, 10: τὰ προφαινόμενα νῦν ἀπὸ τῆς ἑσπέρας νέφη.

[7] For the Aetolian losses see Klaffenbach, *IG*, XI, 1², introd. p. xxxii; cf. Flacelière, 294 *seq.*

greater part of Thessaly. True, by his financial bargain to assist Philip's naval programme, Aratus had saved Achaea from the fate planned by Apelles; but the wearing campaigns on two fronts had weakened the League, and for some time the decision had been wholly in Philip's hands.[1]

Indeed, perhaps the most striking feature of the war was the rapid increase in Philip's stature. From a stripling to be despised,[2] he had, by his boldness, skill and indefatigable energy, made himself the decisive force in the Balkan Peninsula. He had shown himself to be master over his own court and army, and had rapidly outgrown his political apprenticeship under Aratus and the Apelles group. In Greece his prestige was enormous;[3] to the Symmachy he was the 'darling of Hellas',[4] while Crete, united with few exceptions in a single confederacy, had already elected him president (προστάτης).[5] Thus to Philip Naupactus was the end of an epoch.[6] It marked the transition of his interests and ambitions from the restricted sphere of Greece to the west; from now onwards his part was cast in the great Mediterranean conflict between Carthage and Rome.

[1] Similarly, it was Philip, not the Symmachy, who took all the decisive steps towards the peace; cf. Holleaux, 163, n. 2.

[2] Cf. Polyb. IV, 3, 3; 5, 3; 22, 5; V, 18, 6; Plut. Arat. 46, 2. On Philip's position in 217 see (with certain qualifications on the role there given to hostility towards Rome) Holleaux, 164–5.

[3] Examples of dedications to Philip, put up about this time, are IG, IV, 1, 427 (inscription on a statue by Thoenias, son of Teisicrates, erected to Philip at Sicyon) and IG, IV², 1, 590 A (inscription at Epidaurus, in honour of Philip's victories over Sparta and Aetolia in 218; cf. Hiller von Gaertringen, Hist. Gr. Epig. 103). See Dow and Edson, Harv. Stud. XLVIII, 1937, 131–2.

[4] Polyb. VII, 11, 8: κοινός τις οἷον ἐρώμενος ἐγένετο τῶν Ἑλλήνων διὰ τὸ τῆς αἱρέσεως εὐεργετικόν.

[5] Polyb. VII, 11, 9; see above, pp. 32–4. The town of Itanus remained Egyptian, and possibly others; Polybius rather exaggerates the completeness of Macedonian control, and it is doubtful whether as προστάτης Philip was in fact much more than an honorary patron (as for instance Ptolemy Euergetes became Hegemon of the Achaean League in 243 (Plut. Arat. 24, 4; Pausan. II, 8, 5), or Attalus of Pergamum Commander-in-Chief of the Aetolians in 210 (Livy (P) XXVII, 29, 10)). See Cardinali, Riv. Fil. XXXV, 1907, 2–5; Holleaux, Klio, XIII, 1913, 145, n. 3; M. van der Mijnsbrugge, 62.

[6] A dedication by Philip at Delos, Syll. 573, ἀπὸ τῶν κατὰ γῆν ἀγ[ώνων] Ἀπόλλων[ι] is usually dated to this period; cf. Vallois, 158; Laidlaw, 117; Durrbach, Choix d'insc. de Délos, I, 72, no. 56. De Sanctis, IV, 1, 9, n. 26, argues strongly, however, for placing it in 201, after Lade, since the wording implies a corresponding dedication from a victory κατὰ θάλασσαν (IG, XI, 4, 1101?). See below, p. 121, n. 1.

Chapter III : Philip Looks West

THE FIRST WAR WITH ROME (217–205)

FOR the moment the war with Rome was overshadowed by the activities of Scerdilaidas. It was on his way to attack this renegade prince that Philip had heard of the news of Trasimene; and now, on his return from Naupactus to Macedon, he learnt that Scerdilaidas had followed up his exploits at Leucas with an invasion of Pelagonia. It is not impossible that the Romans had some responsibility for this diversion[1] in a district so near their own protectorate; but in any case both immediate and ultimate interests obliged Philip to act quickly. The western and north-western frontiers of Macedon were ill-defined, and it was from the Illyro-Dardanian tribes of this district that the invasion had come, which hastened Doson's death. Now Philip learnt of the capture by Scerdilaidas of Pissaeum, probably in Lyncestis, and further west across the great lakes, in Dassaretia, of other towns, Chrysondyum, Gertus and Antipatreia.[2] In the light of his new ambitions, these towns and the valleys of the Apsus and Genusus, which they controlled, were of the utmost importance, and Philip lost no time in marching to recover them. By the end of the season he had not merely got back what he had lost, but had taken in addition Creonium and Gerus in Dassaretia, Bantia among the Caloecini,[3] Orgyssus among the Pisantini,[4] and, near Lake Lychnidus, Enchelanae, Cerax, Sation and Boei.[5]

Few details of this campaign have survived; but it would appear to have vied in speed and skill with Philip's exploits in Triphylia and Thessaly. Obtaining no help from Rome, Scerdilaidas was driven from Pelagonia and Dassaretia, and Philip brought his possessions to the very threshold of the Roman

[1] Holleaux, *Rome*, 166; *CAH*, VII, 855.
[2] Polyb. V, 108, 2; cf. Zippel, 61–3; Holleaux, 166–7.
[3] Perhaps Korça; cf. Fine, *JRS*, XXVI, 1936, 25.
[4] Near Antipatreia (Berat); cf. Livy (P) XXXI, 27, 2.
[5] Polyb. V, 108, 8; cf. Leake, III, 325 *seq.*, who places these towns on the west shore of the lake.

protectorate. It was, undoubtedly, against this Illyrian protectorate that his next steps were directed. He spent the winter
of 217–16 training his men for the sea and building a hundred
light Illyrian galleys (*lembi*) for operations in Illyrian waters.[1]
Macedonian finances did not allow the construction and main-
tenance of a regular fleet;[2] consequently Philip's actions were
automatically circumscribed. He could not hope to face a naval
conflict with Rome; this Polybius specifically states.[3] On the
other hand, with a hundred *lembi* he could rapidly transport a
force of 5000 men,[4] and relying on the Roman preoccupation
with Hannibal, he might hope to seize the Illyrian coast before
the fleet came up from its station off Lilybaeum in western
Sicily.[5] It was here, in Illyria, that Philip's immediate plans
were centred; but once Illyria was in his hands, he undoubtedly
intended to link up his land communications with Macedon down
the newly-won valleys of the Apsus and Genusus, and with
reinforcements to attempt a rapid crossing to south Italy, where
the Greek cities might be expected to welcome him as a second
Pyrrhus.

Such, Polybius tells us,[6] were the dreams in which Philip
indulged, thanks to the persuasive and unrealistic advice of his
counsellor. They were, however, short-lived. Early in the
summer of 216, Philip set out with his new fleet from Demetrias,[7]
rounded Cape Malea, and, hearing at Leucas that the Roman
fleet was still off Lilybaeum, continued his voyage towards
Illyria.[8] But meanwhile Scerdilaidas had sent a desperate appeal

[1] Polyb. v, 109, 1 *seq.*
[2] Cf. Holleaux, 175; De Sanctis, III, 2, 402–3. References: Polyb. v, 1, 6;
1, 11–12; 2, 10; 95, 1; 108, 1; cf. IV, 29, 7.
[3] Polyb. v, 109, 2: τοῦτο μὲν γὰρ οὐδ᾽ ἂν ἤλπισε δυνατὸς εἶναι, Ῥωμαίοις
διαναυμαχεῖν.
[4] Holleaux, 176, n. 1. A *lembus* held about fifty men, and Polybius speaks
only of *lembi*. It does not appear that, in the early stages at least, Philip proposed using the ships which he had mustered in 218 (cf. Polyb. v, 2).
[5] Polyb. v, 109, 6.
[6] Polyb. v, 101, 10–102, 1; 108, 4–5. For Philip's preoccupation with
Roman affairs at this time, see his second letter to Larisa (*Syll.* 543), written
in August 215, in which he supports his instructions to fill up the citizen-
body, with an elaborate, if inaccurate account of Roman policy in founding
colonies and awarding citizenship; cf. Robert-Mommsen, *Hermes*, XVII, 1882,
467 *seq.*; Cavaignac, *Rev. Phil.* XXXIII, 1909, 179–82; Schroeter, 78–9, no. 31.
[7] Where it was most probably built; cf. Holleaux, 176, n. 2.
  Polyb. v, 109, 4–6.

to the Romans, and a squadron of ten ships was at last despatched from Lilybaeum. Philip had reached the island of Sasona, in the bay of Aulon, when he heard of the approach of this squadron, and falsely imagining that the full Roman fleet was sailing to annihilate him, he ordered an immediate retreat; in breathless haste and panic his fleet reached Cephallenia the next day, and from here, after a short stay to save his face, Philip returned to Macedon amid the jibes of the Greeks.[1]

Hitherto Philip's policy had been based on the assumption that the Romans would be too preoccupied in Italy and the west to send ships to Illyria. The debacle of 216 therefore demanded a complete change of plan. If Rome meant to defend Illyria, Philip's *lembi* were inadequate; hence, the sooner some arrangement could be made with Hannibal the better. So long as Philip had hoped to invade Italy himself, negotiations were better delayed until he could approach Hannibal as an equal on Italian soil. But now he must have seen that his hopes of invading Italy were dashed; and the news of the Roman disaster at Cannae[2] and the subsequent dogged resistance of Rome only emphasised the urgency of an agreement with the Carthaginian, while Philip had still something to offer.[3]

It was in the following summer (215), after negotiations lasting throughout the winter and spring and complicated by the Roman capture of Philip's messenger Xenophanes,[4] that the treaty between Philip and Hannibal was signed. Its text,

---

[1] Polyb. v, 110; as Holleaux, 178, n. 2, observes, these jibes are echoed in the criticisms of Polyb. v, 110, 10–11.

[2] August, 216; cf. Hallward, *CAH*, VIII, 54. This news serves also to explain Philip's inaction in the latter part of 216; the prospect of a peace with Hannibal which left Rome free to turn her full forces on Macedon was a sufficient check on an immediate offensive; cf. Holleaux, 179, n. 2.

[3] An invasion of Italy by Philip must have been unwelcome to Hannibal: Livy XXIV, 13, 5 (Tarentum suitable for Philip to land) though perhaps going back through some annalist to Polybius (cf. De Sanctis, III, 3, 362) may be ignored in view of the recorded terms of the treaty.

[4] Livy (A) XXIII, 33; 38; for the date cf. Livy (A) XXIII, 39, 4, and below, Appendix III, p. 299. Xenophanes was probably captured on his return journey, and the Polybian version of the treaty will be a copy of that seized (Polyb. VII, 9; note the reference to Xenophanes in § 1); however, Livy has Xenophanes taken twice, Appian (*Maced.* 1) puts his capture on the return journey, while Justinus (XXIX, 4) and Zonaras (IX, 4) leave the details vague; cf. Holleaux, 183, n. 2; De Sanctis, III, 2, 407, n. 22; Engers, *Mnem.* VI, 1938, 134 *seq.*

preserved by Polybius,[1] shows clearly both its limited scope and the predominant role of Hannibal. In the preliminary clauses Philip, for the Macedonians and Greeks of the Symmachy, and Hannibal, for the Carthaginians and his allies, including those in Gaul and Italy, pledge each other support in general terms; and it is then laid down that Philip shall assist Hannibal ὡς ἂν χρεία ᾖ καὶ ὡς ἂν συμφωνήσωμεν.[2] The right of making peace shall be Hannibal's, but any peace made with Rome must include Philip; further, the states of Corcyra, Apollonia, Epidamnus, Pharus, Dimale, the Parthini and Atintania shall be taken from Rome; and the Romans shall be compelled to return the friends of Demetrius of Pharus, whom they were holding at Rome. Finally, the alliance was to cover mutual defence in the case of a later attack on either party by the Romans, or any other state not exempt by former treaty with Carthage.

The significance of the treaty lies mainly in its omissions.[3] There is no longer any question of a Macedonian invasion of Italy; the fiasco off Sasona and the battle of Cannae have together relegated Philip's share in the war to a mere diversion. Even so, the treaty was valuable; it promised first and foremost that Illyria should become Macedonian (or at least Pharian), and secondly it secured Philip against a Roman war of revenge. For Hannibal it created a new front, with a new offensive against Rome, at the very moment when the Carthaginian policy was to extend the area of the war;[4] at the same time it did not directly

---

[1] Polyb. VII, 9. The versions of Livy XXIII, 33, 9–12; Appian, *Maced.* I, and Zonaras IX, 4, 2–3, are worthless annalistic fabrications. On the details see Holleaux, 181, n. 2; 183, n. 1; De Sanctis, III, 2, 407; Niese, II, 467. Polybius gives the version sworn to by Hannibal: that sworn to by Philip will have differed in phrasing, but scarcely in substance.

[2] Does this clause foreshadow a later συμφωνία, including definite terms for the mutual exchange of help, military or naval? So Holleaux, *Rome*, 183, n. 3, and (less definitely) *CAH*, VIII, 119. But, if so, there is no evidence that this συμφωνία was ever made or put into practice; and if βοηθεῖν (Polyb. VII, 9, 11) *does* imply sending definite help to Italy, it is only to be sent ὡς ἂν χρεία ᾖ i.e. at Hannibal's discretion.

[3] See in general Niese, II, 467; G. Egelhaaf, *HZ*, LIII, 1885, 456 *seq.*; Kromayer, *HZ*, CIII, 1909, 244 *seq.*; Kahrstedt, *Geschichte der Karthager*, III, 449; De Sanctis, III, 2, 407 *seq.*; Holleaux, *Rome*, 179 *seq.*; *CAH*, VIII, 119; Groag, 80 *seq.*; Altheim, II, 97.

[4] Cf. Hallward, *CAH*, VIII, 61. Holleaux, 182, n. 4, even suggests that Hannibal may have taken the initiative; but the treaty was so obviously advantageous to both parties, that this is difficult to decide.

commit him to send to Greece any assistance which he might require elsewhere. Thus, fundamentally, the treaty was a definition of spheres of interest and, even more, of spheres of operation. Its vagueness was the direct result of the circumstances in which it was signed; it depended for its significance on a swift Carthaginian victory, and as this gradually became more remote, so the terms of the treaty grew less substantial, until by the time of Philip's separate peace with Rome it was an almost forgotten fragment of history.

In Greece itself, meanwhile, the unanimity apparent at Naupactus, which sprang mainly from exhaustion, showed signs of imminent disruption; and, shortly after the signing of the treaty with Hannibal, probably in the autumn of 215,[1] this took the form of an outbreak of class warfare in Messene. The details are obscure;[2] but apparently Philip, hearing of the trouble, hurried to the city and, instead of supporting the pro-Achaeans in power,[3] as his obligations to the Symmachy required, cleverly egged on the popular party to massacre the officials and 200 of their supporters,[4] evidently hoping to make private capital out of their accession to power.

Two factors appear to have moved Philip; one was the fear of Aetolia, the other the arguments of Demetrius. Elected general after the agreement at Naupactus,[5] Agelaus was able, for his year of office, to keep in check the gradually growing discontent and economic distress in Aetolia; for the general peace had at one swoop cut off the whole of Greece from those piratical depre-

---

[1] See below, Appendix III, p. 299 seq.

[2] See Seeliger, 12–13; Niese, II, 468–70; De Sanctis, III, 2, 410–11; Holleaux, *Rome*, 197–8; *CAH*, VIII, 120; Ferrabino, 227 seq.; Walbank, 156; Nicolaus, 63; Porter, *Plutarch's 'Life of Aratus'*, introd. xciv.

[3] Plut. *Arat.* 49, 3. The reference here to στρατηγοί suggests a change of constitution since 220, when the officers were called ephors (Polyb. IV, 4, 3; 31, 2). This change, perhaps to be associated with the complete triumph of Gorgus's policy, does not imply a development from oligarchy to democracy; that Gorgus was pro-Achaean may be inferred from Polybius's eulogy (VII, 10) and from his anti-Spartan policy of 218 (Polyb. V, 5, 4), but his wealth and family (Polyb. VII, 10, 2: οὐδενὸς δεύτερος Μεσσηνίων πλούτῳ καὶ γένει) do not suggest the democrat. At the most, his control may have been democratic in relation to the close oligarchy of the neutral party (Polyb. IV, 32, 1: οἱ... προεστῶτες ὄντες ὀλιγαρχικοί). The fragment, Polyb. VII, 10, 1: οὔσης δημοκρατίας παρὰ τοῖς Μεσσηνίοις, probably refers to the conditions established after the events of 215, described above.

[4] Plut. *Arat.* 49, 3; cf. Livy (P) XXXII, 21, 23.   [5] Polyb. V, 107, 6.

dations on which she largely subsisted. The export of mercenaries afforded some little relief,[1] but sooner or later an outbreak
was inevitable. A weak and faction-ridden Messenia offered
the same temptation now as in 220, when the brigandage of
Dorimachus had led to the Social War;[2] and by unofficial intervention in support of a restored oligarchy, the Aetolians might
reinsinuate themselves into the Peloponnese, from which the
recent peace so adequately excluded them.

These fears weighed heavily with Philip,[3] who dreaded a new
eruption of war in the Peloponnese and the consequent dis-
tractions of a Symmachy clamouring for his aid. Demetrius too
saw his Illyrian schemes imperilled; and he found Philip immediately amenable to his suggestion, which was that he should
seize the citadel of Ithome himself, and hold it, along with
Corinth, Heraea, Orchomenus and Triphylia, with a Macedonian garrison. Thus, held, it would effectively control all
communications between Elis and Laconia, and, in short,
render the disastrous combination of Sparta and Aetolia impossible. Thus, under the stress of his new western programme,
Philip found himself compelled to adopt Apelles's old policy of
dominating the Peloponnese, and, as in the days when Apelles
had organised the election of Eperatus, this path took him away
from Aratus and the oligarchs, and towards the party of social
change. The bonds which bound the Greek oligarchies to Pella
threatened suddenly to fall apart.

But Philip had not allowed for the vehemence of Achaean
opposition. The story repeated with slight variations by Polybius
and Plutarch[4] shows this in a vivid form. Reaching Messene
post-haste, the day after the massacre, Aratus and his son[5] at
once reproached the king in the bitterest terms; and when,
shortly afterwards, Philip had sacrificed to Zeus on the summit
of Ithome and had asked, after consulting the entrails, whether

---

[1] Cf. Holleaux, *REA*, XVIII, 1916, 233 *seq.*

[2] See above, pp. 24 *seq.*

[3] Cf. Holleaux, 197–8, for this convincing explanation of Philip's conduct;
contra Porter, *op. cit.* xcv.

[4] Polyb. VII, 12; Plut. *Arat.* 50; cf. Strabo, VIII, 4, 8. The Polybian version
is preferable, that of Plutarch showing the influence of the rhetorical schools.

[5] The tradition which made him a lover of Philip goes back to Polybius
(cf. VII, 12, 9: ἐπιτετιμημένος δὲ μικρῷ μὲν πρότερον ὑπὸ τοῦ νεωτέρου πικρῶς
ἐπὶ τῇ τῶν ἀνδρῶν ἀπωλείᾳ with Plut. *Arat.* 50, 1 *seq.*).

he should keep or relinquish the citadel, the answers he received made him ponder. On the one side stood Demetrius, on the other Aratus; and their replies were in character. 'If you have the mind of a diviner, you will withdraw: if that of a king, you will seize an opportunity such as may never come your way again, and stay'; and Demetrius finished with the pregnant advice to seize the ox by both horns, meaning, Polybius adds, 'by the horns Ithome and the Acrocorinth, and by the ox the Peloponnese'.[1] Aratus, on the contrary, after a slight hesitation, urged Philip to put his trust in the good faith of his allies, that good faith which served as his garrison as far away as Crete.[2] It was not wholly a plea, as Philip realised; he could not afford to garrison Ithome, if that meant leaving behind him an Achaean League that was dissatisfied and ripe to revolt. Perhaps weakly, perhaps in part swayed by his relations with the younger Aratus,[3] Philip withdrew; and for a time the breach was avoided.

But the escapade was never forgotten. The Messenian poet Alcaeus, from his refuge in Aetolia, poured out his vitriolic epigrams against the king who had forced him into exile;[4] and in Achaea there was a swift revulsion against the recent 'darling of Greece',[5] whose debut in 220 had raised such high hopes[6] among the Peloponnesians. Polybius echoes the popular bewilderment of this period, which could only interpret Philip's changed attitude as a moral deterioration, a μεταβολή, due to the corrupting influence of his Illyrian counsellor.[7] Henceforth nothing was too bad for this tyrant, who had ceased to respect the aspirations of the Achaean League; and Aratus withdrew more and more from the Macedonian court into purely Peloponnesian politics. Philip made desperate attempts to win him back, and in the following summer (214) sent him a special invitation to

[1] Polyb. VII, 12, 3.
[2] Plut. *Arat.* 50, 7: whether authentic in detail or not, the reply is characteristic.
[3] See above, p. 73, n. 5.
[4] Cf. Seeliger, 14–15; 32. For his poems see *Anth. Pal.* VII, 238; 247 (cf. Plut. *Titus*, 9); IX, 518–19 (cf. 520 and Plut. *ibid.*); XI, 12; Appendix XVI, 5–6.
[5] Polyb. VII, 11, 8; see above, p. 67, n. 4.
[6] Polyb. IV, 27, 10; see above, p. 35, n. 2.
[7] Polyb. VII, 11, 10; 13, 7 (after his first taste of human blood he resembles a werewolf); 14, 6 (importance of friends).

accompany him on his latest expedition against Roman Illyria; but it was refused, and Philip found himself without any influence over his former counsellor.

After leaving Messene, Philip had spent the winter of 215–14 at home, planning another naval expedition in the west.[1] Since the fiasco of 216 there had been two important changes; first, Philip was now an ally of Hannibal, and secondly, the Romans had at last awakened to the situation in the Balkans. Since the previous autumn a squadron of fifty ships had been stationed first off Tarentum, and later off Brundisium, under the command of M. Valerius Laevinus, and manned by troops sufficient to be accounted a *legio classica*;[2] and Laevinus had specific instructions 'not merely to guard the shores of Italy, but in addition to investigate the Macedonian war'.[3] Thus Philip's chances in Illyria were distinctly less than two summers ago, when the nearest Roman fleet had been at Lilybaeum. Against this fact how much was the Carthaginian alliance worth? What help had Hannibal to offer, and what form would it take?

The events of the expedition help to furnish an answer to these questions. Significantly, Philip made no move at all until August.[4] In this month he set sail with some 120 *lembi*[5] and, presumably,[6] about 6000 men, and quickly succeeded in taking the town of Oricus, at the head of the bay of Aulon. Then, leaving a small garrison, he continued north, ascended the Aous and began to besiege Apollonia. The Illyrians at once sent an

[1] For the supposed expedition of 215 against Corcyra, mentioned in Appian and Zonaras, see below, Appendix III, p. 299.

[2] Livy (A) XXIII, 38, 7–10 gives 55 ships by mistake; cf. Holleaux, 187, n. 1; Holleaux, *ibid.*, n. 2, rejects the existence of the *legio classica*, but in view of the frequent references to it (Livy (A) XXIV, 11, 3; 44, 5; XXVI, 1, 12; 28, 9; XXVII, 7, 15—the last possibly an error) and De Sanctis's arguments for the authenticity of the legion lists (III, 2, 317–27) it seems preferable to follow the latter (III, 2, 411) and Hallward (*CAH*, VIII, 76) in accepting Livy's testimony.

[3] Livy (A) XXIII, 38, 9: *sed explorare de Macedonico bello.*

[4] His expedition is subsequent to Hannibal's first attack on Tarentum, which was late summer: Livy (A) XXIV, 20, 15: *iam enim aestas exacta est*; cf. Holleaux, 189, n. 1.

[5] Livy (A) XXIV, 40, 2, calls them *biremes*, i.e. there were two men to an oar; cf. Tarn, *JHS*, XXV, 1905, 208, n. 94. The main authority for this expedition Livy (A) XXIV, 40 (cf. also Zonaras IX, 4, 4 and Plut. (P) *Arat.* 51, 1) is very unreliable in detail; cf. Scott, 190, n. 5; De Sanctis, III, 2, 362; 412; Holleaux, 190, n. 5.

[6] So Holleaux, 191, n. 5 continued from p. 190.

appeal to Laevinus, and he, without delay, brought his forces across the straits, recovered Oricus and blocked the mouth of the Aous with his own squadron;[1] further, he may have inflicted some sort of defeat on Philip in a surprise attack, though no confidence is to be placed in the rhetorical account of Livy's annalistic source. In any case, Philip was trapped in an awkward position; the tribes north of Apollonia, Illyrians and Dardanians, were hostile, and there was a real danger that he might be cut off from Macedon by land as well as by sea. Reluctantly, but apparently without hesitation, therefore, Philip burnt his fleet on the spot and retreated over the mountains into Macedonia.[2] For the second time his Illyrian schemes had ended in humiliation and disaster.

Somewhere Philip's calculations had led him astray; and almost certainly this was in his estimate of the help he could expect from Carthage. Not that he anticipated actual naval reinforcements from his ally: such help was not specified in the treaty and Hannibal was in no position to furnish it.[3] True, Philip could not hope to cross over to Italy without naval help; but there is no evidence that Hannibal ever intended him to cross over.[4] The help Philip might hope for lay rather in the paralysing of Laevinus's squadron, which now lay off Brundisium.[5] Without doubt Philip and Hannibal were in communication during the winter of 215 and the first six months of 214; and from Italy Philip will have learnt of Hannibal's hopes both of an outbreak in Sicily, where Hieronymus of Syracuse had already abandoned his alliance with Rome,[6] and also of a swift success at Tarentum. Sicily or south Italy, either would suffice to distract Laevinus

---

[1] Livy's order of events is more complicated; he introduces an abortive attack on Apollonia by Philip before he takes Oricus: and after Laevinus has recovered the latter, he disembarks his *praefectus socium*, Q. Naevius Crispus, at the Aous mouth, to deliver the surprise attack on Philip; the river is not blocked until Philip has been routed. On the probable reconstruction see Scott, *loc. cit.*

[2] The version of Plut. *Arat.* 51, which sends Philip straight back to the Peloponnese, is abridged; not to have made for Macedon would have been foolhardy.

[3] Livy (A) XXIV, 27, 7; it was not until late in 214 or early in 213 that the Punic fleet appeared off Sicily.

[4] *Contra* Holleaux, 199, and n. 1, quoting Livy (A) XXIV, 13, 5; see above, p. 70, n. 3.

[5] See the excellent comments of Holleaux, 189-90; cf. De Sanctis, III, 2, 412.   [6] Polyb. VII, 5, 1-8.

from the affairs of Illyria, whether his squadron should be required for policing the Gulf of Tarentum, or to support the main fleet at Lilybaeum against Syracuse. It was undoubtedly this consideration that kept Philip inactive until August 214. Unfortunately the evidence is insufficient to explain his move when at last it came. Either Philip became impatient and, seeing Hannibal's promises unfulfilled, decided to take a risk,[1] in the hope that the Romans would not move in time;[2] or else his Italian information misled him into thinking that the situation was more favourable than it actually was. Either explanation implies a miscalculation by Philip; but if in fact he had accurate information from Italy, his behaviour, particularly after the warning of 216, displays for the first time a recklessness and neglect not merely for his own safety, but also for that of his fleet, which would be scarcely credible, were it not paralleled by certain of his later actions.[3] The immediate result of the catastrophe was to put an end to Philip's naval policy, and to establish the Roman detachment permanently in Illyria;[4] though for some time the Senate failed to take any energetic steps towards an offensive in Greece.

Philip, meanwhile, was quick to readjust himself to the new situation; and, as a preliminary to resuming his attacks on Illyria on the landward side, he resolved to carry through his plans for the seizure of Messene, which Aratus had persuaded him temporarily to postpone. With his fleet Philip had lost control of the straits which separated Aetolia from the hostile states in the Peloponnese; and perhaps too his indecision of a year ago had alienated the popular party in Messenia.[5] At all events, he now resorted to methods characteristic of Aratus's heyday. Demetrius of Pharus was sent with a detachment by night, and dawn

---

[1] So Holleaux, Rome, 190; CAH, VIII, 122.
[2] De Sanctis, III, 2, 412; but can it seriously be contended that Philip contemplated the possibility of losing his fleet? Yet De Sanctis claims that 'il quale (sc. Filippo) neppure avrebbe arrischiato la sua spedizione se le posizioni da lui in precedenza occupate...non gli avessero assicurato in ogni caso la salvezza per la via di terra'.
[3] E.g. in his policy from 205 to 200; see below, pp. 135 seq.
[4] Laevinus winters at Oricus 214–13: Livy (A) XXIV, 40, 17; cf. Polyb. VIII, 1, 6; and henceforth his province is Graecia Macedoniaque: Livy (A) XXIV, 44, 5. See further Holleaux, 193, n. 2.
[5] So De Sanctis, III, 2, 411.

revealed him within the walls of Messene;[1] however, the towns-people rallied and drove the invaders out, Demetrius himself perishing in the *mêlée*. The news of this disaster, coming so soon after the loss of his fleet, drove Philip to a savagery of behaviour which was reminiscent of his conduct at Thermum, or at Messene itself the previous year, without revealing the definite policy which had explained, if not justified, these incidents; it showed in Philip an uncontrollable temper, which Tarn has acutely traced to his Epirote ancestors.[2]

Following up Demetrius's death with fresh intervention in Messene,[3] but no longer assisted by parties within, Philip could only vent his fury on the plain outside; and this he wasted far and wide, sparing nothing sacred or profane.[4] It was the method of sheer violence and terrorism, employed without hope of gain, since the Messenians merely became more alienated, and their town and citadel were impregnable, except against a surprise attack.[5] Whether the parties united in a war coalition,[6] or whether, as seems less probable, the extreme oligarchs seized the moment to recover power,[7] is not recorded; but Messenia now turned in a general revulsion from Philip and the Symmachy to an Aetolian alliance.[8] And in Achaea the bitterness of 216 was redoubled when, as a grand finale to his Messenian campaign, Philip carried off Polycrateia, the wife of Aratus's son, to Macedon, and it became widely known that he had already used his

---

[1] Polyb. III, 19, 11; Pausan. IV, 29, 1–5; 32, 2 (very unreliable, confusing Demetrius with Philip's son of that name). Pausanias states that Demetrius landed in the Argolid and marched across country to Messene, a most improbable story; cf. Niese, II, 472, n. 2. The version which puts Demetrius's death during a pirating expedition in the Adriatic (Appian, *Illyr.* 8; Zonar. VIII, 10, 13) may be neglected.

[2] *CQ*, XVIII, 1924, 23.

[3] Polyb. VIII, 8, 1–2; 12, 1; Plut. *Arat.* 51, 2 (actual invasion); Polyb. VIII, 8, 3–9 (later traditions, justifying Philip). For the chronology of this attack and that of Demetrius, I have followed Seeliger, 14, and Holleaux, 202, n. 3, against Niese, II, 471–2. De Sanctis, III, 2, 413, leaves the order of the two events undecided. See below, Appendix III, p. 300.

[4] That Philip here employed the methods of destruction that later made him so detested at Athens and Pergamum (see below, pp. 119; 140) is to be deduced from Polybius's use of the words ἀσέβεια and παρανομία (VIII, 8, 4); cf. Polyb. XVIII, 54, 7, for the same words applied to Dicaearchus's piracy in 205.

[5] Polyb. VIII, 12, 1.   [6] So Holleaux, 203.   [7] Seeliger, 16.

[8] Polyb. IX, 30, 6 (date 210); but the alliance was probably in existence some years before then; cf. Holleaux, 203, n. 3, against Seeliger, 16.

position as guest to seduce her in Aratus's own house.[1] To this winter too is probably to be attributed the murder of Chariteles, a guest-friend from Cyparissia, whom Philip is said to have poisoned at a banquet;[2] and the Achaeans pointed with regret to the declining influence of Chrysogonus and Alexander and the continued power of less sympathetic figures such as Taurion, the commissioner for the Peloponnese.[3]

Some allowance must be made for Achaean bias in judging a tradition that is hostile in all our surviving sources; Polybius, for instance, indicates that there were other historians who appraised Philip very differently.[4] When, in the course of the Achaean year 214–13,[5] Aratus died, it is unlikely that he was, as he believed, the victim of Philip's poison cup;[6] far more probably he died a natural death, and the advances of Taurion, which had aroused his fevered suspicions, were the signs of an indirect attempt of Philip to recover a little of the support which experience showed him to be necessary, if the Achaeans were to remain loyal. However, the year 214 had undoubtedly been doubly disastrous for Macedon; it had seen the establishment of a permanent Roman squadron in Illyria, the loss of Philip's fleet, and the hardening of the opposition states against him, at the same time as his friends were alienated: and, finally, his trusted Demetrius had perished in a foolhardy raid on Messene. It is not surprising that such a plethora of disaster, coming as his first real setback, should have caused a passionate outbreak in Philip; more important and more typical is the doggedness with which he set about making good his losses.

[1] Plut. *Arat.* 51, 2–3; Livy (P) xxvii, 31, 8; xxxii, 21, 24.

[2] Livy (P) xxxii, 21, 23, coupling this murder with the Messenian incident; cf. Alcaeus, who probably refers to it in the lines:

πίομαι· ὡς ὄφελόν γε καὶ ἔγκαρον ἐχθροῦ ἀράξας
βρέγμα Φιλιππείης ἐξέπιον κεφαλῆς,
ὅσπερ ἑταιρείοιο παρὰ κρητῆρι φόνοιο
γεύσατ' ἐν ἀκρήτῳ φάρμακα χευάμενος.   (*Anth. Pal.* IX, 519.)

[3] Polyb. VII, 11, 6; 14, 6. For Chrysogonus cf. Polyb. v, 17, 6; 97, 3; for Alexander, Polyb. IV, 86, 5; V, 96. For the change of influence see Polyb. IX, 23, 9.

[4] Polyb. VIII, 8, 3 *seq.*

[5] Now running autumn to autumn; see below, Appendix III, p. 300, n. 3.

[6] Polyb. VIII, 12, 2–8; Plut. *Arat.* 52, 1 (based on Polybius with slight additions from the rhetorical schools or family sources); Pausan. II, 9, 4. See Niese, II, 472, n. 4; Nicolaus, 69–70; De Sanctis, III, 2, 413, n. 31; Holleaux, 225. The poisoning is accepted by Freeman, 466. Achaean tradition made the younger Aratus, who died soon after, also Philip's victim (Plut. *Arat.* 54, 2–3).

At Rome the Senate showed itself slow to grasp the essentials of the Balkan situation; partly because it relied upon Laevinus and his squadron to protect south-east Italy as well as Illyria,[1] but mainly through sheer incomprehension, it allowed Philip to operate unchecked for two years, before taking the elementary step of securing allies among the disaffected Greeks. And Philip employed those two years (213–12) to good purpose. From the meagre records that survive it is, unfortunately, impossible to decide to which of the two years particular incidents are to be allotted. However, the main lines of Philip's advance are clear.[2] Keeping well away from the coast, where such towns as Dyrrhachium and Apollonia were safely held by Laevinus,[3] he systematically subdued Atintania, the Dassaretae and the Parthini,[4] thus gradually cutting away the hinterland from the Roman protectorate; among the inland towns thus taken was Dimale, a Roman possession since the recent Illyrian War.[5] Philip then struck north against Scerdilaidas's Illyrian tribes, compelled the submission of the Ardiaei, or at least their southern branches,[6] and by a brilliant surprise attack recovered access to the Adriatic at Lissus, near the mouth of the Drilo.

The taking of Lissus is the only incident of these campaigns of which a clear picture has survived.[7] With its citadel of Acrolissus, it had the reputation of being impregnable, and it seemed at first as if the many refugees who fled before the

[1] Cf. Holleaux, 193, n. 2; 199, n. 1. The fall of Tarentum in 213–12 (Polyb. VIII, 24, 4 *seq.*; Livy (P) xxv, 7, 10 *seq.*) was caused in part by the transference of Laevinus.

[2] Zippel, 69–70; Niese, II, 473–4; De Sanctis, III, 2, 413–14; Holleaux, 199, n. 2.

[3] Laevinus wintered at Oricus in 214–13 (see above, p. 77, n. 4) and probably at Corcyra in 213–12, as he did in 212–11 (Livy (P) xxvi, 24, 16).

[4] Atintania: Livy (P) xxvii, 30, 13; xxix, 12, 13; Dassaretae: Polyb. VIII, 38; the town of Hyscana, which was also mentioned in this book (VIII, 38), probably lay near Lake Lychnidus (cf. Zippel, 69); Parthini: Livy (P) xxix, 12, 3; 12, 13 (for Polyb. XVIII, 47, 12 see below, p. 103, n. 4).

[5] Dimale: taken by the Romans from Demetrius in 219: Polyb. III, 18, 5; now retaken by Philip: Livy (P) xxix, 12, 3; 12, 13. On the situation of this town, among the Parthini, cf. Holleaux, 135, n. 1, against A. Philippson, *P-W*, 'Dimale', col. 646, and Zippel, 56.

[6] Livy (P) xxvii, 30, 13; cf. Polyb. II, 11, 10; 12, 2. See Holleaux, 199, n. 4; Zippel, 70.

[7] On the situation of Lissus (mod. Leš or Alessio) see Fluss, *P-W*, 'Lissus', cols. 731–3.

advance of Philip[1] would be safe within its walls. Indeed, Philip himself is said to have relinquished hopes of taking anything but the town. However, by the device of hiding a number of his light-armed troops in a woody ravine lying between the town and citadel, and then delivering a direct attack and gradually withdrawing his men, he was able to entice out not only the troops in Lissus, but also the garrison from Acrolissus above. Then, at the critical moment, the ambushed troops rushed out, the regular Macedonian forces turned in their steps and attacked, and the Illyrians were forced to take refuge in the city and abandon the citadel. Lissus itself fell the next day after a hard struggle, and with it the whole neighbourhood rapidly submitted to Philip.

Meanwhile, throughout 213, the Romans did nothing to check him, but confined their attention solely to the coast around Apollonia. Philip, without open enemies in Greece, had once more reached the Adriatic. Now, if ever, was the moment to revive his plans for invading Italy. Did Philip in fact do this? The view is popularly held, and has annalistic authority to support it.[2] Furthermore, the capture by the Roman fleet in 212 of a certain Damippus, whom the Syracusans had sent to Philip,[3] suggests that the Sicilians had hopes of some sort of assistance from him. But what were the real chances of Philip's crossing over into Italy? The loss of his fleet in 214 had destroyed every possibility of his going there as an equal. If he went now, it must be on Punic convoys, which would take him where Hannibal chose, and would be his only means of returning to Macedonia. There was little in the naval record of Carthage[4]

---

[1] Polyb. VIII, 13, 8. It is not stated from what point Philip began his two days' march (VIII, 13, 2) to Lissus.

[2] Livy (A) XXIV, 13, 5: Tarentum, a suitable harbour for Philip to land: see also Justin. XXIX, 4, 4; cf. Niese, II, 475; Holleaux, *Rome*, 199–200: 'C'est ainsi que le roi de Macédoine et le général de Carthage ont préparé...leur rencontre en terre italienne'; *CAH*, VIII, 123.

[3] Livy (P) XXV, 23, 8–9.

[4] Even in 213 and 212, years of great Punic naval activity, in which about 185 ships were sent from Carthage (cf. Livy (A) XXIV, 26, 3; 36, 7; XXV, 25, 11–13; 27, 3–4), this fleet never got beyond Syracuse; cf. Kahrstedt, *Geschichte der Karthager*, 481–2; De Sanctis, III, 2, 305; Holleaux, *Rome*, 200, n. 2; *CAH*, VIII, 123. The second expedition of Bomilcar to Carthage and back is probably to be rejected as a doublet from the previous year; cf. Hallward, *CAH*, VIII, 68, n. 2.

to justify any confidence that a fleet would be at hand, if such a return became necessary. Suppose the allied cause failed and evacuation became a desperate matter: who would be sacrificed first, Hannibal or Philip? Finally, if he should enlist as Hannibal's mercenary, what was to be his pay? What was there in the treaty to suggest that he would be allowed any conquests west of the Adriatic? In short, for Philip to press ahead in Illyria and to call for Carthaginian naval help in this task[1] was not only a fair interpretation of the treaty, but was also sound common sense; but to transport the Macedonian army to Italy at the whim of Hannibal—even after first driving the Romans from Illyria— leaving the Symmachy undefended and Macedon itself open to Aetolian or Dardanian attacks—this, so long as Philip had no fleet of his own, was unthinkable.

And, indeed, the fact that until 212 Laevinus took no steps towards securing allies in Greece shows that the Romans at least did not regard Philip as a potential invader. In itself, this proves little, since the Romans were notoriously slow in the diplomatic game; but it is at least worth weighing against the desperate hopes of the Syracusans, or annalistic traditions which were not uncoloured by the fears and lies which circulated at Rome immediately before the second war with Philip, at the end of the century.

However, in 212 Laevinus began a cautious approach to the Aetolian League.[2] Since the Social War and the generalship of Agelaus, the influence of the war party had been gradually growing inside Aetolia; and there already existed the nucleus of a powerful anti-Macedonian *bloc*, including not only Sparta, Elis and Messenia,[3] but also Attalus of Pergamum, who had been the friend of Aetolia since at least 219.[4] Already, it would appear, Attalus had begun the construction of a fleet, and had

---

[1] He almost obtained Punic help in 209 (Livy (P) xxvii, 15, 7; 30, 16) and 208 (Livy (P) xxviii, 7, 17; 8, 8). See below, pp. 90–91 and 96.

[2] Livy (P) xxv, 23, 9; xxvi, 24, 1: *temptatis prius per secreta conloquia principum animis.* For the chronology of this alliance, see below, Appendix III, pp. 301–4.

[3] Elis and Messenia: Polyb. ix, 30, 6; see above, p. 78, n. 8; Sparta joined the Aetolians actively in 210 (Polyb. ix, 28 *seq.*; xi, 18, 8) but an alliance already existed since winter 220–19 (Polyb. iv, 35, 5; ix, 31, 3).

[4] Polyb. iv, 65, 6: gift for the fortifying of Elaus in Calydon: see above, p. 41, n. 7. Cf. Holleaux, 207, n. 3; Klaffenbach, *IG*, ix, 1², introd. p. xxix.

ambitions in the west which could be satisfied only at the expense of Philip.[1] Now, in 212, the crushing of Achaeus by Antiochus of Syria[2] left him free to turn westward to their accomplishment.

Meanwhile Laevinus showed no undue haste, and it was summer 211 before a special Aetolian assembly was summoned and a treaty signed between Scopas, the League general for 212–11, and the Roman proconsul.[3] It is perhaps unfair to refer the whole responsibility for the delay to Laevinus. Admittedly, the Romans were slow to take the obvious step of approaching the Aetolians; but is it so certain, as Holleaux imagines,[4] that the latter jumped at their proposals the moment they were made? Laevinus's reference to the recent fall of Syracuse and Capua,[5] as proof of the rising fortunes of Rome, suggests that the Aetolians had questioned the Senate's ability to provide an adequate *quid pro quo*—a doubt which later history showed to have been fully justified. And certainly the delay of at least a year in concluding a pact which, by Holleaux's hypothesis, was so completely in the interests of both parties, raises a genuine difficulty.[6]

For a Roman alliance this agreement between Laevinus[7] and the Aetolians showed a number of novel clauses, which have their parallel only in Greek international law;[8] it laid down that

---

[1] Cf. Holleaux, 204–6, with notes; Attalus's hostility towards Philip is most plausibly explained as incidental to a scheme of western expansion, and not as the result of fear (so Wilcken, *P-W*, 'Attalos', col. 2163) or as natural enmity towards an Antigonid, as ally of the Seleucids (so De Sanctis, III, 2, 415–16). Philip's marriage-relationship to his foe, Prusias of Bithynia (cf. Polyb. xv,2 2, 1), may, however, have influenced Attalus slightly against him.

[2] Polyb. VIII, 20–21; cf. Niese, II, 395.   [3] Livy (P) XXVI, 24, 1 *seq.*

[4] *Rome*, 208: 'Rien d'étonnant s'il trouve auprès d'eux grand accueil et s'en fait aussitôt écouter.'

[5] Livy (P) XXVI, 24, 2. The impression created by the fall of Syracuse is stressed both by De Sanctis (III, 2, 414) and by Niese (II, 476); the latter is not, however, to be followed, when he gives the initiative in the negotiations to the Aetolians (following Polyb. IX, 37, 8, against Livy (P) XXV, 23, 9); cf. Horn, 23.

[6] Holleaux avoids this difficulty by dating the treaty to autumn, 212; see below, Appendix III, pp. 301–4.

[7] For the extent to which Laevinus arranged this treaty alone, unhelped by the Senate and even hampered by their indifference, see Holleaux, 211 *seq.* (*contra* Horn, 26); this helps to explain the delay before the treaty was signed, and the further delay of two years (Livy (P) XXVI, 24, 14–15: *biennio post*) before it was ratified.

[8] Livy (P) XXVI, 24, 8–13; Justin. XXIX, 4, 5; cf. Polyb. IX, 39, 3 (= Livy XXVI, 26, 3); XI, 5, 5. See Niese, II, 477; De Sanctis, III, 2, 415; Täubler, I, 210–14; 430–2; Holleaux, *Rome*, 210 *seq.*; 217, n. 1; *CAH*, VIII, 125; Heuss,

the war should be shared between the two parties, Aetolia having the command by land and the Romans (who were to provide not less than twenty-five quinqueremes) by sea; the sphere of action was to stretch inland from a point as far north as Corcyra (with the possible exclusion of Epirus),[1] and, of the cities captured, the booty and slaves were to go to the Romans, the land and houses to the Aetolians; in a special clause the Romans undertook to help their allies to acquire Acarnania, while another left it open for Elis, Sparta, Messenia, and the princes Attalus, Pleuratus and Scerdilaidas[2] to become parties to the treaty, if they wished; finally, neither side was to make a separate treaty neglecting the interests of the other. On these terms the Aetolians entered *in amicitiam societatemque populi Romani.*

Immediately the treaty was signed, practical steps were taken to clinch it with a late summer campaign.[3] While the Aetolians made a raid on Thessaly,[4] Laevinus, with his fleet, seized Zacynthus, all but the acropolis, and then the joint forces took the Acarnanian town of Oeniadae and the small island of Nasus in the Gulf of Melite; the two latter, and perhaps Zacynthus too,[5] Laevinus handed over to the Aetolians, before retiring into early winter quarters at Corcyra.

Of Philip's movements during the early part of 211 nothing is known. But when the news of the Aetolian alliance reached him about August,[6] he was at Pella. He quickly realised the change in the situation which the new treaty brought about. His expansion in the west, carried out so successfully during the last two years, must temporarily cease; for by reproducing the conditions of the Social War, Laevinus had saddled Philip with his

37–41; Horn, 22–7; Larsen, *CP*, xxx, 1935, 199–200; 210–12. Holleaux, Täubler and Larsen are to be followed in their view that the treaty initiated a permanent relationship between Rome and Aetolia, against Heuss, who regards it as merely a temporary alliance for a specific purpose.

[1] See below, p. 86, n. 6.
[2] The two Illyrians are Roman clients, while the others come in on the Aetolian side; Livy accidentally omits Messenia (cf. Holleaux, 211, n. 1) and erroneously describes Pleuratus as king of Thrace (cf. Zippel, 71).
[3] Livy (P) xxvi, 24, 15–16; cf. Polyb. ix, 39, 2.
[4] Cf. Niese, ii, 478.
[5] Livy does not actually state that the Aetolians received Zacynthus (as De Sanctis, iii, 2, 418, and Holleaux, *Rome*, 218, n. 3; *CAH*, viii, 126, assume); this is however, probable, and in any case Philip soon recovered it (see below, p. 98); cf. Klaffenbach, *IG*, ix, 1², introd. p. xxx.
[6] See below, Appendix iii, p. 303.

old task of defending the allies in the Symmachy. Macedon itself was safe enough; but the Greeks, as Philip's allies, would furnish the obvious plunder for the Romano-Aetolian pact. It was in Achaea, Acarnania, Euboea and Thessaly that Philip would now be needed; and the price of neglect would be the loss of whatever possessions and influence he had in Greece.

The naval situation had also deteriorated since 214. In that year Philip had lost his fleet and had henceforth been obliged to surrender the command of the western waters to Laevinus. But now, since the new Aetolian alliance, not only would the Romans be likely to venture into the Corinthian Gulf, or even the Aegean, but Attalus of Pergamum, the patron and perhaps already the official ally[1] of Aetolia, might be expected to cross the Aegean with his fleet[2] and join the coalition against Macedon. Since neither time nor resources would allow for the construction of a new Macedonian fleet, Philip's only standby would have to be the faint hope of help from Carthage.

The immediate steps taken by Philip corresponded with the traditional Macedonian policy of securing the northern frontiers, before marching south. He began with a sudden attack on the districts where he had operated the two previous years, no longer with the object of expanding his frontiers, but rather seeking to terrorise and quieten the peoples outside. First the pro-Roman Illyrians of Oricus and Apollonia, around the mouth of the Aous, were defeated and their lands ravaged;[3] then, hastening north-east, past the great lakes and through Pelagonia into Dardania, Philip seized the strategic frontier town of Sintia.[4] From here, continuing his favourite policy of delivering rapid and unexpected blows in the most diverse districts (and perhaps, too, hearing of the Aetolian raid on Thessaly), he hurried his troops south through Pelagonia, Lyncestis and Bottiaea, and

---

[1] See Holleaux, 207, n. 3; the inclusion of Attalus's name in the treaty with Laevinus suggests that he was already allied formally to the League.

[2] Although there is no definite evidence on this point (notwithstanding Holleaux, 205, n. 2), the probability is that by now Attalus already possessed some of the 35 ships which he brought over in 209 (Livy (P) XXVIII, 5, 1).

[3] Livy (P) XXVI, 25, 1–2.

[4] Livy (P) XXVI, 25, 3; Steph. Byz. s.v. Σιντία. The situation of Sintia is doubtful: De Sanctis, III, 2, 418, n. 54, follows Niese, II, 478, n. 3, and puts it between Prilep and Köprülü, in the Pass of Babuna; Kiepert (FOA, xvi, S. 4a) wrongly identifies it with Petritsch on the Strumitsa.

descended by the coast route to Tempe, which he garrisoned with 4000 men under a general named Perseus.[1] Having thus secured Pieria, even should Larisa prove an inadequate bulwark (for it is unlikely that Philip had forgotten Scopas's raid on Dium in 219),[2] he returned through Macedonia into Thrace, where he ravaged the land of the Maedi and besieged Iamphorynna,[3] their capital.

This campaign had been carried out with remarkable speed, for Philip was working against time.[4] And very soon his wisdom became apparent, for hardly had he completed the siege of Iamphorynna, when an urgent appeal reached him from the Acarnanians. The moment Philip had turned north from Tempe, Scopas, the Aetolian general, had mobilised the whole Aetolian army against Acarnania;[5] starved of plunder since the Peace of Naupactus, the Aetolian appetite had been whetted by the gift of Oeniadae and Nasus, and the situation of the Acarnanians was critical. Realising this, they had sent their women and children into the comparative safety of Epirus,[6] despatched their appeal

[1] Probably not a Macedonian; and in any case not to be confused with Philip's young son by Polycrateia, who had probably been born two years before, in 213; cf. Holleaux, *Mélanges Glotz*, 431–8, against Geyer, *P–W*, 'Makedonia', col. 748.   [2] See above, p. 39.

[3] Livy (P) xxvi, 25, 8; 15. It appears as Φόρουννα in Steph. Byz. (= Polyb. IX, 44) and lies probably on the middle course of the Strymon; cf. De Sanctis, III, 2, 418, n. 55. Leake, III, 473 (*contra* Lenk, *P–W*, 'Maidoi', col. 541) suggests an identification with the modern Ivorina on the Morava.

[4] Note in Livy (P) xxvi, 25 the phrases *subitam* (3), *eadem celeritate* (3), *raptim* (4); cf. § 6: *priusquam maioribus occuparetur rebus.*

[5] Livy (P) xxvi, 25, 9–16; Polyb. IX, 40, 4–6 (preceding IX, 28); xvi, 32, 3. Laevinus appears to have taken no part in this campaign.

[6] Was Epirus neutral in this war? So Täubler, I, 218, and Holleaux, 214, n. 2 against Niese, II, 477, n. 3, and De Sanctis, III, 2, 435, n. 91. Twice Polybius includes Epirus among Philip's allies (IX, 38, 5; XI, 5, 4—both in speeches) and Livy (P) xxix, 12, 8, says that the Epirotes mediated in 205 *taedio diutini belli*. Against this evidence, Holleaux stresses the fact that, when attacked in 211 by the Aetolians, the Acarnanians sent their non-combatants to Epirus; and that, moreover, there is no record of any attack on Epirus during this war. The difficulty is real: but Polybius cannot be so easily dismissed. The explanation may be twofold: first, as Holleaux says, the Romans may have deliberately excluded from the agreement with Aetolia a country so near to their protectorate: and, secondly, they may have come to a private agreement with a pro-Roman party inside Epirus to leave the country in effect neutral, while theoretically still a member of the Symmachy. In return for such immunity, the Epirotes would do their best to sabotage Philip's plans, as they had considered doing during the Social War; cf. Polyb. IV, 30, 6–7 (see above, p. 36). But their inclusion in the Peace of Phoenice (Livy (P) xxix, 12, 14) shows that they never openly left the Macedonian alliance.

to Philip in Thrace, and sworn an oath to fight to the last man. The Aetolians had hardly anticipated such resistance: they hesitated and were lost. For news soon came of the approach of Philip, who was already at Dium; and at this the Aetolians abandoned the enterprise and Philip was able to return at length to his winter quarters in Pella.

A large part of Philip's strategy during the Social War had necessarily been devoted to his communications with the Peloponnese;[1] first, in 219, he had concentrated on the western coast road, and later, in 218, his Phocian expedition was intended to eliminate the tedious route through Boeotia, by substituting the short sea voyage from Cirrha or Anticyra to Corinth. The coming struggle was likely to see a resumption of this strategy; and in the first action of the season—the seizure of Phocian Anticyra by Laevinus and the Aetolians[2]—it is not difficult to see a direct move to check Philip's probable line of southern advance. The inhabitants were of course enslaved, and the Aetolians took the town in accordance with the agreement.

Notwithstanding the shock felt throughout Greece at this invasion of barbarians,[3] whose methods of warfare seemed both strange and horrible,[4] the Romans registered swift successes in the Peloponnese. Following the policy of transferring the weight of the Macedonian war as far as possible on to his Greek allies, Laevinus sought to implement the clauses of the Aetolian agreement by bringing in the Spartans, Messenians and Eleans. When in spring 210 Chlaeneas of Aetolia appeared before the Spartans to urge them to join the Roman side,[5] he could speak of the two

---

[1] See above, pp. 41 seq.; 59–60.

[2] Livy (P) XXVI, 26, 2: veris principio (i.e. 210); Polyb. IX, 39, 2. Livy says Anticyra in Locride, but as Salvetti, Studi di stor. ant. II, 1893, 120, points out, this must be a mistake for Phocis, since Locris had been Aetolian for some time; cf. Niese, II, 479, n. 4; De Sanctis, III, 2, 419, n. 57; Holleaux, 232, n. 1; Klaffenbach, IG, IX, I², introd. p. xxx. Boguth, 11, misses the difficulty, but Oldfather, P–W, 'Lokris', cols. 1225–6, defends the Livian reading; he is, however, driven to assuming that Philip took Locrian Anticyra in the Social War, and he admits that the latter was a mere stronghold on the rocks, whereas the one captured by the Romans was specifically a πόλις.

[3] Cf. Polyb. IX, 39, 2 seq.; XI, 5, 6. See Holleaux, 232; Frank, Roman Imperialism, 150.

[4] Cf. Polyb. X, 15, 5: after the Romans have sacked a town one sees not only the bodies of human beings, ἀλλὰ καὶ τοὺς κύνας δεδιχοτομημένους καὶ τῶν ἄλλων ζῴων μέλη παρακεκομμένα.

[5] Polyb. IX, 28 seq.

latter states as already allied to Aetolia;[1] and though the Acarnanians sent their representative to plead the case of the Symmachy, Sparta, under its pro-Aetolian rulers,[2] followed the
expected course and accepted Chlaeneas's proposals.[3] The
Roman policy had triumphed; and when Laevinus returned the
same spring to take up his consulship for 210, his successor,
P. Sulpicius, could be instructed to dismiss all his troops,
except for the *socii navales*.[4]

Meanwhile the capture of Anticyra did not check Philip in
his drive south; and the first step was to secure a route to the
Malian Gulf over Mt Othrys. His attack on Melitaea in 217,
had it succeeded, would have secured him one way, up the
Enipeus valley; the alternative was to press southwards from
Phthiotic Thebes along the coast of the Pagasean Gulf, and so
round towards Thermopylae.[5] The records for this year are
scanty, but this is apparently the course Philip followed; for he
appears, some time during this summer, before the walls of
Echinus,[6] having presumably taken already Pteleum and Larisa
Cremaste. Simultaneously Sulpicius and the Aetolian general,
Dorimachus, arrived with the Roman fleet in the Aegean, and
tried to break the siege of Echinus. Philip had already built an
elaborate siege-work opposite the walls, and was preparing to
take the town by assault, when he was attacked by the enemy from
the sea. However, he was able to drive them back, whereupon
the townspeople lost heart and surrendered.[7] From Echinus, it

---

[1] Polyb. IX, 30, 6. The speeches of Chlaeneas and Lyciscus of Acarnania
are to be regarded as essentially based on a genuine record; cf. (against
Niese, II, 482, n. 3) Holleaux, 16 *seq.*; Treves, *LEC*, IX, 1940, 148, n. 2; 149,
n. 2; 168, n. 1.

[2] From Livy (P) XXXIV, 32, 1, it appears that Lycurgus was now dead, and
his infant son, Pelops, on the throne: the real power lay with the king's
guardian, Machanidas (Diod. XXVII, 1); cf. De Sanctis, III, 2, 421, n. 66.

[3] Whether at once, or after the capture of Aegina (as De Sanctis, III, 2,
421), the evidence does not allow us to say; there is no record of a Spartan
military move this year.

[4] Livy (P) XXVI, 26, 4; (A) XXVI, 28, 2; 10. There seems no reason to question
these annalistic data.

[5] Cf. Stählin, *Philol.* LXXVII, 1921, 201; *Hellen. Thess.* 180. That Philip
first attempted the route via the Enipeus and Xyniae is perhaps to be deduced
from Polyb. IX, 45, 2; and from Polyb. XVIII, 47, 6, Niese, II, 484, n. 1, infers
Macedonian conquests among the Dolopes this year. But in both cases the
evidence is very slight.

[6] Polyb. IX, 41. For the site of Echinus, see Béquignon, *Vallée du
Spercheios*, 299 *seq.*   [7] Polyb. IX, 42.

seems, Philip advanced farther west, and before returning to
Macedon for the winter, made himself master of Phalara, the
port of Lamia.[1] Meanwhile, Sulpicius and Dorimachus sailed
south into the Saronic Gulf and captured Aegina; after the usual
treatment of Roman conquests, this island was handed over to
the Aetolians, who afterwards sold it to Attalus for thirty talents.[2]

In spite of the large coalition now ranged against him, Philip
had scored a number of distinct successes. His coast route
reached as far as Phalara, enabling him to keep in close touch
with Euboea,[3] and also to attack the Aetolians up the Spercheius
valley: it also put him within striking distance of Thermopylae.
However, he owed much to Roman indolence, which allowed
him to set up complicated siege-works at Echinus before striking
a half-hearted blow for its relief; and also to the fact that, as far
as is known, Sparta made no move against Achaea in 210.
Consequently the Eleans and Messenians remained quiet, and
Philip was not distracted by cries for help from the Peloponnese.
But this interlude could hardly be expected to last; and, worse,
in the autumn of this year, the Aetolians elected Attalus of
Pergamum General-in-Chief of the League,[4] a plain indication
that his arrival in Greece was imminent.

The very next spring, attacked by the Spartans under Machanidas,[5] and by the Aetolians from the sea, the Achaean League
appealed for help to Philip.[6] Marching south along his newly
won coast road, Philip was confronted near Lamia by an Aetolian
force under Pyrrhias, strengthened by Pergamenes and Romans;
these he drove back into Lamia after two battles, but paused in
his march to return to Phalara, in order to meet a number of
ambassadors from various neutral powers. There were representatives of Athens, Rhodes, Egypt and Chios—commercial

---

[1] At all events it was his next year; cf. Livy (P) xxvii, 30, 3. See De Sanctis,
iii, 2, 422. On the position of Phalara, at the mouth of the Achelous, south-
east of Lamia, see Stählin, 217–18. Béquignon, *Vallée du Spercheios*, 295–9,
reverts to the identification with Stylida, 15 km. due east of Lamia.

[2] Polyb. ix, 42, 5; xi, 5, 8; xxii, 8, 9. On the Aetolian motives see Flacelière,
300, n. 2. It is not possible to determine with certainty whether the capture
of Aegina preceded or was subsequent to the interference at Echinus.

[3] Polyb. ix, 42, 4: probably his source of supplies during the siege of
Echinus; cf. Holleaux, 239, n. 6.

[4] Livy (P) xxvii, 29, 10; 30, 1. For his expected approach, see Polyb. ix, 30, 7.

[5] Livy (P) xxvii, 29, 9 calls him *tyrannus Lacedaemoniorum*.

[6] Livy (P) xxvii, 29, 9.

states to whom the war meant a dead loss, and who grudged any increase in the power of either Philip or Attalus—and with them came Amynander of Athamania, who more directly represented the interests of Aetolia.[1] To Philip the Greek war was a distraction and a liability; anxious to adopt any means of limiting this conflict, which the Romans sought to extend, he agreed to a truce of thirty days, in order that the question of a Greek peace might be discussed at a general meeting in Achaea.[2]

Then, pausing at Chalcis to fortify it against the possible arrival of Attalus, he came south through Euboea and Boeotia to Argos,[3] where in his pose as Argead he celebrated the Argive Heraea towards the end of June; this over, he went on to the conference, which had been summoned to Aegium. Here, naturally, the danger to Greece was tactfully represented as coming from Pergamum and Rome, and the Macedonians tried to point out how the Romans were exposing their Greek allies to the brunt of the struggle, in order that ultimately they might march in and reap the fruits themselves.[4] Unfortunately, the conference was interrupted by a report that the Romans were at Naupactus, and, equally important, that Attalus had reached Aegina; and the Aetolians, encouraged at this, promptly demanded that the Achaeans should restore Pylus to the Messenians, and Philip give back Atintania to Rome and Ardiaea to Scerdilaidas and Pleuratus of Scodra. Recognising the Roman hand behind these demands, Philip broke off negotiations, at the same time pointing out to the neutrals that the responsibility for the war now lay on his opponents' shoulders. His protestations were partly genuine: on the other hand, Philip was probably not uninfluenced by the report that a Punic fleet was on its way to Greece.[5] Whether, in fact, as Livy says, he proposed challenging the twenty-five Roman ships[6] by sea is questionable;

---

[1] Livy (P) xxvii, 30, 1–5.
[2] Livy (P) xxvii, 30, 6; 12, says *in concilium Achaeorum*; but the rest of his narrative suggests a more general conference; e.g. § 9, *sociorum concilium*, § 15 (*Philippus*) *concilium dimisit*. See above, p. 16, n. 1.
[3] Livy (P) xxvii, 30, 7: Livy gives Philip's route as *per Thessaliam*, but this is evidently an error.
[4] Contrast Livy (P) xxvii, 30, 5 (objects of the neutrals) and 30, 10 (objects expressed at Aegium). See also Polyb. x, 25 (if it refers to this conference).
[5] Livy (P) xxvii, 15, 7; 30, 16.
[6] Cf. Livy (P) xxviii, 5, 1, for this figure.

but, leaving a force of 4000 men with the Achaeans, he took in exchange five of their warships,[1] evidently hoping to make contact with Bomilcar, the Punic admiral.[2] In addition he was expecting a few ships from Prusias of Bithynia. However, Bomilcar never passed Corcyra; and it was probably his recall to Tarentum which had allowed Sulpicius to advance, during the conference, as far as Naupactus.[3] Accordingly Philip drowned his disappointment in debauchery at the Argive Nemea, which was celebrated in July;[4] and Polybius records the hostility aroused by his pretence of democratic behaviour— Philip wore an ordinary citizen's clothes, without his diadem or purple—combined with the caprice of the complete autocrat. The number of women he seduced became an open scandal.

Perhaps Polybius is giving the hostile tradition. For when Sulpicius crossed from Naupactus to raid the coast between Sicyon and Corinth, Philip hastily marched over the hills in time to drive the Romans with considerable losses to their ships; and in the course of the fighting he was thrown against a tree by his horse and had his helmet broken. The battle over, however, he returned, it is said, to his debauchery at Argos.[5]

As in the Social War, Elis constituted the main Aetolian base against Achaea; and, a few days after the Nemea, Philip set out to join Cycliadas, the general for 210-9, near Dyme, with the object of expelling the Aetolian garrison from the city of Elis.[6] After a successful cavalry battle near the river Larisus on the frontier (where Philopoemen distinguished himself as Achaean hipparch),[7] the joint forces advanced on Elis, unaware that Sulpicius had sailed round to Cyllene and thrown 4000 Romans into the town. Upon discovering what had happened, Philip's immediate impulse was to retire (such at least is Polybius's account), but when the battle developed he charged the Romans

---

[1] On the state of the Achaean navy at this time, see Holleaux, 158, n. 6.
[2] Cf. Holleaux, 240, n. 2.   [3] Holleaux, *ibid*.
[4] Polyb. x, 26; Livy (P) xxvii, 31; xxxii, 21, 24; see also Plut. *Moralia*, 760 A for a typical incident.
[5] Livy (P) xxvii, 31, 1-3; 33, 2.
[6] Livy (P) xxvii, 31, 9-11. As De Sanctis, iii, 2, 427, n. 5, and Holleaux, 232, n. 1, point out, the *urbs* of this passage is Elis, and not (as Niese, ii, 483, imagined) Dyme; in 209 Dyme was still Achaean.
[7] Livy (P) xxvii, 31, 11; Plut. *Philop.* 7, 3 *seq.*; Pausan. viii, 49, 7.

in person, was thrown over his horse's head and became the centre of a long and fierce conflict. Eventually, when, after a gallant fight, his position became really critical, he managed to make his escape on the horse of one of his men, and the next day retrieved his defeat in some degree with the capture of the nearby fortress of Phyrcus;[1] like Thalamae in the Social War, this stronghold yielded rich spoils—4000 men and 20,000 head of cattle, sheep and goats.

Suddenly Philip learnt that a band of Illyrians under a leader, Aeropus, was overrunning the territory near Lake Lychnidus; they had seized the town of Lychnidus by treachery, and with Dassaretia in their hands and the Dardanians preparing to join the movement, Macedon itself was threatened. Never prone to underestimate the danger from the barbarians on his northern and western frontiers, Philip left 2500 men under Menippus and Polyphantas, and marched north through Achaea, Boeotia and Euboea, to Demetrias. Here, ten days later, the news was worse; encouraged by a rumour of Philip's death, the Dardanians had already invaded Orestis.[2] However, on Philip's approach, the barbarians retired, though not without heavy booty; Justinus's exaggerated figure estimates their prisoners at 20,000.[3]

Meanwhile Sulpicius for the second time sailed round into the Aegean, to unite with Attalus, and both leaders spent the winter (209–8) on Aegina.[4] The Achaeans, probably aided by the troops Philip had left behind, defeated the Aetolians and Eleans near Messené.[5] Thus the year dragged on to an end, with no essential change in the situation. For Philip it had been a series of setbacks, the strain of which is perhaps reflected in his behaviour at Argos; prevented from continuing his systematic expansion south, thwarted by the failure of the neutral ambassadors to obtain peace, defeated in Elis and, finally, called back to deal with a dangerous invasion of his own kingdom, he could

---

[1] Livy (P) xxvii, 32, 7; cf. Niese, ii, 488, n. 1. There is a MSS. variant, the Puteanus reading *Phyrcum* and the vulgate *Pyrgum*. Thucyd. v, 49, 1, refers to a fort Phyrcus and this is the preferable reading.

[2] Livy (P) xxvii, 33, 1, says that they had reached the *Argestaeus campus*; the position of this is uncertain; cf. Leake, iv, 122; Niese, ii, 488, n. 4.

[3] Justin. xxix, 4, 6.

[4] Livy (P) xxvii, 33, 4–5.   [5] Livy (P) xxvii, 33, 5.

look to little positive accomplishment this season.[1] But worse than any of these blows had been the failure of Bomilcar or the Bithynians to send those ships which alone could enable Philip to meet the Romans on equal terms; and meanwhile Attalus had arrived in the Aegean, and the Romans were for the first time wintering in the same waters.

The war was, in fact, reaching its crisis; and with the coming of spring (208), the dangers to Macedon became increasingly apparent. As Polybius grudgingly admits,[2] it was the kind of predicament in which Philip's finest qualities—his tireless endurance and refusal to admit defeat—had their greatest scope for expression; 'like a wild beast in the chase' he revealed his strength and courage most clearly when exposed to danger on all sides. Philip first of all appointed a date by which his army should assemble at Larisa; then he went south to Demetrias, to meet representatives of the various members of the Symmachy, who had come to pool their information and, more particularly, to ask for assistance.[3] Acarnanians, Boeotians, Euboeans and Achaeans all reported that the successful conjunction of the Roman and Pergamene fleets off Aegina had inspired the Aetolians to new activity; and the Achaeans, in addition, announced that Machanidas was terrorising the inhabitants of the Argive frontier. Philip, meanwhile, was doubly hampered; his own frontiers were threatened by the Illyrians under Pleuratus and Scerdilaidas, and by the Thracian Maedi, whose capital he had taken in 211,[4] and who had been awaiting such a moment: on the other hand, the Aetolians had recently fortified Thermopylae,[5] to prevent him from continuing his coastal drive south

---

[1] Simultaneously, his allies were constantly asking his help or his forbearance. In a letter of September 209 (*Syll.* 552 = *IG*, IX, 78; cf. Schroeter, 79–80, no. 32) Philip grants the people of Abae in Phocis the right of ἀτελεία, and concludes: ὑμῖν βουλόμενος χαρίζεσθαι γέγρα[φ]α τῶι Ἡρακλείδηι μὴ ἐνο[χ]λεῖν ὑμᾶς. This Heracleides, evidently Philip's military representative in the friendly district of Phocis, is probably Heracleides of Tarentum, who had joined Philip after incurring suspicion with both Hannibal and the Romans (Polyb. XIII, 4; see below, pp. 105–7), rather than the Heracleides of Gyrton, mentioned in the account of Cynoscephalae (Polyb. XVIII, 22, 2).

[2] Polyb. X, 41, 7.   [3] Polyb. X, 41; Livy (P) XXVIII, 5, 1–9.
[4] See above, p. 86.
[5] Livy (P) XXVIII, 5, 8; Polyb. X, 41, 5. Throughout Philip's reign Thermopylae was, of course, in Aetolian hands; but the new fortifications are a reply to Philip's advance along the Malian Gulf.

and so establishing an easy route along which to bring assistance.

However, Philip readily promised help to all—Achaeans,
Acarnanians, Epirotes, Boeotians[1] and Euboeans alike;[2] then,
dismissing the envoys, he sat down to wait for his opponents to
move. With the initiative clearly out of his hands, an alert
defensive was the only immediate, realistic policy. Meanwhile,
he despatched a garrison to the island of Peparethos, which was
reported to be threatened by Attalus and the Romans, who,
after a preliminary voyage to Lemnos, were bearing down upon
it;[3] further, Polyphantas was sent south to Boeotia, and Menippus
to Chalcis with 1500 mixed troops, a third of them Agrianians.[4]
This done, Philip joined his main forces at Scotussa, and led
them rapidly down the coast, hoping to catch the Aetolians in
conference at Heraclea; arriving too late, however, he had to
return to Demetrias, having first brought his men back to
Scotussa.[5] His choice of this centre was perhaps guided by the
fear that the Aetolians might attempt a raid on Macedon. The
immediate problem of keeping a close watch on his enemy's
movements he attempted to solve by a system of fire signals,
which would enable his commanders in Phocis and Boeotia and
in Peparethos to communicate with a central beacon on Mt
Tisaeum at the south-west promontory of Magnesia.[6]

At the Aetolian assembly at Heraclea more neutral ambassadors from Egypt and Rhodes pleaded for peace, but to little
effect;[7] they were simply sent on to Philip. And now the allied
fleet scored a success in the capture by treachery of Oreus in
north Euboea; and though Chalcis resisted the enemy's attack,

[1] Flacelière, 317 seq. argues from epigraphical evidence that about this
time the Aetolians obtained temporary possession of Lebadeia in Boeotia;
contra Ferguson, Ath. Trib. Cyc. 121–2.

[2] Polyb. x, 41, 8; Livy (P) xxviii, 5, 9; Justin. xxix, 4, 7 seq.

[3] Polyb. x, 42, 1; Livy (P) xxviii, 5, 10.

[4] Polyb. x, 42, 2; Livy (P) xxviii, 5, 11–12.

[5] Polyb. x, 42, 3–5; Livy (P) xxviii, 5, 13–15.

'Polyb. x, 42, 6 seq.; Livy (P) xxviii, 5, 16–17. On the position of Mt
Tisaeum, the modern Bardzogya, cf. Leake, iv, 397; Stählin, 55.

[7] Livy (P) xxviii, 7, 14; Appian (Maced. 3, confused) probably refers to
the next year (207), not to 208, as Niese, ii, 490, n. 1. In 208 only Egypt and
Rhodes are mentioned, but Athens and Chios may also have sent representatives, cf. Ferguson, Hellen. Ath. 255; Holleaux, 119, n. 1. In the Social
War Athens had been satisfied to secure her own neutrality: see IG², ii,
1304; cf. Ferguson, Ath. Trib. Cyc. 98.

they were able to seize the Locrian town of Opus. To these moves Philip's reply was as decisive as it was spectacular. The defection of Plator, his officer in Oreus, had prevented him reaching that town in time, and, further, his naval inferiority now rendered the Euboean crossing a hazardous enterprise. But immediately his fire signals reported the assault on Chalcis, Philip hurried to Scotussa and led all his forces to its relief. Expecting no movement, the Aetolians were holding Thermopylae carelessly;[1] Philip was able to force the pass and reach Elatea the same day, after a march of over sixty miles.[2] By this time Attalus was busy at Cynus, the port of Opus, levying contributions and dealing with the plunder, which, contrary to the usual practice, had been granted to him by Sulpicius; the Romans had already returned to Oreus. Philip was thus able to pounce upon the Pergamene forces unexpectedly, and Attalus barely escaped to Oreus with his life. To Philip his escape seemed a disaster, and there is a suspicion that he vented his anger upon the Opuntians, who appeared to have been over-ready to surrender to the enemy;[3] certainly he spent some time there, putting affairs in order, for as long as Epicnemidian Locris remained in Aetolian hands, his communications with the Peloponnese rested on the possession of Opus.

Notwithstanding Philip's disappointment, the skirmish on the shore at Cynus proved, however, to have been the turning-point in the war. Shortly afterwards, news of an attack by Prusias— whether stimulated by Philip or not can only be a matter for speculation—recalled Attalus to Asia Minor, and the pressure from the united fleet was relaxed. Once again Philip could risk taking the offensive against the Aetolians.

The short campaign which followed, and which probably occupied the latter half of June and the beginning of July, 208, was plainly influenced by the recent threat to Philip's southern communications. Marching first on Thronium, which was at

[1] Frontinus, I, 4, 6, relates how Philip detained Aetolian envoys, who had been sent to negotiate for peace, and forced the pass unexpectedly. If, as is probable (cf. Niese, II, 487, n. 2), the reference is to this year, we may assume that, as in 209, there was some question of a truce affecting only the Greek war, and not the Romans and Attalus. In view of the previous year's events, Philip would be unlikely to treat any such negotiations over-seriously.

[2] Livy (P) XXVIII, 7, 1–3; Dio, XVII, 57, 57.

[3] Livy (P) XXVIII, 7, 7–8; cf. Polyb. XI, 7, 1.

present occupied by refugees from Phthiotic Thebes, he took it without difficulty; this done, he proceeded to capture Tithronium and Drymaea, two towns to the north of the Cephisus, formerly Phocian, but perhaps at this time incorporated in Doris and under Aetolian influence.[1] An attempt to hold Lilaea, near the head of the Cephisus, failed, and Philip's garrison was ejected by the inhabitants under a certain Patron,[2] helped perhaps by the Aetolians; but it seems likely that all Epicnemidian Locris now fell into his hands.[3]

On his return to Elatea, Philip found the neutral ambassadors still waiting to be heard; but his successes and the departure of Attalus had removed any desire for peace with Aetolia, and upon receiving an appeal for help from Achaea, Philip dismissed the ambassadors abruptly, and set off south with his light troops.[4] Encouraged by their victories of 209, the Achaeans had attempted to usurp the control of the Olympian Games, and Machanidas had gone to the support of Elis.[5] Philip marched to Megara and Corinth, and from there through Phlius and Pheneus to Heraea, only to learn that the Spartan had fled; accordingly he returned to the July *synodos* of the Achaean League,[6] the more readily as he had once more news of possible help from Carthage. Sulpicius's absence in the Aegean had encouraged Bomilcar to cross over to the Oxeae islands off Oeniadae; but on hearing that the united fleet had left Oreus, he was afraid to be cut off, and with characteristic timidity retired, before he had time to connect with the seven quinqueremes and twenty *lembi* which Philip dragged across the Isthmus to meet him.[7]

Though exasperated at this fiasco, coming so soon after his disappointment at Cynus,[8] Philip nevertheless covered his

---

[1] Livy (P) xxviii, 7, 9; 12–13. Daux, 237 *seq.*, shows that these few towns are the only part of Phocis known to be at this time in Aetolian hands; cf. Salvetti, *Studi di stor. ant.* ii, 1893, 121. Flacelière, 287 and 302, n. 2, regards their inclusion in Doris as an error in Polybius's geography.

[2] Pausan. x, 33, 3. For Attalid troops at Lilaea, cf. Daux, *Rev. Phil.* lviii, 1934, 64, and Flacelière, 301, n. 5; for an epigram to Patron from Delphi (*FD*, iii, 1, n. 523) see Wilhelm, *Wien. Anz.* 1931, 78–96 and W. Peek, *Hermes*, lxvi, 1931, 476–7.

[3] Cf. Klaffenbach, *Klio*, xx, 1926, 82; *contra* Flacelière, 308, n. 1. This part of Locris remained in Philip's hands until at least 198 (Livy (P) xxxii, 36, 9).

[4] Livy (P) xxviii, 7, 13–15.   [5] See below, Appendix iii, p. 304, n. 5.

[6] Livy (P) xxviii, 7, 14–17.   [7] Livy (P) xxviii, 7, 17–18; 8, 8.

[8] So Polybius; cf. Livy (P) xxviii, 8, 1.

annoyance in a speech to the Achaeans, in which he not only pointed with some justice to his successes, but also promised to restore to them Heraea and Triphylia, and to give back Alipheira to Megalopolis.[1] Then, taking over six Achaean warships, he joined Nicias, the League general for 209–8, in a raid on the Aetolian town of Erythrae, sailing over to Locrian Anticyra and bringing back considerable spoils. This raid completed, he sent his men north from Corinth by land, while he himself, braving Sulpicius's fleet off Aegina, sailed round Sunium to Chalcis and Oreus, where he ·reinstated the pro-Macedonian party before returning to Demetrias.[2]

The campaign had demonstrated Philip's unquestionable superiority by land; as he boasted at Aegium, his difficulty lay not in defeating his enemies, but in catching them,[3] and there were signs that already the Aetolians were losing their zest for the war. It was not without significance that, even with Attalus in Greek waters, they had been prepared, both in 209 and 208, to consider the proposals of the neutral powers; and if on the former occasion it was they who, under Roman pressure, brought the truce to an end, in the present year Philip had himself been in a position to dismiss the ambassadors, thoroughly defeat the Aetolians and send their patron Attalus scurrying for his life out of Opus. Furthermore, the achievement of Sulpicius had been negligible; his attempts on Lemnos, Peparethos and Chalcis had all failed, and Philip had easily recovered Opus and Oreus. This fact, and the dismal failure of Bomilcar to afford any help—and perhaps, too, the news of the decisive victory obtained this year by the Romans over this Punic squadron[4]—now brought Philip to a new and important decision. He resolved to lay down the keels for a hundred warships at Cassandreia, and, gathering together a host of workmen, prepared to renew his naval policy.[5]

For the rest of the season Philip was occupied with one of his periodic frontier wars against the Dardanians. Of Sulpicius's movements, meanwhile, next to nothing is known. He was at

---

[1] Livy (P) xxviii, 8, 6; the promise was not kept until 199–8; see below, p. 148.
[2] Livy (P) xxviii, 8, 7–13.   [3] Livy (P) xxviii, 8, 3.
[4] Cf. Holleaux, 244, n. 2.   [5] Livy (P) xxviii, 8, 14.

Aegina when Philip returned by sea to Demetrias, in August; but from then on nothing further is recorded of him. It was, however, probably in this autumn that he inflicted a crushing blow on the Achaeans by the capture and sack of Dyme,[1] and the enslavement of its entire population. After this, the Romans were wholly inactive in Greek waters for two years. It was probably in this autumn, too, that Machanidas retaliated on the Achaeans for his fright in July, by seizing Tegea.[2] However, the election of Philopoemen to the generalship of 208–7, and his thorough reorganisation of the League,[3] rendered further appeals to Philip unnecessary; and though this move towards self-sufficiency had within it the seeds of a later cleavage between Achaea and the Symmachy (in effect, between Achaea and Philip, for it was only as a protector of Achaean interests that the League valued the Symmachy), for the present it offered a welcome relaxation of pressure on the resources of Macedon. Meanwhile, Philip's continual solicitude for the Achaeans was demonstrated when, shortly afterwards, he had the enslaved Dymaeans ransomed and restored to their city.[4]

The following spring (207), the inactivity of the Romans put an entirely new complexion on the war. Philip's predominance on land, so evident even at the height of the offensive, could now be transferred to the sea as well, and it was probably this year that he recovered Zacynthus from the Aetolians;[5] no details, however, have survived in our sources. Indeed, almost all that is known of Philip during this year is that he neglected further neutral attempts to make peace, and was able to repeat his exploit of 218, by penetrating to Thermum itself; notwithstand-

---

[1] Livy (P) xxxii, 21, 28; 22, 10; Pausan. vii, 17, 5. Dyme was still Achaean in summer 209 (Livy (P) xxvii, 31, 9), and from then until autumn 208 Sulpicius was in the Aegean. On the other hand, for 207 and 206, *neglectae eo biennio res in Graecia erant* (Livy (P) xxix, 12, 1); hence Holleaux, 232, n. 1, is probably right in his view against De Sanctis, iii, 2, 427, n. 75, that the capture is not later than 208. (In *CAH*, viii, 132, however, he dates it spring 207; and during 207 and 206 Sulpicius probably stayed with a few ships in Illyrian waters.)

[2] Tegea belonged to Sparta in 207 (Polyb. xi, 18, 8); since, however, Philip never tried to help the Achaeans recover it, they will scarcely have lost it before summer 208; cf. De Sanctis, iii, 2, 427, n. 75.

[3] Polyb. xi, 9 *seq.*; Plut. *Philop.* 9; Pausan. viii, 50, 1; Polyaen. vi, 4, 3.

[4] Livy (P) xxxii, 22, 10.

[5] See above, p. 84, for its recovery, Livy (P) xxxvi, 31, 11; cf. Holleaux, 218, n. 6; De Sanctis, iii, 2, 430, n. 87.

ing Sulpicius's absence he did not proceed with his new fleet—probably through lack of the necessary capital.[1]

To the neutral powers the absence of the Romans had seemed to offer new opportunities of peace; and spring 207 saw representatives of Egypt, Rhodes, Byzantium, Chios, Mytilene and perhaps Athens[2] once more appealing to Aetolia. Polybius records the speech of Thrasycrates of Rhodes, analysing the full implications to Greece of the Romano-Aetolian agreement. Abandoned by Rome, the Aetolians were nevertheless not yet prepared for a thorough capitulation; and Philip, with the tide now flowing directly in his favour, was once more able to disclaim responsibility for the continuation of the war. At the price of Zacynthus[3] he bought Amynander's permission to march through Athamania,[4] and so down the Achelous into northern Aetolia; then, taking as in 218 the easier route along the southern shore of Lake Trichonis,[5] he once more penetrated to Thermum and destroyed whatever his former invasion had left intact. This exploit caused widespread panic in central Greece; at Delphi special Messenian forces were called in as a protection against possible attack.[6]

More important, the tenacity of the Aetolians was at last shaken; and an additional blow was the defeat and death of Machanidas at the hands of Philopoemen's new Achaean army at Mantinea, in June.[7] Moreover, the defeat of Hasdrubal at the Metaurus brought no apparent enthusiasm at Rome for helping the Greek allies, and Sulpicius, denuded of troops,[8] remained inactive off Illyria. Consequently, when the neutral powers made further overtures (probably in winter 207-6), and Sulpicius, though he spoke against the peace, could offer no concrete help,[9] the Aetolians were at last driven to accept Philip's terms. These seem to have included the offer of certain con-

---

[1] Cf. Holleaux, 246 and n. 2.
[2] Polyb. XI, 4, 1; Appian, *Maced.* 3; see above, p. 94, n. 7.
[3] And Gomphi? Cf. Niese, II, 589, n. 4, who thinks Philip later took it back. Amynander appointed Philip of Megalopolis, Philip's later enemy (see below, pp. 198 and 200), governor of Zacynthus.
[4] Livy (P) XXXVI, 31, 11. [5] See Woodhouse, 261.
[6] See the inscriptions *FD*, III, 4, 21-4; cf. Flacelière, 305-6; 490.
[7] Polyb. XI, 11-18. [8] Holleaux, 245, n. 3.
[9] Appian, *Maced.* 3, probably refers to this: the reinforcements there mentioned, and the capture of Ambracia, are, however, annalistic fabrications; cf. Holleaux, 245, n. 2.

cessions in Phthiotic Achaea and Phthiotis, including the town
of Pharsalus,[1] but, if so, Philip had no intention of carrying out

[1] The main towns concerned are Echinus, Larisa Cremaste (both taken by
Philip in 210), Phthiotic Thebes (taken in 217) and Pharsalus. In 198 and
197 the Aetolians claimed these four towns κατὰ τὰς ἐξ ἀρχῆς συνθήκας (i.e.
with Rome), insinuating that Philip was holding them unjustly, and Philip
agreed to surrender Larisa and Pharsalus (Polyb. XVIII, 3, 12; 8, 9; 38, 3).
    (a) *Previous history of Pharsalus.* Polybius (V, 99, 3) states that Pharsalus
was Macedonian during the Social War. Therefore it was probably recovered
with Thessaliotis and Hestiaeotis by Doson in 229–8 (see above, p. 11, n. 3).
On the other hand there are two references to Pharsalian *hieromnemones* at
Delphi (*Syll.* 545: archon Polycleitus; *Syll.* 539A, archon Eudemus) for the
period between Philip's accession and the peace of 206. *Either* Polybius is
to be thrown over, and Philip did not obtain Pharsalus till 207 or 206 (Beloch
and De Sanctis) *or* we must assume with many scholars (e.g. Stählin, *Philol.*
LXXVII, 1921, 204 *seq.*; Tarn, *CAH*, VII, 745) that a Pharsalian *hieromnemon*
representing Aetolia does not necessarily imply Aetolian possession of Pharsalus; by the use of exiles, the Aetolians may have maintained their claim to
towns and districts which they had lost, but to which they had not yet
relinquished their claim. The latter view is rejected by Flacelière and Klaffenbach; but neither meets the arguments of Fine, who shows that the Aetolians
maintained at any rate their representation for Thessaliotis and Hestiaeotis
long after it is clear from Polybius (IV, 61, 1; 76, 2; VII, 11) that these districts
had been recovered by Macedon. I therefore accept the second alternative.
    (b) *The four towns and the peace of* 206. Stählin, followed by Holleaux,
suggests that the four towns, which Philip possessed in 206, were promised
to Aetolia in the peace of that year, but never actually handed over. Against
this Klaffenbach and Flacelière point to the existence of Aetolian *hieromnemones* from Phthiotic Thebes under archons Megartas and Philaetolus (*Syll.*
564 and *OGIS*, 234), dated c. 204 and 202 respectively. They suggest that
Philip actually handed over the towns, but seized them again in autumn 202,
encouraged by dissensions in the towns themselves and by the Aetolian rebuff
at Rome. This is a possible theory; but if the argument from the *hieromnemones* is, as it seems, invalid, it has nothing to recommend it over that of
Stählin. It is, as Fine points out, difficult to explain such a concession as is
implied in either giving or promising the towns to Aetolia, when all the cards
were in Philip's hands; but the Aetolian complaint must have had *some*
grounds, and the promise is more easily understandable, if Philip had no
intention of fulfilling it. When in 198 Philip offered to hand over two of the
towns and not the other two, he was evidently attempting to strike a bargain.
    (c) *The question of Xyniae and Cyphaera.* In 198 these towns were Philip's.
When did he acquire them? Again arguing from the Delphic lists (which
show Aristarchus of Cyphaera acting as Aetolian *epimeletes* at Delphi in the
archonship of Archelaus III = 203–2? cf. Roussel, *BCH*, L, 1926, 124, no. 1),
Klaffenbach and Flacelière put their acquisition in 202, when, they claim,
Philip recovered Pharsalus, etc. Stählin, *P–W*, 'Kypaira', dates their capture
210. Either alternative seems possible (assuming again the invalidity of
arguing from Aetolian practice at Delphi). The existence of a *hieromnemon*
from Thaumaci under the archonship of Philaetolus (c. 202) raises no difficulties, since there is no evidence that Philip ever possessed this town.
    For a full discussion of the problem, see Niese, II, 503, n. 1; Bauer, 59 *seq.*;
64 *seq.*; Swoboda, *Klio*, XI, 1911, 455 *seq.*; Stählin, *Philol.* LXXVII, 1921, 199 *seq.*;
Holleaux, *Rome*, 255, n. 1; *CAH*, VIII, 135, n. 1; Costanzi, *Studi Storici*, I,

his promise; and the general form of the peace was probably based upon the *status quo*.[1]

The agreement seems to have been signed in the autumn of 206,[2] and included besides Philip and the Symmachy on the one hand, and Aetolia on the other, the Aetolian allies, Sparta, Elis and Messenia.[3] Since Attalus had been back in Asia for two years, this peace put a virtual end to the Greek war; and though for the Aetolians it probably meant the surrender of all claim to Thessaly[4] (excepting the promised towns of Phthiotic Thebes, Echinus, Larisa Cremaste and Pharsalus, and a few remaining forts like Melitaea and Thaumaci) yet in view of their exhaustion they welcomed it as much as Philip. Indeed, the criticism has been made[5] that Philip would have served his aims better if,

1908, 427 *seq.*; Beloch, IV, 2, 414–17; De Sanctis, III, 2, 430, n. 85; 435, n. 92; Ferguson, *Athen. Trib. Cyc.* 120 *seq.*; Fine, *TAPhA*, LVIII, 1932, 137 *seq.*; Klaffenbach, *IG*, IX, 1², introd. pp. xxxii *seq.*; *Klio*, XXXII, 1939, 203; Flacelière, 307, n. 2; 316, n. 3; 375–6.

[1] Livy (P) XXIX, 12, 1; *quibus voluit condicionibus* (*Philippus*). There are no grounds for Pomtow's theory that Philip ceded part of Phocis to Aetolia (*N. Jahrb. f. Phil.* CLV, 1897, 801–2); cf. Holleaux, 259, n. 2; Daux, 237 *seq.*; Flacelière, 308, n. 2 (who, however, thinks that Philip may have relinquished Tithronium and Drymaea). Similarly, the inclusion of Thronium and Scarpheia in a list of Aetolian towns on a Magnesian inscription (Kern, *Insc. Magn.* 28 = *IG*, IX, 1², 186; cf. *Syll.* 557, appendix; date *c.* 207: cf. Ferguson, *Ath. Trib. Cyc.* 128) is not proof that Philip gave these towns to the Aetolians, as Flacelière, 308, n. 1, claims against Klaffenbach, *Klio*, XX, 1926, 82, n. 2 (but see now *Klio*, XXXII, 1939, 203, n. 2). The fragmentary inscription *IG*, XI, 4, 1066, which concerns Philip, Elis and Amynander, may refer to this peace.

[2] Livy (P) XXIX, 12, 1; XXXVI, 31, 11. See below, Appendix III, pp. 305–6.

[3] As Holleaux, 261 *seq.* points out, these three states could not continue the war alone, and from Polyb. XVI, 13, 3, it is clear that in 205–4 the alliance between them and Aetolia was still in force. Larsen, *CP*, XXX, 1935, 210–12, argues that Elis, Messenia and Sparta had all signed *foedera* with Rome, and did not make peace with Philip until 205. His strongest evidence is Polybius's reference to Elis and Messenia as σύμμαχοι of Rome in 196, while Aetolia is not so described (Polyb. XVIII, 42, 7); but, as Holleaux points out (263, n. 4, ending on 264; cf. Aymard, *Premiers Rapports*, 73, n. 26), the Eleans and Messenians, by reason of the alliance still subsisting between themselves and Aetolia, became once more nominally allies of Rome (in an ill-defined way, which neither side sought to make more precise) with the reinstitution of close Aetolo-Roman relations in 199. If this is so, Polybius may have felt it necessary to mention that Elis and Messenia were Roman σύμμαχοι (a term not to be pressed too closely in this passage), while omitting this detail for the more obvious case of the Aetolians. Flamininus's retort to the Aetolians at Tempe (Polyb. XVIII, 38, 7–9) implies only that the alliance of 211, with its specific terms, no longer existed, not that the Aetolians were not *socii et amici* during the second Macedonian war. Larsen's error is to argue from the term σύμμαχοι to the existence of a *foedus*.   [4] De Sanctis, III, 2, 431–2; Holleaux, 255, n. 1.

[5] By De Sanctis, III, 2, 431.

even at the expense of prolonging the war, he had taken steps
to win Lamia, Heraclea and the Pass of Thermopylae, before
signing terms with Aetolia. The objection is valid to the extent
that Philip's ambitions still centred on Greece proper; as we
have seen, the larger part of his strategy had been directed to
opening or keeping open his lines of communication with the
Peloponnese. But a peace with the Aetolians, which included
Elis, Sparta and Messenia, made those communications less
vital. If Philip had in fact no intention of surrendering the
Phthiotic coastal towns, he was preserving an adequate line of
communications and could afford to dispense with Thermopylae.[1]
And indeed, loyally though he had supported the allies, since
217 Philip's eyes had been on the west. The invasion of Italy
had been a short-lived dream; but some advance in Illyria
was still practicable. Only it must be soon. After Metaurus,
Hannibal's fate was only a matter of time; and in its incalculable
way the Senate might suddenly awake to Philip's activities and
decide to throw large forces across the straits. It was such
considerations as these that determined Philip to strike a peace
with Aetolia as soon as possible, and to concentrate on expansion
in Illyria.

If Philip had time to begin campaigning here in 206, the
account of it has perished;[2] and the following spring, the Romans
at last became alive to what was happening in Greece. Victorious
in Spain, they despatched P. Sempronius Tuditanus with 35
ships and 11,000 men to Dyrrhachium to resuscitate the war,[3]
and he had already engineered revolts among the Parthini and
their neighbours, and begun the siege of Dimale (which had
been Macedonian since 213–12),[4] when Philip arrived by a
forced march at Apollonia and began ravaging the country
round. At the news of the king's arrival, Sempronius relinquished the siege of Dimale and, having failed to persuade the

---

[1] It is worth noting that, throughout two wars, the only occasion when the
Thermopylae route had been really vital to Philip was during the intense
offensive of 208, when he succeeded in forcing it.

[2] Livy (P) XXIX, 12, 3, is spoilt by annalistic contamination, which, in the
interests of Roman policy, tries to run the Aetolian peace and the return of the
Romans as closely together as possible: *vixdum pace facta nuntius regi venit
Romanos Dyrrhachium venisse.*

[3] On the inadequacy of this force see Holleaux, 285 and n. 5.

[4] See above, p. 80, n. 5. Livy (P + A) XXIX, 12, 3, gives the form *Dimallum.*

Aetolians to break the newly made peace, showed himself either unable or unwilling to press ahead with the war alone. Philip, on the other hand, was not in a position to besiege Apollonia,[1] and since Sempronius declined his offers of battle, the situation was a stalemate.

The knot was cut by the Epirotes,[2] who seized this excellent opportunity to approach both sides with peace proposals. Philip agreed to meet first the Epirote generals and later Sempronius himself at Phoenice, then the main city in Epirus; and here, in the presence of neutral ambassadors and Amynander of Athamania, Philip and Sempronius came to terms and, with the Treaty of Phoenice, brought the long war to an end. The clauses of the agreement[3] were that Philip should surrender to Rome the land of the Parthini, Dimale and the now unknown towns of Bargullum and Eugenium;[4] in return he was to have Atintania, subject to the Senate's confirmation, and almost certainly (notwithstanding Livy's silence) the greater part of his Illyrian conquests of 213,[5] together with those parts of northern and western Dassaretia, which he had captured or recovered from Scerdilaidas in 217. The signatories included Prusias, the Achaeans, Boeotians, Thessalians, Acarnanians, Epirotes and probably the Phocians and Euboeans on Philip's side, and on the Roman side Attalus and Pleuratus of Scodra.[6]

---

[1] Livy (P) xxix, 12, 6–7.

[2] On the diplomatic position of Epirus see above, p. 86, n. 6.

[3] Livy (P + A) xxix, 12, 13–15; Appian, *Maced.* 3.

[4] Polyb. xviii, 47, 12 (=Livy, xxxiii, 34, 11) and Polyb. xviii, 1, 14 (=Livy, xxxii, 33, 3) have respectively been used to prove that Philip later possessed the Parthini, and that he recovered them *after* Phoenice: cf. Niese, II, 502, n. 3; III, 15, n. 3; De Sanctis, III, 2, 435, n. 92, following Costanzi, *Studi Storici*, I, 1908, 427 *seq*. As Zippel, 77–8, has shown, it is doubtful if Πάρθον in the first passage refers to the Parthini (cf. Kromayer, II, 10, n. 3; Holleaux, 278, n. 1); while in the second Livy has misunderstood Polybius, who merely refers to the territory held by Philip under the treaty.

[5] See above pp. 68–9; 80–1; cf. De Sanctis, III, 2, 435–6; Holleaux, 278, n. 2. It is not recorded whether or no Philip kept Lissus.

[6] Livy (P) xxix, 12, 14; cf. Appian, *Maced.* 3. The Phocians, Euboeans and Epicnemidian Locrians are probably omitted by mistake (cf. Holleaux, 259, n. 2); Opuntian Locris was at this time part of Boeotia (cf. Holleaux, *BCH*, xvi, 1892, 466–70; Klaffenbach, *Klio*, xx, 1926, 83). As signatories on the Roman side, Livy also gives the people of Ilium, Nabis *Lacedaemoniorum tyrannus*, the Eleans, the Messenians and the Athenians. The validity of this text has been argued *ad nauseam*. The names are accepted in full by De Sanctis, III, 2, 436–9; *Riv. Fil.* LXIV, 1936, 198, n. 1. Niese, II, 502, n. 4, and Larsen, *CP*, xxx, 1935, 193–214; xxxii, 1937, 15–31, reject Ilium and Athens;

The war was over. Apparently the Romans had returned prepared to carry on the war only if the Aetolians could be won back to the offensive; failing this Sempronius must have had instructions to strike as satisfactory a peace as possible. Thus the Peace of Phoenice was in essentials a Roman peace, proposed by the Romans (through the agency of the Epirotes, whose intervention was perhaps spontaneous) and accepted by Philip and the allies. Nevertheless it was a triumph for Philip—a triumph, that is, if the actual course of the war is considered, and not Philip's original ambitions. As an ally Hannibal had proved first too strong, and later too weak; his victory at Cannae, coinciding with Philip's abortive expedition of 216, had thrust Philip into an alliance, designed as a safeguard. But the failure of the Punic fleet, and the formation of a common front between the Senate, Attalus and the Aetolian League had driven him back into a strict defensive. If, after the crisis of 211, Philip was able to carry the war through to a conclusion in which Aetolia was broken and the Romans ready to offer favourable terms and even concessions, then the Peace of Phoenice could justly be counted a victory for Macedon.

An important factor had been, of course, the half-heartedness of the Romans throughout the greater part of the war, from their culpable delay in securing the help of Aetolia to the still more culpable desertion of their ally in the critical years after Attalus's departure.[1] Consequently Philip had never had to face a determined Roman offensive. A second stroke of good fortune had been the unexpected military *risorgimento* of Achaea under Philopoemen, which from 207 onwards released Philip from the necessity of sending help to the Peloponnese. Nevertheless, to have rejected the Epirote proposals would have been to court

while Täubler, I, 214 *seq.* and Holleaux, 258 *seq.* reject also the three Peloponnesian states. Magie, *Buckler Studies*, 161–2, inclines to accept Ilium. Heuss, 40, n. 1, criticises Holleaux's conclusions without committing himself definitely to any view. Bickermann, *Rev. Phil.* LXI, 1935, 59 *seq.*, accepts all the names, and assumes that the peace takes the form of a κοινὴ εἰρήνη, guaranteeing the peace for all states that are 'adscripti'; against this view see Larsen, *loc. cit.* and McDonald and Walbank, *JRS*, XXVII, 1937, 180 *seq.*, where Holleaux's view is defended. The insertion of Ilium and Athens is a fairly obvious case of annalistic fabrication; and the three Peloponnesian states were, as we saw (above, p. 101), included in the separate treaty with Aetolia: they cannot have made peace with Rome twice. Scerdilaidas appears to have died since 208 (Livy (P) XXVIII, 5, 7).   [1] Cf. Holleaux, 251 *seq.*

disaster, to irritate the Senate and invite a Roman invasion of almost unlimited size, the moment Hannibal was disposed of. It has been contested by many historians[1]—and there is evidence among the less reliable authorities to support the view[2]—that in any case they were only waiting for a suitable opportunity for a war of revenge. This theory is completely untenable; without pausing now to discuss the motives which were going to bring the Romans back to Greece within five years of the Senate's ratification of the Treaty of Phoenice, it is sufficient here to insist that, after the exhaustive analysis of Holleaux,[3] there can be little doubt that Sempronius signed this treaty in good faith. The Romans left Greece as they entered it, without imperial ambitions, territorial or commercial, and without any intention of returning. On any other assumption, their neglect of their own interests—their failure to set up permanent relations with the anti-Macedonian states or to support Philip's northern enemies—is inexplicable: and still more inexplicable is why they chose that moment to make a peace which would simply give Philip a respite in which to recover from the strain of the last ten years.

The Romans, then, were ready for peace; and Philip, weary of a war which had proved so disappointing and which, in spite of certain solid gains, seemed unlikely now to yield anything but new hazards, was ready too. On a mere analysis of the situation in Greece his policy would be explicable. But in fact there is evidence that his attention was already directed elsewhere. Just as in 217 the advice of Demetrius of Pharus had suggested wild dreams of conquest in the west, and had led him to the hastily negotiated peace at Naupactus, so now, in 205, a new figure begins to come forward in Philip's counsels.

Heracleides of Tarentum was a man of humble origin,[4] who had come to Philip after a series of adventures, in which he was suspected in turn of betraying Tarentum to the Romans and the Romans to Hannibal. A sharp intellect, and a mixture of audacity and obsequiousness combined with a complete unscrupulousness

---

[1] E.g. Niese, II, 590; Theiler, 4; De Sanctis, III, 2, 439; IV, 1, 25 seq.
[2] Appian, Maced. 3; Justin. XXIX, 4, 11; Zonaras, IX, 15, 1; Livy (A) XXIX, 12, 16; XXXI, 31, 19–20; XXXII, 21, 18.
[3] Rome, 286 seq.
[4] Polyb. XIII, 4, 4 seq.: πεφυκέναι ἐκ βαναύσων καὶ χειροτεχνῶν ἀνθρώπων.

ASIA MINOR
and the
PROPONTIS

Scale of Miles

0 10 20   40   60

of character, fitted him admirably to be Philip's instrument; and his influence at court grew so strong that Polybius claims[1] that he was 'almost the chief instrument in the overthrow of that great kingdom of Macedon'. If anything, this means that Heracleides played a role in Philip's new policy similar to that which Demetrius had played in his last. Our first reference tb Heracleides goes back to the year 209, when he was in command of Philip's forces in Phocis;[2] but it is not until the years following the Peace of Phoenice that he rises to a position of pre-eminence, in the furthering of Philip's new ambitions. It is these ambitions and the policy to which they led that must be considered in the following pages.

[1] Polyb. XIII, 4, 8: ὥστε τοῦ καταστραφῆναι τὴν τηλικαύτην βασιλείαν σχεδὸν αἰτιώτατος γεγονέναι; cf. Diod. XXVIII, 2 seq.

[2] See above, p. 93, n. 1.

Chapter IV : Philip Looks East

THE AEGEAN AND ASIA MINOR (205-200)

IN the winter of 205-4 Antiochus of Syria returned to his capital from a six years' campaign in central Asia. About the same age as Philip, Antiochus had succeeded in 223, and while his rival had been spending year after year struggling against Rome, he had re-established the Seleucid empire to the threshold of India, filled his treasury, and won for himself the title of 'Great King' and a reputation greater than any Greek since Alexander.[1] His career was a matter of deep concern to Philip. Personal jealousy apart—and this cannot have been small —the revival of Syria threatened the balance of power between Egypt, Syria and Macedon, which had been the basis of Hellenistic politics since the wars of the Diadochi. Egypt, torn by internal revolt and controlled by the weak Philopator and his clique of favourites, could offer little resistance, if Antiochus chose to occupy those ancestral possessions in Syria, Asia Minor and Thrace, which, in spite of Egyptian usurpation, he still regarded as his.[2]

This situation cried out for Macedonian interference; for it was only by establishing himself as a factor in the eastern Mediterranean that Philip could hope to meet Antiochus, militarily or diplomatically, on even terms. But it was now more than twenty years since Doson's Carian expedition,[3] and in the meantime Philip had maintained his interest in Delos, alone of all the Macedonian possessions in the Aegean, where, since the decay of his fleet,[4] he had lost any effective influence. For activity in the Aegean the possession of a fleet was imperative; and Philip's first step must therefore be the building of those ships whose keels he had laid down at Cassandreia in 208,[5] but which had remained unfinished through lack of money.

---

[1] Holleaux, *CAH*, VIII, 142.
[2] Cf. Bickermann, *Hermes*, LXVII, 1932, 47-76.
[3] See above, pp. 12-13.   [4] See above, pp. 13, n. 10; 69.
[5] See above, p. 97.

The year 205 was spent in negotiating the Peace of Phoenice and the subsequent settlements;[1] inevitably there must have been a good deal of work on the Illyrian frontier and in Atintania. But in 204 Philip's eastern policy began to take shape. In the first place he needed money; and unable, like the Aetolians,[2] to contemplate radical changes in his internal economy, he was obliged to look to other sources of income. One solution was piracy. This was a well-established practice among the Illyrians and, at times, the Aetolians;[3] but a king of Macedon might be expected to have natural scruples at such an outrage of public opinion[4] throughout Greece, and particularly among his allies in the Symmachy. Nevertheless, under the pressure of circumstances, it was to piracy that Philip now turned. Whether he did so without hesitation the evidence does not permit us to say; certainly his exploits at Thermum and Messene had revealed few traditional scruples. Equally uncertain is the exact part played by Heracleides. Did he suggest to Philip the advantages of a piratical expedition in the Aegean? Were the five counsellors, whom Philip is said to have put to death at his instigation about this time,[5] opponents of this policy or merely rivals for Philip's favour? All that is known is that the Greek tradition seized upon this moment as a further stage in Philip's degeneration and closely associated with it the figure of the Tarentine.[6]

Since Macedon and Egypt had both virtually abandoned their control over the Aegean, the task of policing its waters had fallen to the maritime trading city of Rhodes.[7] As the natural opponents of war and piracy, both of which interrupted normal trade relations, the Rhodians had tried again and again to negotiate a settlement between Philip and the Romans; and now that the

---

[1] The actual ratification at Rome may not have been before spring 204; cf. Matzat, 160; De Sanctis, III, 2, 444.

[2] Polyb. XIII, 1 seq. Since 206, the richer classes in Aetolia had been driven to accept debt-cancellation under Scopas and Dorimachus, and had only prevented Scopas from becoming general and instituting even more radical reforms through the influence of Alexander of Calydon.

[3] Illyrians: Scerdilaidas and Demetrius in 220 (Polyb. IV, 16, 6 seq.); Aetolians: Polyb. IV, 6, 1.

[4] Cf. Holleaux, REG, XXXIII, 1920, 227–8 (important for the chronology and motivation of Dicaearchus's and Heracleides's activities in the Cretan War).

[5] Diod. XXVIII, 2.   [6] Polyb. XIII, 4, 4 seq.

[7] Cf. Costanzi, Klio, XI, 1911, 282–3; Holleaux, CAH, VIII, 143–4.

war was over, they were ready to throw all their efforts into crushing piracy in the Aegean.[1] Accordingly, in 205 or 204 they began to make war upon the Cretans, as the worst of the pirates,[2] and by so doing aroused the double hostility of Philip. For not only was Philip recognised nominally as president by most of Crete,[3] but it was directly in the interests of his new schemes that piracy should be encouraged. Thus prestige, irritation at the persistent Rhodian interference during the recent war, and, above all, the needs of his purse combined to force him to take up the cause of the Cretan pirates.

In a secret agreement Philip undertook to assist the Cretans against Rhodes;[4] and shortly afterwards there appeared in the Aegean an Aetolian named Dicaearchus, ostensibly an independent pirate, but in fact an agent of Philip, whose task was to exact payments from the autonomous islanders and give what help he could to the Cretans.[5] Whether Dicaearchus had previously been a pirate is not recorded;[6] but in any case his connection with Philip was kept a secret for the present.[7] Later, when the truth leaked out, the stories of Dicaearchus's sacrifices to Asebeia and Paranomia, to Impiety and Lawlessness, wherever he landed,[8] were added to the other elements of the anti-Macedonian tradition.

Dicaearchus's piracies were directed mainly against the rich cities of the Troad[9] and the Cyclades; but the general effect was a deterioration of international morality throughout the Aegean. For Nabis, the king of Sparta, joined in the game, working in conjunction with the Cretans[10] and perhaps Dicae-

---

[1] For the Rhodians as uprooters of piracy see Polyb. IV, 19, 8 (opposition to Demetrius of Pharus); Strabo, XIV, 2, 5; *Syll.* 581, lines 51 *seq.*; 79 *seq.* (treaty between Hierapytna and Rhodes).

[2] Diod. XXVII, 3.

[3] See above, p. 67, n. 5.

[4] Polyb. XIII, 5, 1; Polyaen. V, 17 (2).

[5] Polyb. XVIII, 54, 8–12; Diod. XXVIII, 1. On Dicaearchus see W. L. Westermann, *Upon Slavery in Ptolemaic Egypt*, 22–7.

[6] If so, Philip was following the precedent of Antigonus Gonatas, who had similarly employed the Phocian pirate, Ameinias, in his capture of Cassandreia (Polyaen. IV, 6, 18); cf. Ormerod, 123; Griffith, 67; 262.

[7] The twenty ships given to him by Philip (Diod. XXVIII, 1) will not have been part of Philip's regular fleet; cf. Holleaux, *REG*, XXXIII, 1920, 227–8.

[8] Polyb. XVIII, 54, 10; Diod. XXVIII, 1.

[9] Cf. Holleaux, *REG*, XXXIII, 1920, 241.

[10] Polyb. XIII, 8, 2; cf. Livy (P) XXXIV, 32, 18; 35, 9; 36, 3.

archus. And meanwhile[1] Philip planned a direct move against Rhodes. Playing a part for which his past history well fitted him, Heracleides appeared before the Rhodian *Prytaneis*, with a story that he had deserted from Philip;[2] and in support of this he produced a letter, purporting to be from Philip to the Cretans, promising them help against Rhodes. The very boldness of the trick ensured its success: the Rhodians admitted Heracleides to their confidence. In fact Philip—or his agent—had calculated the position to a nicety; almost certainly the letter would prove convincing, since it corresponded so perfectly with Rhodian suspicions; at the same time Philip could disclaim its authorship, denounce Heracleides and so avoid a breach of international law. Similarly in the sequel; for even when Heracleides made a determined effort to burn down the Rhodian dockyards and arsenals, and succeeded in destroying thirteen ships before making his escape,[3] it could not be proved that he was Philip's agent. And Philip, meanwhile, sent fresh envoys to stir up the Cretans still further in their war against Rhodes.[4]

All this time Philip's outward policy gave no indication of the slightest interest in either Antiochus or the Aegean. Of his campaigns in the summer of 204 no consecutive record has survived, but from the fragments in Polybius[5] it is clear that he was busy in Illyria and in Thrace, where he seems to have penetrated as far as the Hebrus[6] and perhaps to have negotiated some kind of agreement with the Odrysae, a Thracian tribe which had recently superseded Cavarus and his Galatians as the chief power in those parts.[7] Further, he made one of his periodic attacks on the Dardanians, inflicting a crushing defeat, and killing, Diodorus claims,[8] some 10,000 of the enemy. In

[1] The chronology here is indefinite. I follow, in general, Holleaux, *REG*, XXXIII, 1920, 223 *seq.*; but Heracleides's raid on the Rhodian dockyards *may* be in 203.   [2] Polyb. XIII, 5, 1–3; Polyaen. v, 17 (2).

[3] So Polyaenus; the account is probably reliable; cf. Holleaux, *REG*, XXXIII, 1920, 237, n. 2, against Niese, II, 572, n. 2, and Fabricius, *P-W*, 'Herakleides', col. 498, who reject it.

[4] Polyb. XIII, 4, 2: παρορμήσοντας ἐπὶ τὸν κατὰ τῶν 'Ροδίων πόλεμον.

[5] Polyb. XIII, 10, including references to places in Crete and Thrace, and to Μελίτουσσα in Illyria.

[6] See Niese, II, 571, n. 2, who places Καβύλη on the Tundscha; cf. Oberhummer, *P-W*, 'Kabyle'.   [7] Polyb. IV, 46; 52; VIII, 22.

[8] Diod. XXVIII, 2; 9. Justin. XXIX, 4, 10 (confused) probably refers to 208; cf. Holleaux, 287, n. 3.

this way Philip not only established a kind of *alibi* as far as the Aegean was concerned, but also ensured security from the barbarians, whenever he openly turned his attention east; his success can be judged from the fact that we have no record of any disturbance on those frontiers until the winter of 200–199. Finally, with the coming of spring 203, Philip set about the construction of a fleet on the proceeds of Dicaearchus's piracy.[1]

At this point, the centre of events shifts to Egypt, where, in the autumn of 204, Ptolemy Philopator had died, leaving the power in the hands of the palace clique which had for some years been managing his affairs; and their leader, Sosibius, fearing an attack from Antiochus, decided to conceal Ptolemy's death as long as possible.[2] His fears were justified; for by the spring of 203 Antiochus had already begun to encroach[3] upon the Ptolemaic empire, and Sosibius was obliged to look around for support. Shortly before Philopator's death, both Philip and Antiochus had made the king offers of help against a native revolt;[4] and this may have suggested to Sosibius the idea of playing off the lesser danger against the greater. At any rate, in the spring of 203,[5] he now opened negotiations with Philip for a match between one of the king's daughters and Ptolemy Epiphanes, the six-year-old son and heir of the dead Philopator. No conclusion had, however, been reached when, in the autumn, Sosibius died and the palace group were obliged to announce the king's death and Epiphanes's succession; and Agathocles, now in charge, despatched Sosibius's son Ptolemy to Philip to hasten the negotiations, and to request the help of Macedon in the event of a Syrian attack on Coele-Syria.

Of Philip's own movements there is once more no record. Probably he continued his intrigues against Rhodes, and pressed ahead with the construction of his fleet. Undoubtedly he maintained an elaborate system of espionage through any areas in

---

[1] Holleaux, 285, n. 5. This fleet does not appear in action until 202, but a considerable time must be allowed for its construction.

[2] For the chronology of Philopator's death and Epiphanes's accession see my discussion in *JEA*, xxii, 1936, 20–34 (slightly modified by C. F. Nims, *JEA*, xxiv, 1938, 73–4); cf., too, Bikerman, *Chron. d'Égypte*, xxix, 1940, 124–31.

[3] Amyzon has now become Syrian: cf. Wilhelm, *Wien. Anz.* lvii, 1920, xxvii–xxvii, pp. 51 *seq.*; Welles, 165 *seq.*   [4] Polyb. xv, 20, 1.

[5] Polyb. xv, 25, 13: τὰ περὶ τῆς ἐπιγαμίας συνθησόμενον: cf. Niese, ii, 574, n. 1; Holleaux, 79, n. 1.

which he was interested,[1] and he was in no hurry to conclude an open alliance with Egypt, until it was clearer where his interests lay. Such an alliance would be a check on Antiochus; but possible concessions in the Aegean were not much use until Philip's fleet was ready to defend them, and there was the further risk that Philip might become involved in a futile and inconvenient war with Antiochus over Coele-Syria. On the other hand a direct rebuff might drive Egypt voluntarily into the arms of Antiochus.[2] Philip therefore gave the Egyptian envoy a warm welcome, treated him kindly, but took care to keep him at the Macedonian court for close on a year, during which time he created the general impression that Alexandria could rely on his help, while he committed himself to no definite promises.

The same winter (203–2) Antiochus approached Philip with the offer of a pact directed against Egypt,[3] and Philip accepted. The bargain was strictly secret, and its exact terms are difficult to sort out from the exaggerated versions preserved in our sources.[4] But, judging from the subsequent behaviour of the two parties, they did not concern Egypt itself; they merely outlined a general division of the Ptolemaic possessions abroad into spheres of Macedonian and Syrian interest. Coele-Syria, as part of the old Seleucid empire, was to go back to Antiochus, and the Egyptian possessions in Thrace and the Aegean were no doubt to be Philip's; whether Asia Minor was included is uncertain, but there may have been an additional clause pledging the signatories to give each other what assistance they could in the carrying out of these designs.[5]

Outwardly, meanwhile, Philip remained friendly towards Egypt, and whereas Antiochus opened his campaign against

[1] Cf. Polyb. XIII, 5, 7, for spies (Damocles and Pythion) at Rome.

[2] See the comments of Holleaux, 290, n. 1.

[3] Polyb. III, 2, 8; XV, 20, 1 *seq.*; XVI, 1, 9; Livy (P) XXXI, 14, 5; Appian, *Maced.* 4, 1; Justin. XXX, 2, 8; Hieron. *in Daniel.* 11, 13. The initiative most probably came from Antiochus; cf. Cary, 93, n. 3.

[4] In Polybius and, particularly, in Appian; cf. McDonald, *JRS*, XXVII, 1937, 182–4. The recent attempt of D. Magie, *JRS*, XXIX, 1939, 32–44, to reject the pact completely as a product of Rhodian propaganda, which imposed both on Rome and (via Rhodian sources) on Polybius, is too radical; that Philip appealed to Zeuxis for help at all is surely evidence for an agreement of some kind (Polyb. XVI, 1, 8; 24, 6).

[5] Polyb. XVI, 1, 8, where Philip requisitions corn from Antiochus's satrap, Zeuxis, supports this view; cf. also Polyb. XVI, 24, 6.

Coele-Syria in the spring of 202,[1] Philip made no hostile move against Egypt, but, on the contrary, continued to entertain the Egyptian ambassador, Ptolemy, in Macedon until the following autumn.[2] At the same time he was now prepared for an offensive against non-Ptolemaic possessions. Two years of intrigue and secret marauding had laid the stage and provided the funds for open aggression; and the general situation appeared to be favourable.[3] Of the other powers with interests in the Aegean, Rhodes was conveniently saddled with the Cretan war, Antiochus was pledged to benevolent neutrality, and Attalus, in alliance with Antiochus,[4] was not likely to reopen the struggle unless his own territory was directly attacked; for, to Attalus, war with Philip involved a definite risk of war with Philip's kinsman, Prusias of Bithynia.[5] On the other hand, Philip could hope for little help from the Greek allies. The Achaeans in particular, since their victory over Machanidas,[6] were dealing with the Spartans quite independently of Philip; but in 204 Machanidas's successor, Nabis, began a desultory frontier war with Megalopolis,[7] which, though it did not require Philip's assistance, was probably sufficient to keep the Achaeans out of any conflicts overseas.

Philip's first direct move was levelled at Aetolia, and threatened not the Aegean, but the Propontis and the Black Sea trade route. Launching his new fleet, he forced the towns of Lysimacheia and Chalcedon to leave the Aetolian alliance[8] and make treaties attaching themselves to Macedon;[9] they were given Macedonian commanders and became virtually part of Philip's kingdom. Perinthus, a Byzantine town on the north shore of the Propontis,

[1] Polyb. XVI, 22a; Justin. XXXI, 1; Hieron. in Daniel. 11, 11 seq.; cf. Holleaux, CAH, VIII, 151–2.
[2] De Sanctis, IV, 1, 4, n. 10, assumes that Ptolemy's presence in Macedon is inconsistent with the signing of the pact with Antiochus before autumn 202; this is to miss the subtlety of the double game of diplomacy that Philip was playing.   [3] See De Sanctis, IV, 1, 4–5.   [4] Polyb. V, 107, 4.
[5] On the relationship see Wilhelm, Jahresh. XI, 1908, 79–81; Holleaux, 207, n. 1.   [6] See above, p. 99.   [7] Polyb. XIII, 8, 3.
[8] They had probably shared this alliance since the last war; see below, Appendix III, p. 306, n. 7.
[9] Polyb. XV, 23, 9; cf. XVIII, 3, 11; 4, 5. For the treaty with Lysimacheia see Oikonomos, Ἐπιγραφαὶ τῆς Μακεδονίας, I, 1915, 2 seq. (also E. Bikerman, Rev. Phil. LXV, 1939, 348–9; cf. Heuss, Stadt und Herrscher, 180). Little weight need be laid on Philip's later claim that he occupied the towns to preserve them from the Thracians.

was also annexed, and after that Philip took Cius, which was being attacked by Prusias;[1] this town, which was also allied to the Aetolians, he completely sacked, and enslaved its population.

Elated at these successes,[2] Philip ignored the consequences; he failed to consider the revulsion that would be inspired by such unjustifiable barbarism perpetrated against free and unoffending Greek states.[3] In particular, he cannot have envisaged the disgust of the Rhodians, and still less their alarm at the threat to the peaceful trading cities implied in Philip's control of the Black Sea corn route; at Athens, for example, the effects of the crisis are to be seen in the appointment of Cephisodorus to the post of ταμίας τῶν σιτωνικῶν.[4] Philip was still outside Cius when envoys arrived from a number of neutral cities, including Rhodes, to plead for the town.[5] Philip put them off with excuses, sent a messenger to speak in the Prytaneum at Rhodes and continued the siege undeterred. From the moment that the news of the fall of Cius reached Rhodes, the Rhodians considered themselves at war with Philip;[6] but, for this season at least, the Cretan war occupied their full attentions, and their hostility remained nominal. Philip was able to hand over the bare site of Cius to a slightly disgruntled Prusias,[7] who rebuilt it under the name of 'Prusa'; and the near-by town of Myrleia, another capture, reappeared later as 'Apamea'.[8]

On his way back from Cius, Philip put in at the free city of Thasos, and having obtained admission on a promise through his general Metrodorus to respect its independence, he promptly seized it and enslaved its inhabitants.[9] Its position off the coast opposite the frontiers of Macedon and Thrace made Thasos a

[1] Polyb. xv, 21; xviii, 3, 12; 4, 7; Strabo, xii, 4, 3. Holleaux, 291, n. 1, thinks our sources exaggerate the completeness of the destruction. On Perinthus see Treves, LEC, ix, 1940, 158.   [2] Polyb. xv, 22, 1.
[3] Tarn, Hellen. Mil. and Nav. Developments, 44, plausibly suggests that Philip's policy of deliberately practising atrocities at this time was a conscious imitation of Roman methods, as observed in the last war.
[4] Meritt, Hesperia, v, 1936, 426, no. 15; cf. McDonald, JRS, xxvii, 1937, 200 seq.; Heichelheim, Aegyptus, xvii, 1937, 63–4.
[5] Polyb. xv, 22, 4–5; 23, 1–5.
[6] Polyb. xv, 23, 6.   [7] Polyb. xv, 23, 10.
[8] Strabo, xii, 4, 3; Steph. Byz. s.v. Προῦσα. Μύρλεια; OGIS, 340; 341. The name Apamea was given later by Prusias's son; cf. Niese, ii, 583, n. 3.
[9] Polyb. xv, 24, 1–3; cf. Livy (P) xxxiii, 30, 3. Beloch, iv, 2, 347, has no grounds for claiming Thasos as Ptolemaic; cf. De Sanctis, iv, 1, 7, n. 20.

valuable link in Philip's schemes, but his action reinforced the hatred aroused by his earlier exploits this year.[1] And meanwhile Philip's intrigues against Rhodes continued with undiminished vigour, not only in Crete but now on the mainland as well. Inscriptions dating from a little before the open breach between Philip and Rhodes,[2] throw light on the activities of a minor dynast, Olympichus, the ruler of Alinda,[3] who was at this time operating under Philip's control, probably directly as his agent; the attacks of his man, Podilus, on Iasus, on the Gulf of Bargylia, were resisted by the Rhodians, who were able to produce a letter from Philip requiring Olympichus to leave the town unharmed. Though appreciably nearer, an open breach had once more been averted.

In Aetolia, meanwhile, there was a renewed hatred of Philip,[4] who, after failing to make good his promises in Thessaly, had now turned to open assault upon cities allied to the League.[5] But the Aetolians were in no state to reply with arms. The social and economic disturbances, which followed the war, had ended, it is true, in the defeat of Scopas by Alexander of Calydon, and in the autumn of 205 Scopas had left for Egypt.[6] Two years later, however, upon the proclamation of Epiphanes's accession, he had returned to recruit an army of mercenaries,[7] and in 202 Aetolia was still exhausted, both militarily and economically. She therefore decided to appeal to Rome; the Senate, it was felt, was certain to view with distaste this recrudescence of Philip's

[1] Polyb. xv, 24, 4–6.
[2] BMI, III, 441 = Hicks, 182; cf. Holleaux, REG, XII, 1899, 25 seq.; REA, v, 1903, 223 seq.; Beloch, IV, 2, 550; and against Beloch, Nicolaus, 76 seq. One of the inscriptions speaks of φιλίαν καὶ εὔνοιαν still existing between Rhodes and Macedon.
[3] An inscription found at Alinda (Demirdji Déré), and published by A. Laumonier (BCH, LVIII, 1934, 291–8, 'Inscriptions de Carie, no. 1'), shows Olympichus acting as στρατηγός of Philip; this change in status was probably subsequent to Philip's invasion of Caria, in which case this decree will date to 201 or 200, not to 202, as Laumonier suggests. It is no proof that Philip inherited Caria from Doson (as Lenschau, Bursian, 1938, 271; P-W, 'Olympichos (1)'). Laumonier makes out a good case for assuming that Olympichus's seat was at Alinda, not at Mylasa (as Beloch thought: IV, 2, 551). The Olympichus of Polyb. v, 90, 1, may be the same man, or possibly his father. [4] Polyb. xv, 23, 7.
[5] The towns of Lysimacheia, Chalcedon and Perinthus were probably united to Aetolia, not as League-members, but by ἰσοπολιτεία; cf. Swoboda, Gr. Staatsaltertümer,[6] 350, n. 5; De Sanctis, IV, 1, 6, n. 14; Flacelière, 312 and n. 3; in this case their secession gave no technical grounds for war.
[6] Polyb. XIII, 2, 1; see above, p. 109, n. 2, and Walbank, JEA, XXII, 1936, 25, n. 8. [7] Polyb. xv, 25, 16.

power. But the Aetolians had miscalculated; their envoys, despatched to Rome in the autumn of 202, were, to their dismay, rebuffed by the Senate in the most brutal terms;[1] the separate peace—theoretically a desertion of Rome—was thrown in their teeth, and Rome made it quite clear that Philip no longer interested her. The news of this reception must have been as welcome to Philip as it was disheartening to the Aetolians; so long as the Senate's interests were not directly challenged—and in his eastward expansion there seemed little danger of that—Rome might henceforth be left out of his calculations.

With its operations in the Propontis and against Thasos, the campaign of 202 had provided a successful trial for Philip's new fleet. In the spring of 201, therefore, he set sail with some forty to fifty cataphracts, a few light vessels and 150 *lembi*, towards the Cyclades and Asia Minor.[2] The islands offered little resistance; many Philip took over, and perhaps garrisoned:[3] but of actual names only those of Andros, Cythnos and Paros survive.[4] The Cyclades were at this time independent, though unofficially under the protection of Rhodes; their seizure was a further challenge to that city. Samos, Philip's next port of call, was, however, Egyptian, and contained a squadron of Egyptian ships, temporarily dismantled; quite obviously the Egyptian commander, ignorant of the pact with Antiochus, was relying on the friendly relations existing between Alexandria and Pella, and expected no attack. And, indeed, Philip did not annex Samos as he had annexed the Cyclades. He temporarily occupied its valuable naval station and even took the liberty of fitting out part of the Egyptian squadron; but his actions were so managed as to avoid a breach with Alexandria. The resistance with which the townspeople met him was locally inspired,[5] and though he

---

[1] Livy (P) XXXI, 29, 4; Appian, *Maced.* 4, 2; see below, Appendix III, p. 310.
[2] Polyb. XVI, 2, 9, gives the figures before the battle of Chios as 53 cataphracts, some light vessels and 150 galleys and beaked ships; this probably includes *some* of the Egyptian ships from Samos: τὰς γὰρ ἐν τῇ Σάμῳ ναῦς οὐκ ἠδυνήθη καταρτίσαι πάσας: cf. Holleaux, *REA*, XXIII, 1921, 181–6. Philip had probably no losses at the battle of Lade. For the chronology of the year, see below, Appendix III, pp. 307 *seq.*
[3] See below, Appendix III, p. 308.   [4] Livy (P) XXXI, 15, 8; 31, 4.
[5] See the decree honouring a doctor who tended the wounded, published by Klaffenbach, *Ath. Mitt.* LI, 1926, 28–33. The resistance may, as Holleaux suggests (*CAH*, VIII, 153), have sprung from fear lest the town should suffer the fate of Thasos.

was forced to seize the surrounding heights and blockade the town before he could force an entry, Samos remained technically Egyptian and its occupation was never treated as a hostile act.[1]

Meanwhile the Rhodians, uncertain of Philip's objective, resolved to sail and meet him; and when Philip crossed the straits from Samos he found their fleet opposing him off the island of Lade,[2] and thus blocking his approach to Miletus and Caria. The ensuing battle was a victory for Philip. One of the Rhodian ships, upon being rammed, raised her jury-mast and put out to sea, whereupon most of the others followed suit and left Philip victorious. All but two quinqueremes escaped and were carried by a favourable wind to Myndus, and from there to Cos and, presumably, home; and Philip, meanwhile, made a triumphant entry into Miletus,[3] where both he and Heracleides, who had played a great part in the victory, were voted crowns. Later in the year Philip was to give the town of Myus to the Magnesians in return for supplies of figs;[4] as Myus had been annexed to Miletus since 228 at the latest,[5] evidently Philip now assumed sovereignty over the Ionian district around Miletus.

The Rhodian defeat and Philip's invasion of the mainland of Ionia created a grave situation for those cities whose main interests lay in trade; and Byzantium, Cyzicus and Cos now made ready to assist in a coalition against Macedon.[6] More important still, the example of Theophiliscus, the Rhodian admiral, who had been personally responsible for sailing to meet Philip off

---

[1] Appian, Maced. 4, 1; Polyb. III, 2, 8; XVI, 2, 4; 2, 9; 7, 6; Livy (P) XXXI, 31, 4. Samos not included in subsequent negotiations: Polyb. XVIII, 2; 44; among the civitates sociae Ptolomaei in 197: Livy (P) XXXIII, 20, 11–12. Cf. McDonald, JRS, XXVII, 1937, 186, n. 41, and for the date, below, Appendix III, p. 309, n. 2.

[2] For the battle of Lade see Polyb. XVI, 10, 1; 14, 5; 15.

[3] Polyb. XVI, 15, 5–6.   [4] Polyb. XVI, 24, 9.

[5] Rehm, Das Delphinion in Milet, n. 148 and pp. 200–1, 347–8; cf. Holleaux, REA, XXII, 1920, 256; Meyer, Grenzen d. hell. Staaten, 78–9.

[6] Cf. Holleaux, REA, XXIII, 1921, 184–5; these states probably gave help in the subsequent battle of Chios. For the part played by Cos in the war, see the Halasarna decree, Syll. 569 (cf. Herzog, Klio, II, 1902, 321–6; Cardinali, Riv. Fil. XXXV, 1907, 8; Holleaux, REG, XXX, 1917, 88–104; Ormerod, 45 seq.; Segre, Riv. Fil. LXI, 1933, 375 seq.), which shows Cos involved in both the Cretan War and that between Rhodes and Macedon; see also Paton and Hicks, Insc. Cos, 10; for Cyzicus: Polyb. XVI, 31, 3 (referring to 200); for Byzantium: Polyb. XVI, 2, 10.

Lade, assisted, probably, by a specific appeal for help, persuaded Attalus of Pergamum to throw himself once more into the war with Philip.

This decision undoubtedly came as a complete surprise to Philip, who regarded it as unprovoked aggression; his own actions, however outrageous, had hitherto respected Pergamene interests. This surprise may explain Philip's immediate and typical reaction. Leaving his fleet in Ionia, he marched his army north towards Pergamum, and, approaching the town, completely routed a force sent out to oppose him.[1] Unable, however, to force a way into Pergamum itself, and prevented by Attalus's foresight from obtaining much real plunder, he was soon in a difficult position; and, as at Thermum, he took revenge upon the statues and sanctuaries outside the walls.[2] Buildings were destroyed to their foundations, their very stones were shattered, and the sacred olive grove at the Nicephorium was cut down; the temple of Aphrodite was similarly pillaged and destroyed.[3] However, Philip soon began to feel the pinch and was forced to leave the immediate outskirts of the town. First he marched east along the Caicus to the neighbourhood of Thyateira, but soon returned past Pergamum to the fertile plain of Thebe, which lay over the hills to the north, near Adramyttium.[4] In both districts he was baulked; what was to prove his main embarrassment throughout the whole of this year's campaigns— the provisioning of his troops—was already troubling him. He had counted, apparently, on living on the land; but the inhabitants had forestalled him by gathering the harvest into the towns,[5] and he was reduced to marching rapidly from place to place, taking what he could find. From the plain of Thebe he

[1] Polyb. XVI, 1, 1: νομίζων οἷον αὐτόχειρ Ἀττάλου γενέσθαι, must refer to a defeat for Attalus, and the easiest assumption is that troops were sent out against Philip and beaten. This would explain Attalus's failure to offer any real opposition throughout this invasion. On the chronology see below, Appendix III, p. 308.

[2] Polyb. XVI, 1, 5; Appian, *Maced.* 4, 1 speaks of violated tombs, but this may cover a confusion with the later depredations in Attica (cf. Livy (P) XXXI, 26, 12); see Holleaux, *REA*, XXIII, 1921, 195–6.

[3] Polyb. XVIII, 2, 2; 6, 4; Livy (P) XXXI, 46, 4; Diod. XXVIII, 5.

[4] Polyb. XVI, 1, 7: ποιησάμενος τὴν ἀναξυγήν to be taken as 'returning'; cf. Holleaux, *REA*, XXIII, 1921, 197 *seq.* On the richness of the plain of Thebe see Livy (P) XXXVII, 19, 17.

[5] I.e. the month was about June; cf. Holleaux, *REA*, XXV, 1923, 351.

returned once more south-east, past Pergamum and Thyateira to Hiera Come,[1] a village some distance north of the Hermus and on the road from Thyateira to Sardes. His object in going inland was to obtain supplies from Zeuxis, Antiochus's governor at Sardes; but the small help received from this quarter[2] soon indicated the real value of the pact, when it was put to the test.

In the meantime, it appears that Philip's fleet was operating with some success among the Sporades. Inscriptions show Cos repelling attacks at this time, and perhaps Calymna too.[3] But the small island of Nisyros, off the promontory of Cnidus, was probably but one of the many to be taken over; here Philip employed a friendly citizen, Callias, to win over the people.[4] Alcaeus's sarcastic verses, written about this time, give bitter expression to the general feeling throughout Greece that Philip was all but invincible.[5] Meanwhile, at Pergamum, Attalus attended to the ravages of Philip's invasion; and Philip himself, returning from Hiera Come to Miletus, rejoined his fleet in readiness for the next move. After the battle of Lade, Polybius claims,[6] Philip's right policy would have been to sail on Alexandria. It is difficult to accept this criticism. Neither now nor at

[1] Holleaux, *REA*, XXIII, 1921, 197 *seq.* follows Imhoof-Blumer's identification of Hiera Come with the Roman Hierocaesarea, which lies 40 km. north of Sardes near the junction of the Hyllus and Lycus. An inscription (published by Foucart, *BCH*, XI, 1887, 104, no. 25; cf. Buckler, *JHS*, XXXVII, 1917, 110, no. 23) has been found near Thyateira, perhaps from the site of Hiera Come, in honour of Philip; cf. De Sanctis, IV, 1, 12, n. 30.

[2] Polyb. XVI, 1, 8–9.

[3] See above, p. 118, n. 6, and, in particular, Segre, *Riv. Fil.* LXI, 1933, 365 *seq. Syll.* 568 and 569 refer to this war (Cos); *Insc. Cos*, 10, refers to the σύμμαχοι and may be a little later in the year; *Insc. Cos*, 11, and *GDI*, 3590 (Calymna), may refer to either this or the Cretan War, which affected Cos and other islands as well as Rhodes; *Syll.* 567 refers to the Cretan War (Calymna). It seems probable that the Cretan War ended about 201; the treaty between Rhodes and Hierapytna will date from about this time.

[4] *Syll.* 572 (Philip's letter to Nisyros; cf. Schroeter, 80, no. 33). The dedication (*Syll.* 673) to an unknown Nisyrian, who had served with the Rhodians during the Cretan and Macedonian wars, goes back to this period, but does not affect the question of who owned the island (cf. Holleaux, *REG*, XXX, 1917, 102 *seq.*; *REA*, XXV, 1923, 344); it does not prove that the island was still Rhodian until after the battle of Chios.

[5] *Anth. Pal.* IX, 518 (cf. Seeliger, 15; De Sanctis, IV, 1, 9–10):

Μακύνου τείχη, Ζεῦ 'Ολύμπιε· πάντα Φιλίππῳ
ἄμβατα· χαλκείας κλεῖε πύλας μακάρων·
καὶ γὰρ χθὼν καὶ πόντος ὑπὸ σκάπτροισι Φιλίππου
δέδμανται· λοιπὰ δ' ἁ πρὸς "Ολυμπον ὁδός.

[6] Polyb. XVI, 10.

any time had Philip the intention of invading Egypt. His agreement with Antiochus would have been futile if it was his intention to precipitate a crisis by invading the country which was deliberately omitted from their compact, and Polybius's criticism merely reveals the extent to which he was imposed on by the popular exaggerated version of the treaty. On this point De Sanctis's criticisms are conclusive.[1]

Philip now began to blockade the city of Chios,[2] sailing northward up the coast from Miletus, and probably taking possession of such towns as the two Colophons on the way.[3] Since the battle of Lade, Chios had joined the anti-Macedonian coalition, along with Rhodes, Pergamum and, probably, Cyzicus, Cos and Byzantium.[4] Philip's unprovoked attack imposed a direct obligation upon the allies to help

[1] De Sanctis, IV, 1, 10 seq. For a dedication of Philip on Delos from this period see above, p. 67, n. 6.

[2] Appian, Maced. 4, 1 (inaccurate); Plut. Moralia, 245 c (relating an apocryphal story that Philip promised the Chian slaves their freedom and their masters' wives, if they enabled him to take the town by deserting); Polyb. XVI, 2, 1 (name of town not mentioned); cf. Holleaux, Klio, IX, 1909, 450–4; REA, XXII, 1920, 252 seq.; Niccolini, 111–12. It is possible that Frontinus, Strat. III, 9, 8, refers to this occasion. For financial assistance afforded later by Attalus in repairing the damage done by Philip to the walls and to a gymnasium which he burnt, see an inscription published by Zolotas, 'Αθηνᾶ, XX, 1908, 163, no. 3; cf. Rostovtzeff in Ramsay Studies.

[3] Seven Teian decrees (Le Bas-Waddington, 65–7, 70, 72–4) show Philip's agent Perdiccas granted Teian citizenship and using his influence to obtain ἀσυλία for Teos from Cretan towns under Philip's control (Axos, Sybrita, Latos, Istron, Arcadia, Allaria, Latos πρὸς Καμάρᾳ); two inscriptions show Hagesander of Rhodes, an agent of Antiochus, doing the same thing at Rhaucus and Lappa (Le Bas-Waddington, 63, 66); while at Eleutherna (Le Bas-Waddington, 71) both appeared. Holleaux, who dates these decrees to this year, assumes that Philip now gained possession of Teos; and De Sanctis, IV, 1, 11, n. 28, puts its seizure immediately before Philip's attack on Pergamum, which is unlikely, since Teos was off the direct route north, and Philip's usual strategy in such cases was to march with all speed on his objective. But, in fact, as Ruge shows (so too Magie), these decrees, like others recording grants of ἀσυλία on the same occasion, are probably to be dated 205–3, and provide no evidence for Philip's possession of the town. Hagesander's presence shows that Teos was at that time in Antiochus's hands; the part played by Perdiccas follows from Philip's position in Crete (see above p. 67, n. 5). Whereas, if Philip possessed Teos, it is hard to see why Hagesander was employed. See Holleaux, Klio, XIII, 1913, 137 seq.; REA, XXV, 1923, 330 seq.; Ruge, P-W, 'Teos', cols. 539 seq. (with full concordance of inscriptions); Magie, Buckler Studies, 168–9, n. 3.

[4] Cf. Syll. 579. For the Rhodian connections of Chios see Holleaux, 35; 87, n. 2; 91, against Beloch, IV, 2, 345, and De Sanctis, IV, 1, 12, who regard it as nominally Ptolemaic.

her; and, accordingly, Philip shortly afterwards found himself threatened by a united fleet of Pergamum, Rhodes and the minor allies,[1] lying opposite Chios, in the bay between the promontories of Argennum and Mesate, and thus cutting him off from his base at Samos.

Philip controlled a fleet of fifty-three large cataphracts, mostly quinqueremes and quadriremes, but including ships of larger dimensions, a number of light ships, not perhaps very many, and finally about 150 galleys, *lembi* and *pristeis* of the Illyrian type; against these his opponents had sixty-five cataphracts and twelve light ships, of which Attalus provided thirty-five cataphracts and the Rhodians twenty to twenty-five. Numerically the sides were approximately equally balanced;[2] but Philip appreciated the superior seamanship of the Rhodians and the skill which had given them the confidence to attack with inferior numbers at Lade, and he resolved to make with all speed for the open sea, south of the straits, and to return to Samos.[3] The allies were sailing in loose order and this manœuvre took them by surprise; nevertheless they put out from the mainland and attacked, Attalus engaging Philip's left wing from the flank.[4] Seeing his move forestalled and afraid to be attacked at a disadvantage, Philip swung the eastern section of his ships round to face the Pergamene fleet, and himself retired to some islands in the middle of the strait, probably those off Cape Argennum.

For some time this conflict between the Pergamene fleet and what was now Philip's right wing was very even;[5] the Macedonian admiral, Democrates, went down with his ship, and Attalus's own commanders, Deinocrates and Dionysodorus both had the narrowest of escapes. The second stage in the battle came with the entry of the Rhodian contingent, which lay farther north on the allied right and, surprised by Philip's sudden move south, had a considerable distance to row before it

[1] Sources for the battle of Chios: Polyb. XVI, 2–9; XVIII, 2, 2; 6, 3; 8, 10; *OGIS*, 283 (cf. Holleaux, *REG*, XI, 1898, 251). The version in Rodgers, 379–85, is vitiated by his assumption that the city besieged by Philip was Pergamum.
[2] For the numbers on either side see Holleaux, *REA*, XXIII, 1921, 183 *seq.*
[3] Polyb. XVI, 2, 4.
[4] See Holleaux, *Klio*, IX, 1909, 452, n. 6, who shows that the terms 'right' and 'left' in Polyb. XVI, 2, 7–8, are used with reference to the later battle order, and require reversing up to the point when the ships wheel round and face the enemy.   [5] Polyb. XVI, 4, 1–2.

could catch up its opponents. The original Macedonian right was now in turn obliged to wheel round and defend itself, and the battle henceforth developed into two separate actions. The Rhodians found themselves hampered by Philip's *lembi*, which were distributed among the warships, where they made impossible the usual naval manœuvre of *diekplous*;[1] and in hand-to-hand combat over the decks the Macedonians soon proved their superiority.[2] On the other hand, the Rhodians were successful in running alongside and breaking the enemy's oar-banks, and they thus put a large number of ships out of action.

Meanwhile, on Philip's right, Attalus was enjoying a definite advantage, when he rashly allowed himself to become separated from the rest of his fleet, in his endeavour to capture a Macedonian ship that was making for the mainland. Seeing his chance, Philip sailed out from his island, and with four warships and three lighter vessels pursued the king ashore.[3] Attalus himself escaped to Erythrae, but lost his royal ship with all its costly furnishings; and the Macedonians obtained a rich haul of plunder. However, on returning to the battle, Philip found that his fleet had suffered heavy losses; and as the flight of Attalus, and the subsequent withdrawal of his fleet, had opened up the way to the south, Philip marshalled whatever of his ships had survived and retired from the battle. The Rhodians also withdrew to Chios, but Philip anchored for the night off Cape Argennum, as a claim to the victory.

In the event both sides claimed to be victorious, Philip on the grounds that he had remained on the site of the battle and had driven Attalus ashore and captured three of his ships, the Rhodians because of Philip's heavy losses.[4] The Macedonian ships sunk and captured amounted to twenty-eight cataphracts, three light vessels and almost half the *lembi*; whereas the enemy had, between them, lost only eight warships and one light vessel, and had taken two of Philip's quadriremes. The result was an unquestioned superiority, so long as their fleets remained united; and this was fully recognised by Philip the next day,

---

[1] This manœuvre consisted of charging through the enemy's line, thus putting his oars out of action, and then ramming him from behind; cf. Tarn, *Hellen. Mil. and Nav. Developments*, 146.

[2] Polyb. XVI, 4, 9–13.   [3] Polyb. XVI, 6, 1–5.

[4] Polyb. XVI, 7; cf. Holleaux, *REA*, XXIII, 1921, 186.

when he declined further battle.[1] Even more depressing to the
Macedonians than the loss of their fleet was the loss of life it
involved. Against the Rhodian and Pergamene losses of 130
men (including Theophiliscus, the admiral) in all, there are said
to have perished, on Philip's side, 3000 Macedonian soldiers
and 6000 sailors; and in addition nearly 3000 men were taken
prisoner.[2] Allowing for probable exaggeration, this was the
greatest loss he had ever sustained in a single battle;[3] and by
anchoring on the scene of battle, its full horror was brought
home to him and caused, Polybius tells us, a feeling of extreme
dejection in Philip and all his men.[4] However, the allied fleet
shortly afterwards separated: the Rhodians and Attalus returned
to their respective homes, and Philip fell back upon his base at
Samos.

The battle of Chios had altered the whole complexion of
Philip's Asiatic campaign; and in this respect the cause of
Philip's defeat—the unforeseen intervention of Attalus—was as
significant as its results. In Greece, too, Philip's position had
been weakened in consequence of his Aegean policy. Achaean
successes, such as the repulse of a Spartan attack on Messene
by Philopoemen,[5] were calculated to increase the growing feeling
in favour of independence from Macedon.[6] And Philip's prestige
suffered a still greater blow when, in the late summer of this
year (201), the news of the Syro-Macedonian pact leaked out. At
Athens, in particular,[7] this callous plot against the patron-state
of Egypt, supervening upon the recent interference with the
Black Sea corn supply, resulted in the abolition of the two 'Mace-

[1] Polyb. xvi, 8, 5.
[2] Polyb. xvi, 7, 5–6. These figures, together with a great part of the account
of Philip's Asiatic campaigns, are from Rhodian sources and exaggerate
Macedonian losses.
[3] Polyb. xvi, 8, 6.   [4] Polyb. xvi, 8, 10.
[5] Polyb. xvi, 13, 3; 16; 17; Plut. Philop. 12, 4–6; Livy (P) xxxiv, 32, 16;
35, 6; Pausan. iv, 29, 10; viii, 50, 5; cf. Syll. 595.
[6] The anti-Macedonian nature of the Achaean revival is reflected in the
(untrustworthy) tradition that Philip tried to have Philopoemen murdered
(Plut. Philop. 12, 2; Pausan. viii, 50, 4; Justin. xxix, 4, 11).
[7] Livy (P) xxxi, 14, 6–8; IG, ii², 2362 (abolition of Macedonian tribes);
cf. Niese, ii, 589; De Sanctis, iv, 1, 21; Ferguson, Hellen. Ath. 268; Ath.
Trib. Cyc. 141, n. 1; McDonald, JRS, xxvii, 1937, 191. The almost certainly
false allegation that Philip poisoned the Athenian statesmen Eurycleides
and Micion (Pausan. ii, 9, 4) probably springs from the anti-Macedonian
propaganda of this time; cf. Treves, LEC, ix, 1940, 147–9.

donian' tribes, Antigonis and Demetrias; and when, in August or September, two Acarnanians were caught trying to enter the Great Mysteries at Eleusis, a wave of popular anti-Macedonian feeling relieved itself in executing them for sacrilege—and, no doubt, as tools of Philip. For all this, there was no conscious direction in this Greek resentment against Macedon. And when, at the time of Philip's attack on Pergamum, Attalus appealed to the Aetolians for a counter-offensive in Greece,[1] he could get no response; the Aetolians were too depressed by their rebuff at Rome the previous autumn to venture on a fresh war with Macedon.

Meanwhile, at Samos, Philip decided to transfer his offensive to Caria;[2] with the war well removed from Pergamum, there was more chance that Attalus would not resume the struggle. Moreover, Caria was an old Macedonian objective; by conquests here, Philip would be developing the interrupted policy of Antigonus Doson. Such an appeal to the past might be a welcome diversion among his men after the bitter disaster off Chios. It was probably in August that Philip opened his campaign,[3] with an attack on Cnidus in South Caria;[4] but after a number of assaults he was obliged to withdraw and content himself with sacking some near-by forts and villas. Next he besieged Prinassus, in the Rhodian Peraea, somewhat to the east of Cnidus;[5] and finding this to be built on solid rock he resorted to the trick of introducing soil from outside by night, in order that he could remove it openly from his mines during the daytime, until eventually the townspeople, convinced that their walls were by this time undermined, were persuaded to surrender. The fall of Prinassus was followed by the subjugation of the Peraea,[6] which formed the chief mainland possession of Rhodes.

Philip's next move is less certain. He may have marched north

---

[1] Livy (P) xxxi, 46, 4.

[2] On the Carian campaign see Holleaux, *REA*, xxii, 1920, 248 *seq.*; xxiii, 1921, 204 *seq.*; xxv, 1923, 348 *seq.*; Ernst Meyer, *Grenzen*, 70–73.

[3] For the chronology see below, Appendix iii, p. 309.

[4] Polyb. xvi, 11, 1, where the Codex Urbinas has the subtitle πε(ρὶ) τῆς Κνίδου πόλεως.

[5] Polyb. xvi, 11, 2–6; Polyaen. iv, 18, 1; Frontin. *Strat.* iii, 8, 1. For the probable position, on the north coast of the Peraea, see Ernst Meyer, *P-W*, 'Peraea (2)', col. 575.

[6] A direct account is lacking; references: Appian, *Maced.* 4, 1; Polyb. xviii, 2, 3; 6, 3; 8, 9; Livy (P) xxxiii, 18, 1; 18, 20.

to take Stratonicaea, and occupy Panamara, to the extreme north of the Peraea;[1] equally possibly, however, this capture was later, and from the Peraea Philip sailed back with his fleet against northern Caria. But whatever his route, he is next discovered attacking Iasus[2] on the Gulf of Bargylia, a town whose integrity he had only a year ago guaranteed, in a letter to the Rhodians.[3] It soon fell, and with it Bargylia;[4] and about this time Philip acquired the inland towns of Euromus and Pedasa, which lay a little to the south-east of the Latmic Gulf, between Heraclea-in-Latmus and Mylasa.[5] With his fleet in the Gulf of Bargylia, he seemed in a strong position to win over all Caria.

But once more an unforeseen factor stepped in. Moved, no doubt, by the exaggerated report of the Syro-Macedonian pact, Attalus re-equipped his fleet and rejoined the Rhodians. Too late Philip found himself trapped within the bay by a preponderant naval force and an enemy determined that this time he should not escape. For the second time this year he was confronted with a sudden change of fortune; and this time he could not, as after Chios, force a way through to his base. Condemned to a winter on the mainland of Asia Minor,[6] he was soon reduced to plundering the country round, to get the barest necessities for his men; his life, Polybius says, became that of a wolf.[7] Sometimes by coaxing and sometimes by threats or even by ravaging the land, he managed to extract corn, meat and figs from the people of Mylasa,[8] Alabanda[9] and Magnesia:[10] the last

---

[1] Stratonicaea: Livy (P) xxxiii, 18, 4–7; 18, 19; 18, 21–2; (A) 30, 11. Panamara: see the three inscriptions published by Cousin-Holleaux, *BCH*, xxviii, 1904, 346 and 354–5 (no. 1), 346 and 356–8 (no. 2), 347 and 358–9 (no. 3); cf. Oppermann, 18–22. The inscription published by Holleaux, *BCH*, xvii, 1893, 53 *seq.* (=Vol. I, 411–15), in which Nicophanes of Rhodes is thanked for his energetic defence of Panamara, may refer to this year or to 197 (see below, p. 175).
[2] Polyb. xviii, 2, 3; 8, 9; 44, 4; Livy (P) xxxiv, 32, 5; cf. Polyb. xvi, 12, 1 *seq.*   [3] See above, p. 116, n. 2.
[4] Polyb. xviii, 2, 3; 8, 9; 44, 4; 48, 1; 50, 1. Livy (P) xxxiii, 18, 19; xxxiv, 32, 5.
[5] Euromus: Polyb. xviii, 2, 3; 44, 4. Pedasa: Polyb. xviii, 44, 4. On the situation of these towns, 20–30 km. from Iasus, see Holleaux, *RÉA*, xxiii, 1921, 208; and for Pedasa, Meyer, *Die Grenzen d. h. Staaten*, 78, n. 1; Ruge, *P-W*, 'Pedasa', cols. 27–8; Magie, *Buckler Studies*, 163, n. 1.
[6] Polyb. xvi, 24, 1.   [7] Polyb. xvi, 24, 5.
[8] Polyb. xvi, 24, 7, attempt by Philocles to seize Mylasa.
[9] Only recently (*OGIS*, 234: date c. 202) Antiochus had guaranteed Alabanda; but this did not restrain Philip. See Magie, *Buckler Studies*, 163, n. 3.   [10] Polyb. xvi, 24, 6; 24, 9.

he rewarded with the town of Myus, taken over at the same time as Miletus.[1] Zeuxis, too, at Sardes, gave him some supplies, but only enough to preserve the letter of the pact.[2]

To add to Philip's discomfort, he was aware that Rhodes and Attalus had followed the Aetolian example and had, this very autumn, sent embassies to Rome to complain against him.[3] The Senate, it was true, were not contemplating a *revanche*: so much had been clear from the rebuff they had given to the Aetolian appeal. Nevertheless, he had every reason to feel uncomfortable at the thought of his enemies relating their twisted versions of his agreement with Antiochus, and working up feeling against him in a Senate which was now finally clear of its war with Carthage, while he himself lay trapped at Bargylia, in a plight unpleasantly reminiscent of the Aous catastrophe of 214[4]—except that this time there was no retreat by land.

Nor were Philip's apprehensions unwarranted. For at Rome, meanwhile, the news brought by the envoys of Rhodes and Pergamum was causing one of the most amazing reversals of policy known to the history of the republic. Suddenly Philip's activities leapt into the forefront of senatorial policy: vivid recollections of the last war and unreasonable panic became in a moment the deciding factors and, at the elections for 200,[5] P. Sulpicius Galba, Laevinus's successor in 210, was chosen consul and given Macedonia as his province.[6] This sudden change from apathy to a passionate concern for eastern affairs has called forth many explanations;[7] imperialism, commercial interests, sentimental politics, real or affected, defensive imperialism to forestall the dangers of an attack by Philip—all these have been at various times propounded and criticised; while, more recently,[8] Bickermann has argued that the Senate was drawn

---

[1] See above, p. 118.   [2] Polyb. XVI, 24, 6.
[3] Polyb. XVI, 24, 3; see below, Appendix III, p. 311.
[4] See above, pp. 75–6.
[5] Probably in November–December, 201; on the Roman calendar at this time see De Sanctis, IV, 1, 368–83.
[6] Livy (A) XXXI, 5, 1; 6, 1.
[7] The most important views are summarised by Scullard, 257. Historians are agreed in rejecting the annalistic data of Livy XXX, 26 (Macedonian help at Zama); 42, 2–6 (embassy of M. Aurelius, etc.); XXXI, 3, 4–6 (return of Aurelius); 3, 3; 5, 5 (Laevinus off Macedonia with 38 ships).
[8] *Rev. Phil.* LXI, 1935, 59–81; 161–76; criticised by McDonald and Walbank, *JRS*, XXVII, 1937, 180–1; 205–6.

unwillingly into war through commitments under the treaty of Phoenice, which he interprets as a κοινὴ εἰρήνη, in which Philip and the Romans jointly guaranteed the security of all signatories.

The most satisfactory explanation, however, remains that of Holleaux.[1] Almost meaningless though it had by this time become, Philip's pact with Antiochus was represented by the envoys of Rhodes and Pergamum as a direct threat to Rome herself; and they were no doubt at pains to describe Antiochus's successes in Central Asia and his victorious advance (with Philip's connivance) against the Syrian provinces of Egypt, and to impress the Senate with the popular, if inaccurate, picture of the king as a second Alexander, insatiable in his lust for conquest. It was to this sinister figure that Philip had allied himself; could the Senate doubt that the ultimate victim was destined to be Rome? Moreover, a second factor weighed heavily with them.[2] Philip, whose ambition to play the part of a Pyrrhus had occasioned the first Macedonian War, had now rebuilt his fleet, and by its aid had acquired Caria and the Rhodian Peraea; he had defeated the Rhodians at Lade and, in spite of his losses, could claim a technical victory at Chios. Was this fleet to become the instrument of a Syro-Macedonian invasion of Italy?

Such considerations as these, fostered perhaps by individual senators who welcomed a war with Philip, proved conclusive in the eyes of the Senate. With the least possible delay the motion for war was submitted to the centuries for the necessary assent of the people—and was rejected.[3] Clearly there was strong popular opposition to a new military venture, which could only be broken down by persistent propaganda of the type represented by the speech which Livy puts in the mouth of Sulpicius.[4] In the meantime the Senate took more direct steps, by sending out a senatorial commission, consisting of C. Claudius

[1] *Rome*, 312 *seq.*; *CAH*, VIII, 155 *seq.*

[2] Cf. Griffith, *CHJ*, v, 1935, 1–14, who points out that when the Roman decision was taken, the news of Lade and Chios would be available, but not Philip's plight in the Gulf of Bargylia.

[3] Livy (A) XXXI, 6, 3. On the technical issues involved in the declaration of war, and the status of the embassy subsequently sent out to Greece, see Walbank, *JRS*, XXVII, 1937, 192–7.

[4] Livy, XXXI, 7, a passage which is, however, of annalistic origin and very unreliable in detail. T. Frank, *Buckler Studies*, 87–8, claims to detect traces of interventionist propaganda in Plautus, *Cist.* 198–202.

Nero, P. Sempronius Tuditanus and the youthful M. Aemilius Lepidus,[1] to Greece and the Near East, with the double object of sounding Antiochus on his intentions towards Rome and taking the preliminary steps towards raising up a coalition of Greek states against Philip, or at least (as in the case of Achaea) securing their neutrality. This commission visited Phoenice, the capital of Epirus, Amynander of Athamania, Naupactus and Aegium;[2] at each place the commissioners intimated the nature of the ultimatum which they intended presenting to Philip, concealing, of course, the fact that technically they were unauthorised to present a formal *indictio belli*. Eventually, about the end of April 200, they reached Piraeus.

Throughout the whole of this critical winter Philip was chafing within the Bay of Bargylia; and it was not until spring that he succeeded by means of a trick in catching his warders off their guard. He first of all sent an Egyptian 'deserter' to the enemy camp to inform Attalus that he was proposing to attempt a sea-battle the next day; then having lent weight to this information by the old device of lighting watch-fires, he managed to slip out of the gulf unnoticed and make his escape home, closely pursued by the Rhodian and Pergamene fleets.[3] His possessions in Asia Minor he left well garrisoned under a general, Deinocrates,[4] and some subordinates.

On reaching Macedon, Philip found Acarnanian envoys waiting to ask his help in reprisals against Athens for the incident at Eleusis the previous autumn.[5] Irritated at the fiasco in which his recent campaign had ended, and glad to find a scapegoat in the Athenians, who had insulted him by their abolition of the 'Macedonian' tribes, Philip readily offered his help; and, shortly afterwards, Attica was exposed to the ravages of an Acarnanian army, reinforced by Macedonian auxiliaries. At the same time a squadron of Macedonian ships approached the Piraeus, and

---

[1] For a detailed discussion and justification of the present version of the events of 200, see below, Appendix III, pp. 311–17; cf. McDonald and Walbank, *JRS*, XXVII, 1937, 180–207.

[2] Polyb. XVI, 27, 4.   [3] Polyaen. IV, 18, 2.

[4] Livy (P) XXXIII, 18, 6. The three inscriptions from Panamara (see above, p. 126, n. 1), dating from 201, and 200–199 (twenty-third year of Philip's reign) are an epigraphical record of the continued Macedonian occupation of parts of Caria.

[5] Livy (P) XXXI, 14, 9.

carried off four of their warships from before the very eyes of the indignant Athenians.[1]

At this moment the Rhodian and Pergamene fleets came to the rescue; putting out from Aegina, where they had retired after their failure to catch Philip, they divided up the work, the Rhodians recovering the warships with their crews, while Attalus patrolled the Attic coast in case of Macedonian ravages. When eventually the danger seemed to have been averted, the Rhodians probably went forward to recover some of the Cyclades;[2] and Attalus returned to Aegina, where the Athenians, jubilant at the recovery of their ships and the protection of their coast from the imminent threat of Macedonian raids, had despatched messengers to thank him and invite him across to Athens.

It was at this juncture that the Roman commission reached Piraeus, in time to witness the enthusiastic reception given to Attalus. Quickly realising the possibility of exploiting the king's popularity, they had an interview with Attalus and, having explained the Roman position, arranged for him to use his influence to enlist Athenian support for the forthcoming war with Philip.[3] The guests were then received at Athens in high style, particularly Attalus, who was honoured by having a new tribe named Attalis after him, in addition to all the usual distinctions; and finally, in response to his appeal and that of the Rhodians, whose envoys now appeared on the scene, the Athenians declared war on Philip. The Rhodians then received their share of honours before sailing away to Ceos, from whence they systematically annexed the rest of the Cyclades, with the exception of Andros, Paros and Cythnos, where Philip's garrisons held out against them;[4] and Attalus returned to Aegina.[5]

The failure of his ships to achieve anything substantial off Attica, and the news of the Athenian declaration of war together stirred Philip to immediate reprisals. He sent a reliable commander, Nicanor,[6] to ravage Attica with a body of troops, and

---

[1] Livy (P) xxxi, 15, 5; cf. McDonald, *JRS*, xxvii, 1937, 188–9.
[2] Polyb. xvi, 25, 1; cf. Livy (P) xxxi, 14, 11–12.
[3] Polyb. xvi, 25, 3–4; cf. McDonald, *JRS*, xxvii, 1937, 190.
[4] Polyb. xvi, 25, 5–26, 10; cf. Livy (P) xxxi, 15, 1–8.
[5] Livy (P) xxxi, 15, 9.
[6] Perhaps the Nicanor of Polyb. xviii, 24, 2 (cf. Livy (P) xxxiii, 8, 8), who was nicknamed 'the elephant'.

established Philocles as governor of Euboea, the most convenient base for operations against Athens. Meanwhile, the
Romans had not yet left when they received the embarrassing
news that Nicanor was at the Academy. Their diplomacy
had been too successful: and notwithstanding their limited
competence and the adverse decision of the Roman people,
there was no way out of delivering their ultimatum. Having
flaunted it in Epirus, Athamania, Aetolia and Achaea, they
could scarcely withhold it from the enemy himself, when he
threatened the very gates of Athens. And so the ultimatum
was delivered to Nicanor, who naturally bore it back to Philip.
The commissioners, perhaps alarmed at their own action,
sailed at once for Rhodes, to await further news from the
Senate.[1]

The terms of the ultimatum were these:[2] Philip was to make
war on no Greek state, and was to submit the question of the
injuries done to Attalus to an impartial tribunal (δίκας ὑπέχειν
ἐν ἴσῳ κριτηρίῳ); if he refused these conditions, he might consider himself at war with Rome. To Philip, in his present mood of
anger and frustration, they were the proverbial red rag to a bull.
By what right did the Romans set up as protectors of the Greeks,
of states not bound to them by any bond of friendship or alliance? And, granted their common alliance with Attalus in the
last war, why should they speak of injuries done to him, when it
was Attalus who, quite unprovoked by Philip, had answered
the Rhodian appeal and entered into a war that did not concern
him? In sheer irritation Philip took up the challenge which
his cooler judgment would have rejected, and sent Philocles
from Euboea, with a force of 2000 infantry and 200 cavalry, to
ravage Attica.[3]

The Athenians, naturally, looked for help to their benefactors,
Attalus and the Rhodians, who had instigated them to declare
war: Cephisodorus was sent to Egypt, Rhodes, Pergamum and
even to Crete and Aetolia to beg for assistance, but without

[1] Polyb. XVI, 27, 1–5.   [2] Polyb. XVI, 27, 2–3.
[3] Livy (P) XXXI, 16, 2: *ne Romano quidem, quod imminebat, bello territus.*
If Appian, *Maced.* 4, 1, hides a misplaced and distorted reference to this raid
(as McDonald, *JRS*, XXVII, 1937, 197, n. 119, suggests), the words ἑτέρῳ μέρει
στρατοῦ may have originally been applied to the division of forces in summer
200 between Philocles and Philip.

concrete result.[1] The Aetolians, in particular, had only just shown, by rejecting a second appeal from Attalus,[2] that they were resolved to take no part in the war. Consequently, the Athenians were reduced to defending themselves throughout the summer against constant raids, as best they could. The fact was, both Attalus and the Rhodians were exhausted by their last season's efforts, and their winter watch near Bargylia. In Attalus's case, this had already been evident in his long absence from the joint campaign throughout the months separating the battle of Chios from the blockade of Philip; and the Rhodians, having recovered most of the Cyclades, were not equal to challenging Philip's troops in the Peraea, still less operating vigorously off Attica or in the northern Aegean, where Philip himself now turned his attention. Both allies felt that the matter might advantageously be left to Rome.[3] As for Egypt, the Syrian War effectively hindered the sending of any direct help; but there is a report (of questionable authenticity)[4] that an embassy was sent from Alexandria to invite the assistance of Rome. And, eventually, the Athenians too, despairing of help from these more usual sources, sent Cephisodorus to Rome, where he arrived in July, just in time to find the issue of war finally decided.[5]

Meanwhile, notwithstanding his recent reverses, Philip's conduct was in marked contrast to the lack of vigour displayed by his opponents.[6] While Philocles ravaged Attica, he himself, with a similar force of 2000 infantry and 200 horse, and in conjunction with the fleet under Heracleides, proceeded to a fresh campaign in Thrace.[7] Having decided to ignore the Roman demands, which were palpably unjust and based on no kind of legal right, his obvious course was to proceed with his

---

[1] Pausan. I, 36, 5; cf. McDonald, *JRS*, xxvii, 1937, 198–9. Coins struck on the Athenian pattern at Cnossus, Cydonia, Gortyn, Hierapytna, Polyrrhenia, Lappa and Priansus, about this period, tend to confirm Pausanias's statement that an alliance was actually made. Head, 475, thinks that their origin was commercial; but both Hill, 80, and Seltman, 261, connect the issue with the actual sending of troops to help Athens. If such troops *were* sent, they have escaped mention in our literary sources.

[2] Livy (P) xxxi, 15, 9–10.   [3] Polyb. xvi, 28; Livy (P) xxxi, 15, 10–11.

[4] Livy (A) xxxi, 9, 1; see below, Appendix iii, p. 313.

[5] Pausan. I, 36, 5–6; cf. McDonald, *JRS*, xxvii, 1937, 200.

[6] Poiyb. xvi, 28, 3: τὸ Φιλίππου βασιλικὸν καὶ μεγαλόψυχον καὶ τὸ τῆς προθέσεως ἐπίμονον.

[7] Livy (P) xxxi, 16, 3.

plans as if the ultimatum did not exist. Whether in fact Philip knew of the lack of popular support for the war at Rome, and hoped by calling the commissioners' bluff to escape both diplomatic and military defeat, there is unfortunately no evidence to say. Strategically, however, the campaign in Thrace was designed to carry his power indisputably to the Propontic shores of Asia, thus giving him a more vice-like grip on the Pontic corn supply (and so striking at Athens), and also facilitating his advance by land into Asia, if the Roman war-cloud should, after all, blow over.

Philip's advance was swift. Maronea he took by storm, Aenus was betrayed by Callimedes, the Egyptian governor. Then followed a host of smaller towns and forts, Cypsela, Doriscon, Serrheum, and, on the Chersonese, Elaeus, Alopeconnesus, Callipolis, Madytus, Sestus and others whose names have not survived.[1] Most of these were Egyptian; now that Philip's pact with Antiochus was public knowledge, there seemed little sense in trying to keep the friendship of Alexandria, and the Thracian Chersonese was invaluable to his plans. Master of this, he crossed over into Asia, about the end of August, and, with growing confidence at his own success and the failure of the Rhodian and Pergamene fleets to offer any effective opposition, he there began the siege of Abydus. Of the Roman commission he had heard not a word.

At Abydus, however, Philip encountered unexpected resistance.[2] Reinforced by troops from Pergamum and Rhodes, and two warships from Rhodes and Cyzicus,[3] the townspeople offered the most determined resistance to his double assault by land and sea, destroying his siege-engines by means of catapults, and compelling the Macedonian ships to withdraw. However, so long as the allies were afraid to enter the Hellespont, the fall of the city could only be a question of time;[4] and when Philip undermined the walls, and the defenders were driven back on a second wall hastily thrown up to stem his advance, it was resolved to offer a surrender on terms. But Philip would be content with

[1] Livy (P) xxxi, 16, 4–6. For Sestus see Polyb. xvi, 29, 3; Holleaux, *REG*, XXXIII, 1920, 229.
[2] Polyb. xvi, 30–3; Livy (P) xxxi, 16, 6–17, 11.
[3] Polyb. xvi, 30, 7; 31, 3.
[4] Polyb. xvi, 34, 1 (Attalus at Tenedos); Livy (P) xxxi, 16, 6–8.

nothing less than an unconditional capitulation; whereupon the citizens decided to fight to the bitter end, and took an oath to kill all their women and children and destroy their valuables rather than surrender to Philip. There then ensued a most courageous resistance, in which the second wall fell, and the majority of the defenders perished. But, with the coming of night, the survivors wavered at the thought of putting the rest of the plan into execution, and a deputation was sent to surrender the city and beg Philip's mercy.

At this moment M. Aemilius Lepidus arrived from Rhodes.[1] The report of the events in Attica and of the beginning of Philip's Thracian campaign had turned the balance at Rome, and towards the end of July the centuries had finally authorised the war.[2] News of this vote had reached Rhodes about the time that the Rhodian forces off the Hellespont sent their report of Philip's actions at Abydus, and the commissioners, in accordance with senatorial instructions, had despatched their youngest member, M. Aemilius Lepidus, to deliver the ultimatum to Philip in person.

At an interview with the king, Lepidus delivered the declaration of war (for in effect it was no less). In addition to the demands made at Athens, two additional clauses now required Philip to refrain from touching Ptolemy's possessions and to submit to a tribunal the question of the damage done to Rhodes, as well as Attalus. The clause concerning Egypt was the reply to Philip's campaign and new conquests in Thrace; while the championing of Rhodes will reflect the Rhodian influence under which the commissioners had been since they left Athens, and also, perhaps, the establishing of relations of friendship between Rhodes and Rome. When Philip pointed out that the Rhodians were themselves the aggressors (as technically they were),[3] Lepidus interrupted with references to Cius, Athens and Abydus; whereupon the king, realising that the Romans were determined

---

[1] Polyb. xvi, 34, 1; cf. Livy (P) xxxi, 18, 1; Diod. xxviii, 6; Appian, *Maced.* 4, 1.

[2] See below, Appendix iii, p. 316 for the chronology; for the question of fetial procedure, important as a clue to the motives of the Senate throughout 200, see Walbank, *JRS*, xxvii, 1937, 192–7.

[3] The intrigues in the Cretan war and Heracleides's attempts at arson could not be laid with certainty at Philip's door.

to evade the technical aspect, and had, in fact, constituted themselves protectors of Hellas as a whole, independently of any
rights and treaties, gave Lepidus a courteous and ironical reply,
saying that he pardoned his outburst because of his youth and
inexperience; he stood upon his treaty rights and requested the
Romans to respect these; but if they were bent on war, he
accepted their challenge and would give a good account of himself.[1] At this, Lepidus returned to Rhodes, in time to hinder an
Achaean attempt to persuade the Rhodians to make peace; and
from Rhodes the envoys went on to interview Antiochus (whom
they found very ready to give the required assurances). The
Egyptians, whom they visited next, not aware that they had been
sacrificed to Syria, and seeing in the Romans only their defenders against Philip, also gave them a warm welcome. And
finally, in the spring of 199, they returned to Rome.[2]

Meanwhile, Philip entered Abydus, only to find its inhabitants
completely demoralised, and massacring themselves and their
families. He therefore withdrew, ironically announcing a three
days' respite, for all who wished to commit suicide;[3] and when this
time was up, he took full possession of the city. It was now early
September, however, and in the face of the Roman ultimatum
Philip decided to press on no farther into Asia, but to return to
Macedon. Accordingly he re-established some sort of order in
Abydus, and set out along the Thracian coast. He had not quite
reached Macedonia when messengers met him with the news
that a Roman army had landed at Apollonia.[4]

This moment marked the end of Philip's eastern plans, and
brought to a close the epoch which had opened five years previously at Phoenice. These five years had seen important developments in Philip's character and in his ambitions. After every
allowance has been made for the hostility of the Achaean
historian,[5] and of the Rhodian sources upon which, in part, he
drew,[6] they undoubtedly show in Philip a growing inability to
subordinate passion to policy. Soured by long campaigns,
punctuated with constant cries for assistance from his Greek

---

[1] Polyb. XVI, 34, 1–7; Livy (P) XXXI, 18, 1–4.
[2] On the later movements of the embassy see below, Appendix III, pp. 316–17.
[3] Polyb. XVI, 34, 7–12.   [4] Livy (P) XXXI, 18, 9.
[5] E.g. Polyb. XIII, 3; XV, 20; 22; XVI, 1; 10, 1; cf. Diod. XXVIII, 2 seq.
[6] See below, Appendix I, p. 280.

allies, he had suddenly felt himself free to consider only Macedon and himself; and driven by the needs of his new eastern policy to adopt the methods of piracy which so scandalised the Greeks, he had gradually given freer rein to that side of his character, which had already shown itself at Thermum and Messene, until finally he had apparently come to find pleasure in the mere outraging of Hellenic sentiment. What part Heracleides and Dicaearchus played in this psychological progress is not recorded; but it is known that Heracleides was an important agent in the manœuvres against Rhodes, and that he was with Philip in Asia Minor in 201 and in Thrace in 200.

However, the question is not merely one of morals. For the increase of violence and treachery, which showed itself in Dicaearchus's piracy, Heracleides's attempt on the Rhodian dockyards, the taking of Cius, Chalcedon, Perinthus and Thasos, the ravaging of Pergamum, Philocles's attack on Mylasa, the invasions of Attica and the seizure of Abydus—this surrender to passion led Philip to political miscalculations of a serious kind. In the first place, he failed to estimate the amount of provocation and frightfulness the Greeks would endure. For this mistake he paid in the campaign in which Rhodes and Attalus (not to mention a number of smaller states) took the sea against him, robbed him of his naval preponderance and trapped him at Bargylia throughout the critical winter of 201–200; and he was shortly to pay for it still more dearly, when the members of the Symmachy abandoned him in his struggle with Rome.

With regard to Rome Philip's miscalculation was of a different kind, since his spies must have kept him permanently informed of the Senate's lack of interest in the east.[1] Here his error lay rather in not realising the effect that his secret pact with Antiochus would create at Rome; and it is perhaps questionable whether he could have been expected to foresee the garbled version in which Attalus and the Rhodians brought it to the Senate's ears. The ironical feature of this pact was Philip's failure to draw any appreciable advantage from it until it had already ruined him; for by his over-subtle policy of keeping the friendship of Alexandria, while bargaining with Antiochus, he gained absolutely nothing beyond the trifling aid afforded by

[1] See above, p. 113, n. 1.

Zeuxis, yet gave his enemies in Asia a weapon to use against him at Rome.

However, perhaps Philip's worst error was in his attitude towards the Roman ultimatum, which in his indignation he chose to ignore. Technically the Romans had no justice whatever behind their demands (though Philip was scarcely in a strong moral position to dwell upon this); but even after his limited success in the former war, against a small section of the Roman forces, Philip must have realised that the nation that had crushed Hannibal would have no difficulty in crushing him. He may, as De Sanctis suggests,[1] have hoped vaguely that the Senate was still not too much in earnest, that the Greeks—for all his flouting of their sensibilities—might rise at last against the greater danger, or even that the war would be the signal for a revolt in Carthage. But such hopes were all very slight; and the real explanation seems to be that Philip had worked himself into a state of indignation in which his prevailing impulse was to accept the Roman challenge. Family pride and the realisation that to accept the ultimatum was virtually to surrender his freedom of action in foreign affairs combined to drug the acute judgment which he unquestionably possessed. Deliberately he forwent the possibility of an immediate capitulation, which might have been obtained on very easy terms, and would have enabled him to build up a strong coalition with which to challenge Rome on more even terms at a later date. Instead, with a curious blend of heroism and stupidity, he voluntarily drew upon himself the full force of the Roman army and prepared to meet it single-handed.

[1] See IV, 1, 36, where there are some very just remarks on Philip's policy.

Chapter V : Defensive

THE ROMANS AGAINST PHILIP (200–196)

IT was already mid-September when P. Sulpicius reached Apollonia with his two legions, amounting to perhaps 20–25,000 men, and a fleet of fifty ships.[1] On landing he was met by an Athenian deputation asking help,[2] and accordingly a squadron of twenty ships was sent round to Piraeus under C. Claudius Cento; the rest of the fleet remained for the winter at Corcyra. At Piraeus Cento joined the three Rhodian and three Athenian vessels, which were trying to cope with the constant raids from Chalcis, and was able to put an end both to these and to the regular raids over the Isthmus from Philip's garrison post on the Acrocorinth.[3]

Sulpicius, meanwhile, established the main Roman camp on the Apsus,[4] and sent his lieutenant, L. Apustius, up the river to ravage Macedonian Dassaretia;[5] some forts were taken,[6] including the important town of Antipatreia, where the walls were razed and the male population massacred, and on his return Apustius defeated a Macedonian force under Athenagoras, which tried to take him by surprise at a ford.[7] But in view of the advanced season, Philip was concentrating his efforts for the remainder of the year on Greece. From Macedonia he had come south, and was stationed with a large force of 5000 light-armed

[1] Date: see below, Appendix III, p. 317; army: Livy (A) XXXI, 8, 5–6; (P) 14, 2; fleet: Livy (A) XXXI, 14, 2; cf. (A) XXX, 40, 12; 43, 1; see Kromayer, II, 95–6.
[2] Livy (P) XXXI, 14, 3; the Athenians had already sent one embassy to Rome, under Cephisodorus, which arrived just after the passing of the war vote; see above, p. 132, n. 5.
[3] Livy (P) XXXI, 22, 4–8; cf. McDonald, *JRS*, XXVII, 1937, 197.
[4] Probably at Kuçi, some 25–30 km. from the mouth of the river; cf. Veith, *Der Feldzug von Dyrrhachium zwischen Caesar und Pompejus*, 61–2.
[5] Livy (P) XXXI, 27, 1; Zonaras, IX, 15, 2, states that Sulpicius was ill (cf. Kromayer, II, 10; rejected by Holleaux, *BCH*, LVI, 1932, 538, n. 3).
[6] Livy (P) XXXI, 27, 2, gives Corrhagus, Gerunium and Orgessus (? = the Gerus and Orgyssus taken by Philip in 217: see above, p. 68). After Antipatreia Apustius got possession of Codrione and Cnidus.
[7] Livy (P) XXXI. 27, 6–8.

infantry and 300 cavalry at Demetrias, when suddenly bad news reached him from Chalcis.

Guided by refugees, Cento and the Rhodians had sailed up the Euripus by night, seized Chalcis and, after destroying granaries and arsenals and releasing prisoners, had returned unhindered to Piraeus; Sopater, Philip's Acarnanian governor, had perished in the fight,[1] and only shortage of men had prevented the Romans from occupying the town. Though he set out at once, Philip was too late to catch his enemy, and therefore advanced with his usual speed through Boeotia to take his revenge on Athens. But the warning of a scout saved the Athenians from the fate of the Chalcidians, and when Philip approached the Dipylon he found the walls manned and a large force, including a Pergamene garrison, drawn up within the gate.[2]

Now that he was actually before the city which had become almost a symbol of all his hatred for Attalus, Rhodes and the Romans, Philip was filled with a wild elation. Casting caution to the winds, he led his men at the gallop into the space between the two gates, straight into the trap that was laid. But fortune was with him. After a fierce hand-to-hand battle he was able to make his way out again, and, pitching camp at Cynosarges, to the east of the city, from here plundered the Lyceum, and any other shrines and tombs outside the walls on which he could lay his hands.[3]

Next day reinforcements reached Athens from the Romans and from Attalus's garrison on Aegina, and Philip, having first withdrawn to a point three miles from the city, suddenly decided to make a surprise attack on Eleusis; and when this failed he

---

[1] Livy (P) xxxi, 23, 1–12; cf. De Sanctis, IV, 1, 47, n. 85, who suggests that Livy's account exaggerates the Roman success.

[2] Livy (P) xxxi, 24, 1–9.

[3] Livy (P) xxxi, 24, 10–18; Diod. xxviii, 7 (who states that Philip ravaged the Academy). On the topography see Baedeker, *Greece* (English edit. 1909), 70–1; Middleton, *Plans and Drawings of Athenian Buildings*, 24 (Hellen. Soc. supplementary paper iii, 1909); Judeich, *Topographie von Athen*², 93 *seq.* (ravaging), 135 *seq.* (Dipylon), 415 *seq.* (Lyceum), 422 *seq.* (Cynosarges). In general, see Ferguson, 275–6. Pausan. i, 30, 4 speaks of Antigonus Gonatas ravaging the holy grove of Poseidon at Colonus, and Beloch (IV, 1, 590, n. 2) suggests that this was actually the work of Philip V, and has been attributed to his grandfather by a confusion. More probably, however, Tarn, 305, n. 90, is correct in questioning the whole story.

marched to Corinth, and from there to the Achaean assembly which was in session at Argos.[1] Here Philip's object was to test the loyalty of the Hellenic Symmachy; the new Achaea, in particular, might prove a valuable ally in the coming war. However, he found the Achaeans discussing Nabis, who had recently resumed his attacks,[2] and, seeing here a chance to further his own ends, Philip offered to invade Laconia on the League's behalf, if they in turn would lend him men to garrison Oreus, Chalcis and Corinth against Roman attacks. In this way he hoped to involve Achaea in a war with Rome;[3] but Cycliadas, the general, seeing the implications, put Philip off with a technical objection and the Achaeans voted to carry on the war alone. Philip had to return to Corinth with nothing beyond a few Achaeans who volunteered to join his army.[4]

Upon arriving in Attica, Philip now joined forces with Philocles, the governor of Euboea, who had brought 2000 men over Cithaeron to operate against Eleusis.[5] After their combined attack on this citadel was cut short by the arrival of some Roman ships from Piraeus, Philip planned for himself and Philocles to make separate assaults on Athens and its port; but these, as well as a subsequent combined action against the city alone, ended in complete failure. In a conflict amid the ruins of the Long Walls Philip was repulsed; and, in exasperation, he once again divided forces with his lieutenant and indulged in a campaign of sheer barbarism throughout the villages of Attica. With the aid of Philocles's Thracians he proceeded to burn their temples and shrines, and took a savage pleasure in shattering the very stones of which they were composed. Finally, when he could find no further material for his wrath, he retired through Boeotia to his winter quarters in Macedon.[6] The Athenians took their revenge the next spring by a decree which eliminated any reference not only to Philip, but to the whole royal house of Macedon from all statues and inscriptions within the country, and imposed the

---

[1] Livy (P) XXXI, 25, 1-2; Diod. XXVIII, 7.
[2] He had been encouraged by the weakness of the new general Cycliadas (Livy (P) XXXI, 25, 3); earlier in the year he had been defeated by Philopoemen (Polyb. XVI, 36-7).
[3] Livy (P) XXXI, 25, 4-8.
[4] Livy (P) XXXI, 25, 9-11.   [5] Livy (P) XXXI, 26, 1-4.
[6] Livy (P) XXXI, 26, 5-13; 30, 2-11 (Athenian complaints).

death penalty on anyone who should at any future time speak in its favour.[1]

Both at Pella and on the Apsus the winter of 200–199 was spent in war preparations. To the Roman camp flocked Philip's enemies, Pleuratus of Scodra (the son of Scerdilaidas), Amynander of Athamania, who had already thrown up his recent friendship with Macedon,[2] and Bato, the chief of the Dardanians; and Pergamene envoys arranged for joint naval action on the old basis, from Aegina.[3] Amynander's help was particularly welcome, for the influence he had in Aetolia,[4] whose support Sulpicius was anxious to obtain; and at the League meeting which took place early in the spring every effort was made by the Roman envoy, L. Furius Purpurio, and by the representatives of Athens, to persuade the Aetolians to join in the war. Philip, however, sent his men too, to counter this move, and whether by bribery, as Polybius alleges,[5] or by argument, he succeeded in persuading the general, Damocritus, to have the matter postponed, on technical grounds, to an assembly specially convened to discuss it.[6]

This decision represented a setback to Sulpicius's plans, which were for a triple invasion of Macedon, in which his own advance up the valley of the Genusus (the easier and more northerly of the two main routes from Illyria into Macedon) was to be supported by simultaneous invasions of Macedon by the Dardanians and Illyrians, and by the Aetolians via Thessaly; at the same time the fleet was to operate against the Macedonian coast.[7]

Meanwhile, Philip was condemned to a defensive,[8] since he could not tell beforehand which route the Romans would follow, that past Lake Lychnidus and through Lyncestis, or the more southerly one up the Apsus and through the modern Tsangon

---

[1] Livy (P) xxxi, 44, 2–9.   [2] See above, p. 99.
[3] Livy (P) xxxi, 28, 1–3; cf. 45, 7.
[4] Livy (P) xxxi, 28, 3.   [5] Livy (P) xxxi, 32, 1.
[6] Livy (P) xxxi, 29–32: the Macedonians spoke first, then the Athenians and finally the Romans. On the technical question see Nissen, 128; Holleaux, BCH, xxix, 1905, 362–72; Aymard, Assemblées de la Conf. Ach. 408, n. 2.
[7] Cf. Kromayer, ii, 11 seq.; Sulpicius's proposed route was that of the later Via Egnatia. Theiler, 39, questions whether the Dardanian invasion was part of the Roman plan; Bato's presence at Sulpicius's camp suggests that it was.
[8] Kromayer, ii, 17 seq.; De Sanctis, iv, 1, 47 (preferable to Theiler).

Pass to Celetrum and Beroea. In spite of the failure of the now moribund Symmachy to send help, Philip could put an army in the field which almost equalled that of Sulpicius in number;[1] on the other hand, it lacked the training and discipline of its opponents, its equipment was inferior to their heavy arms and Celtiberian swords, and, as Niese points out, its numbers were probably a maximum, which Philip's treasury, already strained by the cost of maintaining so many mercenary garrisons, was not capable of supplementing by hired reinforcements.[2] Philip's best policy, then, was to harass the Romans among the central mountain ranges, avoid a pitched battle and attempt to wear down Sulpicius by guerilla tactics. Against the allied fleets of Pergamum and Rome he did not dare to take the sea; his own fleet under Heracleides remained at Demetrias, and the towns of Sciathos and Peparethos were destroyed, lest they should become naval bases for the enemy.[3] And meanwhile, foreseeing a move from the north, Philip sent a force of men under the nominal command of his thirteen-year-old son, Perseus, to garrison the Axius route against the Dardanians.[4]

Towards the end of May,[5] Sulpicius ascended the valley of the Genusus and reached Lyncestis without any opposition. Here he fell in with the forces of Philip, who had hastened up from Pella immediately he heard of Sulpicius's approach; and the indecisive cavalry skirmish which now took place gave Philip information that convinced him of the need of every man he could raise on the main front. Accordingly he recalled Perseus's detachment from Pelagonia, thus leaving the way into Macedon

---

[1] Livy (P) XXXI, 34, 7; in Lyncestis in 199 Philip had 20,000 infantry and 2000 cavalry (not 4000 cavalry, as Kromayer, II, 19; correct, II, 95).

[2] Niese, II, 600, n. 2; the more important garrisons were Corinth, Orchomenus, Demetrias, other Thessalian towns and Triphylia; Chalcis, Eretria, Oreus, Carystus, Andros and Cythnos; Cassandreia, Thessalonica, Amphipolis, Abdera, Aenus, Maronea, Thasos, Lysimacheia, Perinthus, Abydus, and Myrina; and the Carian towns. Niese estimates the number of men involved at 20–30,000; Griffith, 71–2, adopts a somewhat smaller figure, putting the number of *mercenaries* at 15,000.

[3] Livy (P) XXXI, 28, 6 (cf. Polyb. XVI, 29, 1); 33, 1–2.

[4] Livy (P) XXXI, 28, 5; 33, 3: *faucibus ad Pelagoniam...interclusis.* It is doubtful whether the pass of Köprülü or that of Demir-Kapu is meant (cf. Kromayer, II, 28, 1; De Sanctis, IV, 1, 50); it cannot be one leading into Lyncestis (as Leake, III, 320, and Niese, II, 600, n. 5, suggest).

[5] For the chronology of this year's campaign see below, Appendix III, p. 317 *seq.*

open to the Dardanians,[1] in order to bring his forces up to 22,000.[2] Philip now fortified a camp in south Lyncestis, on a hill called Athaeus, and after some days' skirmishing, which were perhaps more favourable to Macedon than our sources suggest, Sulpicius withdrew to Ottolobus,[3] some seven and a half miles to the north, in order to forage without interruption. Philip, however, seized a favourable moment to cut off a number of foragers among the marshes of the Erigon,[4] and with his Cretan mercenaries scored a considerable success, until his men, pursuing the enemy over-rashly, ran into the main forces which Sulpicius was bringing up, and were completely routed. Philip himself was thrown from his horse, and only saved by one of his cavalry, who gave up his own mount for the king.[5]

After this skirmish Philip decided to withdraw temporarily into the hills of Banitza, to the south of Lyncestis. Although it affected only part of his forces, the defeat had dealt a severe moral shock to the Macedonians. Furthermore, outside Macedon and particularly in Aetolia, such a defeat inflicted on a king of Macedon, within his own frontiers, seemed almost the portent of a new order in the affairs of the Greek world. Eager, there-fore, for a breathing-space, Philip took advantage of Sulpicius's failure to follow up his victory and, asking for a truce to bury his dead, used the night to retire over the hills.[6]

However, when the Romans, instead of following Philip, remained for some days where they were, and then marched north to Stuberra, he soon returned to Bryanium in Lyncestis;[7]

---

[1] Livy (P) xxxi, 33, 6–34, 6; Diod. xxviii, 8. Livy's (=Polybius's) stress on the effect of the Spanish sword upon Macedonian morale is probably exaggerated (cf. Nissen, 128; Kromayer, ii, 19, n. 2).

[2] Livy (P) xxxi, 34, 7.

[3] Livy (P) xxxi, 34, 8–36, 6: cf. Kromayer, ii, 20. The position has not been identified.

[4] The modern Tserna; cf. Kromayer, ii, 20–1.

[5] Livy (P) xxxi, 36, 7–37, 12; Dio, xvii, 58, 1–4 (inaccurate account that Philip was wounded).

[6] Livy (P) xxxi, 38, 1–39, 2: the statement that the news of an Illyrian and Dardanian attack influenced Philip's decision is contradicted by the fact that he returned almost at once into Lyncestis. Frontin. ii, 13, 8, probably refers to this incident. For the topography of these manœuvres see Kromayer, ii, 22 seq.

[7] Bryanium and Stuberra both lie on the Erigon to the north of Lyncestis (Strabo, vii, 7, 9) and the latter is perhaps to be identified with Tsepikovo; cf. N. Vulić, Mélanges Glotz, 875.

and upon Sulpicius's returning south to Pluinna, Philip probably scored some sort of success over him.[1] By this time it was August, and Sulpicius now resolved to try to force his way farther eastward, out of Lyncestis. Philip accordingly took up a position in the pass to the south of Banitza, the modern pass of Kirli-Derbend, through which the railway up to Monastir now runs, and which controls two routes—the southern one into Eordaea, and the road east through Ostrovo and Edessa to the central Macedonian plain.[2] On the woody and uneven ground Philip's phalanx was of little use, and his single Cretan cohort made little impression upon the heavy-armed Romans. Hence, after a short struggle, the Romans forced the pass, and advanced unimpeded, not eastwards on Pella, however—for Philip still held the heights above Ostrovo—but south into Eordaea, where they plundered the fields far and wide.[3]

Though not a major engagement, this fight for the pass of Banitza was the most important battle in the war, excepting, of course, the final battle of Cynoscephalae.[4] On the other hand, when Sulpicius took the southern road into Eordaea, Philip could breathe again, knowing that for this season at least the serious danger was past. He therefore left the Romans to advance south, unhindered, probably as far as the modern Kosane, in Elimiotis, before retiring gently up the Haliacmon to Celetrum (mod. Kastoria). This town Sulpicius compelled to surrender, and then, marching through the Tsangon pass, he descended the Apsus to Apollonia; on the way he took a town Pelion, probably near the modern Korça.[5]

Simultaneously with these campaigns in Lyncestis and Eordaea, the Roman fleet had been operating in the Aegean. Apustius had sailed round from Corcyra early in May,[6] and in

[1] Livy (P) XXXI, 39, 5: *terrorem praebuit subitum hosti*; these words probably conceal a Roman defeat; cf. Kromayer, II, 22, n. 4; *contra* De Sanctis, IV, 1, 54, n. 103.

[2] Livy (P) XXXI, 39, 6–9; cf. Kromayer, II, 23 *seq.* The same pass was forced by Brasidas in 423: Thucyd. IV, 127–128.

[3] Livy (P) XXXI, 39, 10–40, 1.

[4] Cf. Polyb. XVIII, 23, 3; Livy (P) XXXII, 21, 19.

[5] Livy (P) XXXI, 40, 1–6. Pelion is variously identified: Wace, *BSA*, XVIII, 1911–12, 168, puts it near Pliasa, a Vlach village between Lastona and Biklishta, De Sanctis, IV, 1, 56, and Hammond, *BSA*, XXXII, 1931–2, 145, on the site of Korça.

[6] See below, Appendix III, p. 318.

company with Attalus had spent some time at Athens, where, as related, measures were passed against Philip. From Piraeus he sailed against Andros, which fell after a short resistance;[1] then, after a vain attempt on Cythnos, he sent twenty Illyrian *lembi*, which had joined him off Prasiae, to ravage Carystus, while the main squadron waited for a Rhodian contingent off Geraestus. Eventually the combined fleet, including twenty Rhodian ships, sailed north and, after plundering what was left of Sciathos, put in at Mende on the promontory of Pallene. Scattered, however, by a storm and driven off from Cassandreia, they achieved little beyond the sacking of Acanthus, before finally returning by way of Sciathos to Euboea.[2]

It was already August, and in Aetolia feeling was beginning to grow in favour of intervening against Philip. Accordingly, from Euboea Attalus and Apustius now came to a conference with Pyrrhias, a leading Aetolian, at Heraclea in Oetaea. At first there were difficulties; Attalus, who still remembered bitterly his rebuffs of 201 and 200, flatly refused Pyrrhias the help he demanded in return for an Aetolian war-measure. But Apustius had the sense to make unlimited promises; and Pyrrhias's report, which reached Thermum[3] simultaneously with the news of Ottolobus, of an invasion of Illyrians and Dardanians into north Macedonia, and of the Roman siege of Oreus (which directly followed the conference at Heraclea), turned the scale in favour of war. A motion was carried, in the name of the general Damocritus, that they should join the Romans on the same terms as in the previous war.[4]

The force of the Dardanian raid through the gap left in Philip's defences by the withdrawal of Perseus from Pelagonia was, in fact, already spent at the time of the battle of Banitza; and though it provided one reason why he did not pursue Sulpicius south into Eordaea,[5] Philip contented himself with sending Athenagoras with a force of light infantry and most of the cavalry to pursue the retreating foe. The Dardanians suffered considerable losses of booty, if not of men.[6] Meanwhile, Philip heard of the Aetolian war-motion and its sequel: in conjunction with Amy-

---

[1] Livy (P) xxxi, 44, 1–45, 8. [2] Livy (P) xxxi, 45, 9–16.
[3] Livy (P) xxxi, 46, 1–5. [4] Livy (P) xxxi, 40, 9–10.
[5] Livy (P) xxxi, 40, 7. [6] Livy (P) xxxi, 40, 8; 43, 1–3.

nander, the Aetolians had destroyed Cercinium, near Lake Boebe, in Pelasgiotis, and Chyretiae in Perrhaebia; Malloea, close by, had surrendered,[1] and only Amynander's personal desire to obtain Gomphi had turned the Aetolians aside from invading southern Macedonia.[2] Philip resolved to make one of his sensational marches. Following the same route as the Romans into Elimiotis, he turned south-east over the Haliacmon and the Pass of Portaes into the upper Europus valley. The next day at midday he fell upon the Aetolians near Pharcadon, when they were in complete disorder, and routed them with severe losses. Amynander, more circumspect, had encamped on a hill a mile away, and escaped the general rout; consequently he was able to help the remaining Aetolians to safety during the night, and to guide them back along the difficult route towards Aetolia.[3]

Meanwhile the allied fleet was laying persistent siege to Oreus, which controlled the entrance to the Pagasean Gulf and Philip's southern route through Euboea;[4] and, while it still held out, subsidiary expeditions were sent to seize Larisa Cremaste and Pteleum on the coast, towns which Philip had possessed since 216.[5] Both fell (but very soon appear once more in Philip's hands),[6] and after them Oreus; whereupon, as it was autumn, the allied fleet retired. Apustius left thirty ships at Piraeus and sailed with the rest to Corcyra, the Rhodians returned home, and Attalus, after attending the Eleusinian Mysteries, went back to Pergamum.[7]

Before returning to Macedon, Philip made one further attempt to secure the southern frontier of Thessaly, by an assault with siege-engines on Thaumaci, a natural fortress which commanded the western Thessalian plain and what has always been the main

[1] On the position of Cercinium see Stählin, 103; it is uncertain whether it lay at Petra by the lake, or in the foothills west of Gerli. On Chyretiae (so inscriptions: Livy has Cyretiae) see Stählin, 25; it is the modern Domeniko. For Malloea see Stählin, 29.

[2] Livy (P) xxxi, 41, 1–6; see above, p. 99, n. 3.

[3] Livy (P) xxxi, 41, 7–42, 9. The position of Pharcadon is uncertain; against Kromayer, ii, 29, who puts it on the Pindus slope, see Stählin, 116, who identifies it with Klokotos, on the left bank of the Peneius.

[4] Livy (P) xxxi, 46, 6–11; for its fate in the former war see above, pp. 94 and 97.

[5] Livy (P) xxxi, 46, 12–13; see above, p. 88.

[6] Polyb. xviii, 3, 12; 8, 9, for Larisa. Perhaps Philip took them after defeating the Aetolians.

[7] Livy (P) xxxi, 46, 14–16. Fränkel connects Attalus's dedication, OGIS, 284, with the capture of Oreus, which he received.

road over Mt. Othrys into central Greece.[1] However, the Aetolians, after a minor internal crisis due to Scopas's attempt to carry off their best men as mercenaries to Egypt,[2] were once more ready to fight, and under Archedamus threw a relieving force into Thaumaci. Unable to break a way in and influenced by the approach of winter, Philip abandoned the siege, and returned to Macedon, there to review the season's campaigns and to plan the next year's strategy.

He could regard the year's record as a qualified success.[3] The Romans had failed to reach the heart of Macedon; and, constantly in fear of being separated from their base, and harassed by Philip's guerilla tactics, they had suffered from a shortage of food that was only finally removed when their victory at Kirli-Derbend opened the way into Eordaea.[4] The strain of the campaign showed itself the same autumn at Apollonia, shortly after Sulpicius had been relieved by the new consul, P. Villius, when a mutiny broke out and was only put down after Villius had promised to attend to the grievances of his men.[5] Against this Philip had to reckon the ravaging of Macedonian territory and probably the loss of parts of Dassaretia, the effect of which on the morale of his people was a factor he could not afford to neglect. Against the Dardanians and Aetolians too, his success had come only after northern Macedonia and Thessaly had suffered considerable ravaging; and Heracleides, with a fleet of not more than twenty-five warships and perhaps eighty galleys and light vessels, had not dared to come out of Demetrias to oppose a united enemy, who, even without Attalus's squadron, could count some twenty galleys and seventy warships.[6] True,

[1] Livy (P) XXXII, 4, 1; on the site (mod. Domoko) see Leake, I, 458; Stählin, 155-7.

[2] Livy (P) XXXI, 43, 4.

[3] For an estimate of Philip's campaign of 199 see Kromayer, II, 30-3; Theiler, 39-41 (unconvincing); De Sanctis, IV, 1, 59 and n. 116.

[4] E.g. Livy (P) XXXI, 33, 4; 36, 5; 38, 1; 39, 4; 40, 1, for references to foraging, etc.

[5] Livy (A) XXXII, 3, 1-7; rejected by Niese, II, 608, n. 5, but unjustly (cf. De Sanctis, IV, 1, 62, n. 118). The reinforcements mentioned in Livy (A) XXXI, 1, 3 are to be rejected; cf. Kromayer, II, 96 seq.

[6] Philip's numbers after Chios: Polyb. XVI, 7, 1 seq. (and see above, pp. 121-2 and 123). Allies: Rome: Livy (A) XXXI, 14, 2; cf. XXX, 40, 12; 43, 1; Rhodes: Livy (P) XXXI, 46, 6; Illyrian galleys: Livy (P) XXXI, 45, 10. (There is no direct evidence that Attalus took part in this season's campaigns.) Heracleides's inactivity: Livy (P) XXXI, 46, 8.

the allies had accomplished very little off Chalcidice; but the
moral effects of offering no opposition may have been considerable.[1] Such at least is suggested by the recall and arrest of
Heracleides this winter, a concession, we are told, to the Macedonians who hated him.[2]

However, if Macedonian morale was affected, the signs of this
were small; and throughout the winter Philip drilled his army
vigorously, and, as part of his policy of concentration, he evacuated Lysimacheia on the Thracian Chersonese.[3] More important
was the diplomatic aspect of the season's campaigns. To the
opposition of Aetolia Philip had perforce to be resigned. But
the Achaeans were still maintaining a precarious neutrality, and,
particularly since the departure of Philopoemen for Crete,[4] were
likely to be sensitive primarily to their own material interest. It
was with an eye on Achaean loyalty that Philip this winter
restored to the League Orchomenus, the long-promised town of
Heraea, and the district of Triphylia, and gave Alipheira to
Megalopolis;[5] and his new strategy for 198 was based on the
need to give every encouragement to the pro-Macedonian party
in Greece.[6]

The two main routes from Illyria into Macedonia are that
following the Skumbi, past Elbasan and the lakes, and that along
the Devol through Berat and Korça. There is, however, a third
way along the valley of the Viossa (Aous), which runs from
Apollonia south-east to Metsovo, and forms the main route
from Albania into Thessaly; its tributary, the Drynos, carries
an alternative route to Jannina and Epirus. Now the coming in

---

[1] Livy (P) XXXII, 5, 3, states that Philip feared *nunc sociorum, nunc popularium
animos* (i.e. in Macedon) *ne et illi ad spem amicitiae Romanorum deficerent, et
Macedonas ipsos cupido novandi res caperet.*

[2] Livy (P) XXXII, 5, 7. Heracleides was held responsible for Philip's execution of five of his statesmen in or about 205 (Diod. XXVIII, 2). Arvanitopullos, Γραπταὶ στῆλαι, 96, connects his downfall with a conjectured Roman
naval attack on Demetrias in 199.

[3] Polyb. XVIII, 4, 5–6 (it was soon after occupied by Thracians); Livy (P)
XXII, 5, 8. For this policy of concentration in 199 cf. Livy (P) XXXI, 34, 6
(recall of Perseus from Pelagonia).

[4] In autumn 199; cf. Plut. *Philop.* 13, 1.

[5] Promised (except Orchomenus) in 208: Livy (P) XXVIII, 8, 6 (see above,
p. 97). Polyb. XVI, 38, referring to Philip's anti-Roman propaganda in Achaea,
probably dates to this winter; cf. De Sanctis, IV, 1, 118. On the question of
Heraea, Orchomenus and Triphylia see further Aymard, *Premiers Rapports*,
59, n. 53 (but cf. above, p. 17, n. 2).   [6] Cf. Plut. *Flam.* 2, 3.

1. Looking north towards Tepeleni (the site of the battle according to De Sanctis)

2. Looking south-east towards the entrance of the Klisoura Gorge, where Philip had his lines.

The Valley of the Viossa (Aous) near Tepeleni.

of Aetolia offered the Romans the chance of a base in central
Greece, cutting off Philip from Phocis, Locris, Boeotia, Euboea
and Achaea, and the seizure of Oreus had shewn that they realised
this. Philip therefore judged it probable that their advance
would be in the direction of Thessaly and, taking a bold chance,
he resolved not, as last year, to wait for the enemy to penetrate
his own territory, but to occupy a strong defensive position as

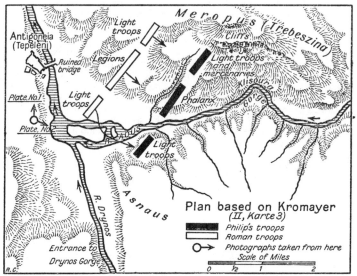

The Battle in the Aous Pass.

far west as he could, and so hold up their advance. Accordingly,
in April, as soon as the mountains were passable, he sent Athenagoras with his light-armed troops over the Furka Pass and down
the Aous to occupy the pass near Antigoneia;[1] and arriving a

[1] Livy (P) XXXII, 5, 9–11; Plut. *Flam.* (P) 3, 4–5, 1. For this position see
Kromayer, II, 40 *seq.* (with map); Leake, I, 71; 385 *seq.*; De Sanctis, IV, 1, 60,
n. 117. The confluence of the Viossa and Drynos is about 2.5 km. south of
Tepeleni (Antigoneia), which overhangs the left bank of the river (Plate, No. 1).
Above the confluence, both rivers run through gorges, that of the Viossa (the
gorge of Klisoura) being of considerable length and very narrow, that of the
Drynos short but twisting. Kromayer (modifying Leake's view, and followed
by Tarn, 264, n. 15 and (formerly) Holleaux, 109) puts Philip's position in
the entrance of Klisoura, where by the threat of a flank attack he could control
the Drynos route into Epirus, as well as that into Thessaly (Plate, No. 2); and
the expression τὰ Στενά (cf. Livy (P) XXXII, 5, 9) most naturally fits this gorge.
However, its use elsewhere to denote a pass connecting Illyria and Epirus

few days later with the rest of his forces, he fortified a strong position between the two hills Asnaus and Meropus, astride the river, just above the point where the Drynos joins it. Athenagoras and the light troops were placed on the slopes of Asnaus, while the king himself pitched his main camp, with his own tent prominently in the forefront, on the side of Meropus (mod. Trebeszina); the position was further assisted with entrenchments, towers, catapults and other artificial defences.

Villius heard of Philip's move from Charops, an Epirote chieftain, while still at Corcyra,[1] and, as Philip had hoped,

proper (e.g. Polyb. II, 5, 6; 6, 6: τὰ παρ' 'Αντιγονείαν στενά) proves either that it included both the Viossa and the Drynos forks, or that the στενά lay below the confluence of the two streams. De Sanctis (followed by Holleaux, *CAH*, VII, 830, n. 1; VIII, 168, n. 1, and Scullard, 262) takes the second view, and establishes Philip on the river at Tepeleni, where there is an appreciable narrowing of the valley (Plate, No. 1): he points out (a) that the pass in question is called the *fauces* or *claustra Epiri* (Livy (P) XXXII, 21, 14; 21, 20; XXXIII, 4, 2) and τὰ κατὰ τὴν "Ηπειρον στενά (Polyb. XXVII, 15, 2) (add Polyb. XVIII, 23, 4, where Flamininus speaks of τὰς ἀπηλπισμένας ἐν 'Ηπείρῳ δυσχωρίας); hence Philip bestrode the pass leading into Epirus; (b) that after the battle the Romans advanced through the same pass (*postero die per ipsas angustias, quas inter valle se flumen insinuat, hostem insequitur*: Livy (P) XXXII, 13, 1; *faucibus quas fuga hostium aperuerat*: Livy (P) XXXII, 14, 5) *into Epirus*!

Neither argument is cogent. The first falls on the fact that Tymphaea and Parauaea were at this time part of Epirus (cf. Livy (P) XXXII, 5, 9, *auxilia... in Chaoniam per Epirum...misit*; 13, 3; and see Fine, *TAPhA*, LVIII, 1932, 126–9, whose argument is not vitiated by his failure to mention the difficulties of this site); hence the term *fauces Epiri*, etc. could apply equally well to Klisoura. Secondly, the passage from Livy (P) XXXII, 14, 5, states only that Philip's flight opened up the route to Epirus; here *faucibus* might well mean the Drynos gorge. On the other hand, the confusion displayed in Livy (P) XXXII, 13, 1 (where *hostem sequitur*, even on De Sanctis's view, only applies to the 2.5 km. between Tepeleni and the river confluence!) suggests that Polybius himself had no clear picture of the geography of the site, and probably that he was misled by the use of the term τὰ στενά to cover both the Drynos gorge and that of the Viossa (as Leake so acutely saw, I, 71). After personally examining both suggested positions, I am convinced that τὰ παρ' 'Αντιγονείαν στενά must be, not the slight narrowing of the valley beneath the hill of Tepeleni, but the gorges which begin a mile and a half higher up. (North of Tepeleni there is no further narrowing of the river till Lundschi, 16 miles downstream.) But the decisive argument against De Sanctis is the complete omission of any reference to Antigoneia in Livy, though with Philip's lines directly in front of the town, it must have played a vital part in the defences. No less decisive, too, is the comparison of the pass occupied to Tempe, in a passage (Plut. *Flam.* 3, 5–6) which, for all its confusion between the Aous and the Apsus, comes directly from Polybius (cf. Nissen, 135; 290), and is only omitted by Livy because of its irrelevance to a Roman reader. The only gorge comparable to Tempe in this part of Albania is that of Klisoura on the Viossa.

[1] Livy (P) XXXII, 6, 1.

accepted the challenge. After the autumn mutiny he dared not face the hazards of Sulpicius's route, and though only the threat of a flank attack covered the Drynos route into Epirus, the risk of such an advance into new lands, where the people favoured Macedon,[1] leaving an undefeated army between himself and his base, was, as Philip had estimated, too great for a mediocre commander to take. Villius reconnoitred, and was sitting down to consider whether to try to force the pass or, after all, to risk taking one of the northern routes, when news came that the new consul for 198 was on his way to succeed him and had already reached Corcyra.[2]

With Titus Flamininus a new and ambitious figure entered the war. Unwilling to give Villius the consideration that the latter had given Sulpicius,[3] the new consul hastened out as soon as he could leave Rome, and took over his command in May. He at once dismissed any notion of advancing along one of the northern routes, realising that Philip had to be defeated, not merely out-manoeuvred,[4] and set about forcing the pass with the help of large reinforcements, nearly 9000 in all.[5] But for all his efforts, he could not break through, and forty days passed in minor attacks without effect.[6]

At the end of this time the Epirotes, weary of the duel on their soil, made overtures such as they had made before Phoenice, and eventually a conference between Philip and Flamininus was arranged near Antigoneia,[7] with the river between the two parties. Flamininus's proposals, however, showed up the conference as being, from his point of view, merely a clever manœuvre. Philip was to withdraw his garrisons from all Greek towns, give reparation to all whose land he had ravaged (i.e. Pergamum, Rhodes and Athens in particular) and submit his other disputes to arbitration. These terms were important primarily for their

---

[1] Livy (P) XXXII, 14, 5: *probe scit cui parti Charopo principe excepto favissent.*
[2] Livy (P) XXXII, 6, 1–4; even Livy (XXXII, 6, 5–8) rejects Valerius Antias's story of a victory in the pass by Villius. On the chronology of the year see below, Appendix III, p. 319.   [3] Cf. Plut. *Flam.* 3, 2.
[4] Livy (P) XXXII, 9, 8–11; Plut. *Flam.* 4, 1.
[5] Livy (A) XXXII, 8, 2; 9, 1; 9, 6; cf. Plut. *Flam.* 3; these figures, though rejected by Niese, II, 610, n. 1, are to be accepted: see De Sanctis, IV, 1, 62, n. 120; Kromayer, II, 62.   [6] Plut. *Flam.* 4, 2.
[7] Livy (P) XXXII, 10, 1–8: *ubi in artissimas ripas Aous cogitur amnis*, probably refers to the narrowing of the valley near Tepeleni; see above, p. 149, n. 1.

clear formulation of the Roman claim already implicit in the ultimatum at Abydus;[1] henceforth the Romans set themselves up (without any right in international law) as the protectors of Greek freedom. The enunciation of this well-worn principle, which was designed to prevent either Philip or Antiochus from developing Greece as a base for an eventual attack on Rome, was just now particularly useful for its propagandist value among the Greeks. In reply, Philip went to the limit in concessions. Driven from the start to act on the defensive, the most he could hope from the war was not to lose it; and he now declared himself ready to surrender all that he had ever taken personally; but the possessions he had inherited he would not give up: and he was willing to accept arbitration on all the questions outstanding between himself and his enemies.[2] When, however, Flamininus, with an insolence similar to that of Lepidus at Abydus, declared airily that in such obvious cases of aggression arbitration was superfluous, and suggested that the freeing of the cities began with Thessaly, Philip lost his self-control and, with the words 'What terms more harsh could you impose, T. Quinctius, if I were already beaten?' rushed from the conference, held back, the Livian account states, from a personal attack on the consul only by the fact that the Aous lay between.[3]

The next day the fighting continued, but still the Romans could not force an entry into the gorge; until, at length, by the help of Charops, a shepherd was found to lead a body of 4000 Romans round the hill of Meropus, a three days' journey. Arriving in sight of their own camp, these men gave out smoke signals, Flamininus then drew out the unsuspecting Macedonians from behind their defences, and the special force attacked them in the rear.[4] In this way the pass was at last taken, and with it Philip's camp, full of valuable spoils. Fortunately for Philip the phalanx seems to have offered some sort of a stand, until the light-armed troops could retire up the gorge,

---

[1] The terms were clearly sanctioned by the Senate; cf. Frank, *Roman Imperialism*, 161, n. 29.

[2] Livy (P) XXXII, 10, 4–6; these concessions show that Philip genuinely sought peace; *contra* Homo, *Rev. Hist.* CXXI, 1916, 243.

[3] Livy (P) XXXII, 10, 7–8.

[4] Livy (P) XXXII, 11, 1–12, 10; Plut. *Flam.* 4, 2–6; Appian, *Maced.* 6; Zon. IX, 16; Auctor *de vir. ill.* 51; Ennius, fr. 334 (Vahlen²). The date was June 25th (see below, Appendix III, pp. 319; 321–2).

and their disciplined resistance kept his losses down to 2000, a small figure in view of his very unequal situation.[1] Assembling his troops at a point five miles up the gorge, Philip then proceeded rapidly upstream, camping that night at the so-called 'Camp of Pyrrhus'; and the next day he reached the '*montes Lyncon*'. Neither place can be identified with certainty,[2] but the second is probably Metsovo. Here Philip spent some days pondering on his next move.

His final decision was to descend into Thessaly. To return at once to Macedon was to sacrifice the natural defences of Pindus and Olympus.[3] Advancing therefore by Tricca, Philip now proceeded to plunder his way through the cities of Thessaly.[4] Phacium, Peiresia,[5] Euhydrium,[6] all towns near the Enipeus, and then Eretria and Palaepharsalus[7] were in turn laid waste: their inhabitants were made to leave their homes and follow Philip, and the towns themselves were burnt. At Pherae Philip found the gates shut against him, and rather than delay in the siege of one of his own cities, he returned through Larisa to Tempe, leaving the route over from Metsovo guarded by a strong garrison of 2000 at Phaloria and probably another at Aeginium.[8]

[1] Cf. Kromayer, II, 47, n. 2, who quotes Livy (P) xxxII, 4, 3, against the rhetorical account of Philip's disordered flight (Livy (P) xxxII, 12, 8–10).

[2] Kromayer, II, 50 *seq.*; Leake, I, 398; De Sanctis, IV, I, 65, n. 123; Hammond, *BSA*, xxxII, 1931–2, 145. Kromayer and Leake put the Camp of Pyrrhus at Ostanitza, 50 km. up the Viossa from the battlefield, and the *montes Lyncon* at Metsovo; Hammond agrees in general, and suggests that the *castra Pyrrhi* was probably at Mesogéphyra. De Sanctis thinks these distances too great, and puts the Camp of Pyrrhus some 15 km. south-east of Premeti, opposite the confluence of the Viossa and Langaritza, the *montes Lyncon* near Konitza, where the fork up to the Furka Pass will explain their description as *interiecti Macedoniae Thessaliaeque*. However, Konitza in its valley scarcely fits Livy's description of *summa iuga* with their *campos patentes*, and Kromayer's identifications are on the whole preferable.

[3] Livy (P) xxxII, 13, 5; Plut. *Flam.* 5, 2; Polyb. xvIII, 3, 9. See Kromayer, II, 51.

[4] On his route see Leake, IV, 492–3; Stählin, 133–4; Béquignon, *BCH*, LII, 1928, 444 *seq.*; cf. Livy (P) xxxII, 13, 5–9.

[5] MSS. *Iresiae*; cf. Kip, 139; Stählin, 135.

[6] For its position between Hadjobachi and Simikli see Stählin, 143, n. 2, and n. 6, against De Sanctis, IV, I, 66, n. 124, who emends to *Methydrium*; cf. Béquignon, *BCH*, LVI, 1932, 122–91, who identifies it with Kturi.

[7] So Livy; but cf. Béquignon, *BCH*, LII, 1928, 22–8, who claims that Palaepharsalus is merely the oldest quarter of Pharsalus itself.

[8] Livy (P) xxxII, 15, 1; 15, 4; 15, 9; xxxIX, 25, 8. The resistance of Pherae was in keeping with its anti-Macedonian record (cf. Stählin, 105) but does not imply revolt: the town was Macedonian in 197; cf. Polyb. xvIII, 19; Livy (P) xxxIII, 6.

Philip's behaviour on this occasion was in many ways more shocking than anything he had done before, for the very reason that these were virtually his own subjects. If, as Kromayer thinks,[1] his object was simply to replenish an empty treasury, it would indeed seem as if Philip had become completely divorced from all moral sense. However, Livy, transcribing Polybius, states that Philip destroyed the towns unwillingly,[2] and with the object of preserving his allies from the enemy; and the refugees were allowed to bring as many moveable goods as they could transport. Hence his motive was probably the strategic one, of hindering the advance of Flamininus by making the district in which he would operate a desert,[3] and so, as in his garrisons on the upper Enipeus, of holding up the advance towards Tempe or any of the other gateways to Macedon as long as possible. However, a further motive of equal weight was undoubtedly Philip's personal reaction to the conference at Antigoneia, which broke up on the question of the Thessalian towns. After his defeat Philip realised that with his military inferiority Thessaly could no longer be defended. It might be sound to oppose Flamininus on the southern side of the Olympus-massif, but the flat plains east and west of Karadagh would inevitably fall to the Romans the moment they cared to take them. In this situation, the sacking of the cities was a psychological gesture in the face of Flamininus; however rationalised as a strategic move, it was, in fact, meant to show the world that the cities were Philip's, to protect and, if he could not protect them, to destroy. Needless to say, the personal feelings of their inhabitants, torn up from their homes and transferred to new habitations far away, were matters which never even came into Philip's consideration.

Meanwhile, Flamininus's victory on the Aous soon stirred up Philip's enemies to action. The Aetolians sent a raiding party

[1] II, 52; without further evidence, Kromayer's other argument—that the towns sacked were pro-Aetolian—is unacceptable.

[2] Livy (P) XXXII, 13, 8: *haec etiam facienti Philippo acerba erant, sed e terra mox futura hostium corpora saltem eripere sociorum volebat*; cf. also Polyb. XVIII, 4, 2 (Philip's own statement).

[3] Béquignon, *BCH*, LII, 1928, 445, sees a broad scheme of defence for Thessaly at Phaloria, Thaumaci (unfortunately not taken) and Phthiotic Thebes; but the ravaging surely shows Philip resigned to the loss of the Thessalian plains.

into western Thessaly.[1] They advanced through the Spercheius
valley, where they sacked Sperchiae and Macra Come, towards
Metropolis, taking Ctimene and Angeia on the way. Unable to
capture either Metropolis or Callithera however, they returned
along the edge of the hills, where they took Teuma, Celathara
and Acharrae; finally they came back over the pass of Xyniae,
sacking the deserted town of Xyniae and capturing the fortress
of Cyphaera.[2] Amynander, too, obtained some men from
Flamininus, captured Phaeca, which controlled the route from
Athamania to Thessaly, and besieged Gomphi. The fall of this
town was followed by the wholesale surrender of a number of
other places in the neighbourhood.[3] In the meantime Lucius
Flamininus, the consul's brother, had been appointed to the
command of the fleet, and having taken over from C. Livius off
Cephallenia,[4] he sailed round via Piraeus to join Attalus and the
Rhodians at Eretria. They had attacked the town after an attempt
on Carystus had been thwarted by Macedonian reinforcements
from Chalcis; but now the combined fleets had no difficulty in
repulsing Philocles's relieving force, and the townspeople were
already negotiating with Attalus when the Romans forced an
entry by night and the town fell.[5] Carystus now capitulated and
the garrison of 300 Macedonians was allowed to leave without
arms on a ransom of 300 sesterces per head. From here the fleets
sailed to Cenchreae, arriving a little before the autumn equinox.[6]

[1] Livy (P) XXXII, 13, 9–15; cf. Béquignon, *BCH*, LII, 1928, 446 *seq.*; *Vallée du Spercheios*, 320 *seq.*; 333 *seq.*; De Sanctis, IV, 1, 66, n. 124; Flacelière, 22; 23; 26; 344. For the sites (which cannot all be identified) see Stählin, 122–4 (Sperchiae and Macra Come); 148–9 (Ctimene and Angeia); 128 *seq.* (Metropolis); 132–3, 165 (Callithera, Teuma—not *Peumata*, as Holleaux, *BCH*, XXVIII, 1904, 357, n. 1—Celathara, Acharrae); 159–60 (Xyniae, Cyphaera); with the criticism of Béquignon. Ctimene and Angeia were both Dolopian towns (cf. Kip, 126 *seq.*); they may have been taken by Doson along with Thessaliotis and Hestiaeotis, or by Philip at some time during the first war with Rome; cf. Flacelière, 304, n. 2.
[2] On Cyphaera (inscriptions have Κύπαιρα and Κύφαιρα) see further Béquignon, *Vallée du Spercheios*, 336–7, and Roussel, *BCH*, L, 1926, 130, n. 2, who identify it with the acropolis of Palaeokaitsa. See above, p. 100, n. 1 (c).
[3] Livy (P) XXXII, 13, 15–14, 3. The places (sites unknown) are Argenta, Pherinium, Timarum, Ligynae, Strymon, Lampsum *aliaque castella iuxta ignobilia*; cf. Stählin, 127–8.   [4] Livy (P) XXXII, 16, 1–3, reading *Samen* for *Zammam*.
[5] Livy (P) XXXII, 16, 4–17; Zon. IX, 16, 2; Pausan. VII, 8, 1 (confused).
[6] For the chronology see below, Appendix III, p. 320. Polyb. XVIII, 45, 5, suggests that Oreus and Eretria were soon recovered by Macedon (cf. Livy (P) XXXIII, 31, 3); but Holleaux, *REG*, XXXVI, 1923, 129, n. 3, argues that Polybius is mistaken; *contra* Aymard, *Premiers Rapports*, 11, n. 29.

Flamininus, meanwhile, did not pursue Philip up the Aous valley, but advanced instead along its tributary, the Drynos, into Epirus. He rightly conjectured that the effect of Philip's defeat and the influence of Charops would be sufficient to secure him the support of the Epirote people; and to this end he refrained from plundering the countryside.[1] July Flamininus spent in Epirus,[2] winning over the tribes and reconditioning his forces with voluntary supplies of food; then, at the beginning of August he marched over the Mitschikeli range from near the site of Jannina, and crossing the Zygos Pass from Metsovo descended by the same route as Philip into Thessaly. At the *mons Cercetius*,[3] he was joined by Amynander, who had just taken Gomphi, and also enrolled large numbers of Epirotes in his army.

In Thessaly Flamininus first of all stormed Phaloria, and sacked and burnt it; Aeginium, the modern Kalabaka, he left untouched—it was almost impregnable—and, having received the submission of Cierium and Metropolis,[4] he went on to Gomphi, where he waited while provisions were brought over from the Ambracian Gulf.[5] From Gomphi he proceeded to the siege of Atrax, a stronghold on the right bank of the Peneius, about ten miles west of Larisa. And meanwhile, from behind the defences of Tempe, Philip sent out occasional help to various parts of Thessaly, but wisely refrained from confronting Flamininus face to face in the plain.[6] Largely because of the vigorous resistance of the Macedonian garrison, in phalanx formation,

---

[1] Livy (P) xxxii, 14, 4–6; Plut. *Flam.* 5, 2 (not clearly referring to Epirus).

[2] See below, Appendix III, p. 319.

[3] Livy (P) xxxii, 14, 7–8. Following Pliny, *N.H.* iv, 30, De Sanctis, iv, 1, 67, n. 128 and Stählin, 123, both place this mountain in Thessaly, and their view is preferable to that of Kromayer, who puts it immediately east of Jannina (ii, 54–5); it probably lies near the Zygos Pass. Since Tymphaea was at this time Epirote, the Epirote enrolments offer no difficulty (cf. Livy (P) xxxii, 13, 3, for *montes Lyncon* in Epirus). On Flamininus's route see Niese, ii, 613, n. 2, against Leake, iv, 528.

[4] In view of the bad Aetolian reputation in Thessaly, this town was evidently ready to surrender to Romans rather than Aetolians; cf. Niese, ii, 613.

[5] Livy (P) xxxii, 14, 7; 15, 1–7. Arrangements had been made for L. Flamininus to leave them here.

[6] Livy (P) xxxii, 15, 9; on the positions of these towns see Stählin, 121–4 (Phaloria and Aeginium); 130 *seq.* (Cierium); 124–6 (Gomphi); 100 *seq.* (Atrax).

after the walls had fallen, the Romans failed to take Atrax; and as it was already September, Flamininus, with his eye on winter quarters, decided to abandon the assault for this season. The town which appeared to offer the best communications with the fleet was Anticyra in Phocis; but first Phocis had to be conquered, in order to render the position secure. Phanoteus, Ambrysus, Hyampolis, and Anticyra itself, presented no difficulties, and Daulis too fell after a short resistance; but Elatea closed its gates and demanded a longer siege. Meanwhile, news arrived of important developments in Achaea.[1]

Encouraged by the attitude of Aristaenus, the Achaean general for 199–98, L. Flamininus and Attalus had gone to a conference, summoned at the consul's request to Sicyon, where Rhodian and Athenian envoys were present at a discussion of Achaean policy in respect to the Roman war and the activities of Nabis. The alliance with Philip had become not a help, but a danger. The presence of a Roman admiral at Cenchreae must have reminded the Achaeans of the sack of Dyme in the previous war; but this time Philip could send no aid. He was virtually a prisoner behind Tempe and, in any case, his recent policy in Thessaly had created a painful impression in Achaea; and to complicate the issue, there was Nabis, whom the Romans might use as a weapon against them, if they persisted in a neutral course. When these questions were thrashed out at Sicyon,[2] a vital cleavage of opinion became evident. Speeches were heard from all the envoys, including representatives of Philip; but the decisive influence on the one side was the speech of Aristaenus, who made a strong appeal to Achaean interest—and to anyone considering soberly the fate of Phocis and Thessaly, self-interest could give only one answer.[3] However, the opposition from the representatives of Dyme, Megalopolis and Argos, cities bound by old ties of friendship or gratitude to Macedon,[4] was so strong that it was only after their attempts to have the discussion

[1] Livy (P) XXXII, 17, 4–18, 9. For an analysis of the Roman offer to the Achaeans see De Sanctis, IV, 1, 68–9; Aymard, *Premiers Rapports*, 1 *seq.*; 50 *seq.*; 83 *seq.*

[2] Livy (P) XXXII, 19–21; Appian, *Maced.* 7; Plut. *Flam.* 5, 3; Zon. IX, 16, 3; Pausan. VII, 8, 2.

[3] For Polybius's judgment see Polyb. XVIII, 8.

[4] Livy (P) XXXII, 22, 10–11; see also, for Megalopolis, Polyb. II, 48, 2; for Argos, whence *se Macedonum reges...oriundos ferunt*, Livy (P) XXVII, 30, 9.

ruled out of order had failed by one vote, and they had themselves left the assembly, that Aristaenus's policy prevailed.

The Achaeans now allied themselves with Rhodes and Attalus, and with Rome, subject to the agreement of the Roman people.[1] This step tore away the last shreds of the Symmachy. It was, as Niese points out,[2] the fruits of the same military weakness that had originally sent Aratus to Antigonus Doson. But it was a weakness no longer due merely to negligence, but one that was, in the face of the Roman attack, fundamental. Armed to her utmost capacity and led by Philopoemen, the League could not have hoped to resist Rome. The causes of the Achaean betrayal (if betrayal it was) lie in the whole past history of the League, which was based on the particularism of the federal state and had resisted to the utmost Macedonian attempts at centralisation.[3] Like the smaller nations of modern Europe, Achaea could never aspire to a role fully independent of the large powers.

The Achaeans now joined L. Flamininus and Attalus in a siege of Corinth,[4] which they hoped to acquire as a reward for their alliance.[5] But when the townspeople rallied round the Macedonian governor, Androsthenes, and Philocles succeeded in getting a relieving force of 1500 across from the Perachora peninsula to Lechaeum, the siege was abandoned, Attalus retiring to Piraeus and the Roman fleet to Corcyra. Meanwhile, the proximity of Philocles stirred up pro-Macedonian feeling at Argos; and after a conflict with a League official on the technical question whether Philip's name was to be read out on a public proclamation, Philocles was called in by night, and occupied the citadel with a garrison. The majority of the Achaean defence force of 500 were allowed to leave the city, but their leader, Aenesidemus of Dyme, and a few others insisted on dying at their post.[6]

In Phocis, meanwhile, after some resistance, the city of Elatea

Livy (P) xxxII, 23, 1–2; Polyb. xvIII, 42, 6 (later details).
II, 618.
[3] For example, Aratus's resistance to Apelles; see above pp. 45 seq.
[4] Livy (P) xxxII, 23, 3–13; Pausan. vII, 8, 2; Zon. ix, 16; Appian, Maced. 7.
[5] L. Flamininus apparently gave definite, if unofficial, guarantees to this effect (Polyb. xvIII, 45, 12: διὰ τὰς ἐξ ἀρχῆς ὁμολογίας: Appian, Maced. 7); cf. Aymard, Premiers Rapports, 99–100.
[6] Livy (P) xxxII, 25, 1–12. On this incident see Edson, HThR, xxvI, 1933, 324–5, who shows that no question of worshipping Philip was involved.

had fallen before the attack of the consul; it was plundered, but the people were granted their freedom and the Macedonian garrison allowed to leave unharmed.[1] This capture gave the Romans control of most of Phocis and eastern Locris;[2] and it was followed by an invitation to take over the town of Opus. Thanks to the richer party, the Aetolians were excluded from the operation, and Flamininus was about to blockade the citadel, when a herald arrived from Philip asking for a conference.[3]

Reviewing the position at leisure within Tempe, Philip had realised that in the face of the overwhelming superiority of the Romans a peace on terms offered him the best chance of a favourable issue to the war; and just now the resistance of Corinth and the revolt of Argos both strengthened his hand for bargaining. And, as it happened, Flamininus saw in a conference just before the time of the Roman elections a means of shaping the course of the war to his own ambitions; if his command was renewed, he wanted to fight Philip to a finish, but if another was to reap the fruit of his campaign, he might prefer to recommend terms with Macedon.[4]

The conference was held towards the end of November in Locris; it lasted three days, the first two days' proceedings being on the shore of the Malian Gulf near Nicaea, at the eastern end of Thermopylae, those of the third day a little further east near Thronium.[5] Flamininus was accompanied by representatives of Pergamum, Rhodes, Achaea, Aetolia and Athens,[6] and by Amynander of Athamania; Philip, who came with five galleys and a *pristis* from Demetrias, had with him Apollodorus and Demosthenes, his secretaries, Brachylles of Boeotia (who

---

[1] Livy (P) XXXII, 24; Pausan. X, 34, 3–4. Cf. P. Paris, *Élatée*, 17 *seq.*

[2] Livy (P) XXXII, 21, 7; 32, 1; but Philip still had some garrisons: Polyb. XVIII, 10, 4.

[3] Livy (P) XXXII, 32, 1–6; Plut. *Flam.* 5, 4.

[4] Livy (P) XXXII, 32, 6–8: the word *gravate* can only refer to an assumed reluctance, as the rest of the passage shows. On this conference and Flamininus's intrigues see Holleaux, *REG*, XXXVI, 1923, 115–71; Aymard, *Premiers Rapports*, 114–27. For the chronology see below, Appendix III, pp. 320–1.

[5] Sources: Polyb. XVIII, 1–10 (very full and detailed); Livy (P) XXXII, 32, 9–36, 10; Plut. *Flam.* 5, 6; Appian, *Maced.* 8; Zon. IX, 16, 4; Justin. XXX, 3, 8 (all deriving ultimately from Polybius).

[6] Polybius omits the Athenians; but Cephisodorus was afterwards sent to Rome (Polyb. XVIII, 10, 11). Aymard, *Premiers Rapports*, 115, n. 5, questions the presence of the Athenians.

had been governor of Sparta under Doson)[1] and Cycliadas of Achaea, who had been expelled at the time of the move towards Rome.[2]

The first day Philip refused to come ashore, on the grounds that he could not trust the Aetolians; and to Flamininus's suggestion that the risk was the same for all he made the characteristic retort that the Aetolians could always elect a fresh general, whereas, if he perished, there was none to fill the throne he left.[3] At his request Flamininus then stated the Roman demands: Philip was to hand over all prisoners and deserters and withdraw from the whole of Greece, and he was to surrender those parts of Illyria which he had kept by the treaty of Phoenice[4] and restore all towns taken from Epiphanes. The other allies then made their claims; if Amynander spoke, his speech has not survived, but Dionysodorus, for Attalus, demanded the restoration of the ships and prisoners taken at Chios,[5] and the repair of the Nicephorium and temple of Aphrodite near Pergamum, destroyed by Philip in 201; Acesimbrotus of Rhodes demanded the evacuation of the Peraea, with the garrisons at Iasus, Bargylia and Euromus,[6] and Perinthus, Sestus, Abydus and all other ports and harbours in Asia; Perinthus was to resume its association with Byzantium; the Achaeans required Corinth and Argos, and the Aetolians reiterated the general demand for the evacuation of Greece, with particular stress on the restoration of such cities as had been members of their League.[7]

The formal claims were followed by a general discussion, in which Philip replied to a vigorous attack from Alexander of Aetolia, defending his actions at Cius and Lysimacheia, and neatly turning the Aetolians' own privateering practices against his opponent; Phaeneas's interruptions he warded off with a jest at the general's bad sight, and he aroused Flamininus's laughter by demanding that the Aetolians define this Greece that

---

[1] Polyb. xx, 5, 12. [2] Livy (P) xxxii, 19, 1–2.

[3] Polyb. xviii, 1, 5–9: cf. Livy (P) xxxii, 32, 12–16.

[4] Polyb. xviii, 1, 14: ὧν γέγονε κύριος μετὰ τὰς ἐν Ἠπείρῳ διαλύσεις: cf. Livy (P) xxxii, 33, 3. On the meaning see Zippel, 73; Holleaux, REG, xxxvi, 1923, 123, n. 6.

[5] Polyb. xvi, 6, 2; 6, 5; 6, 10; 7, 3, imply, however, that Attalus lost no men as prisoners at Chios!

[6] Polybius omits Pedasa; cf. Polyb. xviii, 44, 4.

[7] Polyb. xviii, 1, 10–2, 6; Livy (P) xxxii, 33, 1–8.

he was to evacuate: the Aetolians themselves were not, he said, for the most part Greeks![1] For all that Rhodes and Pergamum were the aggressors, he was willing, he continued, to hand back the Peraea to Rhodes and his ships and men to Attalus; as for the temples and their precincts, he would do his best to restore them by sending gardeners! Encouraged by the good reception of this second jest by Flamininus, Philip went on to the other claims. The Achaeans, notwithstanding their ingratitude— which he stressed at length—should have Argos; but he would confer privately with Flamininus about Corinth, and, meanwhile he wished to know definitely whether the evacuation of Greece was to include only the towns he himself had taken, or those he had inherited as well. Significantly, Flamininus gave no immediate reply; and though, when Philip asked for a written statement of the demands 'because, having no one to consult, he wished to think them over', he taunted him with having murdered all his friends, this sally was designed to cover his good humour to his allies rather than to insult Philip, who, Polybius states, smiled sardonically and said nothing.[2]

As it was now evening Philip took the copy and departed. No arrangement had been reached, but he had reason to regard Flamininus's attitude as encouraging. The next day, arriving late, he opened by requesting a private interview with the consul, and upon the allies assenting, he came ashore and held a long conference alone with Flamininus, after which the latter reported the king's willingness to restore Pharsalus and Larisa Cremaste to the Aetolians, the Peraea to Rhodes, and Argos and the town of Corinth[3] to Achaea. To Rome he had offered the Illyrian possessions and all prisoners, and Attalus was to recover his ships and the survivors from Chios. When the allies protested that there were no guarantees to evacuate Greece, Flamininus at once acceded to Philip's request for an adjournment.[4]

---

[1] Polyb. XVIII, 3, 1–5, 9; Livy (P) XXXII, 33, 9–34, 6.
[2] Polyb. XVIII, 6, 1–7, 6; Livy (P) XXXII, 34, 7–35, 1; Plut. *Moralia*, 197 C.
[3] In view of later discussions, only the town and not the Acrocorinth can be meant; cf. De Sanctis, IV, 1, 70, n. 140. It is plausibly suggested by Aymard, *Premiers Rapports*, 119, n. 16, that until now the exact meaning of 'Corinth' had been deliberately left vague both by the Achaeans (who feared to anticipate a Roman ruling which might be against them) and by Philip (who hoped to use this issue to force a break in the front against him).
[4] Polyb. XVIII, 7, 7–9, 3; Livy (P) XXXII, 35, 2–36, 3.

The next day all met again at Thronium, and Philip asked to be allowed to send an embassy to Rome if the outstanding differences could not be settled; and as Flamininus favoured the suggestion, the allies agreed to it, on condition that they should also send their own representatives to Rome to put their case. Upon his undertaking to evacuate completely Phocis and Locris, Philip was granted an armistice of two months; and meanwhile Flamininus sent Amynander, along with certain trusted officers, to Rome, to work with his supporters there who were trying to secure the renewal of his command. Embassies were also despatched by the allies, including Athens.[1]

Philip's calculations had rested so far on the assumption, deliberately fostered by the consul, that the latter was favourably disposed towards him; it was because of this and, almost certainly, at Flamininus's suggestion, made during the secret interview, that he proposed the unusual course of an embassy to Rome, rather than an immediate compact to be later ratified by the Senate. Polybius repeatedly emphasises Flamininus's guiding influence, and the success of his manoeuvres.[2] However, once the embassy reached Rome, and Flamininus's party had ensured the reassignment of the province of Macedon to its present commander,[3] Philip's envoys realised how they had been duped. For at once Flamininus's representatives raised the question of the so-called 'fetters of Greece'—Chalcis, Acrocorinth and Demetrias; and when the Macedonians confessed to having no instructions on a point on which Flamininus must undoubtedly have given Philip private guarantees, they were dismissed, and the war was resumed.[4]

By his readiness to sacrifice both the promised freedom of the Greeks and the proper interests of Rome to his own insatiable ambition, Flamininus had outwitted Philip; and the material cost of the latter's diplomatic defeat was the loss of his remaining

---

[1] Polyb. XVIII, 9, 4–10, 11; Livy (P) XXXII, 36, 3–10.

[2] E.g. Polyb. XVIII, 10, 1; 10, 3: τοῦ...πράγματος...κατὰ τοὺς ἐξ ἀρχῆς διαλογισμοὺς προκεχωρηκότος: 12, 2.

[3] Livy (A) XXXII, 28, 3–8: it was decided that both consuls should remain in Italy.

[4] Polyb. XVIII, 11, 1–12, 5; Livy (P) XXXII, 37, 1–6. The one flaw in Flamininus's plan was, as Holleaux points out, the fact that if the Senate had decided to supersede Flamininus against the propaganda of his party, they would almost certainly have continued the war; this was a risk Flamininus had to take.

hold on Phocis and Locris—perhaps no great tragedy from the military point of view.[1] It now remained for Philip to make what provisions were still possible for continuing the unequal struggle. In Macedon itself, the strain of the war is perhaps reflected in the revolt of parts of Orestis at this time;[2] and Philip, busy reorganising his forces, was not in a position to put it down. Throughout the length and breadth of his country he held levies to recruit new forces, and was compelled by shortage of manpower to enrol even boys of seventeen and retired veterans; the constant wars, decade after decade, had been disastrous to the population of Macedon.[3]

Meanwhile, Philip was also taking important diplomatic steps in the Peloponnese. The revolt of Argos, however welcome as a gesture of loyalty, had given Philip an awkward outpost to defend; and Philocles, one of his most reliable generals, could ill be spared from his duties in central Greece. Philip therefore decided on a pact with Nabis, the king of Sparta, with whom he had already had some dealings in the course of the Cretan War. Philocles was instructed to meet the king and arrange to hand Argos over to him, on the condition that if Philip won the war it should be returned, but that if not Nabis should keep it.[4] The proposal was accompanied by gifts and the offer of a marriage alliance between Philip's daughters[5] and Nabis's sons. At first

[1] Cf. De Sanctis, IV, I, 71; Holleaux, *REG*, XXXVI, 1923, 151, n. I, rates the loss more seriously.

[2] Polyb. XVIII, 47, 6; Livy (P) XXXIII, 34, 6. From Livy (P) XXXIX, 23, 6; 28, 2, it appears that the revolt of Orestis was at this time; cf De Sanctis, IV, I, 55, n. 106, against Nissen, 222–3. Polyb. XVIII, 11, 10: κατὰ γῆν πλείστων αὐτοῖς χορηγιῶν ἐκδεδαπανημένων is, however, from a speech made by Flamininus's agents at Rome, and cannot be used (as by Kromayer, II, 58, n. 3) as evidence on the internal state of Macedon. The Romans appear to have started a new era in Orestis from this date or, more probably, from 196. An inscription from Orestis, published by A. M. Woodward, *JHS*, XXXIII, 1913, no. 17, pp. 337–46, refers to a Junius Rufinus as governor of Macedon in the year '340'; Woodward dates the inscription A.D. 194, but (as Mr C. F. Edson points out to me in a letter) the governor mentioned must be the Junius Rufinus who was proconsul of Macedon under Hadrian (cf. *P–W*, 'Junius (Rufinus)', no. 138). Calculating the era in Orestis from 197 or 196, the year '340' works out at A.D. 143 or 144, early in the reign of Antoninus Pius.

[3] Livy (P) XXXIII, 3, 1–4.

[4] Aymard, *Premiers Rapports*, 133–4, n. 9, points out the disadvantages of this agreement, which gave Nabis an interest in Philip's defeat. He suggests that the restoration, if it took place, was to be compensated by the cession of other Achaean territory to Nabis.

[5] Philip had at least two daughters; see below, p. 261, n. 3.

Nabis demanded a plebiscite of the Argives;[1] but when it became evident that there was a strong hostility in the city, he abandoned this gesture, and was introduced secretly by Philocles at night. At once he instituted the programme of the social revolution, cancelling debts, dividing up the land, and winning the support of the poorer classes.[2]

This bargain with Nabis was a gross miscalculation on Philip's part. Primarily it is interesting as a further development in Philip's attitude towards the social question in Greece. The split between rich and poor, which the third century had seen accentuated,[3] and which had resulted at Sparta in the growth of a demagogic movement combining a return to the 'Lycurgan' forms of communal life (based of course on the helots) with an aggressive imperialism, did not directly concern Macedonia, which was still at a much earlier stage of economic development; to Philip the social question in Greece was merely a fact to be exploited in the support of political ends. Nevertheless, since the time when Doson, in opposition to Cleomenes, had consti-tuted himself protector of the *status quo* in Achaea, and had set up the Symmachy as the political expression of that relationship, there had been a change in the direction of Macedonian support; and, not unnaturally, this change went step by step with a decline in the influence of the Symmachy. The stages by which Philip was led to this change of policy are all, individually, capable of explanation along the normal lines of power-politics. Thus his recommendations to Larisa,[4] though their effect was to break down oligarchic exclusiveness in the matter of citizenship, were primarily military in origin. His first tentative approach to the socially dissatisfied element in Achaea had been part of Apelles's scheme to secure the election of Eperatus as a weapon against Aratus, in whom he saw the main obstacle to Macedonian expansion in the Peloponnese;[5] and the ineffectiveness of Eperatus had quickly forced the king back into the arms of Aratus. Philip's interference at Messene, four years later,[6] may

[1] Such a plebiscite might later have been used as a pretext for not restoring the town to Philip; cf. Aymard, *Premiers Rapports*, 135, n. 14.

[2] Livy (P) xxxii, 38, 1–9; Justin. xxx, 4, 5. On Nabis and his policy see Mundt, 39 *seq.*; Ehrenberg, *P–W*, 'Nabis'; Hadas, *CW*, xxvi, 1932, 65–8; 73–6.

[3] See above, p. 17.　　　　　[4] See above, pp. 35 and 69, n. 6.

[5] See above, pp. 47–8.　　　　[6] See above, pp. 72 *seq.*

have been actuated by his fear of Aetolia; his demagogic behaviour at Argos[1] was perhaps little more than a debauch at
festival time in a city which the kings of Macedon regarded as
their special preserve; and his toleration in Boeotia of the paying
of poor relief and the institution of communal dining clubs—
a state of affairs which led to the return of Megara to the
Achaean League in 206–5[2]—was probably due to indifference.
But, taken together, these incidents involved a move away
from the possessing classes, towards the securing of popular
support,[3] and this development now found its logical climax in
the end of the Symmachy and the compact with Nabis.

De Sanctis claims that this compact caught Philip in a
dilemma;[4] either he must continue to support the possessing
classes and thus oppose the social revolution, or he must turn
to the poor and, by combining a national with an economic
appeal, become a dangerous demagogic rival to his new ally.
This opposition is over-formal; in effect, Philip's breach with
the possessing classes had been a gradual process, stretching
over some fifteen years, and had already reached its culmination
in the Achaean agreement with Rome. Moreover, the Romans
were (in general)[5] to base their support on that section in each
state *cui salva et tranquilla omnia esse magis expediebat*,[6] and thus
to close the ears of that element to the influence of Macedon.
Finally, Philip's support of the ὄχλοι, the κακέκται, remained
subordinated to Macedonian policy; an encouragement from
without rather than an organising from within,[7] it was hardly
likely to lead to direct rivalry with Nabis.

Philip's error was, in fact, of quite another calibre. Whether he

---

[1] See above, p. 91 (Nemea of 209); Philip's Argive supporters, moreover,
were not limited to the poor: the town was handed over to him in 198 *per
quosdam principes...temptatis prius animis plebis* (Livy (P) XXXII, 25, 1); cf.
Aymard, *Premiers Rapports*, 110; 135 *seq.*

[2] Polyb. XX, 6, 1–4; XXII, 4, 3; cf. Heracleides, *Desc. Graec.* I, 14 *seq.*
Geog. gr. min. (ed. Mueller), I, 103); defection of Megara, Polyb. XX, 6,
7–12 (for the probable date see Aymard, *op. cit.* 14, n. 7; cf. L. Robert,
Rev. Phil. LXV, 1939, 97–122).

[3] Holleaux, 228–9; Aymard, *op. cit.* 64 *seq.*   [4] De Sanctis, IV, I, 74.

[5] Passerini, *Athen.* XI, 1933, 309–35, demonstrates that this Roman support
of the rich is not a rigid and invariable rule applied in every state.

[6] Livy (P) XXXIV, 51, 6.

[7] No evidence for Philip's encouragement of the πολλοί in Thessaly can
be drawn from Livy (P) XXXIV, 51, 4, where the disorder is easily explained as
due to the ravaging of the recent war.

ever imagined that Nabis would keep faith to the extent of handing back Argos is questionable; the marriage alliance may have been designed to that end, but more probably the clause was a mere sop to Argive loyalty. Philip was not, in fact, very concerned with the sequel to a possible victory; he wanted to be free of the responsibility of Argos, and rather than hand it back to the treacherous Achaeans, he gave it to their enemy Nabis. What he did not foresee was that Nabis would immediately open negotiations with his enemies.[1] At a conference at Mycenae it was agreed between Attalus, Flamininus, Nicostratus, the Achaean general for 198–7, and Nabis, that the Spartan should send 600 Cretan archers to the allied army; and meanwhile he and Nicostratus arranged an immediate truce—for four months, according to Livy. A quarrel between Nabis and Attalus over Argos was left undecided.[2]

From Mycenae Attalus returned to Aegina through Achaea, where his many gifts were rewarded with the decree of a golden herm and an annual festival;[3] Nabis went back to Sparta, leaving his wife and an agent, Timocrates, to carry on his ravages in Argos;[4] and Flamininus, after pausing at Corinth for an indecisive interview with Philocles, rejoined his forces at Anticyra, having meanwhile despatched his brother Lucius to win over Acarnania.[5] Shortly afterwards Flamininus marched with a legion to Thebes, to attend a meeting of the Boeotian League, and in the general commotion 2000 of his men slipped into the city and brought it over to Rome.[6] This success, which involved the

[1] Livy (P) xxxii, 39, 1–2. For a discussion of these negotiations and the meeting at Mycenae see Aymard, *Premiers Rapports*, 141–54.

[2] Livy (P) xxxii, 39, 3–40, 4. There is, however, reason to question Livy's statement—four months being a limitation in no one's interest, and a figure which coincides suspiciously with the period from this date until the battle of Cynoscephalae (June 197). If these doubts, raised by Aymard, *Premiers Rapports*, 148, n. 54, are correct, the armistice was probably concluded 'until the end of the war'.

[3] Polyb. xviii, 16; Livy (P) xxxii, 40, 8–9.

[4] Polyb. xviii, 17; Livy (P) xxxii, 40, 10–11.

[5] Livy (P) xxxii, 40, 5–7. Was Flamininus's avoidance of Achaea, where the agreement of Mycenae must have been far from popular, deliberate? See Aymard, *Premiers Rapports*, 152–3.

[6] Livy (P) xxxiii, 1–2. The subsequent meeting in Thebes was marked by the collapse of Attalus, who had a stroke and died a little later at Pergamum. He was succeeded by his son Eumenes (Polyb. xviii, 41; Livy (P) xxxiii, 2, 1–3; 21, 1–5).

triumph of the pro-Roman Zeuxippus and Peisistratus in Boeotia, over Brachylles, removed Philip's last ally in central Greece. Except in Acarnania (which held out until L. Flamininus stormed Leucas) the Greeks were now all won over, and with the coming of spring Philip had to face not only the Roman army, but a Greece united behind it, as far north as Thessaly.

Two courses lay open. To attempt to hold the passes from northern Thessaly into Macedonia, as he had held the Aous pass the year before, was desperate strategy, since the passes were many and not comparable to those in Albania as defensive positions. Alternatively he might stake all on a battle in Thessaly. This, though also a desperate course, had the moral advantage of the offensive; it reasserted Philip's claim to Thessaly, and kept the war from Macedonian soil. Following this second plan, therefore, Philip advanced to Dium, about the time of the equinox.[1] About the same time Flamininus marched north from Elatea along the coast route through Thermopylae to Heraclea, where the Aetolian assembly,[2] notwithstanding Scopas's recent levies, voted a force of 6000 foot and 400 horse;[3] under Phaeneas, these troops joined the Romans a day or two later at Xyniae, and shortly afterwards, in Phthiotis, Flamininus was reinforced by 500 Cretans from Gortyn, 300 Apollonians and 1200 Athamanians under Amynander.[4]

Flamininus now commanded an army of about 26,000 men,[5] over 8000 of them Greeks; the other 18,000 were the remainder of the Roman army, after deductions for casualties and, more important, for garrison work in Illyria[6] and central Greece. Philip's forces were about the same size;[7] his phalanx amounted

---

[1] Livy (P) XXXIII, 3, 5.

[2] Probably a regular assembly; see Holleaux, *BCH*, XXIX, 1905, 371, n. 4.

[3] Livy (P) XXXIII, 3, 6–7; 3, 9; Plut. *Flam.* 7, 2. Livy gives the Aetolian forces as only 600 foot, an error accepted by Kromayer, II, 102 *seq.*; cf. De Sanctis, IV, 1, 78–9, n. 159.

[4] Livy (P) XXXIII, 3, 10. The Cretans are probably part of the 600 offered by Nabis at Mycenae (Livy (P) XXXII, 40, 4); in this case the Apollonians are from Illyria, not from Apollonia in Crete; cf. Aymard, *Premiers Rapports*, 431 (addenda to p. 148, n. 52).

[5] Plut. *Flam.* 7, 2; cf. Livy (P) XXXIII, 4, 4–6.

[6] Kromayer, II, 102–3, does not allow for garrison work, and is thus led to reject the account of Roman reinforcements in 197 (Livy (A) XXXII, 28, 10; cf. 27, 2, giving 6000 foot and 500 cavalry in all).

[7] Plut. *Flam.* 7, 2: ἦν δὲ καὶ τοῦ Φιλίππου τὸ στράτευμα παραπλήσιον. Numbers in Livy (P) XXXIII, 4, 4–5.

to 16,000 men, and, in addition, there were 2000 peltasts, 2000 Thracians and the same number of Illyrians, 1500 mixed mercenaries and 2000 cavalry—in all 23,500 foot and 2000 horse. Philip, too, was considerably handicapped by the large number of his men (chiefly mercenaries) required for garrison duty.[1]

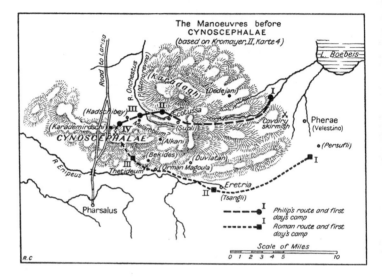

One of Flamininus's immediate objectives was the isolation of Demetrias; and to this end he advanced north-east from Xyniae on Phthiotic Thebes, and waited some time, hoping to take the town with help from within. But when news arrived that Philip was already in Thessaly—it was now May—and Thebes still held out, he advanced with his allies to Pherae and encamped about six miles south of the town.[2] Meanwhile, after a speech of exhortation to his men,[3] Philip came south through Tempe to Larisa, and from here, learning that Flamininus was at Phthiotic Thebes, he continued along the eastern Thessalian plain towards Pherae,[4] and encamped about three and a half miles north of the

---

[1] See above, p. 142, n. 2.   [2] Polyb. XVIII, 18; Livy (P) XXXIII, 5.

[3] The Polybian version (Livy (P) XXXIII, 3, 11–14, 3) stresses the undoubted fact that the outcome of a full clash between legion and phalanx had not yet been tried.

[4] Polyb. XVIII, 19, 3; Livy (P) XXXIII, 3, 11–14, 3; 6, 3 (mistranslating Polybius).

town. The next day advance forces of the two armies made contact in the pass between Thebes and Pherae; and the day after that a cavalry skirmish occurred near Pherae, in which the Aetolians drove back Philip's men. This skirmish showed that the terrain here was unsuited to a pitched battle, and Philip set off the next morning towards Scotussa, where he hoped first to revictual his army and afterwards to find suitable ground for fighting. Suspecting his object, Flamininus set out in the same direction, intending to destroy the corn at Scotussa before Philip could get there.[1]

There now followed three days' marching, with the hills of Cynoscephalae between the two armies, effectively preventing them from a clear understanding of what their opponents were about.[2] On the first day Philip advanced to the river Onchestus

---

[1] Polyb. XVIII, 19, 4–20, 3; Livy (P) XXXIII, 6, 4–8.

[2] On this march and the battle-site see Leake, IV, 457 seq.; 473 seq.; Kromayer, II, 63 seq. (with map); De Sanctis, IV, 1, 85, n. 166; Stählin, P–W, 'Κυνὸς Κεφαλαί'; Das Hellenische Thessalien, 111; 141. De Sanctis, following Leake, puts the battlefield between Supli and Duvlatan, Stählin a little further west, near Alkani. Against Kromayer's reconstruction (substantially that adopted above) De Sanctis urges that when, on the third day, Philip, καταννύσαι σπεύδων ἐπὶ τὸ προκείμενον, ἀναξεύξας προῄει (Polyb. XVIII, 20, 8), he cannot yet have reached Scotussa, since he intended to revictual near that town; and Stählin claims that, as Philip's camp the second night was ἐπὶ τὸ Μελάμβιον προσαγορευόμενον τῆς Σκοτουσσαίας, his first night's camp must have been well to the east of Scotussan territory. Neither argument is cogent. Philip's object was twofold—to revictual near Scotussa and to find a suitable battle-ground. Having revictualled the second day—the whole of which was spent in marching from the camp on the Onchestus to that near Melambium (which was still in Scotussan territory)—Philip was free to carry out the second part of his programme. The words τῆς Σκοτουσσαίας are attached to Melambium for two reasons, first to define further a little known village (note the expression προσαγορευόμενον and the absence of any other reference to the place in extant texts and inscriptions) and secondly for stylistic reasons, to balance the phrase τῆς Φαρσαλίας, which is attached to the Thetideum, reached by Flamininus the same night. Two further objections to putting Philip's first night's camp much east of Scotussa are (a) that Philip camped near the river Onchestus; as Kromayer points out, the only river worthy of the name in this district is the Platanorevma: yet Stählin has to assume that Polybius is referring to one of the dried-up becks near Dedejani; (b) that Stählin admits that the marches are described 'in streng Gleichmässigkeit'; yet from the Roman camp near Persufli to Eretria is about twelve and a half miles, roughly the same distance as from Philip's camp to Supli. This is surely a minimum day's march in view of Philip's eagerness to revictual; and though Stählin assumes part of the first day spent on 'Erntearbeit', Polybius speaks only of corn ἐν τῇ Σκοτουσσαίᾳ. There is also controversy concerning the site of the Thetideum, which Kromayer identifies with the ruins one and a quarter miles south-west of Alkani. De

(probably the modern Platanorevma) immediately to the north-west of Scotussa, a distance of about twelve and a half miles, while Flamininus reached Eretria (mod. Tsangli); on the second Philip, who was probably busy revictualling his army, advanced only as far as Melambium, a hamlet still in the territory of Scotussa, while his opponent reached a point just west of the Thetideum, in the district of Pharsalus, a temple which lay most probably on a small hill to the north of the modern Orman Magoula. Still neither commander knew the whereabouts of the enemy, and when, on the third morning, Philip broke camp early with the object of reaching the level ground near Pharsalus, he found the whole countryside enveloped in a thick mist, after a night's heavy thunder-rain, so that progress was impossible. He therefore pitched a fourth camp (probably between Had-schibey and Karademirdschi, somewhat east of the modern route from Pharsalus to Larisa) and sent out an advance force to hold the summits.[1]

From this action the battle developed.[2] For it happened that simultaneously Flamininus sent out ten cavalry squadrons and almost 1000 light troops in the direction of the pass over the hills,[3] and the two forces unexpectedly encountered each other. The first shock over, they called for reinforcements; and when

Sanctis, basing his view on a misunderstanding of the position during the battle between Pelopidas and Alexander of Pherae in 364, imagines the Thetideum to have lain on the Scotussan side of the main ridge, an impossible position, since Polybius describes it specifically as τῆς Φαρσαλίας. The view of Leake (IV, 472) and Stählin (141) is preferable. They put the temple in the Enipeus valley, between Orman Magoula and Bekides. Flamininus's camp will have been a little to the north-west of the Thetideum, not perhaps so far as Kromayer's map indicates. From here Flamininus sent his forces *forward* (Polyb. XVIII, 21, 1: δέκα προθέμενος οὐλαμούς), i.e. in the same north-westerly direction in which he had been marching from Eretria; and since his purpose—for he could no longer hope to forestall Philip in reaching Scotussa—must now have been to head him off from the plain near Pharsalus, his natural objective would be the gap between the hills, where the modern Larisa-Pharsalus road now runs. Thus Kromayer's position for the battle is substantially correct.

[1] Polyb. XVIII, 20, 4–9; cf. Livy (P) XXXIII, 6, 9–7, 3. Plut. *Flam.* 7, 7, has an apocryphal anecdote of Philip's addressing his men from a hillock, which later proved to be a grave (from the battle of 364?).

[2] On the battle see Delbrück, I[3], 424 *seq.*; Kromayer, II, 78 *seq.*; De Sanctis, IV, 1, 82 *seq.* Authorities: Polyb. XVIII, 21–7; Livy (P) XXXIII, 7, 4–10, 10; Plut. *Flam.* 8; Justin. XXX, 4; Zon. IX, 16.

[3] Polyb. XVIII, 21, 2: ὡς ἐπὶ τὰς ὑπερβολάς—probably where the Larisa-Pharsalus road now runs.

some 2000 foot and 500 horse, under the Aetolians, Archedamus and Eupolemus, and two military tribunes, joined in, the Macedonians, at first victorious, began to give way and retire uphill towards the crest. Having recalled all his foragers, Philip now sent forward his Macedonian and Thessalian horse under Leo and Heracleides of Gyrton, and with them all his mercenaries except the Thracians, under Athenagoras, with the result that the Romans were in turn forced to fall back and were only steadied by the courageous resistance of the Aetolian cavalry.[1]

By this time, however, both generals realised that the skirmish was turning into a full-dress encounter; and while Flamininus drew up his whole battle-line along the south of the hill, Philip on the north, in response to the encouraging reports from his messengers, was making up his mind to bring his phalanx into action, rough ground or no. From the camp he led out the right wing of his phalanx, together with his peltasts, leaving Nicanor to follow up the hill with the left wing; reaching the top of the pass, he wheeled left on to the summits from which his mercenaries had advanced against the enemy. But in the meantime, after a short address, Flamininus, leaving his right wing stationary, with the elephants in front of it, had led his left up the hill and driven back Philip's mercenaries in disorder.[2]

It was this scene that met the king's eyes, as he reached the summit: it left him no choice but to bring into action, without waiting for Nicanor, the wing of the phalanx that was already available. Posting his retreating forces on the right, he commanded his main force of phalangites and peltasts to double its depth to sixteen men, close up and charge the approaching enemy. Under the massed attack the Roman left gave way; but Flamininus, rapidly transferring the assault to the right, advanced against Nicanor's wing before it could deploy from marching into fighting line, and with the help of the elephants drove it back in complete confusion towards the Macedonian camp.[3]

With each side victorious on one flank, honours were momentarily even; the balance was turned by the initiative of an unknown tribune on the Roman right, who wheeled his twenty maniples

[1] Polyb. XVIII, 21, 1–22, 6; Livy (P) XXXIII, 7, 4–13.
[2] Polyb. XVIII, 22, 7–24, 7; Livy (P) XXXIII, 8, 1–10.
[3] Polyb. XVIII, 24, 8–26, 1; Livy (P) XXXIII, 9, 1–7.

round, and attacked the Macedonian right in the rear and left flank. His action determined the issue. Philip, seeing his men throwing down their shields, withdrew to watch the conflict from a distance; then, when he saw the day was lost, he gathered together what Thracians and Macedonians he could and fled. The disastrous delay in bringing up the other wing can be appreciated from the fact that the extreme left never reached the summit at all, but was cut down by Flamininus's pursuing Romans before it had time to strike a blow.[1] As Polybius points out,[2] the result of the battle was a remarkable vindication of the superior mobility of the Roman legion when face to face with the late Hellenistic phalanx. Unbeatable on its own ground, the latter had no defences, once a gap had appeared in its front, and it was always an easy victim to a flank attack.

Retreating at once towards Tempe, Philip passed one night at the so-called Tower of Alexander, and paused the next day at Gonnus to gather up his stragglers.[3] The enemy spent some time plundering, the Romans being particularly annoyed that the Aetolians had been first in the Macedonian camp; but after a night in their own quarters they advanced towards Larisa. Philip, however, had already sent one of his Royal Hypaspists there to destroy all the royal correspondence and official documents, thereby showing a prudence and adaptability to his changed fortunes that called forth the admiration of Polybius.[4]

Flamininus had not been long at Larisa, when Philip sent a herald to ask for a truce to gather up his dead, and at the same time to discover whether the Roman general was disposed to allow the sending of envoys to discuss making peace.[5] Flamininus granted both requests and in addition 'bade Philip be of good cheer',[6] a reply calculated to irritate the Aetolians as much as it encouraged Philip. Indeed, his information on the strained relations between the Romans and the Aetolians may have helped to determine Philip's new policy. He had staked Thessaly on a

---

[1] Polyb. xviii, 26, 2–12; Livy (P) xxxiii, 9, 8–10, 5.
[2] Polyb. xviii, 28–32.
[3] Polyb. xviii, 27, 1–5; Livy (P) xxxiii, 10, 6–7. For the position of Gonnus see Stählin, 33 seq.
[4] Polyb. xviii, 33, 1–7.
[5] Livy (P) xxxiii, 11, 3–4; omitted from our text of Polybius; cf. Holleaux, Rev. Phil. LVII, 1931, 193 seq.
[6] Livy, ibid.: bono animo esse regem ut iuberet.

pitched battle and had lost. Now he could either try to hold up the enemy on his own frontiers, or make as favourable a peace as the Romans would grant; and wisely he chose the second course. Nor was this all; with a complete reversal of his whole policy since the days of Demetrius of Pharus, he now resolved not merely on peace, but also upon positive collaboration with the Romans.

Various factors contributed to Philip's decision. First, since the Romans had the upper hand, if peace was to be made it must be made with a good grace. Secondly, Philip had observed the growing animosity of the Aetolians towards Flamininus, whom they accused of filching the glory of *their* victory at Cynoscephalae, and of failing to consult the allies on matters of common policy.[1] This bitterness the Roman commander both felt and resented. He had a proud disposition easily stirred to hatred; the verses of the Messenian Alcaeus on Cynoscephalae, though aimed at Philip, incensed Flamininus even more, because they praised the Aetolians first[2]—and the Roman's anger was all the more noticeable in the face of Philip's cool and ironical retort.[3] His reasons for restraining the Aetolians were thus partly personal, but partly, too, political; it was not senatorial policy that the Aetolian League should take the place of Macedon.[4]

[1] Polyb. XVIII, 27, 4; 34, 1 *seq.*; Livy (P) XXXIII, 9, 3–10; Plut. *Flam.* 9, 2–5.
[2] Plut. *Flam.* 9, 2 (cf. *Anth. Pal.* VII, 247): μᾶλλον ἡνία τὸν Τίτον ἢ τὸν Φίλιππον. The verses ran:

> Ἄκλαυστοι καὶ ἄθαπτοι, ὁδοίπορε, τῷδ' ἐπὶ νώτῳ
> Θεσσαλίης τρισσαὶ κείμεθα μυριάδες,
> Αἰτωλῶν δμηθέντες ὑπ' Ἄρεος ἠδὲ Λατίνων,
> οὓς Τίτος εὐρείης ἤγαγ' ἀπ' Ἰταλίης,
> Ἠμαθίη μέγα πῆμα. τὸ δὲ θρασὺ κεῖνο Φιλίππου
> πνεῦμα θοῶν ἐλάφων ᾤχετ' ἐλαφρότερον.

These verses and subsequent events (Livy (P) XXXVI, 8, 3–5; Appian, *Syr.* 16) show that Philip, having obtained the real object of his herald's visit, did not care to face the public humiliation of a return to Cynoscephalae to bury the dead, but preferred to endure the private censure of his people: cf. Holleaux, *Rev. Phil.* LVII, 1931, 193 *seq.* See further W. Peek, *P-W*, 'Philippos', col. 2303 (out of place).
[3] Plut. *Flam.* 9, 3 (cf. *Anth. Pal.* Appendix XVI, 26 B).

> Ἄφλοιος καὶ ἄφυλλος, ὁδοίπορε, τῷδ' ἐπὶ νώτῳ
> Ἀλκαίῳ σταυρὸς πήγνυται ἠλίβατος.

—and in coarser vein (probably by Philip, cf. Holleaux, *CAH*, VIII, 736, bibliography); *Anth. Pal.* IX, 520:

> Ἀλκαίου τάφος οὗτος, ὃν ἔκτανεν ἡ πλατύφυλλος
> τιμωρὸς μοιχῶν, γῆς θυγάτηρ ῥάφανος.

[4] Livy (P) XXXIII, 11, 9.

Nor could the Senate afford to crush Macedon completely; for not only did the kingdom of Macedon provide a northern bulwark between Greece and the Balkan tribes,[1] who, though useful as occasional allies of the Senate, could not be allowed to run wild over Greece, but—what was more important— Flamininus had his eyes already fixed on Syria,[2] where Antiochus had been using the interval since 200 to make great strides towards the recovery of the ancient bounds of the Seleucid empire.[3]

By 198 Antiochus had been in a position to invade Egypt. But instead he had utilised Philip's resistance to make headway in Asia Minor. Advancing along the Cilician coast with a mixed fleet of 300 ships, he was met at Coracesium by a Rhodian ultimatum, forbidding him to pass the Chelidonian Islands. Not only the Rhodians, but Flamininus too, were afraid that he was coming to the help of Philip[4]—notwithstanding the assurances given to Lepidus and his colleagues in 200; hence there was widespread relief when the news of Cynoscephalae eased the tension. The Rhodians allowed Antiochus to pass, provided that he left certain Ptolemaic towns untouched, and for a time the crisis was averted.

In the Roman hostility towards Aetolia and alarm at the movements of Antiochus Philip saw a more fruitful means of salvaging his empire than in a futile continuation of the struggle. That he at once resolved to join Rome in her ultimate war with Antiochus is unlikely: in the last resort his policy must necessarily be determined by the balance of forces. But in the meantime, in case the clash came soon, it was plainly better for him to be independent, master of his own lands, however reduced, and able to strike a free and equal bargain with the Syrian, rather than fighting for survival on the Haliacmon and the slopes of Olympus, forced to take as charity what help Antiochus might deign to grant.

---

[1] Polyb. XVIII, 37, 7–10; on this argument, minimised by Holleaux, *CAH*, VIII, 177, n. 1, see De Sanctis, IV, 1, 90.

[2] Polyb. XVIII, 39, 3; cf. 43, 2, where Flamininus placates the Aetolians διὰ τὸ προορᾶσθαι τὸν Ἀντίοχον. These passages contradict the theory of Passerini, *Athen.* X, 1932, 105 *seq.*, that Flamininus opposed the ten commissioners sent out from Rome, because he believed that there was no danger from Antiochus.

[3] Cf. Holleaux, *CAH*, VIII, 173–4. [4] Livy (P) XXXIII, 19, 11; 20, 3.

Meanwhile Cynoscephalae had been accompanied by disasters on other fronts. In Acarnania, the capture of Leucas followed by the news of Philip's defeat had together brought about the surrender of Philip's most faithful allies.[1] About the same time, the Achaeans, who had sent no troops into central Greece, took their share in the victory by defeating Androsthenes, Philip's governor at Corinth, in a major battle near the Nemean beck.[2] Philip had strengthened his vital fortress of Acrocorinth by seizing a number of prominent hostages from the lower town, and increasing his garrison of 1300 with mixed troops, to a total of 6000, of whom 1500 were Macedonians. The defeat of this force by Nicostratus, the Achaean general, when it was out ravaging the land around Pellene, Phlius, Cleonae and Sicyon, meant the end of the war in Achaea. In Asia Minor, too, the Rhodians now sent Pausistratus to continue the attacks on Philip's garrisons in Caria and the Peraea;[3] with the help of 1900 Achaeans and other reinforcements they recovered Tendeba, a little place near Stratonicaea, and after a two days' battle near Alabanda, drove the Macedonian forces, under Deinocrates, back to the coast at Bargylia. However, they lost the chance of taking Stratonicaea, preferring to recover the smaller fortresses in the Peraea, and Deinocrates was able to throw a relieving force into the town. Shortly afterwards the initiative here was to pass to Antiochus.[4]

Thus, though he did not yet know it, the outcome of the struggle fully justified Philip's decision. He now sent a delegation of Demosthenes, Cycliadas and Limnaeus to confer with the Roman general and arrange for an armistice of fifteen days.[5] Flamininus's instructions to the allies to meet at the entrance of Tempe for such a conference caused a new outbreak among the Aetolians, who even began to circulate the preposterous rumour

[1] Livy (P) xxxiii, 16–17.
[2] Livy (P) xxxiii, 14–15. Philocles had probably returned to his post at Chalcis: see Aymard, *Premiers Rapports*, 165, n. 21.
[3] Livy (P) xxxiii, 18. The Rhodians had operated here consistently since 201, and under Nicagoras had already recovered the territory of Pisye, Idymus and Cyllandus (*Syll.* 586; cf. Hiller von Gaertringen, *P–W*, Suppl.-B. v, 'Rhodos', col. 788); the men of Pisye were among Pausistratus's forces this year (Livy (P) xxxiii, 18, 3); cf. Meyer, *Die Grenzen der h. Staaten*, 54 *seq.*; 72.
[4] Livy (P) xxxiii, 18, 22.   [5] Polyb. xviii, 34, 4–5.

that Philip had bribed him;[1] and at a preliminary meeting, after Amynander had as usual shown himself ready to leave the decision with the Romans, the Aetolian representative, Alexander, urged that Philip be deposed. To this the proconsul replied that for general reasons of policy the Romans were resolved to come to terms with Philip, and interrupted Phaeneas's attempts to continue the argument with the demand that he should 'cease talking nonsense'.[2]

At the conference in Tempe, the next day, Philip at once showed his new policy by offering to accept in full the demands made at Nicaea,[3] and to submit all other questions to the Senate. This recognition of the Roman right to negotiate the peace was a tactful approach to Flamininus, particularly in view of the dispute with the Aetolians. The latter were quick to reiterate their claim to Larisa Cremaste, Pharsalus, Phthiotic Thebes and Echinus, but when Philip bade them take the towns, the Roman interposed an arbitrary veto, granting them only Thebes; and when Phaeneas spoke of their rights under the original treaty (of 211), he was quickly reminded of the separate peace of 206. Thebes, however, could be regarded as the fair spoil of war; and having full rights over it, the Romans might graciously bestow it upon whom they pleased.[4] Philip was now granted a four months' truce, and on his agreeing to pay an immediate indemnity of 200 talents and send hostages, including his younger son, Demetrius, to Rome, he was granted permission to send representatives to the Senate; if they rejected his terms, the money and hostages were to be returned.[5]

From Tempe he had to hasten north to attend to a Dardanian invasion, which closely followed the report of Philip's defeat in

[1] Polyb. xviii, 34, 6 seq.; Appian, Maced. 9, 1.
[2] Polyb. xviii, 36–7; Livy (P) xxxiii, 12, 1–13. The representatives of the rest of the allies were given no opportunity to put their case; see Aymard Premiers Rapports, 170, n. 12.   [3] See above, p. 160.
[4] Polyb. xviii, 38, 1–9; Livy (P) xxxiii, 13, 1–13 (misunderstanding Polybius in section 8). Thebes had come over to Rome, not voluntarily, but as a result of Philip's submission after Cynoscephalae (see above, p. 168); logically, however, this did not give the Aetolians any claim to it, or indeed place it in a different category from the towns which had made a deditio. See Täubler, 213; Aymard, Premiers Rapports, 171, n. 21.
[5] Polyb. xviii, 39; Livy (P) xxxiii, 13, 13–15; Appian, Maced. 9, 2; Plut. Flam. 9,4–5; Dio, xviii, 60 (absurd motivation attributed to Flamininus); cf. Zon. ix, 16.

Thessaly. Rapidly levying an army of 6000 infantry and about 500 cavalry, Philip marched to defeat it at Stobi in Paeonia; and with this success to give his people new heart, he returned to Thessalonica, there to arrange for the sending of envoys to Rome.[1]

Meanwhile, Antiochus's advance in Asia Minor,[2] now in collusion with the Rhodians, was rendering peace as urgent a matter for the Senate as for Philip. From Lycia he had proceeded to annex the coastal towns of varied political status; to Rhodes he gave Stratonicaea, and also granted her a kind of protective custody over Samos, Myndus and Halicarnassus, and let her buy Caunus from Ptolemy.[3] Advancing up the coast, Antiochus seized town after town[4] until, with the surrender of Abydus, his forces lay on the Hellespont.[5] When, however, he sent troops against Lampsacus in Aeolis and Smyrna in Ionia, which still held out against him, at the suggestion of Eumenes of Pergamum these towns sent a direct appeal to Rome, to be 'included' in the treaty with Philip.[6] Thus the Senate were constantly being reminded of the danger from Antiochus; so long as Philip remained technically at war, they had not scotched the threat which the war had been designed to eliminate.

When the various envoys were heard at Rome, the elections were already over, and C. Claudius Marcellus, the consul designate,[7] who hankered after a cheap triumph, vigorously opposed the granting of terms to Philip. However, both Senate and people agreed to ratify peace on the terms offered; and the agreement was signed by the Macedonian representatives.[8] Of the specific terms there is no record, but there are clear indications that they were in essentials the fulfilment of the claims made at Nicaea.[9] However, for the detailed regulation of the

---

[1] Livy (P) XXXIII, 19, 1–5.   [2] Cf. Holleaux, *CAH*, VIII, 178–9.

[3] Polyb. XXX, 31, 6; Livy (P) XXXIII, 20, 12; cf. (P) XXXVII, 16, 2.

[4] Iasus (and so probably the other towns; cf. Heuss, *Stadt und Herrscher*, 220; 230, n. 1) was nominally freed (*OGIS*, 237); but it received a Syrian garrison (Livy (P) XXXVII, 17, 3). For Ephesus see Polyb. XVIII, 41 A.

[5] Livy (P) XXXIII, 38, 4.

[6] *Syll.* 591; cf. Holleaux, *REA*, XVIII, 1916, 1 *seq.*; Bickermann, *Philol.* LXXXVII, 1932, 277–99.

[7] Livy (A) XXXIII, 24, 5; cf. Polyb. XVIII, 42, 1 (inaccurate over-compression, cf. Niese, II, 646, n. 2).

[8] It is clear from Polybius that the final ratification was not left to Philip and the ten commissioners; cf. Larsen, *CP*, XXXI, 1936, 342–8.

[9] Cf. Polyb. XVIII, 38, 2.

various clauses, and of any other outstanding problems, such as
the Messenian claim for Asine and Pylus against the Achaeans,
or that of the Eleans for Triphylia,[1] a commission of ten senators
was set up, and given a *senatus consultum* defining in general
terms its joint duties along with Flamininus.[2]

For the latter the winter was mainly distinguished by a series
of unfortunate incidents in Boeotia. While in winter quarters at
Elatea,[3] Flamininus had received a Boeotian request to secure
from Macedon the return of Brachylles and the other Boeotians
serving with Philip; and because he saw in Boeotia a possible
centre of disaffection he undertook this office, hoping to win
favour. To his annoyance, the Boeotians promptly elected the
pro-Macedonian Brachylles Boeotarch and sent their thanks not
to Flamininus, but to Philip.[4] The reply of the pro-Roman party
in Boeotia was to plot with Flamininus and the Aetolian general,
Alexamenus, to secure the murder of Brachylles. In the outcry
that followed this outrage, Peisistratus, one of the leaders of the
party, was executed, though his colleague Zeuxippus escaped.
More important, a widespread massacre of Romans, claiming
500 victims, took place throughout Boeotia; and when the heavy
reparations demanded by Flamininus—500 talents and the surrender of those guilty—were not forthcoming, the proconsul
invaded the country. However, on the appeal of the Achaeans,
the indemnity was reduced to thirty talents, and the incident
was smoothed over.[5]

Shortly after these happenings, which must have been particularly galling to Philip, in view of the longstanding friendship
between his family and that of Brachylles,[6] the Senatorial
Commission reached Elatea, with the decree of the Senate.

---

[1] Polyb. xviii, 42, 6–8; the Achaeans were seeking a formal alliance with
Rome; on the other claim (that of Aetolia to Heraea) see above, p. 17, n. 2.
De Sanctis, iv, 1, 104, n. 207, suggests a mistake of Polybius or his epitomator for 'Phigaleia'; however, Livy certainly read Heraea (cf. Livy (P)
xxxiii, 34, 9) and such an error is very difficult to explain. There is no
evidence that Aetolia ever possessed Heraea; but Philip may have promised
her the town in the peace of 206, without intending to hand it over—just as
he promised it in 208 to Achaea.

[2] Polyb. xviii, 42, 5; cf. 44, 1: τὸ τῆς συγκλήτου ⟨δόγμα⟩.

[3] Polyb. xviii, 43, 1; cf. Livy (P) xxxiii, 27, 5.

[4] Polyb. xviii, 43, 1–4; Livy (P) xxxiii, 27, 5–9.

[5] Polyb. xviii, 43, 5–13; Livy (P) xxxiii, 27, 10–29, 12.

[6] Cf. Polyb. xx, 5, 13.

This document,[1] which has frequently, but erroneously, been identified with the actual peace treaty, contained, in fact, a number of clauses regulating the application of that treaty. Its importance lay, politically, in the fact that the Roman claim to organise the affairs of Greece, and to secure Greek freedom, made originally in the ultimatum at Athens, was now substantiated; even for the fulfilment of those clauses that concern the allies, Philip is in the main responsible directly to the Senate.

The document opened with a general statement that all the Greeks of Asia and Europe, not included in Philip's domains, were to be free.[2] Secondly, the cities and fortresses that Philip had held were to be handed over to the Romans in accordance with the treaty, before the Isthmian Games. Thirdly, as an exception to clause two, the towns of Euromus, Pedasa, Bargylia, Iasus, Sestus, Abydus, Thasos, Myrina and Hephaestia on Lemnos, and Perinthus were to have their Macedonian garrisons withdrawn, leaving them free;[3] and, as an appendix to this, Flamininus was to negotiate with Prusias for the freedom of Cius. Fourthly, all prisoners and deserters were also to be handed over before the Isthmia.[4] Finally, advantage was taken of Philip's agreement to leave the final settlement in the Senate's hands, to impose upon him certain additional burdens; his fleet, with the exception of five light ships and one large warship (a 'Hekkaidekeres' dating back to the time of Demetrius Poliorcetes),[5] was to be surrendered to the Romans before the Isthmia, and he

[1] Polyb. XVIII, 44; Livy (P) XXXIII, 30; Appian, *Maced.* 9, 3; Plut. *Flam.* 10, 1; Justin. XXX, 4, 17; Zon. IX, 16. See Niese, II, 648; De Sanctis, IV, 1, 95, n. 185; Nissen, 146 *seq.*; Täubler, I, 228 *seq.*; Holleaux, *CAH*, VIII, 180; *Rev. Phil.* LVII, 1931, 1 *seq.*; Klotz, *Hermes*, L, 1915, 481 *seq.*; Larsen, *CP*, XXXI, 1936, 342–8; Aymard, *Premiers Rapports*, 272–87. The terms of the *senatus consultum* are best set out by Täubler, *loc. cit.*

[2] Not merely 'those states now occupied by Philip, for which specific arrangements were not made' (Larsen's interpretation, *CP*, XXXI, 1936, 345).

[3] Polybius omits Sestus and Hephaestia (cf. Polyb. XVIII, 2, 4; 48, 2); Stratonicaea was already in Rhodian hands (see above, p. 177) and is therefore omitted. But of the other towns in Asia Minor, which are mentioned, only Bargylia was now in Philip's hands (Polyb. XVIII, 48, 1; cf. Livy (P) XXXIII, 35, 2). Hence this clause of the *senatus consultum* is to be regarded as directed mainly against Antiochus.

[4] It is uncertain whether allied, as well as Roman, deserters and prisoners are indicated.

[5] Cf. Plut. *Demet.* 20, 7; 43, 5. For the history of this ship see Tarn, *Hellen. Mil. and Nav. Developments*, 133, n. 5.

was to pay an indemnity of 1000 talents, half at once and the rest in ten yearly instalments.[1]

This document did not set out to cover every clause in the treaty. Thus there is no reference to the ceding of Illyria, since this was no doubt already in Roman hands. On the other hand, Polybius only claims to give τὰ συνέχοντα τοῦ δόγματος (XVIII, 44, 2), and certain details seem to be omitted. Lysimacheia had already been evacuated and was by this time in Thracian hands;[2] but the omission of any reference to Aenus, Maronea and the other Ptolemaic possessions, later visited by L. Stertinius,[3] suggests that our text has lost a clause dealing with the cities that had formerly been Ptolemy's. It is strange, too, that there is no mention of the payment of reparations to Eumenes (who had recently succeeded his father Attalus); Larsen suggests[4] that Attalus's captured ships are included in the clause demanding the surrender of Philip's navy, but as there is no reference to the restoration of the Pergamene temples either, it seems more likely that here too a clause has been lost.

The moment the Senate's decree was published, the Aetolians seized upon a very definite and grave omission. Philip's remaining possessions in Greece, Demetrias, Chalcis and Corinth —the old 'fetters of Greece'—together with Oreus and Eretria, were to be handed over, in accordance with the treaty and the *senatus consultum*, to the Romans. But, the Aetolians argued, the Senate had not announced that they were to be free: were they then merely to exchange one tyranny for another? And had the Romans unshackled the feet of the Greeks only to put a collar around their neck?[5]

It was in this atmosphere of recrimination that Flamininus and the Commissioners reached Corinth. Here the problem of the 'fetters' was discussed at length. In view of the Syrian question, the Commissioners had been given an open mandate, but Flamininus, who urged that it would be no defence against

---

[1] The further clauses in Livy, XXXIII, 30, 6; 8–11, are recognised to be annalistic falsifications; see Nissen, 145, and De Sanctis, IV, 1, 96, n. 185.

[2] Polyb. XVIII, 4, 5; 51, 7.

[3] Polyb. XVIII, 48, 2; Livy (P) XXXIII, 35, 2.   [4] *CP*, XXXI, 1936, 346.

[5] Polyb. XVIII, 45, 1–6; Livy (P) XXXIII, 31, 1–3; Plut. *Flam.* 10, 1–2. Polybius's reference to Oreus and Eretria is perhaps a mistake; see above, p. 155, n. 6.

Antiochus to leave the Aetolians in a position to make capital out of their complaints, won his colleagues over to the policy of complete evacuation. That Flamininus's tactlessness and pride had already rendered the Aetolians unwilling to be placated by any such concessions, was a misfortune for which Rome was later to pay in full. Meanwhile the town of Corinth was handed at once to the Achaeans; the three fortresses proper were reserved for a more sensational pronouncement.[1]

The declaration, made at the Isthmus, with all the theatrical trimmings calculated to impress the multitude and bring glory to Flamininus, was in essentials the reaffirmation of the policy of a free Greece, which Rome had propounded in 200. It ran: 'The Roman Senate and T. Quinctius the proconsul, having conquered King Philip and the Macedonians, leave free, without garrisons, liable to no tribute and subject to the laws of their countries, the Corinthians, Phocians, Locrians, Euboeans, Phthiotic Achaeans, Magnesians, Thessalians and Perrhaebians.'[2] This proclamation, which automatically included the 'fetters', was greeted with unprecedented enthusiasm: it was followed by the less sensational work of putting the new system into operation.

To the representatives of the various states the Commissioners now proceeded to announce their decisions for the organisation of the territories that had belonged to Philip. Macedonia itself remained untouched, except for Orestis, which received its independence.[3] In Thessaly, the Perrhaebians and Magnesians were shorn from the central state and shortly afterwards constituted as separate leagues; Dolopia was also separated, but joined the Aetolian confederacy. Phthiotic Achaea was left as part of Thessaly, with the exception of Thebes and Pharsalus, the fate of which, in response to the vehement claims of Aetolia, was referred to the Senate. Shortly afterwards, Thessaly (including Achaea) was constituted as a league, like the other Thessalian

[1] Polyb. XVIII, 45, 7–12; Livy (P) XXXIII, 31, 4–11. On the somewhat 'doctrinaire' attitude of Flamininus, who insisted on fulfilling Roman undertakings to the letter, perhaps at the expense of the security which the war had been fought to obtain, see the acute observations of McDonald, *JRS*, XXVIII, 1938, 155.

[2] Polyb. XVIII, 46; Livy (P) XXXIII, 32–3; Plut. *Flam.* 10–11; Appian, *Maced.* 9, 4; Val. Max. IV, 8, 5.

[3] Polyb. XVIII, 47, 6; Livy (P) XXXIII, 34, 6. It had revolted in winter 198–7; see above, p. 163, n. 2.

provinces. It was evidently the Roman policy to hinder the formation of a strong, independent state in Thessaly, which, in combination with Aetolia or Macedon, might tilt the delicate balance which it was the Senate's object to establish.[1]

Farther south, Phocis and eastern Locris were assigned to the Aetolians;[2] Achaea was confirmed in her possession of Corinth, Triphylia and Heraea;[3] and the Euboean cities including Carystus (and also Oreus and Eretria, which the Senate later freed against the proposal of some of the Commissioners to award them to Eumenes) were reformed into another league.[4] Finally, on the western frontiers of Macedon, Pleuratus was granted the districts round Lake Lychnidus,[5] and Amynander allowed to keep the forts he had taken from Philip.[6] The town of Leucas, though claimed by Aetolia, was awarded to the Acarnanians, who, like the Achaeans, probably became official allies of Rome.[7]

---

[1] Polyb. XVIII, 47, 6–8; Livy (P) XXXIII, 34, 6–7. On the Leagues see Niese, II, 653, nn. 1–4; Kip, 111 seq. (Perrhaebians); Holleaux, REG, X, 1897, 304 seq. (= I, 256 seq.); Kip, 87 seq. (Magnesia); De Sanctis, IV, I, 102, nn. 200–1. Thebes went to Aetolia (Salvetti, 124; questioned by Flacelière, 349 and n. 3), but the Senate referred the question of Pharsalus to Flamininus; the Aetolians do not seem to have received it (Livy (P) XXXIV, 23, 7; XXXVI, 10, 9), and perhaps it became a free city, separate both from the Thessalian League and Macedonia (Henze, De civitatibus liberis, Diss. Berlin, 1892, 29; Stählin, 137). The Aetolians may also have kept Thaumaci and one or two such frontier posts as Xyniae and Cyphaera; cf. Flacelière, 349, n. 2.

[2] GDI, 1983; 2125; 1969 (Phocis); cf. Daux, 224. The part of Locris around Larymna and Halae was left, by exception, to Boeotia; cf. Klaffenbach, Klio, XX, 1926, 83.

[3] Polyb. XVIII, 47, 10; Livy (P) XXXIII, 34, 9. For the claims of Elis to Triphylia and of Aetolia to Heraea (Phigaleia?) see above, p. 178, n. 1. Asine and Pylus were probably awarded to Achaea too; see Head, 418, for Achaean coins from Asine.

[4] Polyb. XVIII, 47, 10–11; Livy (P) XXXIII, 34, 10. See Niese, II, 653; De Sanctis, IV, I, 103, n. 203.

[5] Polyb. XVIII, 47, 12; Livy (P) XXXIII, 34, 11. Polybius states that Pleuratus also received Πάρθον, which Livy translates by Parthini; it is, however, improbable that Philip possessed the Parthini, who were ceded to Rome at Phoenice, or that, if he had in fact recovered this territory, for example, in the autumn of 200 against Apustius, the Romans would now have granted this once Roman province to Pleuratus. See above, p. 103, n. 4. Zippel, 77–8, puts both Λυχνίδα and Πάρθον in northern Illyria (contra Fluss, P-W, 'Lychnidus', col. 2112).

[6] Polyb. XVIII, 47, 13; Livy (P) XXXIII, 34, 11. These forts are given as Aeginium, Ericinium (perhaps = Eritium: see below, p. 202, n. 3), Gomphi, Silana, Tricca, Meliboea and Phaloria (Livy (P) XXXVI, 13, 6).

[7] On the granting of a foedus to Achaea see Holleaux, REG, XXXIV, 1921, 400–22 (date 196: refuting Täubler, 219–28); Horn, 33 seq. (date uncertain); Larsen, CP, XXX, 1935, 212–14 (date uncertain); Aymard, Premiers Rapports, 261–7 (probably 194–3).

These arrangements completed, the Commissioners separated and went to supervise their carrying out in the various districts. Thus P. Lentulus sailed to Bargylia, and L. Stertinius visited Thasos, Hephaestia on Lemnos, and the Thracian coastal cities, to attend to their liberation. A final interview also took place, about the beginning of September, in Tempe, between Philip and Cn. Cornelius, one of the Commissioners. The king was informed of the Senate's arrangements and advised to send to Rome to ask for an alliance, so as to leave no room for doubting his goodwill, advice which Philip at once adopted.[1] Cornelius then went on to the Aetolian autumn meeting at Thermum, and after hearing further complaints, urged the assembly to send an embassy to Rome—a course which was followed without any substantial advantage being obtained.[2]

For Philip the war was now over. It had established Rome as the decisive influence in the peninsula, and had cut down the kingdom of Macedon to its original bounds. Thessaly was a group of self-governing, hostile leagues, Orestis was independent, and the Great Lakes once more formed the western frontier of Macedon.[3] To the east, Abdera was again the limit of Philip's realm, and his overseas possessions in Asia Minor and the Aegean had all vanished. His fleet too, useless though it had proved, had been confiscated under the Senate's decree; the authorities at Rome had not forgotten the apparent threat of 201, after Philip's victory at Lade. True, since 200, this fleet had been confined in Demetrias, leaving the initiative by sea completely to the superior fleets of Rome and her allies; in fact, the war at sea had been of such little consequence that no records of it survive at all for the year 197. Perhaps Cythnos and Paros, which had resisted the Rhodians in 200, were now at last taken by the allies; certainly the mass of the Cyclades had by this time thrown off the Macedonian yoke.[4] None the less it was the Senate's policy to allow

---

[1] Polyb. XVIII, 48, 1–5; Livy (P) XXXIII, 35, 1–7; (A) 44, 16. De Sanctis, IV, 1, 105, n. 213, doubts whether Philip obtained full *societas*, or merely came to an arrangement to give military assistance; in the circumstances of 196, the former seems by far the more probable; cf. Heuss, 37; Aymard, *Premiers Rapports*, 219, n. 24.

[2] The complaints were referred back to Flamininus, who took no steps to placate the League (Livy (A) XXXIII, 49, 8; (P) XXXIV, 23, 7).

[3] On the position of this frontier see Zippel, 75–6.

[4] See above, p. 130, n. 4. Cythnos had been attacked again in 199 (Livy (P) XXXI, 45, 9).

not even the ghost of a challenge to its naval superiority,[1] and it had the foresight to confiscate the bulk of what ships were left to Philip after the battle of Chios. Henceforth Macedon, the important source of pitch and timber, was a realm without a fleet.

Philip's behaviour under these new conditions was in marked contrast to his wild policy of the years immediately preceding the war. By his outrageous breach of all forms of international law during his suicidal career of 205–200, and even in his fool-hardy neglect of the ultimatum presented to Nicanor at Athens, Philip had brought down on himself the full weight of the Roman legions. But after Cynoscephalae he displayed sound statesman-ship, by subordinating his private feelings—and his loathing of Rome must now have been a hundred times greater than before—to the necessity of salvaging whatever he could by placating the Senate. How far this change from the years when he had sacri-ficed advantage after advantage to mere passion and caprice is to be connected with the fall of Heracleides, it is impossible to say; certainly the decline of his influence is a factor easy to underestimate.

Both militarily and diplomatically Philip had shown himself inferior to Flamininus. Twice on the field, at Antigoneia and Cynoscephalae (where the superior flexibility of the legion, as against the phalanx, had been triumphantly demonstrated),[2] and once in conference at Nicaea, Philip had paid the price of being outwitted by his opponent; but fundamentally his mistake was ever to accept the Roman challenge. Once the war had started, it had only been a question of how long he could hold out.

And now Philip's immediate need was to repair his kingdom and by close co-operation with the Senate to build up a force capable of playing an active part in the coming clash between Rome and Syria. Towards Antiochus Philip must have felt both dislike and resentment; that contrast which had been so marked in 205 was doubly accentuated now by his rival's victorious advance and his own crushing defeat. As he saw the Syrian fleet and army approaching the Hellespont, and Antiochus's eyes

[1] See Griffith, *CHJ*, v, 1935, 11 *seq.*
[2] Cf. Tarn, *Hellen. Mil. and Nav. Developments*, 29.

directed towards Europe, Philip's jealousy must have turned to a hatred which he could only store up against the time when the breach with Rome widened into war.

Meanwhile, Philip's policy of collaboration with the Senate robbed him of his initiative of action. For a number of years he was to play a minor role in events, the motive force behind which lay elsewhere. For Philip it must have been a difficult and galling part, but on it for the time being rested the only hope of reconstructing Macedon; its main disadvantage, politically, lay in the fact that it depended for its success so entirely on external factors, on Antiochus's merits as a diplomatist, and, above all, on the arbitrary decisions of the Roman Senate.

Chapter VI : Collaboration

THE ROMANS AGAINST ANTIOCHUS
(196–188)

So long as Philip was still in arms, the Senate had continued to treat Antiochus with consideration; an embassy sent by him to Rome in 198 had returned with the usual decrees and pledges of friendship the following spring.[1] But after Cynoscephalae the Roman attitude underwent a decided change; for in spite of the assurances brought back in 199 by Lepidus and his colleagues, Antiochus's advance in Asia Minor had thoroughly alarmed the Senate. Accordingly, when Syrian envoys presented themselves at the Council of Corinth in 196,[2] an opportunity was taken to send word that Antiochus was to keep his hands off those towns that were autonomous (such as Smyrna and Lampsacus), and to withdraw from whatever towns of Philip and Ptolemy he had occupied; further, he was to refrain from crossing over into Europe with an army, since the Greeks were now guaranteed against attack. The Commissioners also stated that they would send an ambassador to his court.

Meanwhile Antiochus himself had already crossed over into the Chersonese, where city after city readily accepted his garrisons;[3] Lysimacheia was restored and its old inhabitants brought back; and an expedition was undertaken against the Thracians before Antiochus returned to this fortress about October, to meet the Roman representatives.[4] The interview was a diplomatic triumph for the king. To the Roman claim that he should surrender the cities that had belonged to Ptolemy or Philip, and refrain from attacking those that were autonomous, Antiochus replied by challenging their right to speak for the towns of Asia: let the Romans leave him to mind his own business in Asia as he left them to mind theirs in Italy; the Chersonese he claimed

---

[1] Livy (P) xxx, 20, 8; cf. Holleaux, *REA*, xv, 1913, 2 *seq.*
[2] Polyb. xviii, 47, 1; Livy (P) xxxiii, 34, 2–3.
[3] Livy (P) xxxiii, 38, 8–9; Appian, *Syr.* i.
[4] Polyb. xviii, 49, 1–50, 3; Livy (P) xxxiii, 38, 10–39, 2.

as part of the territory of his ancestor, Seleucus Nicator;[1] and as for Ptolemy, he had only just concluded a marriage alliance with him!

Somewhat taken aback, the Romans sought to shift the ground of the discussion by calling in the representatives of Smyrna and Lampsacus; but Antiochus, stating that on this question he would accept Rhodian, not Roman arbitration, broke up the conference. When the rumour of Epiphanes's death, which had influenced him in this course, proved to be false,[2] he returned to Antioch, and in the winter of 196–5 sent a further embassy to Flamininus, to propose an alliance; it was referred to Rome, but probably went straight back to Antiochus instead.[3] Clearly neither side was anxious for war; but from Pella, Philip must have watched with interest and amusement how a combination of the Senate's nervousness—the characteristic which had proved his own undoing—and Antiochus's persistence in what he judged to be his rights, was leading inevitably to the conflict, in which he hoped to justify his present distasteful policy of co-operation with Rome.

Meanwhile, in Greece, the outstanding problem of Argos offered the chance to settle a private score.[4] By his agreement with Nabis, Flamininus had virtually recognised the latter's right over Argos; on the other hand, to leave the town in his hands was out of the question. If Flamininus's proclamation at the Isthmus was to count for anything, and the Achaeans were not to be driven over to the side of his Aetolian critics, Argos must be allowed to join the Achaean League as a free state. Further, a powerful Nabis might renew the old Aetolian alliance, and become a dangerous factor in the new eastern question. Accordingly, the whole matter was referred to the Senate by the Commissioners, who returned to Rome in autumn, 196;[5] but the Senate decided to leave the solution to the discretion

[1] This claim, it is argued, was a just one by Hellenistic international law; cf. Bickermann, *Hermes*, LXVII, 1932, 50–3 (not adequately refuted by Heuss, *Stadt und Herrscher*, 227, n. 1; cf. also Magie, *Buckler Studies*, 168, n. 1).
[2] Livy (P) XXXIII, 41, 1–9; Polyb. XVIII, 52; Appian, *Syr.* 4.
[3] Livy (P) XXXIII, 41, 5; XXXIV, 25, 2. On the date see below, Appendix III, pp. 325–6.
[4] On the war against Nabis see Aymard, *Premiers Rapports*, 184–247.
[5] For the date see below, Appendix III, p. 324.

of Flamininus,[1] whose command was extended for a further year.

After a winter spent in reorganisation[2] the proconsul summoned the allies to Corinth to discuss the question of Argos; and, except for the Aetolians, who regarded the whole scheme as a Roman pretext for prolonging their occupation, they decided to declare war on Nabis, if he did not surrender the town.[3] In the subsequent campaign[4] Nabis had little or no chance; faced by an army of some 27,000 men, he offered a stout resistance, but after an attempt at negotiation, which failed, perhaps because Nabis saw that the terms Flamininus proposed were the maximum he cared to inflict,[5] he was compelled to surrender, as an alternative to seeing Sparta sacked. A truce was made on the terms suggested, and when these were carried out, the allied forces withdrew.[6] The coastal towns which Nabis surrendered were put under the Achaeans;[7] and at the subsequent Nemean games, Argos was declared free, and reunited with the Achaean League.[8] This done, Flamininus returned to winter quarters at Elatea, to continue the work of establishing Roman influence in the new leagues, and ejecting the supporters of Macedon.[9] And

---

[1] Livy (A) XXXIII, 45, 3; (P) XXXIV, 32, 5; Justin. XXXI, 1, 5–6. Here the annalistic version is preferable to the Polybian; cf. Nissen, 157; De Sanctis, IV, 1, 105. For the alarm at Rome, at the possibility of a Sparto-Aetolo-Syrian alliance, see Livy (A) XXXIII, 43, 6; 44, 5.

[2] Livy (P) XXXIV, 22, 4. The new leagues in Thessaly and Euboea probably now began to function (see above, pp. 181–2).

[3] Livy (P) XXXIV, 22, 6–24, 7.

[4] Livy (P) XXXIV, 26, 11–41, 7; Plut. *Flam.* 13, 1–4; Zon. IX, 18; Diod. XXVIII, 13; Justin. XXXI, 3, 1; Auct. *de vir. ill.* 51, 3. See Niese, II, 655–63; Mundt, 50 *seq.*; De Sanctis, IV, 1, 105; Holleaux, *CAH*, VIII, 188–91.

[5] Livy (P) XXXIV, 35, 2 *seq.*; Nabis was to hand over Argos to the Romans within ten days; restore their slaves to the Argives, and their ships to the maritime towns; reduce his navy to two sixteen-oared *lembi*; restore all prisoners and deserters; compensate the Messenians for his attack in 201; restore their wives and children to the Spartan exiles; restore their property to any mercenaries who had gone over to the allies; sever relations with Crete and hand over any towns he possessed there to Rome; refrain from any hostilities or the establishment of any kind of armed force abroad; give five hostages including his own son; and pay an indemnity of 500 talents, 100 now and the rest in eight yearly instalments. See further, Aymard, *Premiers Rapports*, 244–5. [6] Polyb. XXI, 3, 4; Livy (P) XXXIV, 52, 9.

[7] Livy (P) XXXV, 13, 2; XXXVIII, 31, 2. The exact status of these towns within the League is uncertain: see De Sanctis, IV, 1, 110, n. 224; Niccolini, 131, n. 1; Aymard, *Premiers Rapports*, 252; A. Gitti, *Rend. Linc.* s. VI, XV, 1939, 189–203.

[8] Livy (P) XXXIV, 40, 5–41, 7; Plut. *Flam.* 12 (inaccurate).

[9] Livy (P) XXXIV, 41, 7; 48, 2; cf. *Syll.* 593, for a letter from Flamininus to Chyretiae, dating from about this period.

meanwhile, at Rome, the peace with Nabis was ratified,[1] and, notwithstanding the opposition of Scipio Africanus, who in view of the threat from Antiochus wanted Macedonia as his province, it was decided to withdraw from Greece the following summer.[2]

Apart from sending 1500 troops—his first action as a Roman ally[3]—Philip had played no part in the summer's events; but he had no reason to be dissatisfied with the course they had taken. Not only had he assisted in the humiliation of the faithless Nabis, but to the irritation of the Aetolians he now saw added the resentment of the Achaeans, that Nabis should still possess his throne.[4] Still more important was the news brought by P. Villius to Flamininus at the time of the first negotiations with Nabis—news that had been a decisive factor in persuading the proconsul to come to terms. Antiochus had once more crossed over into Thrace, to operate against the native tribes and annex the Greek cities on the Pontus;[5] and, upon his return to Ephesus, he had been joined by Hannibal himself, now a refugee from Carthage and the machinations of the Senate.[6] To Philip, of course, Antiochus's material successes must have been bitter; but the collapse of negotiations between Syria and Rome, and the drift towards war, now accentuated by the presence of Hannibal, were creating a situation from which he could reasonably hope to profit.

The following spring (194), in a final speech to the representatives of the allies at Corinth, Flamininus gave his reasons for sparing Nabis, announced the forthcoming evacuation of Chalcis and Demetrias, and handed over the Acrocorinth to the Achaeans; in conclusion, he appealed for the ransoming of any Roman prisoners of war from Carthage, who were slaves in Greece.[7] Then, sending his army direct to Oricus, he himself made a

---

[1] Livy (A) xxxiv, 43, 1–2.

[2] Livy (A) xxxiv, 43, 3–8 (cf. Nissen, 160); Diod. xxviii, 13; Justin. xxxi, 3, 2.

[3] Livy (P) xxxiv, 25, 1–26, 10.   [4] Livy (P) xxxiv, 40, 4.

[5] Livy (P) xxxiv, 33, 12; Appian, *Syr.* 6; on the chronology see below, Appendix iii, p. 326. Appian runs the two summers' campaigns into one.

[6] Livy (P) xxxiii, 49, 5–8. See Holleaux, *CAH*, viii, 191–2; *Hermes*, xliii, 1908, 296–9. It was this news that moved Scipio to demand that Macedon remain a province.

[7] Livy (P) xxxiv, 48, 3–50, 11; Plut. *Flam.* 13, 6–8; Diod. xxviii, 13; Val. Max. v, 2, 6. The Achaeans alone spent 100 talents on redeeming prisoners.

detour through Chalcis and Demetrias into Thessaly, where he set up a government of oligarchic bias, having previously weeded out all pro-Macedonian elements as 'scum'.[1] He then rejoined his forces at Oricus, and transported them back to Brundisium, loaded with every kind of plunder, taken mainly from the Thessalian cities that had been Philip's.[2] The spoils exhibited at Flamininus's triumph were some indication of the price paid by Philip and the Greeks for Roman intervention: there were arms of all kinds, bronze and marble statues, 43,270 pounds of unwrought silver, various *objets d'art* including ten silver shields, 84,000 coined Attic tetradrachms, 3714 pounds of gold, 14,514 'philippi' and 114 golden crowns (given by the cities), a sum amounting in all to over 1200 Euboean talents,[3] and extracted mainly from Thessaly, Phocis, Euboea and Laconia. In the triumphal procession there marched as hostages Armenes, the son of Nabis, and Demetrius, the younger son of Philip.[4]

The same summer Antiochus again invaded Thrace, and, continuing his advance, subdued a number of cities along the north shore of the Aegean as far west as Aenus and Maronea, and took steps to secure the friendship of Byzantium and the Danubian Celts.[5] Though this brought his frontiers close to Macedon, Philip wisely made no move; that winter, however, (194–3) when the Senate had the task of ratifying Flamininus's *acta*, he despatched envoys to Rome.[6] These found themselves in the company of representatives of most of the Greek states[7] affected by the new dispensation, and an embassy consisting of Menippus, Lysias and Hegesianax, whom Antiochus had sent to ask for an alliance; an incidental commission held by Menippus,

---

[1] Livy (P) xxxiv, 51, 4–6: *civitates...ex omni colluvione et confusione in aliquam tolerabilem formam redigendae*; cf. Plut. *Flam.* 12, 4; *Syll.* 674, lines 51–4.

[2] Livy (P) xxxiv, 52, 5; xlv, 39, 1; Plut. *Flam.* 14, 1–3; Val. Max. v, 2, 6; Cic. *pro Murena*, 14, 31; *in Pisonem*, 25, 61.

[3] De Sanctis, iv, 1, 112. It is possible, however, that this figure included the 930 talents already collected as indemnity from Philip (200, 500, 50, 50 talents), Nabis (100 talents) and Boeotia (30 talents); cf. Larsen, *Economic Survey of Ancient Rome*, iv, 317–18.

[4] Livy (P) xxxiv, 52, 9.

[5] Appian, *Syr.* 6 (see above, p. 189, n. 5). Were the Byzantines given additional territory? Βυζαντίοις ἐχαρίζετο πολλά, ὡς ἐπίκαιρον ἐπὶ τοῦ στόματος πόλιν ἔχουσι.

[6] Diod. xxviii, 15; cf. Livy (P) xxxv, 31, 5.

[7] Livy (A) xxxiv, 57, 1–3; Diod. xxviii, 15; Appian, *Syr.* 6.

to ask the Senate to grant immunity to the town of Teos, suggests that the Teians at least expected the embassy to be well received.[1]

However, if Antiochus genuinely desired the Senate's friendship (having now reached the frontiers he had proposed), his opponents still clung to the nervous policy that had driven them into war with Philip. As in 201, they had friends at Pergamum, who had every reason to mistrust Antiochus's plan to re-establish the traditional frontiers of Syria. There is no record that Eumenes actually intrigued with the Senate; it seems probable, however, that his messengers, and perhaps Philip's too, kept the Romans closely informed on Antiochus's movements, and supplemented the information which their own officers would naturally send, so long as Flamininus was in Greece. But, whatever their information, the Senate showed themselves unexpectedly friendly towards the Greeks and Philip. Indeed, provided he gave the Romans his full support, the latter was promised the return of his son Demetrius, and the cancellation of the outstanding part of his tribute; and, in addition, whether by hints or direct promises, he was led to entertain hopes of recovering Magnesia, with the key fortress of Demetrias.[2]

The reception given to the Syrian envoys was in marked contrast.[3] To Flamininus and the ten Commissioners, who on the Senate's instructions received the embassy, Menippus's proposals that the Roman people should strike an alliance with Antiochus, and abandon their claim to arbitrate on the freedom of the Greek cities in Asia, seemed to confirm all the Senate's suspicions. Hence, like the reply of Lepidus to Philip in 200, that of Flamininus made only the thinnest pretence to justice: in the illogicality of its two alternatives it revealed the spirit of self-preservation which actuated Roman policy. If Antiochus would withdraw from Europe, the Senate would not press its claims in respect to the cities of Asia: alternatively, he might continue to operate in Thrace, in which case the Romans retained their right to act on behalf of these cities. Though, in fact,

[1] *Syll.* 601; cf. Holleaux, *Klio*, XIII, 1913, 158–9.
[2] Livy (P) xxxv, 31, 5; Diod. xxviii, 15.
[3] Livy (P) xxxiv, 57, 4–59, 3; Appian, *Syr.* 6; Diod. xxviii, 15. For once, Diodorus gives the more reliable version of Flamininus's reply; cf. Holleaux, *REA*, xv, 1913, 18.

a slight withdrawal from the demands made at Lysimacheia, the alternatives were none the less intolerable; in effect, they were a demand for the evacuation of Thrace, and the envoys naturally declined to consider friendship on such a basis. The most Menippus could do was to induce the Senate to send an embassy to interview Antiochus; and the Senate, by no means anxious to force the issue, appointed P. Sulpicius, P. Villius and P. Aelius to this office.[1]

In Greece, meanwhile, a more bellicose spirit was already apparent. Breaking their journey in Aetolia,[2] the returning Syrian envoys found the war party in power, with Thoas, one of its leaders, general for 194–3.[3] The Aetolians had hoped to have Philip deposed and their League rendered the most powerful force in Greece: instead they saw Philip still reigning at Pella and the Romans beginning to promise him concessions, while they themselves had gained little but Dolopia. Thessaly, with its independent leagues set up under Roman patronage, was now effectively placed beyond their grasp; and meanwhile peace was putting its usual strain upon the economy of a people who lived largely on plunder. At a meeting at Naupactus (193), the new leaders took a decisive step; they would build up a coalition to throw off the Roman yoke. And to this end they despatched Damocritus to Nabis, Dicaearchus, the general's brother, to Antiochus, and Nicander to Philip.[4]

With a ready response, Nabis set about the recovery of the coastal towns of which Flamininus had deprived him. The Achaeans were thus obliged to throw reinforcements into Gytheum (to which Nabis laid siege during the winter of 193–2); they also sent complaints to Rome.[5] Philip, however, proved less susceptible: references to the magnitude of his fall, to the

---

[1] Livy (P) xxxiv, 59, 4–8; Appian, *Syr.* 9; Polyb. III, 11, 1 *seq.*; Justin. xxxi, 4, 4. Appian includes Scipio Africanus in this embassy, and the story of an interview between him and Hannibal is also in Livy (A) xxxv, 14; Plut. *Flam.* 21, 3–5; and *Pyrrh.* 8, 5; Appian, *Syr.* 10. Nissen, 168–9, puts Scipio's embassy in 192, but Holleaux claims (*Hermes*, XLVIII, 1913, 75 *seq.*) that if the incident occurred it was in 193; it is, however, probably to be rejected as apocryphal (De Sanctis, IV, 1, 131, n. 47; Leuze, *Hermes*, LVIII, 1923, 247–68).

[2] Hegesianax was 'proxenos' at Delphi in 193; cf. *Syll.* 585, line 40.

[3] Livy (P) xxxv, 12, 1–2.   [4] Livy (P) xxxv, 12, 1–6.

[5] Livy (P) xxxv, 12, 7–9; 13, 1–3. On the chronology of Nabis's outbreak and the siege of Gytheum see below, Appendix III, p. 327.

past triumphs of the Macedonian people and the might of Hannibal, now adviser at the court of Syria, and the suggestion that he should leave the initiative to Antiochus merely demonstrated the tactlessness of Aetolian diplomacy. Philip, who disliked the Aetolians, could scarcely relish hearing Nicander elaborate upon his losses and urge him to give his support to two rivals, both of whom had failed him in time of need. Moreover, his latest reports from Rome suggested the approaching success of his policy of collaboration. Therefore, although Nicander apparently made a good personal impression upon him, Philip declined to take part in the Aetolian scheme.[1] This did not, however, prevent Dicaearchus from later assuring Antiochus that he had the support of both Philip and Nabis.[2]

Meanwhile the Roman ambassadors reached Asia Minor. From Pergamum, where Eumenes strongly urged a policy of war, two of them went on to interview Hannibal at Ephesus, and from there Villius continued to Apamea, whither Antiochus (who had just celebrated the marriage of his daughter Cleopatra to Ptolemy Epiphanes)[3] now brought his court. However, the sudden death of Antiochus's son suspended negotiations; and it was some time before they were resumed, at Ephesus, this time not by Antiochus, but by his counsellor, Minnio.[4] The meeting proved as abortive as the previous ones; there was a total lack of understanding of the principles on which the Syrian claim was based. Minnio drew a shrewd but tactless analogy between Smyrna and Lampsacus in Asia and the Greek cities of south Italy and Sicily, and explained that it was on the right of conquest by his ancestors, not abrogated by the interval of *de facto* independence, that Antiochus based his claim. To this Sulpicius made a lame reply, and, following the precedent of Lysimacheia, called in various Greek embassies to make their

---

[1] Livy (P) xxxv, 12, 10–14: Philip's reply is unrecorded, but may be deduced from his later conduct and the statement that, in claiming to have his support, Dicaearchus *libero mendacio abutebatur*. That Nicander created a favourable impression is suggested by his later treatment at Philip's hands: Polyb. xx, 11; Livy (P) xxxvi, 29, 5–11; Zon. ix, 19, 13.

[2] Livy (P) xxxv, 12, 15–18.

[3] Livy (P) xxxv, 13, 4–14, 4; for the dangerous position in which Eumenes was placed see Livy (P) xxxix, 28, 5 (Philip's speech).

[4] Livy (P) xxxv, 15, 1–9.

complaints, whereupon the conference not unnaturally broke up.[1]

The departure of the Romans was followed by a council of war. Already Hannibal had put forward proposals for a Syrian invasion of Greece, supported by a counter-diversion which he himself would organise in Carthage;[2] and in support of this plan he had sent a certain Ariston of Tyre to Carthage to test public opinion. This agent had, however, been driven out by the hostile faction, and the only result had been a complaint to Rome and the sending of an embassy, including Africanus, to Carthage in the summer of 193.[3] Now, however, Dicaearchus arrived from Aetolia, and with his promise of Macedonian support rapidly won over Alexander of Acarnania, a renegade from Philip's court, who was persuaded to recount stories of how Philip had repeatedly prayed to the gods to grant him Antiochus as an ally—stories as gratifying as they were false. However, Antiochus was unconvinced and still wavered between peace and war, not to mention the merits of the rival war plans.[4]

At Rome, too, a similar atmosphere of nervousness and uncertainty pervaded the elections for 192, and subsequent activity. The two praetors, M. Baebius Tamphilus and A. Atilius Serranus, after first being appointed to Spain, were transferred to Macedonia (with the fleet) and Bruttium respectively;[5] and though the return of the commission brought reassuring reports, the panic quickly broke out again as the result of a wild rumour that Antiochus was already in Aetolia and about to sail on Sicily![6] It was decided to send a senatorial commission of Flamininus and three others to Greece, to canvass support; meanwhile Baebius was moved to Tarentum and Brundisium, and a fleet

---

[1] Livy (P) xxxv, 16, 1–17, 2; Appian, *Syr.* 12, states that Antiochus offered to guarantee the freedom of Rhodes, Cyzicus, Byzantium and other Greek cities (but not the Aeolians and Ionians) in Asia, if Rome would make a treaty; but this evidence, alone, is weak.

[2] On Hannibal's plan see Livy (P) xxxiv, 60, 5; xxxv, 42; Justin. xxxi, 4, 1–6, 2; Appian, *Syr.* 7; Zon. ix, 18. For some valid criticisms of the traditional account see De Sanctis, iv, 1, 144, who, however, leaves it somewhat vague against whom the African diversion was to be planned.

[3] Livy (P) xxxiv, 61, 1–62, 18.

[4] Livy (P) xxxv, 17, 3–19, 7. On Alexander see further Kirchner, *P-W*, 'Alexandros (59)'; Treves, *P-W*, 'Philippos (64)', col. 2550.

[5] Livy (A) xxxv, 20, 8–12 (provinces reversed: correctly given in 22, 2).

[6] Livy (A) xxxv, 22, 1–3; 23, 1–3.

sent to guard Sicily; new levies were decreed and the east coast towns garrisoned against a possible invasion.[1]

Spring (192) found Nabis still blockading Gytheum; and under the generalship of Philopoemen, back from Crete, the Achaeans now declared war on Sparta.[2] Their hesitation to act before the return of their envoys from Rome had to give way to the urgency of the situation; and, though Flamininus demanded that they should await the arrival of Atilius and the Roman fleet, they resolved to hazard a naval battle. Philopoemen was no admiral, and was defeated off Gytheum; but he replied with a night attack along the coast, and a raid on Tripolis near the Megalopolitan frontier. However, by the time the Achaean levy had met its Acarnanian and Epirote allies at Tegea, Gytheum had fallen, and Nabis was free to march against them—only to be decisively defeated near Mt Barbosthenes, and penned up in Sparta, while the Achaeans ravaged Laconia for over a month; Atilius and the fleet now arrived and, perhaps assisted by Eumenes, recovered Gytheum and the other coastal towns.[3]

Meanwhile the Roman commission had arrived in Greece, and after visiting Achaea, Athens and Chalcis (where they put the pro-Roman party into office)[4] came to Demetrias. Here a certain Eurylochus brought up the alarming story that the Senate had promised to restore the town to Philip. The charge touched Flamininus's pride on a tender point, particularly as he was not in a position to offer a direct denial: the support of Philip happened to be of more account than the goodwill of the Magnesians![5] So instead he took steps to change the government: Zenon, a supporter of Rome, secured the banishment of Eurylochus, who fled to Aetolia to add fuel to the growing hostility towards Rome.[6]

[1] Livy (A) xxxv, 23, 4–9.   [2] Livy (P) xxxv, 25, 1 seq.

[3] Livy (P) xxxv, 25, 1–30, 13; Plut. *Philop.* 14, 2 seq.; Pausan. VIII, 50, 6; *Syll.* 605 A (if the phrase πλεύσαντες τὸ δεύτερον εἰς τὴν Ἑλλάδα refers to this occasion). The exact time of Atilius's arrival (cf. Livy (P) xxxv, 37, 3) is in doubt: see Holleaux, *CAH*, VIII, 204, n. 2. On Philopoemen's campaign see Aymard, *Premiers Rapports*, 305 seq.

[4] Livy (P) xxxv, 31, 1–2; cf. 37, 4.

[5] Livy (P) xxxv, 31, 7: *ita disserendum erat ne timorem vanum iis demendo spes incisa Philippum abalienaret, in quo plus ad omnia momenti quam in Magnetibus esset*—words which suggest that the rumour had some foundation.

[6] Livy (P) xxxv, 31, 3–32, 2.

At the spring meeting at Naupactus reports were now brought back from Antiochus by Thoas, who had visited him since Dicaearchus; the king, he said, would soon be in Europe, and Menippus, who was also present, confirmed this news with an exaggerated account of Antiochus's forces. Flamininus and the representatives of Athens also attended, but the rude rebuff administered to the Romans showed that there was nothing to be done in Aetolia. Flamininus therefore returned to Corinth, and consoled himself by making a truce with Nabis and so forcing the Achaeans to break off their blockade of Sparta—partly to gratify his jealousy of Philopoemen, partly in order to settle affairs in the Peloponnese before Antiochus came.[1]

For the Aetolian decision, taken in the presence of Flamininus, was to summon Antiochus 'to free Greece and arbitrate between themselves and the Romans';[2] and Damocritus is said to have promised Flamininus an early meeting on the Tiber banks.[3] These gestures were followed by a scheme for a triple attack on the valuable strategic centres of Demetrias, Sparta and Chalcis. Diocles was sent to Demetrias and, under the guise of escorting back Eurylochus, whose restoration had been somewhat unwisely sanctioned, took the town without much trouble—and thereby sacrificed the last chance of winning Philip's support.[4] Thoas's attempt on Chalcis miscarried;[5] but at Sparta Alexamenus, the murderer of the Theban Brachylles, assassinated Nabis and began to ravage Laconia. However, the Spartans rallied and killed most of the invaders, whereupon Philopoemen seized the moment to invade Laconia and, ignoring the presence of the Roman fleet off Gytheum, put the aristocratic, pro-Achaean party into power,[6] confiscated Nabis's property, and brought Sparta into the Achaean League.[7]

---

[1] Livy (P) xxxv, 32, 2–33, 11; Plut. *Philop.* 15, 1–2; Pausan. viii, 50, 10. Livy omits this truce with Nabis; cf. Appian, *Syr.* 21; Zon. ix, 19.

[2] Livy (P) xxxv, 33, 8.

[3] Livy (P) xxxv, 33, 10–11; but this story may have grown out of the details of Damocritus's death (cf. Livy (A) xxxvii, 46, 5): see De Sanctis, iv, 1, 138.

[4] Livy (P) xxxv, 34, 6–12. Philip was further alienated by the masssacre of the pro-Roman (i.e now pro-Macedonian) party.

[5] Livy (P) xxxv, 37, 4–38, 14.

[6] Plut. *Philop.* 15, 3; cf. Livy (P) xxxviii, 31, 5.

[7] Livy (P) xxxv, 37, 1–3; Plut. *Philop.* 15, 4 *seq.*; Pausan. viii, 51, 1.

The Aetolians had thus won Demetrias and considerable popular sympathy; for though it is dangerous to interpret the alignment too rigidly, the upper class in Greece were now generally pro-Roman and the people partisans of Aetolia.[1] On the other hand, they had lost the assistance of Sparta and Macedon, and Alexamenus's troops, 1030 in all, had either perished or been enslaved. Meanwhile Flamininus and Eumenes garrisoned Chalcis; but finding Demetrias strongly defended, they returned to Corinth without attempting its recovery.[2]

Antiochus's movements during the first half of 192 are uncertain. The arrival at Rome in spring of Eumenes's brother, Attalus, with the news that Antiochus had crossed the Hellespont[3] suggests that he undertook another Thracian expedition;[4] on the other hand, the story might easily have arisen out of an advance towards the Hellespont, where Antiochus was now besieging Alexandria Troas as well as Lampsacus.[5] It was probably late summer when Thoas brought his news of the fall of Demetrias and an exaggerated account of the war-spirit and preparations in Greece; he urged him to abandon Hannibal's western scheme, with which he was still toying, and to come over into Greece at once.[6] Antiochus was impressed. His quarrel with Rome was not Hannibal's; his object was not to crush his opponent, but simply to have his rights in Asia and Thrace recognised, and to secure himself in turn against Roman expansion. To this end a war in Greece, which would tire the Romans out, without threatening their own territory, seemed the most practical weapon.[7] In such calculations Antiochus ignored, unfortunately, the sensitiveness of the Senate even to the suspicion of a threat, and its tenacity, once it had decided on any course of military action. Meanwhile the capture of Demetrias seemed proof that the Aetolians were in earnest. And so Antio-

---

[1] Livy (P) xxxv, 34, 3. See above, p. 165, n. 5.

[2] Livy (P) xxxv, 39, 1–8.

[3] Livy (A) xxxv, 23, 10–11: in addition, Alexamenus told Nabis that Antiochus was already in Europe (Livy (P) xxxv, 35, 7).

[4] So Leuze, *Hermes*, LVIII, 1923, 244 *seq.*; Holleaux, *CAH*, VIII, 206.

[5] For the siege of Smyrna, Lampsacus and Alexandria see Livy (P) xxxv, 42, 2; on the Thracian expedition of 192 see below, Appendix III, p. 328.

[6] Livy (P) xxxv, 42, 3–14.

[7] On Antiochus's policy see De Sanctis, IV, 1, 141–7; Bickermann, *Hermes*, LXVII, 1932, 47–76.

chus resolved to strike; and in the early autumn of 192, after
sacrificing at Ilium, he embarked a force of 10,000 foot, 500
horse and six elephants, and with a fleet of forty cataphracts,
sixty smaller ships and 200 transports, crossed to Pteleum at the
entrance to the Pagasean Gulf. From here Eurylochus and the
other Magnesian leaders escorted him to Demetrias.[1]

In a demagogic speech to the Aetolians at Lamia Antiochus
made many promises and explained the smallness of his forces
by the late season: more, he said, would arrive in spring. Phaeneas, the new Aetolian general, had commanded the League's
forces at Cynoscephalae; appreciating more than Thoas and the
others the real strength of the Roman legions, and evidently
not impressed by the Syrian army, he spoke in favour of negotiation. However, Thoas carried the day, Antiochus was elected
στρατηγὸς αὐτοκράτωρ and thirty officials were appointed as
his war council.[2]

After a preliminary rebuff at Chalcis, it was decided to attempt
to win support in Boeotia and Achaea, and to secure the alliance
of Amynander of Athamania: the murder of Brachylles and the
rivalry between Flamininus and Philopoemen might be expected
to count against Rome, while it was hoped to work upon Amynander through his brother-in-law, a certain adventurer from
Megalopolis, the namesake of the king of Macedon, who claimed
descent from Alexander and even had his eyes upon the Macedonian throne.[3] Many years later, Philip claimed that Antiochus
had offered him 3000 talents, forty ships and all the Greek cities
he had formerly possessed, for his alliance.[4] The story was
certainly false: but that Philip considered it plausible enough
to put before the Senate shows the value which his alliance
would have had for Antiochus, and the shortsightedness which
led both him and the Aetolians to sacrifice even the small chance
they had of winning it by such actions as the seizure of Demetrias
and the support of Philip of Megalopolis.

[1] Livy (P) xxxv, 43, 1–6; under Antiochus the fortifications, which had
been demolished by the Romans after Cynoscephalae, were now rebuilt; cf.
Stählin, P–W, 'Magnesia', col. 465; Meyer, Pagasai u. Demetrias, 197 seq.
[2] Livy (P) xxxv, 43, 7–45, 9; Appian, Syr. 12; Zon. IX, 19; Polyb. XX, 1.
[3] Livy (P) xxxv, 46, 1–47, 8; Plut. Philop. 15, 1; Flam. 17, 1; Appian,
Syr. 13.
[4] Livy (P) xxxix, 28, 6. De Sanctis, IV, 1, 153, n. 73, wrongly dismisses
the story as annalistic fabrication; falsehood it may be, but Philip's own.

The Boeotians refused to commit themselves;[1] and though Amynander was easily won, the Achaeans, meeting in November,[2] rejected the Aetolian offer and, at the instigation of Flamininus, forestalled the Romans themselves in declaring war on Antiochus and the Aetolians. Moreover they sent 500 men to Chalcis and 500 more to Piraeus, to prevent an anti-Roman rising.[3] However, Antiochus now at last scored a success: Menippus succeeded in wiping out a garrison of 500 Romans in the precincts of the temple of Apollo at Delium, on the coast near Tanagra, before they could reach Chalcis, and notwithstanding the Achaean and Pergamene reinforcements, the town went over.[4] The incident not only brought over the whole of Euboea to Antiochus, but also furnished the Romans with a complete justification for declaring war.

Already the Senate had held its elections, earlier than usual; and by November the praetor urbanus, M. Fulvius, was busy with the construction of fifty new quinqueremes,[5] while Baebius, under orders, had already crossed over to Apollonia with perhaps 2000 men.[6] Shortly afterwards the new consuls took office, and war was declared on Antiochus and the Aetolians; M'. Acilius Glabrio, who obtained Greece as his province, was granted two legions and prepared to cross over as soon as the season would allow.[7] In Greece, meanwhile, Cato was carrying on propaganda for Rome at Athens, Patrae, Aegium and Corinth;[8] and on the other side, from Chalcis, Antiochus despatched military help to Elis and messengers to Epirus, and after a personal visit to Thebes persuaded the Boeotians to join the alliance.[9]

The liberators now called a conference to Demetrias, to discuss in particular the question of Thessaly and Macedonia.[10]

[1] Polyb. xx, 2; Livy (P) xxxv, 50, 5.
[2] On the date see below, Appendix III, p. 330.
[3] Livy (P) xxxv, 48, 1–50, 4; cf. Polyb. III, 3, 3; xxxIx, 3, 8.
[4] Livy (P) xxxv, 50, 6–51, 10; Zon. IX, 19, 5; Diod. xxIx, 1; Appian, *Syr.* 15; Plut. *Moralia*, 197 C.   [5] Livy (A) xxxv, 24, 1–8.
[6] Appian, *Syr.* 15–16; Livy (A) xxxvi, 1, 7; Zon. IX, 18, 7; 19, 1. The two legions given to Baebius in Livy (A) xxxv, 20, 11; 24, 7, are to be rejected; cf. Niese, II, 696, n. 1; De Sanctis, IV, 1, 156, n. 75; Aymard, *Premiers Rapports*, 327, n. 14.
[7] Livy (A) xxxvi, 1–3.
[8] Plut. *Cat. Mai.* 12, 4–5; see Aymard, *op. cit.* 329–30.
[9] Polyb. xx, 3; 7, 3–5; Livy (P) xxxvi, 5, 1–6, 5; Appian, *Syr.* 13.
[10] Livy (P) xxxvi, 6, 6.

This conference was remarkable chiefly for the speech of
Hannibal, who, after a period of unpopularity, had now been
recalled to favour.[1] Memories of Philip's first war with Rome
had given Hannibal a considerable respect for his old ally; and
this had not been diminished by the weakness of the Greek
response to Antiochus, and the inadequacy of the king's own
forces. Seeing this, and not realising the extent to which Philip
had already been alienated, Hannibal now urged above all things
the need of a Macedonian alliance. Failing that, Philip must be
neutralised, if necessary by an attack through Thrace under
Antiochus's son Seleucus; and meanwhile the rest of the Syrian
forces should be brought over to Greece, and marched into
Epirus, and while part of the fleet attempted a diversion on the
Italian coast, the other half should lie off Corcyra, to prevent
the Romans from crossing. This bold plan, not the least important feature of which was its criticism of the passive Syrian
policy towards Philip, was rejected. Polyxenidas was sent back
to Asia for reinforcements, while Antiochus prepared for a
combined invasion to 'free' Thessaly.[2]

Hitherto Philip had remained technically neutral:[3] a minor
incident now persuaded him to give the Romans his active
support. While Antiochus awaited Amynander and the Aetolians
at Pherae, Philip of Megalopolis, seeking to curry favour in
Macedonia, undertook the burial of the dead who had lain on
the field of Cynoscephalae for nearly six years. This action,
deliberately calculated to damage Philip in the eyes of his people,
merely irritated the Macedonians and drove Philip into the arms
of Rome.[4] Previously, no doubt, Philip had been waiting for
definite concessions—for example in Thessaly and Magnesia—
and for the remission of his tribute and the restoration of his son,
before making any move in practical support of his Roman
alliance. Now, his pride hurt at a tender spot, he sent word at
once to Baebius at Apollonia, reporting the enemy's invasion of

---

[1] On Hannibal's new plan (Livy (P) XXXVI, 7, 17–20; Appian, Syr. 14) see
Passerini, Athen. XI, 1933, 10 seq.; contra De Sanctis, IV, 1, 155, n. 74;
Riv. Fil. LXII, 1934, 126–7.   [2] Livy (P) XXXVI, 7, 1–8, 1.
[3] The account of the embassy through which Philip offered the Senate
money, men and provisions, only to have his advances gracefully rejected
(Livy (A) XXXVI, 4, 1; 4, 4) is to be regarded as apocryphal.
[4] Livy (P) XXXVI, 8, 3–6; Appian, Syr. 16. On Philip of Megalopolis see
further Treves, P-W, 'Philippos (12)', cols. 2331–2.

Thessaly, and proposing a discussion for joint action.[1] The Cynoscephalae incident had precipitated Philip's decision; but sooner or later that decision had been inevitable, since, for all its risks, the policy of whole-hearted co-operation with Rome was the only means to re-establish Macedonian influence in any part of its former sphere. The real danger, as De Sanctis points out, lay in the fact that in weakening Aetolia Philip was also weakening any forces in Greece which might ultimately be brought to support a Macedonian *revanche*, and was thus rendering more difficult the ultimate end to which he looked forward beyond his immediate policy. In later years, Philip would have to face this problem and attempt a solution for it; for the present, he had no choice but to play for immediate gains and the destruction of those powers whose claims clashed so directly with his own. Accordingly, at a meeting held in Dassaretia, Philip and Baebius shortly afterwards came to an agreement, by which Philip was to keep any possessions he might win from the Aetolians and their allies.[2]

Antiochus, meanwhile, assisted by Amynander and the Aetolians, was advancing almost unresisted through Thessaly; town after town had fallen to their forces, the Aetolians had ventured into Perrhaebia, where they had seized Malloea and Chyretiae,[3] and Antiochus himself was preparing a final assault on Larisa, when the sight of a multitude of watch-fires on the heights above Gonnus convinced him that a full Roman army was at hand. He therefore withdrew to Demetrias, and Appius Claudius was able to enter Larisa unopposed, with a mere 2000 men, and plant a garrison there.[4] The following months of

[1] Livy (P) XXXVI, 8, 6. While uttering a much-needed warning against accepting the trivial and personal causes which ancient authorities frequently attribute to important decisions, De Sanctis, IV, 1, 153, n. 72, seems in this case to make inadequate allowance for Philip's pride. Otherwise his comments on Philip's policy at this juncture are excellent.

[2] Livy (P) XXXVI, 10, 10; Zon. IX, 19, 3; Appian, *Syr.* 16; for the terms, later confirmed by Acilius, see below, p. 207, n. 2. As Philip was already a Roman *socius*, pledged to give help, this arrangement with Baebius must have been in the nature of an informal agreement, not a signed compact; it is this fact that places Philip in so weak a position, when the Thessalians later challenge his right to the towns he has occupied (see below, pp. 227 *seq.*).

[3] Livy (P) XXXVI, 9, 1–10, 6. For the places seized see Stählin, 104 (Pherae); 109 (Scotussa); 111 (Crannon); 129 (Metropolis: cf. also 27, n. 2); 131 (Cierium); 100 (Atrax); 91 (Gyrton); 117 (Pellinaeum).

[4] Livy (P) XXXVI, 10, 6–14; Appian, *Syr.* 16.

February and March Antiochus spent at Chalcis, where he married the daughter of one of the citizens;[1] and in the meantime Acilius, the Roman consul, crossed over into Epirus with the main Roman army.

In March (191), Antiochus opened the season with an expedition against Acarnania, designed to crush the opposition in the west and so gain the confidence of the Aetolians. Medeon he took by treachery, but hearing that Acilius had crossed over he abandoned his siege of Thyrrheum and returned to Chalcis.[2] Simultaneously, Philip and the Roman troops under Baebius had been operating in Thessaly. Splitting forces they advanced, Philip against Malloea and Baebius against Phacium; operating from Atrax, the latter took Phacium and Phayttus, and then, returning north, seized Chyretiae and Ericinium before rejoining Philip, who was still blockading Malloea with little success.[3] The town gave way before the joint attack, and the two commanders then advanced against the towns in western Thessaly, held by Amynander. Aeginium, Eritium, Gomphi, Tricca, Silana, Meliboea and Phaloria fell in rapid succession, and probably Eurymenae and other forts;[4] then, when Pellinaeum, where Philip of Megalopolis was stationed, resisted the joint attack, to save time Baebius remained, while Philip went on to besiege Limnaeum.[5]

A success here would have gone far towards consoling Philip for his undistinguished delay at Malloea; but at this moment the

[1] The stories of debauchery may, like the similar tales of Hannibal at Capua, be disregarded; see De Sanctis, IV, 1, 157, n. 79 (with authorities).

[2] Livy (P) XXXVI, 11, 1-12, 11; Appian, Syr. 16.

[3] Livy (P) XXXVI, 13, 1-4. For the position of Phayttus (Livy: Phaestus) and Ericinium (Livy: Eritium), see Stählin, 115 (Phayttus), 28, n. 2 (Ericinium). Stählin plausibly suggests a reversal of the two names Eritium and Ericinium in sections 4 and 6 of Livy, XXXVI, 13; from inscriptions (cf. Kip, 121) Ericinium is known to be in Perrhaebia (against De Sanctis, IV, 1, 158, n. 91); whereas the fortress near Gomphi is not mentioned elsewhere.

[4] Livy (P) XXXVI, 13, 5-6; XXXIX, 25, 3. Silana, Eurymenae and Meliboea are otherwise unknown, but must lie near Gomphi; the two latter are not to be confused with the Magnesian towns of the same name (an error made in the case of Eurymenae by Niese, III, 24, n. 1, and De Sanctis, IV, 1, 158, n. 82: rightly placed in Hestiaeotis by Stählin, 127, n. 16; Fine, TAPhA, LVIII, 1932, 131, n. 32; and Daux, 306, n. 1). It is not possible to decide which of these places Amynander had taken the previous winter, and which he had held since the peace of 196.

[5] Livy (P) XXXVI, 13, 7-9. For Limnaeum see Stählin, 83.

consul reached Larisa, with a force of 20,000 foot, 2000 horse, fifteen elephants and Illyrian reinforcements,[1] and at once joined Philip in time to receive the surrender of Limnaeum. Together Acilius and Philip returned to Pellinaeum, which now also surrendered, and gave Philip an opportunity to vent some of his spleen on his namesake of Megalopolis. As the adventurer was led out of the city, preparatory to being sent to Rome in chains, Philip, in words which Livy condemns as lacking in dignity, but which were very typical of his humour, greeted him as brother, and bade his men salute him as king. The rest of the garrison, 4000 Syrians and Athamanians, were handed over to Philip.[2]

After the surrender of Cierium and Metropolis, Acilius returned to Larisa; and a few days later he moved south, taking over town after town until Antiochus was driven back on Thermopylae, where he hoped that his forces would be able to hold the pass until Polyxenidas sent him more men. The speed of Acilius's operations caught many of the Syrian garrisons unprepared; as prisoners they were allowed to choose what they would do, and a thousand, who did not wish to rejoin Antiochus at Demetrias, chose to enrol with Philip.[3] Meanwhile, only 4000 of the Aetolians rallied at Antiochus's summons to Lamia; already he seemed a broken reed, and in the meantime Aetolia itself was being threatened by Philip.

From Pellinaeum, encouraged by his personal triumph, Philip had advanced against his old enemy, Amynander; and following the example of Antiochus and Acilius, he dismissed his Athamanian prisoners without ransom, thus winning a some-what novel reputation for clemency. Amynander, in alarm, fled with his family to Ambracia, and Philip took over the country— a proceeding which must have alarmed the Aetolians, who still remembered the invasion of 207, and may go far towards ex-plaining their absence from Thermopylae. However, a slight illness prevented Philip from either invading Aetolia or joining

---

[1] Livy (P) xxxvi, 14, 1; Appian, *Syr.* 17; Justin. xxxi, 6, 4. For Acilius's march cf. Béquignon, *Vallée du Spercheios*, 280–81.

[2] Livy (P) xxxvi, 14, 2–5.

[3] Livy (P) xxxvi, 14, 6; 14, 10–15; 15, 2–5; 17, 1; Appian, *Syr.* 17; Zon. ix, 19. Xyniae may now have joined the Thessalian League (Livy (P) xxxix, 26, 2); cf. De Sanctis, iv, 1, 159, n. 86. Proerna will have joined Antiochus together with Pharsalus (Livy (P) xxxvi, 14, 2).

Acilius; and a lull in the war left the stage clear for the clash
between Rome and Syria within the historic pass of Thermopylae.[1]

The Roman victory was complete. Antiochus fled with the
remains of his army to Chalcis, and took ship to Ephesus;[2]
and Acilius, after taking over Phocis, Boeotia and Euboea,
returned to Thermopylae, and began the siege of Heraclea.[3] In
three months the Syrian threat had been eliminated. Once more
the preponderant influence in the peninsula, the Romans had
only the residue of the Aetolian war to disturb them. The campaign had brought Philip both gains and misgivings. Of the
cities captured along with Baebius, he is known to have kept
Malloea, Ericinium, Tricca, Phaloria and Gomphi;[4] and he
probably kept many if not all of the others, in accordance with
the compact made in Dassaretia with Baebius, and renewed,
doubtless, with Acilius outside Limnaeum. In addition,
Athamania was a valuable prize. Nevertheless, with the solitary
exception of his minor triumph over Philip of Megalopolis, his
campaigns in Thessaly had involved him in humiliation. Twice,
at Malloea and Limnaeum, a Roman force had snatched the
victory out of his hands, thus demonstrating both the military
and political superiority of Rome. Philip's absence from Thermopylae may thus have had more behind it than a slight illness;
perhaps wounded pride decided him to leave the major issue to
Acilius, while he himself looked after his own advantage.

Indeed there is reason to think that after his invasion of
Athamania Philip resuscitated an old and favourite scheme, the
acquisition of the Pagasean coast road. For it was perhaps in
May of this year, while Acilius was occupied in Chalcis and
Boeotia, that he recovered Alope, Larisa Cremaste, Antron,
Pteleum[5] and (less certainly) Halus and Phthiotic Thebes;[6] but

[1] Livy (P) XXXVI, 14, 7–9; 25, 1; Zon. IX, 19.
[2] For the battle see Niese, II, 704–6; Kromayer, II, 134 seq.; De Sanctis,
IV, 1, 160–5 (references, 164, n. 87); Holleaux, CAH, VIII, 213–15.
[3] Livy (P) XXXVI, 20, 1–21, 6 (includes later naval activity); App. Syr. 20.
[4] Livy (P) XXXIX, 25, 3; 25, 16 (Philippopolis is Gomphi; cf. Stählin, 126).
[5] Livy (P) XLII, 42, 1; 56, 7; 67, 9–10. See De Sanctis, IV, 1, 165, n. 89.
[6] Phthiotic Thebes had gone to Aetolia in 196 (see above, p. 182, n. 1), but
in 185 it appears to be Thessalian (Livy (P) XXXIX, 25, 9, where the Thessalians
complain that Philip had diverted its trade to Demetrias); thus, if Philip took
it now, it reverted very soon to Thessaly. On the whole it seems likelier that
it passed straight from Aetolia to Thessaly. See De Sanctis, IV, 1, 165-6, n. 89.

if so, he probably did not recover control over the whole length of the road.[1] Regarding it as perhaps impolitic to be too long away, he returned to the Malian Gulf and, meeting Acilius on his way back from Chalcis, arranged that he should blockade Lamia, and the Romans Heraclea.[2]

The twin blockade lasted throughout June;[3] and as the two towns lay only seven miles apart, on the opposite slopes of the Spercheius valley, the operations took on the form of open rivalry between the Macedonian and Roman troops. While Acilius attacked the walls with siege works of every description, Philip unwisely decided upon mining Lamia; and since the town lay mainly upon bedrock, he made little headway. Meanwhile persistent attacks night and day, crowned by a cleverly planned midnight assault, gave the consul Heraclea; and—probably as a result of the truce now concluded with the Aetolians—Philip was obliged to withdraw from Lamia.[4]

The fall of Heraclea and the capture of Damocritus there had temporarily broken the resistance of the Aetolians; without further thought for an embassy which they had only recently sent to Antiochus, asking for help, they obtained a ten days' truce from Acilius, and at a meeting with L. Valerius Flaccus at Hypata decided after some discussion to entrust themselves *in fidem populi Romani*. Failing to realise that this was the equivalent to absolute surrender, they were shocked when the consul began to lay down certain unconditional demands, and

Halus is known to be Thessalian in 184–3 (*IG*, IX, 2, 107), but may have been taken from Philip at the conference of Tempe in 185. Coroneia in Phthiotic Achaea (exact situation unknown: cf. Stählin, 167, n. 2; 185, n. 3) may now have become Macedonian: it issued coins showing (apparently) Philip's head; see Graindor, *Rev. Belge*, XVIII, 1939, 85–91.

[1] The fate of Echinus, for instance, is uncertain (see above, p. 176); the Aetolians did not receive it, and it may have formed part of Phthiotic Achaea. From *Syll.* 692, lines 9–10, Stählin, 186, n. 7, argues that Echinus joined Malis in 189.

[2] Livy (P) XXXVI, 25, 1–2. An alternative explanation is that Philip's captures along the Malian coast road were in August, when he marched this way from Lamia to Demetrias; see below, p. 207.

[3] See below, Appendix III, p. 331.

[4] Livy (P) XXXVI, 22, 1–25, 8; Zon. IX, 19, 13; Phleg. Trall. *FGH*, II B, 257, F. 36, III, 1; Plut. *Flam.* 15, 3; Appian, *Syr.* 21; Polyb. XX, 11, 3. Livy makes the truce follow Philip's withdrawal, but the reversed order best explains Acilius's action; cf. De Sanctis, IV, 1, 166. For Philip's resentment see Livy (P) XXXIX, 23, 9. On Heraclea and Lamia see Stählin, 207 *seq.*; 213 *seq.*; Béquignon, *Vallée du Spercheios*, *passim*.

had their representatives, including Phaeneas the general, thrown into chains when they remonstrated; accordingly the whole people boycotted the assembly called to consider the situation, and the war continued as before.[1]

Philip had taken only an indirect part in these events. Among the Aetolian envoys to Antiochus had been the same Nicander who had approached Philip in 193.[2] Arriving at Phalara on his way back, Nicander managed to convey the money Antiochus had sent into Lamia, though Philip and his army were not far away, and Acilius was still at Heraclea. But on trying to reach Hypata between the two armies, he was taken by Macedonian sentries and his capture announced to Philip. The king not only treated him well, but in a personal interview[3] pointed out the mistakes of Aetolian policy in calling in first the Romans and then Antiochus, and impressed upon him the advantages of a rapprochement with Macedon. Coming from the ally of the Senate, this appeal may have rung oddly; it was none the less a foreshadowing of new and important alignments. The demand that Philip withdrew from Lamia, made with typical Roman tactlessness, indicated clearly that he was near the limit of the gains to be made through co-operation with Rome. The Romans were in fact in the difficult position of having bought Philip's help by an agreement which in principle ran counter to the Isthmus proclamation; and the incident of Lamia showed how reluctant Acilius was to honour it. Meanwhile Philip foresaw that the peace would so reduce the power of the Aetolian League that its interests were no longer likely to clash with his own, but that, on the contrary, in their common hostility to the new leagues of Thessaly, he and the Aetolians might well find a common bond. Until peace was made, this was a situation still hidden in the future; and in the meantime Aetolia and Macedon were ranged in opposite camps. But it says much for Philip's political sense that he was already alive to such developments and the possibilities they held out.[4]

For the moment, the report of Nicander—sent by Philip to

---

[1] Polyb. xx, 9, 10; Livy (P) xxxvi, 27, 1–29, 2.
[2] See above, p. 193.
[3] Polybius's account probably derives from Nicander himself; see Woodhouse, 258, n. 1. On Nicander see F. Stähelin, P-W, 'Nikandros', cols. 247–9.
[4] Polyb. xx, 11; Livy (P) xxxvi, 29, 3–11.

Hypata—and the money from Antiochus encouraged the Aetolians to continue the struggle. The federal forces gathered at Naupactus, where they were attacked by App. Claudius with a force of 4000, and later besieged by the consul. During the two months' siege of Naupactus (August–September, 191) the war was brought to a finish in the Peloponnese and, thanks to Flamininus, Messenia was made a member of the Achaean League. Zacynthus, however, which the Achaeans had bought from Amynander's treacherous governor, was detached from the League by Flamininus and became a Roman possession.[1]

Philip, meanwhile, had the good sense not to imperil his gains by a breach with the Romans. With the permission of Acilius, carefully but tactfully obtained beforehand to avoid ambiguity, he advanced along the Malian road to Demetrias, taking many of the towns on the way.[2] Abandoned by both Syrians and Aetolians, the Magnesian citadel surrendered immediately, Eurylochus, the Magnesian general, preferring suicide to capture. Philip sent Antiochus's garrisons under escort by land to Lysimacheia, and also let go the few Syrian ships stationed there. He himself advanced west into Dolopia and Aperantia, but then, instead of assisting Acilius by continuing down the Achelous to repeat his raid on Thermum, he once more showed his consideration of the Aetolians by returning north into Perrhaebia, where he recovered the few towns that still held out.[3]

The knowledge of these successes, which were near to restoring to Philip his old strangle-hold on Thessaly, contributed to Acilius's decision to come to terms with the Aetolians in Naupactus. In particular, Flamininus, arriving from the Pelo-

[1] Livy (P) xxxvi, 30–1; Plut. *Flam.* 17, 4. Asine, Pylus (see above, p. 178) and Cyparissia (cf. Polyb. xi, 18, 2; Livy (P) xxxii, 21, 23) had been Achaean since the end of the third century, and there is evidence that Corone, Colonides and Mothone now entered the League as separate cities (Plut. *Philop.* 18, 5; Livy (P) xxxix, 49, 1; Head, 433). Abia, Thuria and Pharae remained Messenian possessions (cf. Polyb. xxiii, 17, 1). See further Aymard, *Premiers Rapports*, 347, n. 16.
[2] See above, p. 205, n. 2. According to Livy (P) xxxix, 23, 10, the agreement was that any towns taken by the Aetolians from the Thessalians should go to Philip, if he captured them; later it was interpreted (Livy (P) xxxix, 25, 5) to refer only to such towns as were 'originally' Aetolian.
[3] Livy (P) xxxvi, 23, 1–7; cf. (P) xxxix, 23, 10; 28, 3, where, however, the capture of Athamania is placed after the siege of Lamia. Philip's march from Aperantia to Perrhaebia may have touched on Athamania; but the district had been taken the previous April (see above, p. 203).

ponnese, commented on the folly of continuing a siege that was profiting no one but Philip; and with Acilius's permission he negotiated a truce with Phaeneas, to allow the Aetolians to send an embassy to Rome. The Romans now went into winter quarters in Phocis and Philip, his conquests automatically cut short, returned to Macedon. Once more Flamininus had displayed his gifts as a diplomat. Pending the settlement of the main issue in Asia, the Greek situation had been, as it were, petrified: the truce was designed not only to hinder the Aetolians from helping Antiochus, but also to check Philip's unwelcome conquests, until such time as the Romans were free to return and settle the outstanding account in Aetolia. As the main victims of this diplomacy, the Aetolians were only paying the price of their policy since Cynoscephalae: but Philip, too, was learning the limits of profitable collaboration.[1]

At Rome winter brought numerous embassies to interview the Senate. The Epirotes, whose recent conduct had not been beyond suspicion, were sent home with a pardon; and Philip's envoys, who had instructions to congratulate the Senate on the victory at Thermopylae, and ask for permission to sacrifice on the Capitoline and dedicate a golden crown of a hundred pounds to Juppiter Optimus Maximus, received a warm welcome. Above all, the prince Demetrius was now sent back to Pella, and it was promised that if Philip remained loyal, the balance of his tribute — some 250 talents, if the instalment for 191 was already paid— would be remitted.[2] An embassy sent by the new pro-Achaean government at Sparta to plead against any restoration of exiles, a measure which, they claimed, would result in fresh political and economic disturbances, was, however, sent back very dissatisfied; indeed by choosing this very moment to release the Spartan hostages held at Rome since the defeat of Nabis, the Senate showed itself not unwilling to cause deliberate embarrassment to the newly-united Peloponnese.[3]

[1] Livy (P) XXXVI, 34, 1–35, 6; Plut. *Flam.* 15, 4; Zon. IX, 19, 14.

[2] Livy (P) XXXVI, 35, 8–14; Polyb. XXI, 3. For the later co-operation of the Epirotes see Polyb. XXI, 26; Livy (P) XXXVIII, 3, 10 *seq.*; Zon. IX, 19, 14.

[3] Polyb. XXI, 1; 3, 4. Early in 191, an incipient revolt, inflamed by Flamininus and the Achaean general, Diophanes, had only been put down by the tact and courage of Philopoemen (Plut. *Philop.* 16, 1–2; Pausan. VIII, 51, 1; cf. De Sanctis, IV, 1, 170; Aymard, *Premiers Rapports*, 330–8); and when

In central Greece, meanwhile, Acilius spent much of the winter at Delphi, working against Aetolian influence inside the Delphian Amphictyony; and in the town a burst of anti-Aetolian feeling expressed itself in the dispossession of absentee Locrian landlords and in certain frontier adjustments.[1] Simultaneously, the Aetolian embassy at Rome was presented with the harsh alternatives of unconditional surrender or an indemnity of 1000 talents and an alliance with Rome; not unnaturally the terms were rejected and the war continued.[2]

Nevertheless, for all their harshness towards the Aetolians, the Senate could only regard the war in Greece as a distraction; for they were now planning an invasion of Asia Minor, where they hoped finally to extinguish the danger from Syria. The news of a naval victory over Antiochus off Corycus—the first round in a protracted struggle for the Hellespont—had reached Rome in time to encourage them in their preparations for the next season's campaign.[3] L.Scipio had been allotted the province of Greece, on the understanding that Africanus should accompany him as *legatus*; and, on 18 March 190, he marshalled his reinforcements (8000 foot and 300 horse) at Brundisium and crossed over into Illyria.[4] From Apollonia the Scipios ascended the Aous, crossed the Zygos Pass, and descended through Thessaly to Hypata and Amphissa, where their first action was to try to call a halt in the Aetolian war, which was once more in full swing.[5] Africanus's first offer was identical with that of the previous winter and was rejected; but eventually it was arranged that there should be a six months' armistice from May to October, and that envoys should be sent to Rome to try to

Flamininus and Acilius visited the Achaean assembly in autumn (Livy (P) XXXVI, 35, 7; Plut. *Philop.* 17, 4), they failed to settle either the question of the Spartan exiles, or that of Elis's membership of the Achaean League. That Elis joined the League before Diophanes's term of office expired is clear from Pausan. VIII, 30, 5 (statue to Diophanes as the founder of Peloponnesian unity); see too Livy (P) XXXVIII, 32, 5 (League assembly at Elis; cf. Aymard, *REA*, XXX, 1928, 4–24; *Mélanges Glotz*, 59, n. 4).

[1] *Syll.* 609; 610; cf. Daux, 225 *seq.*
[2] Polyb. XXI, 2; cf. Livy (P) XXXVII, 1, 1–6; Diod. XXIX, 4; Zon. IX, 19, 14.
[3] Livy (P) XXXVI, 41, 1–45, 8; Appian, *Syr.* 21–2; Justin. XXXI, 6, 6. For the figures of the Roman fleet see De Sanctis, IV, 1, 173; the news arrived about the time the Aetolians were being heard (Polyb. XXI, 2, 1).
[4] Livy (A) XXXVII, 1, 7–2, 3; 4, 1–4; on the date see below, Appendix III, p. 332; for Scipio's forces see Kromayer, II, 206–7.
[5] Livy (P) XXXVII, 6, 1–2.

obtain more favourable terms.[1] The Aetolians having been thus once more immobilised, Acilius returned to Rome, and the Scipios marched back into Thessaly, preparatory to their advance through Macedonia and Thrace to the Hellespont.

Since his return to Macedon the previous autumn, nothing is recorded of Philip's movements. His agreement with the Romans covered only Aetolian possessions, and so offered him no incentive for a campaign towards the Hellespont; and discouraged perhaps by the frequent rebuffs he had received the previous season, he seems to have taken no part in the short campaign which preceded the truce of Amphissa. But if the impossibility of making further acquisitions had brought his activity to a sudden halt, the return of his envoys from Rome, bringing Demetrius and the Senate's promise to remit his tribute, was a sufficient deterrent against a break with Rome; for he must have had a shrewd suspicion that the fulfilment of this promise would turn on his treatment of the Roman army in its advance through his territory.

The importance of Philip from this aspect was also clear to the Scipios; and accordingly, to avoid all risks, Ti. Sempronius Gracchus was sent post haste to Pella, to catch Philip unawares and so, if possible, to discover his intentions.[2] Having covered the 200 miles from Amphissa in three days, Gracchus found Philip banqueting and somewhat drunk, a circumstance which he interpreted as a reassuring proof that he had no immediate designs against the Roman army. Philip was sufficiently sober to welcome his unexpected visitor, and the next day, when both had rested, he gave him full particulars of his preparations— supplies of corn laid in, rivers bridged and roads repaired. Quite plainly negotiations had been going on before between Pella and Rome upon this question; possibly the envoys who brought back Demetrius carried instructions; but it was reassuring to the Scipios upon their arrival at Thaumaci to receive the first-hand account of Gracchus that these instructions had been fulfilled.[3]

---

[1] Polyb. XXI, 4–5; cf. Livy (P) XXXVII, 6, 1–7, 7; Appian, *Syr.* 23; Zon. IX, 20, 1.

[2] Livy (P) XXXVII, 7, 8–12. There is nothing inherently impossible in the anecdote, which, however, Niese, II, 724, dismisses as worthless and non-Polybian; it is understandable that the Scipios would wish to take every precaution before entrusting their army to Philip's protection.

[3] Livy (P) XXXVII, 7, 13–14.

As the Romans advanced farther north, they were met by Philip, who quickly discovered in Africanus a man whom he could admire; the Roman in turn found something congenial in Philip's courteous and chivalrous behaviour, springing from qualities which he himself shared.[1] The two men struck up a close friendship, which they later maintained by correspondence,[2] and which undoubtedly contributed to the readiness with which Philip assisted the Romans in Macedonia and Thrace,[3] even permitting his own citizens to volunteer in the Roman forces.[4] His reward came when, at the end of the march through Macedonia, Africanus announced the Senate's definite decision to cancel the remainder of his tribute.[5]

Meanwhile the fight for the Hellespont had recommenced, and reached its crisis in August, when a Rhodian victory off the Lycian promontory, over a new Syrian fleet under Hannibal, gave the allies full control of the Aegean.[6] At the same time the Scipios thwarted Antiochus's attempt to retrieve his position diplomatically by securing the alliance of Prusias of Bithynia; in a letter they pointed out how his kinsman Philip had profited by his friendship with Rome, and refuted the current Hellenistic notion that it was the Senate's policy to overthrow all autocratic rulers throughout the world.[7] And the next month, in a final attempt to recover naval superiority, Polyxenidas received a crushing defeat, with the loss of forty-two ships, off Myonnesus, between Teos and Samos.[8]

Myonnesus obliged Antiochus to abandon the defence of the Hellespont and evacuate Lysimacheia: though it was nothing

---

[1] Livy (P) XXXVII, 7, 15: *dexteritas et humanitas, quae commendabilia apud Africanum erant, virum...a comitate...non aversum*; cf. Livy (P) XXVIII, 18, 6: *tanta inerat comitas Scipioni atque ad omnia naturalis ingenii dexteritas*.

[2] Cf. Polyb. X, 9, 4, where Scipio describes his exploits at New Carthage in a letter to Philip; there is no reason to put this correspondence before the meeting (so Schur, 84): in any case, it could not be before 205.

[3] Livy (P) XXXVII, 7, 15; cf. (P) XXXIX, 28, 8–9; Appian, *Syr.* 23; Mac. 9, 5; Zon. IX, 20, 1.

[4] Livy (P) XXXVII, 39, 12: *duo milia mixtorum Macedonum Thracumque, qui voluntate secuti sunt.*

[5] Appian, *Syr.* 23; if the instalment for 190 had been paid, the balance came to 200 talents.

[6] Livy (P) XXXVII, 9–24; Polyb. XXI, 6–8; 10; Appian, *Syr.* 24–5.

[7] Polyb. XXI, 11; cf. Livy (P) XXXVII, 25, 1–14; Appian, *Syr.* 23.

[8] Livy (P) XXXVII, 26–30; Polyb. XXI, 12; Appian, *Syr.* 27. Prusias probably remained neutral, though Appian says he joined Rome.

but reprehensible negligence that let him leave its supplies intact for the approaching Romans.[1] Meanwhile Regillus, the Roman admiral, sent half his ships, along with the Rhodian fleet, to the Hellespont, and with the rest took Phocaea, where he had decided to make his winter quarters.[2]

The Scipios heard of the victory of Myonnesus in October, when they were near Aenus and Maronea.[3] Pressing on to Lysimacheia, they halted here a while to wait for stragglers, before crossing the straits. Religious tabu kept Africanus on the European side for thirty days,[4] during which time the army waited for him on the Asiatic coast; and Antiochus used this breathing space to offer terms, by which he should surrender his claim to Lampsacus, Smyrna and Alexandria Troas, and pay half the costs of the war. But the Romans demanded a full indemnity and the surrender of all Syrian territory west of Taurus, and the campaign continued. The end came shortly afterwards on the plains of Magnesia, with the crushing defeat of the Syrian army, and the surrender of most of the cities of western Asia Minor. Until Antiochus's envoys could be sent to Rome, Scipio imposed a preliminary set of terms similar to the demands made at the Hellespont, with the addition that a specific sum was mentioned as indemnity, and the king was required to surrender certain individual 'trouble-makers', including Thoas the Aetolian and Hannibal.[5]

All this time Greece was enjoying the Aetolian armistice; and the Senate, anxious to prolong this welcome pause as long as possible, appear to have waited until after its expiration in October, before giving the Aetolian embassy an audience.[6] But their opportunism became clear when they repeated their former offer without concessions, and upon its rejection ordered the envoys out of Italy within fifteen days. The same winter, before

[1] Livy (P) xxxvii, 31, 1-2; Appian, *Syr.* 28; 37; Diod. xxix, 5; Zon. ix, 20. De Sanctis, iv, 1, 193, suggests that Antiochus may have been moved by humanitarian motives!

[2] Livy (P) xxxvii, 31, 4-32, 14.

[3] See below, Appendix iii, p. 332, n. 7.

[4] As Salian priest he might not move; Livy (P) xxxvii, 33, 6-7.

[5] Polyb. xxi, 13-17; Livy (P) xxxvii, 3-45; Appian, *Syr.* 28 *seq.* Details and minor authorities in Niese, ii, 737-45; Kromayer, ii, 162-95; De Sanctis, iv, 1, 193-205; Holleaux, *CAH*, viii, 222-5.

[6] Diod. xxix, 9; Livy (P) xxxvii, 49.

the envoys returned, but well after the expiry of the truce, the war blazed up again with a successful attempt by Amynander to recover his kingdom from Philip, who had held it since spring 191.[1] Macedonian rule was unpopular; and in December 190, after negotiations with the inhabitants of Argithea, the capital, Amynander arranged that he should invade the country with 1000 Aetolians, while risings against the Macedonian garrisons took place simultaneously in the four largest citadels of Argithea, Heraclea, Theudoria and Tetraphylia. Everything went according to plan. Xenon, the Macedonian commander at Theium, got wind of the plot and was able to hold out longest; but soon the whole country but for the frontier post of Athenaeum, above Gomphi, was back in the hands of Amynander.[2]

The loss took Philip by surprise. Relying on the Aetolian truce, and perhaps, as De Sanctis suggests,[3] on the election of Nicander of Trichonium to the Aetolian generalship of 190–89, he had not anticipated any resumption of hostilities before spring. Nevertheless, this was the kind of situation he understood. Taking 6000 men, he marched with the utmost speed to Gomphi,[4] and leaving 4000 here he advanced with the rest to the Athenaeum, to ascertain the extent of the revolt; finding it to be complete, he returned to Gomphi and, with his whole force, invaded Athamania in the direction of Argithea. Sending Xenon (who had joined him after the fall of Theium) ahead with 1000 men to seize the fortress of Aethopia,[5] which commanded the capital, Philip himself encamped near the temple of Zeus Acraeus;[6] but the rain delayed him, and on the third day he found the enemy controlling both sides of the rocky pass ahead. Realising the danger of being trapped in this difficult country, Philip retired with all speed; but unfortunately for him the

---

[1] See above, p. 203.
[2] Livy (P) xxxviii, 1. For Argithea see Leake, iv, 272; Stählin, 127, n. 6 (mod. Knisovo); for Athenaeum, Leake, iv, 525; Stählin, 125, n. 3; for Theudoria, Leake, iv, 212 (mod. Theodoriana; Sp. Lambros prefers the identification with Vulgareli; cf. Wilhelm, *GGA*, 1898, 217, n. 1). From Livy (P) xxxix, 25, 17, it appears that in 185 Philip also possessed Poetneum, an Athamanian fortress near the modern village of Tyrna, at the head of the river Portaikos (Stählin, 125, n. 8).
[3] iv, 1, 209.   [4] Livy (P) xxxviii, 2, 1: *ingenti celeritate*.
[5] Probably on the slopes of Mt Tsuka; Stählin, 127.
[6] Near the modern Vatsinja: Stählin, *ibid.*

arrival of Aetolian reinforcements enabled the Athamanians to hurry ahead by mountain tracks, and harass his line from above, while the Aetolians harried the rear. The Macedonians fled in panic, and eventually, in the utmost disorder, reached a river which led them down in safety to Gomphi;[1] and meanwhile Xenon was expelled from Aethopia and, after losing most of his men among the rocks, at length reached Gomphi with a bare handful. Philip later buried his dead under a truce; and Amynander sent a message to the Scipios at Ephesus, announcing the recovery of his throne, making certain vague accusations against Philip and asking for peace.[2]

Philip's discomfiture encouraged the Aetolians to attempt the recovery of those northern provinces which had fallen to Macedonia in summer, 191;[3] rallying the whole federal army, Nicander marched along the Acarnanian frontier to Amphilochia, which had evidently seceded when Philip took the intervening land of Aperantia.[4] Both in Amphilochia and Aperantia the people rose to meet the Aetolians, and after wavering a little the Dolopians followed suit;[5] thus in a little over a month Philip's possessions southwest of Thessaly had all gone. However, the rising Aetolian hopes were quickly dashed by the news of Magnesia and the rejection of their embassy; already, they learnt, M. Fulvius Nobilior, the consul for 189, was on his way to Greece with a new army. Further misfortunes awaited them; for the envoys, whom they now sent to plead their case once more at Rome, were captured by the Epirotes and held to ransom until the Romans intervened, and Damoteles, whom they sent in their place, soon returned on learning at Leucas that Fulvius was already in Epirus.[6]

As he advanced southward, Fulvius was in much the same position as Philip had been in 219;[7] and just as then the Epirotes had urged Philip to take Ambracus, so now with equal success

[1] Not the Portaikos (so Leake, IV, 526; Niese, II, 763, n. 1) but the river on which Musaki now stands. Cf. Livy (P) XXXVIII, 2, 10.

[2] The dating of the campaign depends on the arrival of this embassy in January, 189; Livy (P) XXXVIII, 2, 1–3, 2; Polyb. XXI, 25, 1–2.

[3] See above, p. 207.

[4] Cf. Salvetti, 126; Oberhummer, 181; Klaffenbach, IG, IX, 1², introd. p. xl.   [5] Polyb. XXI, 25, 3–7; Livy (P) XXXVIII, 3, 3–5.

[6] Polyb. XXI, 25, 8–11; 26, 7–19; Livy (P) XXXVIII, 3, 6–8.

[7] See above, pp. 38 seq.

they persuaded Fulvius to lay siege to the larger fortress of Ambracia, Pyrrhus's old capital on the Arachthus, which had been Aetolian since the fall of the Epirote monarchy.[1] Fulvius's full scale investment of the town met, however, with firm resistance; and although a plan for a two-fold attack on the Romans from within and without failed owing to the non-arrival of the main Aetolian army, the Aetolians were nevertheless able to throw two separate relieving forces, 1500 men in all, into the city.[2]

At the same time minor raids and depredations from both sides accompanied the siege. The Aetolians counter-attacked in Acarnania, and Perseus, Philip's eldest son, began a campaign to recover Dolopia and Amphilochia; indeed it is suggested in Livy that Nicander's failure to co-ordinate with the forces inside Ambracia may have been due to the news that some important town, perhaps Amphilochian Argos,[3] was being besieged by Perseus. His presence so far west suggests that the prince had recovered Dolopia; but on Nicander's approach, he abandoned the siege and returned ravaging to Macedonia. And Nicander, in turn, was drawn away from Ambracia once more by a joint Achaean and Illyrian raid on the Aetolian coast.[4]

Eventually, notwithstanding the very keen resistance of the Ambracians, Nicander, whose natural inclination, no less than his recent dealings with Philip, inclined him towards compromise, decided that the League could not support a war on three fronts, and envoys were sent to approach Fulvius.[5] After some Aetolian hesitations, the Roman terms were accepted: and these, thanks to the intervention of the Athenians and Rhodians and of Amynander (who, significantly for Philip's future relations with Rome, was now in favour with his late enemies, and prepared to speak for the Ambracians, with whom he had lived during his short exile), were reduced to an indemnity of 500 talents, 200 to be paid at once and the rest in six yearly instalments, the surrender of all prisoners and deserters, and the exclusion from the

---

[1] Cf. Niese, II, 267. Ambracia is the modern Arta.
[2] Polyb. xxi, 26, 1–6; 27; Livy (P) xxxviii, 3, 9–5, 10; Zon. ix, 21.
[3] Cf. Oberhummer, 184, n. 1; Klaffenbach, *IG*, ix, 1², introd. p. xlii.
[4] Livy (P) xxxviii, 6, 1–7, 3.
[5] Polyb. xxi, 28; Livy (P) xxxviii, 7, 4–8, 7; Polyaen. *Strat.* ii, 7, 14; Zon. ix, 21, 4. For Nicander's later support of Macedon see Polyb. xx, 11, 9 *seq.*

League of any towns that had been taken by the Romans, or had entered into alliance with them since the arrival of the Scipios; and Cephallenia was to be omitted from the peace. A gift of 150 talents to Fulvius saved Ambracia from being sacked; and after arranging for the sending of an Aetolian delegation, including Nicander, to Rome, for the final ratification of the peace, the consul proposed to cross over to Cephallenia.[1]

Already, meanwhile, Philip was having further proof of the Senate's consistent lack of consideration for his interests or even his personal feelings. Until spring 189 Syrian garrisons had managed to keep their hold on the Thracian towns of Maronea and Aenus; and when Q. Fabius Labeo, the new Roman admiral, sailed north from Crete, where he had been operating, to remove these garrisons,[2] Philip not unnaturally anticipated that the help he had given to the Scipios would now be rewarded by a favourable readjustment of his eastern frontiers. Fabius, however, took as the new frontier an inland road, which skirted the Thracian hills behind Maronea, and so excluded both towns from Philip's territory.[3] A further insult was the favour now shown to Amynander,[4] who had so recently expelled Philip ignominiously from Athamania. And, finally, in the terms offered to the Aetolians Philip saw no guarantees that he was to recover Amphilochia and Aperantia.

Immediately after his loss of Dolopia and Athamania in the spring, he had taken the precaution of sending agents to Rome.[5] But the early part of the summer had passed in the settlement of the affairs of Asia and the hearing of the host of embassies from interested parties.[6] Hence, though Philip's representatives had succeeded in accentuating the dislike already felt for the Aetolians, they had made no real progress towards interesting the Senate in Philip's own claims. Therefore, when the matter came up in the autumn, it was not very difficult for the Athenians to persuade the Senate to grant Aetolia terms only a little more

---

[1] Polyb. xxi, 29, 1–30, 16; Livy (P) xxxviii, 8, 8–10, 2. On the slight discrepancy in the Livian version (T. Quinctius for L. Cornelius Scipio) see Vollgraff, Rev. Phil. xxvii, 1903, 236 seq.; Nissen, 203 note; Niese, ii, 767, n. 2; De Sanctis, iv, 1, 214, n. 157; Klaffenbach, IG, ix, 1², introd. p. xlii.
[2] Livy (P) xxxvii, 60, 2–7.   [3] Livy (P) xxxix, 27, 10.
[4] Polyb. xxi, 29, 6 seq.; Livy (P) xxxviii, 9, 4 seq.
[5] Polyb. xxi, 31, 3–4; Livy (P) xxxviii, 10, 3.
[6] Polyb. xxi, 18–24; Livy (A) xxxvii, 52, 1–6; (P) 52, 7–56, 10.

stringent than those proposed by Fulvius; she was given a *foedus iniquum* and became a Roman ally.[1]

This same autumn and winter saw the pendant to the Aetolian War, in the Roman attack on Cephallenia. This island, with its strong strategical position, commanding the Corinthian Gulf, had been stormed unsuccessfully by Philip in 218.[2] The Romans now crossed over and annexed it; but while the details of the surrender were being negotiated, the town of Same revolted, and held out against a persistent siege from October to the end of January. During this time Fulvius visited the Peloponnese to deal with a dispute between Achaea and Sparta, and also returned to Rome to hold the elections; and it was not until he arrived back in Same, that the town fell and the whole island was reduced.[3]

The following summer (188)[4] Cn. Manlius Vulso, Fulvius's colleague in the consulship of 189, held a final conference at Apamea to settle the reorganisation of Asia Minor. Large tracts of Antiochus's former possessions were now made over to Rhodes and Pergamum, and he himself, on certain conditions, was accepted as a Roman ally.[5] Thus by autumn 188 Manlius was free to evacuate Asia Minor, and lead his troops back through Thrace and Macedonia to the Adriatic. After crossing the Hellespont with the help of the Pergamene fleet (the Roman had already returned to Greece), he rested for a time at Lysimacheia before attempting the passage through Thrace. The next stage

[1] The terms were: all deserters, fugitives and prisoners in the possession of Aetolia, with the notable exception of those who had been enemies of Rome when the Aetolians were her allies (for instance any Macedonians taken during the Roman war with Philip!) to be surrendered to the chief magistrate at Corcyra within 100 days; an indemnity fixed at 500 talents, 200 to be paid at once, the rest in yearly instalments of 50 talents; forty hostages to be given; Cephallenia to be exempt from the treaty; all towns and villages taken from Aetolia by the Romans since the consulship of 192 to be exempt from Aetolian annexation; and Oeniadae to be Acarnanian. (Polyb. xxi, 31-2; Livy (P) xxxviii, 10, 4-9; Cicero, *pro Balbo*, 16, 35).

[2] See above, p. 53.

[3] On the chronology see below, Appendix iii, p. 333, and works there quoted. References: Livy (P) xxxviii, 28, 5-29, 13; cf. (A) 35, 1-3; Polyb. xxi, 32 *b*; Zon. ix, 21, 4.

[4] The summer of 189 had been occupied by a punitive expedition against the Galatians (Polyb. xxi, 33-9; Livy (P) xxxviii, 12-27).

[5] Preliminary settlement at Rome: Polyb. xxi, 24; cf. Livy (P) xxxvii, 55, 4-7. Final settlement in Asia: Polyb. xxi, 45; Livy (P) xxxviii, 38-9; Appian, *Syr.* 39; Diod. xxix, 10.

of his march was marked by an attack from four Thracian tribes in a narrow pass, where he lost many men and a large part of the Asiatic booty. A second attack beyond Aenus was beaten off, and eventually the army reached the safety of the Macedonian coast, and from there crossed the mountains to Apollonia, where Manlius spent the winter.[1]

This disastrous march across the Balkans did much to strain the friendship between Philip and the Romans. Unlike the Scipios, Manlius had taken no steps to secure Philip's invaluable assistance; consequently rumour was quick to insinuate that the Thracian attacks had actually been stimulated from Pella.[2] There can be little doubt as to Philip's justifiable bitterness towards Rome. In Asia, where he had given no assistance, he could expect no rewards; but it must have irritated him to see Eumenes succeeding Antiochus as master of the Thracian Chersonese and most of the Syrian possessions in Europe,[3] and he resented his own deliberate exclusion from Aenus and Maronea, which were to be left as no man's land to tempt Thracian marauders down on to the coast. Nearer home, he had been bitterly disappointed at the failure of the Romans to grant him Orestis, which he had never recovered since its revolt during the truce of 198–7.[4] In Greece itself, partly as a result of the Isthmus proclamation, but even more because of the Senate's veiled hostility, the policy of collaboration, faithfully adhered to since Cynoscephalae, had brought quite insignificant advantages. The independent Thessalian League still controlled Melitaea, Thaumaci, Lamia, Malis, Xyniae and the small plain of Parachelois in the hills beyond Metropolis;[5]

---

[1] Livy (P) xxxviii, 40–41.   [2] Livy (P) xxxviii, 40, 8.
[3] Polyb. xxi, 45, 9; Livy (P) xxxviii, 39, 14.
[4] See above, p. 163, n. 2; cf. Livy (P) xxxix, 28, 2. Benecke, *CAH*, viii, 245, claims that Philip's grievances are mere guesses 'since the king is not likely to have announced them publicly in this form'; but in fact he *did* announce them in precisely this form at Thessalonica in 185; cf. Livy (P) xxxix, 28, 2 (Orestis; cf. 23, 6); 28, 3 (Lamia; cf. 23, 9); 28, 4 (loss of Thessaly, Perrhaebia and Athamania; cf. 23, 10–11)—as Benecke himself later describes, *ibid.* 250.
[5] References: Melitaea: *Syll.* 647 = *IG*, ix, 2, 89; Thaumaci: *IG*, ix, 2, 218, dated a little after 178; Xyniae: Livy (P) xxxix, 26, 2; see above, p. 203, n. 3; below, p. 231, n. 1; Lamia: *IG*, ix, 2, 64, dated about 186–5; Parachelois: Livy (P) xxxix, 26, 2. See in general Niese, iii, 19; De Sanctis, iv, 1, 232–3; Kip, 47–9. On the position of Parachelois (mod. Nevropolis) see Leake, iv, 272 *seq.*; Stählin, 146, n. 18.

and though, as we saw, Philip had acquired Magnesia with
Demetrias, and most of the towns along the Malian coast,[1]
including Larisa Cremaste, yet so long as Lamia was in Thessalian hands and the route over Mt Othrys closed to him, there
was little possibility of a vigorous Hellenic policy.

Thessaly, in fact, for all that Philip controlled many of the
towns of Perrhaebia and the western plain, such as Tricca,
Gomphi, Phaloria or Malloea,[2] and such important fortresses
as Gonnocondylus,[3] was rapidly coming to occupy the place of
Aetolia as Philip's chief enemy in the south. The Aetolian League
had now been considerably mutilated. To Thessaly, as we saw,
she had lost her possessions around Mt Othrys, Thaumaci,
Xyniae, Lamia and Malis; in the west Ambracia, Cephallenia
and Oeniadae were gone; Phocis had once more become an
independent and united state;[4] and Dolopia was probably
retained by Philip. On the other hand, Aetolia still remained the
largest state in north Greece, and controlled Amphilochia and
Aperantia (with the Agraei), the town of Stratus, Doris, Aeniania,
east and west Locris,[5] and the town of Heraclea, which the
Senate allowed her to keep as an exception to the general
ruling.[6]

Amphilochia and Aperantia apart—and these were in fact old
Aetolian possessions, the loss of which Philip held against Rome
rather than Aetolia—there was no longer any dispute outstanding
between Philip and the League. Consequently the settlement of

[1] See above, p. 204; Livy (P) XXXIX, 23, 12.
[2] See above, pp. 202; 204, n. 4. The status of Aeginium is uncertain. It
had fallen to Philip and Baebius in 191 and in 168 it was in Perseus's hands
(cf. Livy (P) XLIV, 46, 3; XLV, 27, 1 seq.); but it was not among the towns
Livy mentions as claimed by the Thessalians in 185 (see below, p. 228)—
perhaps because, as a border town, its original status was in question. Strabo,
VII, 7, 9, reckons it under Tymphaea (cf. Stählin, 123; N. G. L. Hammond,
BSA, XXXII, 1931–2, 146); though, as Tymphaea was now Epirote, this would
give Philip no obvious claim to the town.
[3] Livy (P) XXXIX, 25, 16.
[4] See above, p. 182, for the position of Phocis under Aetolia; for its
independence and constitution as a league see Syll. 647. Cf. Swoboda, Gr.
Staatsalt.⁶ 321 seq.; De Sanctis, IV, 1, 233, n. 208.
[5] In the Amphictyonic list of 178 (Syll. 636) both Locrian votes are held
by Aetolians.
[6] See Daux, Delphes, 671 seq.; BCH, LVIII, 1934, 163–4; against Vollgraff,
Rev. Phil. XXVII, 1903, 240–4, who makes it Macedonian; and against Dittenberger, Syll.² 293, n. 12, and De Sanctis, IV, 1, 233, n. 207, who make it independent.

189 soon had its sequel in the already foreshadowed rapprochement between Macedonia and Aetolia,[1] against the common enemy, Thessaly. It was in the manœuvres around Delphi that this new alignment was to become most apparent. The immediate breach between Delphi and Aetolia, which had been inspired by Acilius in the winter of 191–0,[2] and had been attended by the expropriation of Aetolian landowners, the assassination of Delphians and the threat of an Aetolian invasion of the sacred city,[3] had given way to more cordial relations from autumn 190 onwards.[4] Nevertheless, the Aetolian hegemony had ended, and a reshuffle of seats on the Amphictyonic Council now took place; and though, unfortunately, the exact form in which it was reconstituted in 190 is not preserved, a later inscription points clearly to a protracted struggle between the Thessalians on the one hand, and Philip and the Aetolians on the other, for the control of the council. Philip had, it is true, no direct representation; but his vassals in Dolopia and Magnesia could, like the Aetolian subject peoples of Aeniania, Doris, Locris and Oeta, carry on a vicarious struggle for power inside the Amphictyony.[5] In this way Philip took up in a modified form one of his oldest ambitions, which had figured as a cardinal point in the programme of the Social War.[6]

But in other respects Philip was far from reverting to the hopes and ambitions of old policies. The frontiers of Greece established after the Syrian War ruled out the resumption of activity in the Peloponnese, as completely as did the settlement after Cynoscephalae. Central Greece and Thessaly Philip might still regard as his sphere of interest, but the Romans had cut off the Peloponnese from Macedon even more effectively than Aratus's recovery of the Acrocorinth had done in the time of Antigonus Gonatas, half a century before;[7] and Philip, like his grandfather, had to reconcile himself to the loss. Though now

---

[1] See above, p. 206.   [2] See above, p. 209.
[3] *Syll.* 611, lines 10–11; 16–21.
[4] There is no evidence, however, that the Aetolians continued to hold meetings in Delphi; Daux, 269 *seq.* against Niese, III, 14, n. 1; Pomtow, *Klio*, XVI, 1920, 119 *seq.*; Roussel, *BCH*, LVI, 1932, 26 *seq.*
[5] *Syll.* 613, dealing with affairs from 186 onwards; see Daux, 280, and below, pp. 225 *seq.*
[6] Polyb. IV, 25, 6 *seq.*; see above, p. 32.
[7] Tarn, 405.

fifty years of age, and embittered at the injustice he had suffered at the hands of Rome, he nevertheless set to work with tireless energy to rebuild and consolidate his country within its present boundaries. His plans for expansion in the south, in the west and in the east had all in turn foundered, and a *pax Romana* blocked his further hopes in all three directions; therefore, as a result partly of this logic of elimination, but even more of the prominence which his northern neighbours naturally assumed, the moment internal consolidation became his immediate interest, Philip now adopted a northern policy. Thus, for the first time since the days of Philip II, Balkan questions took precedence at Pella over the affairs of Greece and the Hellenistic states; and Philip, who had begun his reign as the sympathetic protégé of Aratus, was to end it in a way that displayed him as the least Hellenic of all the Antigonids.

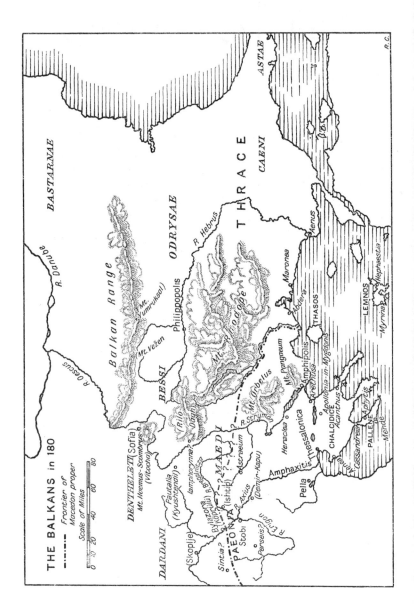

THE BALKANS in 180

- - - Frontier of
Macedon proper

Scale of Miles
0 10 20 40 60 80

BASTARNAE

R. Danube

R. Oescus

Balkan Range

Mt. Yumruksal)

Mt. Vežen

ODRYSAE

BESSI

Philippopolis

R. Hebrus

Mt. Rhodope

THRACE

CAENI

ASTAE

R.B.

Maronea

Abdera

THASOS

LEMNOS

Myrina

Hephaestia

DENTHELETII (Sofia)
Mt. Haemus-Scomius
(Vitocho)

DARDANI

(Skopje)

Paudalia
(Kyustendil)

Iamphorynna

R. Begbunitsa

Bylazora
R. Kopriula
(Ishtip)

Mt. Orbelus

R. Strymon

Astraeum

(Denir-Kapu)

PAEONIA

Stobi

R. Erigon

Perseis?

Sintia?

M A E D I

Rilo

Odoph

Mt. Pangaeum

Heraclea

Amphipolis

Arethusa

Apollonia-in-Mygdonis

Acanthus

CHALCIDICE

Cassandrea

PALLENE

Mende

Amphaxitis

Thessalonica

Pella

R. Axius

Aenus

R.C.

Chapter VII : Philip Looks North

THE RECOVERY OF MACEDON (187–179)

PHILIP'S first and immediate task was the reorganisation and consolidation of the territories which he now held; and this must have involved investigations into the internal affairs of such cities as those in Thessaly, which were being at present governed as mere acquisitions of war, probably with garrisons and military governors. There was a vast amount of work to be done, weeding out hostile elements and systematising the methods of administration in Dolopia, Magnesia or Perrhaebia; and this undoubtedly began as soon as the Roman army was safely out of the way.

However, Philip's anger against Rome soon took him beyond mere consolidation. Probably in 187, but certainly, at the latest, in 186, he seized the Thracian coastal cities of Aenus and Maronea, which Q. Fabius Labeo had so carefully left as neutral territory between the frontiers of Philip and Eumenes.[1] By the simple device of moving the road, which Fabius had laid down as the boundary, Philip appears to have established a shaky title not only to Maronea, but also to many of the surrounding lands and villages under her control;[2] but for Aenus, fifty miles farther east, he must have dispensed with even this slight camouflage. Later he claimed that the towns were split between Macedonian and Pergamene factions; and it is fairly certain that this *stasis* had been a useful instrument in their annexation.[3]

In Philip's seizure of these towns there is, however, no reason to see the beginnings of a new policy of expansion. It is rather the logical extension of his scheme for consolidating Macedon: knowing from experience the folly of leaving an independent strip, to attract the inroads of the Thracian barbarians,[4] Philip

---

[1] See above, p. 216.   [2] Livy (P) XXXIX, 27, 10.

[3] Livy (P) XXXIX, 23, 13—if the *quasdam urbes in Thracia* are in fact Aenus and Maronea, and not smaller towns recovered earlier; cf. Livy (P) XXXIX, 24, 9, for Maronean exiles.

[4] Cf. Polyb. XVIII, 51, 7, where the departure of the Macedonian garrison was the signal for a Thracian raid on Lysimacheia.

was merely rounding-off his possessions before Eumenes fore-stalled him from the other side. In any case, in the years immediately following the Roman withdrawal, this policy of consolidation rapidly came to involve more than the systematisation of government in the outer provinces. In Macedon itself, Philip set about replenishing his depleted treasury by an increase in the revenue from agricultural produce and harbour dues;[1] new mines were sunk and old ones reopened, and very soon large issues of coins were being made, not only by Philip's royal mint, but also by the Macedonians as a body, as well as by certain regional groups and even (as in Thessaly)[2] by separate cities.[3] By these issues, the first in Macedonia since a series of commemorative tetradrachms struck about 212,[4] Philip plainly sought to utilise the silver resources of Macedon to the full in building up the economic life of the country.

The cognate problem of repopulating Macedon, after the losses in man-power of thirty years' warfare, Philip approached in two ways. By a policy of encouraging large families and compelling people to rear what children were born, he set about his main purpose of increasing the native population;[5] at the same time he effected an immediate strengthening by the importation of Thracians from the districts he had annexed.[6]

His policy aroused the hostility of both Eumenes and the

[1] Livy (P) xxxix, 24, 2: *vectigalia regni... fructibus...agrorum portoriisque maritimis auxit.* The double form of tax laid the burden both on the countryside and on such coastal towns as Cassandreia. In the case of the harbour dues, the fresh revenue seems perhaps to have been obtained by an increase of trade as well as by an increase in the rate of tax (see below, p. 229): whether similarly the actual production from the land was stimulated, or whether the rate of the land-tax was merely increased, the evidence does not allow us to determine.

[2] Cf. Head, 291.

[3] For the numismatic evidence and a discussion of the significance of this administrative innovation, see below, pp. 265 *seq.*

[4] Mamroth, *ZN*, xl, 1930, 292–3; Seltman, 224, however, places this issue in *c.* 201, connecting it with Philip's eastern policy, and his attempt to repair the ravages of twenty years' constant warfare.

[5] Livy (P) xxxix, 24, 3: *cogendis omnibus procreare atque educare liberos.* The details of this campaign are unfortunately not recorded; probably definite decrees enforced the rearing of children born, while a system of rewards and penalties was employed to encourage marriage and parenthood. The Greek custom of exposing children is not likely to have been common except in the coastal cities.

[6] Livy (P) xxxix, 24, 4. On the further development of this policy, see below, pp. 243–4.

Thessalians. To Eumenes, the seizure of Aenus and Maronea was a direct threat to his own new possessions in the Chersonese; and the Thessalians, after their long subjection to Macedon, necessarily regarded any increase in Macedonian strength as a threat to their independence. Not only Philip's internal reforms, but his interpretation of the peace settlement, and the agreement with the Romans, under which he had recovered parts of Thessaly, aroused deep suspicions among the Thessalians; and their hostility is, as we saw, reflected in the struggle for control of the Delphic Amphictyony. A decree of 184,[1] marking the reconstitution of that body, and celebrating the good offices of Nicostratus, a Thessalian from Larisa, who had been sent to the Pythiad festival of 186, refers specifically to an Amphictyonic Council composed of autonomous peoples and democratic cities;[2] and this formula certainly covers an attack by the Thessalians (and probably the Athenians, who are mentioned as collaborating with them)[3] upon such states as the Magnesians and the Dolopians, who, as Philip's vassals, could claim neither title, and upon the Aetolian vassals of Aeniania, Doris, Locris and Oeta, all of which appear in the later Amphictyonic list of 173,[4] but would be unable to comply with these conditions.[5]

The re-establishment of the Council seems to have been effected through a body of non-Amphictyonic Greeks,[6] sitting at Delphi, and in the decision to revert in constitution εἰς τὸ ἐξ ἀρχῆς κατὰ τὰ πάτρια,[7] there was scope enough for ambiguity and

[1] Syll. 613; see Daux, 281 seq.
[2] Id. lines 4–5: ἔδοξ[εν τῶι κοι]νῶι τῶν Ἀμφικτιόνων τῶν ἀπὸ τῶν αὐτονόμων ἐθνῶν καὶ δημοκρατουμένων πόλεων. Plainly no city within Philip's frontiers, whatever degree of relative independence it might obtain, could be said to be 'democratic'—a word which here seems to be used without any implied contrast to 'oligarchic', but almost as a synonym for 'self-governing'; cf. note 6, below. An example of what 'democratic' signified at this time is furnished by the Achaean League, which had no difficulty in reconciling a claim to that title (Polyb. II, 38, 6; 44, 6; IV, 1, 5; XXII, 12, 6; XXIII, 12, 8; Syll. 665) with a choice of officials πλουτίνδα καὶ ἀριστίνδα (IG, VII, 188, line 8); see Aymard, Assemblées, 56, n. 4; 137; 335 seq.
[3] Syll. 613, lines 9, 15.   [4] Syll. 636.
[5] So Daux, 281 seq., against Roussel, BCH, LVI, 1932, 28–30.
[6] Syll. 613, lines 19-20: τοῖς ἄλλοις Ἕλλησιν τοῖς αἱρουμένοις τὴν ἐλευθερίαν καὶ δημοκρατίαν.
[7] Id. lines 11-12. Whether this reversion to the 'original' form (i.e. probably that before the third Sacred War in the fourth century) involved the exclusion of the Delphians themselves is uncertain.

intrigue. Nicostratus was chosen to go along with Menedemus of Athens as envoy of the Council to Rome, perhaps in the winter of 186; and the anti-Macedonian alignment is clearly shown again in the inscription, when it speaks of Nicostratus carrying out his duty οὔτε κακοπαθίαν οὔτε κίνδυνον ὑποστελλόμενος τὸν ἐσόμενον ὑπὸ τῶν ἐπιβουλευόντων αὐτῶι[1]—a scarcely-veiled reference to Philip.

However, it was not through the Amphictyonic Council alone that the Thessalians worked against Philip at Rome. In the winter of 186–5 embassies also arrived in Rome from the Thessalians and Perrhaebians, from the Athamanians and from Eumenes, to lay various complaints against Philip; and Philip himself sent his own representatives to reply.[2] The Senate listened to the Thessalian complaints unmoved; and it was only when Eumenes's envoys announced the seizure of the Thracian towns, and refugees from Maronea related how their city and that of Aenus had fallen into Macedonian hands that they became alarmed.[3] The ownership of a few cities in Perrhaebia was a matter of indifference to the Senate; in any case, as Philip's envoys pleaded,[4] the Thessalian accusations were probably distorted, and the king's actions in accordance with the agreement made with Baebius and Acilius. The grievance of the Athamanians, who affirmed that Philip's continued occupation of Poetneum and the Athenaeum gave him control over their whole country,[5] was on a similar plane. But the seizure of Maronea and Aenus, represented no doubt by the Pergamene envoys in the most lurid light, must have seemed the proof of a new plan of expansion, perhaps even a renewal of that eastern policy which had led to the panic of 201 and the Second Macedonian War. At the very least, Philip was defying a Roman decision and once more pursuing an independent course; and since it was now a fundamental axiom of Roman policy to prevent

---

[1] Syll. 613, lines 33–5. Similar accusations that Philip attempted to interfere with embassies are made by the Thessalians in 185; cf. Livy (P) xxxix, 25, 10.

[2] Livy (P) xxxix, 24, 6–12; Polyb. xxii, 6 (abridged; cf. Nissen, 223); Zon. ix, 21, 5. Amynander has now disappeared (for Livy (P) xxxix, 24, 11, is retrospective).

[3] Livy (P) xxxix, 24, 7: maxime moverat senatum quod iam Aeni et Maroneae adfectari possessionem audierant: minus Thessalos curabant.

[4] Livy (P) xxxix, 24, 10–12.   [5] Livy (P) xxxix, 24, 8; cf. 25, 17.

the rise of an independent power in the Balkan peninsula, a drastic remedy was required. Accordingly, a commission of three, consisting of Q.Caecilius Metellus, M. Baebius Tamphilus and Ti. Sempronius Gracchus, was sent out to Greece in the spring of 185, to hear the various complaints and Philip's justification.[1]

From Apollonia the commissioners went over into Thessaly, and arrangements were made for all the interested parties to meet in the vale of Tempe;[2] and here, Livy tells us, Philip sat like a defendant in a court of law, to hear the charges of his accusers before his Roman judges.[3] The main point upon which the claims of the Thessalians and Perrhaebians[4] turned was the interpretation of the agreement under which Philip had co-operated with the Romans against Antiochus and the Aetolians. Throughout the year 191 he had operated, first with Baebius and later with Acilius; and though our first reference to a specific agreement[5] is at the time of Philip's advance on Demetrias, there can be little doubt that from his first meeting with Baebius in Dassaretia it was understood that whatever he took from the Aetolians he should keep. It was indeed because of this compact that Flamininus had pressed for the ending of the siege of Naupactus.[6] But now the Thessalians were claiming, evidently with encouragement from Rome, that the agreement, rightly interpreted, gave Philip only such towns as had been Aetolian of old, and not towns that were in reality Thessalian (or Per-rhaebian) and had been forcibly absorbed into the Aetolian

[1] Polyb. xxii, 6, 6; Livy (P) xxxix, 24, 13. Baebius was the commander who co-operated with Philip in 191 (see above, pp. 201 seq.). Polybius gives the third name as Τεβέριον Κλαύδιον, but that the mistake is that of his epitomator, and not Livy, is shown from the repetition of Ti. Sempronius in Livy (P) xxxix, 33, 1; see De Sanctis, iv, 1, 240, n. 8.

[2] Livy (P) xxxix, 24, 14.   [3] Livy (P) xxxix, 25, 1–2.

[4] Livy (P) xxxix, 25, 6, suggests that the Magnesians joined in the confer-ence. They are not, however, included when the specific complaints are made, or in Philip's reply; and they had sent no representatives to Rome the previous winter. Therefore (as Stählin, P–W, 'Magnesia', col. 466, argues against Niese, iii, 23) the Magnesians were probably not present at Tempe, parti-cularly as they were not at this time an independent people, but part of Philip's empire. If Livy's mistake goes back to Polybius, it may have arisen from a confusion of the Eurymenae and Meliboea taken by Philip (see above, p. 202, n. 4) with the towns of the same name in Magnesia.

[5] Livy (P) xxxix, 23, 10; see above, p. 207, n. 2.
[6] See above, p. 208.

League. In particular, they were entitled to Gomphi, Tricca, Phaloria, Eurymenae and other towns in western Thessaly, which Philip had admittedly captured from the Aetolians, but were originally Thessalian.[1]

The first of the Thessalian speakers adopted a conciliatory manner, urging Philip to act as their friend and ally, and to emulate the Romans in using the weapon of kindness rather than terror;[2] but this approach showed little understanding of Philip's disposition. Evidently this was realised by the later speakers, for with a sudden change of front they proceeded to a bitter attack on Philip's methods and good faith. Even if Philip was compelled to evacuate these towns, he was certain to sack them before handing them over,[3] just as he had done in 198; and had he not carried off five hundred leading Thessalians to Macedon and enslaved them?[4] His bad faith was evident from his attacks on envoys sent by them to Flamininus;[5] and by diverting trade from Phthiotic Thebes to Demetrias, he had done his best to ruin them commercially.[6] In short, the whole of Thessaly was terrified of Philip, and unless the Romans took some steps to tame this unruly steed, their gift of freedom would have been little more than empty words.[7]

Even in the sympathetic account of Polybius, as recorded in Livy, the weakness of the Thessalian case is apparent. For some of their complaints there may well have been a solid foundation. Thus the accusation that Philip had interfered with envoys,

---

[1] Livy (P) xxxix, 25, 3–6. Philip had taken these towns in March 191 (see above, p. 202), apparently from Amynander (Livy (P) xxxvi, 13, 5–6); that they are now said to have been Aetolian is perhaps to be explained by the fact that Amynander and the Aetolians were acting in concert throughout the 191 campaign; see Fine, *TAPhA*, lviii, 1932, 150 *seq.* The new formulation makes no allowance for towns which might be shown to be originally Thessalian, but to have joined the Aetolians voluntarily.

[2] Livy (P) xxxix, 25, 14–15.   [3] Livy (P) xxxix, 25, 7.

[4] Livy (P) xxxix, 25, 8: *et quae reddiderit coactus Thessalis, inutilia ut redderet curasse.* This can only refer to July 198, when he sacked the towns of Thessaly (see above, pp. 153 *seq.*). The abduction of the 500 leading citizens may be a distortion of the fact that Philip on the same occasion forced the populations of these cities to accompany him back to Macedon; or it may refer to the weeding out of the anti-Macedonian party leaders in the cities possessed by Philip since 192. Since no reference to the charge occurs in our version of Philip's reply, the former explanation is the more probable.

[5] Livy (P) xxxix, 25, 10: probably referring to some unrecorded incident in 191.

[6] Livy (P) xxxix, 25, 9.   [7] Livy (P) xxxix, 25, 11–13.

though undoubtedly designed to appeal to the well-known moral scruples of the Romans, who had entered the Illyrian War against Teuta on such a pretext,[1] nevertheless gains support from the similar insinuations of the Amphictyonic Council.[2] The diversion of trade from Phthiotic Thebes, and its harbour of Pyrasus,[3] to Demetrias, is credible as another incident in the long rivalry that had existed between these two cities, ever since Demetrius Poliorcetes had founded Demetrias in 293, as a counter-blast to Cassander's attempted synoecism of the surrounding townships into an enlarged Thebes;[4] it also throws an interesting side-light upon Philip's reorganisation of Macedon.

The cosmopolitan nature of Demetrias in the second century is clearly revealed by the contents of a cemetery, excavated by Arvanitopullos,[5] in which, out of 250 gravestones, dating from 200–150 B.C., there are those of men from Magnesia itself, Macedon, the islands (including those as far afield as Sicily), Asia Minor, Syria and Phoenicia. Further, the existence of the un-Thessalian office of the νομοφύλακες,[6] which later spread to Gonnus,[7] Stählin attributes[8] to the influence of Plato coming through Demetrius of Phalerum, rather than to the nearest local equivalent, the πολιτοφύλακες of Larisa. Thus archaeology confirms the view that when Philip set about restoring the economic prosperity of Macedon by regular taxes and an adequate coinage, he also resolved to make the favourite citadel of

---

[1] Cf. Holleaux, *CAH*, VII, 832.

[2] See above, p. 226, n. 1.   [3] Cf. Stählin, 173.

[4] On the rivalry between Thebes and Demetrias (and its forerunner, Pagasae) see Stählin, 67; Westlake, 5, n. 5. One of these two towns—both of which had easy access by sheltered waterways to south Greece—would always be the main export harbour for the corn and meat which Thessaly produced. (*Corn*: Xen. *Hell.* V, 4, 56; VI, 1, 11; Ephippus, fr. 1 (Kock); Philostr. *Vit. Soph.* p. 225, 526 (II, 39, ll. 8 *seq.* Kayser); inscr. published by Segre, *Riv. Fil.* LXII, 1934, 169–93. *Meat*: Hermippus, fr. 66, line 6 (reading Θετταλίας); Plut. *Moral.* 193 D. In spite of the lack of evidence, hides and wool must have been exported from the large Thessalian ranches; and the timber of Pelion is not so inaccessible as Westlake, 7, suggests—though here again there are no records of export trade.)

[5] Cf. Stählin, 74; *IG*, IX, 2, 1172 *seq.*; cf. Ἀρχ. Δελτ. I, 1915, 57 *seq.*; Πρακτικά, 1912, 186–9; 1920, 4 *seq.*; list of nationalities given by A. J. Reinach, *REG*, XXIV, 1911, 320; Arvanitopullos, Γραπταὶ στῆλαι, 91 *seq.*

[6] *IG*, IX, 2, 1108; 1109; *IG*, V, 2, 367, lines 24, 45; for the νομοφυλάκιον see *IG*, IX, 2, 1106, line 6; 1126, line 3.   [7] See Stählin, 34, n. 11.

[8] *Id.* 74. On the Athenian νομοφύλακες see De Sanctis, in *Entaphia Pozzi*, Turin, 1914, 3 *seq.*

the Antigonids, Demetrias, the chief port for Thessaly on the Pagasean Gulf. The Thessalian complaint suggests the use of unfair methods; but the most effective way of diverting trade from Thebes would be to establish good trading facilities, a sound coinage, no troublesome regulations and fair treatment for resident aliens.[1] We have already seen Philip's emphasis on coinage at this time; and the encouragement of settlers is confirmed not only by Arvanitopullos's excavations, but also by its consistency with Philip's policy of importing foreigners from Thrace[2] which, though partly military in design, was also intended to replenish a depleted population.

Otherwise, however, the Thessalian case rested on a mixture of possibilities and very ancient history: what Philip had done in 198 was no evidence for what he would do now, and neither was relevant to the pivot of the whole complaint, the nature of Philip's compact with the Romans in 191. This was also the point at issue in the Perrhaebian claim to Malloea, Ericinium and Gonnocondylus (the fortress above Gonnus, which Philip had rechristened Olympias to show its affinities with Macedon).[3] In both cases the frequency with which the towns had changed hands between Thessaly and Aetolia made it very difficult to determine the 'original owners':[4] but it was no doubt hoped that the Senate would cut the Gordian knot by an award against Philip. Finally, the Athamanians repeated their charges, and demanded the evacuation of Poetneum and the Athenaeum.[5]

It was now Philip's turn: and he, tired of the role of defendant, and acting on the principle that attack was the best form of defence, retaliated with a series of counter-accusations, many of them as irrelevant as those of his accusers. The Thessalians, he alleged, were themselves guilty of seizing the fortress of the Menelais in Dolopia: and in company with the Perrhaebians they had occupied Petra in Pieria.[6] In addition they had taken possession of Xyniae, which was unquestionably an Aetolian

[1] Cf. [Xenophon], *De vect.* III, 6.
[2] See above, p. 224.
[3] Livy (P) XXXIX, 25, 16; see Stählin, 9, on the significance of the original name of Gonnocondylus (Clenched-fist-before-Gonnus) and that given by Philip; also E. Kirsten, *P-W*, 'Olympias' (3), cols. 175 *seq.*
[4] Livy (P) XXXIX, 25, 6.   [5] Livy (P) XXXIX, 25, 17.
[6] Livy (P) XXXIX, 26, 1. For the Menelais, see Stählin, 147; for Petra, a frontier station north-west of Olympus, *id.* 37-8.

town, and had annexed the fertile valley of Parachelois, which formed part of Athamania.[1] In his reference to the last two places, it was Philip's object to turn the tables on his accusers by showing that it was they who had seized Aetolian and Athamanian territory rather than had their own towns occupied (as they claimed of the towns round Gomphi) by these peoples; and undoubtedly his new relations with Aetolia made Philip the more ready to adopt this line of argument.

Its futility was plain: only the weakest logic could justify the playing off of Xyniae and Parachelois against Gomphi, Tricca and Phaloria; and if Philip attempted this, it can only be because he believed the Romans to be already committed to the Thessalian interpretation of his compact with Baebius.[2] Despondent of his chances on the main issue, he sought to confuse it. With the minor charges he was more at home. It was indeed, he said, absurd, if he was to be held responsible for what ports sailors and merchants chose to frequent; and the Thessalian charges of assaults on envoys were refuted by the very number of embassies that had gone with complaints against him to Roman commanders and to the Senate, without any suggestion of interference. And now there was this charge of attacking envoys sent to Flamininus, a vague and unsupported accusation, in itself an insult to the Roman people, who had to indulge the Thessalians, while they constantly made themselves drunk on freedom, taken neat; they were like manumitted slaves, who only employed their liberty to insult their master. Finally, for his own part, he concluded, adapting a line of Theocritus, 'the sun of all his days was not yet set'.[3]

This outburst did Philip's case no good. An uproar followed his last words, which not only the Thessalians, but the Roman

[1] Livy (P) XXXIX, 26, 2. For Parachelois, see above, p. 218, n. 5. On the fate of Xyniae, Livy is slightly ambiguous (XXXIX, 26, 2): speaking of the Thessalians, Philip says: *Xynias quidem, haud dubie Aetolicum oppidum*, sibi contribuisse eos; *et Paracheloida, quae sub Athamania esset, nullo iure Thessalorum formulae factam*. In this context, however, *sibi contribuisse eos* must mean 'the Thessalians had annexed' (Niese, III, 19; De Sanctis, IV, 1, 232, n. 201; Stählin, 161, n. 3) and not 'the Romans had united it with him (*sc.* Philip)' (Benecke, *CAH*, VIII, 248).

[2] As Baebius himself was one of the commission, his demeanour will have given Philip an easy clue which way the Roman verdict was likely to go.

[3] Livy (P) XXXIX, 26, 3–9; Diod. XXIX, 16; cf. Theoc. I, 102: ἤδη γὰρ φράσδῃ πάνθ' ἅλιον ἄμμι δεδυκεῖν;

commissioners themselves took as a threat; and his reply to the
Perrhaebians and Athamanians did little to mend the harm done.
The towns under discussion, he said, had been given him by
Acilius and the Romans; if, unjustly, they chose to take them
back, he had no choice but to yield. But the Romans would be
making a great mistake in sacrificing a faithful ally to the gratifi-
cation of peoples who did not understand the nature of freedom.[1]
The threat, which this criticism concealed, indicated Philip's
irritation at having to bandy arguments with people whom he
had always regarded as his subjects.[2] And though the issue was
in any case prejudged—for Baebius was in as good a position as
anyone to assess Philip's rights—the king's attitude destroyed
any chance he might still have had. The Commission decreed
that the Macedonian garrisons should be withdrawn from the
cities under discussion, and Macedon should be limited to its
'ancient boundaries'; and machinery was to be set up to deal
with what disputes still remained. This decision, reminiscent
in its ambiguity of the definition of Masinissa's kingdom in
201,[3] would logically have involved the complete expulsion of
Philip from Thessaly; but in practice he continued to hold
Demetrias, a large part of Magnesia and Dolopia, and some of
the towns of Phthiotic Achaea, such as Larisa Cremaste, Alope,
Pteleum and Antron.[4] With these minor exceptions, however,
the Thessalians were now able to round off their frontiers.

From Tempe the commissioners accompanied Philip to
Thessalonica for a further conference on the Thracian question.
Here Eumenes's envoys and the exiled Maroneans[5] repeated the
arguments of the previous winter, the Pergamenes demanding

---

[1] Livy (P) xxxix, 26, 10–13.   [2] Cf. Polyb. iv, 76, 2.
[3] Polyb. xv, 18, 5: the Numidian decision was of course designed to encourage subsequent expansion; but in both cases the clause was framed so as
to permit a later Roman reinterpretation.
[4] See Livy (P) xl, 54, 2 (Demetrias); (P) xliv, 13, 1 (Meliboea in Magnesia; cf. Stählin, 80: but in 171, at least, parts of Magnesia, including the
south bank of the Peneius, were not under Macedonian control: cf. Livy (P)
xlii, 39, 2; 67, 2); (P) xlii, 56, 7; 67, 9 (Alope, Pteleum and Larisa Cremaste).
In addition, Aeginium, which was at this time counted as part of Tymphaea,
may have remained Macedonian (Livy (P) xliv, 46, 3; cf. Stählin, 122); see
above, p. 219, n. 2.
[5] Livy (P) xxxix, 27, 7, calls them simply *legati Maronitarum*: but they
undoubtedly represent the faction that had appeared at Rome the previous
winter (Livy (P) xxxix, 24, 9).

that Aenus and Maronea should be declared free or, better still, assigned to Eumenes in return for the services of his house to Rome; this gift, they claimed, had been implicit in the award of Lysimacheia and the Chersonese, an area to which Aenus and Maronea formed a logical appendix.[1] They were supported by the exiles, who declared Maronea to be full of Macedonians: in addition to the normal garrison, the whole administration of the town, its council and its law-courts, were in the hands of the party that toadied to Philip, and his opponents were either silenced or, like themselves, in exile. They also repeated the story of the shifting of the frontier.[2]

Philip's reply was more cautiously phrased than at Tempe: none the less it was a strong indictment of his treatment at the hands of Rome. Beginning with the revolt of Orestis in 198–7 and the Roman decision to leave this district independent after the Syrian War, he outlined his various grievances down to the recent decisions at Tempe, which had robbed him of those territories in Thessaly, Perrhaebia and Athamania which Acilius had let him acquire in compensation for the loss of Lamia. And now Eumenes was claiming Aenus and Maronea, although in fact the Romans had saved Eumenes from destruction by joining in the war against Antiochus, whereas he had fought voluntarily and at considerable personal disadvantage as their faithful ally, rejecting the most munificent offers from Antiochus; and later he had been mainly responsible for the successful transport of the Roman army across the Balkans. What justice was there in Eumenes's claim? Was not the Roman award specifically limited to the Chersonese and Lysimacheia? In short—and here, under the influence of his emotions, Philip reverted to the defiant attitude of Tempe—if the Romans wanted him as an enemy, let them continue in their present path: if as a friend, let them grant him justice.[3]

Perhaps a little alarmed,[4] the commission hesitated to force a crisis by another adverse decision; instead they gave a studied

[1] Livy (P) xxxix, 27, 2–6: *quae...velut appendices maioris muneris essent.*
[2] Livy (P) xxxix, 27, 7–10 (see above, p. 223): these incidents must already have been retailed at Rome in winter 186–5.
[3] Livy (P) xxxix, 28, 1–14: on the alleged offer of Antiochus see above, p. 198.
[4] Livy (P) xxxix, 29, 1: *movit aliquantum oratio regis legatos.*

answer, carefully phrased to produce an appearance of impartiality, referring the whole matter back to the Senate, but meanwhile —and here the mailed fist showed itself beneath the glove—requiring the withdrawal of Philip's garrisons from both Aenus and Maronea.[1] This done, Metellus went on to the Argive Nemea— for it was now July—to look into further differences which had arisen out of the relations of Sparta, Messenia and Achaea.[2] But at the beginning of the next consular year, after their return to Rome, all the same arguments on the Thracian question once more came up before the Senate, the commission reporting, and the envoys of Philip, Eumenes and the exiles reiterating their respective claims.[3] On the basis of the settlement, the Senate's decision was a just one: Aenus and Maronea were to remain independent, and a fresh commission was to go out, not only to supervise the evacuation of the Thracian coast, but also to see if Philip had carried out the decisions of the recent commission in Thessaly, Perrhaebia and Athamania.[4]

The Senate were in fact in a difficult position; justice to Philip and justice to the Greeks were incompatible, and the ambiguity in both the terms and the interpretation of the agreements with Baebius and Acilius had brought unnecessary complications. The Romans were, as usual, frankly opportunist. In 191, when Philip's help was needed, the Isthmus declaration could be ignored, and even if it proved expedient to give their late enemy an occasional rebuff, the Senate were quite prepared to compensate him in Thessaly, Perrhaebia and Athamania. But now, when Macedon was once more rearing its head, they chose to remember their obligations towards a free Greece, obligations that forced them to interpret the bargain with Acilius and the peace settlement in more rigid terms.

In Philip's eyes, however, all their talk of freedom for the Thessalians was only designed to thwart his own ambitions, and

---

[1] Livy (P) xxxix, 29, 1–2.

[2] Polyb. xxii, 10, 1. On the Spartan problem see Niese, iii, 42–8; De Sanctis, iv, 1, 237–40.

[3] Polyb. xxii, 11, 1–2; cf. Livy (P) xxxix, 33, 1–3. Polybius mentions exiles from Aenus as well as Maronea; but the restriction of the subsequent massacre to Maronea perhaps suggests that opposition from Aenus had been less strong.

[4] Polyb. xxii, 11, 3–12, 10; cf. Livy (P) xxxix, 3–8. The commission had also duties in the Peloponnese.

to withdraw concessions that Roman generals had already
granted;[1] and the report of the Senate's resolution overwhelmed
him with feelings similar to those he had experienced after his
interview with Flamininus at Antigoneia in 198, and his subsequent defeat in the Aous pass. Giving way, as then, to a fit
of uncalculating passion, he resolved that others should not enjoy
what he could not, and planned a summary vengeance on the
remaining members of the opposition in Maronea. Assisted by
Onomastus, the governor of Macedonian Thrace, who in turn
worked through Cassander (perhaps the *epistates* of Maronea),[2]
Philip had a band of Thracian mercenaries introduced into the
town by night, to carry out a large-scale massacre: and, perhaps
using this as a pretext, he still kept his garrisons in Maronea
and Aenus.[3]

When in the spring of 184 App. Claudius and his colleagues
reached Macedon, Philip blandly disclaimed all responsibility
for the massacre, attributing it to local factions within the town;
and relying on the fear of the survivors, he offered to allow the
commissioners to carry out any interrogations they wished.
Apparently disconcerted by this bluff, the Romans made the
unconvincing reply that they knew very well who had perpetrated the massacre, and broke off negotiations for the day;
but having presumably discussed the position overnight, they
opened the next day's proceedings with the demand that Philip
should send Onomastus and Cassander to Rome.[4] It was now
Philip's turn to be taken aback; but he eventually persuaded
App. Claudius to excuse Onomastus, and was freed from the
danger of Cassander's evidence when, shortly after the departure
of the commission for the Peloponnese, Cassander died suddenly
and conveniently in Epirus, while on his way to Rome. Not
unnaturally Philip was accused of adding one more to the long
list of victims of his poison-chest.[5]

The visit of App. Claudius proved a turning-point in Philip's
policy. At a private conference with his two most intimate

---

[1] Polyb. XXII, 13, 1–2; Livy (P) XXXIX, 34, 1.
[2] See above, p. 2, n. 6.
[3] Polyb. XXII, 13, 3–7; Livy (P) XXXIX, 34, 2.
[4] Polyb. XXII, 13, 7–14, 1; Livy (P) XXXIX, 34, 3–6. For stylistic reasons Livy
obscures this night's break in the proceedings.
[5] Polyb. XXII, 14, 2–6; Livy (P) XXXIX, 34, 7–10; Zon. IX, 21.

friends, Apelles and Philocles,[1] he now confessed the seriousness
of his breach with Rome; further, he asserted his conviction that
a clash was inevitable: it was only a question of being prepared
at the right moment to meet it. Macedonia was not yet equal
to either an offensive or a defensive war; therefore they must
play for time. It was a reasonable deduction from the Roman
attitude towards Philip since the Syrian War. Decision after
decision had gone against him, penalising him, it seemed, rather
than rewarding him for his help. Small wonder, therefore, if
Philip applied to his own case the then popular view[2] that it was
the ambition of the Senate to root out all autocratic rulers, and
became convinced that he was being weakened step by step as a
preliminary to his final extirpation. It is fairly certain that in
this view Philip was mistaken: the Senate's decisions were based
on definite principles, even if Roman policy demanded that these
should be interpreted more or less rigidly at different times:
they were not part of a diabolical plan to eradicate the Antigonid
dynasty. None the less, the experience of Carthage forty years
later was to show that the policy Philip feared was not alien to
Roman methods:[3] Philip's estimate of Roman character was
sound if his interpretation of the immediate facts was amiss.

For the consolidation of Macedon Philip required two things,
man-power and money: and something had already been done
to acquire both. The great reservoir of available man-power
lay, however, in Thrace,[4] and it was towards the subjection of
Thrace that Philip's next moves tended. There were three ways
of attacking the Thracian tribes, by an alliance with the Scordisci and Bastarnae,[5] their enemies on their northern frontiers,

---

[1] Polyb. XXII, 14, 7 *seq.*; cf. XXIII, 1, 5. On the importance of this conver-
sation, for which Polybius's source was most probably Macedonian, see
Walbank, *JHS*, LVIII, 1938, 65. Whether this Philocles is the general of the
Carian campaign and the second war with Rome (cf. Polyb. XVI, 24, 7; Livy
(P) XXXI, 16, 2; 26, 1; XXXII, 25, 1; 38, 2 *seq.*) is unknown; the two are identified without hesitation by P. Schoch, *P–W*, 'Philokles', cols. 2491–2.
[2] See above, p. 211, n. 7.   [3] See Hallward, *CAH*, VIII, 475–84.
[4] Cf. Livy (P) XLII, 12, 12: *iuventutem, ut iam Macedonia deficiat, velut ex
perenni fonte unde hauriat, Thraciam subiectam esse.*
[5] Whether the Bastarnae (or Peucini: cf. Tacit. *Germ.* 46, 1) were Germans
or Celts is much disputed: see Niese, III, 30, n. 2 (Celts); A. J. Reinach,
BCH, XXXIV, 1910, 249–53 (Celts); De Sanctis, IV, 1, 256 (Germans); Bauer,
Wien. S. B. CLXXXV, 1918, Abt. 2 (Celts); Much, *Germ. Forsch.* 1925, 7 *seq.*
(Germans). That they were in fact Germans seems proved by the following
epitaph on one of Nero's *corporis custodes* (*Dess.* 1722): *Nereus nat(ione)
German(us) Peucennus.*

by a direct expedition from Macedonia and, finally, by way of Byzantium. To the Byzantines Thrace offered a constant problem,[1] which they solved now by paying tribute to whatever tribe was at the moment paramount, and now by the assistance and protection of any state they could enlist in their service. For many years they had paid an annual tribute to Cavarus, the king of the Thracian Gauls;[2] and later, when his kingdom fell,[3] they had come under the patronage of Antiochus.[4] Now, in 184, their difficulties with a neighbouring king, Amadocus, gave Philip a chance to offer his help; and in a single campaign, in the summer, he served both his own interests and those of Byzantium by defeating the Thracians and taking prisoner Amadocus himself.[5]

Meanwhile Philip still maintained his garrisons in Aenus and Maronea;[6] and in pursuance of his wider schemes in Thrace, he sent messengers to the Bastarnae, who were at this time settled about the Danube mouth, to incite them to migrate farther west. That in 184 Philip was planning an invasion of Italy round the north of the Adriatic is, in spite of Polybius's testimony,[7] highly improbable. As later events showed, his sole intention was probably to annihilate the Dardanians, who were a constant danger to his frontiers on the upper Axius, and to settle a friendly tribe in their place.[8] Perhaps at the same time he began negotiating with the Scordisci, who lay beyond the Dardanians, south-west of the Danube above the site of Belgrade, and succeeded in making the agreement recorded by Justinus.[9] The seriousness with which Philip regarded this activity in the north is shown by his readiness to give one of his daughters in marriage to a certain Teres of Thrace,[10] who was perhaps, as Reinach

---

[1] Cf. Polyb. IV, 45 seq.　　[2] Polyb. IV, 46, 4.　　[3] Polyb. VIII, 22.
[4] Appian, Syr. 12; see above, p. 190, n. 5.
[5] Polyb. XXII, 14, 12; Livy (P) XXXIX, 35, 4. Amadocus was king of the Astae, in the immediate hinterland of Byzantium, or of the Caeni, a little to the north-west.
[6] Livy (P) XXXIX, 46, 9; Polyb. XXIII, 1, 4 (abridged).
[7] Livy (P) XXXIX, 35, 4: *ut in Italiam irrumperent* (cf. (P) XL, 57, 4-9). The phrase is Polybian, though the compressed version of Polyb. XXII, 14, 12, has only χάριν τῆς προκειμένης ἐπιβολῆς: it reflects the current Roman apprehension at Philip's reorganisation of Macedon (cf. Walbank, *JHS*, LVIII, 1938, 66, n. 53). Reinach, *BCH*, XXXIV, 1910, 265, accepts the Polybian view. See also C. Patsch, *Wien. S. B.* 214, 1 (1933), 10.
[8] Cf. Livy (P) XL, 57, 5.　　　　　　　[9] Justin. XXXII, 3, 5.
[10] Diod. XXXII, 15, 7.

suggests,[1] Amadocus's successor, and whose friendship Philip now sought to secure.

Meanwhile, it was obvious that these schemes would be regarded in the worst light at Rome.[2] Accordingly Philip devised a plan to soothe the apprehensions of the Senate. Aware that his younger son, Demetrius, who had spent the years 197–1 at Rome,[3] enjoyed great favour there, he resolved to send him to Rome the following winter, to offer a defence against the charges which he had reason to anticipate, and also to ask the Senate's pardon if he had inadvertently acted against their wishes.[4] This scheme, which represented a change of tactics rather than heart, offered great potentialities: its disastrous failure is to be attributed mainly to the weaknesses in Demetrius's character.[5]

There was, in fact, an unprecedented gathering of embassies at Rome during the winter of 184–3. In addition to the Achaeans and Messenians, and four separate bodies of Spartan exiles, there were embassies from Pergamum, Thessaly, various Thessalian towns, Perrhaebia, Athamania, Epirus and Illyria, and finally the Macedonians, including Demetrius and Philip's two intimate friends, Apelles and Philocles.[6] Clearly the Roman decision, that machinery should be set up to arbitrate on all questions still outstanding,[7] had been a direct encouragement to the former subject peoples of Thessaly to bring forward all the complaints they could find.[8]

After a purely formal audience to Eumenes's brother, Athenaeus, worth noting mainly as an indication of their friendly attitude towards Philip's most persistent enemy, the Senate proceeded to the serious business. The various embassies were invited to recite their complaints in turn before Demetrius; and the long list of charges took three days to present and elaborate. There were complaints about territory and the seizure by Philip

---

[1] *BCH*, xxxiv, 1910, 266, n. 1.

[2] One may compare the alarm caused at Rome by Antiochus's similar activities: see above, pp. 190 *seq.*

[3] See above, pp. 176 and 208.

[4] Polyb. xxii, 14, 9–11.   [5] Polyb. xxiii, 3, 5 *seq.*

[6] Polyb. xxiii, 1, 3–6; Livy (P) xxxix, 46, 6; 46, 9; Appian, *Mac.* 9, 6; Justin. xxxii, 2, 3.   [7] See above, p. 232.

[8] Polyb. xxiii, 1, 2; Livy (P) xxxix, 46, 6–8. κατὰ τὸ σύμβολον refers, not to the treaty between Philip and Rome, but to conventions governing the arbitration between Philip and the various towns; cf. Polyb. xxiii, 1, 12.

of slaves and cattle, and allegations that he had bribed the judges in the courts of arbitration; and out of the medley of charges, prompted by a mixture of truth and falsehood, malice and good faith, it was almost impossible to sift the facts.[1] Unable itself to reach any decision, the Senate appreciated the impossibility of Demetrius's dealing with the charges in detail, particularly in a formal speech. He was therefore asked if he had any instructions from Philip, and upon his somewhat naively producing a notebook with instructions inside, he was told to give the substance of Philip's answers.[2]

A little nervously Demetrius read out Philip's memorandum, the gist of which was that notwithstanding the unfair treatment accorded him by the Romans—a point stressed again and again— all their demands had been carried out; and where his opponents were bringing charges against him, they were in fact themselves the guilty parties. The Senate was, as usual, concerned with policy rather than justice; but the presence of Demetrius, whom they knew and liked, had suggested a change in method. Philip's claims were no longer rejected: instead, the Senate were pleased to accept Demetrius's statement unconditionally, to trust Philip either to have done right or to be prepared to do right, simply because it was Demetrius who pleaded his case. And the following summer a new commission should be sent out, not merely to supervise the carrying out of details, but to explain to Philip that he owed this indulgence to Demetrius.[3]

The studied insolence of this reply probably galled Philip more than the now customary rebuff could have done. It would have been quite easy to hear Demetrius's speech and accept his arguments, however badly made; instead, the Senate had deliberately called for the reading of Philip's memorandum, so that they might emphasise the snub to Philip by contrast with the favour shown to Demetrius. By their decision, moreover, the Senate for the first time jettisoned all pretence of justice in their dealings with Philip; henceforward, he was to hold his position only by virtue of Demetrius's popularity at Rome.

---

[1] Polyb. XXIII, 1, 7–13; Livy (P) XXXIX, 47, 2.
[2] Polyb. XXIII, 2, 1–5; Livy (P) XXXIX, 47, 1; 47, 3–4; plainly Philip was forewarned as to the accusations his embassy was to be called upon to meet.
[3] Polyb. XXIII, 2, 6–11; Livy (P) XXXIX, 47, 5–11.

Nor was this all. Demetrius appears to have been a youth easily corrupted by flattery and favour; and the Senate's attitude turned his head. In a private approach, Flamininus was able to win from him the secrets of the Macedonian court, by suggesting that the Senate intended him as Philip's successor; and a little later, Flamininus wrote a letter to Philip, urging him to send Demetrius, with as many of his friends as possible, back to Rome. However, in these manœuvres Flamininus miscalculated. By favouring Philip solely as the father of Demetrius, no doubt he and the Senate sought to intimidate him into making Demetrius his heir; but, as events proved, these schemes had, as their only result, the turning of Philip against his younger son.[1]

Eumenes's envoys had still to be heard. They had two complaints: first that Philip had sent armed assistance to Prusias, during a recent war with Pergamum,[2] and secondly that he was still maintaining garrisons in Aenus and Maronea.[3] In reply, Philocles spoke at some length, after which the Senate announced that if the next year's commission found their instructions still neglected, they would no longer tolerate disobedience.[4] With this ultimatum the Macedonians returned to Pella, leaving the Senate to deal with the problems of the Peloponnese;[5] and shortly afterwards Q. Marcius Philippus was appointed as legate to Macedonia and Greece.[6]

The triumphant return of Demetrius, followed by Flamininus's letter, appears to have led to the first internal crisis in Macedon since the conspiracy of Leontius and Apelles in 218.[7] Without exception, the sources for Philip's last years go back to a tainted source, and have to be approached with the utmost caution.[8]

---

[1] Polyb. xxiii, 3, 4–9; cf. Livy (P) xxxix, 48, 1; xl, 11, 1 (Perseus's speech).

[2] This war, which broke out (probably) in 186, involved the Galatians, and Hannibal, who commanded Prusias's fleet; it ended with Roman intervention in 184; see Niese, iii, 70–2.

[3] Polyb. xxiii, 3, 1; Livy (P) xxxix, 46, 9; Appian, Mac. 9, 6.

[4] Polyb. xxiii, 3, 1–3. Polybius adds: καὶ πάσας τὰς πόλεις εἰς τὴν τοῦ Εὐμένους πίστιν ἐγκεχειρισμένας, but the Senate's decision had been that the cities were to be free (see above, p. 234); and in 168–7 Aenus and Maronea were still independent (Polyb. xxx, 3, 3). Either Polybius or his excerptor has made an error.

[5] Polyb. xxiii, 4; Livy (P) xxxix, 48, 2–6.

[6] Polyb. xxiii, 4, 16; Livy (P) xxxix, 48, 5.   [7] See above, pp. 45 seq.

[8] For Polybius's attempt at a 'tragic' interpretation, based on an inadequate understanding of Philip's aims, see Walbank, JHS, lviii, 1938, 55–68.

Nevertheless, certain conclusions can be drawn; and it seems evident that, as a result of the Senate's policy, Demetrius was able to win many adherents to the idea of subservience. In the first place, some of Philip's most loyal friends may have felt that the policy of collaboration with Rome had not yet completely failed, or that its small yields were the fault rather of Philip's pride than of the policy itself. The reception accorded to Demetrius must have seemed—as the Senate meant it to seem— a confirmation of the view that Philip had more to gain as a client prince than as a stubborn, independent monarch.

There thus sprang up a body of opinion, perhaps not so unanimous as Polybius suggests,[1] but considerable in numbers and influence, which began to turn to Demetrius as the future king of Macedon. Popular gossip whispered (without foundation) that Perseus was a bastard, and Demetrius the real heir;[2] and the latter's supporters seized every opportunity to urge his superior merits. All this the shallow Demetrius readily drank in; his house became a centre for the many leading Macedonians who favoured a policy of subservience to Rome,[3] until it seemed to Philip almost like a rival court, and Perseus began to grow alarmed for his inheritance. His fears had no basis, however; for Philip maintained unshaken confidence in his elder son who, like himself, could see no virtue in making himself a second Eumenes.

With the arrival of Q. Marcius Philippus and his entourage in the spring of 183, the cleavage became still further accentuated.[4] Philip was now at last compelled to evacuate Aenus, Maronea and the neighbouring Thracian coastal towns, and to carry out, with certain additions, the decisions of the former commissioners; but, even more irritating, he had to watch Demetrius spending his time in the company of the Romans and showing himself daily more and more the Senate's man. Nevertheless, Philip mastered his anger, realising that he was not yet ready to face a war; but, if there is any truth in a somewhat odd story in

---

[1] Polyb. XXIII, 7, 2–4 (compressed; cf. Livy (P) XXXIX, 53, 1–11) contrasting οἱ μὲν Μακεδόνες and ὁ δὲ Φίλιππος καὶ Περσεύς.

[2] Livy (P) XXXIX, 53, 3 (cf. Polyb. XXIII, 7, 6); XL, 9, 2; XLI, 23, 10; cf. Plut. Arat. 54, 7; Aem. Paull. 8, 11–12; Aelian, V.H. XII, 43.

[3] Livy (P) XXXIX, 53, 3–8.

[4] Polyb. XXIII, 8, 1–2; Livy (P) XXXIX, 53, 10–11.

Livy,[1] to the effect that he did not allow a day to pass without having the terms of his treaty with Rome read out twice, he never let himself forget the chafing injustice under which he suffered. Meanwhile, as soon as the Romans had gone, with the double object of furthering his northern policy and, by winning some inland victories which might compensate for his defeat in the diplomatic game of the coastal towns, of thus restoring the unity of the Macedonian people, Philip directed an expedition against the tribes of Thrace.[2]

The chief people in central Thrace were the Odrysae, with whom Philip had formed an alliance in 204;[3] their territory stretched from what is now Bulgaria to Odessus, where they touched the area occupied by the Bastarnae. On the head waters of the Hebrus, west of the Odrysae, lay the Bessi, and farther west again, beyond the Strymon and the Oescus, the Dentheleti. Between them, these tribes controlled the Hebrus route from the Propontis to the Danube, an essential line of communication for the domination of Thrace.[4] Advancing now against the Odrysae, Philip defeated them and took possession of the all-important frontier town of Philippopolis (mod. Plovdiv), a foundation of Philip II. Then, leaving a garrison here,[5] he marched farther up country against the Bessi and the Dentheleti, and through their territory into Paeonia. He was still eager to open up this district for the Bastarnae, whom he hoped to tempt into an expedition against the Dardanians, and for this purpose he resolved to found a new town in the Axius basin, that would control the district around, as Philippopolis controlled the upper valley of the Hebrus. Accordingly, he crossed the Strymon, probably

[1] Livy (A) XLIV, 16, 5–7; but the source is suspect, and quotes the anecdote as proof of Philip's loyalty and peaceable nature; if true, the story must be interpreted in the opposite sense (cf. Nissen, 262).

[2] Polyb. XXIII, 8, 2–3; Livy (P) XXXIX, 53, 12. Polybius's motivation—the desire to mislead the Romans—is deduced from the false premise that Philip was at this time planning an aggressive war on Rome; cf. Walbank, *JHS*, LVIII, 1938, 64 *seq.*   [3] See above, p. 111, n. 7.

[4] For further details and a discussion of the probable frontier between the Odrysae and Bessi, see Reinach, *BCH*, XXXIV, 1910, 268; Lenk, *P–W*, 'Thrake', col. 436.

[5] Polyb. XXIII, 8, 4–7; Livy (P) XXXIX, 53, 12–13. The garrison was soon expelled by the Odrysae; but their rising was evidently put down, since, in the reign of Perseus, Cotys, the king of the Odrysae, is among the most loyal supporters of Macedon (Livy (P) XLII, 29, 12; cf. Polyb. XXVII, 12; Livy (P) XLII, 67, 3).

at Pautalia (mod. Kyushtendil), and, reaching the Axius at Stobi, founded his new city near here; and as a sign of his confidence in his eldest son, he named it Perseis.[1]

Although it had proved a military success, this campaign, which was designed, by its identification with the name of Perseus, to reassert Philip's authority in Macedon, was nevertheless followed by a still greater outburst of disaffection. For in the autumn of this year (183) Philip instituted a policy which had been unpopular in the days of Philip II.[2] By the wholesale transport of the inhabitants of the coastal towns to the Paeonian frontier, and the introduction of Thracians into the districts thus evacuated, he served a double object: by Macedonising the valleys of the Erigon and Axius, he consolidated his defence against the Dardanians, and at the same time he acquired bodies of Thracian and other barbarian troops, responsible directly to himself, in the parts of Macedon whose loyalty he had reason to suspect.[3] Whether the barbarians thus transferred came as mercenaries or as settlers it is not easy to decide. At an army review held by Perseus in 171 there were Thracian *incolae* serving along with the Paeonians and Agrianians;[4] and after

---

[1] Livy (P) XXXIX, 53, 14–6. On the site of Perseis see Desdevises-du-Dezert, *Géographie de la Macédoine*, 316; Heuzey-Daumet, *Mission archéologique de Macédoine*, 322–33; Reinach, *BCH*, XXXIV, 1910, 269; Geyer, *P–W*, 'Makedonia', col. 667. It lay in the district of Deuriopus (Steph. Byz.: Δουρίοπος—the form accepted by Beloch, IV, 1, 8), which an inscription shows to have been in the north of Lyncestis (cf. Kromayer, II, 22, n. 1), and also not very far from the Erigon and Stobi. Reinach plausibly suggests that Perseis was on the site of the modern Prilep, but confuses the issue by defending Heuzey's identification of Prilep with Stuberra: this is ruled out by Strabo, VII, 7, 9, who states that πᾶσαι αἱ τῶν Δευριόπων πόλεις lie ἐπὶ τῷ Ἐρίγονι (cf. Kromayer, *loc. cit.*).

[2] Justinus relates how, after the Sacred War, in 346, Philip *reversus in regnum, ut pecora pastores nunc in hibernos, nunc in aestivos saltus traiciunt, sic ille populos et urbes, ut illi vel replenda vel derelinquenda quaeque loca videbantur, ad libidinem transfert* (VIII, 5, 7); *alios populos in finibus ipsis hostibus opponit; alios in extremis regni terminis statuit; quosdam bello captos in supplementa urbium dividit* (VIII, 6, 1). These measures, by which Philip II sought to unify Macedon, are thus remarkably paralleled by the reorganisation of Philip V; see Zancan, 140. They acquire additional significance, in view of the later Philip's interest in his namesake and supposed ancestor; see below, p. 258, n. 3.

[3] Polyb. XXIII, 10, 4; Livy (P) XL, 3, 3–4. For Polybius's moralist, non-historical treatment of these events, and the relation between the Polybian and Livian accounts, see Walbank, *JHS*, LVIII, 1938, 59 *seq.*

[4] Livy (P) XLII, 51, 5.

the breaking up of Macedon by the Romans in 167 the 'third region' is said to have contained *incolas quoque permultos Gallos et Illyrios, impigros cultores*.[1] The probability is, as Griffith suggests,[2] that the barbarians now introduced into Macedon came originally as mercenaries, perhaps with the promise of land once they had completed their service.

This transfer of populations also served to rid Philip of a dangerous section of political opposition.[3] For it was in the large coastal towns particularly, where the inhabitants were nearer in outlook to the Greeks than elsewhere, and where the bond of Macedonian nationality was least strong,[4] that Philip's Thracian policy and stubborn resistance to Rome were most unpopular. To speak of a trading party in these towns would be an anachronism: all the same, it was here, and not in Pella or Beroea, that the prosperity of Pergamum and Rhodes, basking in the favour of the Senate, will have been most apparent; and there must have been some resentment, too, at the new harbour taxes, exacted to enable Philip to rebuild a treasury emptied by constant warfare. Undoubtedly the hostility spoken of by Polybius was the result of the transfer of families to the bare plains of Paeonia: but the transfer was itself a sequel to previous disaffection.

This disaffection reached its height in about autumn 183, in a conspiracy against the throne. This conspiracy is never directly described in our somewhat fragmentary tradition, but is clearly indicated by subsequent events. For Polybius recounts how, shortly before 182,[5] Philip was obliged to execute a group of Macedonian nobles,[6] including Admetus, Pyrrhichus and his

---

[1] Livy (P) XLV, 30, 5; the 'third' region included the coastal plain of Pella, Edessa and Beroea.   [2] *Mercenaries*, 73; 77–8.

[3] Polyb. XXIII, 10, 4: τοὺς πολιτικοὺς ἄνδρας...ἀναστάτους ποιήσαντα. This, too, had been a policy of Philip II; cf. Momigliano, *Filippo*, 138, 146, n. 1.

[4] Cassandreia was constantly hostile to the Antigonids (cf. Tarn, 186, n. 82); and it is significant that the family mentioned in Livy (P) XL, 40, 4 (story of Theoxena), is from Thessalonica, which was normally remarkable for its loyalty. The existence of a Sarapeum in Thessalonica as early as the reign of Philip (cf. Pelekides, 3 *seq.*) may indicate its cosmopolitan nature. On the early spread of the Egyptian cults in Macedon see, however, Makaronas, *AE*, 1936, app. 9, for a second-century dedication to Sarapis, Isis and Anubis found near Kosane.

[5] Polyb. XXIII, 10, 9; Livy (P) XL, 3, 7. Niese's identification (II, 570, n. 1) of these men with the five counsellors executed about 205 (see above, p. 109, n. 5) must be rejected; see Walbank, *JHS*, LVIII, 1938, 66, n. 56.

[6] Polyb. XXIII, 10, 11: τὰς τῶν πατέρων προαγωγάς.

own foster-brother, Samus,[1] the son of Chrysogonus, for some unrecorded offence. Taking this execution in conjunction with the hostility to Philip, one may infer that it was the sequel to some kind of conspiracy, probably to remove Philip and replace him by Demetrius. The conspiracy was discovered in time; but beyond doubt it had a permanent effect in embittering Philip and in bringing out those characteristics which, while most apparent during the years of his eastern campaigns, were never very far below the surface.

The outcry caused by the transfer of populations convinced Philip that the execution of the ring-leaders in the conspiracy was not enough. Shortly afterwards he had their children arrested and imprisoned,[2] an action which, if Polybius is to be believed, stirred up hostility among the ordinary citizens of Macedon; and the Polybian tradition gives prominence to one particularly sensational incident, when a certain Theoxena, whose husband and father had both perished at different times at Philip's hands, hearing of the new decree, attempted to sail with her children in a small boat from Aenea in Chalcidice to Euboea, but was pursued by royal guards and killed herself and all her children rather than be overtaken.[3] How far such stories represent merely the atrocity propaganda of a hostile tradition it is difficult to say. In any case, Philip had taken the trouble in time; the clash between Perseus and Demetrius was still to come to a head in a violent, personal tragedy, but henceforth there is no suggestion of a serious threat to the throne.

At Rome, meanwhile, Q. Marcius Philippus reported Philip's grudging withdrawal of his garrisons from the Thracian coastal towns, and confirmed the view now prevalent in Rome that Philip was merely awaiting a convenient moment for revenge. Philip's envoys, who had been sent as usual for a winter audience, were therefore formally thanked but also instructed to warn Philip against any action that might be interpreted as hostile to

[1] It was Samus who adapted the verse at Thermum in 218 (Polyb. v, 9, 4). His death is mentioned by Plut. *Moral.* 53 E. See further Corradi, *Studi ellenistici*, 275–6, for his position as Philip's σύντροφος.

[2] Polyb. XXIII, 10, 10; 10, 15 (the children were not killed as the second passage states). Philip is said to have quoted a line from Stasinus: 'A fool is he who slays the father and leaves alive the sons'—νήπιος ὃς πατέρα κτείνας υἱοὺς καταλείπει. Cf. Clem. Alex. *Strom.* VI, ii, 19, 1. See Walbank, *JHS*, LVIII, 1938, 61, n. 30.

[3] Livy (P) XL, 4.

Rome.[1] This message Philip treated as a respite, in which to develop his Thracian schemes a step further; and this same spring (182) his envoys returned from the Bastarnae, accompanied by ambassadors of high standing, one of whom offered his sister in marriage to one of Philip's sons.[2] Such an offer can scarcely have come uninvited from a Bastarnian, however noble; and it is probably a fair assumption that one of the tasks of the envoys sent by Philip, who had been with the Bastarnae since autumn 184,[3] was to ask for a marriage alliance. Philip now accepted the offer, and—notwithstanding the reluctance of the bridegroom—the marriage took place between the Bastarnian princess and the crown prince Perseus.[4] It offers further proof of the importance that Philip attributed to his Thracian schemes; in fact, after his vain efforts at empire in Greece and Asia Minor, he appears to have now been planning what might eventually have proved the first Balkan Empire.

Shortly afterwards, the rivalry between the two princes burst out into open hostility. The occasion was the annual festival of purifying the Macedonian army,[5] when it was the custom first for the whole army, led by its king and preceded by the royal standards from the earliest times, to march in ceremonial fashion between the two halves of a sacrificial dog; this over, a tournament was held, in which two sections of the army were led by Perseus and Demetrius. Incited by the situation, the two princes rapidly converted the tournament into something very like a real battle, in which blood was shed; and in the evening

---

[1] Polyb. XXIII, 9, 4–7; cf. Livy (P) XL, 3, 1–2.
[2] Livy (P) XL, 5, 10.   [3] See above, p. 237.
[4] Livy (P) XL, 5, 11: *quid ista prosunt?* etc.; see Reinach, *BCH*, XXXIV, 1910, 270 seq. Livy never states that Perseus is the son in question; but it is his opinion on the marriage that is quoted, and we know of no other son of Philip besides Perseus and Demetrius. (The Philip of Livy (P) XLII, 52, 5, is probably a son of Perseus, not of Philip; see below, p. 261, n. 3.) Moreover, Perseus was married when he ascended the throne (Livy (P) XLII, 5, 3), but his wife either died, or was, as Livy (P) says, put away, since he soon afterwards married Laodice of Syria (Polyb. XXV, 4, 8; Livy (P) XLII, 12, 3; cf. Appian, *Mac.* 11, 2).
[5] This festival, in honour of the god Xanthus, took place in the month of Xandicus (see Hesych. *s.v.* Ξανθικά; Suidas *s.v.* ἐναγίζων), at this time equivalent to March (see Ideler, *Handbuch der Chronologie*, 396; Reinach, *BCH*, XXXIV, 1910, 270, n. 1). On its significance and probable origin in human sacrifice preceding a military campaign, see Nilsson, *Griech. Feste*, 405; Hellmann, *Arch. Rel.* XXIX, 1931, 202–3; cf. Granier, 22 seq.

Perseus, who had been worsted, declined to join his brother's banquet. At the feast drinking led to high words, and one of Perseus's men, who had gone as an observer, was assaulted; and when, later, Demetrius led his party, by this time drunk, to call up his brother, some, fearing trouble, slipped weapons under their cloaks. Meanwhile Perseus, learning from his spy what had happened, locked his doors on the revellers, who, after shouting for a while, had to return. The next day Perseus denounced his brother to Philip on a charge of attempted assassination; and reluctantly the king admitted his two sons to an audience, at which he delivered a long harangue on the virtues of brotherly love, and the princes made their respective accusations and defence.[1] The upshot was that Perseus's immediate charge fell through; but henceforth Philip regarded Demetrius with even more suspicion than before.[2]

Such is Livy's account, derived in the main from Polybius, but no doubt embellished rhetorically. The detail in which the incident is described points to an informant in close touch with the Macedonian court;[3] and though the speeches are largely an artificial composition, there may be a basis of fact behind Perseus's complaints at the interference of Flamininus, and Demetrius's rather weak attempts to saddle Philip with the responsibility for his pro-Roman policy, since it was he who had sent him as his representative to the Senate. Quite plainly the incident of the banquet was a mere pretext, and the real charge against Demetrius was not fratricide, but high treason. The sequel was that Philip despatched Apelles and Philocles to Rome on a purely formal visit, which would give them the opportunity to investigate privately the attitude of Flamininus and his circle towards Demetrius and the Macedonian succession;[4] and Demetrius retired more than ever from close contact with his father, trying however to avoid suspicion by refraining from any mention of or communication with the Romans.[5]

---

[1] Polyb. XXIII, 1; Livy (P) XL, 6, 1–15, 16.
[2] Livy (P) XL, 16, 1–3.   [3] See Walbank, *JHS*, LVIII, 1938, 65.
[4] Livy (P) XL, 20, 3–4: the statement that Philip regarded these two men as impartial, but that they were in fact in Perseus's confidence, is to be dismissed as part of the pro-Demetrian source (probably Achaean in origin; cf. Walbank, *JHS*, LVIII, 1938, 65, n. 51) used by Polybius for his account of Demetrius's death.   [5] Livy (P) XL, 20, 5–6.

These domestic conflicts and perhaps the marriage of Perseus to the Bastarnian princess[1] prevented Philip from marching into Thrace in 182. He continued his negotiations with the Bastarnae, however, and it was probably in this year that he first sent a leading Macedonian, named Antigonus, back with Cotta, one of the Bastarnian envoys, to make further approaches to the chieftain Clondicus on the subject of a westward migration against the Dardanians.[2] Meanwhile, in central Greece, an Amphictyonic decree in honour of Eumenes[3] shows the anti-Macedonian forces still holding Delphi, and that with the co-operation of Rome. In its naive distinction between 'the bad kings, who plot against the Greeks'[4] and merit reproof (i.e. Philip), and good kings like Eumenes himself, it forms an interesting contrast to a contemporary inscription of the Aetolians,[5] who in granting Eumenes similar honours omit the references both to Rome and to the good and bad kings. Whether the distinction goes back to the original letters sent by Eumenes to the two bodies, or to an excision of what they did not like by the Aetolians, these two documents illuminate the diplomatic alignment of the majority on the Amphictyonic Council, Eumenes and, to some extent, the Senate, against Philip: equally clearly, the Aetolians, though willing to grant honours to Pergamum, were not prepared to offend Pella. On the other hand, Philip's interest in the Amphictyony was now limited to the extent to which it concerned itself with his fragmentary possessions in Dolopia, Magnesia and Phthiotic Achaea.

The following spring (181) Philip led a second expedition into Thrace. Assembling his troops at Stobi in Paeonia, he led them through the Maedi and the desolate territory beyond, and in seven days reached the foot of a mountain which Livy, following Polybius, calls Mt Haemus.[6] From its summit, rumour had it, the Black Sea, the Adriatic, the Danube and the Alps were all visible; and Philip, evidently impressed by the story, and realis-

---

[1] This is the suggestion of Reinach, *BCH*, xxxiv, 1910, 270.
[2] This was the first of many visits by Antigonus to the Bastarnae, during the next two years; cf. Livy (P) xl, 57, 3: *Antigonus...(in 179)...saepe cum ipso Cottone legatus ad concitandos Bastarnas missus.*
[3] *Syll.* 630; latest edition in Daux, 293 *seq.*   [4] *Ibid.* line 8.
[5] *Syll.* 629; better *IG*, ix, 1², 79 (Klaffenbach) or Daux, 298–301.
[6] Livy (P) xl, 21, 1–2; 22, 1.

ing how his Thracian schemes would profit from such a bird's-eye view, had resolved to climb to the top.[1] After a necessary rest of a day, the ascent began; easy at first, it grew more difficult as the band of selected troops reached the higher slopes, where the dense forest often blocked out the sky and there was a constant blanket of mountain mist. At last they reached the summit, only to discover the fruitlessness of the errand; and after sacrifices to Zeus and Helios, they made their way down again. When they reached their base camp two days later, exhausted by the unusual exertion and the bitter cold of the nights (though it was July), they found supplies running short, and Philip was driven to plundering the adjacent territory of the allied Dentheleti; subsequently he returned into Maedica and forced the surrender of Petra, the chief town of the district, before returning to Macedon.[2]

The identification of Mt Haemus has raised considerable difficulty.[3] The mountain to which Polybius refers is probably not any peak in the Balkan range, but Vitocha (2100 m.; the ancient Scomius or Scombrus),[4] which lies at a distance of

[1] Livy (P) XL, 21, 2; Polyb. in Strabo, VII, 5, 1. The suggestion in Livy that Philip's object was to avert suspicion at Rome from the war he was planning against her may be disregarded.   [2] Livy (P) XL, 22, 1–15.

[3] Niese, III, 29 (followed by Heiland, 24, n. 6), identifies it with Dunax; but this is mentioned shortly afterwards (Livy (P) XL, 58, 2) under its own name, where the reference is probably to Rila Planina (2680 m.); see Lenk, P–W, 'Thrake', col. 437. Oster, ZDOeA, 1886, 263–72, thinks Haemus is the peak Muss Alla in the Rilo Dagh (2930 m.), but Oberhummer, P–W, 'Haimos', col. 2222, points out that Livy's description does not tally with the bare slopes of Muss Alla (which he himself identifies with Dunax, in Wien. Anz. 72, 1935, 2 seq.). Followed by Cary and Warmington, Anc. Greek Explorers, 116, and Scullard, 289, he identifies Haemus with Mt Vežen (2200 m.) or Mt Yumruksal (2375 m.) in the Balkan range, north of Plovdiv; and De Sanctis, IV, 1, 255, and Lenk, P–W, 'Thrake', col. 436–7, also accept the identification with the Balkan. However, from Stobi to the foot of Vežen is 150 miles as the crow flies, to Yumruksal is 170; for an army these figures represent at least 200 and 225 miles respectively, either of which is far more than a normal seven days' march. (There is no reason to think that Philip proceeded by forced marches, when admittedly a distance of up to 50 miles a day was possible: cf. Tarn, Hellen. Mil. and Naval Developments, 40, n. 2.) Moreover, as Heiland, loc. cit., points out, the Hebrus valley, through which this range is approached, does not fit Livy's desolate territory beyond Maedica; the Hebrus valley is particularly fertile, and a food shortage would scarcely occur there in July. The most probable identification is therefore that of Leake, III, 472–4 (followed by Reinach, BCH, XXXIV, 1910, 272), whose view is adopted above.

[4] Thucyd. II, 96, 3–5; Aristot. Meteor. I, 13, 350 b, 17 (ed. Fobes).

100 miles as the crow flies from Stobi, between Sofia and Kyush-tendil. From Stobi Philip will have marched north-east up the Bregalnitza, past the site of Ishtip, and over into the middle valley of the Strymon,[1] at the point where the Bregalnitza valley turns south; the last part of his journey, north to Mt Vitocha, thus coincides with the route of the modern railway from Skoplje to Sofia. The expedition against the Dentheleti must have been to the north-west of Vitocha,[2] and apart from the question of supplies, it served the same military purpose as Philip's campaigns of 183; as to the genuineness of Philip's *pudor* in ravaging, some doubt may thus reasonably be felt.[3]

The Haemus expedition saw yet a further step in the family breach between Perseus and Demetrius. Both sons had ac-companied Philip to Stobi, but from here he sent Demetrius back to Macedonia, ostensibly to avoid involving the whole dynasty in an enterprise of some risk, but actually because of the mistrust he now felt for his younger son.[4] Didas, the governor of Paeonia, who accompanied Demetrius, is stated to have been an agent of Perseus, and to have used this opportunity to worm secrets out of Demetrius;[5] and shortly afterwards, while Philip was still at Petra, reports from Didas revealed that Demetrius was planning to flee to Rome. In great anguish of mind, Philip had his son's chief friend, Herodorus, thrown into prison, but awaited the return of Apelles and Philocles from Rome before taking any action against Demetrius himself.[6]

---

[1] It was here, according to Strabo, VII, fr. 36, that the Maedi were situated; but their territory probably included the valley of the Bregalnitza; cf. Lenk, *P-W*, 'Thrake', col. 434.

[2] Not to the south-east, as Leake, III, 474. The Dentheleti lay north of the Oescus-Strymon line; south of it were the Bessi (see above, p. 242).

[3] Livy (P) XL, 22, 11; the ravaging of the territory of the Dentheleti was carried out *non sine magno pudore regis*.

[4] Livy (P) XL, 21, 2–7. If Philip really believed the story of the panorama to be obtained from the summit of Vitocha, he may, as stated in Livy, have hesitated to allow Demetrius to share in the view; for though it is improbable that there is any truth in the story of Philip's plan for an invasion of Italy round the north of the Adriatic (see above, p. 237), the consolidation in Thrace was bound, directly or indirectly, to take on an anti-Roman shape. It is perhaps of interest that Petrarch's ascent of Mt Ventoux (April 1336) was inspired by Livy's account of the Haemus expedition (*Epist. ad Fam.* IV, 1; cf. Carducci, *Opere* (Ed. naz.), XI, 103–12).

[5] Livy (P) XL, 21, 8–11.

[6] Livy (P) XL, 22, 15–23, 5; Justin. XXXII, 2, 9; Zon. IX, 22, 1. Zonaras's version includes a plot against Philip's life, but this is probably a distortion.

When at length the envoys returned, after some months, they brought with them a sealed letter purporting to be from Flamininus. This document, states Livy, deprecated any actions undertaken by Demetrius in his desire for the throne; and for such actions Flamininus disclaimed all responsibility. Perseus's accusations thus seemed to be confirmed; and Philip had Herodorus tortured to death in the hope of securing a confession, though to no purpose. It is stated in Livy that the letter was a forgery; but Apelles's later flight to Rome makes this extremely unlikely. In any case, as Edson points out,[1] the authenticity of the letter, dealing with events at Rome of two years previously (184–3), was irrelevant to the immediate question of Demetrius's attempt on Perseus and his proposed flight. However, equal difficulties stand in the way of accepting the letter as genuine— at any rate in Livy's version.[2] For if the Romans were using Demetrius as their tool, why should Flamininus send a letter virtually admitting his guilt? The likeliest explanation is that Polybius was here employing unreliable evidence, probably of Achaean origin,[3] and that Flamininus's letter, though genuine, was couched in much more guarded terms than our source suggests. To Philip in his present state of distrust and anguish anything less than a complete denial must have seemed sufficient to damn Demetrius.

Perseus now once more took up the charge, pointing to the proposed flight through Paeonia to Rome, and the letter from Flamininus; and reluctantly Philip at last resolved to sacrifice his feelings as a father to state policy.[4] The following spring (180), upon leaving Thessalonica, where the second investigation had been carried out, for Demetrias, he sent Perseus to receive Thracian hostages at Amphipolis, and Demetrius along

[1] *Harv. Stud.* XLVI, 1935, 198.

[2] *Contra* Edson, *op. cit.* 200, who claims that 'even as given by Livy, this is exactly the sort of letter which might be expected under the circumstances'.

[3] See Walbank, *JHS*, LVIII, 1938, 65, n. 51.

[4] Livy (P) XL, 24, 1 *seq.*; cf. Polyb. XXIII, 3, 9; Zon. IX, 22, 2. An interesting side-light on Philip's sense of duty is revealed in a letter from him to his local *epistates*, Archippus, recently discovered between Kosane and Verria (Makaronas, *AE*, 1934–5, 117–27); cf. Welles, *AJA*, XLII, 1938, 248–9). Written in December 181 (year XLII, Aydnaeus), at the very crisis of Philip's domestic tragedy, it shows him giving personal attention to such a question as the allotment of a piece of land of specific size, to enable the tetrarch, Nicanor, and his staff to perform their religious duties.

with Didas to Astraeum in Paeonia.[1] What followed is uncertain. According to Polybius's version, which was, however, only one of many which were later circulated in Achaea,[2] Didas summoned Demetrius to a sacrifice at Heraclea, and there administered poison to him; the prince, realising what had happened, retired to his room, where, shortly afterwards, he was smothered by Thyrsis of Stuberra and Alexander of Beroea. This account in itself suggests a combination of two alternative stories, in which Demetrius met his death by poison and smothering respectively. All that is known with certainty is that sometime during the summer of 180 Demetrius was quietly removed before he could become a real danger in the Senate's hands. Vain and ambitious, he had lent himself to clumsy manœuvring by Flamininus and his circle, and had himself to thank for his untimely end; Philip could not afford to let him live on as a Roman pretender.[3]

There was, however, a sequel. Wintering at Demetrias in 180–79, Philip turned in his distress to a certain Antigonus, the son of Echecrates and nephew of Antigonus Doson.[4] An avowed enemy of Perseus, this man appears in our anti-Persean tradition as the flower of incorruptibility. His real character emerges only from what little of his actions is revealed in the distorted pages of Livy. By playing upon Philip's feeling of remorse for Demetrius's death, he gradually insinuated himself into his counsels, and fostered the story that Apelles and Philocles had forged the letter from Flamininus. Philip, who even in his prime had always proved over-ready to listen to the favourite of the moment, was easily won over by Antigonus; and when, a

---

[1] This town (mod. Stromnitsa) lies on a tributary of the Strymon; cf. Leake, III, 466. Heraclea, where Demetrius died, is also near the Strymon, either at Zervochori (Leake, III, 226 seq.), or at Vetrina, five miles north-east of Demir-Hissar (Kiepert); see also P. Collart, *Philippes, ville de Macédoine* (Paris, 1937), 503; Ernst Meyer, *Gnomon*, XV, 1939, 555–6.

[2] Cf. Livy (P) XLI, 23, 10–11; 24, 3–5, where Callicrates's version corresponds in broad outline to that of Polybius.

[3] On Demetrius's death see Polyb. XXIII, 7; 10–11; Livy (P) XL, 5–16; 20, 3–24, 8; 54–6; Diod. XXIX, 25; Justin. XXXII, 2–3; Plut. *Arat.* 54, 7; *Aem. Paull.* 8, 9 seq.; Zon. IX, 22. For modern discussion: De Sanctis, IV, 1, 253; Edson, *Harv. Stud.* XLVI, 1935, 191–202; Benecke, *CAH*, VIII, 254 (with my criticisms, *JHS*, LVIII, 1938, 55 seq.).

[4] Livy (P) XL, 54, 6, classes him *ex honoratis Philippi amicis*—a translation, as Holleaux points out (*BCH*, LVII, 1933, 32), of the technical expression τῶν τετιμωμένων φίλων. See too Momigliano, *Athen.* XI, 1933, 137.

little later, a certain Xychus, who had been to Rome as secretary to Philocles and Apelles, was arrested and, under threat of torture, confessed their guilt, Philip's remorse was complete. Of the two counsellors, Philocles was arrested; Apelles, more fortunate, escaped in time to Italy.[1]

As Edson has seen,[2] little sense can be made of this confused and biased account, based upon rumour and gossip. The confessions, if confessions there were, prove nothing, and Apelles's flight to Italy certainly argues a clear conscience in respect to Rome. Equally untrustworthy is the story that Philip now resolved to make Antigonus his heir and, after denouncing Perseus, took his successor round the cities of Macedon, 'commending' him to the leading citizens.[3] The account may be true; Philip was now undoubtedly a worn-out, disillusioned man, full of remorse and bitterness and nearing his end. On the other hand, such a story may well have been fostered in pro-Roman circles, both in Greece and Italy, in order to discredit Perseus's right to the throne.[4]

However, Antigonus's triumph was short-lived. While Perseus attended to affairs in Thrace, Philip set out on a tour of his kingdom. From Demetrias he went north to Thessalonica, and after spending some time there, continued his journey east. However, at Amphipolis he fell seriously ill. Since Demetrius's death and the revelations of his 'innocence', Philip had been tortured by mental anguish and sleeplessness, and was in no state to resist sickness. For a time he lingered, not even his physician, Calligenes, regarding his condition as serious; but when suddenly signs of his approaching end appeared, Calligenes sent messengers hastily to summon Perseus, and loyally concealed Philip's death until his son's arrival. Thus Antigonus was thwarted, and Perseus succeeded peacefully to the throne.[5]

The death of Philip in the summer of 179 came dramatically at a moment when his Thracian schemes were nearing fruition.

---

[1] Livy (P) XL, 54, 1–55, 8. There are two versions of Philocles's death, one that he confessed his guilt, the other that he died proclaiming his innocence; Perseus was later accused of recalling Apelles from Italy only to murder him (Livy (P) XLII, 5, 3).

[2] *Harv. Stud.* XLVI, 1935, 199–200. [3] Livy (P) XL, 56, 7: *commendare.*

[4] In this connection one may recall the accusations that Perseus was of bastard birth.

[5] Livy (P) XL, 56, 1–57, 1.

Since 184 he had been in close touch with the Bastarnae, and his expeditions of 183 and 181 had paved the way militarily for their advance south. Now, in 179, ignorant of Philip's death, and relying on his guarantees of a safe passage, they crossed the Danube, sending Antigonus, the Macedonian envoy, and Cotta ahead to announce to the king their approach. The intention was[1] for the Bastarnae to wipe out the Dardanians, Philip's old enemies to the north of Paeonia, and occupy their land. That more than this was planned is unlikely. The sources speak of a further advance north-west through the land of the Scordisci[2] (with whom Philip had certainly some arrangement)[3] and across the north shore of the Adriatic upon Italy, thus causing a diversion which might be employed by Philip to recover his possessions in Greece. The story is improbable and no doubt reached Polybius from Roman or pro-Roman sources. But the annihilation of the Dardanians was a long-cherished scheme of Philip's, and one which would lead to a new era of security for Macedon.

However, the report of Philip's death, which reached Antigonus and Cotta near Amphipolis, transformed the situation. Apart from the immediate problems of the succession and a distaste for the Thracian policy, which was shortly to become more evident, Perseus lacked the skill and personal force to hold such a movement as this within bounds. Very soon the arrangement with the Thracians broke down, the Bastarnae took to plunder and then open warfare, until eventually, attacking the Thracians about Mt Dunax, they were overwhelmed by a storm and routed in a manner reminiscent of the rout of the Gauls at Delphi a century before. The expedition now split up; some 30,000, under Clondicus, continued against the Dardanians, while the rest returned north. The sequel hardly concerns us here; they carried out some operations against the Dardanians, and many of them perished some time later when the ice broke beneath them, as they crossed the frozen Danube.[4] Lacking the direction of Philip, the whole movement dwindled into one of

---

[1] See above, p. 237.

[2] Livy (P) XL, 57, 7 *seq.*   [3] Justin. XXXII, 3.

[4] Livy (P) XL, 58, 1–8; XLI, 19, 4 *seq.*; 23, 12; Appian, *Mac.* 11, 1; Orosius, IV, 20, 34. On this expedition see further C. Patsch, *Wien. S.B.* 214, 1 (1933), 9–14.

the shapeless and unimportant tribal migrations, which afflicted the Balkans for centuries.

Perseus, meanwhile, at once took the wise precaution of executing Antigonus, the son of Echecrates, and sent envoys to Rome to renew the pact of friendship with the Senate and obtain recognition of his accession. Whatever the Senate's previous intrigues, they granted these without hesitation, and Perseus was free to guide Macedonia along whatever path seemed good to him.[1] The path he chose interests us here mainly by its divergence from that along which Philip had moved during his last years. Without surrendering his hold on Thrace[2] or allowing the strength of his empire to decline, Perseus adopted a policy of reconciliation towards the internal enemies of the regime and, in particular, towards the Greeks. Debtors and exiles were pardoned and recalled;[3] a marriage alliance was made with Laodice of Syria—the Bastarnian queen having either died or been discarded;[4] and in the new constitution of the Delphian Amphictyony the king of Macedon once more appeared with a preponderance of Macedonian votes.[5] It was perhaps natural that Perseus, half Greek by birth, should once more embrace a Hellenic policy. Philip's last decade had thus proved an incident, an experiment in policy, not indeed without results (as the part played by the Bastarnae in Perseus's last struggle with Rome clearly shows), but none the less barren, in so far as he had sought to turn the face of a Hellenised Macedon away from the Mediterranean.

Throughout this last decade Philip had displayed remarkable perseverance. In the face of an overbearing Senate and the intrigues of Flamininus, he had kept a tight rein on his violent temper and shown both foresight and organisational skill. Convinced that Rome was preparing his ultimate annihilation, he fought his case diplomatically, step by step, only rarely letting such outbursts as those at Tempe or Maronea provide

---

[1] Livy (P) XL, 58, 9; XLI, 24, 6; Diod. XXIX, 30; Zon. IX, 22, 2.
[2] Perseus energetically repulsed the attack of the Sapaei under Abrupolis on Pangaeum; see Livy (P) XLII, 41, 11.
[3] Polyb. XXV, 3.
[4] Livy (P) XLII, 5, 4 *seq.*; cf. *Syll.* 639.
[5] *Syll.* 636; edited by Daux, *BCH*, LVIII, 1934, 161–4; see also Roussel, *BCH*, LVI, 1932, 29–31; Daux, *Delphes*, 303 *seq.*

his enemies with a weapon against him. Thus Polybius,[1] usually a hostile critic, comments on the way in which, when faced by ill fortune, he became the most moderate of men—πάντων μετριώτατος—and set about the repair of his kingdom. And since it was the Macedon of this decade's work that Perseus inherited and ultimately brought into the war with Rome, it is by Philip's success in reconstruction that these years are most fairly to be judged.

For all their exaggeration, Eumenes's complaints to the Senate[2] on the eve of the Third Macedonian War give some indication of the fruits of Philip's consolidation: 30,000 infantry, 5000 cavalry, hoards of grain sufficient to last the army ten years, without drawing on harvests inside or outside Macedon, enough cash to hire 10,000 mercenaries for ten years, and in addition the revenue of the mines, arms for three such armies as Perseus possessed in his armouries, and Thrace as a perpetual recruiting ground—this was Eumenes's estimate of Macedonian assets. And in fact the forces actually put in the field by Perseus amounted to 43,000 men, of whom 29,000 were Macedonians.[3] In 224 Doson's national army in the Peloponnese had comprised 20,000 foot and 1300 horse, probably a maximum levy:[4] at Sellasia he had 13,300 Macedonians and 5300 mercenaries (6900 if the Illyrians were mercenaries, and not allies).[5] At Cynoscephalae, Philip put on the field an army of 18,000 Macedonian foot, 2000 cavalry and 5500 mercenaries—in all 25,500, which is probably again a maximum force.[6] Thus the consolidation of the years of peace had increased the national levy by about 9000 men, and, equally important, had brought sufficient resources to hire at least 18,000 mercenaries,[7] 9000 for field service and 9000 for garrison work;[8] and after Perseus's fall, notwithstanding the outlay of the war and the traditional poverty of Macedonia, Aemilius Paullus found some 6000 talents still left in the royal

[1] Polyb. xxv, 3, 9.
[2] Livy (P) xlii, 12, 7 seq.; cf. Griffith, 73 seq.   [3] Livy (P) xlii, 51, 3 seq.
[4] Plut. Arat. 43, 1.   [5] Polyb. ii, 65, 2–4.
[6] At the beginning of the war Philip had employed about 15,000 mercenaries on garrison duty (see above, p. 142, n. 2); but many of these had been recalled or had passed out of service before Cynoscephalae.
[7] Perseus's garrison figures were probably upwards of 15,000, about 9000 of them mercenaries; Kromayer, ii, 339–40.
[8] For a detailed analysis of these figures see Griffith, 75.

treasury.[1] Viewed in the light of the position in 189 and the subsequent hostility of Rome, this is a substantial accomplishment; and even though a good deal must go to the credit of Perseus, there is little doubt that the foundations of this work were laid by Philip, and that, as Alexander's conquests had behind them the solid achievement of his father's Thracian campaigns, so now Philip V, by his conquests and consolidation in the north, provided the basis for the ultimate struggle between Perseus and Rome.[2]

[1] Polyb. XVIII, 35, 4; cf. Livy (A) XLV, 40, 1 *seq.*, where Valerius Antias suggests that a similar sum had been expended during the war, or lost in the flight after Pydna.

[2] This analogy is drawn by Griffith, 73.

Chapter VIII : Conclusion

ORTY critical years of Mediterranean history separated
the 'darling of Greece' from the old man who died, worn-
out and disillusioned, at Amphipolis: each of those years
bore Philip's mark and had in turn impressed its mark on him
and on his policy. Hence, his career does not lend itself to
analysis into any simple scheme of aims and accomplishments.
In the conditions of the late third and early second centuries,
his life was necessarily a ding-dong struggle, demanding a
constant readaptation of both ends and means, in which changing
circumstances again and again suggested new objectives. Thus
the superficial impression is one of discontinuity and purpose-
lessness; and it is only by passing behind or rising above the
confusion of detail that one begins to discern the essential con-
tinuity. It is first of all in the personal character of Philip himself, and secondly in the objective role which his realm played
in the history of his time that it is possible to detect the unity
which gives meaning to his career.

To Philip's character heredity offers a clue. The blood of the
fiery Pyrrhus, descending through two grandparents and his
mother Phthia, may help to explain the passionate outbreaks to
which he was liable,[1] just as the knowledge of this ancestry
perhaps rendered him more ready to adopt Demetrius of Pharus's
grandiose schemes for western expansion. But in practice it was
his much more dubious descent from Philip II and Alexander
that Philip preferred to stress;[2] literary evidence and the findings
of archaeology[3] alike indicate that the Antigonids claimed descent
from the more famous Argeads, and that, like their rivals in

[1] So Tarn, *CQ*, XVIII, 1924, 17–23; cf. Fine, *CQ*, XXVIII, 1934, 99 *seq.*
[2] Polyb. V, 10, 10; Livy (P) XXVII, 30, 9; XXXII, 22, 11.
[3] See Edson, *Harv. Stud.* XLV, 1934, 214 *seq.*, who mentions literary texts,
epigrams, coins and, in particular, a line of statues erected in the portico of
Antigonus Gonatas on Delos, which began with Heracles, as evidence for the
Antigonid claim to Argead ancestry. Heracles is commonly found in connection with all the Antigonids. A further proof of Philip's interest in his namesake and supposed forbear is the statement in Photius (*Bibl.* 176, p. 121*a*, 35)
that Philip ὁ πρὸς Ῥωμαίους πολεμήσας made an abridgement from Theopompus of all the details concerning Philip II, reducing them to the compass
of sixteen books. See also above, pp. 243–4; and Treves, *LEC*, IX, 1940, 168–9.

Syria and Egypt,[1] they had already set up this claim shortly before the end of the fourth century. Whether, as Edson believes,[2] this family connection had any basis in fact, the evidence no longer allows us to say; but by Philip's time not even the worst enemies of the house thought to question it.[3] And, real or no, it is important as a source of convictions by which Philip sought consciously to guide his behaviour and his policy.

Of this policy, the permanent as well as the most important instrument was warfare. Out of a reign of forty-two years, Philip spent at the most only eight at peace;[4] and it is, therefore, not strange that his greatest personal qualities were those of a soldier. In campaign after campaign he displayed both speed and indefatigable energy, refusing either to desert his allies or to admit defeat. In his early years in particular he won himself a name by the rapidity of his marches. His conquest of Triphylia, his campaign of 218, when, after a lightning thrust at Thermum, he appeared less than a fortnight later above Sparta, his swift descent from Bylazora to Phthiotic Achaea in 217[5]—these represent a military technique which combined the sustained marches of Philip II and Alexander[6] with the swift stab so dear to Aratus. The same methods appear in the whirlwind campaign of late summer 211, when Illyria, Dardania, Thessaly, Thrace and south-east Macedonia were in turn swept by a Macedonian army within the space of a few short weeks, and in the sixty-mile race to catch Attalus at Cynus in 208 or the invasion of Pergamum in 201.[7] In siege-craft, too, Philip was almost alone among the

---

[1] Cf. Tarn, *JHS*, LIII, 1933, 60.   [2] Edson, *op. cit.* 221–6.

[3] Lycophron, *Alexandra*, 1446–50 (accepting the interpretation of Ziegler, *P–W*, 'Lykophron', cols. 2354–81; but cf. Edson, *op. cit.* 224, n. 1) makes Philip the 'sixth from Alexander', thus omitting all rulers between Alexander and Antigonus I. Seneca, *de ira*, III, 23, 1 (of dubious historical value; cf. Edson, *CP*, XXIX, 1934, 254–5), makes Alexander the nephew of Antigonus. Hence Tarn suggests (*JHS*, LIII, 1933, 60) that a supposed relationship between the two became an article of faith at an early date. Edson, *Harv. Stud.* XLV, 1934, 226, however, regards the relationship as a genuine one dating back to the fifth century.

[4] I.e. 221, 196, 194–2, 188, 185, and 182. In addition there is no record of open warfare in 203; but any of these years may have seen fighting on the northern frontier.

[5] See above, pp. 45 *seq.* (Triphylia), 54 *seq.* (Thermum and Laconia), 63 (Bylazora and Thessaly).

[6] Cf. Tarn, *Hellen. Mil. and Nav. Developments*, 40.

[7] See above, pp. 85–7 (campaign of 211), 94–5 (Attalus), 119 (Pergamum).

later Hellenistic monarchs to achieve any success;[1] for even though he met with set-backs—as for instance at Melitaea, Cephallenia or Chios—and though the fiasco at Lamia marked a deterioration in technique since the time when he employed a piece of brilliant trickery to secure the capitulation of Prinassus in almost parallel circumstances, nevertheless the seizure of Psophis, Alipheira, Lissus and Phthiotic Thebes are outstanding achievements.[2] In each case success was the fruit of storming, not of a protracted blockade; and though there is a wide gulf between Philip's seizure of Psophis and Aratus's capture of Sicyon or the Acrocorinth,[3] the value that Philip attached to taking his enemy unawares may well be an inheritance from the tactics of the Achaean.

A first-class soldier, Philip fell short, however, of the qualities that make a great statesman or even a great general. He could not take the long view of a Hannibal or a Napoleon[4] and weigh in advance the factors, military and political, on which success would depend. Often cruel and always unscrupulous, he was never handicapped by sentiment; but this same wilfulness was liable to blind him to the psychological reactions of the Greeks, whose help was for many years all-important. This defect of character became most apparent in the excesses of the eastern policy, when Philip launched himself recklessly into a programme of atrocities and breaches of established custom, paralleled hitherto by the Romans alone. As in the later massacre at Maronea, passion had the better of reason; and Philip revealed that failure to relate his actions to the concrete possibilities of each situation, that was to prove wholly disastrous in the larger aspects of his policy. His western schemes, for instance, reflect not a sober estimate of the opportunities afforded by the Hannibalic War, but the romantic traditions of a house which had always, as Polybius says,[5] coveted universal dominion. Consequently, when Philip sailed with his 150 *lembi* to Apollonia,

---

[1] On Hellenistic siege-craft see Kromayer-Veith, *Heerwesen und Kriegführung der Griechen und Römer*, 227 seq.

[2] See above, pp. 43 (Psophis), 46 (Alipheira), 53 (Cephallenia), 63–4 (Melitaea and Thebes), 80–1 (Lissus), 121 (Chios), 125 (Prinassus), 205 (Lamia). Among other successes of Philip were Echinus (and the coastal towns of Phthiotic Achaea), Thronium, Cius and Samos.

[3] Cf. Walbank, 33; 46.   [4] De Sanctis, IV, 1, 254.

[5] Polyb. v, 102, 1: ἣ μάλιστά πως ἀεὶ τῆς τῶν ὅλων ἐλπίδος ἐφίεται. On the phrase see Edson, *Harv. Stud.* XLV, 1934, 222, n. 1.

his recklessness was rewarded with the complete destruction of his fleet; and indeed, after the trial of the first war, it is doubtful, as De Sanctis points out,[1] whether, even as late as 200, Philip appreciated the magnitude of the struggle on which he had encouraged the Romans to embark.

Philip's personal character reveals a similar lack of proportion. This shows itself in the licentiousness and heavy drinking in which he provides so marked a contrast to his son and successor, Perseus;[2] even allowing for uniformly hostile sources, it is not easy to discount entirely the stories of the Argive Nemea of 209,[3] when his conduct alienated the governing classes in Achaea; and when Gracchus visited Pella in 190,[4] he found the king indulging in one of the traditional drinking bouts of the Macedonian court. A more serious sign of this weakness is, however, to be seen in Philip's encouragement of favourites; and it is an important matter to determine to what extent these favourites used Philip or allowed him to use them. The early struggle between Aratus and Apelles reflected Achaean and Macedonian particularism, and the triumph of Aratus was in some degree the triumph of a Hellenic policy. But very soon Demetrius of Pharus appeared, to carry the struggle with Aratus one step further by confronting him with a rash expansionist programme which satisfied his own political needs and the romanticism of Philip. Polybius does not hesitate to attribute Philip's deteriora-

---

[1] IV, I, 254.   [2] Cf. Polyb. XXV, 3, 7.

[3] See above, p. 91. It is not however fair to include the seduction of Polycrateia, the wife of the younger Aratus, as evidence of licentiousness, since, as Beloch shows (*Riv. Stor. Ant.* VI, 1901, 3 *seq.*; cf. *Griech. Gesch.* IV, 2, 139 *seq.*), Philip made her his queen, and her son, Perseus, his heir. We may summarise Philip's family connections here (cf. Holleaux, 79, n. 1; Beloch, IV, 2, 139 *seq.*). As far as is known, he had two sons and two daughters; Perseus was the son of Polycrateia, who died about 209. Of the mother of Demetrius, who was five years younger than Perseus (cf. Livy (P) XL, 6, 4), nothing is known, nor even if the two daughters, who married Teres of Thrace (Diod. XXXII, 15, 5) and Prusias II of Bithynia (Livy (P) XLII, 12, 3–4; 29, 3; Appian, *Mith.* 2: her name was Apame: cf. Wilhelm, *Jahresh.* XI, 1908, 80–1) were Demetrius's full sisters. Livy (P) XLII, 52, 5 (corrupt), speaks of a third son, Philip, whom Perseus adopted after his father's death and made heir to the exclusion of his own son, Alexander. The object of such an action is not clear (the two boys were much of an age), and Beloch has shown (IV, 2, 141; *contra* Cardinali, *Riv. Fil.* XXXIX, 1911, 10, n. 1; De Sanctis, IV, I, 252, n. 304; Edson, *Harv. Stud.* XLVI, 1935, 202) that this son, if Philip's, must have been born posthumously in 178; Beloch therefore seems to be right in suspecting the story and making this Philip a son not of Philip V, but of Perseus.

[4] See above, p. 210.

tion to the bad influence of Demetrius, which he sees reflected
in the sacrilege at Thermum and the ravaging of Messenia; and
in the incident on Mt Ithome he gives the clash dramatic
expression. Thus the war with Rome appears as the fruit of
Demetrius's supremacy, just as the Social War was the handi-
work of Aratus; and so long as the Roman war lasts, no further
favourite appears in Polybius's pages—though an inscription
shows Heracleides of Tarentum already holding Macedonian
commands as early as 209. However, Heracleides's hey-day
coincided with the eastern policy; and to Polybius his influence
was comparable only to that of Demetrius.[1] The deliberate
application of Roman methods of terrorism during the years
205–0 cannot be dissociated from Heracleides's name; on the
other hand, his removal by Philip at the end of 199 shows his
influence scarcely outlasting the period of eastern expansion.
From that time onward, no figure of note arises until the last
decade of Philip's life, when the crown prince Perseus, now in
his twenties, captures his father's confidence, and when beneath
the persons of Perseus and Demetrius there is played out the
conflict between a national and a pro-Roman policy. Of the
final influence, that of Antigonus, the son of Echecrates, too little
reliable information exists; and in any case, little of value can be
deduced from the behaviour of the broken-down Philip of 180.[2]

This close correspondence between fresh favourites and fresh
policies is curious; but it would be dangerous to use it as a basis
for generalisations on Philip's character. The conflict between
Aratus and Apelles was a legacy from Doson's reign, and there
is nothing odd in a young man's being influenced by the elders
about him—nor for that matter in his rejecting their influence
as soon as he has the strength to stand alone. Moreover, there
was no favourite during the years following Heracleides's
disgrace, when Philip independently initiated his policy of co-
operation with Rome. True, Demetrius and Heracleides had both
enjoyed considerable influence; but neither can be shown to have
done more than help him towards policies which he was quite
capable of adopting independently.

Nor do Philip's other personal relations suggest the weak tool

[1] Polyb. XIII, 4, 8; cf. Diod. XXVIII, 2 *seq.*
[2] See Edson, *Harv. Stud.* XLVI, 1935, 199 *seq.*

of favourites. Notwithstanding his long hostility to the Senate, Philip was on friendly terms with many eminent Roman families. The friendship struck up with Scipio Africanus in 190 was maintained afterwards in correspondence;[1] and there were close connections between the family of Philip and that of Q. Marcius Philippus, the senatorial commissioner of 183, who later jested to Perseus on the coincidence in the two names.[2] Even Flamininus, judging by Polybius's record of the Council in Locris, found something congenial in his opponent's manner, and the two men appreciated each other's irony and the cynical mood in which both approached the interview. Philip's sense of ironical humour, which came out so clearly at this conference as to call forth the mild reproof of Livy,[3] displays itself later in the verses in which he replied to Alcaeus's taunts after the defeat of Cynoscephalae.[4] Indeed this capacity for coolness and grim humour when his luck was against him provides a remarkable contrast to the impetuosity and careless romanticism with which he would fling himself, without proper consideration, into the most hazardous exploits. It is not strange that Polybius comments on the new prudence Philip displayed after Cynoscephalae,[5] and on the steadfastness with which he faced the setbacks of his last ten years.[6] Great personal courage and enthusiasm in whatever he undertook, and a cool head to meet its failure—these were far too often the qualities that had to compensate for Philip's lack of a genuine grasp of the political situation and the acute mind of the first-class diplomat and statesman.

On the other hand, Philip's qualities were not unsuited to the Macedon he was called upon to govern. Here courage and a strong personality were the first essentials to win the respect of this people of fighters, hunters and peasants. The three epigrams written by Samus,[7] on the bull that Philip had slain on Orbelus in Thrace, indicate what deeds the Macedonians expected from their king. He must ride hard and fight hard: he must be better

---

[1] See above, p. 211, n. 2.
[2] Livy (P) XLII, 38, 7 *seq.*; cf. Münzer, *P-W*, 'Marcius (Philippus), No. 79', col. 1574.
[3] Livy, XXXII, 34, 4 (not in Polybius): *et erat dicacior natura quam regem decet, et ne inter seria quidem risu satis temperans.*
[4] See above, p. 173.   [5] Polyb. XVIII, 33, 7.
[6] Polyb. XXV, 3, 9.   [7] *Anth. Pal.* VI, 114–6.

264 CONCLUSION

than the men he led to the chase or the battle. ἃ πολύολβος 'Ημαθί' ἃ τοίῳ κραίνεται ἀγεμόνι.

Within Macedon, then, Philip's popularity depended largely on his success in maintaining the role traditionally associated with its king. But there were other factors influencing his relations with the assembly in arms, which deserve attention. What was in fact the development of the Macedonian κοινόν, which Doson's death left in a somewhat undefined form? Did the powers of the people increase, or did they disappear in the course of Philip's reign? The answer is much disputed. Holleaux[1] takes the second view against Beloch,[2] who indeed goes as far as to suggest that in his later years Philip instituted some form of popular representation. To speak of 'popular representation' is certainly to go beyond the evidence: on the other hand, Holleaux's argument from the formulae on Delian inscriptions is unconvincing. On two dedications, probably from the first half of Philip's reign,[3] Holleaux points out, instead of the formula βασιλεὺς καὶ Μακεδόνες (frequently found on inscriptions from the reigns of Doson, Philip and Perseus)[4] the form used is βασιλεὺς Μακεδόνων, a phrase which is, he claims, without parallel after the reign of Cassander.[5] This change, Holleaux argues, was permanent; and the remaining evidence from Philip's and Perseus's reigns he disallows on the grounds that it is of non-Macedonian origin and tells us nothing of the style affected by the kings themselves. This theory has been severely shaken by the recent researches of Edson and Dow[6] into the royal style of the Antigonids, which show quite convincingly that there was no such thing as a style peculiar to each king. Indeed, the only important distinction is that between inscriptions which refer to the king alone, and those which refer to the king and the Macedonians (i.e. the army assembly). Therefore, although the only certain reference to the κοινόν[7] is in the

[1] BCH, XXXI, 1907, 97 seq.; so also Treves, LEC, IX, 1940, 149–57.
[2] IV, I, 383. 'Erst nach Kynoskephalae scheint Philippos den Makedonen eine Art von Volksvertretung verliehen zu haben.'
[3] Syll. 573 (to be dated 201: see above, p. 67, n. 6); 574 (dedication of Philip's portico: perhaps c. 211; see below, p. 269).   [4] See above, p. 4, n. 1.
[5] Cf. Syll. 332. The formula appears elsewhere; e.g. IG, VII, 3055, line 8 (Amyntas IV); Welles, Royal Correspondence, 118 seq., no. 25 (Ziaëlas of Bithynia); Treves, op. cit. 152–4, n.   [6] Harv. Stud. XLVIII, 1937, 128–40.
[7] There are no literary references to the κοινόν; on Diod. XVIII, 4, 3; Polyaen. IV, 6, 14, and Arrian, Anab. VII, 9, 5, see Tarn, JHS, XLI, 1921, 16–17. The inscriptions IG, XI, 4, 1103–4, are too fragmentary to be used.

inscription which Vallois, on epigraphical grounds, dates to the beginning of Philip's reign,[1] it is no longer possible to follow Holleaux in his assumption that a period of attempted absolutism, revealed by a change of formula, brought the κοινόν to an end.

In any case, during the last decade of Philip's reign the relations between king and people entered a new phase, in which the whole tendency was towards a greater degree of local autonomy. To secure the whole-hearted co-operation of the people in his policy of economic reorganisation Philip was evidently led to make certain concessions in kind. From 187 onwards,[2] copper coins begin to be minted in Macedon not merely by the king, but also by various local groups and even individual cities. Besides an issue under the name of the Macedonians, coined in Philip's royal mint at Amphipolis, there is now evidence of at least four other regional issues, those of the Amphaxians, coined at Thessalonica, those of the Bottiaeans, coined at Pella, and those of two Paeonian peoples, the Doberes and Paroreians. In addition, many cities also minted in their own names: examples are known from Amphipolis, Aphytis in Chalcidice, Apollonia in Mygdonis, Pella and Thessalonica.[3] It is quite clear that a concession of this magnitude—for hitherto not even the Greek trading cities had been allowed separate coining rights—represents a definite political readjustment between the authority centralised in the king and the local units which had never been wholly absorbed into Macedon.[4]

Before following Gaebler[5] in characterising Philip's policy as weak, we must attempt, however, to analyse more closely both the exact nature of the concession and the conditions that led him to make it. We have already traced[6] how the strongest op-

---

[1] *Syll.* 575; cf. Vallois, 156.
[2] See above, p. 224.
[3] For the evidence see Gaebler, *ZN*, xx, 1897, 169–92; xxxvi, 1926, 111–16 and 183–98 (summed up in *Die antiken Münzen Nord-Griechenlands*, vol. iii, Part i (1906), pp. 1–3, 26–52; Part ii (1935), pp. 1–5, 33, 46, 93, 117, 189–94); Mamroth, *ZN*, xxxviii, 1928, 1 *seq.*; xl, 1930, 207–303; xlii, 1935, 219–51; Perdrizet, *Rev. Num.* vii, 1903, 320–25. Some of the evidence is in Head, 232–4, 242–3, 891 (addenda).
[4] The exact nature of this political readjustment and degree of independence achieved by the cities is still problematic; it may be observed that, *pace* Pelekides, 25, there is still no definite proof of the existence of *politarchai* as city magistrates anywhere in Macedon prior to the Roman conquest.
[5] *ZN*, xx, 1897, 173.   [6] See above, pp. 243 *seq.*

CONCLUSION

position to Philip's policy of consolidation, heavy taxation and resistance to Roman influence arose mainly in the coastal towns, and how it was crushed, partly by drafting the disaffected sections of the population to the inland frontiers, and replacing them by Thracian garrisons, and later by the suppression of Samus's conspiracy. Now it is significant that of the five towns that are known to have been granted autonomous currencies, Amphipolis, Aphytis and Thessalonica lay on the coast, Apollonia, though inland, was the most important town on the direct trade route between Amphipolis and Thessalonica, on what was later to become the Via Egnatia, while the fifth was the royal town of Pella, which had enjoyed comparative independence even in the third century.[1]

The Antigonids had always set their face firmly against granting coining rights to the cities.[2] But Philip was wise enough to see that though methods of absolutism might be effective in camp, during a successful campaign, they would never secure ready collaboration in building up the realm. Some degree of regional autonomy for the districts and special consideration for the trading cities of the coast[3]—this is the meaning of the separate coinages. Now it may be that objectively these concessions tended to produce the conditions for the eventual break-up of the Macedonian monarchy. But the strength or weakness of Philip's policy is to be judged not *in vacuo*, but in relation to the course actually open to him; and the concessions he made were in fact forced upon him by the economic problem of consolidating Macedon. The success he achieved in that policy can be measured by the prosperity of Macedon and the loyalty of the people; and our review of the conditions on the eve of the Third Macedonian War, together with Philip's ruthless suppression of Samus and Admetus, suggest that his concessions weakened neither nation nor monarchy. They simply substituted a looser form of organisation, the success of which is shown in the continued loyalty of the Macedonian people under Perseus, or in the fact that even in 150 Andriscus had only to raise his standards under the

[1] See above, p. 7.
[2] Tarn, 197; exceptions existed outside Macedon, e.g. Gonnus in Thessaly (Stählin, 35, n. 12).
[3] Compare the special treatment afforded to Demetrias (above, pp. 229 *seq.*).

name of Philip to rally all four Macedonian republics behind him.[1]

Thus its results fully justified Philip's programme of consolidation. Of its thoroughness an interesting example has survived in an inscription which also illuminates the important part played by religion as an instrument of domestic policy. This document, recently found at Salonica, contains a special διάγραμμα of the king, in which the revenues of the Sarapeum in that town are protected (in the royal interest) against sequestration by the municipal authorities.[2] The date of the διάγραμμα, which was communicated to the priests of the temple, is Daesius of Philip's thirty-fifth year, i.e. May 187, and thus links up with the new economic policy of the last decade. As an individual, Philip seems to have held the conventional view of religion;[3] unlike Gonatas, his grandfather, he was no philosopher, and shows no acquaintance with the teaching of the schools. On the other hand, our sources never show him accepting the cruder forms of superstition,[4] and he usually figures as an orthodox character, directing the spring-ceremony of the Macedonian army,[5] dedicating the fruit of the chase to Heracles,[6] granting a tetrarch land for the carrying out of religious rites,[7] sacrificing to

[1] Cf. Benecke, *CAH*, VIII, 276: Andriscus was followed by other pretenders; 'anyone who could put forward a claim to belong to the royal house could still count on some support'.

[2] Pelekides, 6–23. Whether the διάγραμμα referred to Sarapea in various Macedonian towns, or only that in Thessalonica is uncertain. On the nature of the διάγραμμα, which was a royal proclamation (not a letter), which laid down certain instructions with the force of law, and invoked certain sanctions for their transgression, see Makaronas, *AE*, 1934–5, 120; Heuss, *Stadt und Herrscher*, 78 *seq.*; and particularly Welles, *AJA*, XLII, 1938, 245–60, and Bikerman, *Rev. Phil.* LXIV, 1938, 295–312.

[3] It is an odd coincidence that two inscriptions connect Philip with the cult of the Egyptian gods—that here mentioned and one (cf. Perdrizet, *BCH*, XVIII, 1894, 416) in which the worship of Philip is combined by a Greek of Amphipolis with that of Isis and Sarapis. But it would be dangerous to conclude that Philip had a particular leaning towards these cults.

[4] The story of the mound at Cynoscephalae (above, p. 170, n. 1) is apocryphal.

[5] See above, p. 246.

[6] Samus, *Anth. Pal.* VI, 114–16. For the particular interest shown by the Antigonids in the cult of Heracles see above, p. 258, n. 3. Further confirmation—again in connection with hunting—comes from a dedication to Heracles by Philip, recently discovered at Pella by Mr C. F. Edson, who will shortly publish it in a report for the Berlin Academy.

[7] In the letter to Archippus; see Makaronas, *AE*, 1934–5, 117–27.

Zeus on Ithome,[1] to unspecified gods on the hills Euas and Olympus at Sellasia,[2] or to Zeus and Helios on the summit of Haemus;[3] and in such a remark as that 'he feared nobody but the gods'[4] he reveals the traditional Greek attitude in orthodox phraseology.

When, however, one turns to Philip's relations with the international cults of the Greek world, at once, as Glotz observes,[5] religious and political motives intermingle. The desire to secure prestige and popularity over a wide sphere undoubtedly influenced Philip's patronage of the lesser shrines, two examples of which come from Lindus on Rhodes and Panamara in Caria. The Lindian *Temple Chronicle* of Timachidas[6] catalogues a gift of ten shields, ten spears and other (undecipherable) objects to Lindian Athena; and there is a similar record of vases and a wine-vessel dedicated to Carian Zeus at Panamara.[7] In the same way, in 209–8, Philip exerted his influence to persuade the people of Chalcis to send representatives to the new festival of Artemis Leucophryene at Magnesia-on-the-Maeander;[8] and in 205–3 his agent Perdiccas appears in Crete, working to obtain the rights of ἀσυλία for Teos.[9] Philip's most important politico-religious activity was, however, on Delos, where his particularly lavish gifts to Apollo may have been designed to compensate for his exclusion from an Aetolian Delphi.[10] Delos formed part of Philip's inheritance, and one of his first acts there was perhaps the completion of his guardian's dedication for the victory of 'Antigonus and the Macedonians and the Allies' over Cleomenes of Sparta at Sellasia.[11] From this time onward his association

---

[1] Polyb. VII, 12, 1.   [2] Polyb. V, 24, 9.   [3] Livy (P) XL, 22, 7.
[4] Polyb. XVIII, 1, 7: φοβεῖσθαι μὲν ἔφησεν ὁ Φίλιππος οὐδένα πλὴν τοὺς θεούς. The story of Philip's praying for Antiochus's help (Livy (P) XXXV, 18, 7), though invented, was no doubt true to character.   [5] *REG*, XXIX, 1916, 301.
[6] Ed. Blinkenberg, 337–8, no. XLII; cf. Holleaux, *REG*, XXVI, 1913, 44–5 (= Vol. I, 405–6); Hiller v. Gaertringen, *P–W*, 'Rhodos', Suppl.-B. V, col. 787. The date of the dedication is uncertain; if the restoration Α[ἰτω]λ[ούς] is accepted, the Social War seems a probable date, but Ad. Wilhelm (*Wien. Anz.* LIX, 1922, 70–72; LXVII, 1930, 102) reads νικάσας Δα[ρ]δ[ανί]ου[ς καὶ Μαίδας or Παίονας]. In either case, the date will scarcely be later than Philip's breach with Rhodes in 202; cf. Treves, *LEC*, IX, 1940, 150, n. 1.
[7] Cousin-Holleaux, *BCH*, XXVIII, 1904, 346–7, 354–9 (nos. 1–3): the dedication is of φιάλας καὶ κάδον.
[8] *Syll.* 561, referring to a letter from Philip; cf. Ferguson, *Ath. Trib. Cyc.*, 128, n. 1.   [9] See above, p. 121, n. 3.
[10] After 189 Delphi was independent, but Macedon got no direct footing there until the time of Perseus (see above, p. 248).   [11] *Syll.* 518.

with Delos was constant throughout the whole of his reign, as numerous inscriptions show.[1]

Of all Philip's gifts to the shrine, the most important were the magnificent portico overlooking the Sacred Harbour, and the institution of the *Philippeia* vase-festival; unfortunately, the date of neither can be established with certainty. References to the *Philippeia* on two mutilated inventories, and under the names of eight different archons in the inventory of Stesileus,[2] show that the festival was instituted early in Philip's reign; but as Stesileus gives the beginning of none of the festivals he mentions, it is uncertain whether the *Philippeia* commemorated its founder's accession[3] or the conclusion of the Social War.[4] A more concrete testimony to Philip's patronage was the portico. This flanked the left-hand side of the avenue along which pilgrims passed from the harbour to the sacred precinct, and confronted the slightly earlier portico of Attalus. Its Doric colonnade, over seventy metres long, made an impressive approach to the site; and its effect[5]—probably deliberately planned—must have been to mask the portico of Attalus and hide it from pilgrims arriving on the quay. Because of its position, Vallois suggests that it was built soon after the breach between Pergamum and Macedon, following on the entry of Attalus's allies, the Aetolians, into the First Macedonian War on the side of Rome.[6] In any case, it is improbable that the portico was begun after Philip's definite loss of naval command in 200; and its style shows affinities to earlier buildings dating from *c.* 230.[7]

Philip's loss of naval power did not, however, sever Macedonian relations with Delos; on the contrary, these continued

[1] For two of these—Philip's dedication after Lade and that from the κοινὸν Μακεδόνων—see above, p. 264, n. 3; for Philip's connections with Delos see Schulhof and Havelin, *BCH*, XXXI, 1907, 50, n. 1; Holleaux, *BCH*, XXXI, 1907, 105, n. 1; Schulhof, *BCH*, XXXII, 1908, 101 *seq.*, commenting on the inventory of Stesileus (*ibid.* insc. 21, p. 83); Durrbach, *BCH*, XXXV, 1911, 19 n.; *BCH*, XL, 1916, 317–19; Glotz, *REG*, XXIX, 1916, 281–325; Vallois, *passim*; Laidlaw, 115–18.
[2] *Insc. de Délos*, 361, line 21 (=Homolle, *Archives*, LXX); 363, line 29 (=Homolle, *Archives*, LXXIII); 366, lines 59, 62, 82, 83, 86, 87 (=Schulhof, *BCH*, XXXII, 1908, 83 *seq.*). [3] Tarn, 391, n. 65.
[4] Laidlaw, 117: 'possibly 216' (given inconsistently on p. 278 as '213?', qualified as 'the year of Philo II'). [5] Vallois, 163; Laidlaw, 118.
[6] This breach was, of course, in 211.
[7] Cf. Laidlaw, 137, n. 16. Vallois, 159, considers the possibility that the building was not completed until towards the end of Philip's life, and that the crown then granted him was to commemorate this.

into the reign of Perseus.[1] Moreover, the inventory of Demares, dating probably to the year 179,[2] refers to a crown presented by the Delians to Philip a little before his death, which Glotz estimates to have cost some 2000 drachmae;[3] this crown, for which they were still paying when Philip died,[4] was, it is suggested, a return for concessions in the purchase of Macedonian pitch and timber— concessions reflected in the drop in the price of pitch on Delos in 179 from 14 drachmae 3 obols to 9 drachmae per *metretes*.[5]

With fuller records, such details as these could no doubt be paralleled from most of the shrines of international repute in the Hellenistic world.[6] But it is only necessary to recall Philip's conduct at Thermum, Messene, Pergamum and Athens, or his patronage of the blasphemous Dicaearchus, to realise how little they reveal of Philip's personal attitude towards religion. Their significance is political, not moral; and it is against the background of Philip's foreign policy that they are most profitably considered.

To any king of Macedonia the first and most fundamental question was that of the northern frontiers. 'It was in warding off the assaults of the northern hordes from Greece and in the consequent preservation of Hellenic culture, that the historic task of the Macedonian monarchy at all times lay; and to this task, consciously or unconsciously, the Antigonids applied themselves with complete success.'[7] Circumstances, it is true, thrust this knightly function upon Philip and his predecessors; but their service to Greece was recognised in their own time, and adduced by Flamininus himself as an argument against the destruction of the Macedonian realm after Cynoscephalae.[8]

[1] Cf. *Syll.* 639 (Delian inscription honouring Laodice, Perseus's queen).
[2] So Laidlaw, 276 (following Durrbach) and Dinsmoor, 503.
[3] Glotz, *REG*, XXIX, 1916, 300–2.
[4] Glotz, *ibid.*; Durrbach, *BCH*, XL, 1916, 317–19.
[5] Glotz, *ibid.* His attempt to link this up with the political situation must, however, be read with caution. See, too, above, p. 269, n. 7.
[6] The statue erected to Doson and Philip (Pausan. VI, 16, 3) points to connections with Olympia, at least at the beginning of Philip's reign. For a dedication to Juppiter Optimus Maximus at Rome (191–0) see above, p. 208. M. Robertson, *JHS*, LIX, 1939, 203 (cf. Lemerle, *BCH*, LXII, 1938, 479) now records a newly-discovered letter of Philip to the Athenians in Hephaestia, from the sanctuary of the Cabiri at Chloi on Lemnos, which 'recalls the protection exercised over the sanctuary by the royal house of Macedon, especially Philip V'.
[7] Fellmann, 40; cf. Tarn, 202.
[8] Cf. Polyb. IX, 35, 2 *seq.* (Lyciscus of Acarnania's speech); Polyb. XVII, 37, 9; Livy (P) XXXIII, 12, 10 (Flamininus).

Macedon was in fact the natural bulwark against the Gauls, Dardanians, Bastarnians and Thracians who lived a semi-nomadic life in the northern Balkans and around the Danube and its tributaries; and these peoples necessarily played a prominent part in Philip's policies. Relations were normally hostile. A crisis in Macedon—war with Aetolia (219), a rumour of Philip's death (209), the Roman offensive of 199 or the defeat of Cynoscephalae—would be a signal for the Dardanians or their neighbours, the Illyrians, to advance plundering across the northern frontiers; and later Philip in turn would take revenge in a punitive expedition, occasionally seizing a key point such as Bylazora, Sintia or Iamphorynna. Up to the end of the second war with Rome, his reign is a constant record of this kind of desultory warfare. But after that, from 197 until 184, the frontier is apparently quiet; and Philip's part in the Roman march through Thrace in 190 certainly points to some agreement with the tribes in that area. When, however, the northern question reappeared, in 184, it was as a major part of Philip's programme. As in 208 and 204, he once more took the offensive, both militarily and in his schemes for replenishing his population from Thrace and settling the Bastarnae in the place of the Dardanians. But whatever Philip's plans in the Balkans, Perseus reverted to a Greek and Mediterranean policy, and Macedon remained a Hellenistic power.

In its move towards the Greeks, the opening of Perseus's reign was only paralleling that of Philip's. For notwithstanding the conflict between Aratus and Apelles, and, subsequently, the growth of Demetrius's influence, the Social War was in essence Philip's Greek apprenticeship: he fought as the president of Doson's Symmachy and his mentor was Aratus. The Peace of Naupactus was his political coming of age and, thanks to the Pharian, took him away from the traditional channels of Macedonian policy. At this juncture two events stood out; on the one hand, Philip's western schemes and, on the other, a situation in Syria, which was to send his young rival Antiochus eastward to the triumphs of an Asiatic 'anabasis', together combined to postpone the duel for which their similar ages and fortunes seemed already to have marked them out. And, in the meantime, the progressive decay of the Ptolemaic Empire under

Philopator ensured that the duel, when it came, would mark the end of the century-old balance of power.

It was not until 205, when the struggle with Rome had served to develop his skill and endurance as a general, but had brought none of the fruits anticipated in 217, that Philip once more reverted to the Aegean and the east. And this time the imminent clash with Syria was turned off by the thieves' compact of 203–2. Neither Philip nor Antiochus was in a position to foresee the ironical chain of events by which a Greek world, stirred beyond endurance by the application of Roman methods of warfare by Philip, would represent their compact as an anti-Roman measure, and so involve Macedon in a second and this time decisive struggle against the Roman legions. Thus the twice-postponed duel never took place; and, not through any superior skill in manœuvring—far from it—but because Philip, in learning from Laevinus, had forgotten the lessons of Aratus, the Senate was able to crush a Hellenistic world already divided within itself, putting down first Philip and then Antiochus, the one with the connivance, the other with the active assistance of his rival.

In 200 Philip lost the initiative of action that he had enjoyed, with short exceptions, since 217; and for that loss he had, in the long run, himself to blame. His two great errors during the earlier period were the adoption of a western policy in 217 and the use of methods of barbarism in his eastern campaigns. The exact details by which these two errors brought about the second war with Rome were perhaps unforeseeable; but the general implications of arousing first the hostility of Rome and then of all the Greeks should not have been hard to discern. That Philip missed them is another proof of that short-sightedness and lack of psychological acuteness which later let him be outmanœuvred by a Flamininus or a Nabis.[1]

After 200, first in the war and then in the peace, Philip was much more limited by circumstances, and his policy of supporting Rome was undoubtedly wise. Cynoscephalae had not destroyed the fundamental cleavage of interest between himself and Antiochus, which demanded that he should take the Senate's side against a Syrian invasion of Greece. All the same, the logic

---

[1] On the question of Argos (Nabis) and at the conference of Locris (Flamininus).

of collaboration did not resolve the contradictions inherent in that policy. For whatever arrangement he entered into and whatever course of action he adopted from time to time, the constant thread running through Philip's policy from 217 to his death was one of hostility to Rome. It is this that makes it so difficult to decide whether Philip was planning a war with Rome during his last decade. In fact, he seems to have been consolidating his kingdom in opposition to Rome, in the belief that Rome was herself plotting his destruction; his new Macedon was to be based on the unlimited resources of a friendly Balkan hinterland; but he did not plan the war with Rome that Polybius attributes to him.

Partly, the Senate was itself responsible for sending Philip north. For the peace that followed Cynoscephalae marked the end of his relations with southern Greece, now effectively cut off behind Thermopylae; it destroyed the last relics of the Symmachy. Philip's relations with the Greeks of the Peloponnese are a history of his relations with the Symmachy, which, after long being moribund, finally fell apart in 196. Within that period, the dividing line, political in origin, though the ancients regarded it as psychological, is laid down by the events at Messene. As Philip's attitude towards the Symmachy changed, and he came to regard it not as an ideal, but as an instrument of his own ambitions, he was less and less willing to tolerate in it what was to him a petty opposition. And since, like the leagues composing it, the Symmachy was part of the machinery of oligarchic domination, the instinct to obtain a weapon against the paramount authorities in, for example, the Achaean League, led Philip to play the demagogue at Messene or Argos. Thus the fundamental economic conflict within third and second century Greece, though suppressed inside Achaea itself, had its reflection in the relations between Achaea and Macedon; and, acting from purely personal motives, Philip eventually found himself, in his alliance with Nabis, supporting the very cause of the social revolution.[1] The fact was that after the Peace of Naupactus the Symmachy had ceased to correspond to the real relations between Philip and the Leagues;[2] and though it had supported the

---

[1] See above, pp. 164–5.
[2] It still continued to exist, however: cf. Polyb. VII, 9, 1; 9, 7; IX, 38, 5; XI, 5, 4; Livy (P) XXVII, 30, 9; etc.; *contra* Heuss, *Stadt und Herrscher*, 163.

intolerable strain of the war with Rome, thanks mainly to the loyal military support which Philip furnished whenever it was required, it is small wonder that it failed to weather the outburst of anti-Macedonian feeling which followed upon the Aegean expeditions of 204–1. After a little hesitation the Achaeans went over to Rome; and in the declaration of Corinth in 196 Flamininus put an end to what had become an anomaly. Henceforth Philip's relations with Greece were restricted to Thessaly and the central states.

The declaration of Corinth also put an end to the equilibrium which had succeeded to Alexander's empire, thus marking the end of an epoch in the history of Hellenism. Looking back on that century, we can see it to-day as the bridge between classical Greece and Rome, as the vital link in the transmission of Greek culture. Against this background, the importance of Macedon—an importance already hinted at[1]—lay in its position as a bulwark of Hellenism against the northern hordes, which enabled it to stand for a hundred years between Greece and barbarism. But the equilibrium which facilitated this task was already doomed when Philopator ascended the throne of Egypt. To the balance of power there were two alternatives—a succession of internecine wars, such as had followed Alexander's death, leading to a permanent dimming, if not extinction of Hellenic culture, or the rise of one power capable of imposing order and herself taking over that heritage.

In Rome such a power did in fact arise. And Philip V of Macedon gains his place in world history from the part he played in relation to Rome and the Hellenistic world. Quite involuntarily and even unconsciously, Philip became the historical instrument of Roman expansion eastwards; and while faithfully preserving his own realm, and with it Greece, from any repetition of the barbarian inroad of 279, he was at the same time responsible for bringing into Greece not only the Roman legions, but also such commanders as Flamininus and the Scipios, who fell a swift prey to the culture of their conquered foes. The second century is the story of the advance eastward of Roman arms; but it is no less the story of the advance westward of Greek culture. The two movements are parallel and complementary, and together provide the all-important features of the century,

[1] See above, p. 270.

in the light of subsequent history; it is thus inevitable that all other events in the Hellenistic world should fall into relation with them. But the clear logic of world movements emerges only from out of an infinite variety of minor streams, a host of contingencies, conflicting ambitions and cross-currents: what in the light of centuries proves all-important may be regarded as little more than an accident, or may even pass unnoticed by the uncomprehending gaze of its contemporaries.

This is above all true in the case of Philip. That his life is a succession of paradoxes is due to the discrepancy between the immediate and contradictory aims of Macedonian, Syrian and senatorial policy and the firm lines of Roman expansion, laid down by the military preponderance of the Roman legions. From this discrepancy sprang the ironical situation of 201, when Philip in turning his back on Rome brought down on himself the full weight of her military machine; it explains too why, throughout the vital last seventeen years of his life, Philip, though passionately hostile to Rome, pursued a sober policy of loyal co-operation with the Senate, in the face of numerous insults and injustices; and how, dying, he left to Perseus a kingdom that was both strengthened and doomed. For it was these same factors, operating within the politico-economic sphere, that obliged Philip, in order that he might consolidate the wealth and loyalty of Macedon, to sponsor and encourage a movement towards local and urban autonomy, which was eventually to facilitate the dismemberment of the country.

But perhaps the greatest irony of all lies in this, that the king of Macedon who was renowned above all for his energy, speed and enterprise, who opened his reign as the 'darling of Greece', but later turned his ambitions to Italy and Asia in turn, who more than once drove his country to the edge of bankruptcy in his attempt to maintain a fleet and army simultaneously, and who died with his eyes fixed upon the Balkans, where he perhaps envisaged a new and formidable empire, should claim his place in world history, not for any of these things which he initiated, but solely as the unwitting instrument that enabled the culture of Greece to spread along the paths of the legions to Rome, and so to the western civilisation that grew up after her.

APPENDICES

Appendix I : A Short Survey of the Sources

In spite of the contributions of archaeology, a history of Philip V must still rely primarily on Polybius's account. Hence, at the outset, two main problems emerge: first to isolate and reconstruct the Polybian version from the fragments which are all we possess from Book V onward and from later writers such as Livy, Diodorus and Plutarch, who draw upon it: and secondly, to assess the value of this version in the light of Polybius's own historical principles, sources of information and possible bias, together with such outside checks as we have. This done, it remains to attempt some assessment of the relevant non-Polybian matter in the sources.

POLYBIUS

Born in 208 at Megalopolis, of a well-known family, Polybius spent his first forty years acquiring the military and political experience of an Achaean statesman.[1] In 168 he was sent as one of the Achaean hostages to Rome, where he lived in contact with the most prominent circles of Roman society until 151, when he was allowed to return. The rest of his life he spent either at home or in travel in all parts of the Mediterranean, dying eventually from a fall off his horse in 117.[2] Polybius's *Life of Philopoemen*[3] and his manual on *Tactics*[4] date to the earliest of these three periods; but the idea of a universal history, showing the rise of Rome to world dominion,[5] cannot have occurred before the stay at Rome; and though it is uncertain how many books were finished by 151,[6] traces still remain of the earlier scheme carrying the history down to 167, on which Polybius later superimposed the design of descending to the destruction of Corinth and Carthage in 146. Slight inconsistencies of this kind suggest that the work was left without a final revision.

To Polybius it was the function of history to furnish examples of moral and political conduct to help his readers to face the vicissitudes of their own lives;[7] and for a history capable of doing this there were

[1] For the date see Beloch, IV, 2, 228 (but it is questioned); for offices held by Polybius cf. Polyb. XXIV, 6 (diplomatic mission—later cancelled—to Egypt); Polyb. XXVIII, 6 (Hipparch); Plut. *Philop.* 21, 5 (carrying of Philopoemen's ashes).
[2] [Lucian], *Macrobioi*, 22.　　　　　　　　　　[3] Polyb. X, 21, 5.
[4] Polyb. IX, 20, 4; cf. contents of IX, 12–20.　　[5] Polyb. I, 3, 1; IV, 2, 4.
[6] Cf. Bury, *Ancient Greek Historians*, 192 ('at least 15 books'); Christ-Schmid, *Gesch. d. gr. Litt.* II, 1, 383 *seq.* ('books I–XXIX').
[7] Polyb. I, 1, 2.

three prerequisites.[1] First, the historian must make a critical study of memoirs and documents; second, and most important, he must 'see for himself', visit places, carry out personal research and enquiry, using his eyes as well as his ears, to come at the truth (αὐτοπαθεία);[2] finally, he must be a man of action, capable of assessing events from his own similar experience.[3]

How far did Polybius put these principles into practice? For the introductory chapters (II, 37–71), covering a period for which the most conscientious personal investigation must have rested on ἀκοὴ ἐξ ἀκοῆς, he was content to follow the *Memoirs* of his fellow-Achaean, Aratus.[4] But for the later years—those of the history proper—his most important evidence comes from eye-witnesses, including, on occasion, himself.[5] Three stages may be traced in the accumulation of this material. Prior to 167, Polybius is unlikely to have done more than assimilate from the sources open to a son of Lycortas the history of the previous fifty years as it appeared to Achaean eyes. Then, when his exile had converted him into a keen pro-Roman, his plan for a universal history must have led to more systematic enquiries at Rome, where he was more fortunate in having not only the Romans to draw on, but also a circle of prominent exiles, including a thousand of his countrymen.[6] Finally, after 151, came his wider researches; but by now the majority of his informants on the years previous to 179 would be dead. We may therefore conclude that Polybius's investigations about Philip were mainly at Rome, and that these, along with his own earlier notes and recollections, form the basis of his account.

Where monographs existed, Polybius was prepared to use them critically. Thus in discussing[7] the treatment of the battles of Chios and Lade and of Nabis's attack on Messene in the Rhodian historians Zeno and Antisthenes, he speaks of other authors who were

[1] Polyb. XII, 25e.
[2] Polyb. XII, 4c, 4; 25h, 4; 27, 6: ἡ δὲ πολυπραγμοσύνη πολλῆς μὲν προσδεῖται ταλαιπωρίας καὶ δαπάνης, μέγα δέ τι συμβάλλεται καὶ μέγιστόν ἐστι μέρος τῆς ἱστορίας.
[3] Cf. Polyb. XII, 25e, 7, criticising Timaeus, the armchair historian.
[4] On Aratus's *Memoirs* see Walbank, 11–12; Porter, xv–xvi.
[5] Polyb. IV, 2, 2.
[6] Since in sixteen years their numbers fell from 1000 to 300 (Pausan. VII, 10, 12), and they are not likely to have been ill-treated, most of them were evidently well beyond middle age in 167, and so valuable informants. Woodhouse, 258, n. 1, makes out a good case for regarding Nicander of Trichonium as an eyewitness source for Polybius's account of Philip's invasion of Thermum in 218 (Polyb. v, 6–14), and for other events (cf. Polyb. xx, 11 ; XXI, 25).
[7] Polyb. XVI, 14, 1–2: ἐπεὶ δέ τινες τῶν τὰς κατὰ μέρος γραφόντων πράξεις γεγράφασι καὶ περὶ τούτων τῶν καιρῶν...βούλομαι βραχέα περὶ αὐτῶν διαλεχθῆναι. ποιήσομαι δ' οὐ πρὸς ἅπαντας, ἀλλ' ὅσους ὑπολαμβάνω μνήμης ἀξίους εἶναι καὶ διαστολῆς. Cf. also VIII, 8, 3, where he speaks of writers on Messenian affairs and τοὺς γράφοντας τοῦ Φιλίππου τὰς πράξεις, whose works are mere panegyrics (the reference is to Philip V, though in going on to criticise Theopompus, Polybius switches over to Philip II).

not worth his attention. Such sources[1] were probably few and unimportant, however, and can scarcely have included any major writer.[2] Perhaps more important was Polybius's use of popular editions of speeches, pamphlets and the other propaganda material which no doubt circulated widely at this time.[3] He also referred occasionally to original documents;[4] though his irony at Timaeus's expense[5] is a warning against expecting too much research of this kind. One passage (xvi, 14 *seq.*) shows Polybius to have had access to the records in the Prytaneum at Rhodes, and Schulte professes to see this source in use elsewhere.[6] Similarly, the texts of the treaties between Rome and Carthage,[7] Philip and Hannibal,[8] Rome and Aetolia,[9] and Rome and Antiochus[10] point to a use of Roman records; and from various exceptions to his usual strict avoidance of hiatus, it has been deduced that at the points where these occur Polybius is adhering rather closely to some official record.[11] Finally, there were records kept in Achaea, certainly at Aegium, and probably at towns like Argos and Megalopolis;[12] and though the use of these cannot be definitely traced in any one passage, they must have been frequently consulted by Polybius, particularly after 151, to supplement the findings of αὐτοπαθεία and personal enquiry.[13]

Polybius's trustworthiness is usually accounted high, notwith-

[1] One may be the Straton (of Rhodes?), who wrote on the wars of Philip and Perseus against Rome (Diog. Laert. v, 61), and is perhaps the object of Polybius's polemic in III, 32, 8 and XXII, 18; see Laqueur, *P–W*, 'Straton', col. 274.

[2] Apart from Phylarchus, used in Polyb. v, 34–9; cf. Walbank, 14.

[3] This may have been his source for many of the speeches he reproduces (e.g. see above, p. 66, n. 5; 88, n. 1).

[4] See Klotz, *Phil. Woch.* 28, 1908, 446; A. Schulte, *De ratione quae intercedit inter Polyb. et tabulas publicas*, Diss. Halle, 1909; J. M. J. Valeton, *De Polyb. fontibus et auctoritate*, Traiecti ad Rhenum, 1879.

[5] Polyb. XII, 10, 4; 11, 2.

[6] Schulte, 35–9: cf. Polyb. IV, 56, 2–3; v, 88, 5; XVI, 7, 1; 26, 8–10; XVIII, 2, 3; XXXI, 31, 1. In all these, however, the source may be Zeno or Antisthenes, whom, however, Polybius probably knew only via Zeno; cf. Schwartz, *P–W*, 'Antisthenes', col. 2537–8.   [7] Polyb. III, 26, 1.   [8] Polyb. VII, 9.

[9] Polyb. XXI, 32, 2–14; cf. 30, 1–5, for a different authority.

[10] Polyb. XXI, 43; cf. 17, 3–9. Appian, *Syr.* 39, records that this treaty was set up in bronze on the Capitol.

[11] Cf. Schulte, 18–24. Schulte, 40, it is true, regards the text of the treaty between Philip and Hannibal as a product of the Macedonian royal record office, and is at pains to point out that the burning of documents mentioned in Polyb. XVIII, 33, 2, only included letters and commentaries; but as there is no other evidence that Polybius ever had access to this office, and it is known that the first version of the treaty was intercepted by the Romans (see above, p. 70, n. 4), it is almost certainly the latter that Polybius reproduces.

[12] Polyb. XXII, 9: προφερομένου τοῦ στρατηγοῦ πάσας τὰς συμμαχίας—where προφερομένου must mean 'producing from the record office' and scarcely, as has been suggested, 'reciting from memory'.

[13] Nissen, 106, n.; cf. Holleaux, *REG*, xxxvi, 1923, 115, n. 1, suggesting that Polybius's account of the conference of Locris (XVIII, 1–12) derives from an official Achaean memorandum.

standing his concession in one passage to the claims of patriotism.[1] Unfortunately, in the case of Philip V, he is hampered by a fundamental lack of understanding. The ideas of the Greek and Achaean world he was familiar with from childhood, and he learnt to appreciate the Roman attitude from associating with Scipio Aemilianus and his circle; but of the Macedonian stand-point he has no inkling.[2] In his pages Philip is portrayed as a study in psychology, not as a political force: he is the young philhellene who deteriorates into a tyrant, until, like a figure from some ancient tragedy, he brings down his whole house in destruction.[3] Unable to appreciate either Philip's aims or the logic that strung together his actions and their results, Polybius falls back on the τύχη of Demetrius of Phalerum,[4] which elsewhere he dismisses as 'a cheap explanation'.[5] It is important to recognise Polybius's failure here, for this means that however closely and confidently he is followed for his account of Philip's actions, his motivation must be questioned at every step.

To revert now to our first problem: how far can Polybius be recovered? The first five books survive intact, the rest only in fragments of unequal value, from various sources.[6] Of these the collection in the Codex Urbinas is wholly reliable, the passages in the Constantinian excerpts[7] less so; for in the latter, which are grouped according to subject matter, the beginning and end of a passage have often suffered at the hands of the excerptor,[8] so that Livy gives a more accurate notion of the original.[9] Finally, to these must be added a miscellaneous assortment of fragments from Suidas, Athenaeus, Hero and Stephanus of Byzantium, which cannot always be identified, still less placed, with accuracy.

Most of the fragments therefore demand great caution in the reader. Since they are uncontaminated, they are generally safe evidence that

[1] Polyb. XVI, 14, 6: ἐγὼ δὲ διότι μὲν δεῖ ῥοπὰς διδόναι ταῖς αὑτῶν πατρίσι τοὺς συγγραφέας, συγχωρήσαιμ' ἄν, οὐ μὴν τὰς ἐναντίας τοῖς συμβεβηκόσιν ἀποφάσεις ποιεῖσθαι περὶ αὐτῶν: contrast XXXVIII, 4. On his toleration of superstition and the 'political lie' as a means of disciplining the masses (cf. VI, 56; XVI, 12, 9–11) see B. Farrington, *Science and Politics in the Ancient World* (London, 1939), 166–8.

[2] See the passage (XXXVI, 17, 15) in which he confesses himself unable to explain the support given to Andriscus, except as δαιμονοβλαβεία.

[3] See further Walbank, *JHS*, LVIII, 1938, 55–68.

[4] E.g. Polyb. XXIII, 10; XXIX, 21 (on Perseus).

[5] Polyb. XXXVI, 17; II, 38, 5: φαῦλον γάρ.

[6] See Nissen, 1–17; 312–23; Büttner-Wobst, ed. Polybius, introd.

[7] There are four sections of these, under the headings 'On Embassies', 'On Virtue and Vice', 'On Opinions', and 'On Plots'; of these the 'Embassy' fragments are nearest to the original text.

[8] E.g. Polyb. X, 26, 1; αὖθις εἰς "Αργος ἐπανῆλθε (the Nemea being at this time held at Argos).

[9] E.g. compare Polyb. XXII, 6 and Livy, XXXIX, 24, 6; Polyb. XXIII, 7, and Livy, XXXIX, 53; Polyb. XXIII, 10 and Livy, XL, 3, 3, where the Polybian fragments have suffered from abridgement.

a fact (but not necessarily a judgment) was in Polybius; on the other hand, the omission from the fragments of a fact recorded by Livy is not evidence that Livy has supplemented Polybius from another source. Usually probability is the only criterion whether Livy is giving more than Polybius, or the fragments less; and, indeed, for the fullest conception of the text it is necessary to turn from the fragments themselves to the later writers who reproduced Polybius.

LIVY[1]

For the period after 200, Livy's source for events in Greece and the eastern Mediterranean is almost exclusively Polybius.[2] The relevant passages of Books XXXI–XL (and XLI–XLV carrying the account down to Pydna) are, indeed, a paraphrase of Polybius, altered stylistically to suit the contemporary notion of history as an *opus oratorium*. In the course of this adaptation, Livy was quite ready to omit what he judged to be uninteresting or irrelevant to Roman affairs, to add explanations for his Roman readers and either to expand or condense incidents in order to render them more dramatic.[3] For example, Perseus's two embassies to Rhodes and Boeotia (Polyb. XXVII, 4–5) have been compressed into one in Livy (XLII, 46, 7); and similarly the account of Cynoscephalae diverges at many points from the Polybian original.[4]

At what point in his history Livy began using Polybius is uncertain; but the Greek events of Books XXIII and XXIV have no resemblance to the Polybian account, and they are followed by silence about Greece until Book XXVI[5] when Polybius is plainly being used. It has been suggested[6] that Livy began using as his sources for the first Macedonian war the annalists whom he was following for events in Italy, but, on realising their deficiencies, put aside the whole of the Greek events until he had finished with the Hannibalic War, when he returned to insert from Polybius the Greek chapters of Books XXVI–XXIX. Whatever the truth of this, the narrative suffers from annalistic accretions,[7] and Livy's annalistic sources also play a large part in Book XXX and the

---

[1] For Livy's sources see Nissen, *op. cit.*; De Sanctis, III, 2, 176–95, 355–79, 638–56.　　　　[2] Nissen, 19–85 and *passim*.

[3] Moreover, Livy displays the characters of his main figures, not by direct comment, like Polybius, but indirectly, by placing such comments in their own mouths or those of their contemporaries, or by describing others' reactions to what they did; cf. Bruns, *Die Persönlichkeit in der Geschichtsschreibung der Alten* (Berlin, 1898), 12–42.

[4] Polyb. XVIII, 18–40; Livy (P) XXXIII, 5–12. For other examples of compression and alteration by Livy see Nissen, 29; Holleaux, *REG*, XXXVI, 1923, 141, n. 1; *Rev. Phil.* LVII, 1931, 204, n. 8.

[5] Livy (P) XXV, 23, 9, is a minor exception.

[6] By Soltau, *Livius' Geschichtswerk, seine Komposition und seine Quellen* (Leipzig, 1897), 48 *seq.*

[7] E.g. Livy (P) XXIX, 12 (peace of Phoenice).

beginning of xxxi;[1] and in general the Polybian tradition for Greece in the third decade of Livy is much more abbreviated and less reliable than for the years following 200.

In estimating the value of the parts of Livy derived from the annalists, a distinction must be made between the simple, straightforward and, for the later years, well-informed works of such early writers as L. Calpurnius Piso, and the florid productions of the post-Gracchans.[2] Of the latter, Q. Claudius Quadrigarius and Valerius Antias are of paramount importance for the non-Polybian part of Livy's narrative;[3] and whereas Claudius seems to have made some use of Polybius, to his gain, Valerius's work contained the wildest exaggerations, particularly in the matter of figures, as Livy himself came to realise.[4] However, in dealing with eastern affairs, Livy restricted himself to Polybius; and it is only in his treatment of negotiations in Italy, for which he made no use of Polybius until 193,[5] that his annalistic sources achieve any great importance for Macedonian affairs. Fortunately, Livy's time-allowance of from two to three months a book (and that spent mostly on polishing the speeches)[6] gave him little opportunity for source contamination, and he usually seized on one source and transcribed him for long sections at a time. Within certain limits, these sources can thus be isolated and some sort of index of credibility set up. In general, it appears that details of legion lists, commanders, elections, etc., which come from the older annalists, are reliable,[7] but that parts derived from Antias and Claudius, and all details of negotiations, motivation of actions and the like are subject to grave suspicion, and are not to be accepted unless there is confirming evidence or, alternatively, they contain a strong inherent degree of probability.

With these provisoes, Livy is to be regarded as the most important secondary source; taken as a whole, his relevant books are fuller and more complete than Polybius, and, indeed, at times nearer to him than the fragments themselves. With these fragments, Livy forms the main approach to the original Polybian tradition, and our substitute for it where this is lost.

[1] E.g. Livy, xxx, 26; 42, which are derived from the anti-Macedonian propaganda of the years 200–199; cf. also xxxi, 1, 6–2, 4; 3; 5–9, where Antias is probably to be detected.
[2] See Nissen, 86–109; T. Frank, *Life and Literature in the Roman Republic*, Cambridge, 1930, 169 *seq.*; H. Stuart Jones, *CAH*, vii, 312 *seq.*
[3] The Greek events of Livy xxiii and xxiv probably go back to Valerius Antias (though Kahrstedt attributes xxiv, 40, to Coelius Antipater).
[4] See A. A. Howard, *Harv. Stud.* xvii, 1906, 161–82.
[5] I.e. until Livy, xxxiv, 57, 4.
[6] Cf. Cavaignac, *Rev. Phil.* xxxix, 1915, 1 *seq.*
[7] See Hallward, *CAH*, viii, plan facing p. 104, and authorities there quoted; also the evidence on Roman family tradition in Münzer, *op. cit.*

MINOR AUTHORITIES

In the lesser writers it is frequently impossible to trace the method in which Polybius has been used; often the most that can be done is to try to isolate the Polybian tradition from a contaminated account, and use the extent to which it has been followed as a measure of credibility.

Livy's contemporary, DIODORUS SICULUS,[1] dealt with the period of Philip's life in Books XXVI-XXX of his history; but Schwartz shows from a study of the fragments of these books that they were a mere abridgement of Polybius without independent value. The problem of the *Philippic Histories* of TROGUS POMPEIUS,[2] the only other Augustan source (and our only substantial Latin source besides Livy) is less simple. Trogus only survives in his *Prologi*, and in the second-century abridgement of JUSTINUS:[3] but from these it appears that in the relevant parts at least (Books XXVIII-XXXII) he drew on Polybius, not directly, but via the work of Timagenes of Alexandria,[4] a first-century historian mentioned by Horace (*Ep.* I, 19, 15). The title of Trogus's work, the omission from it of Roman history prior to Roman contact with the east, and the view that the second war with Philip was a war of revenge[5] all support this theory; and though Livy may be used occasionally, and there are traces of annalistic contamination,[6] the main source is undoubtedly to be sought outside Italy. Justinus contains more than Diodorus; but his work is further from Polybius, and carelessly transcribed,[7] so that he is generally to be rejected where his version clashes with that of Polybius or Livy.

Five of PLUTARCH's *Lives* are relevant, those of *Aratus, Flamininus, Philopoemen, Aemilius Paullus* and *Cato*. Of these, the *Aratus*, from chapter XLVII (where it begins to concern Philip) to the end, is, as Schulz has shown, a précis of Polybius;[8] two slight discrepancies are

---

[1] See E. Schwartz, *P-W*, 'Diodoros', giving a full concordance of Diodorus and Polybius; cf. Nissen, 110-13.

[2] See Nissen, 305-7; Schanz-Hosius, *Gesch. d. röm. Litt.* II, 1, 445.

[3] See R. B. Steele, *AJPh*, XXXVIII, 1917, 19 seq.

[4] See Gutschmid, *Rhein. Mus.* XXXVII, 1882, 548 seq. (=*Kl. Schriften*, V, 218 seq.); Wachsmuth, *Rhein. Mus.* XLVI, 1891, 477; Schanz-Hosius, II, 1, 450; Momigliano, *Rend. Lomb.* LXVI, 1933, 983-6.

[5] Cf. Justin. XXIX, 4, 11: *contentis* interim *bellum Macedonicum distulisse*; XXX, 3, 6: *statim igitur* titulo *ferendi sociis auxilii bellum adversus Philippum decernitur*. See also XXXI, 1, 7 seq. (Roman fear), XXXI, 3, 3-4 (praise of Philopoemen).

[6] E.g. Justin. XXX, 2, 8; 3, 4; XXXI, 1, 2 (Aemilius Lepidus's guardianship of Epiphanes, a story in neither Livy nor Polybius).

[7] E.g. Justin. XXX, 4, 12 (Philip in 197 is *puer inmaturae aetatis*); XXXI, 6, 3 (Antiochus's sloth after his marriage; Justinus does not make it clear that he is in Europe); XXXII, 3, 5 (tribes instigated by Philip are called the Scordisci: Trogus, *Prol.* XXXII, following Livy, has *Basternae*).

[8] *Quibus ex fontibus fluxerint Ag. Cleom. Arat. vitae Plutarcheae*, Berlin, 1886. See Walbank, 18-19; Porter, XIX-XX.

due to Plutarch's use of popular, or perhaps family versions of famous incidents.[1] The *Philopoemen*, which is richer in detail than Polybius, draws for its main source, not on the *Histories*, but on the Polybian *Life of Philopoemen*;[2] in addition it uses the *Laconica* of a certain Aristocrates of Sparta, who writes with an anti-Achaean bias, and, in the last chapter, for events later than Philopoemen's death, Polybius's *Histories*. This *Life* has little directly concerning Philip, but is valuable for contemporary events in the Peloponnese. For the sections in the *Flamininus* (or *Titus*) which refer directly to Philip, the main source is again Polybius's *Histories*. But here, as in the earlier chapters of the *Aratus*, an attempt to combine the use of a large number of sources[3] has resulted in chronological confusion; and perhaps some of the most important information in this *Life* lies in the anecdotes which are interspersed and which probably come from some collection.[4] The *Aemilius Paullus* contains an interesting résumé of Macedonian history from the time of Gonatas, which is certainly not derived directly from Polybius;[5] but whether the source is Poseidonius, as Nissen imagined, or an unknown writer, who contaminated Polybius with a monograph on Perseus,[6] is of small importance here, since the little that concerns Philip (ch. VIII–IX) tallies with Polybius. Finally, the *Cato*[7] has also two chapters relevant to Philip (XII–XIV), and here the source appears to be an account by Cato himself; it adds a little to what is known from Livy, but may, as Plutarch recognised,[8] slightly exaggerate Cato's own achievements.[9]

The next source in chronological order is APPIAN,[10] an Alexandrian who composed a Roman history on ethnographical lines in about the middle of the second century; the relevant passages are Book IX (*Macedonica*) and parts of the Illyrian and Syrian sections. These

---

[1] *Arat.* 50, 3 *seq.*; cf. Polyb. VII, 11 (incident on Ithome); *Arat.* 52, 2 *seq.*; cf. Polyb. VIII, 14, 2–5 (poisoning of Aratus).

[2] Polyb. X, 21, 5; cf. Nissen, 280–90.

[3] E.g. Cicero's *De Senect.* (ch. 18, 3 *seq.*); Livy (ch. 18, 9: containing references, from Livy, to Cato and Valerius Antias); two unnamed authorities (ch. 20, 9); οἱ περὶ Τουδιτανόν (ch. 14, 2: Tuditanus or οἱ περὶ τὸν Τίτον, i.e. Livy); Λεύκιος (ch. 20, 10 = Λίβιος (Stephanus), Πολύβιος (Nissen) or ᾿Ακίλιος (Kümpel; accepted by Holleaux, *Hermes*, XLVIII, 1913, 81, n. 4)). See Nissen, 290–2.   [4] I.e. 7, 4; 9; 10; 12, 4–8; 21.

[5] It mentions Doson's name, absent from Polybius, calls Cynoscephalae 'Scotussa' and dismisses the accusation of Perseus's bastardy as gossip.

[6] So Rosenberg, *Einleitung und Quellenkunde zur römischen Geschichte*, Berlin, 1921, 217 *seq.* See also Nissen, 298; Schwarze, *Quibus fontibus Plutarchus in vita L. Aem. Paull. usus sit*, Leipzig, 1891; C. Liedmeier, *Plutarchus' biographie van Aemilius Paullus*, Utrecht, 1935.

[7] Nissen, 181–2; 292–8.   [8] Plut. *Cato*, 14, 2.

[9] On the *Flamininus*, *Aemilius Paullus* and *Cato* see now R. E. Smith, *CQ*, XXXIV, 1940, 1–10.

[10] Nissen, 114; E. Schwartz, P-W, 'Appianus'; Christ-Schmid, II, 2, 751.

survive only in the fragments of the Constantinian collection and in Suidas, and their source is problematical. Various theories attempt to explain the discrepancies between Polybius and Appian,[1] and the bias which the latter shows against Flamininus.[2] Thus Rosenberg[3] suggests that Appian is following a first-century annalist, who in turn used both earlier annalists and Greek sources; and Schwartz, denying any direct use of Greek authorities, suggests as Appian's source a post-Livian annalist, who contaminated Livy and the earlier annalists, and only gradually came to realise the superior merits of Polybius. All that can be said with certainty is that Appian's main immediate source was Latin,[4] that through this he draws on a tradition in which Polybian and annalistic strains are contaminated, and that one of these annalistic strains appears to go back to some second century source hostile to the Quinctii. The result is often useful, but Appian frequently offers worthless explanations,[5] and his general reliability is small.

The *Periegesis* of PAUSANIAS,[6] written shortly after Appian's history, contains material of a very uneven character, sometimes valuable, but often merely fantastic.[7] Apart from incidental references, there are two continuous passages of some importance, giving the history of the Achaean League (VII, 7–16) and the life of Philopoemen (VIII, 49–52). Of these the first, covering the period from Philip's reign to 146, is, in spite of many absurdities, of some value as being derived from a non-Polybian, though markedly pro-Achaean source;[8] for the life of Philip, however, it offers no check on the main anti-Macedonian tradition. The second extract is based on Plutarch's *Philopoemen*;[9] and the possibility of testing Pausanias's many errors is useful as an index to his reliability elsewhere. On the other hand much in Pausanias is derived from personal observation,[10] and in these

[1] E.g. *Mac.* 1; cf. Polyb. VII, 9; *Mac.* 3; cf. Livy (P + A) XXIX, 12; *Mac.* 4; cf. Polyb. XVI, 34, 2–3; *Mac.* 9, 2; cf. Polyb. XVIII, 38, 2; 39, 4–7 (negotiations leading to peace of 197); *Syr.* 23; cf. Polyb. XXI, 11.

[2] E.g. *Maced.* 9, 3: τὰς δὲ προτάσεις τὰς Φλαμινίνου σμικρύνασα καὶ φαυλίσασα (sc. ἡ σύγκλητος), ἐκέλευσε τὰς πόλεις ὅσαι ἦσαν Ἑλληνίδες ὑπὸ Φιλίππῳ, πάσας ἐλευθέρας εἶναι.   [3] Rosenberg, 203 *seq.*

[4] The Greek prophecy in verse in *Maced.* 2 (cf. Pausan. VII, 8, 9) seems to point to some immediate Greek source however.

[5] E.g. *Maced.* 12, on Perseus's character; and cf. Nissen, 116.

[6] See Frazer's edition; Christ-Schmid, *op. cit.* IV, 2, 755. For the relevant passages see below, Bibliography, p. 351.

[7] E.g. IV, 29, 1 (confusion of Demetrius of Pharus with Philip's son); VII, 7, 3 (Doson handed over the throne to Philip when he came of age); VII, 8, 2 ('Otilios' for P. Villius).

[8] So Wachsmuth, *Leipz. Stud.* X, 1887, 260–98; cf. Baier, *Studien zur achäischen Bundesverfassung*, 1886.

[9] Nissen, 287–90; *contra* Rühl, *N. Jahrb. f. Phil.* CXXVII, 1883, 37, who claims that Polybius's *Philopoemen* was used direct.

[10] E.g. VI, 16, 3 (statue of Philip at Olympia); I, 36, 5 (Cephisodorus's tombstone).

cases he merits greater respect, although taken as a whole, he ranks low among the minor sources.

The work of CASSIUS DIO[1] has survived in fragments from the Constantinian excerpts and also in the abridgement of Johannes Zonaras, a twelfth-century Byzantine monk; and though for the parts relevant here[2] (covering the period from the time when Demetrius of Pharus joined Philip until the latter's death) it is the abridgements that are more considerable, the two writers are most conveniently considered together. For the period prior to 200 (Dio XVII, 57, 57; Zon. VIII, 20–IX, 11) the source is non-Polybian in origin;[3] for the years after 200 Polybius is all-important, but whether he was used solely via annalists, as Schwartz believes, or directly, in addition to the annalists, as Rosenberg claims, it is difficult to determine. Certainly the source is not Livy, since in some cases Dio gives a Polybian version where Livy is following an annalist,[4] and in others Dio's account is non-Polybian where Livy is transcribing Polybius.[5] Over Dio's merits there is fortunately less controversy. Thoroughly unreliable,[6] he is given to explanations that are too absurd to be misleading, and as an authority he is to be accounted third-rate.

The remaining literary sources are incidental references in a large selection of writers, including Strabo and Polyaenus; a list is given below (pp. 351–2) and the more important passages have already been mentioned in the footnotes. It will be sufficient here to refer to the poems of Alcaeus, Samus and Philip himself, preserved in the *Palatine Anthology*, which offer valuable contemporary evidence on various incidents in Philip's life.

NON-LITERARY SOURCES

Most of the large number of inscriptions which directly or indirectly supplement the literary evidence have been quoted in the footnotes. One may notice here the *Lindian Temple Chronicle* of Timachidas,

[1] Schwartz, *P-W*, 'Cassius Dio Cocceianus'; Christ-Schmid, II, 2, 795; Rosenberg, 260; Holleaux, *CAH*, VIII, 138, n.
[2] Dio, XVII, 57, 57; 57, 77; 58, 1–4; XVIII, 60; XIX, 62; Zon. VIII, 20–IX, 22.
[3] E.g. Dio gives an annalistic version of Philip's treaty with Hannibal.
[4] E.g. Zon. IX, 15, 2; cf. Polyb. XVI, 27; 34 (Livy, XXXI, 3, is annalistic).
[5] E.g. Zon. IX, 16, 1; contrast Livy XXXII, 12, which is Polybian (cf. Plut. *Flam.* 4). Sometimes Dio's non-Polybian authority is also Appian's; e.g. Zon. IX, 18, 13–14=Appian, *Syr.* 9 (cf. Claudius in Livy, XXXV, 14); Zon. IX, 20, 10=Appian, *Syr.* 29 (cf. Polyb. XXI, 45, and Livy, XXXVIII, 38; 39, 7–17).
[6] E.g. Zon. IX, 15 (Sulpicius's illness in 200, to explain the lack of events in his consulship); Zon. IX, 16 (Flamininus 'consul' in 197; cf. Justin. XXX, 34); Dio, XVIII, 60 (absurd motivation and traces of an anti-Flamininus source); Zon. IX, 18 (reference to Taygetus; contradictions in Roman attitude towards Antiochus).

288 APPENDICES

the particularly valuable collection of letters and διαγράμματα sent by Philip to various bodies and individuals,[1] and also two fragments dealing with the organisation of the Macedonian army, which probably date to the reign of Philip.[2] The importance of the Macedonian coinage as throwing light on internal affairs, and of Philip's building on Delos as an indication of religious policy has already been discussed. The general position is that though occasionally archaeology has acted as a corrective to our literary sources, it has more often confirmed and amplified the information they give.

[1] The following letters and διαγράμματα of Philip are either in existence or referred to:

A. *Surviving*:
  (a) *Syll.* 543; to Larisa, 220 (Schroeter, 78–9, no. 30).
  (b) *Ibid.*; second letter to Larisa, 215 (Schroeter, 78–9, no. 31).
  (c) *Syll.* 552; to the Abaei, 209 (Schroeter, 79–80, no. 32).
  (d) *Syll.* 572; to the Nisyrii, c. 201 (Schroeter, 80, no. 33).
  (e) *IG*, XII, 5, 125; to the (Parians?) a little after the first sack of Thermum (fragmentary).
  (f) *AE*, 1934–5, 117; to Archippus.
  (g) *Ibid.* 119; fragmentary letter (?) found at Banitza.
  (h) Pelekides, 6; to Andronicus, for the priests of Sarapis, Thessalonica.
  (i) Ἑλληνικά, VII, 1934, 177–208 (= *IG*, XII, Suppl. 644): army code at Chalcis (see above, p. 52, n. 3).
  (j) Fragments of an army code found at Amphipolis (see below, n. 2).
  (k) Unpublished letter to the Athenians in Hephaestia on Lemnos (cf. *BCH*, LXII, 1938, 479; *JHS*, LIX, 1939, 203).

B. *References*:
  (a) *Syll.* 561; to Chalcis, on behalf of Magnesia-on-the-Maeander.
  (b) *AE*, 1913, 36, n. 165 B, line 21; 43, n. 172; 44, n. 173; 46, n. 174; letters (?) to the Gonnians.
  (c) Oikonomos, Ἐπιγραφαὶ τῆς Μακεδονίας, I, 1915, 2–7; reference to διάγραμμα.
  (d) *IG*, VII, 21; διάγραμμα at Orchomenus.
  (e) *Syll.* 552; reference to letter to Heracleides.
  (f) Polyb. IV, 67, 8; to Achaean general and cities.
  (g) *Insc. Magn.* no. 24; letter to the Magnesians: very fragmentary.
  (h) *BMI*, III, 441 (Holleaux, *REG*, XII, 1899, 25 *seq.*; *REA*, V, 1903, 223–8); reference to letter received by Rhodes on the subject of Iasus.

[2] *Rev. Arch.* III[6], 1934, 39 *seq.* (ed. Roussel); *ibid.* VI[6], 1935, 29–68 (ed. Feyel); cf. De Sanctis, *Riv. Fil.* LXII, 1934, 515; Segre, *Riv. Fil.* LXIII, 1935, 222–5; Kougeas, Ἑλληνικά, VIII, 1935, 149–50; Welles, *AJA*, XLII, 1938, 245–60.

Appendix II : Notes on the Army under Philip V[1]

With the campaigns of 224–2 details of the army of the Antigonids first appear in our literary sources: they reveal a marked change of emphasis since the time of Alexander. In 334 Alexander had crossed the Hellespont with foot and horse in the proportion of 6 : 1;[2] at Sellasia Doson had only 1200 horse to 27,600 foot, and of these only 10,000 phalangites, 3000 peltasts and 300 horse were national troops.[3] At Cynoscephalae, with a phalanx of 16,000, 2000 peltasts and some 5500 mercenaries, Philip had only 2000 horse.[4] These figures show clearly how little Macedon had been affected by the emergence of cavalry as the decisive arm in Hellenistic warfare, a development which lasted (outside the Greek peninsula) for about a century.[5] As in the days before Philip II, the weight of the army was once more in the phalanx, the massed body of heavy-armed footsoldiers, enrolled territorially from the Macedonian peasantry,[6] and armed with the national weapon, the *sarissa*, now a 21-foot spear.[7] The remaining arms of the phalangite comprised helmet, sword, shield (of eighteen inches diameter), breastplate and greaves.[8] In battle the phalanx formed a solid mass of men, sixteen ranks deep, with an allowance of three feet or even (by the device known as συνασπισμός) of only half that space to each man. The spears of five ranks actually protruded beyond the front of the phalanx, and the remaining eleven ranks merely pushed[9]—a terrifying spectacle for any foe, as Aemilius Paullus bore ample witness at the battle of Pydna.[10] More rigid and more specialised than Alexander's phalanx, its members parts in a machine rather than separate fighting men (the new *sarissa* required

---

[1] For further details reference should be made to the following works (which *throughout this appendix only*.are quoted under the author's name alone): H. Berve, *Das Alexanderreich auf prosopographischer Grundlage*, 1926; J. Kromayer and G. Veith, *Heerwesen u. Kriegführung der Griechen und Römer*, 1928; W. W. Tarn, *Hellenistic Military and Naval Developments*, 1930; also the quoted articles of Roussel, Feyel, Kougeas, De Sanctis and Welles; and Tarn, *Antigonos Gonatas*, 424–8 (Appendix III).

[2] Tarn, *CAH*, VI, 358.

[3] Polyb. II, 65, 2 *seq.* Doson's forces in 224 were 20,000 infantry and 1300 horse (Plut. *Arat.* 43, 1).

[4] Livy (P) XXXIII, 4, 4–5.   [5] Tarn, 11.

[6] Cf. Polyb. V, 97, 3–4: τοὺς ἄνω Μακεδόνας,...τοὺς ἐκ τῆς Βοττίας καὶ τῆς Ἀμφαξίτιδος.

[7] For the various experiments which had been made in the length of the *sarissa* see Kromayer-Veith, 134 *seq.*; Momigliano, *Filippo*, 45, n. 1. In Polybius's own time the length was standardised at 14 cubits, i.e. 21 feet (Polyb. XVIII, 29).   [8] Kromayer-Veith, 133.

[9] Tarn, 27–8.   [10] Polyb. XXIX, 17; Plut. *Aem. Paull.* 19, 2.

both hands to control it), this late Hellenistic phalanx was especially liable to break up on rough ground, and was almost unprotected on the flanks, a weakness which proved its undoing when it met the Roman legions.[1]

In addition to his heavy phalanx Alexander had a second fighting force, his Hypaspists.[2] This term has two distinct meanings, first the king's private bodyguard (when it is equivalent to σωματοφύλακες and is often qualified as βασιλικοὶ ὑπασπισταί),[3] and secondly an infantry force, at Issus about 3000 in number, which fought beside the phalanx in battle, but was at other times employed for ambushes, forced marches and special expeditions, and in short as a 'crack' regiment, which had to bear the brunt of the fighting in all its aspects.[4] Of the hypaspists' armour no definite record survives;[5] and it is by no means certain that it was appreciably lighter than that of the phalangite. General opinion now assumes that in weight it was midway between the armour of the phalangite and that of the 'Iphicratean peltast';[6] at least it seems to be established that Alexander's hypaspists were not peltasts.[7]

Hypaspists in this second sense occur in the national armies of Syria;[8] and it is frequently assumed that they existed in Antigonid Macedon as well. Thus a fierce and indecisive controversy on the tactics of the battle of Pydna has turned on the question whether the *caetrati* of Livy (P) XLIV, 41, 1–2—'Perseus's hypaspists'[9]—are the same as the *leucaspis phalanx* referred to by Livy a few lines below; and Feyel, in the course of his commentary on part of the army code of Philip V, found near Amphipolis,[10] assumes that certain troops there referred to as possessing the armour of a phalangite *without a breast-plate* are necessarily hypaspists, and even goes so far as to suppose that Philip may have had more hypaspists than Alexander![11]

There are, however, extremely full records of the campaigns of Philip V, and the only occasion that a hypaspist is mentioned by a

[1] Cf. Tarn, 29, for the results, tactically, of Cynoscephalae, Pydna, Magnesia and Corinth. [2] Cf. Berve, I, 122.
[3] Hypaspists in this sense are found in Ptolemaic Egypt: cf. Polyb. xv, 25, 3; XVI, 19, 7.
[4] The hypaspists in this second sense had an ἄγημα—an élite troop, quite distinct from the βασιλικοὶ ὑπασπισταί (cf. Arrian, I, 8, 4; see Berve, I, 126).
[5] Berve, I, 125; Kromayer, 109, on the basis of Paeonian coin-representations describes their attire as consisting of shield, short lance, chiton and cap: but this is not certain.
[6] For the latter see Kromayer-Veith, 89. [7] Berve, I, 125; Tarn, 16.
[8] Cf. Polyb. VII, 16, 2; XVI, 18, 7. See Bikerman, *Institutions des Séleucides*, 52–3, 64–5.
[9] So Tarn, 17, who reproves Meyer, *Berlin S.B.* 1909, 794–8 (=*Kl. Schriften* (Halle, 1924), II, 483 *seq.*) for translating *caetrati* by 'Peltasten' when 'he *means* hypaspists' (and in fact he does!).
[10] *Rev. Arch.* VI[6], 1935, 63 *seq.* [11] *Ibid.* 65.

literary source is when, after the battle of Cynoscephalae, Philip sent one to Larisa to burn his state papers.[1] This incident is paralleled by Perseus's sending a σωματοφύλαξ to burn his fleet in similar circumstances;[2] but even without the parallel it is fairly clear that by hypaspist Polybius here means a member of the royal bodyguard.

Inscriptions provide three more examples of hypaspists from the reign of Philip V. In the first fragment of the Amphipolis army code,[3] certain fines are to be paid to the hypaspists if they have been the first to lay information of a given offence before the king; and when the army encamps, the hypaspists' quarters are to be erected immediately after those of the king and his immediate entourage. Here again both De Sanctis and Roussel are agreed in seeing a reference to βασιλικοὶ ὑπασπισταί; and Feyel, who believes the second part of the code to contain an allusion to the hypaspist infantry force, and so, unfortunately, confuses the ὑπασπισταί of the first fragment with the ἄγημα βασιλικόν,[4] makes the acute suggestion that 'the sense of the word (hypaspist) became restricted during the third century, and that the term ὑπασπισταί without further indication refers henceforward to the royal guard'.[5]

Finally, in an inscription dealing with a grant of land to Nicanor,[6] the tetrarch of a garrison at Greia (mod: Koilada, near Kosane), for the use of his πρωτολοχία, a hypaspist is named between the tetrarch and the *lochagos*. Welles[7] compares the peculiar position of this hypaspist with that held by the *speculatores* under the Roman empire. On our present evidence it is not possible to say what his exact function can have been, but in view of Philip's system of divided responsibilities, by which one official was set up to check the work of another—a system clearly revealed both in the fragments of the Amphipolis army code and in the code from Chalcis[8]—it seems at least possible that a hypaspist stationed with a garrison was a liaison-officer, directly responsible to Philip, and instructed to keep a watch on the loyalty and efficiency of troops levied on a local basis.[9] In any case, a βασιλικὸς ὑπασπιστής seems once more to be indicated.

Had Philip, then, no force of hypaspists in the broader sense? He had, only they operated under another name. As Griffith has already suggested,[10] Philip's hypaspists are to be identified in the troops which

[1] Polyb. XVIII, 33, 1–7.   [2] Diod. XXX, 11.   [3] See above, p. 288, n. 2.
[4] See above, p. 290, n. 4.   [5] *Op. cit.* 64.
[6] Makaronas, *AE*, 1934–5, 117 *seq.*   [7] *AJA*, XLII, 1938, 249.
[8] Kougeas, Ἑλληνικά, VII, 1934, 177–208; cf. Welles, *op. cit.* 252 *seq.*
[9] In this case Nicanor's πρωτολοχία consists of τῶν...στρατευομένων Εὐϊεστῶν (lines 13–14), i.e. troops levied in the Dassaretian town of Εὐϊα (cf. Livy (P) XLII, 51, 4, where Makaronas emends the corrupt *Eulyestae* to *Euiestae*; Diod. XIX, 11, 2; Claud. Ptol. III, 12, 29).
[10] *Hellenistic Mercenaries*, 319. This is, of course, not the same as saying that Alexander's hypaspists were peltasts.

Polybius calls 'peltasts'. Philip's peltasts were, like Alexander's hypaspists, a 'crack' corps of Macedonians,[1] probably 3000 in number;[2] though by the time of the third Macedonian war this number had grown to 5000.[3] Like the hypaspists they had an *agema*,[4] closely associated with them; and the fact that they are always mentioned in thousands suggests that they were organised in chiliarchies.[5] Concerning the hypaspists Berve speaks of[6] 'ihre Verwendung, meist zusammen mit den Agrianen und Bogenschützen, häufig auf Streifzügen und anderen Einzelunternehmungen...obgleich sie in der Schlacht dieser (*sc.* der Phalanx) zugerechnet wurde(n) (Arr. III, 11, 9).' Similarly, Philip's peltasts formed part of the phalanx at Cynoscephalae, where they shared in its manœuvres both immediately before and during the shock;[7] and at Pydna too they were either part of the phalanx[8] or immediately on its left.[9] Otherwise they were used, as Alexander used his hypaspists, for special action, particularly in conjunction with light troops and mercenaries. Here are the main recorded occasions:

Polyb. IV, 64, 6: the peltasts are sent first across a river to secure the crossing for the rest of the army (cf. Arr. I, 6, 6).

Polyb. IV, 75, 4: Philip advances on Thalamae with mercenaries, peltasts and εὔ3ωνοι.

Polyb. V, 4, 9: peltasts used as shock troops in storming Cephallenia.

Polyb. V, 13, 5–6: peltasts used along with Illyrians for an ambush on the way from Thermum. (But where there is an acute risk of danger and no *active* counter-measures to be taken, the peltasts are protected along with the phalanx: Polyb. V, 7, 11; 13, 1).

---

[1] Polyb. V, 26, 8: τῶν τε πελταστῶν καὶ τῶν ἄλλων τῶν ἐπιφανεστάτων συστημάτων.

[2] Cf. Polyb. II, 65, 2 (3000 at Sellasia); IV, 67, 6 (2000 in Peloponnese, winter 219); X, 42, 2 (1000 sent to Euboea in 208); Livy (P) XXXIII, 4, 4 (2000 at Cynoscephalae).

[3] Livy (P) XLII, 51, 4–5; 2000 of these formed the *agema*: see below, n. 9.

[4] Polyb. V, 25, 1: τοὺς πελταστὰς καὶ τοὺς ἐκ τοῦ λεγομένου παρὰ τοῖς Μακεδόσιν ἀγήματος; cf. Livy (P) XLII, 51, 4: *delecta deinde et viribus et robore aetatis ex omni caetratorum numero duo milia erant: agema hanc ipsi legionem vocabant.* (That *caetrati* are peltasts is clear from Livy (P) XXXI, 36, 1.)

[5] For the chiliarchies of the hypaspists see Berve, I, 127.

[6] I, 125.

[7] Polyb. XVIII, 24, 8: τοῖς τε πελτασταῖς καὶ τοῖς φαλαγγίταις παρήγγελλε διπλασιά3ειν τὸ βάθος καὶ πυκνοῦν ἐπὶ τὸ δεξιόν. In the next sentence the peltasts are included in τοῖς φαλαγγίταις in contrast to τοῖς εὐ3ώνοις, the light-armed, who have been driven back.

[8] So Meyer, *Berlin S. B.* 1909, 794 *seq.* (= *Kl. Schriften*, II, 485 *seq.*).

[9] Kromayer, II, 310 *seq.*; De Sanctis, IV, 1, 324. No clear distinction is made in our sources for the battle of Pydna between the peltasts (*caetrati*: Livy (P) XLIV, 41, 2) and the *agema* (Plut. *Aem. Paull.* 18, 7: ἄγημα τρίτον οἱ λογάδες: 19, 1: τοὺς ἐν τοῖς ἀγήμασι Μακεδόνας: 21, 6: οἱ τρισχίλιοι λογάδες) though the distinction was in fact clear (cf. Livy (P) XLII, 51, 4–5, where the *agema* and *ceteri caetrati* have separate leaders).

Polyb. v, 22, 9: in the attack on the Menelaeum Philip uses mercenaries, peltasts and Illyrians; and a little later (23, 8), along with εὔзωνοι and cavalry, the peltasts cover the passing of the phalanx.

Polyb. v, 27, 4: peltasts are sent to Triphylia (in this case a ruse to enable Philip to execute their captain, Leontius).

Polyb. vii, 13 seq.: in the attack on Lissus peltasts operate with εὔзωνοι.

Polyb. x, 42, 2: 1000 peltasts are sent along with 500 Agrianians to Euboea (cf. Arrian, iii, 29, 7; iv, 3, 2; v, 13, 4).

Livy (P) xxxi, 36, 1; peltasts are used for an ambush in Lyncestis.

Of the armour worn by Philip's peltasts no clear indication has survived. On one occasion, however, Polybius refers to them with the words τὴν τῶν βαρέων ὅπλων ἔφοδον:[1] and their position in battle formation suggests that they were not much more lightly armed than the phalangites. It is at least possible that they kept the shorter *sarissa* of Alexander's time; and if they are the troops referred to in the second fragment of the Amphipolis code,[2] they wore a kind of protective belt of cloth or leather instead of a breastplate.[3]

Together the peltasts and phalanx formed the main bulk of the citizen army. Of its organisation almost nothing was formerly known;[4] now, as a result of the discovery of the Amphipolis code, which dates to the reign of Philip V,[5] some details are available. From this code and some indications in the literary sources it appears that the tactical unit of the army was the σπεῖρα,[6] which, if it is equivalent to the σύνταγμα of Alexander's army,[7] comprised 256 men, capable of forming a square sixteen deep; this unit was under a σπειράρχης. As a subdivision of the σπεῖρα we find the τετραρχία, under a τετράρχης, consisting of four λόχοι, each of sixteen men, including a λοχαγός.[8] There were thus four *tetrarchiae* to a σπεῖρα; and in turn four σπεῖραι formed a χιλιαρχία, under an officer who in Macedon appears to have been called not a *chiliarch*, but simply a *hegemon*.[9] (The term *hegemon*

---

[1] Polyb. v, 23, 4, describing the attack on the Menelaeum.

[2] Feyel, *op. cit.* col. i, lines 11 *seq.*; but Feyel is much too dogmatic in claiming (p. 63) that the absence of a breastplate is the distinction between phalangite and hypaspist. Peltasts were certainly used for garrison duty in the towns; e.g. the 2000 at Thessalonica in Perseus's reign (Livy (P) xliv, 32, 6).

[3] The term used is κότθυβος, which Feyel identifies with κόσσυμβος, a word found in Hesychius and meaning περίзωμα αἰγύπτιον (cf. Polyb. vi, 25, 3; ii, 9, 3).

[4] The indications in Asclepiod. *Tact.* ii, though now to some extent confirmed, are nevertheless over-schematic. [5] See above, p. 288, n. 2.

[6] Cf. Polyb. xi, 11, 6 (at Mantinea Philopoemen arranged his phalanx κατὰ τέλη σπειρηδόν ἐν διαστήμασιν); v, 4, 9 (peltasts at Cephallenia); xviii, 28, 10 (φαλαγγιτικὴ σπεῖρα in Pyrrhus's army).

[7] Feyel, 42–7; the σύνταγμα is never mentioned on the Greek continent, the σπεῖρα never in Alexander's army or in Egypt.

[8] Cf. Welles, *AJA*, xlii, 1938, 248–9.

[9] Feyel, 54: the term *chiliarch* seems in Macedon to have acquired the sense of viceroy. We have here some analogy for the similar change over to the more general term in the case of the peltasts.

was also used in a general sense to cover speirarchs and tetrarchs.) Finally four *chiliarchiae* formed a στρατηγία, an army corps of something over 4000 men, under a *strategos*. Alongside the military hierarchy there seems also to have been an administrative organisation, partly parallel, partly subordinated at the various levels to the corresponding military officials. According to the scheme proposed by Feyel[1] there was a *grammateus* for each *strategia*, an *archyperetes* for each *chiliarchia*, and a *hyperetes* for each *speira*. At present, however, this is still a hypothesis to be confirmed or modified by later discoveries. Meanwhile, the code discovered at Chalcis[2] reveals a similar parallelism in the staff of the permanent garrisons: here the military φρούραρχος has his counterpart in the administrative οἰκονόμος and his underlings (line 9: οἱ διὰ τῶν οἰκονόμων χειρισταί). In general, any such schematic arrangement as is here outlined must have been subject to considerable local variations in number and organisation, when applied to a citizen army enrolled upon a regional basis.

To supplement and to some extent to spare their national forces all Hellenistic kings and governments made use of mercenaries. In this Philip was at the mercy of his purse.[3] During his early campaigns his extreme poverty[4] restricted the numbers he could afford to hire, and the largest figure recorded is 1200 in his campaigns of 218.[5] The proceeds of the years 205–200 evidently strengthened Philip's hiring powers, since the second war with Rome involved him without financial disaster in a vast system of garrisons, which Griffith estimates to have required 15,000 mercenaries, apart from those he used in the field. After Cynoscephalae Philip had no further need of hired troops on a considerable scale.

---

[1] *Op. cit.* 61–2.
[2] Kougeas, Ἑλληνικά, VII, 1934, 177–208; cf. Welles, *op. cit.* 251 *seq.*
[3] For full details of Philip's use of mercenaries see Griffith, 70–3.
[4] Cf. Polyb. v, 1, 10.   [5] Polyb. v, 2, 11.

Appendix III : Some Chronological Problems

1. PHILIP'S BIRTH, ACCESSION AND DEATH

Philip died in the consulship of Q. Fulvius and L. Manlius, A.U.C. 575 = 179 (Julian).[1] Porphyry gives the month as the fifth of Olymp. 150, 2, i.e. *c.* November–December, 179;[2] and this is supported by his allowance of a reign of ten years eight months to Perseus (from his accession to Pydna in June 168).[3] But the Bastarnian invasion which coincided with Philip's death (Livy (P) XL, 57, 2 *seq.*) will hardly have been so late as November;[4] and the sequence in Livy (P) XL, 54–6—winter quarters at Demetrias, 180–79, vindication of Demetrius, coldness towards Perseus, Philip's tour of Macedon, his death at Amphipolis—suggests that he died in the summer or early autumn of 179.[5] Porphyry (*FGH*, II B, 260, F. 3, 17) states that he was then aged 58, in which case his birth was in 238–7; and this is confirmed by Polybius's statement that he was seventeen in autumn-winter 221 and late summer 220.[6] If, as seems likely, the second of Polybius's dates is a repetition of the first, we may perhaps put Philip's birth in late summer 238.

The evidence for dating his accession is as follows:

(*a*) Philip is stated by Porphyry (in Eusebius) to have reigned 42 years (*FGH*, II B, 260, F. 3, 17) or 42 years 9 months (*Ibid.* F. 31, 9). Calculating from August–September 179, this brings his accession to August–September 221 and November–December 222 respectively.

(*b*) Porphyry (*FGH*, II B, 260, F. 31, 6) gives Doson a reign of nine years, ending in Olymp. 139, 4, i.e. 221–20. If Doson acceded in spring 229, when the Romans crossed to Illyria (Polyb. II, 44, 2),[7] his

---

[1] Livy (P) XL, 54, 1. The consular year was running Dec.-Dec.; cf. De Sanctis, IV, 1, 369; *contra* Beloch, IV, 2, 113; 256; Dinsmoor, 509, who claim that it began in August.

[2] *FGH*, II B, 260, F. 31, 9; cf. Durrbach, *BCH*, XL, 1916, 318.

[3] De Sanctis, *loc. cit.*; *contra* Beloch, *Klio*, XV, 1918, 413 *seq.*

[4] Beloch, IV, 2, 113.

[5] Cf. Bergk, *Philol.* XLII, 1884, 253; Niese, III, 34, n. 7; Glotz, *REG*, XXIX, 1916, 20, n. 1; Durrbach, *BCH*, XL, 1916, 318. From Livy (P) XL, 54, 1: *Demetriade hibernabat*, De Sanctis, IV, 1, 254, n. 28, assumes that Philip died in winter; these words, however, merely indicate the point at which the narrative is resumed.

[6] Polyb. IV, 5, 3; 24, 1. Justinus's statement that he was fourteen (XXVIII, 4, 16; XXIX, 1, 2) may be ignored; cf. Fine, *CQ*, XXVIII, 1934, 100.

[7] Tarn, *CAH*, VII, 834, n. 1; Holleaux, *REG*, XLIII, 1930, 255 *seq.* against Beloch, IV, 1, 637; IV, 2, 112; 120–1. Treves, *Athen.* XII, 1934, 386, puts the accession a little earlier; and Dinsmoor, applying Beloch's Roman Calendar of 200 B.C. to a period thirty years earlier (contrast Beloch himself, IV, 2, 271) favours autumn 230.

reign ended spring 220. But Porphyry may be giving a round figure representing eight years *x* months.

(c) Polybius (v, 34, 1) clearly believed Philip's accession to have preceded the death of Ptolemy Euergetes.[1]

(d) On the other hand, H. Frank has calculated[2] that Euergetes's death was certainly prior to May 221[3] and probably (from the evidence of papyri) between Choiak 13 and Tybi 12, i.e. *c.* February 221.

(e) Doson's death was preceded by Philip's visit to the Peloponnese (Plut. *Arat.* 46, 2–3), probably the last event mentioned in Aratus's *Memoirs*.[4] Thus the statement that the Messenian events of mid-summer 221, which form the opening of Polybius's fourth book, are συνεχῆ τοῖς τελευταίοις τῆς παρ' 'Αράτου Σικυωνίου συντάξεως (1, 3, 2; cf. IV, 2, 1) is true only if the gap between these and Philip's visit is small.

(f) Four dated letters from Philip may, from internal evidence, lend some help. These are the two to Larisa (*Syll.* 543) dated Hyperberetaeus 21 of year II and Gorpiaeus 13 of year VII, that to the Abaei (*Syll.* 552) dated Hyperberetaeus of year XIII, and that to Archippus (*AE*, 1934–5, 117–27) dated Aydnaeus of year XLII.

Polybius contradicts himself. For if Doson's death in fact preceded that of Euergetes, not only is Philip's visit to the Peloponnese ruled out,[5] but also Polybius's claim that his history follows straight after the *Memoirs*; nor can Doson's death be used to motivate the Aetolian aggression in Messenia.[6] It is more likely, however, that Polybius has reversed the order of the two kings' deaths than that he is deliberately and pointlessly misrepresenting the relation of his work to that of

[1] From Polyb. v, 35, 2 (and its adaptation in Plut. *Cleom.* 34, 1) Niese, II, 348, n. 6, and Beloch, IV, 2, 113, argue that Euergetes died before Doson. The passage will not support this interpretation. On the other hand, the words μεταλλάξαντος τοῦ πατρός (Polyb. v, 34, 1) rule out Dinsmoor's theory (*op. cit.* 487–9; 509) that Doson's death preceded Philopator's accession to co-regency with his father in Sept. 222. (H. Frank, *Arch. Pap.* XI, 1935, 42–7, questions the very existence of such a co-regency.)

[2] *Op. cit.* 34 *seq.*; confirmed by Henne, *REA*, XXXVII, 1935, 21–33. Dinsmoor, *loc. cit.*, also dates Euergetes's death after 28 January 221.

[3] Polyb. v, 42, 5, must, he shows, refer to Philopator, and is to be dated May 221. *Contra* Beloch, IV, 1, 689, n. 2; Tarn, *CAH*, VII, 724, n. 1; Holleaux, *Mél. Nicole*, 273 *seq.*, who explain the passage as a mistake of Polybius.

[4] After chapter 46, the *Aratus* becomes a précis of Polybius.

[5] There is no time for Doson's northern campaign, his illness and Philip's visit to the Peloponnese in the six months following Sellasia, which was in July 222 (Niese, *Hermes*, XXXV, 1900, 60–9; Tarn, *CAH*, VII, 863; Beloch, IV, 2, 219; Frank, *op. cit.* 53–5; Henne, *op. cit.* 21–33; Porter, lxxv; Aymard, *Assemblées*, 65, n. 3). Following Ferrabino, 268, I formerly (*Aratos of Sicyon*, 172; 195) dated Sellasia July 223; for a good criticism of this view (since followed, unfortunately, by Theunissen, 262 *seq.*, and Koster, introd. LXXX) see Porter, *Hermathena*, XLVIII, 1933, 266.

[6] Cf. Polyb. IV, 3, 2: ἕως 'Αντίγονος ἔζη, δεδιότες Μακεδόνας ἦγον ἡσυχίαν.

Aratus; and since Porphyry dates Doson's death in the Olympiad year 221–20, we may neglect Polyb. v, 34, 1, and provisionally place it in or subsequent to July 221—remembering that the greater the gap between Euergetes's death and Doson's, the harder Polybius's error is to explain.

To extract any help from the letters, it is first necessary to consider how the Macedonian royal year was calculated.[1] If it was reckoned from the actual date of accession, the calendar would be complicated by a new year every reign, and an unfinished year at the end of every reign; Makaronas therefore concludes that royal years, like Macedonian calendar years, ran from Dius to Hyperberetaeus.[2] Which then was a king's first year, that from his accession to the end of his first Hyperberetaeus, or that beginning with his first Dius 1? Makaronas is undoubtedly right in adopting the former hypothesis. A new king would be unlikely to date by his predecessor, even for a few months only, and the contemporary Egyptian system[3] provides an analogy for counting year 1 from the accession to the end of the first civil year.

The task then is to discover whether the letters contain internal evidence which can fix the beginning of Philip's *second* year in October 221 or October 220. The normal view, which assigns the Larisean letters to 219 and 214,[4] implies the later date, with Philip's accession subsequent to September 221;[5] and Makaronas, who is concerned chiefly with the letter to Archippus, does not dispose of this. In December 180 (on this basis the date of the Archippus letter) Philip was, he claims, at Demetrias, a dying man, and the minor details of this letter would certainly have been left to a representative at Pella; further, if it came from Demetrias, the letter would say so.

[1] See Makaronas, *AE*, 1934–5, 124 *seq.*

[2] I.e. October–September. For the Julian equivalents, deduced from the Florentine-Leyden *Horologium*, see Bischoff, *P-W*, 'Kalender', cols. 1586 *seq.* It is, as Dow and Edson, *Harv. Stud.* XLVIII, 1937, 176, n. 1, point out, true that we have no synchronisms to give us accurate information about the Macedonian calendar in the third century. We know, however, that up to Alexander's death it was running true to the sun (Dinsmoor, 474), and that even in Egypt, where it was superimposed upon the native calendar, it ran true until 268 (Dinsmoor, 478). In the following calculations it is assumed, therefore, that in the absence of evidence to the contrary we may take it that the Macedonian calendar continued to run more or less true during the third and second centuries; if subsequently discovered synchronisms should reveal a disordered calendar, the results would of course require modification.

[3] Walbank, *JEA*, XXII, 1936, 23, n. 9: in Egypt a king's first year was calculated from his accession to the fifth epagomenal day following it, and his second and subsequent years began on Thoth 1.

[4] E.g. Mommsen, *Hermes*, XVII, 1882, 467 *seq.*; Hiller in *Syll.* 543.

[5] This would fit Niese, II, 348, and Treves, *Athen.* x, 1932, 198–9, who both date the accession winter 221–20.

These arguments are plausible but inconclusive: for in 179 Philip was still strong enough to make a tour of his kingdom.[1] Similarly, the letter to the people of Abae, a city in the part of Phocis loyal to Philip, might have been written in either 209 or 208; and it is, indeed, only from the first letter to Larisa that any positive evidence emerges.[2] But first one must turn to Polybius.

In summer 219 news of a Dardanian invasion recalled Philip to Macedon from Acarnania; but when, on arriving, he found that the invasion had been abandoned, he sent his men to gather in the harvest and himself went to Thessaly, where he spent τὸ λοιπὸν μέρος τοῦ θέρους at Larisa (Polyb. IV, 66, 7). The references to the end of the Olympiad year (IV, 66, 11) and to the July harvest[3] fix the beginning of Philip's stay at Larisa beyond question. According to Polyb. IV, 67, 6, when the winter was already advanced (τοῦ χειμῶνος ἔτι προβαίνοντος), and shortly before the winter solstice (67, 7) Philip set out for the Peloponnese ἀπὸ Λαρίσης. It is not certain, but at least highly probable that he had spent the intervening months in that town. On the usual dating of *Syll.* 543, however, he returned to Pella in time to send a letter to Larisa on Hyperberetaeus 21. The letter itself, however, makes it clear that Philip had no personal acquaintance with the position in Thessaly: his knowledge is derived from three Thessalians, ὡς ἀπὸ τῆς πρεσβείας ἐγένοντο,[4] and his proposals are merely provisional (ἕως ἂν οὖν καὶ ἑτέρους ἐπινοήσωμεν ἀξίους τοῦ παρ' ὑμῖν πολιτεύματος, ἐπὶ τοῦ παρόντος κρίνω...); they are certainly not consistent with the view that Philip has himself just returned from a two to three months stay at Larisa. We may, therefore, conclude that the first letter to Larisa was an emergency measure of September (Hyperberetaeus) 220, when the declaration of war on Aetolia made it essential to protect the approaches to southern Macedonia through Tempe. His stay at Larisa the following summer was undertaken after Scopas's raid on Dium had shown the inadequacy of the preliminary measures.

From this it follows that Philip's accession was between July and October 221, probably, since the Messenian events followed Doson's death,[5] in July; and also that the second letter to Larisa was written in August 215. What then was the expedition for which Philip was then preparing?[6] The usual view identifies it with Philip's disastrous

[1] Livy (P) XL, 54 *seq.*
[2] The Carian inscription, *BCH*, XXVIII, 1904, 346, 2, dated to Philip's twenty-third year, is of no help; similarly, the Sarapeum inscription (see above, p. 267), dated Daesius of year XXXV, might be either May 186 or May 187.
[3] For the date of this harvest see Kromayer, 21, n. 2.
[4] On this phrase see Herzog, *Hermes*, LXV, 1930, 465.
[5] See above, p. 296, n. 6.
[6] *Syll.* 543, lines 37-8: ἕως ἂν ἐγὼ ἐπιστρέψας ἀπὸ τῆς [στρατ]είας ἀκούσω.

expedition to the Aous, of summer 214;[1] but the date proposed above
rules this out. There are three possible answers. The word [στρατ]είας,
Makaronas argues,[2] may be neglected as a mere restoration of Lolling;
this is true, but on the other hand no one has suggested an alternative.
A second solution would be to identify the στρατεία with the expedition against Corcyra, mentioned in Zonaras and Appian,[3] immediately
after Philip's alliance with Hannibal. Both Niese and Geyer accept
the tradition;[4] but Zonaras and Appian, alone, are wretched authorities, and Livy states[5] that *prius se aestas circumegit, quam movere ac
moliri quicquam rex posset.* There is, in fact, little doubt that the
expedition is a doublet from 216.[6] The third and, I believe, correct
solution is to accept what the inscription says and nothing more—
that in August 215 Philip was contemplating an expedition. This
may have been some raid on the Dardanians, which, as so often, at
the last moment proved unnecessary, or which took place, yet failed
to be recorded by our sources; alternatively, it may have been a
proposed Illyrian expedition, abandoned before it was begun. The
only certain conclusion is that it has no reference to the Aous expedition of 214.

Thus Philip was born in late summer 238, acceded *c.* July 221,
and died in early autumn 179, after a reign of a little over 42 years.

2. PROBLEMS OF THE FIRST WAR WITH ROME

The chronology for the years immediately after 217 suffers from the
fragmentary state of Polybius and the absence for some years of a
corresponding version in Livy. Some dates can be determined with
certainty. Thus Philip's Pelagonian operations were in autumn 217
(Polyb. v, 108), and he spent the winter of 217–16 building a fleet
(v, 109); his Aous expedition was June-August 216.[7] From Polyb.
vii, 9, the treaty between Philip and Hannibal is limited only to the
period between 216 and 214; but there is no reason to question Livy's
annalistic dating of it (xxiii, 33; 39, 4) to A.U.C. 539 = 215 (Julian).
Livy may also be followed when he dates Philip's second Illyrian
expedition (Livy (A) xxiv, 40) to A.U.C. 540 = 214 (Julian), and the
month was probably August.[8]

The Messenian Events (Ithome incident: Polyb. vii, 10–14; Plut.
Arat. 49, 2–50; the ravaging: Polyb. viii, 8; Plut. *Arat.* 51, 2). The

---

[1] Livy (A) xxiv, 40.   [2] *AE*, 1934–5, 126.
[3] Zon. ix, 4, 2; Appian, *Maced.* 1.
[4] Niese, ii, 468; Geyer, *P-W*, 'Makedonia', col. 747.
[5] Livy (A) xxiii, 39, 4.
[6] So Boguth, 7, n. 8; Holleaux, 185, n. 1.
[7] Polyb. v, 109, 4: ἀρχομένης θερείας, cf. De Sanctis, iii, 2, 440 *seq.*
[8] Holleaux, 189, n. 1, against Zippel, 66 *seq.*, who puts it in autumn 215.

Ithome incident comes immediately after the treaty with Hannibal in the fragments of Polybius, and was probably, therefore, in the same year, 215 (though it may be winter 215–14 or even spring 214).[1] The ravaging was prior to Aratus's death (Polyb. VIII, 12), which fell in his sixteenth generalship;[2] and since that probably began in autumn 214,[3] the Messenian incursion may be either in the spring of 213, or in autumn 214, after Philip's Aous disaster. If the Polybian version of Plutarch (*Arat.* 51, 2) is accepted rather than the annalistic account in Livy (XXIV, 40, 17),[4] the ravaging will be in autumn 214; and the carrying off of Polycrateia of Argos will fall about the same time.[5] Whether the attack on Messene in which Demetrius of Pharus perished (Polyb. III, 19, 11; cf. Pausan. IV, 29, 1; 32, 2 (confused)) is before or after the events of autumn 214 is uncertain. Niese, II, 472, claims that it may be as late as 212, but more probably it precedes and explains Philip's attack.[6]

The Siege of Lissus and Acrolissus (Polyb. VIII, 13–14) fell in 214–12, after the ravaging of Messenia and Aratus's death (probably spring-summer 213) according to the order of the Polybian fragments. It may be in the summer of either 213 or 212.[7]

The Campaigns against Atintania, the Ardiaei, Parthini and Dassaretae (Livy (P) XXVII, 30, 13; XXIX, 12, 3; 12, 13; Polyb. VIII, 14a, 1; 14b, 2) are also spread over the two years 213 and 212, and cannot be separated into distinct campaigns.[8]

Note on Walek's Chronology (*Rev. Phil.* LIV, 1928, 5 *seq.*).

On the basis of Plut. *Arat.* 53, 1, who states that Aratus died during his seventeenth *strategia*, Walek brings his death down to the Achaean

---

[1] Holleaux, 197, n. 4.   [2] Walbank, 174–5 (but see the next note).
[3] In 217 the Achaean general entered office in May (Polyb. IV, 37, 2; V, 1, 1, stressing τότε; V, 30, 7), in 207 (cf. Polyb. XI, 11 *seq.*) and throughout the second century at the autumn equinox (cf. Aymard, *REA*, XXX, 1928, 1–2). When was the change made? Probably in 217, when Timoxenus was elected immediately after the Peace of Naupactus (Polyb. V, 106); so Niese, II, 461 (giving earlier views); Nissen, 137; De Sanctis, III, 1, 221; Holleaux, *REG*, XLIII, 1930, 251, n. 4; and the main difficulty (Aratus's probable unwillingness to agree to a curtailment of his year of office) disappears in view of the fact that Timoxenus was one of his own supporters (Polyb. IV, 82, 8), who had on a former occasion (225: Plut. *Arat.* 38, 2) held office for his leader. It is not, however, impossible that the change was not made until Aratus's death (so Clementi, 58) or even later. For a full discussion see Aymard, *Assemblées*, 238–47.
[4] Holleaux, *Rome*, 202, n. 1; *CAH*, VIII, 122, accepts 214 (so also Seeliger, 13–14; Nicolaus, 68–9); De Sanctis, III, 2, 440, prefers 213.
[5] Accepting the theory of Beloch, IV, 2, 139 *seq.*, that Polycrateia was the mother of Perseus, who was born in 213.
[6] So Holleaux, 202, n. 3.
[7] Cf. Niese, II, 474, and Holleaux, *Rome*, 199; *CAH*, VIII, 123 (213); De Sanctis, III, 2, 44, and Walek, *Rev. Phil.* LIV, 1928, 9 (212).
[8] Cf. Niese, II, 474; Holleaux, 199.

year 212–11 (autumn-autumn); and since it closely followed the ravaging of Messenia (Polyb. VIII, 12, 2: μετ' οὐ πολύ), he dates the latter spring 212, before the expedition against Lissus. To the empty year he assigns provisionally the death of Demetrius. The problem of Aratus's seventeen terms of office is, however, far from insuperable without assuming a *strategia* in 212–11.[1] Moreover, Aratus's death is described in Polyb. VIII, which covers Olymp. 141, 3–4 = 214–13 and 213–12. Hence Walek has to assume that it is described prematurely, as a pendant to the Messenian events, and compares Polyb. III, 118, 6, where Postumius's death is given as a pendant to Cannae. But there is really no analogy. The death of Aratus, the greatest hero of Achaea, was not an event that an Achaean historian would introduce casually and incidentally, as a tail-piece to something else. On the contrary, if it occurs in Book VIII, it may be assumed that it fell within the period 214–12; and Walek's theory and all its implications may safely be discarded.

The Roman Alliance with Aetolia (Livy (P) XXVI, 24–6, 4).

Livy (A) XXVI, 22–3 gives the Roman elections of autumn 211 for the year 210; Livy (P) XXVI, 24 states that *per idem tempus M. Valerius Laevinus, temptatis prius* (i.e. presumably in 212 and 211; cf. Livy (P) XXV, 23, 9) *per secreta conloquia principum animis, ad indictum ante ad id ipsum concilium Aetolorum classe expedita venit.* After speaking at this meeting of the fall of Capua and Syracuse (211), with the help of Scopas, *qui tum praetor gentis erat* (24, 7), and Dorimachus, *princeps Aetolorum*, Valerius negotiated a treaty between Rome and Aetolia. After this, *extemplo* (24, 15), both allies levelled an offensive, the Romans taking Zacynthus, Oeniadae and Nasus, before returning to Corcyra. The news of the alliance reached Philip *Pellae hibernanti*, and he made an expedition against the Illyrians and Dardanians, in preparation for the next season when, *primo vere*, he should march into Greece (25, 1 *seq.*); after a visit to Thessaly, he went on to take Iamphorynna in Thrace before returning to Pella (25, 17). *Veris principio* (26, 1) Laevinus joined *Scopas Aetolique* in taking Anticyra, and about this time learnt that he had been elected consul in his absence. Falling ill, he arrived home later than was expected (26, 4), and so, *magna parte anni circumacta* ((P) XXVI, 40, 1), he finally reached Sicily, his province for 210.

In general this chronology is confirmed from Polybius, who in Book IX (covering Olymp. 142, 1 and 2 = 212–11 and 211–10) deals with Agrigentum (taken by the Romans, 210), the speeches of the Aetolian and Acarnanian envoys at Sparta (where the capture of

---

[1] For various suggestions see Klatt, *Quellen und Chronologie des Kleomenischen Krieges*, Berlin, 1877, 122; Tarn, *CAH*, VII, 863; Walbank, 174; Porter, lxxx.

Oeniadae and Nasus is referred to as quite recent; IX, 39, 2), Philip's siege of Echinus and Sulpicius's counter-efforts along with Dorimachus, ὁ τῶν Αἰτωλῶν στρατηγός, and Sulpicius's occupation of Aegina. Thus the events at Echinus and Aegina appear to be in 210, and the presence of the envoys at Sparta in the same year.[1]

Two difficulties emerge: (1) Dorimachus is Aetolian general for 211–10 (Polyb. IX, 42, 1); then presumably Scopas, in whose *strategia* the alliance was concluded, is general for 212–11. Livy, however, says that the treaty was signed in the autumn (*per idem tempus* as the Roman elections) and the following spring it is still *Scopas Aetolique* who meet Laevinus at Anticyra. (2) News of the Treaty, signed in autumn, reaches Philip in winter, *Pellae hibernanti*; yet he proceeds to an immediate expedition in the, for winter, difficult districts of Illyria and Thrace.

Are these difficulties more easily resolved by putting the alliance in 212 or in 211?[2] The first certainly disappears, if the earlier date is adopted; on the other hand, this view neglects Livy's consistent account of Laevinus's movements, and leaves unexplained the reference to the fall of Capua and Syracuse in Laevinus's speech. Moreover, Laevinus's successor was Sulpicius Galba (Livy (P) XXVI, 26, 4), who was consul in 211 (Livy (A) XXV, 41, 11), when, by the earlier dating, he will have come out to Greece; but not only does Livy make it clear that he went out as proconsul ((A) XXVI, 22, 1), but he also states that no 'consular leader' held a command in the war in Greece ((P) XXXII, 21, 17, where Aristaenus says: *nec duce consulari nec exercitu bellum gesserunt*).[3] One apparent inconsistency—that Marcellus, whom Laevinus succeeded, returned to Rome, after the capture of Syracuse, in winter 211–10 ((P) XXVI, 21, 1) —springs from the fact that Livy related the capture of Syracuse, which was actually in 211, a year earlier in 212.[4] Certainly Livy believed the Romano-Aetolian alliance to have been in 211.

How then, keeping the 211 date, are the two difficulties to be resolved? The words *per idem tempus* are, as De Sanctis rightly argues,[5] not to be interpreted over-rigidly. If one assumes that the treaty

---

[1] The last event mentioned by the envoys at Sparta is the Roman capture of Anticyra (Polyb. IX, 39, 2: κατέσχον δὲ πρῴην τὴν τῶν ταλαιπώρων ᾿Αντικυρέων πόλιν) in spring 210 (Livy, 26, 1: *veris principio*). The Aetolian alliance with Elis and Messenia is also prior to this embassy (Polyb. IX, 30, 6), but whether it preceded the alliance with Rome is not indicated.

[2] For 212 see Oldfather, *P-W*, 'Lokris', col. 1225; Kahrstedt, *Gesch. d. Karth.* III, 284; Niese, II, 477; Holleaux, *Rome*, 209, n. 2; *CAH*, VIII, 124; Klaffenbach, *IG*, IX, 1², introd. p. xxx; Flacelière, 298. For 211, Clementi, *Studi di stor. ant.* I, 1891, 57; De Sanctis, III, 2, 441; Walek, *Rev. Phil.* LIV, 1928, 9 *seq.*

[3] The few months spent by Laevinus awaiting his successor would be ignored in such a context.

[4] De Sanctis, III, 2, 330–34.   [5] III, 2, 440 *seq.*

was signed before the equinox of 211, Scopas is still general; and when *Scopas Aetolique* meet Laevinus the next spring at Anticyra Scopas is no longer general, but only *princeps Aetolorum*[1]—the general being now Dorimachus (Polyb. IX, 42, 1), who was *princeps Aetolorum* the previous year (Livy (P) XXVI, 24, 7). As to the winter campaign, the words *Pellae hibernanti* are a mistranslation of some such phrase as ἐν Πέλλῃ διατρίβων; and Philip's winter campaign in reality precedes the autumn equinox of 211, while Scopas's counter-invasion of Acarnania is about the time of the change of generals in Aetolia (Livy (P) XXVI, 25, 9).

Walek, however,[2] in view of Perseus's campaign of 170–69 and Caesar's of 49–8, prefers to take Livy's account as it stands; and since this, and a rigid interpretation of *per idem tempus*, will bring the alliance later than the autumn equinox of 211, then plainly Scopas, *qui tum praetor gentis erat*, was the general for 211–10. For 210–9, however, the general was unquestionably Pyrrhias:[3] therefore, in Walek's chronology, Dorimachus's *strategia* must drop out.[4] What then of Polybius's statement that Dorimachus was στρατηγός at Echinus (IX, 42, 1)? The word στρατηγός, Walek replies, had a double meaning in Aetolia: it could connote either the General of the League or the officer in command of a detachment of Aetolian or allied troops: and Dorimachus is στρατηγός only in the second sense.[5] Unfortunately, in the first of the three examples quoted to support this theory (Polyb. IV, 77, 6), Dorimachus was in fact general of the League (cf. IV, 67, 1). The other two, which go together (Polyb. V, 30, 2; 94, 1), describe the position held in Elis by Pyrrhias and Euripidas in turn; in the first Pyrrhias is specifically called ὁ παρὰ τῶν Αἰτωλῶν ἀπεσταλμένος στρατηγὸς τοῖς Ἠλείοις, so that all ambiguity was out of the question. That στρατηγός has the general sense of 'commander' no one has ever doubted:[6] the point is whether by ὁ τῶν Αἰτωλῶν στρατηγός Polybius would be likely to mean anything but 'General of the League'.[7] And this seems very improbable.

[1] Cf. Polyb. IV, 5, 1, where Dorimachus and Scopas act for the general Ariston, who is ill.   [2] *Rev. Phil.* LIV, 1928, 9 *seq.*

[3] Livy (P) XXVII, 30, 1: *duce Pyrrhia qui praetor in eum annum cum absente Attalo creatus est.* (Yet Walek, *Rev. Phil.* LIV, 1928, 13, states that Attalus was not elected general till his arrival in Aetolia in 209!)

[4] Clementi, *Studi di stor. ant.* I, 1891, 57, also omits Dorimachus's generalship.

[5] The description of Sulpicius in this context as στρατηγός (*praetor*), though he was in fact proconsul, is irrelevant: looseness on Roman technicalities does not mean that a Greek historian would make a similar mistake in using the more familiar terminology of the Greek Leagues.

[6] E.g. Polyb. XV, 23, 9.

[7] Polyb. II, 53, 2: μετὰ Τιμοξένου τοῦ στρατηγοῦ, where Timoxenus held a *de facto* command (cf. Tarn, *CAH*, VII, 863), is in fact a special case, since Aratus was at this time στρατηγὸς αὐτοκράτωρ of the Achaean League.

This disposes of the attempt to date the alliance after the equinox of autumn 211. And though it is still possible to argue for placing it immediately before the elections, and keeping the winter campaign, once the attempt to prove Livy wholly consistent has failed, it seems more logical to follow De Sanctis in moving Philip's winter campaign some months forward, along with the alliance. Livy probably assumed that the account which he found in Polyb. IX under Olymp. 142, 2 (211–10) referred, as so often,[1] to events subsequent to the end of the previous campaigning season. Philip, who was inactive at Pella, had, he imagined, already gone into winter quarters; hence the ensuing campaign was in winter. Such is at least a consistent explanation of *per idem tempus* and *hibernanti*, and it is the one adopted above.

The Events of 209 and 208.

These Livy relates[2] under the years A.U.C. 546 and 547 = 208 and 207, as references to the Heraea, Nemea and Olympia show. This error was probably due to failure in co-ordinating Polybius and the annalistic account he was following for non-Greek events.[3] Since the Nemea of 209 was preceded by a thirty days truce (Livy, XXVII, 30, 6), which included the Heraea (in June), Philip's Malian campaign (30, 1) will be May–June, and the Spartan and Aetolian attacks on Achaea earlier in the year (29, 9). Philip's campaign in Elis and his return to meet the Dardanians (32, 9) will coincide with Sulpicius's arrival in the Aegean (33, 4), about August. In 208, Philip reached the Aetolian congress in May,[4] about the time of the Roman attack on Peparethos (XXVIII, 5, 10). For the remaining events, the dividing line is Machanidas's attack on the Achaeans in July, a little before the Olympian games;[5] after it came Philip's Aetolian campaign, along with Nicias, the Achaean general for 209–8, his return to

[1] Cf. De Sanctis, III, 1, 219–221.
[2] Livy (P) XXVII, 29, 9–33, 5; XXVIII, 5–8.
[3] See De Sanctis, III, 2, 443, with the valid criticisms of Walek, *Rev. Phil* LIV, 1928, 13 *seq.*
[4] Livy (P) XXVIII, 5, 15: *segetibus...quae iam prope maturitatem erant.*
[5] Livy (P) XXVIII, 7, 15: *nuntius adfertur Machanidam Olympiorum sollemne ludicrum parantes Elios adgredi statuisse.* There is some mistake, as the Eleans were allies of Machanidas (cf. Niese, II, 492, n. 1). Walek, *Rev. Phil.* LIV, 1928, 16, n. 5, thinks their previous year's defeat had induced the Eleans to revolt from Aetolia; but this is unlikely at the height of the Romano-Aetolian offensive. The likeliest solution is that the Achaeans usurped Olympia, and Machanidas attacked them on behalf of his allies; this explains why, on the flight of Machanidas, Philip went on to Aegium, instead of marching into Elis, to strengthen her resistance against Machanidas, as Walek's hypothesis would lead one to expect. On the prestige of holding the games cf. Plut. *Arat.* 28, 5–6, where Aratus in 235 holds a rival Nemea at Cleonae.

Chalcis and recovery of Oreus (XXVIII, 8, 13) and eventually, after his naval activity at Cassandreia, the expedition against the Dardanians (August–September).

Philip in Aetolia.

From Polybius (XI, 7, 2) it is clear that Philip invaded Aetolia in 207. But Livy recounts ((P) XXXVI, 31, 11) how Philip gave Zacynthus to Amynander *ut per Athamaniam ducere exercitum in superiorem partem Aetoliae liceret, qua expeditione fractis animis Aetolos compulit ad petendam pacem* (cf. (P) XXIX, 12, 1). Was this the expedition of 207? Or were there, as Niese thinks (II, 495; 500), two separate invasions?[1] The real difficulty is the gap between an invasion in 207 and a peace signed, according to Livy ((P+A) XXIX, 12, 3: *vixdum pace facta*), in 205. To surmount this, De Sanctis (III, 2, 430; 444) has the following suggestion: Livy's statement that Sempronius returned immediately after the Aetolian peace is annalistic exaggeration; the immediate effect of Philip's invasion of 207 was to depress the Aetolian morale and lead to appeals for help to Rome (cf. Livy (P) XXXII, 21, 17: *ut Philippus Aetolos nequiquam opem Romanorum implorantes depopularetur*); when in 206 no help arrived, and neutrals again put in a plea for peace,[2] the Aetolians resolved to offer peace on terms;[3] Sempronius did not arrive until spring 205, and the negotiations at Phoenice were the same autumn—though, as Sempronius was elected consul for 204 *absens, cum provinciam Graeciam haberet* (Livy (A) XXIX, 11, 10), they may have dragged on into the winter, or even into spring 204.

Walek has three unsuccessful criticisms of this chronology. If peace with Aetolia was made in 206, why did not Philip attack the Roman possessions in Illyria? He had not necessarily sufficient time left in 206, however, and in 205, notwithstanding the arrival of Roman forces, he did in fact attack Apollonia (Livy (P) XXIX, 12, 5–6). Secondly, the Roman forces (Livy (P) XXIX, 12, 2: 11,000 men and 35 ships) were inadequate, unless Sempronius was relying on Aetolian help: hence, in spring 205 the Aetolians had not yet made peace! Quite obviously Sempronius *was* relying on Aetolia, and his whole policy was to try to bring her back into the war or, failing that, to

[1] So too Geyer, *P-W*, 'Makedonia', col. 749; Walek, *Rev. Phil.* LIV, 1928, 20, postulates three invasions, because Polyb. XI, 7, 2, shows Philip in 207 mutilating the statues ὅσα πρότερον ἀπέλιπε τῶν ἀναθημάτων, i.e. in 208. But the reference is obviously to the invasion of 218 (cf. Polyb. V, 9 *seq.*). Walek's version is further vitiated by his apparent ignorance of the passage, Livy (P) XXXVI, 31, 11, cited above.

[2] Appian, *Maced.* 3.

[3] For the concessions Philip probably made (on paper) see above, p. 100, n. 1.

make peace with Philip (as he did); but this does not mean that the Aetolians were still in a state of war. Finally, Walek asks, if Philip had made peace with Aetolia in 206, why is there no reference to his fleet? The probability is that the fleet begun in 208 (Livy (P) XXVIII, 8, 14) was never completed, and that Philip's naval policy was not resumed until winter 204–3.[1]

None of these criticisms is very pertinent; and De Sanctis's chronology may be accepted as satisfactory.

3. THE EASTERN POLICY

The years 204 and probably 203 contained Philip's campaigns against the Illyrians, Dardanians and Thracians.[2] For his activity in Asia Minor the dividing line is the accession of Epiphanes in Egypt in about September 203,[3] followed by the anti-Egyptian pact with Antiochus the following winter.[4] Holleaux has shown[5] that Dicaearchus's plundering expedition in the Cyclades preceded Heracleides's attempts to burn the Rhodian dockyards, but leaves its date open between 205 and 204. The signing of the Peace of Phoenice in 205 is rather against the earlier date, and further, as the proceeds of the raids were probably used for Philip's naval programme, if these were in 205, it is odd that there are no signs of a fleet until 202.[6] The seizure of Lysimacheia, Cius and Chalcedon—Aetolian allies, probably since the time of the first Macedonian war[7]—the Byzantine town of Perinthus and the independent state of Thasos falls in 202; Niese and De Sanctis[8] claim that Philip also took Sestus this year, but more probably it fell along with Abydus in 200 (cf. Polyb. XVI, 29, 3). The following year's events have been exhaustively treated by Holleaux,[9] certain details of whose reconstruction, however, require reconsideration.

[1] Holleaux, *CAH*, VIII, 145, n. 2.   [2] See above, pp. 111 seq.
[3] See Walbank, *JEA*, XXII, 1936, 20–34. Bikerman, *Chron. d'Égypte*, XXIX, 1940, 124–31, puts Epiphanes's accession between March 12 and September 8, 204.
[4] See above, p. 113, n. 3.   [5] *REG*, XXXIII, 1920, 223 seq.
[6] Polyb. XV, 24, 1: κατὰ τὸν ἀνάπλουν.
[7] When an Aetolian alliance was an obvious reply to the threatening compact of Philip and Prusias: cf. De Sanctis, IV, 1, 6, n. 14. Polyb. XV, 23, 8–9, is no evidence one way or the other, however; and Holleaux mistranslates when he assumes that Philip 'had entered into friendship and alliance with Aetolia, Lysimacheia, etc.' (*REG*, XXXIII, 1920, 229; *Rome*, 291, n. 2). Philip's peace with Aetolia did not render him her ally. Niese, II, 581, dates the alliance of these towns with Aetolia subsequent to Phoenice.
[8] Niese, II, 582; De Sanctis, IV, 1, 7, n. 20. For the 200 dating see Holleaux, *REG*, XXXIII, 1920, 229.
[9] *Klio*, IX, 1909, 450–60; and more exhaustively, *REA*, XXII, 1920, 237 seq.; XXIII, 1921, 181 seq.; XXV, 1923, 330 seq.

The Battles of Chios and Lade.

Niese and Holleaux[1] place these two battles in this order, which is that given by Polybius in his polemic against Zeno and Antisthenes.[2] However, Polyb. XVI, 10, 1, states that after Lade, τὸν Ἄτταλον μηδέπω συμμεμιχέναι: and from this De Sanctis[3] deduces that since Attalus fought at Chios, Lade must be the earlier battle. And he gives as his order for the main events of early 201: (1) battle of Lade, (2) ravaging of Pergamum, (3) battle of Chios; for, he argues, after his repulse at Chios, Philip would scarcely have dared to leave his fleet and attack Pergamum. The words μηδέπω συμμεμιχέναι do not alone rule out Holleaux's argument that after his partial defeat at Chios Attalus returned home, only to rejoin his allies in the autumn. On the other hand, the fact that Polybius contemplates Philip's sailing for Egypt after Lade is in itself an argument for putting that battle first; for it implies that the Aegean is under Philip's control, hence that Attalus has not yet joined in the war. With Attalus only temporarily out of action, the Egyptian expedition would be sheer madness: but if Rhodes had been defeated at Lade, and Attalus was not yet at war, the scheme was, if bad politics, at least within the bounds of possibility. Moreover, Chios so weakened Philip's fleet,[4] that even the victory at Lade would not have sufficed to make the attack on Alexandria plausible.

Another argument for the priority of Lade is Polybius's eulogy on Theophiliscus, the Rhodian navarch who perished at Chios.[5] By beginning hostilities (ἀρχὴν πολέμου ποιήσας) i.e. at Lade, Theophiliscus had forced Attalus to join in the war (μὴ μέλλειν καὶ παρασκευάζεσθαι τὰ πρὸς τὸν πόλεμον, ἀλλὰ πολεμεῖν ἐρρωμένως καὶ κινδυνεύειν). True, he is referred to as κατὰ τὸν κίνδυνον ἀγαθὸς γενόμενος; but the word κίνδυνος covers all the events of that critical year, right up to the battle of Chios, which brought the danger to an end.

Holleaux adduces two other small objections. Whereas the Macedonian admiral at Chios was Democrates,[6] who perished in the battle, the post was held not only in 200 and 199,[7] but also at Lade,[8] by Heracleides of Tarentum; and the command is likely to have been continuous. This argument neglects the fact that Heracleides was no

---

[1] Niese, II, 583 *seq.*; Holleaux, *REA*, XXII, 1920, 244, giving other views; followed by Hiller v. Gaertringen, *P-W*, 'Rhodos', Suppl.-B. v, col. 788; Starr, *CP*, XXXIII, 1938, 63–4; Magie, *JRS*, XXIX, 1939, 37, n. 25.

[2] Polyb. XVI, 14, 5.

[3] IV, 1, 10, n. 27; followed by Griffith, *CHJ*, V, 1935, 1 *seq.*; McDonald and Walbank, *JRS*, XXVII, 1937, 186.

[4] Polyb. XVI, 7, 1–2: Philip lost in all 100 ships of various kinds.

[5] Polyb. XVI, 5, 1; 9, 1.   [6] Polyb. XVI, 3, 6.

[7] Livy (P) XXXI, 16, 2; 33, 2; 46, 8.

[8] Polyb. XVI, 15, 6, where he is voted a crown by the Milesians διὰ τὴν ἔφοδον.

professional admiral, but Philip's confidential friend:[1] there may have been excellent reasons why his command was temporarily interrupted—assuming that διὰ τὴν ἔφοδον *necessarily* means that he was admiral at Lade. Similarly, because Polybius does not name the Rhodian navarch at Lade,[2] it does not follow that he was the Cleonaeus of Polyb. XVI, 9, 1, and *IG*, XII, 3, 103,[3] and not Theophiliscus. Neither argument is of the sort to damage the chronology which De Sanctis has established.

The Ravaging of Pergamum (Polyb. XVI, 1, 1–8).

This De Sanctis places between the two naval battles,[4] Holleaux subsequent to both.[5] Holleaux is, however, quite correct in pointing out that Attalus and Rhodes were accounted technically aggressors in the war,[6] and that therefore some hostile act of Attalus must have preceded the ravaging of Pergamum. But such an act may well have been a declaration of war on Philip, at Theophiliscus's instigation;[7] neither this nor yet the expression νομίζων οἷον αὐτόχειρ 'Αττάλου γενέσθαι in Polyb. XVI, 1, 1, need refer to the battle of Chios. Indeed it is doubtful if Philip would have been in a position to undertake an expedition so far from his fleet after Chios.[8] On the other hand, in his reference to Philip's acting like a madman after Lade,[9] Polybius is undoubtedly thinking of the invasion of Pergamum.

Philip and the Cyclades.

Philip's lack of interest in and control over the Aegean[10] during the early part of his reign is shown by his welcome to Demetrius of Pharus, after the latter had carried out a plundering expedition in the Cyclades.[11] Free from the supervision of either Macedon or Egypt,[12] from about 220 onwards the islands enjoyed a period of relative and uneasy independence, which was broken in 204 by Dicaearchus's raids, and shortly afterwards by Philip's conversion of the Aegean into a 'Macedonian lake'.[13] In spring 200 the Rhodians took into their

---

[1] Polyb. XIII, 4, 8.

[2] Polyb. XVI, 15, 8: τῆς ἐπιστολῆς...τῆς...ὑπὸ τοῦ ναυάρχου πεμφθείσης.

[3] So Holleaux, *REG*, XXX, 1917, 98.

[4] IV, 1, 10, n. 27.   [5] *REA*, XXII, 1920, 238.

[6] Theophiliscus persuaded Attalus to open hostilities; and Philip is never contradicted when he accuses him of the initiative: Polyb. XVI, 34, 5; XVIII, 6, 1–2.

[7] Polyb. XVI, 9, 4 (quoted above, p. 307).   [8] See above, p. 307.

[9] Polyb. XVI, 10 (1 *a*), 1.   [10] See above, p. 108.

[11] See above, pp. 28–30.

[12] Holleaux, *BCH*, XXXI, 1907, 94 *seq.*; Tarn, 466; Laidlaw, 115.

[13] Holleaux, *BCH*, XXXI, 1907, 114; *REG*, XXXIII, 1920, 223 *seq.* (with bibliography).

confederacy all the Cyclades except Andros, Paros and Cythnos, where Macedonian garrisons still held out; Attalus took Andros in 199, but failed at Cythnos.

With the possible exception of Andros, which may have been inherited from Doson,[1] the probability is that all these islands were taken by Philip in 202 or 201—probably in the latter year, before the seizure of Samos.[2] For it is unlikely that such an expedition was subsequent to Philip's disembarking in Asia Minor.[3] The annexation was apparently swift, and only in Andros, Paros and Cythnos were adequate garrisons established. What few islands Philip kept throughout the second war with Rome must have been taken from him after Cynoscephalae.

Philip's Imprisonment at Bargylia.

Polybius XVI, 24, 1, shows Philip blockaded at Bargylia τοῦ χειμῶνος ἤδη καταρχομένου, καθ' ὃν Πόπλιος Σολπίκιος ὕπατος κατεστάθη ἐν 'Ρώμῃ, i.e. in October 201.[4] The expedition against Pergamum, sandwiched between Lade and Chios, had been in June[5] and July; and in August are to be placed the attack on Cnidus, the siege of Prinassus and the invasion of Caria, and in September the conquest of the Peraea, the attack on north-west Caria and the siege and capture of Iasus and Bargylia.[6] Once blockaded, Philip did not escape until the end of winter 201–200; for his arrival in Greek waters, pursued by Attalus, was only a little before the Romans appeared at Athens in the spring of 200.[7]

[1] Holleaux, *BCH*, XXXI, 1907, 106; De Sanctis, IV, 1, 8, n. 22.
[2] See above, p. 117. Samos was probably occupied early in 201, since Philip was unable to fit out all the ships there in time for the battle of Chios (cf. Holleaux, *REA*, XXII, 1920, 250 *seq.*; De Sanctis, IV, 1, 8, n. 22); and this date is, if anything, confirmed by the coupling of the taking of Samos with Chios, in Appian's inaccurate account, *Maced.* 4, 1, that Philip Σάμον καὶ Χίον εἷλε. Passerini, *Athen.* IX, 1931, 265, takes the 202 date. That Samos was not formally annexed is recognised by Holleaux, 318, n. 2, 'moins conquise...qu'occupée à titre provisoire'.
[3] Cf. Holleaux, *REA*, XXV, 1923, 340.
[4] The expression χειμὼν καταρχόμενος denotes the beginning of the bad season, about October: Polybius employs no word for autumn. See Holleaux, *REA*, XXV, 1923, 354.
[5] Philip counted on living on the harvest.
[6] Polyb. XVI, 11–12 (according to Holleaux's chronology).
[7] Polyb. XVI, 25; cf. Holleaux, *REA*, XXV, 1923, 355, n. 4.

4. THE PRELIMINARIES OF THE SECOND WAR WITH ROME

It is of importance to establish the authenticity and dates of the various embassies which preceded the war.

The Aetolian Embassy (Appian, *Maced.* 4, 2; Livy (P) XXXI, 29, 4; perhaps (A) XXX, 26, 2).

Though Philip had been expanding at their expense in 202, the Aetolians in summer 201 rejected Attalus's appeal for a counter-move against the Macedonians in Greece;[1] it is in this context that the Senate's rejection of an Aetolian[2] appeal must be considered. Appian dates this Aetolian appeal after the embassies of Rhodes and Athens and before the despatch of the Roman commission to Greece; but it is difficult to see why,[3] if it connects with Philip's aggression in 202, it should have been so long delayed, or, equally, to imagine the Romans rejecting in 201–200 help they were so soon to be soliciting.[4] Holleaux therefore dates the appeal after Zama, in autumn 202.[5] Carcopino[6] and De Sanctis[7] set it before Zama, and explain its rejection by the Roman preoccupation with Africa; but, alone, this is insufficient to explain the *bitterness* of the rebuff, which could only indicate that the Senate had still no thought of a fresh war against Philip.[8]

Little can be said for the theories of Passerini, who dates the appeal 205–4,[9] and Walek, who would bring it up to 206 or 205.[10] The former bases his case on an assumption that the Syro-Macedonian pact was already common knowledge in 202, and that Scopas's recruiting drive for Egypt at that time proves that the Aetolian government had then no aggressive intentions. In fact, the pact was not made public until late summer 201;[11] the federal government had probably no powers to prevent Scopas recruiting;[12] and it is a confusion to regard an Aetolian appeal against aggression as itself a sign of a policy of aggression. Indeed Passerini's arguments hardly approach the real question; and both he and Walek, with their various explana-

---

[1] Livy (P) XXXI, 46, 4.   [2] Livy (P) XXXI, 29, 4.
[3] Cf. Holleaux, 293, n. 1. Appian's chronology is accepted by Nissen, 325; Van Gelder, 124; Bouché-Leclercq, *Hist. des Lagides*, I, 355; Ferguson, 270 and Bickermann, *Rev. Phil.* LXI, 1935, 59.
[4] Polyb. XVI, 27, 4.
[5] Zama was probably in October 202; cf. De Sanctis, III, 2, 599–600; Scullard, *Scipio Africanus in the Second Punic War*, 327–8.
[6] *Points de vue sur l'impérialisme romain*, 62 (= *Journ. Sav.* 1924, 26).
[7] IV, 1, 39.   [8] See McDonald, *JRS*, XXVII, 1937, 184–5.
[9] *Athen.* IX, 1931, 266–9.   [10] *Eos*, XXXI, 1928, 369 *seq.*
[11] See McDonald, *JRS*, XXVII, 1937, 191: this connects with the abolition of the 'Macedonian' tribes at Athens.
[12] Cf. Mommsen, I, 691.

tions of the object of the Aetolian appeal, ignore Livy (P) XXXI, 29, 4, where a Macedonian, pleading for Aetolian help (which he fears may be refused), argues that the Romans, after formerly refusing the Aetolians assistance, have now had to come begging it—the implication being that if the Aetolians now refuse help to Macedon, *they* may later come asking it in vain. The logic of this passage rests on the view that the Aetolian embassy was sent to Rome to ask for help against aggression.

Thus it seems certain that the Aetolian appeal was made in autumn 202 against Philip's seizure of Lysimacheia, Chalcedon and Cius;[1] but whether it was prior or subsequent to Zama the evidence is not sufficient to determine.

The Embassies of Rhodes and Pergamum (Livy (A) XXXI, 2, 1; Appian, *Maced.* 4, 2).

It was probably these embassies that caused Philip's alarm at Bargylia in the winter of 201–200.[2] Hence they will have been despatched in the autumn of 201; and upon the Rhodians informing the Senate of the Syro-Macedonian pact,[3] the Romans in turn sent a commission to the east. The route and objects of this commission will be considered below.

The Athenian Appeal to Rome (Livy (A) XXXI, 1, 10; Appian, *Maced.* 4, 2; Florus, I, 23, 7).

One of Livy's three causes of the second Macedonian war was the appeal of the Athenians *quos agro prevastato (Philippus) in urbem compulerat*; and Appian states that ἐπὶ τοῖς ʻΡοδίων, Athenian ambassadors complained at Rome of the siege of their city. What is the truth behind this tradition?

Philip's first act of provocation against Athens was to lend auxiliaries to his allies, the Acarnanians, for an expedition sent to carry out reprisals for the execution of two Acarnanian youths who had been caught violating the Eleusinian mysteries.[4] The sacrilege must have been at the Great Mysteries of August-September 201, and the execution connects with the strong anti-Macedonian feeling in Athens at this time.[5] But in view of the difficulty of sending messages to Philip both before and during his confinement in Bargylia,

---

[1] So Holleaux, 293, n. 1; cf. Griffith, *CHJ*, V, 1935, 5; McDonald and Walbank, *JRS*, XXVII, 1937, 184.
[2] Polyb. XVI, 24, 3. This passage states that Philip feared the Romans and the Aetolians, but not that the embassies sent to Rome included one from Aetolia.
[3] Appian, *Maced.* 4, 2.
[4] Livy (P) XXXI, 14, 6–9.　　[5] See McDonald, *JRS*, XXVII, 1937, 191.

the Acarnanian raid cannot have been prior to his return from Asia in 200.[1] The compression of Livy (P) XXXI, 14, 10–12, conceals the fact that between Philip's return to Macedon and Attalus's arrival in Piraeus, there had been time for the attempted seizure by the Macedonians and recovery by Attalus of a number of Athenian warships, and hence time too for the Acarnanians to obtain Philip's co-operation in their raid on Athens.[2]

This chronology, however, rules out an embassy reaching Rome at the same time as that from Rhodes (as Appian says); and the Roman commission was in Athens[3] too soon after the raid for any embassy sent as a result to have influenced the Senate's decision. Moreover,[4] Athens had had no diplomatic relations with the Senate previously; and when the Roman commission reached Athens, it was treated with marked coldness, particularly in contrast to the reception given to Attalus. Nor was any but incidental reference made to Athens in the Roman ultimatum at either Athens or Abydus. In short, the hypothesis of an Athenian embassy influencing the Roman decision in autumn 201 must be completely rejected, and with it too the *Atheniensium nova legatio*, which reached Rome[5] with a similar story that Philip was threatening Athens, about the Ides of March, i.e. December–January by the Julian calendar.[6] Both the context and contents of the appeal brand it as wholly unreliable.[7]

That an Athenian embassy under Cephisodorus later visited Rome is, however, clear from Pausanias[8] and from an inscription of 196–5

---

[1] So De Sanctis, IV, 1, 21; Passerini, *Athen.* IX, 1931, 276. Holleaux dates the raid 201–200 in *REA*, XXII, 1920, 77 *seq.*; *Rome*, 276, n. 4; and in spring 200 in *CAH*, VIII, 161. Ferguson, *Athen. Trib. Cyc.* 141, n. 1; *Hellen. Ath.* 268; and Bickermann, *Rev. Phil.* LXI, 1935, 164, n. 3, date it autumn 201.

[2] Cf. McDonald, *JRS*, XXVII, 1937, 191, n. 70.

[3] Polyb. XVI, 25, 2: since their presence at Athens would contradict his annalistic version, which sent them to Egypt only, Livy omits the envoys from his account.

[4] Holleaux's arguments against the authenticity of the appeal are conclusive (*REA*, XXII, 1920, 77 *seq.*); *contra* De Sanctis, IV, 1, 32, n. 65, who fails to shake them. (Summary in Scullard, 463–4.) Bickermann's defence of the appeal (*Rev. Phil.* LXI, 1935, 161 *seq.*) is based on a false interpretation of the Peace of Phoenice.   [5] Livy (A) XXXI, 5, 2–6.

[6] On the calendar see De Sanctis, IV, 1, 368; Holleaux, *BCH*, LVI, 1932, 531 *seq.*

[7] Cf. De Sanctis, IV, 1, 32, n. 65; Holleaux, 271, n. 1. Livy mentions the embassy along with *litterae ab M. Aurelio legato et M. Valerio Laevino propraetore adlatae*—part of the faked annalistic tradition, which also appears in XXX, 26, 2–4; 40, 4; 42, 1–10; XXXI, 1, 9–10; 3, 3–6.

[8] Pausan. I, 36, 5, based on the inscription on Cephisodorus's tomb; cf. Niese, II, 590, n. 1; Ferguson, 269, n. 1; De Sanctis, IV, 1, 21, n. 53; Larsen, *CP*, XXX, 1935, 212, n. 82; XXXII, 1937, 21, n. McDonald, *JRS*, XXVII, 1937, 198 *seq.* refutes Holleaux's view (*REA*, XXII, 1920, 77 *seq.*) that the journey to Rome was that of 198–7 (Polyb. XVIII, 10, 11).

recently published by Meritt,[1] which together show that an Athenian appeal to Rome was made in the late summer of 200, after Cephisodorus had tried with little success to secure help from Egypt, Crete, Pergamum and Rhodes against the Macedonian attacks. This embassy must have reached Rome before the army left, if one is to explain the annalistic tradition, which magnified it into a major cause of the war[2] (though in fact the war-vote was passed before its arrival). Incidentally, there is no reason to think that the deputation that met Sulpicius in Illyria in September went on to Rome,[3] or that it had anything to do with the embassy of Cephisodorus.

The Egyptian Embassy (Livy (A) XXXI, 9, 1).[4]

An Egyptian embassy is said to have arrived in Rome in 200, when the state was *in ipso apparatu belli*; though suspect in details,[5] this annalistic account is probably based on an actual incident. Pausan. 1, 36, 5 refers to Cephisodorus's appeal for Egyptian help; and it is not impossible that Egypt passed on the appeal to the Senate. The date at which this embassy reached Rome is about July 200;[6] and as in the case of the Athenian embassy, which arrived a little later, its effect on Roman policy will have been negligible.

The Roman Embassy of 200.[7]

To the Rhodian and Pergamene envoys the Senate promised only a Roman investigation:[8] meanwhile C. Claudius Nero, M. Aemilius Lepidus and P. Sempronius Tuditanus were sent, nominally to Ptolemy to thank him for his loyalty and to beg him to maintain it in the event of a Roman war with Philip.[9] Since the Ptolemy in question

---

[1] *Hesperia*, v, 1936, 3, 424–5; 427; cf. Larsen, *CP*, XXXII, 1937, 21 n.; McDonald, *JRS*, XXVII, 1937, 200 *seq.*; Heichelheim, *Aegyptus*, XVII, 1937, 63–4.

[2] Cf. McDonald, *JRS*, XXVII, 1937, 203.

[3] Livy (P) XXXI, 14, 3; so Larsen, *CP*, XXXII, 1937, 23, assumes; cf. Passerini, *Athen.* IX, 1931, 282.

[4] The Egyptian ambassador sent to Rome in late 203 (Polyb. XV, 25, 14; cf. Walbank, *JEA*, XXII, 1936, 34), shortly after Epiphanes's accession, may be the basis of Justinus's strange story (XXX, 2, 8—3, 4) that the Senate was asked to appoint a guardian for Epiphanes, and did in fact appoint M. Aemilius Lepidus (cf. Otto, 27 *seq.* with full bibliography); but this embassy had nothing to do with the second war with Philip.

[5] Nissen, 124; McDonald, *JRS*, XXVII, 1937, 203, n. 146; cf. Walek, *Eos*, XXXI, 1928, 383, who points out that in 200 Egypt could scarcely have offered to make war on Philip on Athens's behalf.

[6] See below, p. 316.

[7] See in general McDonald and Walbank, *JRS*, XXVII, 1937, 189 *seq.* against Bickermann, *Rev. Phil.* LXI, 1935, 161 *seq.*

[8] Livy (A) XXXI, 2, 2: *curae eam rem senatui fore*.

[9] Livy (A) XXXI, 2, 3.

was the boy Epiphanes, this reference to his past loyalty renders the whole of this annalistic motivation in Livy suspect. And indeed Appian[1] attributes to the embassy the wider task of visiting Antiochus and Philip, and forbidding the former to attack Egypt and the latter Rhodes, Athens, Pergamum ἢ ἐς ἄλλον τινὰ 'Ρωμαίων φίλον; while Polybius[2] suggests that part of its duty was to negotiate a settlement between Egypt and Syria. The actual procedure followed by the envoys[3] demonstrates, however, that they had the more important task of canvassing Greek opinion in preparation for the war with Philip.

This embassy was at Athens in spring 200, at the same time as the Rhodians and Attalus who, as we saw, had pursued Philip from Bargylia;[4] hence it will have left Rome in the late winter or early spring of 200,[5] probably after the consul's entry into office and the presenting of the war-motion to the centuries.[6] Already the Senate had decided upon war,[7] and the putting of the war-motion was the first act of the new consul[8]—who saw it almost unanimously rejected.[9] Whereupon, the annalistic account in Livy records, he harangued the people on the dangers of a Macedonian invasion and was able to carry the war-measure at a second count. There followed three days' *supplicatio*, war preparations were set on foot, the Egyptian ambassadors were received (see above, p. 313), religious rites were fulfilled and Sulpicius crossed over into Illyria,[10] when the season was already *autumno fere exacto*, i.e. mid-September.[11] Now from Sulpicius's election to his arrival in Illyria is 9–10 months; hence the account of a second vote on the war-measure immediately after the first is suspect. The probability is[12] that there was a space between the two votes, which the Senate utilised for war-propaganda. The commission to Greece would be sent by the Senate immediately after the first vote. Quite obviously the Senate, anticipating no opposition, will have wanted its commission authorised to deliver the declaration of war, and would postpone its departure until after the voting; but upon the measure being rejected, it would despatch the commission

---

[1] Appian, *Maced.* 4, 2; Justin. xxx, 3, is vitiated by the 'guardianship' story.
[2] Polyb. xvi, 27, 5.
[3] Polyb. xvi, 25, 2–6; 26, 6; 27, 1–5; 34, 1–7; 35, 1–2.
[4] Polyb. xvi, 25, 2 *seq.*
[5] So Holleaux, *REA*, xxv, 1923, 355–6.
[6] The consuls entered office on the Ides of March (=Dec.–Jan. Julian; see above, p. 312, n. 6).
[7] Livy (A) xxxi, 5, 9 *seq.*   [8] Livy (A) xxxi, 6, 1.
[9] Livy (A) xxxi, 6, 3.   [10] Livy (P) xxxi, 14, 3; 18, 9; 22, 4.
[11] See below, p. 317.
[12] Bickermann's view (*loc. cit.*) that the first vote was not taken until late in the year is ruled out by the allotting of Macedonia as a province to Sulpicius.

to do the preliminary work, until the consent of the centuries could be obtained for a regular declaration of war.[1]

After visiting Epirus, Athamania, Aetolia and Achaea,[2] the envoys reached Athens, probably about the end of April; for Philip's escape from Bargylia, with a fleet in pursuit, will scarcely have been much earlier than March–April, and his arrival in Greek waters was followed by the Acarnanian attack on Athens and certain naval operations on the part of Attalus and the Rhodians.[3] Nicanor's invasion of Attica occurred while the Roman envoys were in Athens, and so was perhaps early May.[4] Driven by circumstances to deliver an ultimatum for which they had no popular authorisation, the envoys at once left for Rhodes,[5] where they spent most of the remaining part of the summer. This is clear from the details of Philip's campaign in Thrace.

Philip's reply to the ultimatum was to send Philocles to ravage Attica;[6] after this he conducted a campaign in Thrace, taking Aenus and Maronea after a long siege,[7] and then a series of other towns and fortresses (including perhaps Sestus)[8] until he was checked by Abydus.[9] The siege of this town must have lasted at least a fortnight, since the news of its real nature (τὸ σαφές)[10] had to reach the Romans at Rhodes before Lepidus sailed up to the straits; then came the conference before, three days later, Philip took the town.[11] There is no evidence that Philip stayed long at Abydus;[12] and on his way back to Macedon he heard of the Roman landing in Illyria.[13]

If Sulpicius's landing was in mid-September,[14] Philip must have

---

[1] For a detailed defence of this view and a consideration of the relevant question of fetial law, see McDonald and Walbank, *JRS*, XXVII, 1937, 189 *seq*. Livy (A) XXXI, 2, 1, which sends the embassy to Egypt only, may be neglected. Scullard, 253, attempts to reconcile this version with the arrival of the embassy in Athens in spring 200, by postulating two embassies with the same personnel, one to announce the conclusion of peace with Hannibal, the other to deliver the ultimatum to Philip.

[2] Polyb. XVI, 27, 4. The view of Meischke, *Zur Gesch. d. Königs Eumenes II*, 6, n. 3; Walek, *Eos*, XXXI, 1928, 369; and Passerini, *Athen.* IX, 1931, 260, that the Romans visited these places after their stay at Athens, may be neglected.

[3] See above, p. 312.   [4] Polyb. XVI, 27.

[5] Polyb. XVI, 34, 2: in spite of Polybius's statement that they left Athens to visit Ptolemy and Antiochus (XVI, 27, 5), they got no farther than Rhodes until autumn.

[6] Livy (P) XXXI, 16, 2. So Holleaux, *CAH*, VIII, 163; other views quoted by McDonald, *JRS*, XXVII, 1937, 192, n. 75.

[7] Livy (P) XXXI, 16, 4.   [8] See above, p. 306, n. 8.

[9] Livy (P) XXXI, 16, 6: *ea oppugnatio diu Philippum tenuit*.

[10] Polyb. XVI, 34, 2.   [11] Polyb. XVI, 34, 10.

[12] Certainly not six weeks, as Bickermann suggests (*Rev. Phil.* LXI, 1935, 174, n. 3); cf. Livy (P) XXXI, 18, 8: *Philippus imposito Abydi praesidio in regnum rediit*.

[13] Livy (P) XXXI, 18, 9.   [14] See below, p. 317.

left Abydus about the same time; thus the siege of Abydus will have been at the end of August and the beginning of September, with Lepidus's ultimatum about September 1st. Now the journey from Brundisium to Epirus required two days,[1] that from Rome to Brundisium about a week,[2] and the expedition was preceded by a three days' *supplicatio*;[3] thus the Roman army was ready to start about the end of August. But how long would the preliminaries require? Bickermann[4] allows ten days, but surely this is too little. More probably they took up the whole of August, in which case the second vote of the Comitia was towards the end of July; allowing three to four weeks for the news to reach Rhodes, Lepidus and his colleagues will have heard of the vote towards the end of August—when, as we saw, they almost immediately sailed north to Abydus.[5]

Upon Lepidus's return to Rhodes, the envoys will have continued their mission to Syria and Egypt (early September). What were their objects here? That they were sent to exchange compliments with Ptolemy and secure his alliance against Philip[6] is an annalistic view that may be rejected at once; in 200 Egyptian help was scarcely worth soliciting. Again Appian's and Justinus's statement that they were to forbid Antiochus to touch Egypt[7] is contradicted by the fact that Rome allowed Coele-Syria to be swallowed up without lifting a finger. We are left with Polybius's view,[8] that the embassy was to arbitrate between Egypt and Syria. If this was so, it had little success. But in fact a glance at Roman policy, and above all at the repercussions of the Syro-Macedonian pact,[9] confirms Holleaux's claim that[10] the real purpose of the commission was to buy Syrian neutrality in the coming war with Philip, at the expense of Egypt.

That the envoys made no concessions to Antiochus (had they done so, these must inevitably have been brought up in the later negotiations between him and the Senate) is to be explained[11] by the fact that upon reaching Syria, they at once discovered how groundless were their fears of a coalition with Philip. Leaving Antiochus on good terms,

[1] Livy (A) XXXI, 14, 2.   [2] Livy (A) XXXVII, 4, 1.
[3] Livy (A) XXXI, 8, 2.   [4] *Loc. cit.*
[5] The chronology of the stay at Rhodes is elastic: the envoys *may* have stayed at Athens till June. The limiting factor is Philip's expedition in Thrace; and in this respect it must be remembered that a fortnight is a minimum for the siege of Abydus. The silence of the embassy at Rhodes is against putting the second war-vote much before the end of July. For a refutation of Bickermann's chronology see Walbank, *JRS*, XXVII, 1937, 194, n. 92.
[6] Livy (A) XXXI, 2, 3–4; followed by Walek, *Eos*, XXXI, 1928, 380 *seq.*, and in part by De Sanctis, IV, 1, 28.
[7] Appian, *Maced.* 4, 2; Justin. XXX, 3, 3.
[8] Polyb. XVI, 27, 5.
[9] Cf. Holleaux, 320 *seq.*; McDonald, *JRS*, XXVII, 1937, 205–7.
[10] *REA*, XV, 1913, 1 *seq.*; *Rome*, 82 *seq.*
[11] So McDonald, *JRS*, XXVII, 1937, 204–5.

they proceeded to Alexandria, where ignorance of their betrayal to Antiochus and knowledge of the terms of the ultimatum at Abydus ensured the envoys a hearty welcome from the Egyptian court. The date of these visits cannot be determined; but the probability is that the commission spent winter in Egypt and returned to Rome in spring 199.

5. THE SECOND WAR WITH ROME

The Campaign of 200.

Polybius knows no season between θέρος and χειμών (beginning about October 1st); hence when Livy states that Sulpicius arrived in Illyria *autumno fere exacto*,[1] this phrase is a Livian adaptation by which must be understood a date about the middle of September.[2] This view is confirmed by Apustius's campaign in the Apsus valley,[3] which can hardly have been subsequent to the autumn rains, which set in early in October. The twenty ships under Cento were sent round to the Aegean at once;[4] and the raid on Chalcis in which they took part must have been about a month after the Romans first landed,[5] and so mid-October. This is confirmed by the fact that at the Achaean meeting, called about ten days later, Cycliadas had succeeded Philopoemen in the generalship.[6]

After a short stay in Macedon[7] Philip marched south, and, reaching Demetrias in time to hear of the fall of Chalcis,[8] pressed on to a further attack on Athens. After a fruitless visit to the Achaean assembly (about ten days after the fall of Chalcis, and so the third week in October) he returned, ravaged Athens again and retired to winter in Macedon about the beginning of November.

The Campaign of 199.

Not knowing which route the enemy would take, Philip necessarily left the initiative to Sulpicius; and he, in view of the nature of the country, postponed moving until May.[9] Lyncestis, where the armies encountered each other,[10] is about 125 miles from the Apsus mouth

---

[1] Livy (P) XXXI, 22, 4.
[2] Cf. Holleaux, *BCH*, LVI, 1932, 533 *seq.*
[3] Livy (P) XXXI, 27.   [4] Livy (P) XXXI, 14, 3.
[5] See Holleaux, *BCH*, LVI, 1932, 537, n. 1, for a detailed proof.
[6] The Achaean elections were between the end of September and the beginning of November: nearer approximation has proved impossible; cf. Aymard, *REA*, XXX, 1928, 2, n. 4; *Assemblées*, 238 *seq.*
[7] Livy (P) XXXI, 18, 9.   [8] Livy (P) XXXI, 24, 1.
[9] On the detailed chronology of 199–7 see in particular Kromayer, II, 106–15.
[10] Livy (P) XXXI, 33, 6: *ad Lyncum.*

and only 60 miles from Pella, clear proof that Philip set out only when he had learnt which route Sulpicius had taken. The skirmish at Ottolobus[1] was early in July, as is evident from Livy's many references to the July harvest;[2] hence it seems that Livy omitted certain intervening events, including perhaps some minor Macedonian successes. After some manœuvring in Lyncestis (including the Roman defeat at Pluinna),[3] the battle of Banitza opened up the route into Eordaea to Sulpicius.[4] If this was at the end of August, September and October can be allowed for the Roman retreat.[5]

The Dardanian invasion must be almost contemporary with Ottolobus,[6] since it followed Perseus's withdrawal from Pelagonia immediately after the first cavalry skirmish in Lyncestis,[7] which was about the middle of June. Philip could not deal with the Dardanians until after Banitza, when Sulpicius's move southward enabled him to send Athenagoras up into the Axius valley,[8] while he himself followed Sulpicius and fell upon the Aetolians in Thessaly.[9]

At the spring Panaetolica,[10] the question of joining in the war had been postponed to a later meeting. Three circumstances persuaded the Aetolians to join Rome, the victory at Ottolobus, the news of the Dardanian invasion and the arrival of the Roman fleet at Oreus.[11] Two of these were in July: what of the third? The siege of Oreus was the last naval event of the year; after this *iam autumnale aequinoctium instabat* (Livy (P) XXXI, 47, 1) and Attalus went on to the Eleusinian mysteries in September. Had the siege of Oreus lasted more than a fortnight, it is probable that our sources would have recorded the fact; hence the meeting at Heraclea which preceded it, and from which the Aetolians departed *cum spe magis, Romanis omnia pollicentibus quam cum auxilio*, will have been in early August.[12] And the alliance with Rome cannot be much before the beginning of September. This view is supported by the full naval programme[13] which preceded the meeting of Heraclea and which is quite sufficient to fill the months from May (when the Romans sailed round into the Aegean)[14] to August.

---

[1] Livy (P) XXXI, 36 *seq.*

[2] E.g. Livy (P) XXXI, 36, 5: *dispersos milites per agros*; 36, 9: *vagos frumentatores*; 39, 4: *frumentum quod in agris erat*. Earlier in the campaign (Livy (P) XXXI, 33, 6), the *horrea Dassaretiorum* will refer to last year's harvest already in granaries; cf. Kromayer, II, 21.

[3] Livy (P) XXXI, 39, 4.

[4] Livy (P) XXXI, 39, 7; cf. (P) XXXII, 21, 19; Polyb. XVIII, 23, 3.

[5] Livy (P) XXXI, 40, 1–6.

[6] Livy (P) XXXI, 40, 7.   [7] Livy (P) XXXI, 34, 6.

[8] Livy (P) XXXI, 40, 8.   [9] Livy (P) XXXI, 41, 10.

[10] Livy (P) XXXI, 29, 1 *seq.*; probably February–March; cf. Holleaux, *BCH*, XXIX, 1905, 362–72.   [11] Livy (P) XXXI, 40, 9.

[12] Livy (P) XXXI, 46, 5. Niese, II, 606, n. 2, accepts this date as probable.

[13] See above, pp. 144–6.

[14] Livy (P) XXXI, 44, 1: *principio aestatis*.

Thus the Aetolian invasion of Thessaly is about the same time as, or just after, the battle of Banitza—not long after, however, or this would be mentioned as influencing the Aetolian decision. After his defeat of the Aetolians near Gomphi,[1] Philip went on to besiege Thaumaci, but without success;[2] and so, probably in October, or late September, he returned to Macedon for the winter.

The Campaign of 198.

At the end of the season of 199, Sulpicius was succeeded by P. Villius;[3] and the next spring Philip took the offensive by marching over Pindus and occupying a position on the Aous.[4] The height of the Pindus passes (over 4500 ft.) makes it unlikely that he crossed before early April;[5] on the other hand, if he was to forestall Villius he cannot have crossed much later. After facing Philip at Antigoneia *per multos dies*,[6] Villius was relieved by Flamininus, who crossed over from Italy *maturato itinere*,[7] and then spent fifty days before finally forcing the pass.[8] The battle enabling him to do this took place when *pernox forte luna erat*.[9]

Kromayer dates this battle June 25th, and so makes Flamininus's arrival in Illyria about the end of the first week in May; and this is the normally accepted chronology.[10] After defeating Philip, Flamininus advanced into Epirus; but before continuing into Thessaly he was joined by Amynander, who had meanwhile carried out a Thessalian campaign of three weeks' duration. For, setting out on the news of the Aous battle[11] (i.e. eight to ten days after it occurred),[12] he would require ten days for his march to and from Thessaly and another ten for operations there.[13] Hence Flamininus must have spent July in Epirus, and his meeting with Amynander *in monte Cercetio* will be early in August. Another fortnight is needed for the taking of Phaloria and Aeginium[14] and the provisioning from Ambracia (in itself a twelve days' journey, there and back); and then came the siege of Atrax,[15] which Kromayer estimates at between one and two months'

---

[1] On his two days' march from Banitza see Kromayer, II, 29.
[2] Livy (P) xxxII, 4.   [3] Livy (P) xxxII, 3, 2.
[4] Livy (P) xxxII, 5, 9: *principio veris*.
[5] Cf. Kromayer, II, 107–8.   [6] Livy (P) xxxII, 6, 4.
[7] Livy (P) xxxII, 6, 4; cf. Plut. *Flam.* 3, 4 *seq.*
[8] I.e. forty days waiting (Livy (P) xxxII, 10, 1), a day or two for negotiations (10, 2 *seq.*), *postero die* an attempt at storming (10, 9), three days marching round (11, 6; 12, 1).
[9] Livy (P) xxxII, 11, 9.
[10] E.g. Kromayer, II, 108; De Sanctis, IV, 1, 385; Holleaux, *CAH*, VIII, 170.
[11] Livy (P) xxxII, 13, 15.   [12] Kromayer, II, 108.
[13] Livy (P) xxxII, 14, 1–3; the assault on Gomphi alone lasted *per aliquot dies*.
[14] Livy (P) xxxII, 15, 1; 15, 4.   [15] Livy (P) xxxII, 15, 8; 17, 4–18, 3.

duration. This is, however, too long; for it involves dating the capture of the towns in Phocis[1] and the siege of Elatea[2] in the latter part of October and early November.

As Holleaux points out,[3] four events follow in close succession: Flamininus's capture of Elatea (Livy (P) XXXII, 24, 1–7), the rising against Philip at Opus (32, 1–2),[4] Flamininus's arrival at Opus (32, 3–4), and the sending of Philip's herald (32, 5). Furthermore, about the time when the siege of Elatea was beginning, attempts were made to win over the Achaeans at Sicyon;[5] these negotiations and, though it is not specifically stated, probably the subsequent attack on Corinth,[6] were under the generalship of Aristaenus.[7] After the attack on Corinth the Roman and Pergamene fleets went into winter quarters,[8] a proceeding which normally took place in mid-September (cf. Livy (P) XXXI, 47, 1–2), but might on occasion be a little later. Combining these data Aymard[9] puts the meeting at Sicyon about the middle, and the fall of Elatea about the end of October, Holleaux[10] about a fortnight earlier; but since the date at which the Achaean general took office is uncertain, and the other evidence is elastic, it is impossible to achieve complete accuracy.

The date when the admiral L. Flamininus crossed to Illyria depends on whether the word *consul* in Livy (P) XXXII, 16, 1,[11] refers to Villius or Flamininus; the description of Lucius immediately afterwards as *frater consulis* suggests the latter, in which case he crossed about the beginning of May. His summer operations in the Aegean ended with the surrender of Eretria and Carystus,[12] after which he sailed back to Cenchreae, evidently in early September, since he attended the Achaean assembly at Sicyon, and Cenchreae had fallen when the Achaeans attacked Corinth about the time of the equinox.[13] Also about this time, and, as far as can be seen,[14] before the change of general in Achaea, Philocles succeeded in detaching Argos from the Achaean League.

---

[1] Livy (P) XXXII, 18, 6–9. [2] Livy (P) XXXII, 18, 9.

[3] *REG*, XXXVI, 1923, 168–71.

[4] Livy states that *hiems iam eo tempore erat*; this is probably a translation of χειμὼν καταρχόμενος, which is roughly October–December; cf. Holleaux, *REA*, XXV, 1923, 353–4.

[5] Livy (P) XXXII, 19, 1; 21, 14. [6] Livy (P) XXXII, 23, 3 *seq.*

[7] Aristaenus was Achaean general, 199–8; see De Sanctis, IV, 1, 403; 406; Aymard, *REA*, XXX, 1928, 1–3.

[8] Livy (P) XXXII, 23, 13.

[9] *Premiers Rapports*, 80–1, n. 49. [10] *Loc. cit.*

[11] *Sub idem fere tempus quo consul adversus Philippum primum in Epiri faucibus posuit castra, et L. Quinctius frater consulis, etc.*

[12] Livy (P) XXXII, 16, 17–17, 3. See above, p. 155.

[13] Livy (P) XXXII, 23, 3.

[14] Cf. Livy (P) XXXII, 51, 1: *adventu in Achaiam Philoclis...non Corinthus tantum liberata obsidione, sed Argivorum quoque civitas...prodita est.*

The conference at Nicaea, which Niese[1] and Matzat[2] place in winter, is rightly assigned by Holleaux[3] and De Sanctis[4] to the middle or end of November. This follows from dating the sending of the Macedonian herald to Opus in October; and it also fits in with Flamininus's manœuvres to secure his re-appointment to the Greek command.[5]

Note on Leuze's Dating of the Battle of the Aous Pass (Hermes, LVIII, 1923, 187 seq.).

This Leuze would put in July, August or even September, for the following reasons. Livy has an annalistic record[6] of how Flamininus, before he left Italy, gave an audience to an embassy from Attalus, complaining of an attack by Antiochus on Pergamene territory at a time when the kingdom was *vacuum...praesidiis navalibus terrestribusque*, and asking either for Roman help or, failing that, permission for Attalus to withdraw his fleet from Greece in self-defence. This embassy was heard early in 198, after the consuls had entered office. And since the attack cannot have been in winter 199–8,[7] when Attalus was back in Pergamum,[8] nor yet in autumn 199—for in that case Attalus must already have withdrawn before his envoys reached Rome—it must have been in spring 198.

Although both Niese and Holleaux[9] reject this embassy as an annalistic invention, Leuze's view is worth examining. If Antiochus's attack has any authenticity, Leuze's date is the right one, since in the previous summer he was still fully occupied with his Syrian war.[10] But this date assumes that Attalus could sail over to Greece, receive news of Antiochus's attack and despatch *legati* to Rome before Flamininus himself left for Greece; and Leuze thus finds himself in difficulties with Livy (P) XXXII, 16, 6, where, after L. Quinctius's arrival at Piraeus, some time after his brother had taken up a position in the Aous valley, has been described, the historian goes on to say that *eodem tempore duae ex Asia classes profectae, una cum Attalo rege*, etc. To this passage, which implies that Flamininus was established

---

[1] II, 620.
[2] *Zeitrechnung*, 181.
[3] *REG*, XXXVI, 1923, 170–1.
[4] IV, 1, 385.
[5] Cf. Polyb. XVIII, 10, 7; 11, 2; Livy (P) XXXII, 32, 7; Plut. *Flam.* 7, 1–3; see Münzer, 119; Holleaux, *loc. cit.* The Ides of March were at this time *c.* December–January (Julian): see above, p. 312, n. 6.
[6] Livy (A) XXXII, 8, 9–16; 27, 1.
[7] Holleaux, *Klio*, VIII, 1908, 279–81.
[8] Livy (P) XXXI, 47, 2: *secundum initia et ipse in Asiam se recepit.*
[9] Niese, II, 607, n. 4; Holleaux, *loc. cit.*, does not entirely rule out the possibility of the attack, but tends to reject it.
[10] Livy (P) XXXI, 43, 5, shows Scopas recruiting in Aetolia in autumn 199 for troops to be used by Egypt against Syria: and from Livy (P) XXXIII, 19, 8, it is evident that this war was not really over until summer 198.

in Greece when Attalus left Pergamum, Leuze gives the unnatural interpretation that the Rhodian and Pergamene fleets left Asia simultaneously *with each other*. The fact is that such phrases as *eodem tempore, eodem fere tempore, sub idem tempus*, etc., are loose transitional expressions, of varying accuracy, but certainly related to what precedes, rather than what follows.

Other arguments produced by Leuze in favour of a late departure for Flamininus are hardly more cogent. The levy held by Flamininus (Livy (A) XXXII, 8, 6), which he regards as proof that it was already spring, was held merely to provide forces for the praetors to take to their provinces, and offers no evidence for the time of year. And Leuze himself admits that the tribunes' statement,[1] that Flamininus had spent the greater part of his year of office in religious duties at Rome, is either part of the vitiated annalistic tradition or else a record of deliberately tendentious statements, designed to secure the prorogation of Flamininus's command. Thus Leuze fails to prove his case for a late departure from Rome. And, on the other hand, Kromayer's analysis of the events from the battle on the Aous to the end of the season suggests that his figure of four months, though probably a maximum, does not allow for much compression. On the whole, therefore, the evidence supports the usual view that the battle on the Aous was about June 24th.

Events of 197.

Cynoscephalae was undoubtedly in June of this year.[2] This is clear from the Polybian account in Livy. Philip rallied his forces in Macedon *primo vere*, i.e. in early March (XXXIII, 3, 1), by which time the envoys sent to Rome after the conference of Nicaea were back in Macedon. *Secundum vernum aequinoctium*, i.e. about March 24th, Philip marshalled his army at Dium (3, 6). Meanwhile, *initio veris*, Flamininus had carried out an expedition against Thebes, and at the time Philip was at Dium (*per eosdem ferme dies*) he marched from Elatea into Thessaly (3, 6). After three days' delay at Heraclea (3, 8) he reached Xyniae, where he waited for some time, at the most a month, for the Aetolians (3, 8)—not longer, since Livy specifically states that *nihil morati Aetoli sunt*. The march from Xyniae, then, will be late April or, at the latest, early May. There was probably a further delay at Phthiotic Thebes (3, 10); and the battle occurred on the seventh day after leaving this town.

Thus, at the latest, the battle was in late May or early June; and this is confirmed by Polybius's statement[3] that Flamininus hastened

[1] Livy (A) XXXII, 28, 3 *seq.*
[2] So Kromayer, II, 109 *seq.*; De Sanctis, IV, 1, 86 n.; 386; Holleaux, *CAH*, VIII, 174; *REA*, XVII, 1915, 165–70.　　　　　[3] Polyb. XVIII, 20, 3.

σπεύδων προκαταφθεῖραι τὸν ἐν τῇ Σκοτουσσαίᾳ σῖτον—for the corn is ripe in Thessaly in July. Moreover, the Ludi Romani, taking place on September 15th (early July (Julian)) are said this year to have been *magnificentius quam alias facti et laetius propter res bello bene gestas*;[1] hence, the news of Cynoscephalae was in Rome by early July, so the battle itself must have occurred at the beginning of June.

There is one difficulty—Livy's statement that news of the battle only reached Rome *exitu ferme anni*;[2] and here there is little doubt[3] that Livy has confused the arrival of the news with that of the various embassies which reached Rome about November–December (Julian) of this year.[4] Two facts confirm this hypothesis: first, the news of the victory was read out by M. Sergius, the praetor,[5] which suggests that the consuls were not in Rome (as they would have been *exitu anni*); and secondly the ten commissioners, whose despatch followed the hearing of the embassies,[6] did not reach Greece until late winter.[7] In short, the news of Cynoscephalae was in Rome by the beginning of July, but the *legati*, in spite of Livy's 'brevi post', did not all arrive until November.

The remaining dates cause little difficulty. The meeting of Attalus, Flamininus and Nabis at Mycenae was a little before the campaigning season, i.e. c. February–March, 197.[8] The taking of Leucas and surrender of Acarnania fall between March and June, the latter event being the direct result of the news of Cynoscephalae;[9] and the tradition that the Achaean victory of the Nemean brook was on the same day as Cynoscephalae[10] shows that the two events were roughly contemporaneous. After the battle and the truce formalities, Philip marched north to deal with the Dardanian invasion, which followed on the news of his defeat;[11] his campaign in the Axius valley will be in July and August, and after this he returned to Thessalonica.

[1] Livy (A) xxxiii, 25, 1. [2] Livy (A) xxxiii, 24, 3.
[3] Nissen, 143; Kromayer, *loc. cit.*; De Sanctis, *loc. cit.*
[4] Polyb. xviii, 42, shows the *legati* being heard by the consuls of 196; Livy (A) xxxiii, 24, 5, however, states that *brevi post (sc. victoriam nuntiatam) legati...venerunt.*
[5] Livy (A) xxxiii, 24, 4. [6] Livy (A) xxxiii, 24, 7.
[7] Polyb. xviii, 44, 1; Livy (P) xxxiii, 30, 1; i.e. after the trouble in Boeotia.
[8] Livy (P) xxxii, 29, 6 *seq.*; cf. Niese, ii, 625, n. 3.
[9] Livy (P) xxxii, 40, 7; xxxiii, 16, 1 *seq.*; 17, 15.
[10] Livy (P) xxxiii, 14–15. [11] Livy (P) xxxiii, 19, 1–5.

6. FROM 196 TO 192

Events of 196.

The senatorial commission reached Greece at the end of winter, 196,[1] shortly after the murder of Brachylles and the Boeotian reprisals.[2] It remained in session at Corinth until the Isthmia of June–July,[3] and for some time afterwards, hearing the Syrian envoys[4] and settling various administrative and territorial problems; finally it broke up shortly before the autumn equinox[5] and the commissioners went on various errands. Cn. Cornelius was sent to interview Philip, and met him at Tempe.[6] There are clear indications that the meeting was short. First, the fact that it took place in Tempe suggests that Philip was either on his way south to meet the Roman, or awaiting the results of the Roman deliberations somewhere near his southern frontier. Cornelius began by giving Philip certain instructions and advice, which he accepted; whereupon Cornelius 'at once took leave of him and proceeded to Thermum', where the Aetolian assembly was actually in session.[7] Thus, with every indication that the meeting at Tempe was brief, we may deduce that the Council of Corinth ended about the second week in September, thus giving Cornelius time to travel via Tempe to the Aetolian autumn assembly at the end of the month.

From Livy[8] it is clear that the commissioners returned to Rome at the end of 196. Niese, however,[9] deduces from two passages that their return was not till 194.[10] In these are mentioned the return to Greece from Thrace of Villius, one of the *legati*, in 195, and the presence of *legati* at a discussion in late summer of the same year. The explanation[11] is that when the rest of the commissioners returned to Rome, P. Villius and P. Sulpicius stayed on in the capacity of lieutenants (*legati*), in accordance with a decision of winter 198–7,[12] taken in view of their special qualifications as ex-consuls who had operated against Philip. In winter 196 Flamininus's command was extended for a further year.[13]

---

[1] Polyb. XVIII, 44: κατὰ τὸν καιρὸν τοῦτον (i.e. the time of Brachylles's death); Livy (P) XXXIII, 30.

[2] Polyb. XVIII, 43; Livy (P) XXXIII, 27, 5–29, 12.

[3] Polyb. XVIII, 46; Livy (P) XXXIII, 32. The commission came straight on to Corinth; cf. Polyb. XVIII, 45, 7: παραυτίκα.

[4] Polyb. XVIII, 47; Livy (P) XXXIII, 34, 1–4.   [6] Polyb. XVIII, 48, 5–6.

[5] Polyb. XVIII, 48, 3–5.

[7] Polyb. XVIII, 48, 5: τοῦ δὲ βασιλέως συγκαταθεμένου τοῖς ὑποδεικνυμένοις, εὐθέως ἀπ' ἐκείνου χωρισθέντες ἧκον ἐπὶ τὴν τῶν Θερμικῶν σύνοδον κτλ.

[8] Livy (A) XXXIII, 44, 5; (P) XXXIV, 25, 2.

[9] II, 661, n. 4.   [10] Livy (P) XXXIV, 33, 12; 35, 1.

[11] Holleaux, *REA*, XV, 1913, 11, n. 2; cf. De Sanctis, IV, 1, 105, n. 209.

[12] Livy (A) XXXII, 28, 12.   [13] Livy (A) XXXIII, 43, 6.

Note on the Conference of Lysimacheia.

From Corinth, in autumn 196, P. Lentulus was sent to free Bargylia, and L. Terentius and P. Villius to interview Antiochus.[1] Since the two latter seem to have delayed some time at Thasos with their colleague L. Stertinius, three separate sets of envoys reached Lysimacheia together: the commissioners L. Terentius and P. Villius from Thasos, L. Cornelius and his entourage, whom the Senate had sent to bring about peace between Antiochus and Ptolemy,[2] and Antiochus's own envoys, Hegesianax and Lysias, from Corinth. The subsequent conference is dated October 196 by Holleaux;[3] Leuze, however,[4] claims that the evidence is not sufficient to determine the month.

Holleaux argues that the report of Epiphanes's death, which broke up the conference,[5] is to be connected with Scopas's revolt, which is in October 196; and also that Antiochus's arrival in Seleuceia for the winter[6] cannot be long after the conference, which must itself, therefore, be towards winter. These arguments Leuze easily refutes. The connection between the Egyptian rumour and Scopas's revolt is a mere guess; and, as is now clear, Scopas's revolt was in fact in autumn 197, not 196.[7] Furthermore, it is unknown at what speed Antiochus came from Lysimacheia to Seleuceia; for once he learnt that the rumour was false, all need for haste was at an end: and the naval revolt off the Eurymedon or the subsequent shipwreck may have delayed him for weeks.[8]

However, Holleaux's third argument for October seems conclusive. The Council of Corinth, as we saw, broke up shortly before the autumn equinox; and though both Lentulus and his colleagues Terentius and Villius were delayed a little on the way, their simultaneous arrival along with Hegesianax and Lysias[9] (who would naturally be all haste to report to the king) shows that this delay was inconsiderable. Leuze's arguments fail to suggest why Cornelius's interview at Tempe should have lasted more than two days at the most; and so Holleaux's date for the conference of Lysimacheia in early October may be accepted.

Events of 195 and 194.

After the conference of Lysimacheia Antiochus sent envoys to Flamininus;[10] they evidently spent the winter in Greece on other

[1] Polyb. xviii, 48, 3; Livy (P) xxxiii, 35, 2.
[2] Polyb. xviii, 49, 2; Livy (P) xxxiii, 39, 1–2; Appian, *Syr.* 2–3 ('Cn. Cornelius' by confusion with the commissioner who visited Philip).
[3] *REA*, xv, 1913, 8–9.   [4] *Hermes*, lviii, 1923, 203–4.
[5] Livy (P) xxxiii, 41, 1.   [6] Livy (P) xxxiii, 41, 9.
[7] Walbank, *JEA*, xxii, 1936, 21, n. 9.   [8] Livy (P) xxxiii, 41, 7.
[9] Polyb. xviii, 49, 4: συνεκύρησαν...εἰς τὸν καιρὸν τοῦτον.
[10] Livy (P) xxxiii, 41, 5.

business, since the Roman reply was not given until spring 195.[1] They were given a hearing *per eosdem dies*[2] as the summoning of the allies to Corinth *hibernis actis*,[3] i.e. March–April. The subsequent campaign against Nabis cannot be dated with certainty, since the Nemea which followed it had been postponed[4] for an unspecified period; nor was the summer necessarily over when Flamininus returned to Elatea.[5] Early in spring 194[6] Flamininus called a conference to Corinth; and then, dismissing his army from Elatea, he sent them back to Oricus through Epirus, while he himself made a détour through Chalcis and Thessaly. His reorganisation there must have occupied a considerable time,[7] and it will have been late summer when he finally crossed over to Italy and triumphed the same year.

Antiochus, meanwhile, spent 195 and 194 in Asia Minor and Thrace.[8] In both summers he invaded Thrace,[9] and at the end of 194 returned to Ephesus. Whether the envoys present at Rome in spring 193, and despatched from Ephesus,[10] were sent in autumn 194 or spring 193 (when Antiochus came back from Syria to Ephesus)[11] is uncertain. Holleaux favours 193, but 194 is probably preferable, in view of the dangers of a winter sea voyage.

Events of 193 *and* 192.

When the Syrian envoys returned in spring 193, Antiochus had already moved against the Pisidians.[12] The Roman *legati* sent in reply[13] came via Pergamum and probably arrived in late summer, since the

---

[1] Livy (P) XXXIV, 25, 2. Leuze, *Hermes*, LVIII, 1923, 205 *seq.* against Holleaux, *REA*, XV, 1913, 8–9, who assumes that the embassy was not despatched until spring 194. There is no evidence that the envoys carried out Flamininus's suggestion to go on to Rome.

[2] Livy (P) XXXIV, 25, 2.   [3] Livy (P) XXXIV, 22, 4.

[4] Livy (P) XXXIV, 41, 1.

[5] But this was *probably* so: Livy (P) XXXIV, 48, 2: *eodem hoc anno...quo in hiberna reduxerat copias.*

[6] Livy (P) XXXIV, 48, 3: *veris initio.*

[7] Livy (P) XXXIV, 51, 4–52, 2.

[8] Leuze, *op. cit.* 205 *seq.*, disproving Niese's attempt (II, 675) to postpone these two years' events until 194 and 193.

[9] Cf. Holleaux, *Hermes*, XLIII, 1908, 299, n. 4.

[10] Livy (P) XXXIV, 57, 4–59, 8; Diod. XXVIII, 15; Appian, *Syr.* 6.

[11] Livy (P) XXXV, 13, 4: *extremo iam hiemis Ephesum pervenit.*

[12] Livy (P) XXXV, 13, 4: *principio veris.*

[13] Livy (P) XXXIV, 59, 8: P. Sulpicius, P. Villius and P. Aelius, *qui Lysimachiae apud eum fuerant.* Sulpicius and Aelius are nowhere else mentioned as having been present at Lysimacheia; but, as Leuze observes (*op. cit.* 215 *seq.*), P. Aelius is never mentioned in the account of the negotiations at Ephesus in this year, though he was present. Similarly, others of the ten commissioners may have attended at Lysimacheia without being mentioned. Certainly there are no grounds for deducing from this minor discrepancy a second conference at Lysimacheia. See also Holleaux, *REA*, XV, 1913, 11 *seq.*

Pisidian campaign was over; their return to Rome was in late autumn, after the elections.[1] In Greece, meanwhile, probably after the Syrian envoys had called in on their way back from Rome, and so in early summer, the Aetolians held an assembly at Naupactus;[2] the result of their decision to send Dicaearchus to Antiochus and Damocritus to Nabis is to be seen in Antiochus's war council, held in autumn, after the Romans had gone,[3] and in Nabis's new outburst.

On receipt of the Aetolian message in summer 193, Nabis at once[4] set about recovering the Lacedaemonian coastal towns; and at once[5] the Achaeans sent a protest and also *auxilia ad Gytheum, quod iam oppugnabatur ab tyranno.* This suggests that the siege of Gytheum began at the latest in early autumn 193; yet in February 192 it is still proceeding.[6] It is more unlikely that this siege lasted a whole winter than that Livy's indications are unreliable:[7] probably Nabis acquired some of the lesser coastal towns in autumn 193, and began the siege of Gytheum in late winter 192.

The Achaean envoys sent to Rome in winter 193–2 returned early the next year;[8] at an assembly at Sicyon the situation was referred back to Flamininus, who had been sent out on the heels of the Achaean envoys, to sound public opinion in the Greek states. However, at the instigation of Philopoemen, the general of 193–2,[9] war was declared, and the subsequent campaigns up to Mt Barbosthenes occupy February, and the siege of Sparta March.[10] This is fixed by the Aetolian spring assembly at Naupactus, which Flamininus visited after he had been to Achaea, Athens, Chalcis, Thessaly and Demetrias.[11] From Naupactus he returned to Corinth and terminated the siege of Sparta, after it had lasted a month. Livy specifically states, moreover, that the Achaean campaign and Flamininus's canvassing were contemporaneous.[12]

The triple Aetolian attack on Demetrias, Chalcis and Sparta,[13] which followed the assembly, occupies the early summer months of 192. A little later Thoas was sent to Antiochus to report on the position in Greece,[14] and found the king besieging Smyrna, Alexandria

[1] Livy (P) xxxv, 20, 14.
[2] Livy (P) xxxv, 12, 3 *seq.*; cf. *Syll.* 585, line 40. Hegesianax, one of the envoys, was *proxenos* at Delphi during the first half of 193.
[3] Livy (P) xxxv, 17, 3.   [4] Livy (P) xxxv, 13, 1.
[5] Livy (P) xxxv, 13, 2.   [6] Livy (P) xxxv, 25, 1.
[7] The Livian chronology is followed by Aymard, *Premiers Rapports*, 298, n. 21; rejected by Meischke, *Symbolae*, 49; Mundt, 71; Niccolini, 134–5.
[8] Livy (P) xxxv, 25, 4.   [9] Livy (P) xxxv, 25, 7.
[10] Plut. *Philop.* 15, 4 *seq.*; Pausan. VIII, 50, 10.
[11] Livy (P) xxxv, 31, 2–32, 1; Holleaux, *BCH*, XXIX, 1905, 362–72, gives good reasons for dating the spring meeting of the Aetolian League in February–March.
[12] Livy (P) xxxv, 31, 1.   [13] Livy (P) xxxv, 34, 4 *seq.*
[14] Livy (P) xxxv, 42, 4.

Troas and Lampsacus (presumably with separate divisions). Whether Antiochus had already invaded Thrace that spring is much debated. Attalus had arrived at Rome in spring with the report that Antiochus had crossed the Hellespont;[1] and Alexamenus the Aetolian had informed Nabis that Antiochus had crossed over into Europe and would soon be in Greece.[2] On the strength of these two passages both Leuze and Holleaux[3] accept a Thracian expedition in spring 192; and certainly, if baseless, the coincidence of the two rumours is odd. However, Livy never states them as facts, and against the theory is his statement that Antiochus *neque ab tergo relinquere* (sc. *tres civitates*) *traiciens ipse in Europam volebat*.[4] Both Lampsacus and Alexandria Troas command the Hellespontine route into Europe; hence, as Antiochus's eyes were now on Greece, it is improbable that the Thracian expedition was more than a rumour that sprang out of a report of his march north to attack these towns.

When Antiochus crossed to Pteleum, it was already autumn, probably late October;[5] for Phaeneas was already Aetolian general for 192–1,[6] and Antiochus spoke of the season as being *ad navigandum immaturo*.[7] About the same time M. Baebius crossed over from Brundisium to Illyria,[8] after the elections, which were held early (perhaps September–October (Julian)).[9]

7. THE SYRIAN WAR

Events of Winter 192–1.

From Antiochus's arrival in Greece in October until he went into winter quarters at Chalcis,[10] his movements cover about three months.[11] The occupation of Demetrias, the Aetolian assembly at Lamia, the first expedition against Chalcis, the sending of envoys to Boeotia and Achaea, the second expedition against Chalcis and setting up of headquarters there, the taking of Euboea, the reception of ambassadors and the journey to Thebes[12]—these events, Kromayer calculates, fill the months of November and December.[13] The subsequent Thessalian

[1] Livy (A) xxxv, 23, 10.   [2] Livy (P) xxxv, 35, 7.
[3] Leuze, *op. cit.* 244 *seq.*; Holleaux, *CAH*, VIII, 206 (formerly, *Hermes*, XLVIII, 1913, 85, n. 1, Holleaux rejected this expedition).
[4] Livy (P) xxxv, 42, 2.   [5] Livy (P) xxxv, 43.
[6] Livy (P) xxxv, 44, 1.
[7] Livy (P) xxxv, 44, 3; cf. Kromayer, II, 220.
[8] Livy (A) xxxv, 24, 7: *in Epirum*. In annalistic passages this frequently signifies Illyria.
[9] Livy (A) xxxv, 24, 1 *seq.* The fact that the consuls for 192 returned to their provinces shows that the year was not very far advanced.
[10] Livy (P) xxxvi, 10, 12 *seq.*: *hiemem instare* is probably a mistranslation of Polybius. Cf. above, pp. 309, n. 4; 320, n. 4.   [11] Kromayer, II, 220 *seq.*
[12] Livy (P) xxxv, 43–51; xxxvi, 5–6; Polyb. xx, 7; Appian, *Syr.* 13.
[13] *Loc. cit.* From Demetrias to Chalcis alone is an eight days' march.

expedition was in mid-winter;[1] it began with a visit to Cynoscephalae, after which a ten days' siege of Pherae[2] was followed by a rapid campaign in Thessaly,[3] which Kromayer estimates to have taken up fifteen days from leaving Pherae. It concluded with the unexpected arrival of App. Claudius above Tempe;[4] and if this was about the end of January, the meeting of Baebius and Philip in Dassaretia[5] will also have taken place earlier that month.

The Campaign of 191.

The chronology of this year turns on the date of Thermopylae, which has been variously placed in April, May and June;[6] since Kromayer[7] showed that the June dating does not leave enough time for the remaining events of the consular year, the issue is, however, now between April and May. Kromayer's argument for April is as follows. Having assembled his men at Brundisium on either January 4th or 27th,[8] Acilius crossed over into Illyria in late February, and, allowing thirty days for the march from Apollonia to Larisa, via Tymphaea and the Zygos Pass, in the snow, arrived in Thessaly March–April. The considerable successes already achieved here by Philip and Baebius since the beginning of spring[9] had been secured rapidly, as Livy's narrative makes clear. From Acilius's arrival at Larisa to the battle of Thermopylae is about a fortnight: hence the date of the latter is late April, April 24th, if one accepts the statement that it was at the time of the new moon.[10]

This date is supported by the fact that Acilius caught Antiochus in Acarnania, which he invaded *principio veris*:[11] he would hardly have risked such an expedition later in the year. Moreover, the later events of the season confirm Kromayer's view. For, from the battle of Thermopylae to the siege of Heraclea[12] occupies a month, allowing for Acilius's march to Chalcis and back, and a few days' stay there. The siege of Heraclea needs another month, since it lasted twenty-four days after all was ready;[13] and a third month will go on the

[1] Livy (P) xxxvi, 6, 10: *ex hieme, quae tum ferme media erat.*
[2] Livy (P) xxxvi, 10, 1.
[3] Livy (P) xxxvi, 10, 6: *his raptim peractis.*
[4] Livy (P) xxxvi, 10, 10; see Niese, II, 700, n. 6.
[5] Livy (P) xxxvi, 10, 10.
[6] E.g. Matzat, 197 (June); Leuze, *op. cit.* 268 *seq.* (May); Kromayer, II, 224 *seq.*; cf. De Sanctis, IV, 1, 389; Holleaux, *CAH*, VIII, 214 (April).
[7] *Loc. cit.*
[8] Livy (A) xxxvi, 3, 13: *idibus Maiis*, i.e. January 4th or 27th (not 26th, as Kromayer, cf. Leuze, *op. cit.* 269, n. 5), accordingly as the year is intercalated or not.
[9] Livy (P) xxxvi, 13, 2: *principio veris.*
[10] Plut. *Cato*, 13, 1.   [11] Livy (P) xxxvi, 11, 5.
[12] Livy (P) xxxvi, 22 *seq.*   [13] Livy (P) xxxvi, 23, 6.

negotiations with the Aetolians (including two truces of ten days each) and the march to Naupactus.[1] The siege of Naupactus itself, until Flamininus's arrival, lasted two months;[2] yet Acilius was apparently still consul after it was over.[3] Therefore, as the consular year began on November 17th (Julian) at this time,[4] the five months in question are, at the latest, June to October. However, from Livy we know that the admiral Livius was held up *per aliquot dies* at Delos during the summer months, owing to the *adversi venti*.[5] At this time Acilius was already besieging Naupactus;[6] therefore, if Kromayer is right in identifying these winds with the Etesians of July and August, the latest date for the siege of Naupactus is August and September, 191.[7] In that case, the five months are from May to September, and Thermopylae falls at the end of April.

Leuze raises various arguments in support of May.[8] Whether true or not, the rumour of Acilius's crossing when the season was *maturum iam ad navigandum*,[9] proves that the crossing was in fact later than the spring equinox; Octavius's further claim,[10] that *in Thessalia castra Romana esse*, refers not to Acilius,[11] but to Baebius. This argument is indecisive. The evidence of a *rumor* is slender; the *castra in Thessalia* may be that of Acilius; and if sufficient time is allowed for the news of Acilius to reach Antiochus in Thyrrheum from Illyria (or Thessaly?), there is no argument against a Roman crossing in February. In any case, the season was reckoned as technically *maturum ad navigandum* as early as February.[12] Secondly, Leuze stresses the length of the campaign carried out by Baebius and Philip between spring and Acilius's arrival in Thessaly. This is, however, no argument for postponing Acilius's arrival, since Livy stresses the speed of their operations, and the towns of western Thessaly may well have come over voluntarily.[13] Thirdly, the Achaeans declared war τετραμήνῳ πρότερον τῆς Ῥωμαίων διαβάσεως;[14] and since it is clear from Livy[15] that this decision was not earlier than the beginning of November, 192, the Roman crossing will have been in March. This objection Kromayer had already forestalled by his assumption of inclusive

[1] Polyb. xx, 9, 5; 10, 12; Livy (P) xxxvi, 27, 3; 28, 8; 30, 4.
[2] Livy (P) xxxvi, 34, 2.
[3] Livy (P) xxxvi, 34, 8; 35, 7; 35, 8; 35, 9. Alone, however, this evidence would not be conclusive: see below, p. 333, n. 9.
[4] Cf. De Sanctis, iv, 1, 389.
[5] Livy (P) xxxvi, 43, 1.   [6] *Ibid.*
[7] So too Aymard, *REA*, xxx, 1928, 7–14; Daux, 225–6.
[8] *Op. cit.* 268 seq.   [9] Livy (P) xxxvi, 12, 11.
[10] Livy (P) xxxvi, 12, 10.   [11] So De Sanctis, iv, 1, 389.
[12] Cf. Pliny, *N.H.* ii, 122: *ver ergo aperit naviganti maria...is dies sextus Februarias ante idus*; xviii, 239; Varro, *de re rust.* i, 28, 1: *a. d. VII id. Feb.*; quoted by De Sanctis, iv, 1, 389.
[13] Livy (P) xxxvi, 13, 6.   [14] Polyb. xxxix, 3, 8.
[15] Livy (P) xxxv, 48–50.

reckoning. Fourthly, the *supplicatio*, celebrating the victory, was held at Rome *per eosdem dies* as the *ovatio* of Fulvius Nobilior,[1] which is known to have been on December 16th (Roman), i.e. August 2nd or 3rd (Julian);[2] this would fit in with the sending of the news by Cato after Acilius's visit to Chalcis (i.e. Thermopylae, end of May; despatch of Cato, late June; arrival in Rome, late July). However, no weight can be placed upon this conjunction, since Fulvius's *ovatio* is given again in another context;[3] and *per eosdem dies* is nothing more than Livy's usual loose copula.[4]

Finally, Leuze would have the *adversi venti*, which kept Livius at Delos, to be not the Etesians, but the equinoctial storms; in this case, Livius's departure is at the end of September, and the battle of Corycus[5] is in October. Against this is the fact that *cum iam hiems appeteret* (describing a time a few days before Corycus)[6] certainly signifies the approach of the autumn equinox;[7] hence Corycus is undoubtedly in September, and the siege of Naupactus August and September at the latest. However, as Leuze points out, the siege of Naupactus may have begun about August 20th, and so coincided with Livius's stay on Delos for some twelve days at the end of the month; and this would give adequate time for the intervening events subsequent to a battle of Thermopylae fought *c.* May 20th.

Thus Leuze fails to refute Kromayer: on the other hand his own theory cannot be fundamentally disproved. It seems preferable, however, to follow Kromayer, on the general grounds that, other things being equal, the earlier date of crossing is the more likely to be correct.[8]

Philip's movements link up with those of the Romans. With Baebius he marched into Thessaly *principio veris*;[9] he was attacking Limnaeum when Acilius joined him in early April. During the days immediately prior to Thermopylae, Philip was busy in Athamania[10] though his absence from the battle itself he explained as due to illness.[11] His siege of Lamia was parallel to that of Heraclea in June; and in the meantime he may have acquired part of the Pagasean coast-road.[12] When on the fall of Heraclea, at the beginning of July, he was

[1] Livy (A) XXXVI, 21, 7–10.   [2] Cf. De Sanctis, IV, 1, 380.
[3] Livy (A) XXXVI, 39, 1.   [4] Cf. De Sanctis, IV, 1, 390.
[5] Livy (P) XXXVI, 45, 6–8.   [6] Livy (P) XXXVI, 45, 8.
[7] Cf. Livy (P) XXXI, 22, 4. See Holleaux, *REA*, XXV, 1923, 354–5; *BCH*, LIV, 1930, 32.
[8] Livy (A) XXXV, 41, 5, stresses the Roman determination to act quickly: *delectum habere L. Quinctius consul iussus, ne quid moraretur, quo minus consul novus...extemplo proficisci posset.* Note too that the army was at Brundisium by the Ides of May (Roman), a date which Leuze, somewhat curiously, in view of his general thesis, equates with January 4th, the earlier date.
[9] Livy (P) XXXVI, 13, 2 *seq.*   [10] Livy (P) XXXVI, 14, 7 *seq.*
[11] Livy (P) XXXVI, 25, 1.   [12] See above, p. 204.

obliged to withdraw from Lamia,[1] he marched by this route to take over Demetrias. During August and September, while the Romans were outside Naupactus, he recovered Dolopia, Aperantia and most of Perrhaebia.[2]

Events of 190.

The Ides of Quinctilis, when Scipio's army marshalled at Brundisium, can be equated with March 18th (Julian);[3] its arrival at Amphissa will therefore be about the end of April,[4] and the subsequent six months' armistice will cover the period from May to October.[5] Setting out north in May, the Scipios reached Lysimacheia about October; for religious tabu kept Scipio stationary throughout the month *a. d. kal. Mart.* to *a. d. kal. Apr.*,[6] that is from October 25th to November 22nd, or November 16th/17th to December 14th/15th (Julian), accordingly as the year was intercalated or not. The battle of Magnesia, some twenty-five days later, was thus *c.* December 20th, 190, or January 10th, 189. The naval battle of Myonnesus, which led to the evacuation of Lysimacheia, will thus have been in September.[7]

Events of 189.

Philip's expulsion from Athamania was followed by the sending of a messenger to the Scipios *Ephesi post magnum cum Antiocho proelium morantes*;[8] it may therefore be dated December, 190–January, 189. However, the Aetolian hopes were quickly dashed by Damoteles's report that Fulvius was already on his way out to Greece[9] (*c.*January–February). A new embassy to Rome fell into the hands of pirates; and Damoteles, sent instead, turned back when he heard that Fulvius was now advancing through Epirus.[10] It was now θέρος,[11] perhaps May–June; and the subsequent siege of Ambracia must have lasted till the autumn equinox,[12] since Nicander, the Aetolian general for 190–89, will not have been sent to Rome until his office had expired.[13]

---

[1] Livy (P) xxxvi, 25, 8. [2] Livy (P) xxxvi, 33, 7.
[3] Livy (A) xxxvii, 4, 1–5. The solar eclipse of *a. d. V id. Quinct.* was on March 14th (Julian).
[4] Polyb. xxi, 4; Livy (P) xxxvii, 6, 2.
[5] Polyb. xxi, 5, 11; Livy (P) xxxvii, 7, 4.
[6] On this question see De Sanctis, iv, 1, 390 *seq.*
[7] Livy (P) xxxvii, 30; cf. 33, 1; *per idem fere tempus* as the fleet was preparing for winter quarters (i.e. late September), the consul heard of Myonnesus and the evacuation of Lysimacheia, while he was near Aenus and Maronea. [8] Livy (P) xxxviii, 3, 1.
[9] Polyb. xxi, 25, 8 *seq.*; Livy (A) xxxvii, 49; (P) xxxviii, 3, 6; Diod. xxix, 9. If there is any truth in Livy (A) xxxvii, 49, 6, the Aetolian envoys had been kept at Rome until after the truce had expired.
[10] Polyb. xxi, 26, 18. [11] Polyb. xxi, 26, 4; Livy (P) xxxviii, 3, 11.
[12] Cf. Holleaux, *BCH*, liv, 1930, 1–41. [13] Polyb. xxi, 30, 15.

Fulvius's siege of Same lasted about four months,[1] roughly October, 189–January, 188.[2]

Some difficulty has been caused by the chronology of Fulvius's visits to Rome and the Peloponnese this same winter. Livy's annalistic statement that Fulvius went on from the Peloponnese to Rome[3] is accepted by De Sanctis;[4] but a letter to the Delphians from C. Livius Salinator,[5] the consul for 189–8, which refers to Same as still under siege, shows that Fulvius must have returned from Rome to finish it off. The visits to both the Peloponnese and Rome involve the difficulty of a long absence from Same; and in any case a Polybian passage in Livy sets the Peloponnesian visit *after* the fall of Same.[6] Thus the probability is that the siege of Same began about October 1st, 189, that Fulvius left for Rome in mid-October, arrived in November, held the elections[7] and returned to complete the siege in January, 188.

Events of 188.

Fulvius's visit to the Peloponnese at the end of January, 188, was the sequel to a Sparto-Achaean outbreak, probably in October, 189; in spite of the Achaean declaration of war, winter had limited operations to a few frontier skirmishes.[8] Fulvius[9] attended two assemblies held in quick succession, first a *syncletos* at Argos, held to discuss changing the meeting-place for *synodoi*,[10] then, a little later, a second *syncletos* at Elis on the Spartan question.[11] At the latter Fulvius ordered envoys to be sent to Rome;[12] if they went at once, they could be back by the first week in April. Philopoemen's spring expedition,[13] which was subsequent to their return, need not have begun before the middle of April. During the autumn of 188, Manlius Vulso, the other consul, returned from Asia; he crossed Macedonia during the summer,[14] and wintered at Apollonia,[15] before crossing to Italy in 187.

[1] Livy (P) xxxviii, 29, 9.
[2] On the chronology of this winter see Aymard, *REA*, xxx, 1928, 4–24; *Mélanges Glotz*, 49–73; Cavaignac, *Mélanges Thomas*, 120–31; Holleaux, *BCH*, liv, 1930, 1–41; lv, 1931, 1–10.
[3] Livy (A) xxxviii, 35, 1.   [4] iv, 1, 396.
[5] Text in Holleaux, *BCH*, liv, 1930, 40 = *Syll.* 611.
[6] Livy (P) xxxviii, 30, 1: *consul compositis rebus Cephalleniae, praesidio Samae imposito, in Peloponnesum...traiecit.*
[7] As instructed; cf. Livy (A) xxxvii, 50, 6. Aymard questions this visit to Rome, but Holleaux is right in accepting it.
[8] Livy (P) xxxviii, 32, 1; the passage, Livy (P) xxxviii, 30, 6–32, 2, is parenthetical and refers to events of the previous autumn and winter.
[9] Wrongly described as *consul* by Livy (P) xxxviii, 30, 1; 30, 4; 30, 5; 32, 3.
[10] Aymard, *Mélanges Glotz*, 49 *seq.*; *Assemblées*, 237, n. 3; 313, n. 1; 323, n. 6, against Holleaux, *BCH*, lv, 1931, 1–10, who regards it as a *synodos*.
[11] Livy (P) xxxviii, 30, 5 (Argos); 32, 3 (Elis).
[12] Livy (P) xxxviii, 32, 4.   [13] Livy (P) xxxviii, 33, 1: *veris initio.*
[14] Livy (P) xxxviii, 40, 3 *seq.*   [15] Livy (P) xxxviii, 41, 15.

8. THE FINAL DECADE

As a result of complaints made at Rome against Philip in the winter of 186–5, a senatorial commission was appointed for the following spring.[1] The actions of Philip which led up to these complaints cannot be dated with certainty; but they were probably not prior to Manlius's departure in autumn, 188. It is likely that Aenus and Maronea were annexed in 187;[2] but Philip's other measures will have been spread over 187 and 186. In 185 he met the commission at Tempe, probably in spring;[3] for a further session took place at Thessalonica, before Metellus returned south to the Argive Nemea of July–August.[4]

Further complaints during the winter 185–4 decided the Senate to send out a fresh commission;[5] and since Philip's massacre at Maronea followed upon his hearing of this decision,[6] and preceded the arrival of Appius Claudius, it was probably January or February, 184. In view of Appius's later programme in Achaea and Crete,[7] his interview with Philip was probably in spring 184. The summer Philip spent fighting with the Byzantines against the Thracians;[8] and his messengers to the tribes across the Danube date to this year.[9]

After Demetrius's visit to Rome in winter 184–3, to answer fresh accusations,[10] a new commission was sent out in 183 under Q. Marcius Philippus.[11] After interviewing him, and so in the summer of 183, Philip carried out the Thracian expedition which concluded with the foundation of Perseis,[12] and his policy of exchanging populations probably dates to this autumn, since Polybius describes it in Book XXIII, and Livy connects it with the report of Marcius Philippus in winter 183–2.[13]

The open breach between Perseus and Demetrius took place in spring 182,[14] at the annual purification of the Macedonian army; and

---

[1] Polyb. XXII, 6, 6; Livy (P) XXXIX, 24, 13.

[2] Cf. Livy (P) XXXIX, 24, 7: *maxime moverat senatum quod iam Aeni et Maroneae adfectari possessionem audierant.*

[3] Livy (P) XXXIX, 25.

[4] Livy (P) XXXIX, 27 *seq.*; Polyb. XXII, 10, 1. Büttner-Wobst, *Beiträge zu Polybios*, 12 (cf. Mamroth, *ZN*, XL, 1930, 282; Gaebler, *ZN*, XXXVI, 1926, 114) puts Caecilius's embassy in 187, and that of App. Claudius in 186; for a refutation of this view see Niese, III, 22, n. 1 and in particular Aymard, *REA*, XXX, 1928, 25–42.

[5] Polyb. XXII, 11; Livy (P) XXXIX, 33, 3.

[6] Polyb. XXI, 13, 1 *seq.*; Livy (P) XXXIX, 34, 1 *seq.*

[7] Polyb. XXII, 15, 2; Livy (P) XXXIX, 35, 8.

[8] Polyb. XXII, 14, 12.   [9] Livy (P) XXXIX, 35, 4.

[10] Polyb. XXIII, 1; Livy (P) XXXIX, 47, 1 *seq.*

[11] Polyb. XXIII, 8, 1; Livy (P) XXXIX, 48, 5.

[12] Polyb. XXIII, 8, 3 *seq.*; Livy (P) XXXIX, 53, 12 *seq.*

[13] Polyb. XXIII, 10, 4; Livy (P) XL, 3, 3.   [14] Livy (P) XL, 5 *seq.*

it will have been in the course of that summer that Philip, after hearing the charges,[1] sent Apelles and Philocles to Rome to investigate them.[2] The imprisonments mentioned in both Polybius and Livy[3] were, most probably, in the winter of 183–2, though they cannot, any more than the execution of the Samus group, be dated with accuracy. The return of Philip's envoys from the Bastarnae will also have been at the same time.[4]

Philip's ascent of Haemus in 181[5] can be dated to July by a reference to the dogstar. In the autumn of this year Apelles and Philocles[6] returned from Rome, and as a result of their information Herodorus was executed.[7] The date of Demetrius's murder is uncertain; the relevant part of Polybius is lost, and Livy (who gives no Macedonian events under the year 180) seems to have compressed the final stages of the feud for dramatic effect. Thus Perseus's fresh accusations[8] may well have been made in the winter of 181–80; and when Philip sets out from Thessalonica to Demetrias, but sends Demetrius to Paeonia and Perseus to Amphipolis, it will be already spring 180.[9] In this case, Philip will have spent 180 in Demetrias, for the words *Demetriade hibernabat*[10] refer to the winter of 180–79. As we saw above,[11] Philip's death was probably in the early autumn of 179, at the time of the Bastarnian invasion; and the events of Livy (P) XL, 54–6 therefore cover the early months of that year, as their position in the text suggests.

---

[1] Livy (P) XL, 8 *seq.*; cf. Polyb. XXIII, 11.   [2] Livy (P) XL, 20, 3.
[3] Polyb. XXIII, 10, 8; Livy (P) XL, 3, 7 *seq.*   [4] Livy (P) XL, 5, 10.
[5] Livy (P) XL, 22, 7: *caniculae ortus.*   [6] Livy (P) XL, 23, 6.
[7] Livy (P) XL, 23, 9.
[8] Livy (P) XL, 24, 1 (i.e. under 181 in Livy).
[9] Livy (P) XL, 24, 3 *seq.*   [10] Livy (P) XL, 54, 2.
[11] See above, p. 299.

Table of Dates

238		Philip born to Phthia-Chryseis and Demetrius II.
222/1	Winter	Philip sent by Doson to the Peloponnese.
221	c. July	Death of Doson: accession of Philip. Dorimachus in Messenia.
	Autumn	Ariston elected Aetolian general: Aetolian aggression at Clarium, in Epirus and on the high seas.
220	Winter	Aetolian inroad into Messenia.
	May	Complaints at Achaean meeting: levy decreed. Aratus, the new general, defeated at Caphyae.
	Summer	Aetolian attack on Cynaetha. Philip at Corinth: war declared on Aetolia. Troops sent to Crete. Massacre of Macedonian party at Sparta.
	September	Philip's first letter to Larisa.
	Autumn	Machatas, the Aetolian, at Sparta.
219	Winter	Philip's alliance with Scerdilaidas. Frontier work. Spartan alliance with Aetolia.
	Spring	Lycurgus of Sparta invades Argolid, declares war on Achaea and invests the Athenaeum.
	Summer	Philip's western expedition in Epirus and Acarnania. Aetolian raid on Aegira: Achaean League hard hit. Scopas's raid on Dium. Philip recalled by Dardanian invasion: joined by Demetrius of Pharus. Philip spends rest of summer and autumn at Larisa.
	Autumn	Aetolian raid on Epirus and Dodona.
219/18	Winter	Philip's winter expedition. Psophis, south Elis and Triphylia subdued. Apelles's first schemes against Achaea.
218	Feb./Mar.	Apelles gets Eperatus elected Achaean general. Expedition against north Elis: Amphidamus clears Aratus.
	May	Philip's naval policy: financial arrangement with Achaea. Apelles goes to Chalcis.
	Summer	Attack on Cephallenia. Invasion of Aetolia. Aetolian countermoves on Messenia and Thessaly. Megaleas condemned. Invasion of Laconia. Court conspiracy: Apelles rebuffed. Rhodian ambassadors.
	Autumn	Philip's Phocian expedition. Execution of the anti-Achaean party.
217	Summer	Capture of Bylazora and Phthiotic Thebes. More neutral envoys. Preparations for expedition against Scerdilaidas.
	July/Sept.	Nemea. News of Trasimene. Peace of Naupactus.
	Autumn	Philip in Pelagonia against Scerdilaidas.
	Winter	Fleet of 100 *lembi* prepared.

216	Early summer	Philip sails via Cephallenia to the Aous, but retires in fear of a Roman attack.
215	Spring–Summer	Philip sends Xenophanes to Hannibal: captured coming back. Treaty between Philip and Hannibal.
	August	Second letter to Larisa.
	Autumn–Winter	Philip in Greece: first trouble at Messene. Incident on Ithome.
214	Late Summer	Philip's expedition to the Aous: forced to burn his fleet and return overland.
	Autumn	Demetrius of Pharus killed attacking Messene. Philip ravages Messenia.
	Winter	Philip's rape of Polycrateia.
213	Summer	Philip overthrows Atintania, the Ardiaeans and the Parthini. Capture of Lissus (or in 212: see above, p. 300). Birth of Perseus.
212	Spring	Damippus taken on his way from Syracuse to Philip.
	Summer	Philip continues his advance in Illyria: Dimale taken. Activities in Dassaretia (events of 212 and 213 indistinguishable). Roman moves towards Aetolia.
211	Summer	Alliance between Rome and Aetolia. Aetolian attack on Thessaly, and joint expedition against Zacynthus, Oeniadae and Nasus. Philip in Aous valley; takes Sintia; garrisons Tempe; takes Iamphorynna; and descends to Dium. Aetolian attack on Acarnania checked.
210	Spring	Laevinus and Scopas take Anticyra. Laevinus returns to Rome. Sparta joins Aetolia. Philip takes Pteleum and Larisa Cremaste; then Echinus.
	Summer	Sulpicius takes Aegina; gives it to the Aetolians. Philip takes Phalara.
	Autumn	Philip garrisons coast-route and returns to Pella.
209	Spring–Early summer	Appeal to Philip from Achaea.
	May/June	Philip marches south along coast: Pyrrhias driven into Lamia. Neutrals at Phalara: 30 days' armistice.
	Late June	Philip goes via Boeotia and Chalcis to Argive Heraea.
	June/July	Conference of Aegium: failure. Attalus at Aegina, Romans off Naupactus, Punic fleet off Corcyra.
	July	Philip at the Nemea. Repulses attack near Sicyon.
	July/Aug.	Operates with Cycliadas in Elis. Recalled by Illyrian invasion around Lychnidus.
	August	Philip repels barbarians, leaving troops in Peloponnese.
	September	Philip's letter to Abae. Sulpicius and Attalus winter at Aegina.
208	Spring	Aetolians fortify Thermopylae.
	May	Philip calls a conference at Demetrias. Defence measures. Aetolian congress at Heraclea: Philip arrives too late.

208	June	Philip sets up fire-signal system. Romans and allies take Oreus and Opus, but fail at Chalcis. Philip attacks Attalus at Cynus; Attalus returns home; Philip recovers Opus.
	June/July	Philip in Phocis and Doris. Successes in Cephisus valley.
	July	Neutrals at Elatea: Philip called away to defend Achaeans against Machanidas. Failure to make contact with Bomilcar. Promises the Achaeans Triphylia, Alipheira and Heraea.
	July/Aug.	Philip and Nicias, Achaean general, raid Erythrae.
	August	Philip recovers Oreus; starts a fleet at Cassandreia.
	Aug.–Oct.	War against the Dardanians: Heracleides in central Greece.
207	Spring	Philip recovers Zacynthus. Neutral intervention; armistice, but without any result.
	June	Philopoemen defeats Machanidas at Mantinea.
	Summer	Philip buys Amynander's support and invades Aetolia through Athamania. Thermum again ravaged.
206		Failure of Aetolian appeal to Rome. Aetolians agree to make peace with Philip.
205	Spring	P. Sempronius arrives in Illyria. Philip ravages district round Apollonia.
	Summer	Epirotes arrange meeting at Phoenice. Peace of Phoenice.
	Autumn	Scopas leaves Aetolia for Alexandria.
204		Philip's expedition against Illyria, Dardanians and Thrace. Alliance with Odrysae. Cretan War breaks out between Cretan cities and Rhodes. Dicaearchus plundering in the Cyclades. Heracleides sent to burn the Rhodian dockyards; Philip stirs up anti-Rhodian feeling in Crete. Nabis begins a border-war against Megalopolis.
203	Winter/Spring	Philip builds a fleet. Suggested marriage between Epiphanes of Egypt and one of Philip's daughters.
	c. September	Epiphanes recognised as King of Egypt. Sosibius's son Ptolemy sent to Philip: Ptolemy the son of Agesarchus sent via Greece to Rome.
203/2	Winter	Syro-Macedonian alliance between Philip and Antiochus directed against Ptolemy Epiphanes.
202		Philip forces Lysimacheia to accept a Macedonian governor. Chalcedon and Perinthus also annexed. Philip and Prusias besiege and sack Cius: Rhodian protests. Myrleia also sacked. Olympichus harries Iasus in Caria for Philip.
	Autumn	Philip seizes Thasos. Return of Ptolemy, son of Sosibius, to Alexandria. Aetolians appeal to Rome for help; appeal rejected.
201	Spring	Philip sails and takes over Cyclades.
	April	Samos temporarily occupied; Egyptian squadron fitted out; no breach with Egypt.

201	April/May	Battle of Lade: Philip defeats Rhodians. Miletus joins Philip. (Myus taken?) Attalus agrees to send help to Rhodes, on the appeal of Theophiliscus.
	May/June	Philip ravages Pergamum. Pergamene appeal to Aetolia rejected. Macedonian fleet in Sporades: attacks on Cos and Calymna: submission of Nisyros.
	June/July	Philip marches on Thyateira: invades plain of Thebe: second march on Thyateira: passes Hiera Come. Has to appeal to Zeuxis in Sardes for food. Return towards Miletus. Fleet ravages other islands?
	Late July	Sailing from Miletus to Chios, Philip takes Teos. Chios blockaded. Battle of Chios. Philip returns to Samos: allies separate.
	Summer	In Greece, Philopoemen repulses Nabis's attack on Messene.
	August	Philip operates with his fleet against south Caria, viz: Cnidus, Prinassus and Rhodian Peraea. (Stratonicaea taken?) Callias at Nisyros.
	September	Philip operates against north Caria, viz: Iasus taken. (Euromus and Pedasa taken?) Philip trapped at Bargylia. Rhodes and Attalus rejoin forces.
	Autumn	Syro-Macedonian pact becomes known. Rhodian and Pergamene envoys sent to Rome. At Athens, the 'Macedonian' tribes are abolished: Acarnanians executed, following violation of Mysteries.
	Aut./Wint.	Philip's attacks on Mylasa, and ravaging of Alabanda. (Stratonicaea taken?)
	Nov./Dec.	Elections at Rome: Sulpicius consul with Macedonia as province.
200	January	War-motion rejected by centuries at Rome.
	End of Winter	Senatorial commission sent to Greece: visits Phoenice, Athamania, Naupactus and Aegium.
	Mar./April	Philip escapes from Bargylia; pursued by Rhodes and Attalus. Grants help to Acarnanians. Raid on Athens by land and sea. Rhodians recover Athenian ships taken by Macedonians, while Attalus protects Attica. Attalus on Aegina; Rhodian successes in Cyclades.
	April/May	Roman commission at Piraeus. Reception to Attalus and Rhodians in Athens. Athens declares war on Philip. Rhodians take over rest of Cyclades, with few exceptions. Romans give ultimatum to Nicanor.
	May	Commission go on to Rhodes. Philocles ravages Attica.
	Summer	Ravaging goes on. Cephisodorus appeals to Egypt, Rhodes, Pergamum, Aetolia, Crete. Philip advances in Thrace, Heracleides controlling the fleet. Fall of Aenus, Maronea, Sestus, etc. Commission report to Rome.

200	July	Comitia pass the war-vote: Egyptian embassy at Rome. Cephisodorus's embassy at Rome. War preparations.
	End of August	Philip besieges Abydus: half-moves from Rhodes and Pergamum. Lepidus delivers ultimatum: Philip rejects it.
	September	Fall of Abydus. Achaean embassy at Rhodes.
	Mid. Sept.	Philip marches west to Macedon. Romans arrive in Illyria under Sulpicius. Ships sent round to Piraeus: camp on Apsus.
	Sept./Oct.	Apustius takes Antipatreia and repulses Athenagoras. Commission goes on to visit Antiochus and Ptolemy.
	October	Athenian raid on Chalcis: Philip descends from Demetrias and attacks Athens. Philip at Dipylon: outskirts plundered. Offers Achaeans help against Nabis, in return for garrison work. Offer rejected.
	Oct./Nov.	Philip and Philocles ravage Attica. Philip winters in Macedonia. Roman commission probably reaches Egypt.
200–199	Winter	Pleuratus, Bato and Amynander with Sulpicius. Aetolians postpone decision.
199	Spring	Perseus sent to garrison the Axius valley.
	May/June	Two sides meet in Lyncestis. Skirmishing.
	July	Roman success at Ottolobus; Philip defeats enemy at Pluinna.
	Late Aug.	Battle near Banitza. Roman advance into Eordaea.
	May–Aug.	Roman and Rhodian naval activity in the Aegean. Macedonian coast raided.
	Late Aug.	Aetolian meeting at Heraclea.
	September	Sulpicius returns through Orestis. Athenagoras sent to drive back the Dardanians. Aetolians decide on war, and invade Thessaly. Philip expels them. Scopas recruiting in Aetolia for Egypt. Oreus taken; fleets retire for winter.
	Autumn	Philip besieges Thaumaci. Returns to Macedon for winter.
	Winter	Villius succeeds Sulpicius. Mutiny among Roman troops.
198		Philip withdraws from Lysimacheia; hands over towns to Achaea; deposes and imprisons Heracleides; and drills his troops.
	April	Philip at the Aous Pass near Antigoneia. Villius fails to penetrate.
	May	Flamininus succeeds Villius: also held up for 40 days.
	June	Aous conference. (June 25th) Battle of Aous Pass. Philip retires into Thessaly.
	July	Philip plunders his way to Tempe. Aetolian and Athamanian raids in Thessaly. Flamininus stays in Epirus.
	May–Sept.	Naval campaign in Aegean; L. Flamininus goes to Cenchreae.

198	August	Flamininus advances into Thessaly. Phaloria and Aeginium taken. Revictualling from Ambracia.
	September	Siege of Atrax. Philip behind Tempe. Flamininus marches into Phocis. Elatea holds out.
	October	Conference of Sicyon. Achaea joins the Romans. Siege of Corinth unsuccessful. Argos goes over to Macedon. Fall of Elatea: rising at Opus calling in Flamininus: ambassador from Philip.
	November	Conference of Locris. Two months' truce. Orestis revolts.
	December	Flamininus's command extended. Philip offered harsher terms, which he rejects. Villius and Sulpicius appointed *legati* in Greece.
197	Winter	Philip's arrangement with Nabis; Nabis takes Argos.
	Feb./Mar.	Conference of Mycenae: Nabis joins Rome, and a four months' armistice between Achaea and Sparta is arranged.
	March	Philip mobilises and reaches Dium at the equinox. Flamininus seizes Thebes: Attalus has a stroke there, and is taken home to die.
	Mar./Apr.	Flamininus advances from Elatea to Heraclea (Aetolian meeting), then to Xyniae.
	Late April	Flamininus fails to take Phthiotic Thebes; waits for allies.
	May/June	Philip descends to near Pherae.
	June	Battle of Cynoscephalae. Philip rallies at Gonnus; burns papers in Larisa. Obtains permission to send an embassy to Flamininus at Larisa.
	Mar./June	L. Flamininus takes over Acarnania, after the storming of Leucas. Achaean victory at Nemean brook. Rhodian success at Alabanda against Macedonian forces. Antiochus's advance towards Hellespont, with Rhodian collaboration. No records of war at sea.
	Summer	Conference at Gonnus. Philip given four months' truce. Demetrius sent to Rome. Other embassies to Rome arranged.
	July/Aug.	Philip defeats an invasion of Dardanians at Stobi, and returns to Thessalonica.
	December	Senate ratifies peace: senatorial commission of ten appointed. Flamininus winters at Elatea: Philip returns Boeotians serving with him.
196	Winter	Brachylles elected Boeotarch: murdered by Aetolians. Reprisals against Romans. Invasion of Boeotia by Flamininus. Affair settled.
	Early Spring	Ten commissioners arrive at Elatea with S.C.
	Spring	Council of Corinth. Philip evacuates the 'Fetters'.
	June/July	Isthmia. Declaration of freedom. Council of Corinth continues through summer.
	September	Cn. Cornelius meets Philip at Tempe. Philip sends to Rome to ask for an alliance. Cornelius

196		at the Aetolian assembly at Thermum, at the equinox.
	October	Council of Lysimacheia. Roman commissioners interview Antiochus. Rumour of Epiphanes's death. Antiochus returns to Syria and sends envoys to Flamininus. Question of Nabis referred back to Senate. Ten commissioners return to Rome (except Sulpicius and Villius).
	December	Flamininus's command renewed: question of Nabis referred back to him. Winter spent in reorganisation.
195	Spring	Flamininus at Corinth. Antiochus's envoys dismissed. War declared on Nabis. Argos resists. Laconia invaded.
	Spring/ Summer	Nabis defeated. Laconia ravaged. Gytheum taken from the sea. Conference with Nabis: terms rejected by Nabis. Attack on Sparta. Nabis capitulates, and is granted terms. Maritime towns under Achaea. Argos rises.
	Autumn	Nemea held late. Argos declared free and rejoins the Achaean League. Antiochus, returning from another invasion of Thrace to Ephesus, is joined by Hannibal.
	Nov./Dec.	Senate decides to evacuate Greece. Flamininus spends winter establishing Roman influence in the cities.
194	Spring	Council at Corinth: Acrocorinth handed over.
	Summer	Flamininus goes via Chalcis and Thessaly to rejoin his troops at Oricus. Antiochus again in Thrace.
	Autumn	The Romans leave Greece. Triumph of Flamininus.
194/3	Winter	Many embassies at Rome. Philip given guarantees about his son, and perhaps Demetrias. Antiochus's envoys given a kind of ultimatum.
193	Spring	Antiochus at Ephesus. Hannibal's plan. Ariston sent to Carthage. Aetolian assembly at Naupactus. Nicander sent to Philip, Damocritus to Nabis and Dicaearchus to Antiochus.
	Summer	Nabis attacks the coastal towns. Scipio's mission to Carthage. Embassy to Antiochus. Conference of Apamea. Conference of Ephesus.
	Autumn	Return of Roman embassy. Antiochus's council of war. Dicaearchus urges war, stating that Philip was supporting Aetolia. Hannibal temporarily out of favour.
	Nov./Dec.	Roman elections. Atilius and Baebius, the praetors, transferred to the command of the fleet and Macedon, and Bruttium respectively. Arrival of the Roman embassy from Antiochus eases the situation.
192	Winter	Sudden panic at Rome. War measures. Flamininus sent to Greece.
	February	Achaeans declare war on Nabis; Achaean naval defeat off Gytheum (besieged by Nabis); fall of Gytheum; Nabis defeated at Mt Barbosthenes.

192	March	Siege of Sparta.
	Feb./Mar.	Flamininus and his colleagues arrive and visit various places; they expel Eurylochus at Demetrias; are insulted at the Panaetolicum. Aetolians decide to call in Antiochus. Flamininus compels termination of siege of Sparta.
	Spring–Summer	Aetolians recover Demetrias: murder Nabis, but are driven out of Sparta (which Philopoemen annexes to the Achaean League); fail to take Chalcis.
	Sept./Oct.	Roman elections held early. Antiochus besieging Smyrna, Lampsacus and Alexandria Troas. Thoas sent to persuade him to cross over to Greece.
	End of Oct.	Antiochus crosses to Europe. Lands at Pteleum, taken to Demetrias. Aetolian meeting at Lamia.
	Oct./Nov.	Baebius crosses to Epirus.
	November	First expedition against Chalcis. Achaeans declare war on Antiochus and Aetolians. Anti-Roman party put down by Flamininus at Athens. Boeotia non-committal. Cato visits various towns.
	December	Second attack on Chalcis. Romans defeated at Delium. Euboea joins Antiochus; so too Boeotia. War declared on Antiochus by Rome.
191	January	Antiochus's conference at Demetrias. Joint attack on Thessaly. Philip of Megalopolis buries the dead at Cynoscephalae. Philip meets Baebius in Dassaretia: agreement for joint action. App. Claudius sent to Larisa. His arrival checks rapid Syrian and Aetolian successes.
	Jan. 27th	(or Jan. 4th) Acilius at Brundisium.
	February	Romans cross to Epirus. Antiochus in winter quarters at Chalcis.
	March	Antiochus's Acarnanian expedition. Philip and Baebius operating in Thessaly; joined at Limnaeum by Acilius.
	April	Philip of Megalopolis taken at Pellinaeum. Philip gets possession of Athamania. Advance south of Acilius.
	April 24th	Battle of Thermopylae. Flight of Antiochus to Asia.
	May	Acilius visits Chalcis.
	June	Acilius besieges Heraclea, Philip Lamia. (Meanwhile Philip has perhaps made acquisitions on the Malian coast road.)
	July	Fall of Heraclea. Aetolians granted armistice. Philip forced to withdraw from Lamia. Nicander taken by Philip and released. Negotiations break down. Aetolians rally at Naupactus. Philopoemen settles incipient trouble at Sparta.
	Aug./Sept.	Two months' siege of Naupactus. Philip recovers coast road, Dolopia, Aperantia and much of Perrhaebia. Flamininus makes Messenia join Achaean League, but vetoes League acquisition of Zacynthus. Livius at Delos: Etesian winds.

191	September	Battle of Corycus. Phocaea garrisoned. Livius goes into winter quarters near Pergamum. Siege of Naupactus raised. Aetolians given truce.
	Autumn	Acilius spends autumn and winter at Delphi.
	Nov./Dec.	Philip's envoys at Rome. Demetrius restored, and remission of tribute promised. Aetolians offered terms, which they reject.
190	Feb./Mar.	Aetolians fortify Corax.
	Mar./Apr.	Acilius sacks Lamia, and blockades Amphissa. Naval activity off Hellespont. Syrian success: Pausistratus, the Rhodian admiral, defeated and killed.
	March 18th	Scipios marshal at Brundisium and cross over. Regillus takes over fleet from Livius: Livius's Lycian expedition.
	April	Scipios march to Amphissa. Six months' armistice with Aetolia arranged.
	May	Scipios set out for Hellespont. Gracchus's visit to Philip. Help and volunteers from Philip.
	May–July	Asia Minor: activity near Pergamum and at sea indecisive.
	August	Scipios in Macedon. Philip's tribute cancelled. Battle of Side: Eudamus defeats Hannibal. Antiochus prevented from getting help of Prusias.
	September	Battle of Myonnesus. Antiochus evacuates Lysimacheia. Regillus takes Phocaea and sends part of his fleet to the Hellespont.
	October	Scipio hears of Myonnesus, while near Aenus and Maronea. Scipio at Lysimacheia.
	Oct. 25th–Nov. 22nd	(Or Nov. 16/17th–Dec. 14/15th) Army delayed at Hellespont for Scipio. Antiochus's offer rejected.
190 or 189	December or January	Battle of Magnesia: defeat of Antiochus.
189	Winter	Preliminary settlement with Antiochus: Eumenes leaves for Rome. Aetolian envoys rebuffed at Rome and expelled from Italy. Philip expelled from Athamania by Amynander: first the Macedonian garrisons are ejected, then Philip's relieving expedition from Gomphi defeated. Amynander sends news of his success to Scipio at Ephesus.
	Jan./Feb.	Aetolians recover Amphilochia and Aperantia; then Dolopia. Embassies sent to Rome.
	Feb./Mar.	Aetolian embassy captured by pirates. Damoteles only gets as far as Leucas.
	April/May	Fulvius Nobilior at Apollonia: decision to besiege Ambracia. Q. Fabius fixes Philip's boundaries west of Aenus and Maronea.
	Summer	Siege of Ambracia. Perseus recovers Dolopia and besieges Amphilochian Argos; retires before Aetolians. Aetolians eventually granted terms.
	Autumnal equinox	Ambracia surrenders. Fulvius bought off from sacking it.

189	Autumn	Philip's envoys at Rome to complain of his losses. Aetolians given peace, Cephallenia excepted.
	October	Siege of Same begins. Anti-Achaean rising at Sparta.
	November	Fulvius leaves for Rome for elections. Achaea declares war on Sparta.
	December	At the end of the month Fulvius returns to Same.
188	Jan./Feb.	Same capitulates: Fulvius comes to Peloponnese.
	February	Achaean meetings at Argos and Elis. Achaean and Spartan embassies sent to Rome.
	April	Achaean invasion of Sparta: Sparta reorganised by Philopoemen.
	Summer	Council at Apamea to settle affairs of Asia.
	Autumn	Manlius's return through Thrace and Macedon: attacks by Thracian tribes. Manlius winters at Apollonia.
187	Spring	Manlius and Fulvius both reach Rome. Philip seizes Aenus and Maronea sometime this year. Policy of removing and exchanging populations begun.
186		Philip busy reorganising Macedon: taxes, mines, population, settlement of Thracians. Perhaps some increase of power in Thessaly, Magnesia and Athamania.
185	Winter	Complaints against Philip at Rome. Senate decides to send out a commission.
	Spring	Negotiations at Tempe. Accusations and Philip's reply. Frontiers restricted.
	May/June	Negotiations at Thessalonica. Decision on Aenus and Maronea withheld.
	July/Aug.	Roman commission at the Argive Nemea.
184	Winter	More embassies at Rome. Decision to send another commission.
	Jan./Feb.	Massacre at Maronea.
	Spring	Appius Claudius visits Philip in Macedon. Cassander to be sent to Rome, but dies in Epirus.
	Summer	Philip helps Byzantium against the Thracians, and takes Amadocus prisoner. He sends messengers to the Danube tribes.
183	Winter	Embassies at Rome from Pergamum and Philip's enemies. Demetrius, Apelles and Philocles sent to reply. Favourable reply as a concession to Demetrius: Flamininus tampers with Demetrius's loyalty (?).
	Spring	Unpopularity of Demetrius in Macedon. Arrival of commission under Q. Marcius. Aenus and Maronea evacuated.
	Summer	Philip's Thracian expedition against Odrysae, Bessi and Dentheleti. Philippopolis garrisoned. Haemus valley controlled. Perseis founded near Stobi.
	Autumn	Philip now concentrates on a policy of exchanging populations between Paeonia and the seacoast towns. Conspiracy of Samus (?).

182	Winter	Further Macedonian envoys at Rome. Philip imprisons the children of those executed, particularly in the Samus conspiracy. The Theoxena story. Growing influence of Perseus.
	Spring	Return of envoys from Bastarnae: offer of a princess in marriage to Perseus.
	Mar./April	Purification of Macedonian army. Quarrel between Perseus and Demetrius. First trial of Demetrius.
	Summer	Perhaps Perseus's marriage to the Dardanian princess.
	Autumn	Philip decides to send Apelles and Philocles to Rome.
181	Winter	Apelles and Philocles at Rome.
	Spring/ Summer	Philip's Thracian expedition from Stobi against the Maedi. Ascent of Haemus. Demetrius sent home.
	July	Dentheleti plundered and Petra taken. Letters from Didas on Demetrius's plan for flight. Herodorus imprisoned.
	Autumn	Arrival of Apelles and Philocles with letters purporting to be from Flamininus. Herodorus tortured to death.
	Winter	Perseus again accuses Demetrius.
180	Spring/ Summer	Philip leaves Pella for Demetrias. Perseus sent to Amphipolis, Demetrius to Astraeum with Didas. Demetrius murdered at Heraclea in Pelagonia.
180/79	Winter	Philip at Demetrias. Influence of Antigonus, son of Echecrates. Remorse for Demetrius's death.
179	Spring	Philocles and Apelles proved guilty by a slave under torture. Philocles executed, Apelles flees to Italy.
	Summer	Perseus in Thrace. Philip tours his kingdom with Antigonus. Visits Thessalonica. Dies at Amphipolis.
	Autumn	Invasion of Bastarnae over Danube. Owing to Philip's death the movement achieves little. Perseus has Antigonus put to death, and sends envoys to Rome to renew friendship.

List of Abbreviations 349

The following abbreviations have been used in the text and bibliography to refer to journals, standard reference works, etc.

Abh. Bay. Ak.	Abhandlung der Bayerischen Akademie der Wissenschaft.
AE.	Ἀρχαιολογικὴ Ἐφημερίς.
Aegyptus	Aegyptus: Rivista italiana di egittologia e di papirologia.
AJA.	American Journal of Archaeology.
AJPh.	American Journal of Philology.
Am. Hist. Rev.	American Historical Review.
Arch. Anz.	Archäologischer Anzeiger (in Jahrbuch des deutschen archäologischen Instituts).
Ἀρχ. Δελτ.	Ἀρχαιολογικὸν Δελτίον.
Arch. Pap.	Archiv für Papyrusforschung.
Arch. Rel.	Archiv für Religionswissenschaft.
Athen.	Athenaeum: Studii periodici di letteratura e storia dell' antichità.
Ἀθηνᾶ	Ἀθηνᾶ. Σύγγραμμα τῆς ἐν Ἀθήναις ἐπιστημονικῆς ἑταιρείας.
Ath. Mitt.	Mitteilungen des deutschen arch. Institutes (Athenische Abteilung).
Att. Acc. Torino	Atti della R. Accademia delle scienze di Torino.
BCH.	Bulletin de correspondance hellénique.
Berlin S.B.	Sitzungsberichte d. preuss. Akademie d. Wissenschaften zu Berlin.
BMI.	Ancient Greek Inscriptions in the British Museum.
BPW.	Berliner Philologische Wochenschrift.
BSA.	Annual of the British School at Athens.
Bull. Ryl. Lib.	Bulletin of the John Rylands Library, Manchester.
Bursian	Bursian's Jahresbericht über die Fortschritte der klassischen Altertumswissenschaft.
CAH.	Cambridge Ancient History.
CHJ.	Cambridge Historical Journal.
Chron. d'Égypte	Chronique d'Égypte. Bulletin périodique de la fondation égyptologique Reine Elisabeth, Bruxelles.
CIL.	Corpus Inscriptionum Latinarum.
CP.	Classical Philology.
CQ.	Classical Quarterly.
CW.	Classical Weekly.
Dess.	Dessau's Inscriptiones Latinae Selectae.
Ἑλληνικά	Ἑλληνικά, ἱστορικὸν περιοδικὸν δημοσίευμα.
Eos	Eos. Commentarii Societatis Philologae Polonorum.
FD.	Fouilles de Delphes.
FGH.	F. Jacoby's Fragmente der griechischen Historiker.
FHG.	C. Müller's Fragmenta Historicorum Graecorum.
FOA.	Kiepert's Formae Orbis Antiqui.
GDI.	Collitz's Sammlung der griechischen Dialektinschriften.
GGA.	Göttingische Gelehrte Anzeigen.
Gnomon	Gnomon: Kritische Zeitschrift für die gesamte klassische Altertumswissenschaft.
Gött. Nach.	Nachrichten von der k. Gesellschaft der Wissenschaften zu Göttingen. Phil.-hist. Klasse.
Harv. Stud.	Harvard Studies in Classical Philology.
Hermathena	Hermathena: a series of papers on Literature, Science and Philosophy by members of Trinity College, Dublin.
Hermes	Hermes: Zeitschrift für klassische Philologie.
Hesperia	Hesperia. Journal of the American School of Classical Studies at Athens.

Hist. Gr. Epig.	Hiller v. Gaertringen's Historische griechische Epigramme.
Historia	Historia. Studi storici per l'antichità classica, Milano.
HThR.	Harvard Theological Review.
HZ.	Historische Zeitschrift.
IG.	Inscriptiones Graecae.
IG².	Inscriptiones Graecae: editio minor.
Insc. Cos	Paton and Hicks's Inscriptions of Cos.
Insc. Magn.	Kern's Inschriften von Magnesia a. Maeander (Berlin, 1900).
Jahresh.	Jahreshefte d. österr. archäol. Instituts in Wien.
JEA.	Journal of Egyptian Archaeology.
JHS.	Journal of Hellenic Studies.
Journ. Sav.	Journal des savants.
JRGS.	Journal of the Royal Geographical Society.
JRS.	Journal of Roman Studies.
Klio	Klio: Beiträge zur alten Geschichte.
LEC.	Les études classiques.
Leipz. Stud.	Leipziger Studien zur classischen Philologie.
Mem. Acc. Torino	Memorie della R. Accademia delle scienze di Torino.
Mnem.	Mnemosyne: Bibliotheca Classica Batava.
NC.	Numismatic Chronicle and Journal of the Numismatic Society.
N. Jahrb. f. Ant.	Neue Jahrbücher für Antike u. deutsche Bildung.
N. Jahrb. f. Phil.	Neue Jahrbücher für Philologie.
N. J. Kl. Alt.	Neue Jahrbücher f. d. klassische Altertum.
OGIS.	Dittenberger's Orientis Graeci Inscriptiones Selectae.
Philol.	Philologus: Zeitschrift für das klassische Altertum.
Phil. Woch.	Philologische Wochenschrift.
Πρακτικά	Πρακτικὰ τῆς ἐν Ἀθήναις ἀρχαιολογικῆς ἑταιρείας.
P-W.	Pauly-Wissowa-Kroll's Real-Encyclopädie der classischen Altertumswissenschaft.
REA.	Revue des études anciennes.
REG.	Revue des études grecques.
Rend. Linc.	Rendiconti della R. Accademia dei Lincei.
Rend. Lomb.	Rendiconti del R. Istituto Lombardo di scienze e lettere.
Rev. Arch.	Revue archéologique.
Rev. Belge	Revue belge de philologie et d'histoire, Bruxelles.
Rev. Hist.	Revue historique.
Rev. Num.	Revue numismatique.
Rev. Phil.	Revue de philologie, de littérature et d'histoire anciennes.
Rhein. Mus.	Rheinisches Museum für Philologie.
Riv. Fil.	Rivista di filologia.
Riv. Stor. Ant.	Rivista di storia antica.
Studi di stor. ant.	Beloch's Studi di storia antica.
Studi storici	Pais's Studi storici per l'antichità classica.
Syll.	Dittenberger's Sylloge Inscriptionum Graecarum, 3rd edition.
TAPhA.	Transactions and Proceedings of the American Philological Association.
Wien. Anz.	Anzeiger d. Akad. d. Wissenschaften in Wien: Phil.-hist. Klasse.
Wien. S.B.	Sitzungsberichte d. Akad. d. Wissenschaften in Wien.
ZDOeA.	Zeitschrift des deutschen und österreichischen Alpenvereins.
ZN.	Zeitschrift für Numismatik.

Bibliography

SOURCES[1]

(a) PROSE AUTHORS

Polybius (ed. Büttner-Wobst): relevant parts of Books II–V; VII–XI; XIII–XVI; XVIII; XX–XXIII; XXV.
Livy[2] (ed. Weissenborn-Müller): relevant parts of Books XXIII–XL.
Diodorus Siculus: fragments of Books XXVI–XXX.
Justinus: Books XXVIII–XXXII (with the *Prologi* of Trogus Pompeius).
Plutarch: Lives of *Aratus* (ch. 47–end), *Philopoemen, Flamininus, Aemilius Paullus* (ch. 8–9) and *Cato Maior* (ch. 12–14); *Moralia*, 53 E, 197 C, 245 C, 760 A.
Appian: fragments of *Macedonica*, 1–10, *Syriaca*, 1–46, *Illyrica*, 8.
Pausanias: I, 36, 5–6; II, 8, 4–9, 5; III, 24, 6; IV, 29, 1 *seq.*; VI, 16, 3; VII, 7, 3–8, 7; 17, 5; VIII, 8, 11; 50, 4 *seq.*; X, 33, 3; 34, 3–4.
Cassius Dio Cocceianus: fragments of Book XVII (57, 57; 57, 77; 58, 1–4); Book XVIII (60); Book XIX (62).
Zonaras: VIII, 20 to IX, 22.
Strabo: VII, 5, 1, C. 312–13; 7, 9, C. 327; VIII, 4, 8, C. 361; XII, 4, 3, C. 563; XIV, 2, 5, C. 652–3.
Polyaenus: *Strat.* IV, 18, 1; 18, 2; V, 17 (2); VI, 17.
Frontinus: *Strat.* I, 4, 6; II, 7, 4; 13, 8; III, 8, 1; 9, 8 (?).
[Auctor] *de viris illustribus*: 51; 54, 1.
Sallust: *Hist. lib.* IV, fr. 69 (Maurenbrecher) = *Epist. Mithr.* 5–7.
Cicero: *Pro Balbo*, 16, 35.
Florus: I, 23–5.
Aelian: *V.H.* XII, 43.
Orosius: IV, 20, 1–3; 5–7; 27–8; 34–5.
Eutropius: III, 12; 13; 14; IV, 1; 2; 3.
Ampelius: *Lib. mem.* XVI, 3.
Johannes Antioch.: fragments 54; 56 (*FHG*, IV, 558).
Valerius Maximus: IV, 8, 5; V, 2, 6.
Hieronymus: *in Daniel.* 11, 11 *seq.*
Tacitus: *Annals*, IV, 8, 5.
Timachidas: *Lindian Temple Chronicle*, XLII (ed. Blinkenberg, *Bulletin de l'académie royale des sciences et des lettres de Danemark*, 1912, pp. 317–457; cf. *Die lindische Tempelchronik* (Lietzmann's *Kl. Texte*, no 131), Bonn, 1915).
Pliny: *N.H.* IV, 8, 30.
Photius: *Bibl.* 176, p. 121 *a*, 35.
Stephanus of Byzantium: Προῦσα. Μύρλεια.
Clement of Alexandria: *Strom.* VI, ii, 19, 1.
Suidas: Φίλιππος.
Phlegon of Tralles: Περὶ θαυμασίων, III (*FGH*, II B, 257, F. 36, III).[3]

---

[1] Excluding chapter I, the sources for which will be found in the footnotes.
[2] Livy's sources are indicated thus: (P)=Polybius; (A)=Annalist(s).
[3] [Auctor] *ad Herenn.* IV, 68, is not to be regarded as a historical reminiscence (as is claimed by Münzer, *Philol.* LXXXIX, 1934, 215 *seq.*).

(b) Verse Authors

Alcaeus of Messene: *Anth. Pal.* VII, 238 (?); 247; IX, 518–19; XI, 12; appendix, XVI, 5–6.
Samus: *Anth. Pal.* VI, 114–16.
Philippus V rex: *Anth. Pal.* IX, 520 (?), appendix, XVI, 26 B.
Sibylline Oracle, apud Pausan. VII, 8, 8–9.
Ennius: fragments 326 *s*, 329, 334 (Vahlen²).
Lycophron: *Alexandra*, 1446–50 (cf. Ziegler, *P-W*, 'Lykophron', cols. 2354–81).[1]

(c) Inscriptions

The most important inscriptions of the period will be found (though not always in their latest editions) in Ditt. *Syll.* 518–636. Detailed references are given in the footnotes. In addition the following inscriptions particularly concern Philip:

Hesperia, V, 1936, pp. 424–5; 427 (ed. Meritt).
Ath. Mitt. LI, 1926, 28 (ed. Klaffenbach).
Oikonomos, Ἐπιγραφαὶ τῆς Μακεδονίας, I, 1915, 2–7; cf. Bikerman, *Rev. Phil.* LXV, 1939, 348–9.
Ἑλληνικά, VII, 1934, 177–208 (ed. Kougeas).
Rev. Arch. III⁶, 1934, 39 *seq.* (ed. Roussel; cf. De Sanctis, *Riv. Fil.* LXII, 1934, 515); *ibid.* VI⁶, 1935, 29–68 (ed. Feyel).
GDI, 1969; 1983; 2125; 3750 (=Hicks, 182).
AE, 1913, 40, no. 170 (ed. Arvanitopullos).
OGIS, 237, 283, 284.
Inscriptions de Délos, 361, line 21; 363, line 29; 366, lines 59, 62, 82, 83, 86, 87.
See also the list of letters and διαγράμματα of Philip, above, p. 288, n. 1.

MODERN WORKS[2]

Altheim, F. *Epochen der römischen Geschichte*, Bd. II: *Weltherrschaft und Krise.* Frankfurt, 1935. pp. 1–148.
Arci, F. *Studi di stor. ant.* II, 1893, 141–55. 'Il Peloponneso al tempo della guerra sociale (220–17 a.C.).'
Arvanitopullos, A. S. Ἀρχ. Δελτ. I, 1915, 57 *seq.* (On cemetery at Demetrias.)
—— Πρακτικά, 1912, 186–9. (On cemetery at Demetrias.)
—— *AE*, 1913, 43–6. 'Θεσσαλικαὶ ἐπιγραφαί: ἐπιγραφαὶ Γόννων, nos. 173–4.'
—— Γραπταὶ στῆλαι Δημητριάδος-Παγασῶν. Athens, 1928.
Aymard, A. *REA*, XXX, 1928, 1–62. 'Les stratèges de la confédération achéenne de 202 à 172 av. J.-C.'

---

[1] S. Schebelev, *Comptes rendus de l'Ac. des Sciences de l'U.R.S.S.*, 1929, 193–200 (in Russian: report by E. Bickermann, *Phil. Woch.* 1930, 242), suggests that the Paean of Isyllus (*IG*, IV², 1, 128, lines 57 *seq.*; cf. J. U. Powell, *Collectanea Alexandrina*, 134, lines 62 *seq.*) refers to Philip V's invasion of Laconia in 218, and that Philip intended to expel Lycurgus from the throne: but the *communis opinio* follows Wilamowitz, *Isyllos v. Epidauros*, Berlin, 1886, in referring the Paean to Philip II's march on Sparta in 338.

[2] Where there is more than one work under an author's name, the use of the name alone in footnotes is to be taken as referring to the first in the list For references in Appendix II see p. 289, n. 1.

Aymard, G. *Mélanges Glotz* (Paris, 1932), 49–73. 'À propos d'une assemblée achaienne (L'assemblée d'Argos: début de 188 av. J.-C.).'
—— *REA*, xxxv, 1933, 445–62. 'Une hypothèse nouvelle sur les assemblées achaiennes.'
—— *REA*, xxxviii, 1936, 265–6, review of Treves's 'Antigono Dosone'.
—— *Les assemblées de la confédération achaienne*. Bordeaux, 1938.
—— *Les premiers rapports de Rome et de la confédération achaienne* (198–89 av. J.-C.). Bordeaux, 1938.
Bauer, E. *Untersuchungen zur Geographie und Geschichte der nordw. Landschaften Griechenlands*. Diss. Halle, 1907.
Beloch, K. J. *Griechische Geschichte*², IV, 1 and 2. Berlin-Leipzig, 1925–7.
—— *Die Bevölkerung der gr.-rom. Welt*. Leipzig, 1886.
—— *Riv. Stor. Ant.* VI, 1901, 1–8. 'La madre di Perseo.'
—— *Hermes*, LVII, 1922, 119 *seq.* 'Die Sonnenfinsternis des Ennius und der vorjulianische Kalender.'
—— *Klio*, XXII, 1929, 464 *seq.* 'Der römische Kalender, Varr. 565 und 566 (189 v. Chr.).'
—— *Klio*, XV, 1918, 382 *seq.* 'Der römische Kalender von 218–168.'
—— *Hermes*, XXXII, 1897, 667–72. 'ΑΙΤΩΛΙΚΑ.'
Benecke, H. *Die Seepolitik der Aitoler*. Diss. Hamburg, 1934.
Benecke, P. V. M. *CAH*, VIII, 1930, 241 *seq.* (ch. 8). 'The fall of the Macedonian Monarchy.' With bibliography, pp. 758–9.
Béquignon, Y. *BCH*, LII, 1928, 444–65. 'La retraite de Philippe V en 198 et l'invasion étolienne en Thessalie.'
—— (cf. *ibid.* 22–8, 'Le champ de bataille de Pharsale' for the problem of Palaepharsalus.)
—— *BCH*, LVI, 1932, 89–191. 'Études thessaliennes.'
—— *La vallée du Spercheios des origines au* IVe *siècle*. Paris, 1937.
Bergk, Th. *Philol.* XLII, 1884, 228–65. 'Die Liste der delphischen Gastfreunde.'
Berve, H. *Das Alexanderreich auf prosopographischer Grundlage*. 2 vols. München, 1926.
Bettingen, W. *König Antigonos Doson von Makedonien* (229–220 v. Chr.). Diss. Jena, 1912.
Bevan, E. R. *The House of Seleucus*. London, 1902.
—— *A History of Egypt under the Ptolemaic Dynasty*. London, 1927.
Bickermann, E. *Gnomon*, VII, 1931, 54–6, review of Horn's 'Foederati'.
—— *Hermes*, LXVII, 1932, 47–76. 'Bellum Antiochicum.'
—— *Philol.* LXXXVII, 1932, 277–99. 'Rom und Lampsakos.'
—— *Rev. Phil.* LXI, 1935, 55 *seq.*; 161 *seq.* 'Les préliminaires de la seconde guerre de Macédoine.'
—— *REA*, XXXVIII, 1936, 96; review of Zancan's 'Monarcato ellenistico'.
—— *See* Schebelev, S.
[Bikerman, E.] *Rev. Phil.* LXIV, 1938, 295–313. 'Διάγραμμα.'
—— *Institutions des Séleucides*. Paris, 1938.
—— *REA*, LX, 1938, 369–83. 'Sur les batailles navales de Cos et d'Andros.'
—— *Rev. Phil.* LXV, 1939, 335–49. 'La cité grecque dans les monarchies hellénistiques.' (Review of Heuss, *Stadt u. Herrscher*.)
—— *Chron. d'Égypte*, XXIX, 1940, 124–31. 'L'avènement de Ptolémée V Épiphane.'
Bilco, J. *BCH*, VI, 1882, 171–5. 'Lettre du roi Philippe aux habitants d'Abae.'
Boethius, A. *Der argivische Kalender*. Upsala, 1922.
Boguth, W. *M. Valerius Laevinus. Ein Beitrag zur Geschichte des zweiten punischen Krieges*. Progr. Krems, 1892.
Bouché-Leclercq, A. *Histoire des Lagides*. Paris, 1903–7.
—— *Histoire des Séleucides*. Paris, 1913.

Bruns, I. *Die Persönlichkeit in der Geschichtsschreibung der Alten.* Berlin, 1898.
Buckler, W. H. *JHS*, XXXVII, 1917, 110. 'Lydian records, no. 23.'
Busolt, G. See Swoboda, H.
Büttner-Wobst, Th. *Beiträge zu Polybios.* Dresden, 1901.
Carcopino, J. *Points de vue sur l'impérialisme romain.* Paris, 1934. Chapter on 'Les débuts de l'impérialisme romain et le livre d'Holleaux', pp. 21–69 (*Journ. Sav.* 1923, pp. 112–21, 173–81; 1924, pp. 16–30).
Cardinali, G. *Il regno di Pergamo.* Rome, 1906.
—— *Riv. Fil.* XXXIII, 1905, 519–51. 'La guerra di Litto.'
—— *Riv. Fil.* XXXV, 1907, 1–32. 'Creta nel tramonto dell' Ellenismo.'
—— *Riv. Fil.* XXXIX, 1911, 1 *seq.* 'Lo Pseudo-Filippo.'
Cary, M. *A History of the Greek World from 323 to 146.* London, 1932.
—— *Mélanges Glotz* (Paris, 1932). 'Sources of silver for the Greek world.' Pp. 133–42.
—— (with Warmington, E.) *The Ancient Greek Explorers.* London, 1929.
Casson, S. *Macedonia, Thrace and Illyria.* Oxford, 1926.
Cavaignac, E. *Histoire de l'antiquité*, vol. III. Paris, 1914.
——*Rev. Phil.* XXXIII, 1909, 179–82. 'Sur un passage de la lettre de Philippe aux Lariséens.'
—— *Klio*, XIV, 1914, 37–42. 'La chronologie romaine de 215 à 168.'
—— *Rev. Phil.* XXXIX, 1915, 1 *seq.*; 21 *seq.* 'Quelques remarques sur l'historicité de Tite-Live.'
—— *REG*, XXXVII, 1924, 164 *seq.* 'Le calendrier romain vers 198.'
—— *Rev. Phil.* L, 1926, 103–9. 'Sur l'économie de l'histoire de Polybe d'après Tite-Live.'
—— *Mélanges Thomas* (Bruges, 1930), pp. 120–31. 'Fulvius Nobilior en Grèce (189 av. J.-C.).'
Clementi, G. *Studi di stor. ant.* I, 1891, 51–79. 'La guerra annibalica in Oriente.'
Colin, G. *Rome et la Grèce de 200 à 146 av. J.-C.* Paris, 1905.
Conway, R. S. *Bull. Ryl. Lib.* X, 1926, 309–39. 'A Graeco-Roman Tragedy.'
Corradi, G. *Riv. Fil.* XXXVII, 1909, 373–9. 'Sulla data della nascità di Filippo V.'
—— *Studi ellenistici.* Torino, 1929.
Costanzi, V. *Studi storici*, I, 1908, 31–45; II, 1909, 214–230. 'Sulla cronologia della prima guerra macedonica.'
—— *Studi storici*, I, 1908, 420–42. 'Le relazioni degli Etoli coi Romani dopo la pace di Fenice.'
—— *Klio*, XI, 1911, 277–83. 'Il dominio egiziano nelle Cicladi sotto Tolomeo Filopatore.'
—— *Athen.* VIII, 1930, 157–67. 'Sulla costituzione macedonica.'
Cousin, G. (with Holleaux, M.). *BCH*, XXVIII, 1904, 345; 353 (nos. 1–3). 'Inscriptions du sanctuaire de Zeus Panamaros.'
Culmann, P. *Die römische Orientgesandschaft vom Jahre 201–200.* Diss. Giessen, 1922.
Curtius, E. *Peloponnesos*, vols. I–II. Gotha, 1851–2.
Daux, G. *Delphes au IIe et au Ier siècle depuis l'abaissement de l'Étolie jusqu'à la paix romaine, 191–31 av. J.-C.* Paris, 1936.
—— *BCH*, LVIII, 1934, 157–67. 'Sosthenis.'
Degen, E. *Kritische Ausführungen zur Geschichte Antiochos des Grossen.* Diss. Zürich, 1918.
Deiters, P. *Rhein. Mus.* LIX, 1904, 565 *seq.* 'Zwei kretische Inschriften aus Magnesia.'
Delamarre, J. *Rev. Phil.* XXVI, 1902, 301–25. 'L'influence macédonienne dans les Cyclades au IIIe siècle av. J.-C.'

Delbrück, H. *Geschichte der Kriegskunst im Rahmen der politischen Geschichte.* Ed. 3. Vol. I. Berlin, 1920.
De Sanctis, G. *Storia dei Romani,* Vols. III, 2, and IV, I. Torino, 1917–23.
—— *Att. Acc.* Torino, LVII, 1921–2, 242–9. 'Una lettera degli Scipioni.'
—— *Compte-rendu du Ve Congrès international des sciences historiques,* Bruxelles, 1923, 464. 'La date d'une dédicace du roi Philippe V à Délos.'
—— *Enciclopedia Italiana,* vol. XV, 1932, 313–15. Art. on 'Filippo V di Macedonia'.
—— *Riv. Fil.* LV, 1927, 489–91. 'Sellasia' (accepting 222 B.C.).
—— *Riv. Fil.* LXII, 1934, 108–09. (Note on Agelaus's speech at Naupactus.)
—— *Riv. Fil.* LXII, 1934, 126–7. Review of Passerini's 'Ultimo piano di Annibale.'
—— *Riv. Fil.* LXII, 1934, 515 *seq.* 'Il regolamento militare dei Macedoni.'
—— *Riv. Fil.* LXIII, 1935, 419–20. Note on Hampl's 'König d. Makedonen'.
—— *Riv. Fil.* LXIII, 1935, 420–421. Review of Treves's 'Antigono Dosone'.
—— *Riv. Fil.* LXIV, 1936, 189–203. Review of Haywood's 'Scipio Africanus'.
Desdevises-du-Dezert, Th. *Géographie ancienne de la Macédoine.* Paris, 1862.
Dinsmoor, W. B. *The Archons of Athens in the Hellenistic Age.* Cambridge (Mass.), 1931.
Dittenberger, W. *Hermes,* XXXII, 1897, 161–90. 'Die delphische Amphictionie im Jahre 178 vor Chr.'
Dow, S. (with Edson, C. F. Junr.). *Harv. Stud.* XLVIII, 1937, 127–80. 'Chryseis. A study of the evidence in regard to the mother of Philip V.'
Droysen, J. G. *Geschichte des Hellenismus.* Ed. 2. Gotha, 1877.
Durrbach, F. *BCH,* X, 1886, 111 *seq.* 'Décrets trouvés à Délos.' (Rhodes and the Cyclades at the end of the second century.)
—— *BCH,* XXXV, 1911, 19 n. 'Fouilles de Délos.'
—— *BCH,* XL, 1916, 298–352. 'La chronologie des archontes déliens' (particularly 317–19, on the date of Philip's death).
—— *Choix d'inscriptions de Délos,* I. Paris, 1921. Pp. 71–3.
Edson, C. F. Junr. *HThR,* XXVI, 1933, 324–5. 'Legitimus honor. A note on Hellenistic ruler-worship.'
—— *Harv. Stud.* XLV, 1934, 213–46. 'The Antigonids, Heracles and Beroea.'
—— *CP,* XXIX, 1934, 254–5. 'The personal appearance of Antigonus Gonatas.'
—— *Harv. Stud.* XLVI, 1935, 191–202. 'Perseus and Demetrius.'
—— *See* Dow, S.
Egelhaaf, G. *HZ,* LIII, 1885, 456–64. 'Analekten zur Geschichte des zweiten punischen Krieges. 2. Der Vertrag Hannibals mit Philippos V.'
Ehrenberg, V. *Der griechische und der hellenistische Staat.* Leipzig-Berlin, 1932. Pp. 66 *seq.*
—— *Alexander and the Greeks.* Oxford, 1938. (Particularly chapter I.)
Engers, M. *Mnem.* (third series), VI, 1938, 121–38. 'Die Vorgeschichte der makedonischen Kriege Roms.'
Fellmann, W. *Antigonos Gonatas, König der Makedonen, und die griechischen Staaten.* Diss. Würzburg, 1930.
Ferguson, W. S. *Hellenistic Athens.* London, 1911.
—— *Greek Imperialism.* London, 1913.
—— *Athenian Tribal Cycles.* Harvard, 1932.
—— *Gnomon,* XI, 1935, 518 *seq.*; review of Granier and Hampl, *op. cit. infra.*
Ferrabino, A. *Il problema dell' unità nazionale nella Grecia antica.* I. *Arato di Sicione e l'idea federale.* Florence, 1921.
Feyel, M. *Rev. Arch.* VI[6], 1935, 29–68. 'Un nouveau fragment du règlement militaire trouvé à Amphipolis.'
—— *REA,* XL, 1938, 191; review of Dow-Edson's 'Chryseis.'

Fine, J. V. A. *TAPhA*, LVIII, 1932, 126–55. 'The problem of Macedonian holdings in Epirus and Thessaly in 221.'
—— *CQ*, XXVIII, 1934, 99 *seq*. 'The mother of Philip V of Macedon.'
—— *JRS*, XXVI, 1936, 24–39. 'Macedon, Illyria and Rome, 220–19.'
—— *CW*, XXXII, 1938, 90 *seq*.; review of Flacelière's 'Aitoliens'.
—— *AJPh*, LXI, 1940, 129–65. 'The background of the Social War of 220–17 B.C.'
Flacelière, R. *Les Aitoliens à Delphes: contribution à l'histoire de la Grèce centrale au IIIe siècle av. J.-C.* Paris, 1937.
Flathe, L. *Geschichte Macedoniens und der Reiche, welche von macedonischen Königen beherrscht wurden.* Vol. II. Leipzig, 1834.
Frank, H. *Arch. Pap.* XI, 1935, 1–56. 'Ein Beitrag zur Ptolemäerchronologie des III. Jahr. v. C.' (Particularly 54–6, for Achaean chronology.)
Frank, T. *Roman Imperialism.* New York, 1914.
—— *A History of Rome.* London. No date (1923).
—— *An Economic History of Rome.* Ed. 2. Baltimore, 1927.
—— *Am. Hist. Rev.* XVIII, 1912–13, 233–52. 'Mercantilism and Rome's foreign policy.'
—— *CP*, IV, 1909, 118–38. 'A chapter in the story of Roman Imperialism.'
—— 'Plautus on Anatolian Affairs' in *Anatolian Studies presented to W. H. Buckler.* Manchester, 1939. Pp. 85–8.
Frazer, J. G. *Pausanias' Description of Greece*, I–VI. London, 1898.
Freeman, E. A. *History of Federal Government in Greece and Italy.* Ed. 2 (J. B. Bury). London, 1893.
Fustel de Coulanges, N. D. *Questions historiques.* Paris, 1893. 'Polybe ou la Grèce conquise par les Romains.' Pp. 121–211.
Gaebler, H. *ZN*, XX, 1897, 169–92. 'Die autonome Münzprägung der Makedonen, Amphaxier und Botteaten.'
—— *Die antiken Münzen Nord-Griechenlands.* Vol. III. *Makedonia und Paionia.* Parts 1 and 2. Berlin, 1906–35.
—— *ZN*, XXXVI, 1926, 111–16. 'Der Prägebeginn in Thessalonike.'
—— *ZN*, XXXVI, 1926, 183–98. 'Die Distrikte Doberos und Paroreia. Das mygdonische Apollonia.'
Gelder, H. van. *Geschichte der alten Rhodier.* Haag, 1900.
Geyer, F. *P-W*, article on 'Makedonia' cols. 744–59, for the history of Philip.
—— *P-W*, article on 'Philippus V'.
Gillischewski, H. *De Aetolorum praetoribus inter annos 221 et 168 a.Chr.n. munere functis.* Diss. Berlin, 1896.
Gitti, A. *Rend. Linc.* S. VI, XV, 1939, 189–203. 'I perieci di Sparta e le origini del ΚΟΙΝΟΝ ΤῶΝ ΛΑΚΕΔΑΙΜΟΝΙῶΝ.'
Glotz, G. *REG*, XXIX, 1916, 281–325. 'L'histoire de Délos d'après le prix d'une denrée.'
Graindor, P. *Rev. Belge*, XVIII, 1939, 85–91. 'Coroneia de Phthiotide et Philippe V de Macédoine.'
Granier, F. *Die makedonische Heeresversammlung. Ein Beitrag zum antiken Staatsrecht.* München, 1931. .
Griffith, G. T. *The Mercenaries of the Hellenistic World.* Cambridge, 1935.
—— *CHJ*, V, 1935, 1–14. 'An early motive of Roman imperialism (201 B.C.).'
Groag, E. *Hannibal als Politiker.* Wien, 1929.
Guarducci, M. *Riv. Fil.* LVII, 1929, 74 *seq*. 'Gli Scipioni in una nuova iscrizione cretese ed in altri monumenti dell' epigrafia greca.'
—— *Riv. Fil.* LVIII, 1930, 67 *seq*. 'Demiurgi in Creta.'
Hadas, M. *CW*, XXVI, 1932, 65–8; 73–6. 'The Social Revolution in Third-Century Sparta.' (Mainly deals with Nabis.)

BIBLIOGRAPHY

357

Hallward, B. L. *CAH*, VIII, 1930, 25–115 (ch. 2–4) on the Second Punic War. Bibliography on pp. 721–9.

Hammond, N. G. L. *BSA*, XXXII, 1931–2, 139–47. 'Prehistoric Epirus and the Dorian Invasion. B. The terrain of Epirus and the Pindus routes.'

Hampl, F. *Der König der Makedonen.* (Diss. Leipzig.) Weida-in-Th., 1934.

Haywood, R. M. *Studies on Scipio Africanus.* Baltimore, 1933. Pp. 59 *seq.*

Head, B. V. *Historia Numorum.* Ed. 2. Oxford, 1911.

Heichelheim, F. *Bericht über griechische Staatskunde von* 1902 *bis* 1932, in Bursian's *Jahresberichte*, 1934, 145–287.

—— *Aegyptus*, XVII, 1937, 61–4. 'Zu *Pap. Michigan*, III, 173, und *Hesperia*, V (1936), 419 ff., nr. 15.'

Heiland, P. *Untersuchungen zur Geschichte des Königs Perseus von Makedonien* (179–68). Diss. Jena, 1913. Pp. 7–13; 24–7.

Heitland, W. E. *The Roman Republic.* Ed. 2. Cambridge, 1923.

—— *Agricola.* Cambridge, 1921. Pp. 112–30.

Hellmann, F. *Arch. Rel.* XXIX, 1931, 202–3. 'Zur Lustration des makedonischen Heeres.'

Henne, H. *REA*, XXXVII, 1935, 21–33. 'Chronique papyrologique.' (Particularly 27–9: 'P. Tebt. III, 815, et la date de Sèllasie.')

Hennebig, J. *L'Orient, la Grèce et l'Italie.* Paris, 1935.

Henze, W. *De civitatibus liberis.* Diss. Berlin, 1892.

Herzog, R. *Berlin S.B.* 1901, 470–94. 'Das Heiligtum des Apollo in Halasarna.'

—— *Klio*, II, 1902, 316–33. 'Κρητικὸς πόλεμος.'

—— *Hermes*, LXV, 1930, 465. 'Griechische Königsbriefe.' (On *Syll.* 543.)

Heuss, A. *Die völkerrechtlichen Grundlagen der römischen Aussenpolitik in republikanischer Zeit.* Klio Beiheft XXXI. Leipzig, 1933.

—— *Stadt und Herrscher des Hellenismus in ihren staats- und völkerrechtlichen Beziehungen.* Klio Beiheft XXXIX, Leipzig, 1937.

—— *N. Jahrb. f. Ant.* I, 1938, 337–52. 'Die römische Ostpolitik und die Begründung der römischen Weltherrschaft.'

Heuzey, L. and Daumet, H. *Mission archéologique de Macédoine.* Paris, 1876.

Hicks, E. L. *A Manual of Greek Historical Inscriptions.* Oxford, 1882.

—— See Paton, W. R.

Hill, G. F. *Historical Greek Coins.* London, 1906. Nos. 78–9 (Philip V and Cretans), no. 80 (Athens and Crete in League against Philip V).

Holleaux, M. *Rome, la Grèce et les monarchies hellénistiques au IIIe siècle av. J.-C.* (273–205). Paris, 1921.

—— *BCH*, XVI, 1892, 466. 'Notes d'épigraphie béotienne.'

—— *REG*, X, 1897, 279–308. 'Deux inscriptions trouvées à Kleitor.' (= Vol. I, 231–60.)[1]

—— *REG*, XI, 1898, 251–8. 'Epigraphica II.' (= Vol. II, 43–9.)

—— *REG*, XII, 1899, 20–37. 'Trois décrets de Rhodes.'

—— *REA*, V, 1903, 223–8. 'Curae epigraphicae.'

—— *BCH*, XXVIII, 1904, 346–7; 354–9; nos. 1–3 (with G. Cousin). 'Inscriptions du sanctuaire de Zeus Panamaros.'

—— *BCH*, XXIX, 1905, 362–72. 'Sur les assemblées ordinaires de la ligue aitolienne.' (= Vol. I, 219–27.)

—— *Mélanges Nicole* (Geneva, 1905), 273–9. 'La première expédition d'Antiochos-le-Grand en Koilé-Syrie.' (Sellasia dated 222 B.C.)

---

[1] References in brackets are to the collected edition of Holleaux's works, published as *Études d'épigraphie et d'histoire grecques* (Paris, 1938–), with notes by L. Robert.

Holleaux, M. *BCH*, XXXI, 1907, 96–114. 'Dédicace d'un monument commémoratif de la bataille de Séllasia.'

—— *Klio*, VII, 1907, 294–5. 'Zum Pylaicum concilium: eine Erwiderung.' (=Vol. I, 229–30.)

—— *BCH*, XXXII, 1908, 266–70. 'Antiochos Mégas.'

—— *Klio*, VIII, 1908, 267–81. 'La chronologie de la cinquième guerre de Syrie.'

—— *Hermes*, XLIII, 1908, 296–9. 'La rencontre d'Hannibal et d'Antiochos le Grand à Éphèse.'

—— *Klio*, IX, 1909, 450–60. 'L'expédition de Philippe V en Asie Mineure. La bataille de Chios (201 av. J.-C.).'

—— *Hermes*, XLVII, 1912, 481–91. 'Ardys et Mithridates.'

—— *REA*, XV, 1913, 1–24. 'Recherches sur l'histoire des négociations d'Antiochos III avec les Romains.'

—— *REG*, XXVI, 1913, 44–5. 'Notes sur la *Chronique de Lindos*.' (=Vol. I, 405–6.)

—— *Klio*, XIII, 1913, 137–59. 'Remarques sur les décrets des villes de Crète relatifs à l'ἀσυλία de Téos.'

—— *Hermes*, XLVIII, 1913, 75–98. 'L'entretien de Scipion l'Africain et d'Hannibal.'

—— *REA*, XVII, 1915, 165–72. 'L'année de la bataille de Cynoscéphalai.'

—— *REA*, XVIII, 1916, 1 *seq.* 'Lampsaque et les Galates.'

—— *Ibid.* 233–47. 'Les Aitoliens auxiliaires d'Achaios (Polyb. VII, 16, 7).'

—— *REG*, XXX, 1917, 88–104. 'Sur la "Guerre Crétoise".'

—— *REG*, XXXIII, 1920, 223 *seq.* 'L'expédition de Dikaiarchos dans les Cyclades et sur l'Hellespont.'

—— *REA*, XXII, 1920, 77 *seq.* 'Le prétendu recours des Athéniens aux Romains en 201–200.'

—— *REA*, XXII, 1920, 237–58. 'L'expédition de Philippe V en Asie en 201 av. J.-C.'

—— *REA*, XXIII, 1921, 181–212. 'L'expédition de Philippe V en Asie en 201 av. J.-C.' (*Cont.*)

—— *REA*, XXV, 1923, 330–66. 'L'expédition de Philippe V en Asie en 201 av. J.-C.' (*Cont.*)

—— *REG*, XXXIV, 1921, 400–422. 'L'alliance de Rome et de l'Achaïe.'

—— *REG*, XXXVI, 1923, 115–71. 'Les conférences de Lokride et la politique de T. Quinctius Flamininus.'

—— *REG*, XXXVI, 1923, 480–98. 'Polybe et le tremblement de terre de Rhodes.' (=Vol. I, 445–62.)

—— *Riv. Fil.* LII, 1924, 29–44. 'La lettera degli Scipioni agli abitanti di Colofone a mare.'

—— *Rev. Phil.* L, 1926, 46–66; 194–218. 'La politique romaine en Grèce et dans l'Orient hellénistique au IIIe siècle.'

—— *CAH*, VII, 822–57 (1928). 'The Romans in Illyria' with bibliography (pp. 931–3). (Chap. 26.)

—— *CAH*, VIII, 116–240 (1930). 'Rome and Macedon' and 'Rome and Antiochus' with bibliography (pp. 730–57). (Chaps. 5–7.)

—— *REG*, XLIII, 1930, 243–61. 'La date de la première guerre romaine d'Illyrie.'

—— *Rev. Phil.* LVI, 1930, 305–9. 'Sur un passage de Phlégon de Tralles.'

—— *BCH*, LIV, 1930, 1–41. 'Le consul M. Fulvius et le siège de Samé.'

—— *BCH*, LV, 1931, 1–10. 'Le consul M. Fulvius et le siège de Samé: note complémentaire.'

—— *Rev. Phil.* LVII, 1931, 1–19; 193–208. 'Notes sur Tite-Live. 1. Les additions annalistiques au traité de 196. 2. Le caducéator envoyé par Philippe V à T. Quinctius Flamininus en 197.'

Holleaux, M. *Mélanges Glotz* (Paris, 1932), 431 *seq.* 'Les deux Perseus.'
—— *BCH*, LVI, 1932, 531–45. 'L'élection au consulat de P. Sulpicius.'
—— *BCH*, LVII, 1933, 6–67. 'Une inscription de Séleucie-de-Piérie.'
Homo, L. *L'Italie primitive et les débuts de l'impérialisme romain.* Paris, 1925.
—— *Mélanges Cagnat* (Paris, 1912), 31 *seq.* 'Les conférences de Nicée et la diplomatie romaine en Grèce.'
—— *Rev. Hist.* CXXI, 1916, 241–79; CXXII, 1916, 1–32. 'Flamininus et la politique romaine en Grèce (198–4 av. J.-C.).'
Homolle, Th. *Les archives de l'intendance sacrée à Délos.* Paris, 1887.
—— *BCH*, XX, 1896, 502–22. 'Le roi Nabis.'
Horn, H. *Foederati: Untersuchungen zur Geschichte ihrer Rechtsstellung im Zeitalter der römischen Republik und des frühen Principats.* Diss. Frankfurt a/M., 1930. Pp. 22–39; 65 *seq.*
Howard, A. A. *Harv. Stud.* XVII, 1906, 161–82. 'Livy and Valerius Antias.'
Jochmus, A. *JRGS*, XXVII, 1857, 1–53. '1. On the expedition of Philip of Macedon against Thermus and Sparta. 4. On the battle of Sellasia.'
Jones, A. H. M. *The Cities of the Eastern Roman Provinces.* Oxford, 1937.
—— '*Civitates liberae et immunes* in the East' in *Anatolian Studies presented to W. H. Buckler.* Manchester, 1939. Pp. 103–17.
Jouguet, P. *L'impérialisme macédonien et l'hellénisation de l'orient.* Paris, 1926.
Judeich, W. *Topographie von Athen.* Ed. 2. München, 1931.
Kaerst, J. *Geschichte des Hellenismus.* Ed. 2. Leipzig, 1917–26.
Kahrstedt, U. *Geschichte der Karthager von 218 bis 146.* Berlin, 1913.
—— *Die Annalistik von Livius, B.* XXXI–XLV. Berlin, 1913.
—— *Gött. Nach.* 1923, 99–100. 'Zwei Urkunden aus Polybios. II. Die "Herren Karthager".'
—— *Gnomon*, X, 1934, 401–3; review of Hampl's 'König d. Makedonen'.
Kip, G. *Thessalische Studien.* Diss. Halle, 1910.
Klaffenbach, G. *Gnomon*, I, 1925, 88 *seq.*, review of Schober's 'Phokis'.
—— *Klio*, XX, 1926, 68–88. 'Zur Geschichte von Ost-Lokris.'
—— *Ath. Mitt.* LI, 1926, 28 *seq.* 'Samische Inschriften.'
—— *IG*, IX, 1², 'Inscriptiones Aetoliae', introduction. Berlin, 1932.
—— *Berlin S.B.* 1935, 691–726. 'Bericht über eine epigraphische Reise durch Mittelgriechenland und die ionischen Inseln.'
—— *Klio*, XXXII, 1939, 189–219. 'Zur Geschichte Aetoliens u. Delphis im 3. Jahrhundert' (review of Flacelière's 'Les Aitoliens à Delphes').
Klotz, A. *Hermes*, L, 1915, 481 *seq.* 'Zu den Quellen der vierten und fünften Dekade des Livius.'
Kolbe, W. *GGA*, 1916, 433–75, review of Tarn's 'Antigonos Gonatas'.
König, W. *Der Bund der Nesioten.* Diss. Halle, 1910.
Koster, A. J. *Plutarchi vitam Arati edidit, prolegomenis commentarioque instruxit.* Leiden, 1937.
Kougeas, S. B. Ἑλληνικά, VII, 1934, 177–208. 'Διάγραμμα στρατιωτικῆς οἰκονομίας τῶν Μακεδονικῶν χρόνων ἐκ Χαλκίδος.'
—— Ἑλληνικά, VIII, 1935, 149–50. 'Περιστεγνοποίας.'
Kromayer, J. *Antike Schlachtfelder in Griechenland: Bausteine zu einer antiken Kriegsgeschichte.* Bd. II. *Die hellenistisch-römische Periode: von Kynoskephalae bis Pharsalos.* Berlin, 1907. Pp. 1–227, with maps.
—— *N. J. Kl. Alt.* XIX, 1907, 681–99. 'Hannibal und Antiochos der Grosse.'
—— *Roms Kampf um die Weltherrschaft.* Leipzig, 1912.
—— *HZ*, CIII, 1909, 237–73. 'Hannibal als Staatsmann.'
—— (with Veith, G.) *Schlachten-Atlas zur antiken Kriegsgeschichte.* II. *Römische Abteilung.* Leipzig, 1922.

Kromayer, J. *Heerwesen und Kriegführung der Griechen und Römer*. München, 1928.
Kubitschek, W. *Grundriss der antiken Zeitrechnung*. München, 1928.
Laidlaw, W. A. *A History of Delos*. Oxford, 1933. Chapter III.
Larsen, J. A. O. *CP*, XXX, 1935, 193–214. 'Was Greece free between 196 and 146?'
—— *CP*, XXXI, 1936, 342–8. 'The treaty of peace at the conclusion of the Second Macedonian War.'
—— *CP*, XXXII, 1937, 15–31. 'The Peace of Phoenice and the outbreak of the Second Macedonian War.'
—— *An Economic Survey of Ancient Rome*, Vol. IV, Pt. 3, 'Roman Greece', pp. 259 *seq*. Baltimore, 1938.
Laumonier, A. *BCH*, LVIII, 1934, 291–8. 'Inscriptions de Carie, no. 1.'
Leake, W. M. *Travels in Northern Greece*. Vols. I–IV. London, 1835.
—— *Travels in the Morea*. Vols. I–III. London, 1830.
Le Bas, P. and Waddington, W. H. *Voyage archéologique en Grèce et en Asie Mineure. Inscriptions du troisième volume*. Paris, 1847.
Lenschau, T. *Bericht über griechische Geschichte*, 1903–6, 1907–14, 1915–25, 1926–31, 1932–4, 1935–7, in Bursian's *Jahresberichte*, 1907, pp. 158–229; 1919, pp. 210–49; 1928, pp. 119–56; 1934, pp. 95–125; 1936, pp. 154–70; 1938, pp. 269–78.
Leuze, O. *Hermes*, LVIII, 1923, 187–229; 241–87. 'Die Feldzüge Antiochos des Grossen nach Kleinasien und Thrakien.'
Levi, M. A. *Att. Acc. Torino*, LVII, 1921–2, 179–85. 'La cronologia degli strateghi etolici negli anni 221–168 *a. C*.'
Liedmeier, C. *Plutarchus' biographie van Aemilius Paullus*. Utrecht, 1935.
Loring, W. *JHS*, XV, 1895, 25–89. 'Some ancient routes in the Peloponnese.'
McDonald, A. H. *JRS*, XXVIII, 1938, 153–64. 'Scipio Africanus and Roman politics in the second century.'
—— (with Walbank, F. W.) *JRS*, XXVII, 1937, 180–207. 'The origins of the Second Macedonian War.'
Magie, D. *JRS*, XXIX, 1939, 32–44. 'The "agreement" between Philip V and Antiochus III for the partition of the Egyptian empire.'
—— 'Rome and the City-States of Western Asia Minor from 200 to 133 B.C.' in *Anatolian Studies presented to W. H. Buckler*. Manchester, 1939. Pp. 161–85.
Makaronas, Ch. I. *AE*, 1934–5, 117–27. 'Ἐπιστολὴ τοῦ βασιλέως Φιλίππου τοῦ Ε΄.'
Mamroth, A. *ZN*, XXXVIII, 1928, 1 *seq*. 'Die Silbermünzen des Königs Perseus.'
—— *ZN*, XL, 1930, 207–303. 'Die Silbermünzen des Königs Philippos V von Makedonien.'
—— *ZN*, XLII, 1935, 219–51. 'Die Bronzemünzen des Königs Philippos V von Makedonien.'
Matthaei, L. E. *CQ*, I, 1907, 182 *seq*. 'On the classification of Roman allies.'
Matzat, H. *Die römische Zeitrechnung für die Jahre 219 bis 1 v. Chr*. Berlin, 1889.
Meischke, K. *Symbolae ad Eumenis II Pergamenorum regis historiam*. Diss. Leipzig, 1892.
—— *Zur Geschichte des Königs Eumenes II von Pergamon*. Progr. Pirna, 1905.
Meritt, B. D. *Hesperia*, V, 1936, no. 3, pp. 424–5, 427. 'Decree in honour of Cephisodorus.'
Meyer, Ed. *Weltgeschichte und Weltkrieg: Gesammelte Aufsätze*. Stuttgart, 1916. 'Die Entwicklung der römischen Weltherrschaft.'
—— *Kleine Schriften*, I (ed. 2) and II. Halle, 1924. (Particularly vol. I, 213–64. 'Der Gang der alten Geschichte: Hellas und Rom.' Vol. II, 463–94. 'Die Schlacht bei Pydna.')

Meyer, Ernst. *Untersuchungen zur Chronologie der ersten Ptolemäer auf Grund der Papyri*. Beiheft zum *Arch. Pap.* 1925.
—— *Die Grenzen der hellenistischen Staaten in Kleinasien*. Zürich-Leipzig, 1925.
—— *See* Stählin, F.
Michel, Ch. *Recueil d'inscriptions grecques*. Bruxelles, 1900.
Mijnsbrugge, M. van der. *The Cretan Koinon*. New York, 1931.
Momigliano, A. *Filippo il Macedone: Saggio sulla storia greca del IV secolo a. C.* Florence, 1934.
—— *Athen.* XI, 1933, 136–41. '*Honorati amici*.'
—— *Athen.* XIII, 1935, 3 *seq*. 'Re e popolo in Macedonia prima di Alessandro Magno.'
Mommsen, Th. *Römische Geschichte*. Ed. 7. Berlin, 1881.
—— (with Robert, C.) *Hermes*, XVII, 1882, 467 *seq*. 'König Philipp V und die Larisäer.' Republished in *Ges. Schr.* IV (= *Hist. Schr.* I), 49 *seq*. Berlin, 1906.
Mundt, J. *Nabis, König von Sparta*. Diss. Münster-in-W., 1903.
Münzer, F. *Römische Adelsparteien und Adelsfamilien*. Stuttgart, 1920.
—— *Die politische Vernichtung des Griechentums*. Leipzig, 1925.
—— *Philol.* LXXXIX, 1934, 215 *seq*. 'Eine Probe rhodischer Beredsamkeit in lateinischer Fassung.'
Niccolini, G. *La confederazione achea*. Pavia, 1914.
—— *Studi storici*, I, 1908, 224–52. 'Gli strateghi della lega achea.'
—— *Studi storici*, II, 1909, 249–347. 'Le relazioni fra Roma e la lega achea.'
—— *Studi storici*, V, 1912, 108–24. 'Quando cominciò la prima guerra macedonica.'
Nicolaus, M. *Zwei Beiträge zur Geschichte König Philipps V. von Makedonien.* 1. *Philippos und Aratos*. 2. *Die Beziehungen Philipps zu Karien*. Diss. Berlin, 1909.
Niese, B. *Geschichte der griechischen und makedonischen Staaten seit der Schlacht bei Chaeronea*. Vols. II and III. Gotha, 1893–1903.
—— *Hermes*, XXXIV, 1899, 549–52. 'Das arkadische Dekret für Magnesia-am-Maeander.'
—— *Hermes*, XXXV, 1900, 60–9. 'Zur Geschichte des Hellenismus. 2. Die Zeit der Schlacht bei Sellasia.'
Nims, C. F. *JEA*, XXIV, 1938, 73–4. 'Notes on University of Michigan Demotic Papyri from Philadelphia. 1. The Chronology of the early years of Ptolemy Epiphanes.'
Nissen, H. *Kritische Untersuchungen über die Quellen der vierten und fünften Dekade des Livius*. Berlin, 1863.
—— *Rhein. Mus.* XXVI, 1871, 241–82. 'Die Oekonomie des Polybius.'
Oberhummer, E. *Akarnanien, Ambrakia, Amphilochien, Leukas im Altertum*. München, 1887.
Oikonomos, G. P. Ἐπιγραφαὶ τῆς Μακεδονίας, I, Athens, 1915. Pp. 2 *seq*.
—— *Ath. Mitt.* LI, 1926, 75–97. 'Bronzen von Pella.'
Oppermann, H. *Zeus Panamaros*. Giessen, 1924. (Vol. XIX, 3, of Religionsgesch. Versuche und Vorarbeiten.)
Ormerod, H. A. *Piracy in the Ancient World*. Liverpool-London, 1924.
Oster, H. E. *ZDOeA*, XVII, 1886, 263–72. 'Eine Bergfahrt König Philipps III. von Macedonien im Jahre 181 v. Chr.'
Otto, W. *Zur Geschichte der Zeit des VIten Ptolemäers*. Abh. Bay. Ak. 1934.
Pais, E. *Storia di Roma durante le grandi conquiste mediterranee*. Torino, 1931.
—— (with Bayet, J.) *Histoire Romaine*. Vol. I. (In Glotz, *Histoire générale*.) Paris, 1926.
Paris, P. *Élatée, la ville, le temple d'Athéna Cranaia*. Paris, 1891.

Passerini, A. *Athen.* IX, 1931, 260 *seq.* 'Le relazioni di Roma con l'Oriente negli anni 201–200 a.c.'

—— *Athen.* IX, 1931, 542–62. 'I moventi di Roma nella seconda guerra macedonica.'

—— *Athen.* X, 1932, 105 *seq.* 'La pace con Filippo e le relazioni con Antioco.'

—— *Athen.* X, 1932, 325 *seq.* 'Lo scoppio della guerra siriaca.'

—— *Athen.* XI, 1933, 10–28. 'L'ultimo piano di Annibale e una testimonianza di Ennio.'

—— *Athen.* XI, 1933, 309–35. 'I moti politico-sociali della Grecia e i Romani.'

Paton, W. R. (with Hicks, E. L.) *The Inscriptions of Cos.* Oxford, 1891.

Patsch, C. *Wien. S.B.* 214, 1 (1933). 'Beiträge zur Völkerkunde von Südosteuropa, V, 1.' Pp. 9–14.

Pelekides, S. Ἀπὸ τὴν πολιτεία καὶ τὴν κοινωνία τῆς ἀρχαίας Θεσσαλονίκης. Salonica, 1934. Pp. 1–23.

Perdrizet, P. *BCH*, XVIII, 1894, 416–19. 'Voyage dans la Macédoine première. I. Amphipolis, inscription no. 1.'

—— *Rev. Num.* (IVᵉ série), VII, 1903, 320–325. 'Notes de numismatique macédonienne. III. Monnayage des Macédoniens sous leurs deux derniers rois.'

Peter, C. *Studien zur römischen Geschichte. Ein Beitrag zur Kritik von Th. Mommsens Römischer Geschichte.* III. *Die macchiavellistische Politik der Römer in der Zeit vom Ende des zweiten punischen Krieges bis zu den Gracchen.* Halle, 1863. Pp. 115 *seq.*

Piganiol, A. *La conquête romaine.* Ed. 2, Paris, 1930.

Pöhlmann, R. von. *Geschichte der sozialen Frage und des Sozialismus in der antiken Welt.* Ed. 3 by F. Oertel. München, 1925.

—— *Grundriss der griechischen Geschichte.* Ed. 5, München, 1916.

Pomtow, H. *N. Jahrb. f. Phil.* CLIII, 1896, 623 *seq.* 'Die dreiseitige Basis der Messenier und Naupaktier zu Delphi.'

—— *N. Jahrb. f. Phil.* CLV, 1897, 801 *seq.* 'Fasti Delphici.'

—— *Klio*, XVI, 1920, 109–59. 'Die Befreiung Delphis durch die Römer.'

Porter, W. H. *Plutarch's Life of Aratus with introduction, notes and appendix.* Cork, 1937.

—— *Hermathena*, XLVIII, 1933, 266 *seq.* Review of Walbank's 'Aratos of Sicyon'.

Powell, B. *AJA*, VIII, 1904, 137–73. 'Oeniadae: history and topography.'

Pozzi, E. *Mem. Acc. Torino*, LXIII, 1913, 319–87. 'Le battaglie di Cos e di Andro.'

Rehm, A. *Das Delphinion in Milet.* (Th. Wiegand, *Milet*, I, iii.) Berlin, 1914.

Reinach, A. J. *BCH*, XXXIV, 1910, 249–330. 'Delphes et les Bastarnes.'

—— *REG*, XXIV, 1911, 319–20. 'Bulletin épigraphique: Thessalie.'

Riemann, O. *BCH*, I, 1877, 87 *seq.* 'Inscriptions grecques de Cyriaque d'Ancone.' (Particularly on *Syll.* 573.)

Robert, C. See Mommsen, Th.

Robert, L. *Rev. Phil.* LXV, 1939, 97–122. 'Hellénica I: 1. Inscriptions de Pagai en Mégaride relatives à un arbitrage.'

Rodgers, W. L. *Greek and Roman Naval Warfare.* Annapolis, 1937.

Rosenberg, A. *Hermes*, LI, 1916, 499–509. 'Amyntas, der Vater Philipps II.' (Particularly 503 *seq.*)

—— *BPW*, XXXVI, 1916, col. 1104–5. Review of T. Frank's 'Roman Imperialism.'

—— *Einleitung und Quellenkunde zur römischen Geschichte.* Berlin, 1921.

Rostovtzeff, M. I. 'Notes on the economic policy of the Pergamene kings' in *Anatolian Studies presented to Sir W. Ramsay.* Manchester, 1923. P. 390.

—— *A History of the Ancient World: Vol. II, Rome.* Oxford, 1927.

BIBLIOGRAPHY 363

Rostovtzeff, M. I. *Am. Hist. Rev.* XLI, 1935–6, 231–52. 'The Hellenistic World: its economic development.'

Roussel, P. *BCH*, XXXIII, 1909, 479–80. 'Fouilles de Délos.' Dealing with a mutilated Ptolemaic inscription on Delos (cf. Tarn, 391.)

—— *BCH*, L, 1926, 124 *seq.* 'Les épimélètes aitoliens à Delphes.'

—— *BCH*, LVI, 1932, 1 *seq.* 'Delphes et l'Amphictyonie après la guerre d'Aitolie.'

—— *Rev. Arch.* III⁶, 1934, 39 *seq.* 'Un règlement militaire macédonien.'

Rühl, F. *N. Jahrb. f. Phil.* CXXVII, 1883, 33–46. 'Der letzte Kampf der Achäer gegen Nabis.'

Salvetti, C. *Studi di stor. ant.* II, 1893, 95–137. 'Ricerche storiche intorno alla lega etolica.'

Schebelev, S. *Comptes rendus de l'Académie des Sciences de l'U.R.S.S.* 1929, 193–200. Note on the Paean of Isyllus (in Russian; cf. Bickermann, *Phil. Woch.* 1930, 242).

—— *Ibid.* 1930, 488–9. Notes on Aetolian decrees (in Russian: cf. Bickermann, *Phil. Woch.* 1931, 1575).

Schober, F. *Phokis.* Diss. Jena, 1924. Pp. 80 *seq.*

Schorn, W. *Geschichte Griechenlands von der Entstehung ḍ. ätol. und ach. Bünde bis auf die Zerstörung Korinths.* Bonn, 1833.

Schroeter, F. *De regum hellenisticorum epistulis.* Leipzig, 1932.

Schubart, W. *Gnomon*, XI, 1935, 513 *seq.* Review of Zancan's 'Monarcato ellenistico'.

Schulhof, E. *BCH*, XXXI, 1907, 50, n. 1; 105, n. 1. 'Fouilles de Délos'; on the date of the Portico of Philip.

—— *BCH*, XXXII, 1908, 83 *seq.* 'Fouilles de Délos'; on the vase-festivals.

Schur, W. *Scipio Africanus und die Begründung der römischen Weltherrschaft.* Leipzig, 1927.

Scott, F. A. *Macedonien und Rom während des hannibalischen Krieges.* Diss. Leipzig, 1873.

Scrinzi, A. *Atti dell' Istituto Veneto*, IX, 1897/8, 1509 *seq.* 'La guerra di Lyttos del 220 av. Cr. e i trattati internazionali cretesi.'

Scullard, H. H. *A History of the Roman World from 753 to 146 B.C.* London, 1935. Pp. 217–89.

—— *Scipio Africanus in the Second Punic War.* Cambridge, 1930.

Seeliger, K. *Messenien und der achäische Bund.* Prog. Zittau, 1897.

Segre, M. *Riv. Fil.* LXI, 1933, 365–92. 'ΚΡΗΤΙΚΟΣ ΠΟΛΕΜΟΣ.'

—— *Riv. Fil.* LXII, 1934, 169–93. 'Grano di Tessaglia a Cos.'

—— *Riv. Fil.* LXIII, 1935, 222–5. 'Εστεγνοποιημένοι.'

Seltman, C. *Greek Coins.* London, 1933.

Serre, P. *Les marines de guerre de l'antiquité et du moyen-âge.* Vol. I, pp. 119 *seq.* (on the battle of Chios). Paris, 1885.

Smith, R. E. *CQ*, XXXIV, 1940, 1–10. 'Plutarch's biographical sources in the Roman Lives.'

Sokoloff, T. *Klio*, VII, 1907, 52–72. 'Die delphische Amphictionie: Nach-schrift.' (On the *Pylaicum concilium*.)

Soltau, W. *Livius' Geschichtswerk, seine Composition und seine Quellen.* Leipzig, 1897.

Stählin, F. *Das hellenische Thessalien.* Stuttgart, 1924.

—— *Philol.* LXXVII, 1921, 199 *seq.* 'Pharsalica II: Die Phthiotis und der Friede zwischen Philippos V und den Aetolern.'

—— (with Meyer, Ernst and Heidner, A.) *Pagasai und Demetrias. Beschreib-ung der Reste und Stadtgeschichte.* Berlin-Leipzig, 1934.

Starr, C. G. Junr. *CP*, XXXIII, 1938, 63–8. 'Rhodes and Pergamum, 201–200 B.C.'

Steele, R. B. *AJPh*, XXXVIII, 1917, 17 *seq.* 'Pompeius Trogus and Justinus.'

Swoboda, H. *Klio*, XI, 1911, 450. 'Studien zu den griechischen Bünden. 1. Zur Urkunde *Insc. Magn.* 28.'

—— *Klio*, XII, 1912, 21 *seq.* 'Studien zu den griechischen Bünden. 3. Die Städte im achäischen Bunde.'

—— *Wien. S.B.* 199 (2), 1924, 59 *seq.* 'Zwei Kapitel aus dem griechischen Bundesrecht. II. Die Sympolitien von Keos und Ost-Lokris.'

—— Hermann's *Lehrbuch der griech. Staatsaltertümer*, Vol. III. Ed. 6. Tübingen, 1913.

—— *Hermes*, LVII, 1922, 529. 'Neue Urkunden von Epidauros.' (Theory that Philip shared the throne with Doson.)

—— (with Busolt, G.) *Griechische Staatskunde*, Vol. II. Ed. 3. München, 1926.

Tarn, W. W. *Antigonos Gonatas*. Oxford, 1913. (Particularly Appendix XIII: The Macedonian protectorate in the Cyclades.)

—— *Hellenistic Civilisation*. Ed. 2. London, 1930.

—— *The Hellenistic Age*. Chapter on 'The Social Question in the Third Century.' Pp. 139 *seq.* Cambridge, 1923.

—— *Hellenistic Military and Naval Developments*. Cambridge, 1930.

—— *The Greeks in Bactria and India*. Cambridge, 1938.

—— *CAH*, VII, 1928, 732–68. (Chap. 23.) 'The Greek Leagues and Macedonia.' (Bibliography on pp. 874–88.)

—— *JHS*, XXV, 1905, 137–56; 205–24. 'The Greek Warship.'

—— *JHS*, XXIX, 1909, 264 *seq.* 'The battles of Andros and Cos.'

—— *JHS*, XLI, 1921, 1–17. 'Alexander's ὑπομνήματα and the 'World-kingdom'.' (Pp. 16–17 on the Macedonian κοινόν.)

—— *CQ*, XVIII, 1924, 17–23. 'Philip V and Phthia.'

—— *CQ*, XXIII, 1929, 140 *seq.* 'Queen Ptolemais and Apama.'

—— *JHS*, LIII, 1933, 57–68. 'Two notes on Ptolemaic history.'

—— 'Phthia-Chryseis' (forthcoming article).

Täubler, E. *Imperium Romanum*, Vol. I. Leipzig-Berlin, 1913.

Theiler, W. *Die politische Lage in den beiden makedonischen Kriegen*. Diss. Halle, 1914.

Theunissen, W. P. *Ploutarchos' leven van Aratos: met historisch-topographisch commentaar*. Nijmegen, 1935.

Treves, P. *Athen.* XII, 1934, 381–411. 'Studi su Antigono Dosone.'

—— *Athen.* XIII, 1935, 22–56. 'Studi su Antigono Dosone.' (*Cont.*)

—— *Athen.* X, 1932, 184–203. Review of Dinsmoor's 'Archons of Athens'.

—— *Athen.* XII, 1934, 324–9. Review of Walbank's 'Aratos'.

—— *LEC*, IX, 1940, 138–74. 'Les documents apocryphes du 'Pro Corona'.'

Tscherikower, V. *Die hellenistischen Städtegründungen von Alexander dem Grossen bis auf die Römerzeit. Philol. Suppl.-B.* XIX, 1. Leipzig, 1927.

Vallois, R. *Le portique de Philippe. Exploration archéologique de Délos*, Vol. VII, 1. Paris, 1923.

Varese, P. *Cronologia romana*. Vol. 1. *Il calendario flaviano*. Rome, 1908.

Veith, G. *Der Feldzug von Dyrrhachium zwischen Caesar und Pompejus*. Wien, 1920. (Pp. 61 *seq.* on the second Macedonian war.)

Vollgraff, W. *Rev. Phil.* XXVII, 1903, 236–44. 'Notes sur la fin et les conséquences de la guerre étolienne. 1. La bonne foi de Tite-Live. 2. À quelle époque Héraclée est-elle sortie de la ligue étolienne?'

Vulić, N. *Mélanges Glotz* (Paris, 1932). 'Une inscription grecque de Macédoine.' Pp. 869–76.

—— *Bull. Acad. Royale Serbe, Sect. Lettres*, 1935, 185–97. 'Les Dardanes.'

—— *Ibid.* 1935, 231–43. 'Première guerre d'Illyrie.'

Wace, A. J. B. *JHS*, XXV, 1905, 88 *seq.* 'Hellenistic royal portraits.'

Wace, A. J. B. (with Woodward, A. M.) *BSA*, xviii, 1911–12, 166–88. 'Inscriptions from Upper Macedonia.'

Walbank, F. W. *Aratos of Sicyon.* Cambridge, 1933.

—— *JEA*, xxii, 1936, 20–34. 'The accession of Ptolemy Epiphanes: a problem in chronology.'

—— *JHS*, lviii, 1938, 55–68. 'ΦΙΛΙΠΠΟΣ ΤΡΑΓΩΙΔΟΥΜΕΝΟΣ: a Polybian experiment.'

—— *See* McDonald, A. H.

Walek-Czernecki, T. *Dzieje upadku monarchji macedońskiej.* (History of the fall of the Macedonian monarchy: with French summary.) Cracow, 1924.

—— *Rev. Phil.* xlix, 1925, 45 *seq.* 'La politique romaine en Grèce et dans l'Orient hellénistique au IIIe siècle.'

—— *Rev. Phil.* liv, 1928, 5 *seq.* 'La chronologie de la première guerre de Macédoine.'

—— *Eos*, xxxi, 1928, 369–404. 'Les origines de la seconde guerre de Macédoine.'

Welles, C. B. *Royal Correspondence of the Hellenistic Age.* Yale, 1934. Pp. 165 *seq.*

—— *AJA*, xlii, 1938, 245–60. 'New texts from the chancery of Philip V of Macedon and the problem of the "Diagramma".'

Westermann, W. L. *Upon Slavery in Ptolemaic Egypt.* New York, 1929. (Particularly pp. 22–7 on Dicaearchus.)

Westlake, H. D. *Thessaly in the fourth century B.C.* London, 1935.

Wilamowitz-Moellendorff, U. von. *Staat und Gesellschaft der Griechen und Römer bis zum Ausgang des Mittelalters.* Ed. 2. Leipzig-Berlin, 1923. Pp. 149 *seq.*

—— *Reden und Vorträge.* Vol. ii, Ed. 4. Berlin, 1926. P. 193, n. 1.

Wilhelm, A. *GGA*, 1898, 217 *seq.* Review of Michel's 'Recueil'.

—— *Jahresh.* xi, 1908, 79–81. 'Eine Inschrift des Königs Epiphanes Nikomedes.' (Relationship of Philip and Prusias.)

—— *BPW*, xxxii, 1912, 314–15. 'Königin Phthia'.

—— *Wien. Anz.* lvii, 1920, xvii–xxvii, 40–57. 'Ein Brief Antiochos' III.'

—— *Wien. Anz.* lviii, 1921, xviii, 1 *seq.* 'Hellenistisches.'

Winkler, A. *Rom und Aegypten.* Diss. Leipzig, 1933.

Witte, K. *Rhein. Mus.* lxv, 1910, 270–305; 359–415. 'Ueber die Form der Darstellung in Livius' Geschichtswerk.'

Wolters, P. *Ath. Mitt.* xxii, 1897, 139–47. 'König Nabis.'

Woodhouse, W. J. *Aetolia, its geography, topography and antiquities.* Oxford, 1897. (Pp. 228–86 for Philip's invasion of Thermum in 218.)

Woodward, A. M. *JHS*, xxxiii, 1913, 337–46. 'Inscriptions from Thessaly and Macedon, no. 17.'

—— *See* Wace, A. J. B.

Wroth, W. *NC*, iv³, 1884, 53–4. 'Cretan coins.' (On a coin of Polyrrhenia.

Zancan, P. *Il monarcato ellenistico nei suoi elementi federativi.* Padova, 1934.

Ziegler, K. *Phil. Woch.* xlviii, 1928, cols. 94–5. 'Zu Lykophron, 1.'

Zippel, G. *Die römische Herrschaft in Illyrien.* Leipzig, 1877.

Much valuable material is to be found in *P-W*, under the relevant headings.

INDEX

Abae, 93 n.1, 288 n.1, 296, 298
Abdera, 142 n.2, 183
Abia (Messenia), 207 n.1
Abrupolis, 255 n.2
Abydus, 133–4, 136, 142 n.2, 152,
  160, 177, 179, 306, 312, 315–17
Academy, Athenian, 131, 139 n.3
Acanthus, 145
Acarnania, in Symmachy, 16; complaints, 32; declares war on Aetolia,
  36; Philip's campaign (219), 39 seq.;
  troops sent to Cephallenia, 53;
  raids, 62; gains in Social War, 66;
  attacked by Rome, 84–5; appeal
  to Philip, 86; pleads at Sparta, 88;
  Aetolian attacks, 93–4; at Phoenice,
  103; two Acarnanians executed
  at Eleusis, 125, 311–12; appeal to
  Philip, 129, 315; L. Flamininus
  sent, 166; joins Rome, 167, 175,
  323; awarded Leucas, 182; help
  to Achaea, 195; Syrian attack, 202;
  Aetolian attacks, 215
Acesimbrotus of Rhodes, 160
Achaea, Achaeans, take Acrocorinth,
  13; war with Demetrius II, 10;
  Roman embassy, 12; Cleomenean
  War, 14–15; in Symmachy, 16;
  Messenian alliance, 25; appeal to
  Philip and Symmachy, 27 seq.;
  troops in Crete, 33; declare war on
  Aetolia, 34; oath to king of
  Macedon, 34; faced with collapse,
  38; appeals to Philip, 39–40; given
  Psophis, 44, 66; Eperatus general,
  48, 164; agreement with Philip,
  50; help to Messenia, 53; regional
  reorganisation, 62; given Phigaleia,
  47 n.3, 66; appeal to Philip (209),
  89, 304; state of navy, 91 n.1;
  Spartan attacks, 93; appeal to
  Philip (208), 96; under Philopoemen, 98; at Phoenice, 103; and
  Sparta, 114; Roman approach,
  129, 131, 315; appeal to Rhodes,
  135; and Philip, 140; recover
  Heraea, etc., 148; join Rome,
  157–8, 165, 274, 320; at conference
  of Locris, 159–61; social problems,
  164; victory of Nemean Beck,

175, 323; troops in Asia Minor,
  175; position in 196, 182; granted
  a foedus (?), 182 n.7; and Argos,
  187–9; declares war on Sparta
  (192), 195; gains Sparta, 196;
  Aetolian approach, 198, 328;
  declares war on Antiochus, 199,
  330; gains Messenia, 207; and
  Sparta and Elis, 208–9; raids
  Aetolia, 215; dispute with Sparta,
  217, 234, 238, 334; in what sense
  'democratic', 225 n.2; source of
  anti-Persean propaganda, 252;
  date of generals' taking office, 300
  n.3; date of elections, 317 n.6
— Phthiotic, 11, 20, 32, 63, 100,
  181, 232, 248, 259, 260 n.2
Achaeus, 83
Acharrae, 155
Achelous, R., 32, 39–40, 54, 99, 207
— (at Lamia), 89
Acilius Glabrio, M'., 199, 202–10,
  220, 226–7, 232–4, 329–30
Acrocorinth, 13, 17, 74, 138, 161 n.3,
  162, 189
Acrolissus, 80–81, 300
Actium, 39–41
Admetus, Macedonian, 244, 266
Adramyttium, 119
Adriatic Sea, 80–82, 217, 237, 248,
  254
Aegae, 35 n.1
Aegaean Sea, 85, 88, 92–3, 108 seq.,
  113, 130–2, 144–5, 211–12, 272,
  308, 317, 320
Aegeira, 38
Aegina, 88 n.3, 92–3, 98, 130, 139,
  141, 166, 302
Aeginium, 153, 156, 182 n.6, 202,
  219 n.2, 232 n.4, 319
Aegium, 25, 34, 50, 62, 90, 97, 129,
  199, 304
Aelius, P., 192, 326 n.13
Aemilius Paullus, L., 4 n.1, 256, 289
Aenea, 245
Aenesidemus of Dyme, 158
Aeniania, 219–20, 225
Aenus, 133, 142 n.2, 180, 190, 212,
  216, 218, 223–6, 233–7, 240–41,
  315, 334